Wiltshire Record Society

(formerly the Records Branch of the Wiltshire
Archaeological and Natural History Society)

VOLUME 75

Published on behalf of the Wiltshire Record Society
by The Hobnob Press,
8 Lock Warehouse, Severn Road,
Gloucester GL1 2GA
www.hobnobpress.co.uk

© Wiltshire Record Society, 2022
c/o Wiltshire and Swindon History Centre,
Cocklebury Road, Chippenham SN15 3QN

www.wiltshirerecordsociety.org.uk

ISBN 978–0–901333–52–0

Typeset by John Chandler

CONTENTS

Maps of Salisbury Streets and Locations	ii
Dedication	viii
Preface	ix
INTRODUCTION	xi
SALISBURY DOMESDAY BOOKS	1
Book One	2
Book Two	16
Book Three	30
Book Four	130
Book Five	170
Witnesses to Documents	338
INDEX ONE General index: persons, places, and subjects	347
INDEX TWO Salisbury: buildings, locations, and institutions	401
List of officers	417
List of members	417
List of publications	420

*This seventy-fifth volume of the Wiltshire Record Society
is dedicated to*
KENNETH H ROGERS
*former Wiltshire County and Diocesan Archivist,
member of the society for over seventy years,
long-serving committee member and volume editor,
and lifelong enthusiast for the county's history
and supporter of its historians.*

PREFACE

A note published in 2012 drew the attention of readers of *Sarum Chronicle* to the importance of the Salisbury Domesday books as a rich source of information about the city's medieval history and topography. Their potential, it suggested, extends well beyond academic interest in the history of Salisbury's economy, topography and society; they can also inform planners and archaeologists concerned with investigating development sites and interpreting the results of excavations. Out of this note stemmed a proposal by Dr Chandler to the Wiltshire Record Society that it might consider an edition of the Domesday books, to be followed up by a synthesis of the topographical and biographical information they provide alongside other documentary sources, as has been attempted for a number of medieval towns and cities. The present volume is the first of a projected trilogy which hopes to achieve this aim.

The editors of this volume, Dr Crowley and Dr Chandler, wish to acknowledge the help that they have been given by the staff of the Wiltshire & Swindon History Centre throughout, and in particular the service that Jane Silcocks has given them in photographing each folio of the books, enabling them to prepare the work remotely. They also wish formally to thank Wiltshire Council for permission to edit them. Dr Chandler is grateful also to Emily Naish, Salisbury Cathedral Archivist, for access to material in her care.

Writing in 1980, the late Helen Bonney of the Royal Commission on Historical Monuments (England), opined that: 'The student of Salisbury history is hampered by lack of early documents, but a lifetime might be spent sorting out evidence which survives from the late 14th century and subsequent periods.' Through their exemplary editing and indexing of the documents, the editors of this volume will have made the student's task far less time-consuming.

Tom Plant
General Editor

known only from the list of contents, contained a further 225 transcripts dating between 1347 and 1362, although there are indications that details of other pertinent documents were never entered and chronological order was disrupted (**318–542**). Book 3 comprises transcripts of 300 documents dated 1361–1381, a will of 1349 and a deed of 1351 (**543–844**). Book 4 is lost, its contents included in the list of contents. It included 811 documents, spanning 1369–1396 (**845–1655**). Book 5 comprises transcripts of 510 documents, 1396–1413, with four earlier deeds, 1361, 1387 and 1395 (**1656–2169**). A further 601 documents, mostly dating between 1413 and 1478 (though nine are earlier) are transcribed in Books 6 and 7.[3]

THE BOOKS IN THE CONTEXT OF SALISBURY'S GOVERNANCE

Medieval Salisbury was the creation of its bishop, who owned the city and exercised authority over all aspects of its governance. His rights, bestowed by the Crown, and the rights and obligations of his citizens, were set out in two charters dating from the first decade of the new foundation. The earlier, granted by Bishop Richard Poore in 1225 to his free citizens, gave them liberty to grant, sell or mortgage their tenements under his bailiff's supervision.[4] Among the provisions of the latter, the 1227 royal charter to the bishop, were two relating to tenure.[5] One was designed to prevent mortmain, by forbidding citizens from granting or selling their tenements to churches or religious houses without episcopal permission. The other permitted the bishop to tallage (that is, to impose a tax on) his citizens when he was himself tallaged by the king. It is likely, therefore, that the bishop's court kept a record of transactions brought to its notice from the outset, although no such document has survived from the thirteenth century. By 1306 it is clear that a register was being kept, and that it was known as Domesday.[6]

The bishop's court continued to exercise judicial rights over his citizens throughout the period covered by the Domesday books and beyond. Its functions included exhibiting wills that had been proved in the subdean's (or during a vacancy the dean's) court, and the public

---

3   These figures replace the estimates given by Hobbs and Chandler (2012), 82.
4   Davies (1908), 187–8.
5   Jones and Macray (1891), 176–7.
6   Davies (1908), 194 (*registro, quod cives ipsi apud se Domus Dei appellant*), discussed by Street, 196–7.

performance of conveyances.⁷ As the city grew in population and prosperity this subjugation to the bishop's authority rankled and was periodically tested by force. Thus in 1344 his bailiff was assaulted by a conspiracy of 33 persons intent on hindering the business of the court, who carried off rolls and memoranda.⁸ Further protests occurred in 1395 and, more seriously, over a protracted period between 1465 and 1474, though in every case the bishop's authority was confirmed.⁹ Through the fourteenth and fifteenth centuries self-government by the citizen body, the mayor and commonalty, increased, and in 1406, confirmed by the bishop in 1412, it was granted permission to acquire and retain property up to a certain value (**1931, 2100**), which power it first exercised in 1413 (**2157–9**).¹⁰ Although tensions between opposing authorities festered, there are also instances to be seen in the Domesday books of co-operation between bailiff and mayor (**399**, also **237, 241, 247**).

The Domesday books, therefore, provided a record for the bishop and his bailiff that property transfers were conducted within the terms of the city's charters, in which their existence was enshrined. But they also afforded protection for the citizens themselves, and so it was in the interest of the city corporation that they be maintained and preserved. In Albert Hollaender's words: 'The city having no court of its own conveyances must needs be effected in one of the ecclesiastical courts, but the citizens no doubt needed a record of these conveyances, if only to prove that the prohibition against alienation in mortmain had not been violated.'¹¹ It is perhaps for this reason that the surviving books are found among the corporation, not the diocesan, records.

PARALLELS ELSEWHERE

It was claimed as early as the 10th century that property transactions witnessed before the borough court of Cambridge had legal validity, in the same way as those of Ipswich, Norwich and Thetford.¹² Rolls and

---

7   Crittall (1962), 95.
8   Street (1916), 224–5. Conceivably the first Domesday book may have been taken (though later returned) and it may be significant that the second book commenced in 1347, immediately after order had been restored.
9   Street (1916), 226, 233–57.
10   Crittall (1962), 101–2.
11   in Rathbone (1951), 64.
12   Martin (1971), 155, citing *Liber Eliensis*.

registers of conveyances survive from the 13th century from Wallingford (1231–2) and London (1252), and from Ipswich (1255) which before 1272 had a custumal called *le Domesday*.[13] By 1300 many towns, including Winchester, Colchester, Exeter and Nottingham, were enrolling property deeds on the general rolls of the city court.[14] Separate registers of deeds, or abstracts of deeds, proliferated during the 14th century, including at Winchester from 1303,[15] and Bristol from 1380.[16] Elsewhere, including Oxford, Canterbury, Dorchester, Gloucester and Ely, cartularies, registers and surveys of major landowners recorded the tenurial history of many city properties.[17] These and other records have been used to relate the topography of medieval cities to their owners and occupants.[18]

RELATED OR RELEVANT SALISBURY ARCHIVES

The Domesday books are the most important, but not the only, source of information about property holding and transfer in the city during the fourteenth and fifteenth centuries. Salisbury Cathedral Archive retains over 330 deeds and similar documents relating to Salisbury earlier than 1500, of which 21 are certainly or probably dated before 1300, approximately 213 are of fourteenth-century date, and 102 of the fifteenth century.[19] They include many which were enrolled in the lost Domesday Books and are now recorded only in the *Kalendare*.

Preserved among the city archives are over 250 bundles of original deeds (WSA, G23/150/1–259), including 34 involving property which extend back before 1500, and two earlier than 1300.[20] There is also a substantial deposit of medieval deeds relating to the city properties of

13   Martin (1971), 155, 158, 166–7; Allen (2000).
14   Keene (1985), 13.
15   BL, Stowe 846, used extensively by Keene (1985).
16   Veale (1931).
17   Salter (1960, 1969); Urry (1967); Mayo (1908); Rhodes (2016); Holton-Krayenbuhl (2011).
18   Winchester: Keene (1985); Bristol: Leech (1997, 2000); Oxford: Salter (1960, 1969); Canterbury: Urry (1967); Gloucester: Rhodes (2016); Chichester: Morgan (1992); Hull: Horrox (1983); York: Raine (1955).
19   SCA, Press I, boxes 9–16. The deeds are arranged chronologically in four sequences, numbered 1/1–117; 2/1–84; 3/1–122; 4/1–42. Some are later than 1500. All have full translations on cards.
20   Apart from G23/150/252 all fall within the range G23/150/5–111.

INTRODUCTION

Trinity Hospital, Salisbury (WSA, 1446/1/1–77);[21] a group of fifteen medieval city deeds acquired by Salisbury Museum (WSA 164/1–15); a collection of leases of Dean and Chapter properties in the city in Salisbury Cathedral Archive (SCA, CO/CH/5/1/1–24); eleven deeds and other instruments relating to Chapter property in Salisbury among the Church Commissioners records (WSA, CC/Chap);[22] a fifteenth-century register of leases of city properties (WSA, G23/1/238); and smaller accumulations, such as those in the parish collections of St Edmund's (WSA, 1901/175–7) and St Thomas's (WSA, 1900/135), and family deposits, such as Eyre-Matcham (WSA, 1369/4/18); and several stray single deeds.

Approximately 100 wills of Salisbury citizens or clergy residing in the city, and proved before 1500, survive as enrolled copies in diocesan and archdiocesan records. Of these 38, contained in Dean John Chandler's register, 1404–17 (WSA, D5/1/1), have been edited and published.[23] A further ten are recorded in a general court act book of the subdeans of Salisbury beginning in 1477 (WSA, D4/3/1). The Prerogative Court of Canterbury proved c.50 Salisbury wills before 1500 and these are now in the National Archives (in TNA, PROB 11) and available for download.

Alongside the restless dynamic of property changing hands may be set the occasional snapshots provided by listings of Salisbury inhabitants or householders for the purpose of taxation. Five such medieval lists have been published, for 1332, 1379, 1381, 1399 and 1455. The 1332 list records contributors to a tax known as a tenth, which was assessed on the movable goods of the laity; those with goods valued less than 6s. were exempt. Salisbury contributors are listed with their contributions by ward, 63 in Market ward, 14 in Meadow ward, 49 in St Martin's ward, 60 in New Street ward, 186 names in all.[24] The 1379 and 1381 lists are returns to the poll taxes of those years, the former including 1,886 names, the latter, which is fragmentary and illegible in places, includes all or part of c.300 names.[25] A list of 1,000 names, arranged by ward and with the amount of tax paid by each, has survived among the city archives. It probably relates to a tenth gathered in 1399 and referred to in the earliest city ledger.[26]

21 Fully catalogued for WSA: see Smith (1983).
22 Documents before 1500 are CC/Chap/43; 48c/1–4; 54a; 64a; 71/1; 76a–b; 83a.
23 Timmins (1984), described on p. xxxvi, and indexed, p. 240.
24 Crowley (1989), 1–3; the original is TNA E 179/196.8, rot. 1.
25 Fenwick (2005), 110–19, 123–5.
26 WSA, G23/1/236, transcribed in Chandler (1983), 262–72, and referred to in Carr (2001) 10–11 (nos. 27, 29).

The fifth listing is a rental (*Rentale Civitatis Sarum de Assisis*) dated 1455, which was compiled for Bishop Richard Beauchamp and is to be found in his *Liber Niger* (WSA, D1/1/5), ff. 155–62. It was edited and published in 1911.[27] This most useful document is arranged by ward, grouping properties by tenant and describing in considerable detail each tenement, often with location, abuttals, and the names of previous tenants. The rent is recorded and sometimes the occupation of the tenant.

POTENTIAL HISTORICAL VALUE OF THE DOMESDAY BOOKS

Henry Hatcher (1777–1846), Salisbury's 19th-century historian, described and used the Domesday Books, devoting a chapter of his history to 'a rapid view, under different heads' of their contents, 'reserving those which it may be necessary to cite at greater length, in elucidation of particular points'.[28] Thereafter the books seem to have been used seldom by historians until the 1960s. Their existence was noted by the Historical Manuscripts Commission in 1907, commenting that they were 'of considerable local interest',[29] and by Hollaender in 1951, who described them in the introduction to his list of Salisbury borough records.[30] They were then used by the Victoria County History editors to elucidate the topography of Salisbury,[31] and by Helen Bonney for the Royal Commission on Historical Monuments, whose inventory of Salisbury buildings made extensive use of them.[32]

So large an accumulation of wills and deeds, extending over so long a period, yields invaluable information about Salisbury's history, topography and citizens. Familial relationships are revealed by the parties to transactions and the beneficiaries of wills. Occupations may be given, and located to specific areas of the city. Notable topographical features and landmark buildings occur and may be described, along with the existence and nomenclature of streets and rows. The tenurial and land use history of individual locatable tenements may be traced over long periods. All in all the evidence to be extracted from the Domesday books offers a barometer

27　Nevill (1911).
28　Benson and Hatcher (1843), 87–102.
29　HMC (1907), 191–2.
30　in Rathbone (1951), 63–4, 80 (no. 145).
31　Crittall (1962), 69–90 *passim*.
32　RCHM (1980), xxvi and *passim*.

of the city's growth and prosperity, during a long period when many of its neighbours were in decline.

THE MEDIEVAL TOPOGRAPHY OF SALISBURY

The principal aim of this project is to use the evidence provided by the Domesday books and other sources to document the microtopography of medieval Salisbury. To this end a second volume, covering books 6 and 7 (1413–78), is in preparation. These will be used, in conjunction with the other sources described above, to produce a third volume, which will aim for a tenement-by-tenement account of the city's tenurial history. Until this can be achieved, and to assist users of the present volume, the accompanying maps with key (before the title page) depict and list the streets and principal landmarks of the city, using their medieval names. Like many other places, Salisbury's street names have changed and evolved. But because of the city's developed grid plan, its nomenclature is peculiarly confusing. Alternative names were sometimes used to denote the whole length of a street and specific sections of it; many modern names were not in use, and some medieval names (including High Street and Winchester Street) later referred to different streets.

METHOD OF EDITING

All the entries in the Domesday Books presented below have been translated from Latin.

The entries taken from book 6 and referring to the contents of books 1, 2, and 4, nos. **1–542** and **845–1655**, are very short and are presented as almost word-for-word translations. In some cases, for the sake of economy, successive entries involving at least one of the same parties, or by means of which the same property was conveyed, have been drawn together.

The entries in books 3 and 5, nos. **543–844** and **1656–2169**, are evidently full transcripts of original charters, deeds, wills, and other writings. They are presented below in an abbreviated form. In the case of charters and deeds, moreover, some formulaic sentences have been omitted. Such sentences include those rehearsing the nature of a quitclaim and those in which a right to keep back or claim back any part of a property was given up. Clauses by means of which one party warranted a property to another party are mentioned but not recounted. In the case of wills the order in which dispositions were recorded by the testator has not been respected. Dispositions of movable possessions have been grouped together as bequests, those of real property, including rent, as devises. The names of men who witnessed documents as officers have been given not in the list of witnesses at the foot of each document but in separate lists below the whole text. The date at which a charter or a deed was perfected, or a will approved, has been omitted from the entry of each individual document and used as a subheading for all the documents perfected or approved at that date. A note on dating appears at the head of the text.

An attempt has been made to give each forename, surname, and place name a standard and modern form and to use it throughout this edition. Forenames given in Latin have been translated wherever possible, Latin common nouns and adjectives used for descriptive or occupational surnames have been translated, and some Latin surnames have been given in their English form. In surnames the word 'de' has usually been translated to 'of', and the word 'le' has been translated to 'the' or omitted. Where the form or spelling of a place name in the original is much different from what it is now, that earlier form or spelling is noted in italics within round brackets. Unidentified place or feature names, and obscure or unmodernized surnames, are set within inverted commas. Dates, most often indicated by reference to religious festivals or saints' days, occasionally by the use of the Roman calendar, have been modernized, and regnal and all other years have been converted to the year of grace as it is now reckoned. Roman numerals, most often used for sums of money, have been converted to Arabic. Square brackets are used to enclose marginal notes and editorial interpolations. Round brackets are used to enclose alternative readings of abbreviated Latin words, to enclose Latin words which may have a meaning different from that ascribed to them by the editors, and for other purposes. Some words which, or the meaning of which, are not clear to the editors are printed, partially or fully, in italics. Where there is a lacuna in an edition of an entry it is denoted by three full points and indicates that a word or words in the original cannot be read.

Abbreviations
BL: British Library
HMC: Historical Manuscripts Commission
RCHM: Royal Commission on Historical Monuments (England)

SCA: Salisbury Cathedral Archives
TNA: The National Archives
WSA: Wiltshire & Swindon Archives

Bibliography

Allen, D. (ed.), *Ipswich Borough Records, 1255–1835*, Suffolk Records Society 43 (2000).
Benson, R. and Hatcher, H. *Old and New Sarum, or Salisbury* (History of Modern Wiltshire, vol. 6, 1843).
Carr, D.R. (ed.), *The First General Entry Book of the City of Salisbury.*
Chandler, J., *Endless Street: a history of Salisbury and its people* (Hobnob Press, 1983).
Crittall, Elizabeth (ed.), *A History of Wiltshire*, vol. 6 (Victoria County History of Wiltshire, 1962).
Crowley, D.A. (ed.), *The Wiltshire tax list of 1332* (Wiltshire Record Soc. vol. 45, 1989).
Davies, J. S. (ed.), *The Tropenell Cartulary*, vol. 1 (Devizes, WANHS, 1908).
Fenwick, Carolyn C. (ed.), *The Poll Taxes of 1377, 1379 and 1381, pt. 3: Wiltshire–Yorkshire* (British Academy, Records of Social and Economic History, n.s. 37, 2005.
HMC, *Report on Manuscripts in Various Collections*, vol. 4 (HMSO, 1907).
Hobbs, S. and Chandler, J., 'The Salisbury Domesday Books: a note', *Sarum Chronicle* 12 (2012), 81–6 .
Holton-Krayenbuhl, Anne, *The Topography of Medieval Ely* (Cambridgeshire Records Soc, 20, 2011).
Horrox, Rosemary (ed.), *Selected Rentals and Accounts of Medieval Hull, 1293–1528* (Yorkshire Archaeological Soc, Record Series 141, 1983).
Jones, W.H. and Macray, W. D. (eds.), *Charters and Documents illustrating the History of . . . Salisbury* (Rolls Series, 1891).
Keene, D., *Survey of medieval Winchester*, 2 parts, Winchester Studies 2 (Oxford: Clarendon Press, 1985).
Leech, R. H., *The Topography of Medieval and Early Modern Bristol*, parts 1 and 2 (Bristol Record Soc. 48 (1997), 52 (2000)).
Martin, G.H., 'The registration of deeds of title in the medieval borough' in D.A. Bullough and R.L. Storey (ed.), *The Study of Medieval Records: essays in honour of Kathleen Major* (Oxford, Clarendon Press, 1971), 151–73.
Mayo, C.H. (ed.), *Municipal records of the borough of Dorchester* (1908).
Morgan, R. R., *Chichester: a documentary history* (Phillimore, 1992).
Nevill, E.R., 'Salisbury in 1455', *Wilts. Arch & Nat Hist. Mag.* 37 (1911), 66–91.
Raine, Angelo, *Medieval York: a topographical survey based on original sources* (John Murray, 1955).
Rathbone, M.G. (ed.), *List of Wiltshire Borough Records earlier in date than 1836* (WA&NHS Records Branch 5, for 1949 (1951)).

RCHM, *Ancient and Historical Monuments in the City of Salisbury*, vol. 1 (HMSO, 1980).

Rhodes, J. (ed.), *Terrier of Llanthony Priory's Houses and Lands in Gloucester, 1443* (Glos Record Series, 2016).

Salter, H.E., *Survey of Oxford*, 2 vols. ed W.A. Pantin and W.T. Mitchell), Oxford Historical Soc., n.s. 14 (1960) and 20 (1969).

Smith, W. 'A medieval archive from Trinity Hospital, Salisbury', *Archives*, 16. No. 69 (1983), 39–46.

Street, Fanny, 'The Relations of the Bishops and Citizens of Salisbury (New Sarum) between 1225 and 1612', *Wilts. Arch & Nat Hist. Mag.* 39 (1916), 185–257, 319–67.

Timmins, T.C.B. (ed.), *The Register of John Chandler, Dean of Salisbury, 1404–17* (Wiltshire Record Soc. vol. 39, 1984).

Urry, W., *Canterbury under the Angevin kings* (London: Athlone Press, 1967).

Veale, E.W.W. (ed.), *The Great Red Book of* Bristol, 5 vols, Bristol Record Soc, 2, 4, 8, 16, 18 (1931–53).

SALISBURY DOMESDAY BOOKS

A calendar of all the charters, wills, and other memoranda entered in the books which, in the city of Salisbury, we call Domesday, from the year 1317–18

A note on dating
Each of the charters, deeds, wills, and other writings copied into Domesday Books 3 and 5, almost without exception, includes the date on which it was perfected and, in the case of the wills, the date on which it was proved in front of an ecclesiastical authority and the date on which it was approved in the city court. The documents were not copied into the books in the order of the dates which they bear and, in the text below, the edited versions of them have been placed in chronological order by the editors. Most of the charters and deeds were dated to a day on which the city court met and were presumably witnessed at court. For the sake of conformity the wills are entered in the chronological sequence according to the day on which they too came before the court. In a few cases the editors have suspected that a date was copied erroneously, and such suspicions have been recorded in the text below.
  The contents of Domesday Books 1–5, and of the first half of book 6, are listed in book 6. The contents of books 1, 2, and 4 are known only from that list, and an edited version of each entry in it relating to a document supposed to have been copied into those three books is given below. None of the entries in the list is individually or fully dated and, because the order of the entries in the list relating to the documents recorded in books 3 and 5 corresponds to the order of the entries in those books, which is known to be unchronological, it seems certain that the entries in the list relating to books 1, 2, and 4 are likewise out of chronological order. In the list of contents, however, dates expressed as regnal years are entered at the tops, or in the margins, of many pages and it can be assumed, from the evidence of books 3 and 5, that most of the documents, although not in chronological order, were perfected in the years indicated by those entries. For that reason the regnal years entered in the list of contents have been given as subheadings in the text below, and the documents which seem to have been ascribed to those years in the list have been entered under those subheadings in the text.
  All, however, is not so simple. In the list of contents regnal years are sometimes intruded out of order, in many cases and for reasons which are obscure the words *eodem anno* were written in the margin beside particular entries, and it was often difficult for the editors to feel confident when assigning an entry, or a succession of entries, to a particular regnal year. Moreover, books 3 and 5 show that some documents entered under one regnal year in the list of contents were in fact dated to another year long before or long after that one. Two notes in the

list of contents suggest how that might have happened. It was recorded that, at the request of John Upton, 24 documents, dating from 1330 or earlier to 1357 or later, were entered as a group in book 2 regardless of chronological order and that six folios in that book were left blank for more of his documents to be entered at his convenience. It was similarly recorded that three other men asked for their records to be entered and that many empty pages were left for them in book 2.

In short, the reader may rely on the dates given for the documents copied into Domesday Books 3 and 5. In respect of books 1, 2, and 4, however, the reader is advised that, in the text below, the documents are probably not listed in chronological order and that, although many documents may have been perfected in the years indicated by the subheadings, it is almost certain that many others were not

BOOK 1
[in the form of a list of contents taken from book 6: WSA G 23/1/214]

20 November 1281 x 7 July 1307
1 A charter of William Montagu and his wife Alice perfected for the master William of Crichel concerning a tenement in the high street

20 November 1304 x 19 November 1305
2 A deed of Emme, the relict of John of 'Hoydon', perfected for the master William of Crichel concerning a tenement and rent of 1 mark

8 July 1313 x 7 July 1314
3 A deed of William Crichel, a clerk, perfected for John Crichel concerning a tenement in the high street

8 July 1316 x 7 July 1317
4 The will of William Pinnock, which includes several tenements. A copy of the will is contained and stitched in the first quire.
5 A writ *ex gravi querela* which John, a son of William Pinnock, brought against John Codford and William Codford concerning a tenement in Salisbury. There follows a record of the plea until it ended in a fine.
6 The will of Alice, the wife of William Scot, dyer, which includes several tenements

8 July 1317 x 7 July 1318
7 A charter of Roger Grew perfected for John Baldry concerning a part of a tenement in St. Martin's Street
8 The will of William Russell, formerly a citizen and merchant of Salisbury, which includes several tenements
9–10 Two writings perfected for Henry of Stoke and his wife Alice concerning a tenement on the way to St. Martin's church: a charter of Isabel, the relict of Henry Ackerman, who held the tenement as dower, and a release of Guy, a son

of Henry Ackerman

11 A charter of Thomas Southmere, of Frome, perfected for Peter of Collingbourne concerning a rent of 6s. 2d. issuing from a tenement in Winchester Street

12 A charter of Alice, the relict of John at the work, of Wootton, and another (*or* others), executors of John, perfected for John White ... [*word(s) illegble*] concerning a corner tenement in Carter Street

13 A release of William Brightwhite, a son of Geoffrey Brightwhite, perfected for Adam of Newnham, a chaplain, concerning a rent of 4s. issuing from a tenement in Minster Street

14 Note: the custom that a wife, after the death of her husband, should hold for her life as dower that of her husband's tenements in which he and she dwelt on the day of his death, notwithstanding any devise. If they did not live in the city the wife should have the best tenement of which her husband died seised, to be held likewise. If the husband held no tenement, but held rent, the wife should hold the rent of one tenement, as is well known. If the husband alienated all his tenements and rent in his lifetime the wife should have nothing of them.

15 ... [*nearly all illegible*] ... against Martin ... and his wife Parnel

16 A deed of release of Hugh 'Chouch' perfected for Edith, the relict of John of Knoyle, concerning a rent of 2 marks, two pairs of hose, and two pairs of shoes issuing from a tenement in Minster Street

17 A charter of Nicholas Aslin perfected for Roger Foliot, of Buckland, concerning a shop opposite the butchers' stalls

18 A charter of William of Berwick perfected for Robert Gould and his wife Alice concerning a piece of land in Gigant Street

19 The will of John Palmer, which includes several tenements

20 A charter of John Walrond and another (*or* others), executors of John Palmer, perfected for John Noble and his wife Alice concerning a corner tenement in Wineman Street and Brown Street

21 Note: the custom is proclaimed that the common seal should be affixed to charters. If anyone does not ... [*MS. illegible*] he is barred from an action.

22 The will of Edward of Woodford, which includes a single tenement

23 A charter of a younger John Callow perfected for William Callow and his wife Isabel concerning a shop in Minster Street

24–5 Two charters perfected for Constance, the relict of Peter of Notley: one of Alice, the relict of Henry Baldry, and another (*or* others), executors of Henry, concerning a tenement in Brown Street, and one of Alice concerning a tenement in Chipper Street and rent of 32s. issuing from various tenements

26 A charter of John of Chirton, dubber, perfected for Thomas Wise and his wife Margery concerning a tenement in Minster Street

27 A release of Richard of Ludgershall, a son of R of Ludgershall, perfected for John Baldry concerning a rent of 7s. 6d. issuing from a tenement in St. Martin's Street

28 A deed of Robert Cheese perfected for Adam Cole and his wife Parnel concerning a tenement (*or* tenements) in Winchester Street and Brown Street [?Cheese Corner]

8 July 1318 x 7 July 1319
70 A charter of Adam of Newnham, a chaplain, perfected for the lord William Paviour, a vicar of the cathedral church, concerning a tenement in Minster Street
71 A plea of land, by means of a writ *de recto*, between Roger Greenleaf and his wife Joan, plaintiffs, and Roger [?*rectius* Robert: *cf.* **67, 90**], a son of William May, in front of the bailiff
72 A charter of Henry of Nursling, called Spicer, perfected for the lord William of Geddington, the rector of Cholderton, concerning a tenement in Brown Street, leading from the canons' close towards St. Martin's church, on a corner
73 The will of William Callow, which includes several tenements
74 A charter of Edith, the relict of William Russell, perfected for Adam of Bridgehampton concerning a rent of 5s. issuing from a tenement in Winchester Street
75 A charter of the lord William Paviour, a vicar of the cathedral church, perfected for Adam Newnham, a chaplain, concerning a tenement in Minster Street
76 The will of Walter of Heytesbury, which includes a tenement beside the grammar school, and a shop
77 A charter of John of Ford and his wife Joan perfected for John of Knighton concerning a tenement in Minster Street towards the bar
78 A charter of William Paviour, a vicar of the cathedral church, perfected for John Springham and his wife Agnes concerning a tenement in Gigant Street
79 The will of Ralph Rise, which includes several tenements devised both to his wife and to his children
80 A charter of John of Halwell perfected for Andrew the hatter and his wife Alice, concerning a tenement in the high street called Carter Street, which includes rent of 20s. a year from Robert of Knoyle
81 The will of Richard of Langford, which includes rent and several tenements [devised] both to his wife and to his children
82 A charter of John Basing perfected for Henry at the weald and his wife Alice concerning a tenement in Freren Street beside a trench
83 The will of William of Upavon, called Cutler, a chaplain
84 The will of Gunhild, the wife of Nicholas of Hinton, which includes 2s. a year to celebrate mass in St. Martin's church on the day of [her] anniversary
85 A charter of Edith, the relict of Robert Jukes, called Brewer, perfected for Henry Bristwin concerning a tenement, beyond the bar, opposite the bishop of Salisbury's land held in villeinage
86 A charter of Adam Sidelinch perfected for Nicholas of Wylye, his wife Isabel, and their son John concerning a tenement in New Street
87 The will of Robert Silvain, called Inways, which includes several tenements and rent; provided that the seisin of six shops in Winchester Street was not released because, after he made the will, he gave those shops to Robert of Knoyle
88 A deed of Thomas at the hope, of Portbury, perfected for Robert of Ann, his wife Christine, and their daughter Gillian concerning a tenement in Minster Street for a term of life, for a rent to be paid to him yearly and for meeting other

charges and rent

89 A charter of Richard of Ludgershall perfected for Henry of Melksham concerning a tenement on the south side of St. Thomas's church in Minster Street

90 The fine of a plea determined between Roger Greenleaf and his wife Joan, and Robert, the son of William May, by means of a writ *de recto*

91 A charter of Edith, the relict of William Russell, perfected for Robert of Knoyle concerning a tenement in Culver Street, three cottages in that street, and a rent of 5*s*. issuing from a tenement in Winchester Street

92 A charter of Reynold Tidworth perfected for John Farthing and his wife Alice concerning a tenement in Butcher Row

93 The record, on an attached schedule, as to how the master Walter Harvey and other canons of Salisbury, on behalf of the dean and chapter, made a complaint in the court concerning the withdrawal of a rent of 10*s*. a year accruing to them from Walter of Hampton's tenement in New Street, which was formerly William Starr's, and how of his own accord Walter [of Hampton] confessed himself the payer of that rent. Afterwards Reynold of Tidworth released his right or claim to it to the dean and chapter.

94 The will of Reynold of Tidworth, which includes various tenements and rent devised in various ways to various people; with an inventory of them

95 A charter of Robert of Knoyle perfected for Roger Foliot, of Buckland, and his wife Edith concerning various tenements in the city

96 A charter of William Keed perfected for Walter of Melbury and his wife Agnes concerning a tenement between New Street on the north side and [St. Martin's] street, leading from the east gate of the Close towards St. Martin's church, on the south side, and how much there in length and width

97 A charter of Richard of Tidworth and another (*or* others), executors of Reynold of Tidworth, perfected for Henry of Figheldean, a citizen of the city, and the lord Henry of Loddington, a chaplain, concerning several various tenements and rent

98 The will of a younger John Whitefoot, which includes various tenements devised to his wife and children

99 A charter of Robert Poulter perfected for Paul of Thatcham concerning a corner tenement opposite the butchers' stalls, and including the charge of various rents

100 A charter of Philip Aubin perfected for Henry Bury concerning a tenement called Bull Hall in Winchester Street

101 The will of Nicholas Stratford, which includes several tenements and rent devised to his wife and others in various ways

102–3 Two charters concerning the halves of a tenement opposite the market place where grains are sold: one of Marion Sprot perfected for John of Langford, and one of John perfected for Hugh of Langford and his wife Marion

104 A charter of Richard Sprot and Roger Tankard, executors of William Sprot, perfected for Hugh Langford concerning a tenement in Nuggeston

105 A charter of John Spicer and his wife Maud perfected for Richard Sealer and his wife Alice concerning a tenement in New Street, paying a rent of 10*s*. a year to the fabric of the cathedral church

106–7 Two writings concerning a tenement in Minster Street: a deed of Thomas at the hope, of Portbury, perfected for Robert of Ann and others for a term of life, and a charter of Richard of Tidworth perfected for Robert and his wife Christine
108 A deed of Roger of Wallop perfected for his daughter Iseult concerning a house, with a room, in Wineman Street
109 A charter of Robert of Lavington perfected for John of Lyneham and Catherine, a daughter in marriage, concerning a tenement in the high street, on a corner
110 A charter of *Galiena*, the relict of Stephen of Harpenden, perfected for Thomas Harpenden and his wife Christine concerning a shop in Minster Street and a portion of land, beyond the bar, on the way to the castle
111 A charter of Thomas Montagu perfected for Margery and Emme, daughters of Robert Ayloff, concerning a cellar in New Street for his life
112 A charter of John Hatter, a chaplain, perfected for William Berwick, concerning a rent of 10*s*. issuing from a tenement in the high street
113 A charter of William Hatter and his wife Edith perfected for William of Berwick and his wife Christine concerning a tenement in Carter Street and a rent of 8*s*. a year, with the reversion of a house within the tenement
114–15 Two writings of John Cheese concerning a messuage in Winchester Street: a quitclaim perfected for Adam Cole and his wife Parnel, and a ratification of that deed perfected for Adam
116 A charter of Stephen Crier and John Botwell, a chaplain, perfected for Stephen Bold concerning a tenement in Butcher Row opposite the butchers' stalls
117 A charter of Ellen Vellard perfected for Richard Tidworth concerning rent of 8*s*. issuing from various tenements
118 A charter of William Santel perfected for Peter Osborne concerning a rent of 2*s*. issuing from two cottages and a yard in Chipper Street
119 The will of Richard of Hawkchurch, which includes a single tenement
120 The will of William Dorchester, which includes a tenement in New Street devised to his wife
121 A charter of Philip Aubin and his wife Alice perfected for William Goldrom and his wife Isabel concerning a tenement in New Street
122 A charter of John Bishop perfected for Roger Cole, of Lymington, and his wife Joan concerning a tenement in the market [place]

8 July 1319 x 7 July 1320
123 A charter of Amice, a daughter of William Cheese, perfected for John Thornhill concerning a tenement in New Street
124 A charter of William of Sutton, a vicar of Salisbury, perfected for Ingram at the brook and his wife Alice concerning a tenement in Winchester Street
125 A charter of Richard Magg and his wife Edith perfected for Robert of Laverstock concerning a rent of 10*s*. issuing from a tenement in Brown Street
126 A writ *de recto* of Richard of Barford which he brought against William

Keynes, with the record and process of it
127 The will of John of Ford, which includes two tenements
128 A charter of John Dolling and his wife Christine perfected for Robert Poulter concerning a piece of land in Brown Street
129 A charter of William Santel perfected for John Knighton concerning a tenement in Gigant Street
130 A writ *de recto*, with the record, which Thomas Harpenden brought against John Noble, of Winterbourne
131 The will of John of Langford, linendraper, which includes two tenements
132–3 Two charters of Thomas of Stratford perfected for Roger of Littleton: one concerning a rent of 14*s*. issuing from a tenement in Wineman Street, and one concerning a rent of 11*s*. issuing from a tenement in Winchester Street
134 A charter of an executor (*or* executors) of John Britford perfected for Robert Baldry concerning a rent of 15*s*. issuing from a tenement in Winchester Street
135 A charter of William Langford, a vicar of the cathedral church, perfected for Richard Breamore concerning a tenement in Culver Street
136 A charter of Robert Sibley, of Homanton, perfected for William Ellis concerning a tenement in New Street

8 July 1320 x 7 July 1321
137 An accusation made in front of the keeper of the king's market by Edith Champness in that year against William Berwick concerning a certain measure in his time in office as mayor. The end of the matter [was] that she, the complainant, should undergo the judgement of the pillory for a false measure.
138 The will of Henry at the bar, a scribe, which includes a tenement from which [is paid] 4*s*. a year to the vicars of Salisbury and 12*d*. to the chief lord
139 The will of John of Alton, which includes the devise of a meadow towards St. Nicholas's hospital
140 A charter of William Keynes and his wife Joan perfected for Parnel, a daughter of William of Eling, concerning a meadow on the way to Ayleswade bridge
141 The will of Lambert of Roscombe, which includes several tenements, made between 8 July 1312 and 7 July 1313

8 July 1321 x 7 July 1322
142 A quitclaim of John, a son of Robert Cheese, perfected for Adam Cole concerning rent of 10 marks and two shops in the high street
143 A writ *ex gravi querela* which John, a son of Richard Pinnock, brought against Richard of Ludgershall concerning two messuages, with the great record and process of that writ
144 Letters of attorney perfected for William Dash by William of Nottingham, the general minister of the order of Franciscans, to sell a tenement which William of Harrowden appointed to those friars in Mead ward
145 The will of John of Bedwyn
146 The will of John of Thornhill, which includes several tenements

8 July 1322 x 7 July 1323
147 A writ *de iudiciale* returned between Henry Bury and John Chantrell
148 The will of Robert Leadbeater, which includes a tenement
149 A charter of Robert Warin, a cook, and his wife Gillian perfected for William of Moredon concerning a tenement in New Street
150 The will of John of Homington, which includes a tenement
151 The will of Lucy Ironmonger, which includes rent and a shop
152 The will of Maud Dovedale, which includes a shop in Minster Street
153 The will of William Pitt, a fisherman, which includes several tenements
154 The will of Isabel, the wife [?*rectius* relict: cf. **59**] of Richard of Christchurch, which includes a single tenement
155 The will of Roger Newman, which includes two tenements
156 The will of Christine, the wife of Robert of Lavington, which includes a tenement
157 The will of Edith Brewer, which includes a tenement
158 The will of Roger of Wight, which includes a tenement
159 A charter of Robert Warin, a cook, and his wife Gillian perfected for William of Moredon concerning a tenement in New Street
160 A charter of Philip Aubin and his wife Alice perfected for Henry Bury concerning a cellar, with a sollar, in Winchester Street
161 There is included a surrender, in court, of 2 acres beyond the bar perfected by Thomas of Harpenden and his wife Christine to the use of Thomas Long and his wife Joan.
162 Also concerning another 2 acres there
163 There is also included a final agreement in the bishop's court, by means of a record sent across from the king's court, between Robert Woodford, plaintiff, and John of Winterbourne and his wife Alice deforciants, concerning a messuage in Salisbury.
164 The will of William Santel, which includes a tenement in Castle Street and a croft opposite the graveyard of St. Edmund's church
165 The will of William of Durrington, which includes a single tenement in St. Martin's Street
166 A charter of Clarice of Wylye perfected for John Knighton concerning rent of 22*s.* issuing from two tenements in the city
167 The will of John of Thornhill, which includes two tenements
168 The will of Robert Fromand, the rector of St. Thomas's church

8 July 1324 x 7 July 1325
169–70 Two charters perfected for Robert of Windsor and his wife Agnes: one of Roger of Littleton concerning rent of 14*s.* issuing from various tenements, and one of John of Nugg concerning a tenement in Chipper Lane
171 The will of Thomas of Berden, which includes fixed rent devised to certain persons to be appropriated, if possible, for an anniversary mass; if not to be sold
172 The will of Robert Marshall, which includes rent of 100*s.* from a tenement (*or* tenements) in Minster Street

8 July 1325 x 7 July 1326
173 The will of Henry of Melksham, which includes several tenements, rent, and shops
174 The will of William of Kilmeston, which includes several tenements, rent, shops, and cottages
175 A charter of William Bishop and his wife Edith perfected for Roger Looseway concerning a tenement in New Street
176 The will of Reynold of Milbourne, which includes several tenements, shops, cottages, and rent devised in various ways
177 A writ *de dote*, with the record and process, which Cecily, the relict of John Cheese, brought against Adam Cole and Stephen Cheese concerning a tenement in Salisbury. Because she held another tenement by a devise of her husband she was excluded from her dower, as it appears.
178 The will of John of Iwerne, which includes two tenements
179 The will of John Cheese, which includes Cheese Corner, with a cellar (*or* cellars) and a shop (*or* shops)
180 The will of Robert Poulter, which includes various tenements and rent
181 The will of John Cupping, which includes a single tenement
182 The will of Isabel of Okehampton, which includes several tenements and rent
183 The will of William of Coleshill, the rector of Kington, which includes a tenement
184 The will of Simon of Oxford, which includes several tenements and rent
185 The will of Robert of Windsor, which includes several tenements and rent
186 The will of Thomas Florentine, which includes several tenements and rent
187 The will of Robert Gould, which includes various tenements
188 The will of William Florentine, which includes various tenements. Other tenements and rent are to be appropriated to a religious house for an anniversary mass to be held, if possible.
189 The will of Peter of Ringwood, which includes a single tenement
190 The will of John Bishop, which includes various tenements, cottages, rent, and meadow
191 The will of Richard Sturmy, which includes two tenements
192 The will of Richard Swift, of Croucheston, which includes various tenements
193 The will of Richard of Lavington, which includes several tenements
194 The will of John Coppiner, which includes several tenements
195 The will of Richard Breamore, which includes several tenements
196 The will of John Gomeldon, which includes a tenement
197 The will of William Scot, a dyer, which includes several tenements and various acres in the field of Old Sarum
198 The will of Gilbert Hubert, which includes a single tenement
199 The will of Joan, the wife of Ellis of Wendover, which includes a tenement
200 The will of Margaret, the wife of Richard Warrener, which includes several tenements
201 The will of Roger Culpriest, which includes several tenements

202 The will of Henry of Winterslow, which includes several tenements
203 The will of Martin Tenterer, which includes the charge of a candle maintained in the cathedral church and several other things bequeathed to the church, and to the chaplains of the college, of St. Edmund
204 A writ *ex gravi querela*, with the record and process, which Sibyl, a daughter of Thomas Martin, brought against John Nugg
205 The will of Adam Brazier, called Bridgehampton, which includes several tenements
206 A writ of the king directed to the mayor and aldermen of London for liberties to be allowed to the city of Salisbury concerning the customs of murage and pannage, on the strength of which it is settled that it was granted that there the citizens of Salisbury were to be quit
207 The will of Nicholas Dyer, glover, which includes a single tenement
208 The will of Alice Shendlove, which includes a tenement
209 The will of Philip Aubin, which includes several tenements, rent, and a shop (*or* shops)
210 A charter of John Everard, his wife Agnes, and others perfected for Robert Russell concerning a tenement in Minster Street

25 January 1327 x 21 June 1377
211 The will of Robert of Winterbourne, which includes several tenements and rent
212 The will of Ralph Ive, which includes a chief tenement
213 The will of Nicholas Plubel, which includes several tenements

25 January 1330 x 24 January 1331
214–15 Two charters perfected for John Knighton: one of William Monk concerning a tenement in Minster Street beyond the bar, and one of Peter Long and his wife Aubrey concerning a corner tenement in Winchester Street and Gigant Street
216 The will of William Brickway, which includes a tenement
217 Letters of attorney for a compact to be made between Southampton and Salisbury in which it is contained that the liberty formerly granted is to be preserved
218 The will of Alice Gould, which includes several tenements
219 The will of Ralph Scriven, which includes a tenement
220 The will of Edith, the wife of Thomas Skinner, which includes a tenement
221 The will of William of Winchester, a dyer, which includes several tenements and rent
222 The will of Robert of Ann, which includes several tenements and rent
223 A writ *de cui in vita*, with the record and process, which Alice, the relict of Philip Aubin, brought against Henry Bury concerning a tenement in Salisbury
224 There is contained in that volume [an entry] concerning the vacancy of the bishopric of Salisbury on account of the death of Roger Martival, and how the citizens were by right to be submissive to the dean and chapter without further

coercion.

225 A charter of Peter Long perfected for John of Knighton concerning a corner tenement in Gigant Street and Winchester Street

226 The will of Henry Fleming, which includes a tenement

227 The will of Agnes, the wife of John of Winterbourne, a clerk, which includes two tenements

228 The will of Richard of Horsted, which includes rent of 13*s*. 4*d*.

229 The will of Richard Blick, which includes various tenements, rent, and gardens

230 The will of William Saucer, which includes several tenements and rent

231 A charter of Denise, the relict of William Saucer, and another (*or* others), executors of William, perfected for John of Knighton concerning a tenement in Minster Street

232 The will of William Rayner, which includes a tenement

233 A quitclaim of John Smith, of Compton Chamberlayne, and his wife Maud perfected for William of Berwick concerning all the tenements which were those of Michael of Barnwell and Robert of Barnwell, of Salisbury

234 A quitclaim of Simon Chelworth and his wife Alice perfected for Thomas of Haydor and his wife Catherine concerning a tenement in Culver Street

235 The will of Walter Harvey, the archdeacon, and a canon, of Salisbury, which includes tenements in the Close and meadow

236 A charter of Nicholas of 'Werton' and his wife Alice perfected for Henry Russell concerning a tenement in Minster Street

237 The record and process of an agreement reached in the presence of the bailiffs and the mayor concerning dower agreed between Amice, a daughter of Hugh Buddle, and John London

238 A writ *de precipe*, with the record and process, [in a cause heard] in front of the king's justices between William, a son of John Chipper, the demandant, and Roger Fowle and his wife Christine concerning a messuage in Salisbury

25 January 1331 × 24 January 1332

239 A charter of Nicholas of Potterne, a chaplain, perfected for Ralph Stoville and his wife Parnel concerning a tenement in St. Martin's Street; also in that charter the charge of a rent of 8*s*. a year to the vicars of the cathedral church

240 A deed of Laurence of Ford and his wife Isabel perfected for Peter of Collingbourne concerning a shop at the butchers' stalls

241 John Legat and his wife Isabel, at a court in front of the mayor and the bailiff, surrendered a messuage towards St. Edmund's church to the use of Roger Looseway.

242 At a court Robert Boyce and his wife Margery surrendered into the hand of the bishop a tenement in St. Martin's Street to the use of William 'Lytebrouth', called Limeburner, and his wife Agnes.

243 At a court John Sherborne, cook, and his wife Edith surrendered into the hand of the lord [bishop] a tenement in Carter Street to the use of Edward Knoyle.

244 The order of fees concerning fines levied in the bishop's court
245 A writ *de dote*, with the record and process, which Gillian, the relict of John Dean, brought against Peter Collingbourne in front of the bailiff
246 The will of Henry of Christchurch, which includes several tenements
247 A writ *conventione*, with the record and process, which Henry Hussey, a smith, his wife Joan, and their daughter Alice brought against Stephen Glendy and his wife Alice concerning a messuage; determined in front of the bailiff and the mayor
248 The will of John Carpenter, a baker, which includes several tenements
249 The will of Nicholas of Hinton, which includes a tenement
250 At a court Gilbert of Bridgehampton brought a deed of quitclaim perfected for him by John, a son of Robert Belter, concerning a tenement in New Street.
251 At a court John, a son of Robert Belter, brought forth a deed of quitclaim perfected for him by Henry Looseway concerning a tenement in New Street.
252 The will of Paul of Thatcham, which includes several tenements
253 The will of Nicholas of Wylye, which includes several tenements
254 The will of Gillian of Ann, which includes several tenements, rent, and reversions
255 A charter of William Ironmonger perfected for Henry Bury concerning the reversion of a tenement opposite the market place where wheelwrights wait
256 The will of Walter of Hampton, a baker, which includes various [?tenements]
257 The will of John of Stratford, which includes two tenements
258 The will of Roger Cole, which includes several tenements
259 The will of Walter Bold, which includes various tenements and shops
260 The will of Adam of Hampton, a skinner, which includes several tenements
261 A writ *ex gravi querela,* with the record and process, which John, a son of John of Wells, brought against William of Abbotsbury, his wife Alice, and others concerning a tenement in Salisbury
262 At a court Gillian, the wife [?relict] of Thomas of Barford, surrendered into the hand of the lord [bishop] a tenement in Minster Street to the use of Ellis Preece, a baker.

25 January 1332 x 24 January 1336
263 The will of Alice, the wife of William of Abbotsbury, which includes various tenements and rent
264 A quitclaim of Simon, a son of Simon of Oxford, perfected for William of Abbotsbury concerning rent of 40s. from various tenements
265 The will of Geoffrey Baldry, which includes a tenement (*or* tenements) and a yard (*or* yards)
266 The will of John FitzPain, which includes several tenements, rent, and a yard (*or* yards)
267 The will of Richard of Studley, which includes several tenements and rent
268 The will of Alexander Parchment, which includes a tenement
269 A writ *de precipe*, with the record and process, which Roger, a son of John Cole, brought against John Stalbridge and his wife Joan in front of the bailiff;

removed from the Common Bench
270 The will of Edith, a daughter of Thomas Barford, which includes a tenement
271 The will of William Cole, which includes a tenement
272 The will of John Stickbeard, which includes a tenement and a barn
273 The will of Roger Upwell, which includes several tenements and shops
274 A writ *de precipe dum infra etatem*, with the record and process, which William Randolph and his wife Lucy brought against Isabel, the relict of Nicholas of Wylye; determined in front of the bailiff
275 The will of John Nugg, which includes several tenements, shops, and rent
276 The will of John of Knighton, which includes several tenements, shops, and rent
277 A writ *de precipe*, with the record and process, which John Dash brought against John Springham and his wife Agnes in front of the bailiff
278 The record concerning the king's pardon perfected for Henry Bury and several others, citizens of Salisbury, on a recognizance perfected in the court of the Exchequer
279 A writ in an assize of novel disseisin, with the record and process, which John Selwood brought against William Whitehorn and others in front of the bailiff
280 The will of John Harnham, which includes a tenement
281 The will of William Holbury, which includes a tenement
282 A writ *ex gravi querela*, with the record and process in front of the bailiff, which John, a son of Robert of Winterbourne, brought against Ralph at the cross and his wife Joan concerning a messuage in Salisbury
283 A writ *de precipe*, which he might return, with the record and process, which John Spicer, of Shaftesbury, brought against John Steed and his wife Margery in front of the bailiff
284 The will of Thomas of Britford, which includes several tenements

25 January 1334 x 24 January 1335
285 A charter of Roger Upwell and his wife Parnel perfected for John of Winterbourne, tanner, and his wife Joan concerning a tenement in New Street

25 January 1338 x 24 January 1339
286 The will of Edith, a daughter of William of Winchester, which includes a tenement
287 The will of John Pierce, which includes a tenement
288 The will of Mabel Durnford, the relict of John Langford, tucker
289 The will of Roger Littlefish, which includes a tenement
290 The will of Henry Winterslow, which includes several tenements
291 The will of John Cupping, which includes a tenement
292 The will of Richard Lavington, which includes several tenements
293 The will of William of Winchester, a dyer, which includes a tenement and several rents
294 The will of Robert Gould, which includes various tenements and racks
295 The will of Alice, the wife of Walter Skutt, which includes several tenements

296 The will of Henry Bunt, which includes several tenements, rent, and a third tenement
297 The will of Nicholas Taunton, a baker, which includes a tenement in Freren Street

25 January 1339 x 24 January 1340
298 The will of John of Tyringham, which includes various rent
299 The will of Alice, the relict of William of Winchester, [which includes] a tenement in Castle Street
300 The will of Alice, the relict of John at the bar, which includes various tenements
301 The will of Roger Mutton, which includes several tenements, rent, and cottages in various streets
302 The will of Agnes, the wife of Nicholas of Breamore, which includes a tenement in Culver Street
303 The will of Hugh of Langford, linendraper, which includes several tenements and rent in various streets
304 The will of William Ellis, which includes several [tenements] and rent
305 The will of John Sorrel, which includes two tenements, one opposite the market place and one in Minster Street
306 The will of Philip Pratt, which includes various tenements, rent, and yards
307 The will of Gilbert Dubber, which includes several tenements and cottages
308 The will of Nicholas Aslin, which includes various tenements and rent
309 The will of John Chandler, which includes a tenement and rent
310 The will of John Whitton, which includes two tenements, one in Gigant Street and one in Winchester Street
311 The will of William Berwick, which includes several tenements and rent
312 The will of Reynold of Milbourne, which includes several tenements and rent
313 The will of Robert of Knoyle, which includes two tenements, one in Carter Street and one in Culver Street
314 The will of Richard Baldry, which includes two tenements in New Street
315 The will of Robert Baldry, which includes several tenements, rent, shops, and cottages
316 A writ of the king directed to the sheriff, the mayor, the aldermen, and the collectors of the murage, pannage, and passage of London concerning the liberty to be allowed to the city of Salisbury
317 There follows concerning a record that the citizens of Salisbury might be immune from chiminage by an allowance of the justice of the forest in his eyre.

BOOK 2
[in the form of a list of contents taken from book 6: WSA G 23/1/214]

In the second book and quire various years, in respect of the enrolments, are not consecutive but are interposed.

25 January 1347 x 24 January 1348
318 A charter of Thomas Marlborough perfected for John Powell concerning a shop in a street where iron is sold
319–21 Three releases perfected for John Clark, of Handley: one of John, a son of Nicholas of Nunton, concerning a corner tenement in New Street which extends as far as Gigant Street, one of Adam, another son of Nicholas, concerning all the land and tenements in the city which descended to him on his father's death, and one of Alice, a daughter of Nicholas, concerning the right to a tenement in New Street

25 January 1348 x 24 January 1349
322 The will of Thomas Thurstan, which includes several tenements
323 The will of Margaret, the wife of John Powell

25 January 1349 x 24 January 1350
324–6 Three charters concerning a messuage, with a yard (*or* yards), in Scots Lane: one of Thomas Erlestoke, a chaplain, perfected for Hugh Boney, one of John Prentice and Catherine, a daughter of William of Moredon, executors of Thomas Thurstan, perfected for Hugh, and one of Hugh perfected for Richard Ryborough

25 January 1350 x 24 January 1351
327 A charter of Roger Edmond, a chaplain, and John Dewey, executors of John Hagbourne, perfected for Richard Ryborough concerning a tenement in Minster Street
328 A charter of Thomas Glendy, of Stratford, perfected for John Salisbury, a clerk, a son of John Nugg, concerning a tenement in Minster Street
329 A charter of John of Woodford, Henry Russell, and others, executors of Robert of Woodford, perfected for the lords Walter Beek and Thomas Erlestoke concerning a messuage and a corner tenement in Wineman Street and Brown Street
330 A charter of the lords Walter Beek and Thomas Erlestoke perfected for John Woodford and his wife Agnes concerning the corner tenement [*as in* **329**]
331–2 Two charters concerning a tenement in New Street: one of of Adam of Barnwell perfected for Richard of Berwick, and one of Richard perfected for Edward of Upton and his wife Agnes
333–4 Two charters concerning a tenement opposite the market place: one of Richard Tidworth perfected for his son John and William of Fisherton, and one of John and William perfected for Richard of Tidworth and his wife Catherine
335 A charter of Richard of Tidworth perfected for John of Oxford concerning two shops in Minster Street and a rent of 4*s*. issuing from a corner shop in New Street and Gigant Street
336 A charter of John of Oxford [?*rectius* Woodford: *cf.* **676**] and his wife Agnes, the relict of Edward Steward, called Upton, perfected for John of Oxford and

his wife Agnes concerning a rent of 18s. issuing from a corner tenement in St. Martin's Street

The following charters and wills are enrolled out of order with regard to the sequence of the years.
337 The will of William of Winchester, which includes several tenements devised to his wife Agnes for life, and afterwards for ever to his son John
338–40 Three writings concerning a chief tenement in Winchester Street and other tenements and rent: a charter of John, a son of William of Winchester, perfected for Thomas Whitton, of Hindon, and his son Thomas, a release of John perfected for Thomas and his son Thomas, and a release of Ellis Sallitt, a kinsman of John, perfected for Edith, a daughter of [?the elder] Thomas
341 A release of William of Lyme perfected for John of Upton and his wife Edith concerning land and tenements which were Adam Winchester's
342 A release of Peter Whitton, a brother and heir of a younger Thomas Whitton, perfected for John of Upton and his wife Edith concerning tenements [*as in* **338–40** *or* **341**]
343 25 January 1356 x 24 January 1357. A charter of John Upton and his wife Edith perfected for John of Westbury, John Richman, and John Powell concerning a tenement in New Street and Carter Street and all their other land and tenements in the city
344 25 January 1357 x 24 January 1358. A charter of John Westbury, John Richman, and John Powell perfected for John Upton and his wife Edith concerning the land and tenements [*as in* **343**]
345 25 January 1329 x 24 January 1330. A charter of William of Winchester, a son of Adam of Winchester, perfected for Richard Piggesden concerning a tenement in New Street and a rent of 20s. issuing from a tenement opposite Cheese Corner
346 25 January 1330 x 24 January 1331. A charter of Richard Piggesden perfected for William of Winchester and his wife Cecily concerning a tenement in New Street and a rent of 20s. [*as in* **345**]
347 25 January 1346 x 24 January 1347. A charter of John Hawk and his wife Agnes, the relict of William of Winchester, perfected for Roger at the well concerning a tenement in New Street and a piece of a yard in Drake Hall Street
348 25 January 1346 x 24 January 1347. A charter of Roger at the well perfected for John Hawk and his wife Agnes concerning two tenements in New Street
349 25 January 1346 x 24 January 1347. The will of Agnes, the wife of John Hawk, approved in that year
350 A charter of John Hawk perfected for Roger Woolmonger and Nicholas Buck, a chaplain, concerning two tenements, one in New Street and the other in St. Martin's Street, and a rent of 20s. [*as in* **345**]
351 A charter of Roger Woolmonger and Nicholas Buck, a chaplain, perfected for John of Upton concerning a tenement in New Street, a portion of a garden in Drake Hall Street, and a rent of 20s. [*as in* **345**]
352–6 Five writings concerning a tenement in New Street: a release of Robert Coleshill perfected for Richard Baldry, a charter of Margaret, Richard's relict,

perfected for William Hark, the will of William Hark, hatter, which includes it, a charter of John Frank and his wife Isabel, an executor of William, perfected for Robert Gore and Thomas Chaplin, and a charter of Robert and Thomas perfected for John Upton

357–8 Two charters perfected for John Upton: one of Thomas Leadbeater and his wife Agnes, a daughter of Thomas Stratford, concerning a tenement in Winchester Street, and one of Peter Bennett concerning seven shops, and cottages, in Winchester Street and Culver Street for a rent of 30s. to be paid to Peter for a term of life

359–60 Two charters concerning a tenement in New Street: one of William Pye perfected for Adam May, and one of Adam perfected for John Upton

Note that in the second book, from which the preceding enrolments are in part drawn, from the will of William of Winchester the charters and wills are enrolled at the petition of John Upton. Six empty folios in that book are reserved for other deeds of his to be enrolled when he brought them together.

25 January 1351 x 24 January 1352
361 A charter of Walter, a son of Thomas Ironmonger, perfected for William of Hook Norton and John Powell concerning a corner shop in Butcher Row

362–3 Two charters concerning three tenements and two shops: one of John of Oxford and his wife Agnes, an executor of John Baldry, and another (*or* other) executor(s) of John, perfected for John Barnaby and Richard Callis, and one of John and Richard perfected for John and Agnes. One of the tenements stands opposite the Franciscans, one in Carter Street, and the third, opposite the east gate of the canons' close, at the end of Drake Hall Street. The two shops stand in Brown Street.

25 January 1352 x 24 January 1353
364 A deed of Robert Godmanstone and R[oger] Tarrant, executors of Robert Lavington, perfected for Richard Ryborough concerning a rent of 7s. issuing from a tenement in Brown Street

25 January 1353 x 24 January 1354
365–7 Three writings perfected for William Wagain: a charter of John Hill, sheather, and his wife Maud, an executor of William Upwell, concerning a mediety of a tenement and garden in New Street, a charter of John and Maud concerning the other mediety, and a release of Nicholas, a son and heir of Joan, the relict of John of Winterbourne, tanner, concerning two tenements in New Street

25 January 1354 x 24 January 1355
368 The will of Alice, the wife of Bertin Spicer and the relict of Richard Lavington, which includes several tenements

369 A charter of Richard Ryborough and Gilbert Whichbury, executors of Alice Bertins, perfected for William Wishford concerning a tenement in Winchester

Street beside the New Inn

370 A charter of John Grew, hatter, perfected for Richard Ryborough concerning three cottages in St. Martin's Street

371–2 Two writings perfected for William of Wishford: a deed of John Spray and Gilbert of Whichbury concerning a tenement in New Street of late Thomas Long's, together with other goods and chattels of late Thomas's, by virtue of an indenture, and a release of Thomas concerning that shop (*or* those shops)

373 A charter of William of Wishford perfected for Richard Ryborough concerning two shops in New Street

374–5 Two charters concerning a rent of 10*s*. issuing from a yard (*or* yards), with a rack (*or* racks), opposite the graveyard of St. Edmund's church: one of Richard Still perfected for Richard Shearer and his wife Alice, and one of Richard Shearer perfected for Richard Ryborough

25 January 1355 x 24 January 1356

376 A writ of the king, directed to the mayor and aldermen of London concerning liberties to be allowed, by means of which the citizens of Salisbury were immune from pontage

377 A charter of William Wishford perfected for Richard Ryborough concerning a tenement [*as in* **369**]

378 A charter of Hugh Boney perfected for Richard Ryborough concerning a messuage [*as in* **326**]

379–81 Three writings concerning a tenement in Minster Street [*as in* **328**]: a release of Thomas Glendy perfected for John Salisbury concerning a rent of 8*s*. issuing from it, a charter of Gilbert Whichbury perfected for Richard Ryborough concerning a rent of 20*s*. issuing from it, and a charter of John Salisbury, a clerk, a son of John Nugg, perfected for Richard

382–4 Three deeds of Thomas Knoyle, a son of Thomas Knoyle: one perfected for Richard Ryborough, his wife Joan, and their sons Peter and John for their life concerning a tenement in Winchester Street and concerning five shops in the butchers' street for a rent of 116*s*. 8*d*. a year therefrom, one perfected for Richard concerning 106*s*. 8*d*. issuing from various cottages in Culver Street and from a tenement in Winchester Street in fee simple, and one, indented, between those same parties on condition that, if Richard, Joan, Peter, and John were to hold the tenement and shops in peace for their life, the grant of the rent of 106*s*. 8*d*. would be void

385 A charter of Philip Aubin perfected for Richard Ryborough concerning a rent of 40*s*. issuing from a tenement in Winchester Street

386–7 Two wills which include several tenements in Salisbury and Old Sarum: that of Joan, the wife of Nicholas Gaunt and the relict of Thomas Long, and that of Nicholas

25 January 1356 x 24 January 1357

388–9 Two writings perfected for Nicholas Buck, a chaplain, and Robert of Harnham concerning a tenement in Minster Street: an indented deed of John

Mariner, hatter, and his wife Agnes for a term of life for a rent of a rose from the tenement, and a release of John's son John

25 January 1357 x 24 January 1358
390–1 Two charters concerning a shop [*as in* **318**] and two shops in Pot Row: one of John Powell perfected for Robert Alwin and Gilbert Whichbury, and one of Robert and Gilbert perfected for Richard Ryborough
392 A release of William Ironmonger perfected for John Powell concerning a shop [*as in* **361**]
393 A charter of John Powell and his wife Emme perfected for Robert Alwin and Gilbert Whichbury concerning a corner shop with a cellar
394 A charter of Peter Bennett perfected for Richard Ryborough concerning a tenement, with a shop (*or* shops) and a cellar (*or* cellars), near the graveyard of St. Thomas's church
395–6 Two writings perfected for Richard Shearer and his wife Alice concerning a tenement in Minster Street: a deed of Walter at the burgh, and a release of Alice, a daughter and heir of Thomas Callow
397–8 Two writings concerning a shop, with a sollar (*or* sollars), in Minster Street: an indenture of Edward Pinnock perfected for John of Wells, tailor, his wife Alice, and their son William for their life for a rent of a rose a year, and a deed of John, Alice, and William, perfected for John of Oxford

26 July 1357
399 A final agreement, made in the bishop of Salisbury's court for Salisbury held on 26 July 1357 in front of Walter at the burgh, the bailiff of the bishop's liberty, John Richman, the mayor of the city, and other faithful subjects of the king, between Walter at the burgh, plaintiff, and Alice Callow, deforciant, concerning a messuage in Salisbury. A plea of covenant was summoned between them in that court by means of a writ of the king in accordance with the bishop's liberty upheld in the king's court in front of the justices of the [Common] Bench. Alice acknowledged the messuage to be the right of Walter. She granted that the messuage, which Peter Mondelard holds for life by a grant of Henry Melksham, of late a citizen of Salisbury, and which on Peter's death should remain to Alice as a daughter and heir of Thomas Callow, should remain immediately on Peter's death to Walter, and his heirs, to be held by them for ever. For that acknowledgement, fine, and agreement Walter gave £20 to Alice. The agreement was made in the presence of Peter, who attorned to Walter.

25 January 1358 x 24 January 1359
400 A charter of John Buddle, called Prentice, and his wife Catherine perfected for Richard Ryborough concerning a messuage, with a yard (*or* yards), in Scots Lane
401 A charter of Richard Shearer and his wife Alice perfected for a younger William Tenterer concerning a tenement [*as in* **395–6**]
402 A charter of John Clark, of Handley, perfected for John of Oxford concerning

a corner tenement in New Street and Gigant Street
403 A release of Edward Pinnock perfected for John of Oxford concerning a shop [*as in* **397–8**]

Note that all the records in the other part of this quire are enrolled at the petition of a younger William Tenterer, William Wagain, and John of Oxford. Many empty folios are reserved there for other records to be enrolled.

25 January 1359 x 24 January 1360
404 A release of Christine, the relict of Peter Bennett, perfected for Richard Ryborough concerning a rent of 20s. issuing from a tenement [*as in* **394**]
405–8 Four writings concerning two messuages, one near the graveyard of St. Thomas's church and one in New Street: a charter of Robert Bunt and George Goss perfected for Richard Ryborough and Robert Alwin, a release of Nicholas, a son of Nicholas Gaunt, perfected for Richard and Robert, a charter of Richard and Robert perfected for John Crichel and Thomas Erlestoke, chaplains, and a release of Peter Bouch perfected for John and Thomas
409 A charter of John, a son of Andrew Bunt, perfected for Joan Brays, his sister, concerning two shops on the way to St. Edmund's church
410 A charter of John at the brook, a son of Ingram at the brook, perfected for Edmund Steercock concerning a cottage (*or* cottages), with a yard (*or* yards), in Winchester Street
411 The will of Hugh Boney, which includes several tenements, shops, cottages, dovecots, rent, and reversions
412 A charter of John Crichel and Thomas Erlestoke, chaplains, perfected for Richard Ryborough concerning two messuages [*as in* **405–8**]
413 A charter of Edith, the relict of Hugh Boney, perfected for Hugh's son John concerning a corner tenement in Winchester Street and Culver Street
414 A charter of John Knoyle, of Ludgershall, perfected for John Hawk concerning five cottages in Culver Street
415 A charter of Stephen Crier perfected for John of Shrewton and John Snel concerning two shops, with a sollar (*or* sollars), at the butchers' stalls
416 A charter of William of Bruton and his wife Agnes perfected for Richard of Berwick concerning a tenement, called Wimpler's Corner, on the way to the upper bridge of Fisherton
417 A charter of John Woodford and his wife Agnes perfected for Richard Ryborough concerning two tenements, in Wineman Street and Brown Street, a messuage in Gigant Street, and a rent of 15s. issuing from a tenement in Wineman Street with the reversion of the tenement on the death of Richard Mealmonger and his wife Christine
418 A charter of John Shrewton and John Snel perfected for Stephen Crier concerning two shops [*as in* **415**]
419 A charter of John of Woodford and his wife Agnes perfected for John of Oxford concerning a tenement in New Street
420 The will of John Powell, which includes several tenements, shops, and

cottages [devised] to his children and godchildren

421 A charter of John Gough, a canon of the cathedral church, perfected, by a licence of the king and a licence of the bishop of Salisbury, for the dean and chapter concerning two messuages, five shops, and a rent of 24s. in New Street and Minster Street, under an ordinance of the foundation

422 A charter of William of Wishford perfected for John Hawk concerning a tenement in St. Martin's Street

423 A charter of George Goss perfected for William of Wishford concerning a corner tenement in Winchester Street and Brown Street

424 A charter of Emme, the relict, and an executor, of John Powell, and another (*or* other) executor(s) of John, perfected for John of Upton concerning a tenement in Minster Street beyond the bar

425 A charter of Roger Tropenell perfected for John of Upton and John of Highworth (*Worthe*), a clerk, concerning a tenement and a conjoined shop in Wineman Street

426 A charter of Christine, the relict of Peter Bennett, perfected for John of Upton concerning a meadow in Drake Hall Street

427–8 Two charters perfected for Robert Bunt and Edmund Bier, a clerk, concerning two tenements in Minster Street and two tenements in Southampton: one of Richard Shearer and his wife Alice, and one, in the form of a release, of Richard and Alice, an executor of John Barnaby, and another (*or* other) executor(s) of John

429 A charter of Nicholas, called Upwell, a son of John of Winterbourne, perfected for William of Sexhampcote concerning a corner shop, with a sollar, in Minster Street near the graveyard of St. Thomas's church

430 A charter of Henry Long perfected for Nicholas Hamish, a chaplain, concerning a tenement in New Street

431 A charter of William Friend perfected for Robert Alwin concerning a piece of a yard in New Street

432 A charter of John Bunt and his wife Alice, the relict of Henry Bunt, perfected for Ralph Shearer concerning a tenement opposite the graveyard of St. Thomas's church

433 A charter of Robert Bunt and Edmund Bier perfected for Richard Shearer concerning two conjoined tenements in Minster Street and a yard in Culver Street

434 A charter of Robert Alwin and Gilbert Whichbury perfected for Richard Ryborough concerning a corner shop, with a sollar, in Winchester Street where smiths wait and a corner shop, with a sollar, in Butcher Row

435 The will of Philip Longenough, which includes several shops and tenements. It includes the release to his wife of a tenement, devised to his daughter, because the wife claimed it as her dower. Also, because Philip's brother was excluded from the keeping of the daughter, ordered in the will, certain matters [are] contrary to the appointments of the will.

436 A writ of the king directed to the sheriff of Wiltshire for a coroner to be chosen in the city, according to the assize of the citizens, on account of the death of John Powell, a coroner

437 A charter of Roger Fowle perfected for Nicholas Best and his wife Agnes concerning a tenement in Minster Street

25 January 1360 x 24 January 1361

438 A charter of John Knoyle, of Ludgershall, perfected for John Paris, the rector of Bruton, concerning a rent of 26s. issuing from a tenement in Winchester Street

439 An indented charter of the dean and chapter of Salisbury perfected for Nicholas Hamish, a chaplain, and Gilbert Whichbury concerning a tenement in Minster Street in fee simple for a rent of 26s. 8d. to be paid for ever, with a clause for recovering the seisin for a default in the payment of the rent

440 An indented deed of the dean and chapter of Salisbury perfected for Nicholas Boor and Adam Gore, vicars of that church, concerning a corner tenement in New Street, adjoining Culver Street, in fee simple for a rent of 26s. 8s. to be paid from it, with a clause for recovering the seisin for a default either in maintenance or in payment of the rent

441 The will of Maud Upwell, which includes two shops in Cordwainer Row

442 A charter of John Hacker and his wife Agnes perfected for Thomas Erlestoke and John Bradwell, chaplains, concerning two shops in Chipper Street

443 Two writings perfected for Walter at the burgh concerning two shops in Cordwainer Row opposite Poultry: a charter of Reynold Calabry, and a release of Nicholas Upwell, a son and heir of John of Winterbourne

444 A charter of William of Wallop, butcher, perfected for Nicholas Russell concerning two cottages in Culver Street

445 A charter of Peter at the hall, of Downton, perfected for Richard Ryborough concerning a tenement in Carter Street and all the shops on either side of the tenement, on a corner

446 A release of Christine, a daughter of Thomas Vellard, perfected for John of Winterbourne and his wife Gillian concerning a toft in Freren Street opposite a close of the Franciscans

447 A release of Robert, a son of Geoffrey Cook, perfected for Agnes, his mother, concerning a tenement in New Street

448 A charter of Agnes, the relict of Walter of Boreham, perfected for Richard Dudmore and his wife Margaret concerning a tenement in Winchester Street

449–51 Three charters concerning a corner tenement, with a dovecot and a yard (*or* yards), opposite St. Edmund's church: one of Joan, the relict, and an executor, of Thomas of Butterley, and another (*or* other) executor(s) of Thomas perfected for the lord John White, the rector of Landford, one of John perfected for Joan, and one of Joan perfected for the lord Nicholas Buck for a rent of 30s. cash from it to be paid for ever to Joan and her heirs, with a clause for re-entry if the rent should be in arrear for a quarter of a year

452–4 Three charters perfected for William Costard: one of Thomas Erlestoke, a chaplain, concerning a tenement in Wineman Street, one of Hugh, the vicar of Shrewton, and Thomas concerning a shop, with a room, in Minster Street, and one of William Chandler, a brother of Laurence Chandler, concerning seven shops in New Street

455 The will of William Higdon, which includes various tenements

456 A charter of Robert Bunt and George Goss perfected for John Deanbridge concerning a tenement in New Street

457 A charter of William Goldston perfected for William of Buckland and his wife Margaret concerning a tenement in Gigant Street and rent of 10s., with the reversion of a tenement in New Street

458 A charter of Joyce Lutwich perfected for John of Haxton concerning a tenement in Nuggeston

459 A charter of Nicholas Buck, a chaplain, and Robert of Harnham perfected for John Mariner, hatter, and his wife Agnes concerning a tenement in Minster Street

460 A charter of John Fish perfected for Nicholas Taylor concerning a shop, with a sollar, opposite the fishermen's stalls

461–2 Two writings concerning a tenement in Winchester Street: a charter of Robert at the mill, of Alderbury, and his wife Edith perfected for William of Wishford, and a note that, on the Wednesday after the feast of the assumption of the Blessed Mary in that year [*assumed to be* 19 August 1360], Agnes, a daughter and heir of Robert and Edith, and Thomas, a son of Reynold Dyne, came [to court] and, by their deed, released their right to it to William

463 A charter of William of Hook Norton, the vicar of Britford, and Thomas Erlestoke perfected for Roger Frank and his wife Emme concerning a corner tenement called Powell's Corner

464 A charter of Richard Martin, of Homington, perfected for Thomas of Erlestoke, a chaplain, concerning two shops in Minster Street

465 A charter of Nicholas Hamish, a chaplain, and Gilbert Whichbury perfected for Adam Haxton concerning a tenement, with shops, in Minster Street

466 A charter of John Tott perfected for William of Bruton concerning a tenement near the graveyard of St. Thomas's church, and that he could build above a stile there

467 A charter of Henry Fleming perfected for William Costard concerning a tenement opposite the Guildhall

468 A charter of Thomas Erlestoke, a chaplain, perfected for William Scammel and his wife Joan concerning a tenement in Carter Street, and concerning a rent of 60s. a year, together with the dyeing of 12 lb. of wool (*tintura xii lb lane*), issuing from a tenement, which William Hurn holds, opposite the market place, and the reversion of that tenement

469 A charter of Gilbert of Wick perfected for William Knight concerning a piece of a yard, taken from his yard in Brown Street, measuring 54 ft. in length

470 A charter of John Godfrey, a fisherman, perfected for Walter Eliot, William Painter, and Edmund Bier, a clerk, concerning a yard (*or* yards) in Freren Street

471–2 Two charters of Henry Fleming perfected for Richard Ryborough: one concerning a rent of 10s. a year to be received from a tenement in Winchester Street, with a clause for distraint, and one concerning rent of 30s., of which 20s. issues from Thomas Durrington's tenement in Castle Street and 10s. from a corner tenement in Endless Street, rent of 23s. 8d. [?*rectius* 23s. 4d.] of which 13s. 4d. issues from a tenement in Winchester Street and 10s. from two shops in Brown Street, a rent of 10s. from a tenement, formerly Stephen Coombe's, called Drake Hall, and a rent of 18s. issuing from a tenement in Drake Hall Street, beside the grammar school, with the reversion of the tenement

473 A charter of Gilbert of Wick perfected for Gilbert Whichbury concerning a tenement in Brown Street

474 The will of Maud Dovedale, the relict of Thomas Netheravon, which includes two tenements. One tenement, in Castle Street, was devised to her daughter Agnes and her issue and, in default, should remain to others. The other, in Scots Lane, was devised to her son John Dovedale and his issue and, in default, should remain to other children.

475 A release of Richard Moyne, a kinsman and heir of William Moyne, perfected for John Everard concerning a tenement in Brown Street, a tenement between a corner tenement etc., and a toft in Gigant Street

476 A charter of William of Bruton perfected for Nicholas Taylor concerning a tenement, in Minster Street between the graveyard of St. Thomas's church etc., which extends as far as the Avon [*margin*: council house]

477–8 Two charters perfected for a younger Walter Park, of Upton Scudamore, and the lord Thomas Erlestoke, a chaplain: one of John of Upton concerning four tenements, two conjoined in New Street, one in the same street beside [the lower] bridge of Fisherton, and the fourth on a corner opposite the tavern called Hott Corner, a shop in Minster Street between that corner tenement etc., and a meadow in Drake Hall Street, and one of John and his wife Edith concerning a corner tenement in Carter Street and New Street, a tenement in Carter Street with a garden, a tenement in Winchester Street near the pillories, a tenement in New Street between Richard of Otterbourne's tenement etc., a corner tenement in Winchester Street and Culver Street, and a garden at the end of Drake Hall Street

479 A release of Richard Ryborough perfected for Robert Alwin and Gilbert of Whichbury concerning a chief tenement in Carter Street and all the other land and tenements which Robert and Gilbert hold by a grant of John Bodenham in the city or elsewhere

480 An indented charter of Christine, the relict of Peter Bennett, perfected for Agnes, the relict of John of Bodenham, concerning three cottages in Culver Street in fee simple, paying a rent of 4s. for Christine's life, with a clause for re-entry if the rent was not paid

481 A charter of a younger William Tenterer perfected for Edward Longenough and Robert Bunt concerning a tenement in Winchester Street

482 Three charters of Robert Alwin and Gilbert of Whichbury: one perfected for Roger of Halwell, called the tanner, and his wife Maud concerning a tenement in St. Martin's Street and another tenement in that street between etc. in fee simple, one perfected for William Knight concerning a tenement in Carter Street, and one perfected for John Chandler concerning half a toft in Freren Street

483 A release of George Lutwich, a taverner, and his wife Margaret perfected

for Richard Ryborough for ever concerning a corner tenement with a shop (*or* shops) in Ironmonger Row opposite the high cross where fruit is sold
484 A charter of Henry Fleming perfected for Robert Bunt concerning three conjoined tenements in Minster Street
485 A charter of John, a son of Walter Ewan, and his wife Joan perfected for John Mount and his wife Joan concerning a shop in Endless Street beside Henry Pope's tenement

25 January 1361 x 24 January 1362
486 A charter of John Mount and his wife Joan perfected for Thomas Grundy concerning a shop in Endless Street [*as in* **485**]
487 A charter of Thomas, a son of John of Homington, perfected for a younger William Tenterer concerning a shop, with a sollar, in Minster Street attached to a tenement in which Peter Mondelard dwells
488 A charter of Ralph Shearer perfected for John Homington, a clerk, concerning a tenement opposite St. Thomas's church
489 A charter of John Hoare, an executor of Maud, the wife of Adam Cole, perfected for Thomas Smith, of Amesbury, concerning a tenement in Brown Street and two other tenements, one in Winchester Street and one in Endless Street, for ever
490 A charter of William of Woodford, called 'Ele', perfected for Gilbert of Whichbury concerning a tenement in New Street
491 A release of Philip Aubin perfected for Alice, the relict of Philip Longenough, concerning three conjoined shops in Carter Street [*referred to in* **1656**]
492–3 Two charters of William of Bruton perfected for Richard Frear concerning premises in Minster Street beyond the bar: one concerning a tenement, with two shops, a yard (*or* yards), and a dovecot, and 11 cottages, with yards and a rack, and one concerning nine shops, with a yard (*or* yards)
494 A charter of Thomas of Hungerford perfected for Richard Frear concerning a tenement, with a garden, in Minster Street, beyond the bar, between Ellis Homes's tenements, and a messuage, with a yard (*or* yards), in Culver Street, with a clause of warranty
495 A deed of William of Harpenden, a son of William of Harpenden, perfected for [Thomas of: *cf.* **656**] Shalbourne, a chaplain, concerning a tenement in Winchester Street; with a release of that tenement given 25 January 1354 x 24 January 1355
496 A charter of Alice, the relict of Philip Longenough, perfected for Philip Aubin, of Winchester, concerning rent of 20*s.* issuing from two shops in Carter Street [*given in full as* **1656**]
497 A charter of John Everard, of Stratford, perfected for John Doder concerning a tenement extending from Brown Street and Winchester Street, and another tenement in Winchester Street
498 A charter of Robert of Kendal perfected for a younger William Tenterer concerning two tenements, with a yard (*or* yards), in St. Martin's Street in fee
499 The will of Edward Longenough, which includes various tenements

appointed in various ways

500 A charter of Peter Bennett perfected for a younger William Tenterer concerning a shop in Minster Street in fee

501 The will of Thomas Hungerford, a citizen of Salisbury, which includes various tenements, cottages, and rent devised in various ways

502 A charter of Walter Park, of Upton Scudamore, and Thomas Erlestoke, a chaplain, perfected for John of Upton concerning five messuages, shops, cottages, and gardens, one messuage of which stands in Carter Street and New Street, one in Carter Street, one in Winchester Street and Fishmonger Row near the pillories, a fourth in New Street, and a fifth in Winchester Street and Culver Street, and a garden of which lies in Drake Hall Street [*described slightly differently in 478*], and five other messuages in various streets, [all] to be held for ever

503 A charter of William Uffcott, a chaplain, perfected for Henry Stapleford concerning a tenement in Minster Street at the bar

504 A charter of John of Woodborough, a son of William of Woodborough, perfected for Robert of Godmanstone and his wife Joan concerning a tenement in Endless Street in fee simple

505 A charter of Thomas of Erlestoke and John of Bradwell, chaplains, perfected for John Marshall, a smith, and James Bromham concerning a corner tenement in Minster Street in fee

506 A charter of Gilbert Whichbury perfected for William Newman, a tanner, and his wife Edith concerning a tenement in Endless Street in fee

507 A charter of Agnes, the relict of Laurence Chandler, and Thomas Erlestoke, executors of Laurence, perfected for Richard Cook concerning two shops, with a garden (*or* gardens) and a plot of land, in Freren Street in fee

508 A charter of Thomas of Erlestoke, a chaplain, perfected for Edmund Steercock concerning a corner tenement in Winchester Street and Culver Street in fee

509 A charter of Henry [Gill], the rector of Fisherton, and others, executors of Thomas of Hungerford, perfected for Robert Godmanstone and his wife Joan concerning a cottage (*or* cottages), with a yard (*or* yards), in Martin's Croft

510 A charter of Thomas of Erlestoke, a chaplain, an executor of Robert of Warminster, a vicar of Salisbury, perfected for John of Essington, taverner, concerning a tenement, with a yard (*or* yards), in Drake Hall Street

511 The will of William Wagain, draper, which includes two tenements in Salisbury and part of a tenement in Southampton

512 A charter of John Florentine perfected for Richard Alden, of Southampton, concerning a corner tenement in New Street and Minster Street called Florentine's Corner, and concerning rent, with the reversion of a shop in New Street

513 A charter of Thomas of Erlestoke perfected for Richard Farley, spicer, and his wife Edith concerning two tenements in New Street in fee

514–15 Two writings perfected for John Crichel, Robert Axbey, and John Cerney, chaplains, concerning a corner yard in Nuggeston and Gigant Street in fee: a charter of Thomas of Erlestoke and William Candelan, chaplains, executors of John, a son of John Nugg, and a release of Henry, a son of John Nugg [?the elder]

516 A deed of grant and release of Henry, a son of John Nugg, perfected for

John Crichel, John Duckman, Walter Charlton, John Dean, Robert Axbey, and Robert Oakford, vicars of the cathedral church, concerning a rent of 2 marks issuing from a tenement in Endless Street, beside a corner tenement of late Edmund Bramshaw's, in fee

517 The will of Stephen Crier, which includes various tenements [and] cottages. Approved

518 The will of William Costard, which includes several and various tenements, cottages, and shops. Approved

519 The will of John Essington, taverner, which includes a messuage, with a yard (*or* yards), in Drake Hall Street. Approved

520 The will of Thomas Smith, of Amesbury, which includes various tenements, cottages, and yards devised to John Hoare and to others. Approved

521 The record as to how Nicholas Boor and Adam Gore surrendered into the hand of the lord [bishop] the seisin of a corner tenement in New Street and Culver Street, which they held by a grant of the dean and chapter of Salisbury, to the use of John Frank and his wife Isabel

522 The record as to how Thomas of Erlestoke, a chaplain, and Thomas of Britford, executors of William Costard, surrendered into the hand of the lord [bishop] the seisin of a tenement, opposite the Guildhall, beside John Nalder's tenement to the use of Thomas of Bridgehampton

523 The record as to how Joan, a daughter of William Bartlet, surrendered into the hand of the lord [bishop] the seisin of a corner tenement in Scots Lane and Endless Street to the use of Thomas of Britford, the lord Nicholas Buck, the lord William Buck, and John Prentice

524 The record as to how Robert Kendal and Richard Still surrendered into the hand of the lord [bishop] the seisin of a tenement in Winchester Street to the use of Richard at the stone

525 The will of John Richman, which includes rent and several and various tenements, shops, and cottages devised in various ways. Approved

526 The will of Andrew of Langford, which includes various cottages, messuages, and rent. Approved

527 The will of William Cavenasser, which includes a tenement in Minster Street and a tenement in Butcher Row. Approved

528 The beginning of the will of Maud, the wife of Stephen Shearer; not, however, extended to the end

529 The will of John Coates, which includes a corner tenement called Ro Corner in St. Martin's Street and Gigant Street devised to his wife Lucy for ever. Not approved

530 The will of James of Bromham, which includes a corner tenement in Minster Street devised to his wife. Approved

531 A charter of John Knoyle, of Ludgershall, John Paris, called Purbeck, William Candelan, and Robert Axbey, chaplains, concerning a shop in Minster Street

532 The title of a charter of Richard Brewer and William Cavenasser perfected for Henry of Stapleford concerning a tenement in Minster Street beyond the bar

533 A charter of John of Westbury and his wife Joan perfected for William, the vicar of Idmiston, John of Upton, George Goss, and John Marshall concerning a corner tenement, called Ive's Corner, in Wineman Street and Mealmonger Street, and a corner tenement in Wineman Street and Brown Street

534 The will of Christine [of] Ann, the relict of Peter Bennett, which includes several tenements and yards, among them a messuage, with a yard (*or* yards), in Nuggeston devised to the mayor and commonalty and their successors. Approved

535 A charter of John Linnier and Thomas Mussel, executors of John Mussel, and of Christine, the relict of John Mussel, perfected for John Upton and William Wishford concerning a tenement in Brown Street, two shops in Butcher Row, and three cottages, with a yard (*or* yards), in Gigant Street in fee

536 The will of Alice, the relict of Philip Longenough, which includes various tenements in Carter Street. Approved

537 A charter of Thomas Erlestoke and John Bradwell perfected for John Hacker and his wife Agnes concerning two shops in Chipper Street

538 A charter of Richard Brewer and William Cavenasser, executors of Walter Cavenasser, perfected for John Marshall concerning a tenement in Minster Street in fee

539 The will of Margaret, the relict of Richard Dudmore, which includes a tenement in Winchester Street. Approved

540 The will of Edmund Steercock, which includes two tenements in Winchester Street and a tenement in Castle Street. Approved

541 The will of Robert Alwin, which includes various tenements, shops, cottages, and gardens in various streets of the city appointed to be sold by his executors. Approved

542 A charter of John of Homington, a clerk, perfected for Nicholas Hamish, a chaplain, concerning a tenement opposite St. Thomas's church in fee

BOOK 3

WSA 23/1/212

5 August 1349, at Salisbury

543 Approval of the will of Ellis Homes, of late a citizen of Salisbury, made on 15 December 1348. <u>Interment</u>: in the church of the Dominicans of Fisherton. <u>Bequests</u>: 12*d.* to the fabric of the cathedral church; 12*d.* to the fabric of St. Thomas's church, 12*d.* to the high altar for his forgotten tithes and lesser benefactions, 6*d.* to the parochial chaplain, and 3*d.* to the deacon; all the expenses incurred with regard to his burial, with the expenses for holding his obit on the 30th day and on the anniversary day, to the order of his executors; a piece of silver to the Dominicans of Fisherton for a chalice to be made for the service of God there and that church; 10*s.* to his daughter Joan; 20*s.* to his daughter Alice; 13*s.* 4*d.* to John, his elder son, of London; his best robe, a cloak *de paele*, and his best coat, with a hood, to Walter Ironmonger; the rest of his goods to his sons Ellis and John to be divided equally between them. <u>Devises</u>: to Ellis and John a chief tenement, in which he dwelt, opposite the market place where pewter is sold, between a tenement then William Chandler's on one side and Robert of Melksham's tenement on the other side, extending in that street as far as Winchester Street; also to Ellis and John cottages, with yards, which he acquired from Richard Rivers and his wife Denise, in Minster Street, beyond the bars, on the way to Old Sarum castle. Those tenements are to be held for ever by Ellis and John and their issue, and if Ellis and John were to die without issue they should be sold by the elder Ellis's executors and by the parson of St. Thomas's church and the mayor of Salisbury for the time being. Half the money received should be paid towards the construction and improvement of St. Thomas's church, half towards the relief of tallage for the benefit of the commonalty of the city, for the salvation of the elder Ellis's soul and the souls of others. Ellis appointed that a tenement in Minster Street, beyond the bar, on the way to Old Sarum castle, with a fish-yard and a dovecot, should be sold by his executors and by the parson of St. Thomas's church and the mayor of Salisbury. The money received should be spent on paying the debts to which he is rightly bound. <u>Executors</u>: the lord Henry [Gill], the parson of Fisherton church, John Hawk, and John Marshall. <u>Proved</u> on 28 December 1348 in front of a commissary of the subdean. The nominated executors declined the administration; in their place the commissary, on 27 January 1349, appointed Robert of Faringdon and William, called Long, citizens of Salisbury, as executors and entrusted the administration to them. <u>Approved</u> at a court held in front of the bailiff, the mayor, and other citizens; the seisin of the tenements was released to the legatees.

28 September 1351, at Salisbury
544 By an indenture it is attested that Richard Ryborough, a citizen of Salisbury, granted to Nicholas of Hampton and his wife Maud a tenement in Minster Street between George Goss's tenement on one side and a tenement formerly Nicholas of Breamore's on the other side. The tenement is to be held for their life, and the life of the one of them living longer, by Nicholas and Maud and their assigns of Richard and his heirs or assigns without causing waste or ruin, paying a rent of 13*s*. 4*d*. cash a year to Richard and his heirs or assigns, rendering to the chief lord and all others the rent and services owed and customary, and at their own expense maintaining the tenement in all things necessary and in a state as good as, or even better than, that in which they received it so that the rent would not be lost. Clause to permit permanent repossession if the rent were in arrear for 15 days or, if Richard and his heirs and assigns preferred, re-entry, distraint, and the keeping of distresses until the unpaid rent and other losses were recovered. Clause of warranty in respect of the tenement for the life of Nicholas and Maud, of acquittance in respect of the rent. Seals: those of the parties to the parts of the indenture in turn and the mayoral seal of the city. Named witnesses: the bailiff, the mayor, the coroners, the reeves, Henry Russell, Adam of Ludwell, Peter Bennett, Philip Longenough, Thomas of Butterley, John of Upton, John Cole, John Fosbury, and the clerk.

17 March 1361
545 By his indented charter John Hawk, a citizen of Salisbury, granted to

Nicholas Holtby a tenement in Minster Street between a tenement formerly John of Lyneham's on one side and a tenement of late that of Robert of Woodford, mercer, on the other side. The tenement was held by John by a grant of John Wallis, an executor of John of St. Honorine, and is to be held for ever by Nicholas and his heirs and assigns, paying a rent of 40s. cash a year to John and his heirs and assigns, and maintaining the tenement in all things necessary at their own expense so that the rent would not be lost. Clause to permit re-entry if the rent were in arrear, distraint, and the keeping of distresses until the unpaid rent was recovered. Clause of warranty and acquittance. Seals: those of the parties in turn and the common and mayoral seals of the city.

5 June 1361, at Salisbury
546 By his charter William Wagain, a merchant, granted to the lord Roger of Clowne, a clerk, his land and tenements in New Street ('the new street of Salisbury'), on the south side, between a tenement of John Crichel, carpenter, on one side and a tenement which was Hugh Boney's on the other side, to be held for ever by Roger and his heirs and assigns. Clause of warranty. Seals: William's. Named witnesses: the mayor, John Upton, John Richman, John of Oxford, and Edmund Steercock.

18 August 1361, at Salisbury
547 [*The substance of the writing is lacking. The named witnesses include*] ... of Upton, Robert of Godmanstone, William of Wishford, Thomas of Britford, George Goss, and the clerk.

(after 11 August 1361)
548 The will of Thomas Quarter, made on 9 August 1361. Interment: in the graveyard of St. Martin's church. Bequests: 6d. to the fabric of the cathedral church; the rest of his goods to his wife Alice. Devises: to Alice a tenement, which he acquired from Peter Bennett, in St. Martin's Street between John Justice's tenement on one side and John Hawk's tenement on the other side, to be held for ever by her and her heirs and assigns. If Alice were to die without issue the tenement should be sold by Thomas's executors, Alice's executors, or their executors. The money received should be laid out on pious uses, such as celebrating masses and charitable almsgiving, on behalf of Thomas's soul, Alice's soul, and other souls. Executor: Alice. Proved on 11 August 1361 in front of an officer of the subdean; the administration was entrusted to Alice.

(after 16 August 1361)
549 The will of Adam of Haxton, a citizen of Salisbury, made on 17 June 1361. Interment: in the graveyard of St. Edmund's church. Bequests: 6s. 8d. to the fabric of the cathedral church; 3s. 4d. to the provost of St. Edmund's church for forgotten tithes, 3s. 4d. to the parochial chaplain, and 40d. to the deacon; 2s. 6d. to the Dominicans of Fisherton to celebrate mass on behalf of his soul; 2s. 6d. to the Franciscans of Salisbury; 40s. for his funeral expenses; 40s. each to his sons James and William; the rest of his goods to his wife Isabel, his son John, and his daughter Agnes to be divided equally among them. Devises: to Thomas

Long a tenement, with [five] shops, in Minster Street between Nicholas Taylor's tenement on the south side and Robert New's tenement on the north side. The tenement was held by Adam by a feoffment of Nicholas Hamish, a chaplain, and Gilbert of Whichbury and is to be held for ever by Thomas and his heirs and assigns. Thomas should pay to Adam's executors, their executors, or the executors of their executors, in St. Thomas's church about Michaelmas 1362 in the presence of the mayor and other honourable men of the city, £80, with all the reasonable expenses and payments incurred by Adam or his executors on the improvement and maintenance of the tenement, or on any defect of it, from when it came into Adam's hand by means of Nicholas's and Gilbert's charter. At the same time Thomas should cause the executors to have the seisin of a tenement, of late Adam's, in the same street, between Thomas of Barford's tenement on the north side and the graveyard of St. Thomas's church on the south side, just as Adam acquired it for himself, it not having deteriorated from when John Tott, of Netheravon, who held it by Adam's feoffment, granted it by his charter to William of Bruton. Adam appointed that, if Thomas were to make the payment of £80, with the expenses and payments, at that time and cause the executors to have the seisin of the tenement between Thomas of Barford's tenement and the graveyard, 100s. of that money should be laid out for a chaplain, to be chosen by his executors, to celebrate mass in St. Edmund's church on behalf of his soul. The rest of the money should be divided equally between Isabel and his children, one part to her and the other part to be divided equally among the children. In such case the tenement near the graveyard should be granted to Isabel for life and, on her death, should remain for ever to Adam's son John and his issue. If John were to die without issue it would remain for ever to Adam's daughter Agnes and her issue, and if Agnes were to die without issue it should be sold by the executors. The money received should be laid out on behalf of Adam's soul and the souls of Isabel and his children. If Isabel, John, and Agnes were all to die before Michaelmas 1362 Adam's executors should sell the tenement and lay out the money in the same way. In the event that Thomas Long does not pay the £80, with the expenses and payments, nor causes the executors to have the seisin of the tenement near the graveyard, the devise to him of the tenement, with the shops, would be void. In that case Adam devised to Isabel the two of the shops which stand conjoined between Adam's shops on the north side and Nicholas Taylor's tenement on the south side to be held for ever by her and her heirs and assigns, paying a rent of 13s. 4d. a year to the dean and chapter of Salisbury and their successors for ever. In the same case Adam devised the chief tenement, between his shops on the south side and Robert New's tenement on the north side, to Isabel for life. On Isabel's death the tenement should remain for ever to Adam's son John and his issue. If John were to die without issue it would remain for ever to Adam's daughter Agnes and her issue, and if Agnes were to die without issue it should be sold by the executors. The money received should be laid out on behalf of Adam's soul, Isabel's soul, and the souls of others. In the same case Adam devised to Agnes the three of the shops which stand conjoined between the chief tenement on the north side and the two shops on the south side to be held for ever by her and her issue, paying a rent of 13s. 4d. to the dean and chapter and their successors for ever. If Agnes were to die without issue the three shops would remain for ever to John and his issue, and if John were to die without issue they should be sold by the executors. The money received should be laid out on behalf of Adam's soul and the souls of others. The 13s. 4d. from the two shops devised to Isabel, and the 13s. 4d. from the chief tenement [?*rectius* three shops], would be paid to discharge a rent of 2 marks with which the chief tenement and the shops were charged to pay to the dean and chapter and which was customarily paid. Executors: Isabel, his brother John of Haxton, John at the wick, John Creed, William Ashley. Proved on 16 August 1361 in front of an officer of the subdean; the administration was entrusted to Isabel and John Creed, reserving the power to entrust it also to John of Haxton, John at the wick, and William Ashley when they might come to seek it.

1 September 1361, at Salisbury
550 Approval of the will of John Poulton, a citizen of Salisbury, made on 1 August 1361. Interment: in the graveyard of St. Edmund's church beside the grave of Edith, of late his wife. Bequests: his second-best belt to the fabric of the cathedral church; the rest of his goods to his daughters Christine and Margaret to be divided equally between them. Devise: to Christine and Margaret a tenement, in which he dwelt, in Wineman Street between a tenement which William Stanley [holds] on one side and a tenement which Roger of Westbury holds on the east side. The tenement was held by John by a feoffment of Henry Bull and is to be held for ever by Christine and Margaret and their issue. If Christine and Margaret were to die without issue the tenement should be sold by William Friend, his executors, or the executors of John's executors. The money received should be laid out on behalf of John's soul, Edith's soul, and the souls of others. Executors: William Gifford and William Stringer; overseer, William Friend. Proved on 9 August 1361 in front of an officer of the subdean; the administration was entrusted to the executors. Approved at a court held in front of the bailiff, the mayor, and other citizens; the seisin of the tenement was released to the legatees.

551 Approval of the will of Robert Osborne, a fisherman, a citizen of Salisbury, made on 29 July 1361. Interment: in the graveyard of St. Martin's church beside the tomb of his wife Catherine. Bequests: 2s. each to the fabric of the cathedral church and the light in front of the great cross there; 20s. for all the basic expenses on the day of his burial; a brass pot, a brass pan, and half a bed to Robert, a son of Peter Needler; the rest of his goods to his wife Margaret [*rectius* Margery: *cf.* **666, 709**]. Devises: to Margery a tenement, beyond the bars, on the way to St. Martin's church, between Roger Mutton's tenement on one side and a tenement formerly William Dogskin's on the other side, to be held for ever by her and her heirs and assigns. Robert devised four cottages in St. Martin's Street, between Agnes Berwick's tenement on the east side and Roger Tanner's tenement on the west side, to his executors to be sold. The money received should be spent on behalf of his soul and the souls of others and on paying his debts. He devised a tenement, which he held by a devise of John Jordan, mercer, between a younger William

Tenterer's tenement on the east side and Roger Tanner's tenement on the west side, to his executors to be sold. The money received should be spent on behalf of the souls of John Jordan and his wife Joan, of Robert's wife Catherine, and of others. Executors: his wife Margery and Peter Needler; overseer, Walter Calne. Proved on 9 August 1361 in front of an officer of the subdean; the administration was entrusted to the executors. Approved at a court held in front of the bailiff, the mayor, and other citizens; the seisin of the tenements was released to the legatees.

552 By his charter Philip Aubin, a citizen of Salisbury, granted to Stephen Haim, a citizen of Winchester, a rent of 40s. a year issuing from a tenement, formerly William Stringer's, in Winchester Street between a tenement, which Richard Ryborough holds, on the west side and a tenement, which William of Buckland of late held, on the east side; also a rent of 20s. a year issuing from a tenement, formerly Walter Boreham's, in Winchester Street between William of Bruton's tenement on the east side and a tenement which William of Buckland of late held on the west side; also a rent of 20s. a year issuing from two shops, with sollars, and a lower shop which stand conjoined in Carter Street in front of a tenement of late that of Alice, the relict of Philip Longenough. The two shops, with the sollars, stand beside a tenement formerly that of a younger Robert Baldry on the south [? *rectius* north] side, and the lower shop stands between the two shops on the north side and the chief entrance of the tenement formerly Alice's on the south side. The rents are to be held for ever by Stephen and his heirs and assigns. Clause to permit entry on the tenements and the shops if any of the rent was in arrear for a quindene, distraint, and the keeping of distresses until the unpaid rent was recovered. Clause of warranty. Seals: Philip's and the common and mayoral seals of the city. Named witnesses: the bailiff, the mayor, the reeves, John of Upton, Robert of Godmanstone, William of Wishford, Thomas of Bridgehampton, and Thomas of Britford.

553 Approval [*dated to the Wednesday after the feast of St. Giles (8 September) probably in error for the Wednesday of that feast (1 September)*] of the will of John of Britford, fisher, a citizen of Salisbury, made on 26 July 1361. Interment: in the graveyard of St. Thomas's church. Bequests: 12d. to the fabric of the cathedral church; 12d. to the fabric of St. Thomas's church, 2s. to the high altar for his forgotten tithes and lesser benefactions, 12d. to the parochial chaplain, and 3d. each to the deacon and the sacristan; a brass pot to John, his servant; ½ mark each to Thomas Bowyer and Edmund Dyer, a clerk; the rest of his goods to his wife Christine to be divided equally between his sons John and Thomas. Devises: to John and Thomas two conjoined tenements, in the street on the way to the church of the Dominicans of Fisherton, between an empty plot formerly John Rich's on the east side and the river Avon on the west side. John held the tenement beside the river, formerly Ingolf at the water's, by a feoffment of Thomas of Bristol, a fisherman, and the other tenement by a grant of Alice, a daughter of Thomas Ironmonger. The two, with a shop (*or* shops), are to be held for ever by John and Thomas and their issue, and if John and Thomas were to die without issue they would remain for ever to the elder John's kinsmen John, a son of Robert of Paxhill, and John, a son of John Bailiff, the elder John's brother, and their issue. If John, the son of Robert, and John, the son of John Bailiff, were to die without issue the tenements should be sold by the elder John of Britford's executors, their executors, or subsequent executors. The money received should be laid out on masses, bread, clothes, shoes, the repair of ways and bridges, and other alms and charitable deeds on behalf of John's soul, Christine's soul, and the souls of others. The chief tenement, beside the river, with a house called Brewery attached to it, is to be held of John's sons by Christine for life as dower as is customary. John devised to John and Thomas a tenement in Minster Street, beyond the bars, between John Richman's tenement on the north side and a tenement of late Richard of Breamore's on the south side. The tenement was held by John by a grant of Robert, a son of Simon Fisher, and a release of John, a son and heir of Simon, and is to be held for ever by John and Thomas and their issue. If John and Thomas were to die without issue the tenement would remain for ever to John, the son of Robert of Paxhill, and John, the son of John Bailiff, and their issue, and if they were to die without issue it should be sold by John of Britford's executors, their executors, or subsequent executors. The money received should be laid out in the way described above and on behalf of the same souls. No tenement should be sold by the executors while any of John's sons John and Thomas, John, the son of Robert of Paxhill, John, the son of John Bailiff, or issue of any of them, was alive. John of Britford devised the keeping of John and Thomas to Christine, she finding security to the mayor for the keeping as is customary. Executors: his wife Christine and Thomas Bowyer. Proved on 3 August 1361 in front of an officer of the subdean; the administration was entrusted to Christine, reserving the power to entrust it to Thomas when he might come to seek it. Approved at a court held in front the bailiff, the mayor, and other citizens; the seisin of the tenements was released to the legatees. *An attached note records that* after the death of Christine, many years having passed, Thomas Bowyer sought the administration and, because it could not rightfully be denied to him, in front of William of Glinton, the subdean, it was entrusted to him.

(after 24 August 1361)

554 The will of Richard Frear, a citizen of Salisbury, made on 11 August 1361. Interment: in the graveyard of St. Edmund's church. Bequests: 2s. to the fabric of St. Mary's church; 20s. both to the Franciscans of Salisbury and the Dominicans of Fisherton; 20s. to Thomas New, a Franciscan friar; the rest of his goods to his wife Edith. Devises: to Edith for her life conjoined cottages, with a garden and a yard (or yards), in Minster Street, beyond the bar, between John Cole's tenement on the south side and Robert Bunt's tenement on the north side, and conjoined cottages, with a garden, a dovecot, a yard (or yards), and a rack (or racks), in the same street, beyond the bar, between a tenement which William Goldston holds on the south side and Richard's own cottage, of late William Lord's, on the north side. All those cottages were held by Richard by a feoffment of William of Bruton, are to be held by Edith and her assigns, and after Edith's death should be sold by Richard's executors, their executors, or subsequent executors. Richard devised to Edith for life three conjoined cottages in Minster Street, beyond the bar, between John Cole's tenement on the north side and the cottages devised to her on the south side. On Edith's death the cottages should remain for ever to Richard's children John, Edith, and Joan and their issue, and if John, Edith, and Joan were to die without issue they should be sold by the executors. Richard devised to his wife Edith for life a cottage, with a yard (*or* yards) and a rack (*or* racks), in Minster Street, beyond the bar, between Henry of Stapleford's tenement on the north side and his own tenement on the south side. On Edith's death the cottage should remain for ever to John and his issue. If John were to die without issue it would remain for ever to Joan and Edith and their issue, and if Joan and Edith were to die without issue it should be sold by the executors. Richard devised to Joan a cottage in Minster Street, beyond the bar, between the cottage devised to his wife Edith on the north side and a tenement which Philip Stint holds on the south side, to be held for ever by her and her issue. If Joan were to die without issue the cottage would remain for ever to John and Edith, the daughter, and their issue, and if John and Edith were to die without issue it should be sold by the executors. Richard devised to his wife Edith for life a tenement in St. Martin's Street between William Fox's tenement on one side and a tenement of the provost of the college of St. Edmund on the other side. The tenement was held by Richard by a feoffment of Thomas Goodyear, a smith, and on Edith's death should remain for ever to John, Edith, and Joan, and their issue. If John, Edith, and Joan were to die without issue it should be sold by the executors. Richard devised to his executors cottages in Culver Street, which he acquired from Thomas Hungerford, to be sold as soon as possible after his death; John Marshall might have the cottages for 14 marks if he wished. After each sale by the executors the money received should be laid out on celebrating masses and doing other charitable deeds on behalf of Richard's soul, the soul of his wife Edith, and the souls of others. <u>Executors</u>: his wife Edith, John Marshall, the lord John of Bradwell, Roger of Kilmeston, and Thomas of Britford. <u>Proved</u> on 24 August 1361 in front of an officer of the subdean; the administration was entrusted to Edith, Roger, and John Bradwell; John Marshall and Thomas, appearing in person, declined it.

15 September 1361, at Salisbury
William Dunkerton received the office of the clerk of the city
555 By his charter Thomas Read, an executor of Margaret, the relict of Richard Dudmore, a taverner, on the strength Margaret's will granted to Robert of Godmanstone and his wife Joan a tenement in Winchester Street between William of Bruton's tenement on the east side and a tenement which William of Buckland of late held on the west side. The tenement was devised by Margaret to be sold after the death of Agnes Borhams and is to be held for ever by Robert and Joan and Robert's heirs and assigns. Seals: Thomas's and the common and mayoral seals of the city. Named witnesses: the bailiff, the mayor, a reeve, John of Upton, William of Wishford, William of Bruton, George Goss, Nicholas Taylor, Robert Bunt, Thomas of Britford, and John of Farnborough.
556 Approval of the will of John Doder, a citizen of Salisbury, made on 30 August 1361. <u>Interment</u>: in the graveyard of St. Edmund's church. <u>Bequests</u>: 20*s*. to the

fabric of the cathedral church; the rest of his goods to his wife Agnes. Devises: a tenement in Winchester Street, in which William Ashley dwells and which he acquired from Walter Cosham, to John Snel, draper, for life, paying 30s. each year for masses to be celebrated and cloth to be handed out to paupers during that John's life. After John Snel's death the tenement should be sold by John Doder's executors or their executors. The money received should be spent on behalf of John Doder's soul and other souls. John appointed that a tenement in Winchester Street, between John Hoare's tenement on one side and the previously mentioned tenement [?Doder's] on the other side, in which Walter Cooper dwells and which he acquired from Walter Cosham, should be sold by his executors or their executors. According to the order of the executors half the money received should be spent on celebrating masses on behalf of John's soul and the souls of others, and half should be handed out to paupers to pray for the same souls. John devised to Agnes the keeping of his son John, with all the tenements in Salisbury and all the goods and chattels remised to him, until he reached his majority. Those tenements should descend to the younger John by way of inheritance and should be held by him and his issue for ever. If Agnes were to die before that John, the elder John devised the keeping to his own executors, finding security to the mayor and bailiffs of the city. Executors: John Oxford, John Snel, draper, and Agnes. Proved on 4 September 1361 in front of an officer of the subdean; the administration was entrusted to the executors. Approved at a court held in front of the bailiff, the mayor, and other citizens. Agnes declined her dower, and the seisin of the tenements was released to the legatees.

557 Approval of the will of William Cofford, a citizen of Salisbury, made on 25 August 1361. Interment: in the graveyard of St. Edmund's church beside the grave of Ellen, of late his wife. Bequests: 13s. 4d. to the fabric of the cathedral church; half of the rest of his goods to his wife Maud, and half to his executors to be laid out on behalf of the souls of those named below. Devises: to Maud a tenement, with shops next to it, in Chipper Street and Minster Street between George Goss's tenement on one side and a tenement of John Hacker and his wife Agnes on the other side, to be held for her life by her and her assigns. After Maud's death the tenement should be sold by William's executors, their executors, or subsequent executors. The money received should be laid out on celebrating masses, giving alms, and doing other charitable deeds on behalf of William's soul, Maud's soul, and the souls of others. William devised to Maud for her life a yard, excluding two racks constructed in it, which he acquired from Thomas of Hungerford, in Martin's Croft between John Richman's yard on the north side and Richard Still's yard on the south side. He devised the racks, with free ingress and egress, to Nicholas Cofford and Edmund Cofford for their life and the life of the one of them living longer. If Maud were to die while Nicholas and Edmund were living the yard would remain to them and, with the racks, be held for their life by them and their assigns. After the death of Maud, Nicholas, and Edmund the yard, with the racks, should be sold by William's executors or subsequent executors. The money received should be laid out on behalf of the souls of those named above. Executors: Maud, George Goss, William of Wishford, John Anger, and John Bosset. Proved on 21 August 1361 in front of an officer of the subdean; the administration was entrusted to the executors. Approved at a court held in front of the bailiff, the mayor, and other officers of the bishop. The seisin of the tenement was released to the legatees.

558 Approval of the will of Agnes, the relict of William Gill, of late a citizen of Salisbury, made on 5 August 1361. Interment: in the graveyard of St. Edmund's church. Bequests: 40*d*. to the fabric of the cathedral church; half of the rest of her goods to her executors to be laid out in the way described below and on behalf of the same souls; the other half to her daughter Agnes if she survived her for six months or, if not, to be laid out by her own executors on behalf of her soul and the souls of those named below. Devise: a chief tenement, in which she dwelt, in Endless Street, and a tenement in Minster Street, with a yard (*or* yards) and a dovecot, to be sold by her executors, their executors, or subsequent executors as soon after her death as it could be done advantageously. Money received should be used for her debts and the debts of William, her husband, to be discharged and for two chaplains, chosen by the executors with the oversight of William's executors, to celebrate mass in St. Edmund's church on behalf of the souls of Thomas Toostrange, his wife Amice, and others, as William provided for in his will. The rest of the money should be laid out, at the discretion of the executors, on masses, alms, and other charitable deeds on behalf of Agnes's soul, William's soul, and the souls of others. The tenement in which Agnes dwelt, between Robert Gore's corner tenement on the north side and Thomas Hutchins's tenement on the south side, was held by William by a feoffment of Thomas Toostrange and Amice. The tenement in Minster Street, between Thomas of Britford's tenement on the south side and a tenement of late Roger of Wallop's on the north side, was held by Agnes by William's devise. Executors: her mother Agnes, William of Wootton, John Prentice, William at the ford, Walter of Deanbridge, Edward of Deanbridge, John the son of Richard Packer, and Thomas Brute, a tanner. Proved in the cathedral church on 1 September 1361 in front of an officer of the subdean; the administration was entrusted to Agnes, the wife of [John of Woodford: *cf.* **664**] and to William Wootton, John Prentice, Edward Deanbridge, Thomas Brute, and John Packer, reserving the power to entrust it to William at the ford and Walter Deanbridge as co-executors when they might come back. Approved at a court held in front of the bailiff, the mayor, and other citizens; the seisin of the tenements was released to the legatees.

29 September 1361, at Salisbury

559 Approval of the will of Alice Bunt, the relict of Henry Bunt, of Salisbury, made at Kintbury on 14 September 1361. Interment: in the graveyard of Kintbury church. Bequests: 3*s*. to the fabric of the cathedral church; her executors should find a priest to celebrate mass on behalf of her soul and Henry's soul for two years. Devise: the rest of her goods, movable and immovable, to Joan, a daughter of her daughter Christine, and Robert March. If Joan were to die, which God forbid, Robert should have Alice's land, rent, and tenements in Salisbury for ever. Executors: Joan and Robert. Proved on 23 September 1361 in front of an officer of Berkshire; the administration was entrusted to the executors. Approved at a court held in front of the bailiff, the mayor, and other citizens; the seisin of the tenements and rent was released to the legatees.

560 Approval of the will of Philip Odiham made on 26 August 1361. Interment: in the graveyard of St. Thomas's church. Bequests: 12*d*. to the fabric of that church; the rest of his goods to his sons Edmund, Philip, and John to be shared equally among them. Devise: to Edmund, Philip, and John a tenement in New Street between William Vellard's tenement on the east side and Richard Hartwell's tenement on the west side, to be held for ever by them, or the one of them living longest, and their issue. If Edmund, Philip, and John were to die without issue the tenement should be sold by the elder Philip's executors or the executors of those executors. The money received should be laid out on celebrating masses, dangerous ways, destitute paupers, and other charitable deeds on behalf of that Philip's soul, his wife's soul, and the souls of others. Executors: Gilbert Baker and Walter Mere; overseer, Thomas Erlestoke, a chaplain. Proved on 28 August in front of an officer of the subdean; the administration was entrusted to Walter. Gilbert, appearing in person, declined it. Approved at a court held in front of the bailiff, the mayor, and other citizens; the seisin of the tenement was released to the legatees.

561 By their charter Margery, the relict of Robert Osborne, a fisherman, a citizen of Salisbury, and Peter Needler, Robert's executors, on the strength of Robert's will granted to a younger William Tenterer, a citizen of Salisbury, a tenement in St. Martin's Street between William's tenement on the east side and Roger Tanner's tenement on the west side. The tenement was held by Robert by a devise of John Jordan, mercer, was devised by him to be sold by his executors, and is to be held for ever by William and his heirs and assigns. Clause of warranty. Seals: those of Margery and Peter and the common and mayoral seals of the city. Named witnesses: the bailiff, the mayor, the reeves, Robert of Godmanstone, William of Wishford, Robert Bunt, Thomas of Britford, and the clerk.

562 By his charter Robert March granted to Robert Play, a smith, of Salisbury, a rent of 6*s*. a year to be received by him and his heirs and assigns from a tenement, which Robert of Boscombe, a tanner, of late held, in Gigant Street between a tenement of late John Baldry's on one side and a tenement in which Thomas Brute now dwells on the other side; also a rent of 8*s*. a year to be received from the tenement in which Thomas now dwells; also a rent of 12*s*. a year to be received from a tenement, which John Poulshot, a carpenter now holds, in the same street. The rents are to be held for ever by Robert Play and his heirs and assigns with the reversion of the tenements when it fell due. Seals: Robert March's and the common and mayoral seals of the city. Named witnesses: the bailiff, the mayor, John of Upton, Robert of Godmanstone, William of Wishford, and the reeves.

563 By his charter Robert March, an executor of Alice, the relict, and an executor, of Henry Bunt, of late a citizen of Salisbury, on the strength of Henry's will granted to Walter Cooper, of Salisbury, a tenement in Winchester Street between a tenement formerly Thomas of Stratford's on one side and a tenement formerly that of Henry at the bar, a clerk, on the other side; also a cottage, with a yard, beyond the bars, opposite the bishop of Salisbury's land held in villeinage in the Old Town, between a tenement formerly Henry Dogskin's on one side and a tenement formerly Matthew Beveridge's on the other side. The tenement and the cottage were devised by Henry Bunt to be sold by his executors or their executors and are to be held for ever by Walter and his heirs and assigns. Seals: Robert's and the common and mayoral seals of the city. Named witnesses: the bailiff, the mayor, John of Upton, Robert of Godmanstone, William of Wishford, and the reeves.

13 October 1361, at Salisbury
564 Approval of the will of John Robet, of Haxton, a citizen of Salisbury, made on 23 December 1360. Bequests: 2s. to the fabric of the cathedral church; the rest of his goods to his executors to do with them, on behalf of the souls of those named below, what seemed best to them. Devises: to his wife Edith a tenement, opposite the market place where grains are sold, between a tenement of late Richard of Tidworth's on the east side and a tenement of late Nicholas Skilling's on the west side, to be held for her life by her and her assigns. After Edith's death the tenement should be sold by John's executors or their executors. The money received should be laid out in the city or elsewhere in Wiltshire on celebrating masses, on other alms, and on doing charitable deeds on behalf of John's soul, Edith's soul, and the souls of others. John devised to Edith a rent of 20s. a year issuing from a chief tenement, formerly John Sorrel's, lying opposite the same market place. The rent was held by John Robet by a feoffment of Henry of Ludwell, of late the vicar of Laverstock, and John of Upton, is to be held for her life by Edith and her assigns, and after Edith's death should be sold by John's executors, their executors, or subsequent executors as quickly as it could be done profitably. The money received should be laid out in the way described above and on behalf of the same souls. John devised to Edith three conjoined shops in Scots Lane between a tenement formerly William Bartlet's on one side and a corner tenement of late Ralph of Langford's on the other side. Those shops were held by John by a grant of Ralph's son John and Hugh Oliver, Ralph's executors, are to be held for her life by Edith and her assigns, and after Edith's death should be sold by John's executors or subsequent executors. The money received should be laid out in the way described above and on behalf of the same souls. John devised to William Duckman, of Devizes, a yard in Nuggeston between a cottage and a yard both Henry Pope's on one side and a cottage and a yard both Maud Haxton's on the other side. The yard was held by John by a grant of Joyce Taverner and his wife Margaret and is to be held for ever by William and his heirs and assigns. Executors: his wife Edith, John at the wick, William Duckman, and Richard Ryborough. Proved on 17 September 1361 in front of Roger of Clowne, the archdeacon of Salisbury; the administration was entrusted to Edith, John, and William, reserving the power to entrust it to Richard when he might come to seek it. Approved on the same day in front of an officer of the subdean; the administration was entrusted and reserved likewise. Approved at a court held in

front of the bailiff, the mayor, and other citizens; the seisin of the tenements and rent was released to the legatees.

565 Approval of the will of Christine, the wife of Robert New, a citizen of Salisbury, made on 4 September 1361. Interment: in the graveyard of St. Martin's church. Bequests: 12d. to the fabric of the cathedral church; 12d. to the fabric of St. Martin's church, 2s. 6d. to the parochial chaplain to celebrate a trental in it on behalf of her soul, and 6d. to the deacon; 2s. 6d. both to the Franciscans of Salisbury and the Dominicans of Fisherton; 2d. each to her godchildren; the rest of her goods to her son Stephen and her daughters Joan and Amice to be divided equally among them. Devise: to Stephen the tenements, shops, cottages, and rent which she held in Salisbury, both by a devise of her father Henry Bunt and by purchase, to be held for ever by him and his issue. If Stephen were to die without issue the premises and the rent should be sold by Christine's executors or their executors. The money received should be spent in Salisbury on the salvation of Christine's soul, Stephen's soul, and the souls of others. Executors: Stephen and John, a son of William Bunt, formerly her husband. Proved on 19 September 1361 in front of an officer of the subdean; the administration was entrusted to John Bunt, Stephen being dead. Approved at a court held in front of the bailiff, the mayor, and other citizens; the seisin of the tenements was released to the legatees.

566 Approval of the will of Edith, the relict of Richard of Farley, spicer, a citizen of Salisbury, made on 4 September 1361. Interment: in the graveyard of St. Thomas's church in the tomb formerly of her father Geoffrey of Warminster, a citizen of Salisbury. Bequests: 10s. to the fabric of the cathedral church; 2s. to the fabric of St. Thomas's church; 12d. to Ayleswade bridge; a trental both to the Dominicans of Fisherton and the Franciscans; 2d. to each priest celebrating mass in St. Thomas's church on the day of her burial; a best gold ring to the image of the Blessed Mary at the west door; 12d. and a second-best kerchief from Worms to Cecily, a daughter of Thomas Mussel; 12d. to Margery, a daughter of John at the wood; 40d., a rosary of amber beads, and a second-best robe to Joan, a daughter of William Stanley; 20s. to William Stanley, 13s. 4d. to his wife Agnes, and 6s. 8d. to his son William; 20s., a coverlet, a tapet being for weaving, and a tapet, with two second-best linen cloths and a blanket, to John, her apprentice; 6s. 8d. each to Richard of Farley, of Stockton, and the lord Thomas Erlestoke, a chaplain; 20s. for her funeral expenses; the rest of her goods to her daughter Alice. Edith appointed that John, her apprentice, should keep up her shop around the Guildhall until the debts of her and her husband Richard were paid with the goods being in the shop and the debts leviable and receivable by them. The goods kept and sold in good faith, the debts paid, and an account concerning the receipts and payments made to John by her executors, Edith, for herself and her executors, released to John the term of his apprenticeship. She appointed that if her daughter Alice were to die under-age, guiltless, and unmarried the goods left to her should be sold by her own executors, their executors, or subsequent executors, or by a keeper who had the keeping of Alice, and laid out on celebrating masses, dangerous ways, destitute paupers, and charitable deeds on behalf of the soul of her husband Richard, the souls of herself and Alice, and the souls of others. Devises: to Alice two tenements in New Street, one between a tenement formerly Robert Painter's on one side and Walter Franklin's tenement on the other side, and the other between Richard Long's tenement on one side and Robert Burgess's tenement on the other side. Those tenements were held by Edith by a devise of her father Geoffrey, are to be held for ever by Alice and her issue, and if Alice were to die issue would remain for ever to Edith's nearest blood relative. Executors: William Stanley and John Warman. Proved on 10 September 1361 in front of an officer of the subdean; the administration was entrusted to the executors. Approved at a court held in front of the bailiff, the mayor, and other citizens; the seisin of the tenements was released to the legatees.

567 Approval of the will of Adam Inways, a burgess of Southampton, made on 17 July 1361. Interment: in the church of the Blessed Mary near Southampton. Bequests: £20 to perform his funeral rites on the day of his burial; 10 marks to be handed out to paupers on the day of his burial; 20s. to the fabric of the church of the Blessed Mary; 6s. 8d. each to the fabric of All Saints' church, Southampton, the fabric of St. Laurence's church there, and the fabric of St. John's church there; 13s. 4d. to the fabric of the church of the Holy Cross there; 10 marks to the fabric of the bell of St. Michael's church there, 40s. to the rector, and 6d. to each priest celebrating mass there; 40s. both to the Franciscans of Southampton and the Dominicans of Salisbury; 20s. in each case to the Franciscans of Winchester, the Dominicans of Winchester, the Augustinians of Winchester, the Carmelites of Winchester, and the Franciscans of Salisbury. The money bequeathed should be paid to those chaplains and friars within a month after Adam's death. Adam bequeathed £20 to a chaplain who would celebrate mass on behalf of his soul and the souls of all the faithful departed for five years in St. Michael's church; 100s. to Adam Hain; 60s. to Andrew Limeburner; 100s. to Thomas of Kington; 10s. and a robe to William, his cook; 6s. 8d. and a robe to John Packer; 40s., a robe, and a feather bed with all the equipment to Richard Pyeleg; four feather beds with all the equipment, two pieces of best silver, and £20 to Alice, the wife of William Bennett; four feather beds with all the equipment, a box full of linen sheets and coverlets, four pieces of best silver, £40, the whole cloth lying above his head in a room, eight silver bowls, and two little mazers to Robert, a son of his deceased brother Adam; 40s. to the lord Stephen Bottlesham, a chaplain; two feather beds with all the equipment, two pieces of silver, and £20 to both Joan and Marion, daughters of Nicholas Wrong; 40s. to Robert Long; 60s. to Nicholas Wrong; 20 dozen cloths of Wells in a bundle, 10 cloths of Winchester in a bundle, and four silver bowls to William Bennett; 40s. each to Christine and William, his servants at Romsey; 100s. and a feather bed with all the equipment to Joan, his servant at Southampton; 10s. to John Alton; 100s. each to Amice Parlabean and Joan, the wife of John Barber, of Romsey; 60s. to Joan, the relict of John Stacy; 20s. to the lord John Donnet, a chaplain; the rest of his goods to be put in order and handed out to paupers and indigent religious men on behalf of his soul and the souls of others. Devises: to Alice, the wife of William Bennett, a tenement, with appurtenant cottages, in Simnel Street, Southampton, opposite Henry Fleming's house in St. Michael's parish, to be held for ever by her and her heirs and assigns. Adam devised to Robert, the son of his brother Adam, two shops in Bull Street, in St. John's parish, Southampton, which he acquired from Thomas Cust; also a corner tenement, which his father Robert Inways devised to him, in Salisbury opposite the market place where fish are sold; also three shops in Winchester Street opposite the [?common trench of] running water and beside Walter Smith's corner [tenement]; also a yard, behind Henry Fleming's shop, touching the town wall of Southampton. The shops, the tenement, and the yard are to be held for ever by Robert and his heirs and assigns. Executors: William Bennett, his kinsman Robert Long, and John Donnet; overseer, Thomas of Kington. Proved on 8 September 1361 in front of the dean of Southampton in St. Michael's church; the administration was entrusted to the executors. Approved at a court held in front of the bailiff, the mayor, and other citizens; the seisin of the tenements was released to the legatees.

568 Approval of the will of William Goldston, a citizen of Salisbury, made on 18 May 1361. Interment: in the graveyard of St. Martin's church near a cross there. Bequests: 3s. 4d. each to the fabric of the cathedral church and the fabric of St. Martin's church; the rest of his goods to his wife Christine. Devises: to Christine a chief tenement, in Winchester Street between John Hoare's tenement on the west side and Richard Still's tenement on the east side, of which William held half by a grant of William Easton and his wife Maud and half by a grant of Joan, the relict of Thomas Gleese. The whole is to be held for her life by Christine and her assigns, and after Christine's death should be sold by William's or her executors or by their executors. The money received should be laid out on celebrating masses, other alms, and charitable deeds on behalf of William's soul, Christine's soul, and the souls of others. A garden in Freren Street, between Agnes Bodenham's cottage on one side and Richard Cook's garden on the other side, should be sold by William's executors immediately after his death. The money received should be used to fulfil his bequests and pay his debts. Executors: his wife Christine and a younger William Buckland; overseer, the lord Thomas, a chaplain of St. Martin's parish. Proved on 21 August 1361 in front of an officer of the subdean; the administration was entrusted to Christine and Thomas, reserving the power to entrust it also to William when he might come to seek it. Approved at a court held in front of the bailiff, the mayor, and other citizens; the seisin of the tenements was released to the legatees.

569 Approval of the will of Richard of Otterbourne, a citizen of Salisbury, made on 16 August 1361. Interment: in the graveyard of the cathedral church in front of the image of the Blessed Virgin on the west side. Bequests: 100s. to the fabric of that church; 2s. 6d. to the fabric of St. Thomas's church, with the 40d. devised by Richard's late wife Joan for a chalice of the high altar to be gilded; 2s. 6s. to the fabric of St. Edmund's church; 2s. to the fabric of St. Martin's church; 40s. to Thomas Chaplin, and a rosary of beryl beads to his wife Joan; 20s. and a rosary of beads of coral mixed with silver to John Winterbourne; a trental to the lord Thomas Enford; ½d. to each pauper on the day of his burial; his other funeral expenses to be laid out by his executors; a bugle-horn for drinking and four silver spoons to John Stallington, a clerk; 5s. to each order of friars in Salisbury; 12d. both to St. Nicholas's hospital and the lepers of Harnham; a trental to the lord Nicholas Boor; the rest of his goods to be divided into three parts, one for masses and other pious alms, one for his two daughters and their mother, and one for his sister Christine, her son Richard, and her four daughters; the keeping of his two daughters, and everything appointed to them, to their mother until their majority; 12d. to Roger, his lad, if he outlived him. <u>Devise</u>: to his daughters Edith and Agnes, and to the one of them living longer, a tenement in New Street between a tenement formerly John of Wells's on the east side and John of Upton's tenement on the west side. If Edith and Agnes were to die without issue Richard devised the tenement for life to his mother Joan, and after her death to the keepers of the fabric of the cathedral church to be disposed of on behalf of Richard's soul for the benefit of the fabric. <u>Executors</u>: the master John of Wilton and Thomas Chaplin. <u>Proved</u> on 19 August 1361 in front of an officer of the subdean; the administration was entrusted to the executors. <u>Approved</u> at a court held in front of the bailiff, the mayor, and other citizens; the seisin of the tenement was released to the legatees.

570 Approval of the will of William Friend, a citizen of Salisbury, made on 13 September 1361. <u>Interment</u>: in the graveyard of St. Edmund's church. <u>Bequests</u>: 6s. 8d. to the fabric of the cathedral church; 12d. to the lord Thomas Skilling, a chaplain; 2s. to William Lord; 40d. each to John Merriott, Alice Merriott, and Roger, his servant; the rest of his goods to his wife Christine. <u>Devises</u>: to Christine a tenement in St. Martin's Street, with adjacent shops in Brown Street, in which Henry, a son of Robert Baldry and his wife Agnes, formerly dwelt, and which at some time was Douce Baldry's. The tenement, with the shops, was held by William by a feoffment of William Chandler and Robert Alwin, executors of Agnes, the relict of Robert Baldry, an executor of Henry Baldry, the son of Robert and her, and of John of Salisbury, formerly the parson of St. Thomas's church, and Adam of Ludwell, of late the mayor, is to be held for her life by Christine and her assigns, and after Christine's death should be sold by William's executors, their executors, or subsequent executors. The money received should be laid out on celebrating masses, giving alms, and doing other charitable deeds on behalf of William's soul, Christine's soul, and the souls of others. William devised to Christine a messuage in Freren Street between a tenement of the college of St. Edmund on one side and William Pain's tenement on the other side. The messuage was held by William by a feoffment of Robert Gore, is to be held for her life by Christine and her assigns, and after her death should be sold by William's executors or subsequent executors. The money received should be laid out for chaplains, to be chosen by the executors, to celebrate mass on behalf of William's soul, Christine's soul, and the souls of others. William devised to Christine, the relict of John Friend, a tenement, with a yard, in New Street between a tenement formerly Robert of Knoyle's on the east side and shops of late Robert Baldry's on the west side. The tenement was held by William, John Steward, and Henry Bull by a grant of John Friend and, with the yard, is to be held for ever by Christine and her heirs and assigns. Before Christine receives the seisin of the tenement she should pay to William's executors £40 or give to them such security for the payment of it as she and they can agree on. If Christine were not to pay the money, nor find sufficient security, the tenement, with the yard, should be sold by those executors or subsequent executors. William bequeathed the money received to Christine except for £40 in which John, of late her husband, is bound to William by the Statute of Merchants, in which case the statute would have no value. Executors: his wife Christine, William Ashley, Thomas Hill, and John Melksham. Proved on 15 September 1361 in front of an officer of the subdean; the administration was entrusted to the executors. Approved at a court held in front of the bailiff, the mayor, and other citizens; the seisin of the tenements was released to the legatees.

571 Approval of the will of Alice, the wife of William of Wootton, dyer, of Salisbury, made on 15 July 1361. Interment: in the graveyard of St. Edmund's church. Bequests: 40*d*. to the fabric of the cathedral church; 40*s*. to William's son John; half of the rest of her goods to William, and half to her executors to find a chaplain to celebrate mass on behalf of her soul and the souls of others for as long as that half would last. Devises: to her husband a chief tenement in Winchester Street between a tenement of late Robert of Knoyle's on the east side and a tenement formerly that of Osmund of Cholderton (*Childryngton*) on the west side. The tenement was of late Gilbert of Bridgehampton's, is to be held for his life by William and his assigns, and after William's death should be sold by his executors, their executors, or subsequent executors. The money received should be laid out on celebrating masses, other alms, and doing charitable deeds on behalf of Alice's soul, William's soul, and the souls of others. Executors: William of Wootton and William Gill. Proved on 12 August 1361 in front of an officer of the subdean; the administration was entrusted to William of Wootton, William Gill being dead. Approved at a court held in front of the bailiff, the mayor, and other citizens; the seisin of the tenement was released to the legatee.

572 By their charter John of Upton and William Pain, executors of Christine, the relict of Peter Bennett, of late a citizen of Salisbury, on the strength of Christine's will granted to Thomas Boyton, bowyer, of Salisbury, a tenement, with shops, opposite the market place where wool is sold, between a tenement of late that of Robert of Woodford, a clothier, on the south side and a corner tenement which John of Beaminster now holds on the north side. In her will Christine devised the tenement, with the shops, to be sold by her executors, and it is to be held for ever by Thomas and his heirs and assigns. Seals: those of John and William. Named witnesses: the bailiff, the mayor, the reeves, Nicholas Taylor, William of Wishford, Thomas of Britford, Robert of Godmanstone, William of Bruton, and the clerk.

573 By their charter John Hoare, a citizen of Salisbury, and his wife Gillian, a daughter of John Durrington, granted to John Cole and John Hawk, citizens of Salisbury, [Chantrell's Corner], a corner tenement formerly John Chantrell's, at the butchers' stalls, between John of Langford's shops on the west side and a street of the city. The tenement was held by William of Stockbridge, ironmonger, and his wife Agnes by a feoffment of William Durrington and descended to Gillian by inheritance if William and Agnes were to have died without joint issue. John Hoare and Gillian also granted to John Cole and John Hawk a tenement in New Street, beyond the bar, between a tenement of late Richard Batt's on the east side and a tenement of late Adam Barnwell's on the west side. The tenement descended to Gillian by inheritance on the death of Agnes, a daughter and heir of John Durrington. The two tenements are to be held for ever by John Cole and John Hawk and their heirs and assigns. Clause of warranty. Seals: those of John Hoare and Gillian and the common and mayoral seals of the city. Named witnesses: the bailiff, the mayor, John of Upton, Thomas of Britford, Robert of Godmanstone, William of Wishford, and George Goss.

17 October 1361, at Salisbury
574 By her letters Alice, the relict of John Tott, of Netheravon, of late a citizen of Salisbury, quitclaimed to her son Thomas Tott and his heirs and assigns her right or claim to a corner tenement in Winchester Street [*rectius* Wineman Street: *cf.* **575, 600, 652, 730**] between a tenement of late John Anger's on the east side and Thomas Hutchins's tenement on the north side. Seals: Alice's and the common and mayoral seals of the city. Named witnesses: the bailiff, the mayor, the reeves, John of Upton, William of Wishford, Robert of Godmanstone, and Thomas of Britford.

19 October 1361, at Salisbury
575 By his charter Thomas, a son and heir of John Tott, of Netheravon, of late a citizen of Salisbury, granted to William of Peakirk, the rector of Dinton, Stephen Newton, the rector of Little Langford, William Dunn, and Walter Kerry a corner tenement in Wineman Street and Endless Street between a tenement of late John Anger's on the east side and Thomas Hutchins's tenement on the north side. The tenement descended to Thomas by right of inheritance on the death of his father and is to be held for ever by the grantees and their heirs and assigns. Clause of warranty. Seals: Thomas's and the common and mayoral seals of the city. Named witnesses: the bailiff, the mayor, the reeves, John of Upton, Robert of Godmanstone, William of Wishford, Thomas of Bridgehampton, Robert Bunt, and George Goss.

20 October 1361, at Salisbury
576 By her letters Alice, the relict of John Tott, of Netheravon, of late a citizen of Salisbury, quitclaimed to the lord William of Peakirk, the rector of Dinton, Stephen Newton, the rector of Little Langford, William Dunn, Walter Kerry, and their heirs and assigns her right or claim to a tenement in Winchester Street [*rectius* Wineman Street: *cf.* **575, 600, 652, 730**] and Endless Street between a tenement of late John Anger's on the east side and Thomas Hutchins's tenement on the north side. Clause of warranty. Seals: Alice's and the common and mayoral seals of the city. Named witnesses: the bailiff, the mayor, the reeves, John of Upton, Robert of Godmanstone, William of Wishford, Thomas of Bridgehampton, and Robert Bunt.

27 October 1361, at Salisbury

577 Approval of the will of John Wallop, a clothier, a citizen of Salisbury, made on 18 October 1361. Interment: in the graveyard of St. Edmund's church. Bequests: 20s. to the fabric of the cathedral church; the rest of his goods should be divided in two, part to John at the wick and Agnes, that John's wife and his own daughter, and part to be handed out among feeble and destitute paupers. Devise: to John at the wick and Agnes a corner tenement, with conjoined shops and yards, in Minster Street and Scots Lane between Richard Ryborough's tenement on the east side and a tenement of the lord Thomas of Erlestoke on the north side. The tenement was of late Thomas Thurstan's, is to be held for ever by John and Agnes and Agnes's issue, and if Agnes were to die without living issue by John would remain to John for his life. After the death of John and, [without issue], Agnes the tenement should be sold by John Wallop's executors, their executors, or subsequent executors. The money received should be laid out as follows: 10 marks on the improvement of ways and bridges, 10 marks on the common affairs of the mayor and commonalty for the time being, and the rest on chaplains, to be chosen by the executors, to celebrate mass in St. Edmund's church on behalf of his soul, the souls of his father, his mother, Edith, of late his wife, and his daughter Agnes, and the souls of others. The tenement should be sold, and the money spent, under the supervision of the mayor for the time being. Executors: his brother Thomas Wallop, John at the wick, and John Bosset. Proved in the cathedral church on 20 October 1361 in front of an officer of the subdean; the administration was entrusted to Thomas Wallop and John at the wick, reserving the power to entrust it to John Bosset when he might come to seek it. Approved at a court held in front of the bailiff, the mayor, and other citizens; the seisin of the tenement was released to the legatees.

578 The will of Joan Butterley, a lady, of Landford, made on 1 September 1361. Interment: [*place unspecified*]. Bequests: 6s. 8d. to the fabric of the cathedral church; 2s. to the church of Christ; a best ox, a best cow, 30 best sheep, and a coverlet for the great cross in St. Andrew's church, Landford, 10 wethers for the maintenance of the light of the Blessed Mary there, 20 best sheep, an ox, a best cow, and 1 qr. of wheat and 2 qr. of barley from the best corn to John White, the rector, for the maintenance of his chancel, a best tablecloth for making two cloths for the high altar, a towel for the hands of the priest, 6 ells of linen cloth for making a vestment, a second-best brass pot for the bell, a quantity of lead for the fabric, 18 sheep for a house and for a light of St. Mary Magdalen in the graveyard, and a small coffer for keeping vestments and necessities in the church; 20s. for the salvation of Joan's soul, and a small maple-wood bowl bound with silver gilt, to John White; 20s. to the lord William of Netton to pray for her soul, 20s. and a piece of silver to make a chalice which will remain to him and his successors to celebrate mass on behalf of the souls of Thomas of Butterley and Joan, a third-best brass pot and a basin with a laver, a coffer standing at the end of her bed for his vestments, and an old maple-wood bowl; a silk belt each to Nicholas Buck and John White; two coverlets with two testers, two linen cloths, a counterpoint, a larger bowl with the furniture, two coffers from Flanders, and a maple-wood bowl to John Butterley; a complete bed with all the equipment, two tablecloths, two lined towels, a small silver bowl with the furniture, a green coffer bound with iron, and a maple-wood bowl to Richard of Knottingley; 20 sheep, an ox, a heifer, 2 qr. of wheat, and 1 qr. of barley to Richard Howes, her bailiff; 4 qr. of wheat, 5 qr. of barley, a cart bound with iron, 3 horses, and a plough with the equipment to her son Thomas of Lea; 4 qr. of wheat, 5 qr. of barley, a gown, a coat with a hood, of one suit, a red coverlet, a blanket, two linen cloths, a parcel of motley wool, a russet, and the white wool which lies beside that russet to Maud Blowers; a complete bed and a brass pot containing 3 gallons to Richard Howes, and three pieces of wool to his wife Maud; a mantle furred with miniver to the friar Thomas Scammel; a mantle furred with budge to the Dominican friars; 3 qr. of barley and 2 bu. of wheat of good measure, for 2 qr. of malt, to Christine at the wood; 2 wethers to Joan's godson Thomas at the wood; 10s. or the value to both John Howes and John Bailiff; 5s. or the value to William Baggs; 2 bu. of wheat and 2 bu. of barley to each of her servants; the rest of her goods, after her grave has been honourably made, to John of Butterley and Richard of Knottingley in equal portions. Devises: to William of Netton for his life a rent of 35s. a year issuing from a tenement, which the lord Nicholas Buck holds, opposite St. Edmund's church, and a rent of 5s. a year issuing from a tenement in Salisbury which Richard Mount formerly held. Joan devised the reversion of the rents to her executors to sell them and to carry out pious uses for the salvation of her soul and the souls of Thomas of Butterley and his former wife Agnes. She devised all her [?other] rent in Salisbury to be sold by her executors. The money raised should laid out on behalf of her soul, the souls of Thomas of Butterley and Agnes, and the souls of the poor and for masses to be celebrated. Executors: John White, John Butterley, and Richard of Knottingley. Proved on 6 September 1361 in the cathedral church in front of Roger of Clowne, the archdeacon of Salisbury; the administration was entrusted to the executors. The executors brought forth the will at the court held on 27 October.

579 The will of William Sexhampcote, made on 19 August 1361. Interment: in the graveyard of St. Edmund's church. Bequests: 2s. each to the fabric the cathedral church, the fraternity of the high cross in that church, and the fraternity of the light of the Blessed Mary at its west door; ½ mark to the fabric of St. Edmund's church, 40d. to the fraternity of the high cross of St. Edmund, 12d. to each chaplain of the college, 6d. a year to each annual chaplain celebrating mass in the church on the day of his burial, and 2s. to the lord John of Bradwell, the parochial chaplain; a trental both to the Dominicans of Fisherton and the Franciscans of Salisbury; 2s. to the fraternity of St. Anne's light at the east gate of the Close; 40d. to the fabric of St. Michael's church, Figheldean [*miscopied as* Fisherton]; 40s. to his brother Robert; 20s. to each of his other brothers; 40s., cash or in service, to his sister Edith; 13s. 4d. to Walter Mere; ½ mark to John, his apprentice; a best coat, with a hood, to Richard, his servant; a second-best robe to Walter, his servant; a best robe to Philip Penn, his servant; 40d. to William Lord; 10 marks to his daughter Agnes; if Agnes were to die before she married

5 of the 10 marks should remain to William's wife, and 5 should be laid out on celebrating masses and doing other charitable deeds on behalf of his soul and the souls of others; the rest of his goods to his wife Joan; [*bequest unspecified*] for a chaplain, chosen by his executors, to celebrate mass in St. Edmund's church for a year after his death. Devises: to Joan a shop in Minster Street, between a tenement of the college of St. Edmund on one side and a tenement of Walter at the burgh on the other side, to be held for her life by her and her assigns. On Joan's death the shop should remain for ever to William's daughter Agnes and her issue, and if Agnes were to die without issue it should be sold by William's executors, their executors, or subsequent executors. The money received should be laid out on behalf of William's soul, the souls of Joan and Agnes, and the souls of others. William devised to Joan a rent of 4*s.* a year issuing from a tenement in Endless Street between John Pannett's tenement on one side and a tenement which Walter Holbury holds on the other side. The rent was acquired by him from William of Bruton, is to be held for her life by Joan and her assigns, on Joan's death should remain for ever to Agnes and her issue, and if Agnes were to die without issue would remain for ever to a kinsman of William's blood. Executors: Joan, Roger Ward, Robert Sexhampcote, and Thomas Sexhampcote. Proved on 28 August 1361 in front of an officer of the subdean; the administration was entrusted to the executors. The executors brought forth the will at the court held on 27 October.

580 The will of John Monkton, a citizen of Salisbury, made on 2 September 1361. Interment: in the graveyard of St. Martin's church. Bequests: 12*d.* to the fabric of the cathedral church; 6*d.* to the fabric of St. Martin's church, 6*d.* to the high altar for his forgotten tithes, 3*d.* each to the deacon and the sacristan, and 7 marks cash for a chaplain to celebrate mass in the church for a year on behalf of John's soul and the souls of others; £10 cash to his son Nicholas, and if Nicholas were to die within a term of 6 years or 10 years the £10 would remain to John's executors or their executors to do with what seemed best to them on behalf of John's soul and the souls of others; two complete second-best beds, a second-best brass pot and a small ewer, a coffer, and two best pans to Nicholas; 2*s.* to the lord Thomas Erlestoke, a chaplain; 5*s.* to the Dominicans of Fisherton to celebrate two trental masses on behalf of his soul and the souls of others; 2*s.* 6*d.* to the Franciscans of Salisbury to celebrate mass likewise; 6*d.* to the lord John Chatt; 10 marks for expenses incurred around his corpse on the day of his burial, as on improving the wax and other matters; 5*s.* and a coat, with a hood made for it, to William Boyland; 5*s.* cash and a coat, with a hood, newly bought, to John Justice; a striped coat to John Newport; a striped coat, with a hood, to Richard Swain; the rest of his goods to his wife Alice and his children. Devise: to Alice for life a tenement, in which John dwelt, in Winchester Street between a tenement of late that of John Springham, draper, on the west side and Gilbert Brazier's tenement on the east side. The tenement was held by John by a feoffment of William Wishford, draper, after Alice's death should be held for life by Nicholas, a son of John and Alice, and after Nicholas's death should remain to John's executors to be sold. The money received should be spent on behalf of John's soul and the souls of others, paying 6*d.* a year for the fabric of St. Martin's church and 6*d.* for the light burning near the cross there. Executors: his wife Alice, William Boyland, and John Justice. Witnesses: John Newport, Richard Swain, and Thomas, a clerk, the scribe. Proved on 6 September 1361 in front of an officer of the subdean; the administration was entrusted to the executors. The executors brought forth the will at the court held on 27 October.

581 The will of William Newman, a citizen of Salisbury, made on 9 July 1361. Interment: in the graveyard of St. Edmund's church. Bequests: 12*d*. to the fabric of the cathedral church, and 6*d*. to the light burning in front of the high cross there; 12*d*. to the fabric of St. Edmund's church; 20*s*. for all the expenses incurred around his corpse on the day of his burial; the rest of his goods to his wife Edith and her daughter Maud; 2*s*. each to Barnabas, a son of Robert Kendal, and Agnes, a daughter of that Robert; 3 dozen shoes to be handed out among paupers on behalf of his soul; 10*s*. to Thomas Bishop, a clerk. Devise: to Edith a tenement in Endless Street, between a tenement of late Hugh Langford's on the south side and William's own tenement, of late Thomas Caws's, on the north side, to be held for her life by Edith and her assigns. On Edith's death the tenement should remain for ever to John, a son of William's brother Henry, and his issue, and if John were to die without issue should be sold by William's executors, their executors, or subsequent executors. The money received should be laid out on celebrating masses, other alms, and doing charitable deeds on behalf of his soul, the souls of Edith and Margery, of late his wife, and the souls of others. Executors: his wife Edith and Thomas Bishop. Proved on 9 August 1361 in front of an officer of the subdean; the administration was entrusted to Edith, Thomas being dead. The executor brought forth the will at the court held on 27 October.

582 Approval of the will of Richard Cook, a citizen of Salisbury, made on 27 August 1361. Interment: in the graveyard of St. Martin's church. Bequests: 2*s*. to the fabric of the cathedral church; 12*d*. to the fabric of St. Martin's church, 12*d*. to the lord Thomas, the parochial chaplain, 12*d*. to the lord John Chatt, and 2*s*. to the high altar for his forgotten tithes; 2*s*. 6*d*. to the Franciscans of Salisbury to celebrate a trental mass; the rest of his goods to his wife Emme. Devises: to Emme a tenement, in which he dwelt, in Freren Street opposite the Franciscans, to be held for ever by her and her heirs and assigns. Richard devised to John Chandler, a citizen of Salisbury, a cottage between his own tenement on one side and the ditch called the Trench opposite the Franciscans on the other side, to be held for ever by him and his heirs and assigns; also to John a garden, which Richard acquired from Philip Odiham, formerly a citizen of Salisbury, in Freren Street between a garden formerly William Goldston's on one side and a garden formerly William Buckland's on the other side, to be held for ever by John and his heirs and assigns. Richard devised to Emme a garden between William Difford's garden on one side and the garden which he devised to John Chandler on the other side, to be held for ever by Emme and her heirs and assigns. Executors: his wife Emme and John Chandler. Witnesses: Thomas, a clerk, the scribe, and the executors. Proved on 5 September 1361 in front of an officer of the subdean; the administration was entrusted to the executors. Approved at a court held in front of the bailiff, the mayor, and other citizens; the seisin of the tenements was released to the legatees.

583 The will of Robert Steed, of Fisherton near Salisbury, made on 3 August 1361. <u>Interment</u>: in the graveyard of the Dominicans of Fisherton. <u>Bequests</u>: 13*s*. 4*d*. for all his funeral expenses except wax, and 3*s*. for wax to be bought; 5*s*. to be handed out among paupers on the day of his burial; a silver bowl to the Dominicans of Fisherton; 12*d*. to the fabric of St. Clement's church, Fisherton; a silver spoon to the friar Richard of Collingbourne; a spoon to the rector of Fisherton church; a muid of iron, an anvil, and a hammer to Robert, a son of John Marshall; a yoke, with its appurtenances, to the vicar of Shrewton; a yoke to his brother; a scythe and 12 horseshoes to William Waite; a tapet and a linen sheet to Hugh, a son of that William; 12 horseshoes to Thomas Thornborough; 12 horseshoes to William Thornborough; a brass pot, a brass pan, a tapet, and three linen cloths to Gillian, his maid; the rest of his goods to his wife Lettice. <u>Devises</u>: to John Marshall, of Salisbury, a rent of 6*s*. a year issuing from a house and a shop, formerly Roger Marshall's, to be held for ever by him and his heirs and assigns. Robert devised to Lettice a rent of 6*s*. a year issuing from the house and the shop, to be held for ever by her and her heirs and assigns; Lettice, or the heir or assign to whom the rent might come, should find a square candle to burn for ever in St. Clement's church in front of the image of St. Thomas of Canterbury. <u>Executors</u>: his wife Lettice and John Marshall. <u>Proved</u> on 27 August 1361 in front of an officer of the subdean; the administration was entrusted to the executors. The executors brought forth the will at the court held on 27 October.

584 The will of Henry Long, made on 28 July 1341. <u>Interment</u>: in the graveyard of St. Swithun's church, Winchester. <u>Bequests</u>: 12*d*. to the rector of St. Laurence's church, and a trental to the Carmelites, in each case to celebrate mass on behalf of his soul. <u>Devises</u>: to his wife Alice for life a tenement in New Street, Salisbury, between Geoffrey Warminster's tenement on the east side and John Fountain's tenement on the west side. Alice should devise the tenement to be sold after her death, and the money raised should be laid out by her executors on masses and alms on behalf her soul, Henry's soul, and the souls of others. Henry devised to Alice half a tenement, that of his brother William Salisbury, which descended to Henry by right of inheritance to be divided between him and his brother Thomas Long according to the custom of the city. Alice should sell the half to discharge Henry's debts on behalf of his soul. <u>Executors</u>: his wife Alice and Philip Hatter, an assistant. <u>Proved</u> on 3 September 1341 in front of the dean of Winchester; the administration was entrusted to Alice. The executors brought forth the will at the court held on 27 October.

585 By their charter Agnes, the relict, and an executor, of John Doder, of late a citizen of Salisbury, and John of Oxford and John Snel, her co-executors, on the strength of John Doder's will granted to the lords John of Bradwell and Nicholas Buck, chaplains, a tenement, with shops, in Winchester Street between John Hoare's tenement on the west side and William of Wishford's messuage on the east side, with a gate in Brown Street next to it. The tenement, with the shops and the gate, was devised by John Doder to be sold and is to be held for ever by John and Nicholas and their heirs and assigns. Seals: those of the grantors and the common and mayoral seals of the city. Named witnesses: the bailiff, the mayor, the reeves, John of Upton, Robert of Godmanstone, William of Wishford, Thomas of Bridgehampton, and Thomas of Britford

586 By his charter John of Upton, a citizen of Salisbury, granted to Agnes, the relict of John Doder, of late a citizen of Salisbury, and to her son John three cottages, with a garden, in Gigant Street between John of Handley's cottages on one side and Agnes's cottage property, of late Robert Baldry's, on the other side. The cottages were held by John of Upton by a grant of John Linnier and Thomas Mussel, executors of John Mussel, an executor of Robert Baldry, of late a citizen of Salisbury, and are to be held for ever by Agnes and John and their heirs and assigns. Clause of warranty. Seals: John of Upton's and the common and mayoral seals of the city. Named witnesses: the bailiff, the mayor, the reeves, Robert of Godmanstone, Nicholas Taylor, Thomas of Bridgehampton, and Thomas of Britford

587 By her charter Agnes, the relict of John Doder and a kinswoman and heir of Alice, a daughter and heir of Robert Baldry, of late a citizen of Salisbury, granted to John of Upton and John of Oxford, citizens of Salisbury, a tenement in Brown Street, in which Philip Longenough and his wife Alice of late dwelt, beside her own tenement, of late that of John Baldry, her father, on the north side; also 11 cottages, with yards, gardens, and a rack. Five of the cottages stand in Brown Street opposite the tenement, between a cottage of late Robert Alwin's on one side and John New's tenement on the other side; three cottages, with a yard (*or* yards) and a garden, stand in Gigant Street between cottages of late Robert Russell's on one side and three cottages, with a garden, now John of Upton's, on the other side; three cottages, with yards and the rack, stand in Mealmonger Street on the way from a gate of the college of St. Edmund towards the south, between cottages of late John Powell's on the north side and Agnes's own cottage, of late that of John Baldry, her father, on the south side. The tenement and the cottages, with the yards, gardens, and rack, descended to Agnes on the death of Alice and are to be held for ever by John of Upton and John of Oxford and their heirs and assigns. Clause of warranty. Seals: Agnes's and the common and mayoral seals of the city. Named witnesses: the bailiff, the mayor, the reeves, Robert of Godmanstone, William of Wishford, Robert Bunt, and Thomas of Britford

588 By his charter John Justice granted to John New, a younger William Tenterer, and Thomas of Bridgehampton, citizens of Salisbury, and to Nicholas Baker a tenement in the street [St. Martin's Street], extending from the east gate of the canons' close towards St. Martin's church, between a tenement of late Ralph of Coulston's on the east side and a tenement of late that of Maud Blicks on the west side. The tenement was held by John Justice by a grant of Thomas Goodyear, a smith, a citizen of Salisbury, and is to be held for ever by the grantees and their heirs and assigns. Seals: John's and the common and mayoral seals of the city. Named witnesses: the bailiff, the mayor, the reeves, John of Upton, Robert of Godmanstone, William of Wishford, and Thomas of Britford

589 By his charter Henry Gill, the rector of Fisherton near Salisbury, an executor of Margery, who was the wife of Robert Steed, of Fisherton, on the strength of

Margery's will granted to John Marshall, a citizen of Salisbury, a conjoined house and shop on a corner of Winchester Street and Minster Street opposite Walter at the burgh's tenement. The house and the shop were devised by Margery to be sold by her executors if her son John had died without issue and are to be held for ever by John Marshall and his heirs and assigns. Seals: Henry's and the common and mayoral seals of the city. Named witnesses: the bailiff, the mayor, the reeves, John of Upton, William of Wishford, Robert of Godmanstone, and the clerk

590 By her charter Agnes, the relict of John of Woodford, a citizen of Salisbury, and an executor of William of Berwick, a citizen of Salisbury, on the strength of William's will granted to Robert of Kendal, a citizen of Salisbury, and his wife Margaret and their heirs and assigns, or to the one of them living longer and that one's heirs and assigns, a garden in St. Martin's Street between a tenement of late John of Bodenham's on one side and Roger Halwell's tenement on the other side. The garden was held by Agnes by a devise of William on the day on which he died and is to be held for ever by the grantees. Seals: Agnes's and the common and mayoral seals of the city. Named witnesses: the bailiff, the mayor, the reeves, William of Wishford, Nicholas Taylor, Robert of Godmanstone, Thomas of Britford, and the clerk

591 By his charter John Cole, a citizen of Salisbury, granted to Agnes, the relict of Richard Fry, of late a citizen of Salisbury, a tenement in Gigant Street between a tenement formerly Michael of Brigmerston's on either side. The tenement was held by John Cole by a grant of Richard of Alderbury and is to be held for ever by Agnes and her heirs and assigns. Clause of warranty. Seals: John's and the common and mayoral seals of the city. Named witnesses: the bailiff, the mayor, the reeves, John of Upton, Robert Godmanstone, William of Wishford, Nicholas Taylor, and Thomas of Britford

10 November 1361, at Salisbury

592 By their charter John Hoare and his wife Gillian, a sister of Agnes, the relict of Thomas Smith, of Amesbury, of late a citizen of Salisbury, appearing at the court held on that day, granted to Robert of Godmanstone and his wife Joan a tenement in Gigant Street between John's garden on the north side and a tenement of John of Woodford, of late a citizen of Salisbury, on the south side. The tenement descended to Gillian on Agnes's death and is to be held for ever by Robert and Joan and Robert's heirs and assigns. Clause of warranty. Seals: those of John and Gillian and the common and mayoral seals of the city. Named witnesses: the bailiff, the mayor, the reeves, John of Upton, William of Wishford, Thomas of Britford, and the clerk

593 By his charter John Hoare, an executor of Thomas Smith, of Amesbury, of late a citizen of Salisbury, on the strength of Thomas's will granted to Robert of Godmanstone and his wife Joan a plot of land, with two racks built on it, in Gigant Street between Robert's tenement, which he held by a grant of John and his wife Gillian, and John's garden. The plot, with the racks, was devised by Thomas to be sold by his executors and is to be held for ever by Robert and Joan and Robert's heirs and assigns. Seals: John's and the common and mayoral seals of the city. Named witnesses: the bailiff, the mayor, the reeves, John of Upton, Thomas of Britford, and George Goss

594 By their charter John Bradwell and Nicholas Buck, chaplains, granted to John of Oxford, a citizen of Salisbury, a tenement in Winchester Street between John Hoare's tenement on the west side and William of Wishford's messuage on the east side, with a gate next to it in Brown Street. The tenement was held by John and Nicholas by a grant of Agnes, the relict, and an executor, of John Doder, of late a citizen of Salisbury, and of John of Oxford and John Snel, Agnes's co-executors, and, with shops and the gate, is to be held for ever by John of Oxford and his heirs and assigns. Seals: those of the grantors and the common and mayoral seals of the city. Named witnesses: the bailiff, the mayor, the reeves, John of Upton, Robert of Godmanstone, Thomas of Britford, and the clerk

595 Approval [*dated to the Wednesday after the feast of St. Martin (17 November) probably in error for the Wednesday before that feast (10 November)*] of the will of John Anger, made on 11 September 1361. <u>Interment</u>: [*place unspecified*]. <u>Bequests</u>: 12*d*. to the fabric of the cathedral church; 6 wethers each to the chapel of Martin and the chapel of Tidpit; 10 wethers to the rector of that church; 5 wethers to the chaplain of Pentridge; 4 wethers to John Young; the rest of his goods to his brother William Anger. <u>Devises</u>: to William a tenement in Wineman Street, between a tenement formerly John Uphill's on one side and Thomas Vellard's tenement on the other side, to be held for ever by him and his heirs and assigns. <u>Executors</u>: Maud Milton and his son Robert. <u>Proved</u> on 18 September 1361 in front of an officer of the archdeacon of Salisbury in the chapel of Martin; the administration was entrusted to Robert, Maud appearing in person and expressly declining it. <u>Approved</u> at a court held in front of the bailiff, the mayor, and other citizens; the seisin of the tenement was released to the legatee.

596 By his charter Peter Needler, an executor of Robert Osborne, a fisherman, of late a citizen of Salisbury, on the strength of Robert's will granted to Andrew Cook and his wife Margery four cottages in St. Martin's Street between Agnes of Berwick's tenement on the east side and Roger Tanner's tenement on the west side. The cottages were devised by Robert to be sold by his executors and are to be held by Andrew and Margery and their heirs and assigns by right of inheritance. Seals: Peter's and the common and mayoral seals of the city. Named witnesses: the bailiff, the mayor, the reeves, John of Upton, William of Wishford, Thomas of Britford, and the clerk

597 By his charter John Ewan, a son and heir of Walter Ewan, of late a citizen of Salisbury, granted to John Warneford a rent of 13*s*. 4*d*. a year issuing from a tenement, which John at the hill holds of him for life, in Endless Street between a tenement formerly Reynold Tidworth's on the north side and Henry Pope's tenement on the south side, with the reversion of the tenement when it fell due on John at the hill's death. The rent and the reversion are to be held for ever by John Warneford and his heirs and assigns. Clause of warranty. Seals: John Ewan's and the common and mayoral seals of the city. Named witnesses: the bailiff, the mayor, the coroners, the reeves, William of Wishford, Robert Bunt, George Goss, and the clerk

598 By their charter Henry Gill, the rector of Fisherton, Thomas of Britford, a citizen of Salisbury, and John of Bradwell, a chaplain, executors of Thomas of Hungerford, of late a citizen of Salisbury, on the strength of Thomas's will granted to John Lokebet two tenements in Minster Street between a tenement of late Thomas of Hungerford's on the south side and a tenement of late Richard Frear's on the north side; also a rent of 24s. a year issuing from a tenement, which Roger of Ringwood holds for life by a devise of Thomas of Hungerford, in Minster Street between the two tenements on the north side and a shop of late Nicholas of Breamore's on the south side. Thomas of Hungerford devised the two tenements to be sold by his executors and the third to be sold after Roger of Ringwood's death. The two tenements, the rent, and the reversion are to be held for ever by John Lokebet and his heirs and assigns. Seals: those of the grantors and the common and mayoral seals of the city. Named witnesses: the bailiff, the mayor, the coroners, the reeves, William of Wishford, Robert of Godmanstone, Robert Bunt, George Goss, and the clerk

(after 7 November 1361)

599 The will of John Deanbridge, made on 30 July 1361. <u>Interment</u>: in the church of the Dominicans of Fisherton. <u>Bequests</u>: 40*d*. to the fabric of the cathedral church; the rest of his goods to his wife Agnes to pay his debts so far as his goods can, and what remains should be laid out as stated below. <u>Devises</u>: to Agnes a tenement, opposite the market place where grains are sold, which he acquired from Peter Bennett and his wife Christine, a tenement which he acquired from William at the bridge, and a tenement in New Street between Richard Ryborough's tenement on one side and Robert Fewster's tenement on the other side. Those tenements are to be held for ever by Agnes and her heirs and assigns on a condition that she would pay John's debts and find a chaplain, to be chosen by John's executors from the Dominicans of Fisherton, to celebrate mass in their church there for the three years following his death on behalf of his soul and the souls of others. If Agnes should decline to accept the tenements on that condition, or if she were to die within a year of his death, John devised the tenements to be sold by his executors or their executors. The money received should be spent on paying his debts, celebrating masses, and doing other charitable deeds. John devised to his father Adam a tenement in the borough of Stockbridge, to be held for ever by him and his heirs and assigns. He devised to Alice Hussey an estate in a shop in Castle Street, in which Walter Millman dwells, which he acquired from her for her life. He devised to the lord John of Wilton, the rector of St. Thomas's church, an estate which John, by his deed, gave to him in a corner tenement [in New Street] beside Black bridge: the estate is to be given back to him and held for nothing. <u>Executors</u>: his wife Agnes, John of Upton, the lord Henry [Gill], the rector of Fisherton, and William Pain. <u>Proved</u> on 27 October 1361 in front of an officer of the dean of Salisbury, the subdeanery being vacant; the administration was entrusted to Agnes, reserving the power to entrust it to the other executors when they might come to seek it. On 7 November 1361 the lord Henry appeared in front of that officer and was entrusted with the administration.

24 November 1361
600 By his charter William Anger granted to William of Wishford, a citizen of Salisbury, a tenement in Wineman Street between a tenement formerly John Uphill's on one side and a tenement of late that of John Tott, of Netheravon, on the other side. The tenement was held by William Anger by a devise of his brother John and is to be held for ever by William of Wishford and his heirs and assigns. Clause of warranty. Seals: William Anger's and the common and mayoral seals of the city

601 By her charter Agnes, the relict, and an executor, of Richard Fry, of late a citizen of Salisbury, granted to William Fairwood, a baker, and his wife Margaret a tenement in Wineman Street, between a tenement of late Philip Kimble's on one side and Agnes's own tenement on the other side, which Richard and Agnes held by a feoffment of Roger of Kilmeston, an executor of Ralph Woolbedding; also a messuage in Culver Street, between John Talbot's tenement on one side and Agnes's own tenement on the other side, formerly that of Thomas Banner, of late a citizen of Salisbury. The tenement and the messuage are to be held for ever by William and Margaret and their heirs and assigns. Clause of warranty. Seals: Agnes's and the common and mayoral seals of the city. Named witnesses: the bailiff, the mayor, the coroners, the reeves, Robert of Godmanstone, William Wishford, Robert Bunt, George Goss, and the clerk. At the court held on that day Agnes surrendered to the lord [bishop] the seisin of the tenement and of the messuage.

602 By their charter William Pain, an executor of Alice, who was the wife of William Whitehorn, of late a citizen of Salisbury, and Agnes, the relict of John Deanbridge, his co-executor, on the strength of William Whitehorn's will granted to William Agodeshalf, a tailor, a tenement, with an adjacent yard, in Gigant Street between a cottage of David the clerk on one side and Richard of Dinton's tenement on the other side. The cottage [?*rectius* tenement] was devised by William Whitehorn to be sold by Alice's executors if his daughter Alice were to die without issue before her and, with the yard, is to be held for ever by William Agodeshalf and his heirs and assigns. Seals: those of William Pain and Agnes and the common and mayoral seals of the city. Named witnesses: the bailiff, the mayor, the coroners, the reeves, William of Wishford, Robert of Godmanstone, Robert Bunt, George Goss, and the clerk

603 Approval of the will of John Wiltshire, a citizen of Salisbury, made on 18 September 1361. <u>Interment</u>: in the graveyard of St. Martin's church. <u>Bequests</u>: 12*d*. each to the fabric of the cathedral church and the fabric of Durnford church; 2*s*. to the fabric of St. Martin's church; 40*d*. to John Nash; the rest of his goods to his son Thomas or, if Thomas were to die within a year of his own death, to his executors or their executors to be administered on behalf of his soul and the souls of others. <u>Devises</u>: to Thomas a corner tenement, with an adjacent yard (*or* yards), beyond the bar, on the way to St. Martin's church, between a tenement of late Edward of Upton's on the west side and a tenement of late Adam of Barnwell's on the east side. The tenement, with the yard(s), was held by John and his wife Maud by a grant of John Poulshot, an executor of his father John

Poulshot, an executor of Walter Poulshot, of late a citizen of Salisbury, is to be held for ever by Thomas and his issue, and if Thomas were to die without issue should to be sold by John's executors, their executors, or subsequent executors. The money received should be laid out on masses and other charitable deeds on behalf of John's soul, the souls of his wives and of his and their children, and the souls of others. Executors: John Chatt, a chaplain, and John Nash; overseer, the lord Thomas of Clifton, a chaplain. Proved on 5 November 1361 in front of an officer of the dean of Salisbury, the subdeanery being vacant; the administration was entrusted to the executors. Approved at a court held in front of the bailiff, the mayor, and other citizens; the seisin of the tenement was released to the legatee.

604 By their charter Gilbert of Whichbury and Thomas Chaplin, citizens of Salisbury, executors of Robert Alwin, of late a citizen of Salisbury, on the strength of Robert's will granted to Agnes, the relict of John of Bodenham, of late a citizen of Salisbury, a tenement in Carter Street between a tenement of late that of John Wallop, carder, on the south side and a tenement, in which Robert of late dwelt, on the south [?*rectius* north] side; also a yard, behind the tenement in which Robert of late dwelt, between a yard of late William Friend's on one side and a yard of late John of Bodenham's on the other side; also two shops and a bakehouse, conjoined in Carter Street, between a tenement of late William Whitehorn's on the south side and a shop of late Andrew Baker's on the north side. The tenement, yard, shops, and bakehouse were devised by Robert to be sold by his executors and are to be held for ever by Agnes and her heirs and assigns. Seals: those of Gilbert and Thomas and the common and mayoral seals of the city. Named witnesses: the bailiff, the mayor, the coroners, the reeves, William of Wishford, a younger William Tenterer, Robert of Godmanstone, Robert Bunt, George Goss, and the clerk

605 By their charter John White, the rector of Landford, John of Butterley, and Richard of Knottingley, executors of Joan Butterley, the relict of Thomas of Butterley, of late a citizen of Salisbury, on the strength of Joan's will granted to William of Wishford, a citizen of Salisbury, a rent of 5*s.* a year issuing from a tenement in Endless Street between a tenement formerly Richard of Tidworth's on the north side and Henry Pope's tenement on the south side; also a rent of 30*s.* a year issuing from a corner tenement opposite the graveyard of St. Edmund's church beside Nicholas Baker's tenement on the south side; also a rent of 20*s.* a year issuing from a tenement in Winchester Street between a tenement of late John Monkton's on the west side and John Cole's tenement on the east side; also a rent of 40*s.* a year issuing from a corner tenement in Winchester Street and Brown Street beside a tenement formerly Adam Ludwell's on the west side; also a rent of 8*s.* a year issuing from a tenement in Winchester Street between John Hoare's tenement on the west side and Richard Still's tenement on the east side; also a rent of 10*s.* a year issuing from a tenement in Minster Street between a tenement formerly Stephen Crier's on one side and a tenement of late John Richman's on the other side. Those rents were devised by Joan to be sold and are to be held for ever by William and his heirs and assigns. Seals: those of the grantors and the common and mayoral seals of the city. Named witnesses: the bailiff, the mayor, the reeves, the coroners, Robert of Godmanstone, and the clerk

8 December 1361, at Salisbury
606 Approval of the will of John Pannett, a citizen of Salisbury, made on 26 November 1361. Interment: in the graveyard of St. Edmund's church. Bequests: 2*s.* to the fabric of St. Edmund's church, 6*d.* to the parochial chaplain, and 3*d.* to the deacon; 2*s.* 6*d.* both to the Dominicans of Fisherton and the Franciscans of Salisbury, in each case to celebrate a trental on behalf of his soul; the rest of his goods to his wife Margery and his daughter Emme to be divided equally between them. Devise: to Margery a tenement in Endless Street between his own tenement, formerly that of his father John Pannett, on one side and a tenement formerly Roger Plummer's on the other side. The tenement was acquired by the younger John from Robert Holbury and is to be held for ever by Margery and her heirs and assigns. Executors: his wife Margery and John Stickbeard. Proved on 5 December 1361 in front of an officer of the dean of Salisbury, the subdeanery being vacant; the administration was entrusted to the executors. Approved at a court held in front of the bailiff, the mayor, and other citizens; the seisin of the tenement was released to the legatee.

607 By their charter Gilbert of Whichbury and Thomas Chaplin, citizens of Salisbury, executors of Robert Alwin, of late a citizen of Salisbury, on the strength of Robert's will granted to Nicholas of Whichbury a tenement in Brown Street between a tenement of late John Luckham's on the north side and a tenement of late Henry Baldry's on the south side; also two conjoined shops in Gigant Street between a tenement of late Henry Baldry's on the north side and John of Oxford's corner tenement on the south side. The tenement and the shops were devised by Robert to be sold by his executors and are to be held for ever by Nicholas and his heirs and assigns. Seals: those of Gilbert and Thomas and the common and mayoral seals of the city. Named witnesses: the bailiff, the mayor, the coroners, the reeves, William of Wishford, a younger William Tenterer, Robert Godmanstone, and the clerk

608 By their charter William of Wootton and his wife Christine, the relict, and an executor, of William Friend, of late a citizen of Salisbury, and William Ashley and John Creed, her co-executors, executors of John Kimble, of late a citizen of Salisbury, on the strength of John Kimble's will granted to Thomas Hill, carpenter, and his wife Joan a tenement in Wineman Street between a tenement of late Ralph Woolbedding's on one side and a tenement of late John Powell's on the other side; also a tenement in Culver Street between a tenement of late Ingram at the brook's on one side and a tenement of late William Fox's on the other side. The tenements were devised by John Kimble to be sold after the death of his daughter Agnes by his executors or their executors and are to be held for ever by Thomas and Joan and their heirs and assigns. Seals: those of the grantors and the common and mayoral seals of the city. Named witnesses: the bailiff, the mayor, the coroners, the reeves, William of Wishford, Robert of Godmanstone, a younger William Tenterer, Robert Bunt, and the clerk

609 By their charter John Crichel and Robert of Axbey, chaplains, granted to

William of Stanley, a citizen of Salisbury, a yard in Nuggeston and Gigant Street on a corner between Christine of Ann's tenement on the east side and Gigant Street on the west side. The yard was held by John and Robert by a grant of Thomas of Erlestoke and William Candelan, chaplains, executors of John Nugg, a clerk, a son and heir of John Nugg, formerly a citizen of Salisbury, was devised by the younger John Nugg to be sold by his executors, and is to be held for ever by William Stanley and his heirs and assigns. Seals: those of John and Robert and the common and mayoral seals of the city. Named witnesses: the bailiff, the mayor, John of Upton, William of Upton, William Wishford, and the clerk

610 By their charter Margery, the relict, and an executor, of John Pannett, the eldest son of John Pannett, formerly a citizen of Salisbury, and John Stickbeard, Margery's co-executor, on the strength of the will of the elder John Pannett granted to George Goss, a citizen of Salisbury, a tenement in Endless Street between a tenement of late Roger Plummer's on the south side and Scots Lane on the north side. The tenement was devised by the elder John Pannett to be sold by the executors of the last descendant of his children and is to be held for ever by George and his heirs and assigns. Seals: those of Margery and John and the common and mayoral seals of the city. Named witnesses: the bailiff, the mayor, the coroners, the reeves, William of Wishford, Robert of Godmanstone, a younger William Tenterer, and the clerk

611 By his charter Gilbert of Whichbury, a citizen of Salisbury, granted to Nicholas of Whichbury two conjoined tenements in Winchester Street, between a younger William Tenterer's tenement on the east side and Richard Still's tenement on the west side, to be held for ever by Nicholas and his heirs and assigns. Seals: Gilbert's and the common and mayoral seals of the city. Named witnesses: the bailiff, the mayor, the coroners, the reeves, William of Wishford, a younger William Tenterer, Robert of Godmanstone, Thomas of Bridgehampton, George Goss, and the clerk

612 By his charter of Gilbert of Whichbury, a citizen of Salisbury, an executor of Parnel, who was the wife of Robert Alwin, of late a citizen of Salisbury, on the strength of the will of Andrew of Sherborne, formerly a citizen of Salisbury, granted to Agnes, the relict of John of Bodenham, a citizen of Salisbury, a tenement in Carter Street between a tenement formerly that of a younger John of Fosbury on the north side and a shop formerly Andrew's on the south side; also a shop, with an adjacent yard, in Carter Street between that tenement and the shops of late Robert's on the south side. The tenement and the shop, with the yard, were devised by Andrew to be sold, if Parnel were to die without issue, by his executors or hers, and they are to be held for ever by Agnes and her heirs and assigns. Seals: Gilbert's and the common and mayoral seals of the city. Named witnesses: the bailiff, the mayor, the reeves, Robert of Godmanstone, William of Wishford, John of Oxford, and the clerk

613 By his charter Richard Still, a citizen of Salisbury, granted to George Goss and John Buddle, called Prentice, a tenement in the street [St. Martin's Street], on the way from the east gate of the canons' close to St. Martin's church, between a tenement of the college of St. Edmund on the west side and a tenement of the choristers of the cathedral church on the east side. The tenement was held by Richard by a feoffment of Nicholas Laurence, of Wilton, and is to be held for ever by George and John and their heirs and assigns. Clause of warranty. Seals: Richard's and the common and mayoral seals of the city. Named witnesses: the bailiff, the mayor, the coroners, the reeves, Robert of Godmanstone, William of Bruton, John Chandler, and the clerk

22 December 1361
614 By his charter Gilbert of Whichbury, a citizen of Salisbury, granted to Nicholas of Whichbury, a citizen of Salisbury, a tenement in Gigant Street between a tenement of the provost of the college of St. Edmund on the north side and Nicholas's shops on the south side. The tenement was held by Edmund Beer and Gilbert by a feoffment of Robert Alwin, of late a citizen of Salisbury, an executor of Agnes Baldry, an executor of Henry Baldry, of late a citizen of Salisbury, was devised by Henry to be sold his executors or Agnes's, and is to be held for ever by Nicholas and his heirs and assigns. Seals: Gilbert's and the common and mayoral seals of the city. Named witnesses: the bailiff, the mayor, the coroners, the reeves, William of Wishford, Robert of Godmanstone, a younger William Tenterer, Robert Bunt, George Goss, and the clerk. At the court held on that day Gilbert surrendered the seisin of the tenement into the hand of the lord [bishop] to the use of Nicholas.
615 By their charter John Cole and John Hawk, citizens of Salisbury, granted to John Hoare, a citizen of Salisbury, and his wife Gillian [Chantrell's Corner: cf. **1727**], a corner tenement formerly John Chantrell's, at the butchers' stalls beside shops of late John of Langford's on the west side; also a tenement in New Street, beyond the bar, between a tenement of late Richard Bunt's on the east side and a tenement of late Adam of Barnwell's on the west side. The tenements were held by John Cole and John Hawk by a grant of John Hoare and Gillian and are to be held for ever by John and Gillian and John's heirs and assigns. Seals: those of John Cole and John Hawk and the common and mayoral seals of the city. Named witnesses: the bailiff, the mayor, the coroners, the reeves, William of Wishford, a younger William Tenterer, Robert of Godmanstone, and the clerk
616 By their charter John of Upton and William Pain, executors of Christine, the relict of Peter Bennett, of late a citizen of Salisbury, on the strength of Christine's will granted to George Goss, a citizen of Salisbury, a messuage, with a yard (*or* yards) and a dovecot, in Nuggeston between a tenement in which William Forest now dwells on the east side and John Cole's yard on the west side. The messuage, with the yard(s) and the dovecot, was devised by Christine to be sold by her executors and is to be held for ever by George and his heirs and assigns. Seals: those of John of Upton and William Pain and the common and mayoral seals of the city. Named witnesses: the bailiff, the mayor, the coroners, the reeves, Robert of Godmanstone, William of Wishford, a younger William Tenterer, and the clerk
617 By their charter Agnes, the relict of John Deanbridge, and William Pain, executors of Alice, the relict of Philip Longenough and of William Whitehorn, a

citizen of Salisbury, on the strength of William Whitehorn's will granted to John of Upton, a citizen of Salisbury, a tenement, with shops and a garden, in Carter Street between John's own tenement on one side and a tenement of late Robert Alwin's on the other side. The tenement was devised by William to be sold after the death of his daughter Alice, if she died without issue, by that Alice's executors or the executors of his wife Alice and, with the shops and the garden, is to be held for ever by John of Upton and his heirs and assigns. Seals: those of Agnes and William and the common and mayoral seals of the city. Named witnesses: the bailiff, the mayor, a coroner, the reeves, William of Wishford, Robert of Godmanstone, George Goss, and the clerk

618 By their charter Agnes of Woodford, an executor of Agnes, the relict of William Gill, of late a citizen of Salisbury, and William of Wootton and John Buddle, citizens of Salisbury, her co-executors, on the strength of Agnes's will granted to Joan, the relict of William Sexhampcote, a tenement, with a yard (*or* yards) and a dovecot, in Minster Street between a tenement of Thomas of Britford on either side, together with a gate in that street between Thomas of Britford's tenement on the south side and a tenement of late Roger Wallop's on the north side. The tenement, with the yard(s), the dovecot, and the gate, and with other tenements, was devised by Agnes, the relict of William Gill, to be sold by her executors and is to be held for ever by Joan and her heirs and assigns. Seals: those of the grantors and the common and mayoral seals of the city. Named witnesses: the bailiff, the mayor, the coroners, the reeves, William of Wishford, Robert of Godmanstone, a younger William Tenterer, and William of Bruton

5 January 1362, at Salisbury
619 Approval of the will of John Paris, otherwise called Purbeck, the rector of Bruton, made on 12 August 1361. <u>Interment</u>: in Bruton church. <u>Bequests</u>: 2*s*. each to the cathedral church and the fabric of Church Knowle church; 12*d*. to the fabric of St. Thomas's church; 20*s*. each to his sister Alice, Joan, a daughter of John Figheldean, and Thomas, a son of John Figheldean; his horse to the master John Corfe; his porteous, his best bed, 20*s*., a book which is called *Innocent*, a pair of decretals, a book which is called *Hugucium*, and a book which is called *Sextus Liber Doctrinalium* to the master William of Affpuddle; 20*s*. and a bed to John Kennet; 13*s*. 4*d*. each to his nephew William and Henry Kilpeck; 2*s*. each to his godson John Cutler and Margery, a daughter of Richard Henshaw; 12*d*. each to John, a son of John Dore, and John, a son of John Swith; 20*s*. to the master Nicholas Damerham; the rest of his goods to be disposed of by his executors on behalf of his soul. <u>Devises</u>: to his executors a rent of 26*s*. 8*d*. a year, which he held by a grant of John Keevil of Ludgershall, issuing from a tenement formerly that of Richard at the oak, of Glastonbury, now John Chalke's, in Winchester Street between a tenement formerly Ellis Homes's on the east side and a lane on the west side to be sold by them at a fair price. The money received should be applied to the fabric of the cathedral church on behalf of John's soul and the souls of the master Henry Ludgershall, his father John Knoyle, his mother Edith, and his brother John, of John's own father and mother John Paris and his wife

Agnes, and of John Corfe and John Figheldean. John devised to John Figheldean and his son Thomas a rent of 10s. a year issuing from a shop, with a sollar and a small room attached to it, which Richard Lyner, his wife Emme, and their son John held in Minster Street between John's own shop, which Philip Montagu and his wife Mabel hold, on the south side and Edward Pinnock's tenement on the north side. The rent is to be held for ever by John and Thomas and their heirs and assigns so that they might cause 20 masses a year to be celebrated in St. Thomas's church on behalf of John Paris's soul and the souls of his kinsmen previously named. Executors: John Corfe, the rector of Radipole, John Figheldean, and William Affpuddle, a clerk. Proved at Bruton on 23 September 1361 in front of William Bide, a commissary general of the bishop of Salisbury; the administration was entrusted to William Affpuddle, John Figheldean having died and John Corfe declining to accept it. Proved on 9 January 1362 in front of an officer of the dean of Salisbury, the subdeanery being vacant; the administration was entrusted to William Affpuddle. Approved at a court held in front of the bailiff, the mayor, and other citizens; the seisin of the rents was released to the legatees

19 January 1362, at Salisbury
620 Approval of the will of Robert Inkpen, a citizen and merchant of Winchester, made on 8 May 1349. Interment: in the north part of the nuns' monastery of the Blessed Mary, Winchester, beside the grave of Henry and the master Peter, his brothers. Bequests: 20s. to the fabric of that church; the rest of his goods, movable and immovable, to John of Inkpen, his brother, without opposition or interference. Devise: to John his rent, land, and tenements in Winchester, Salisbury, and Southampton to be held by him for life. After John's death the rent, land, and tenements should be appropriated to the High Trinity of the Blessed Mary and All Saints and to the keeper or provost of the chapel of the Holy Trinity, founded in the graveyard of the nuns of the Blessed Mary, Winchester, by Robert's parents, and for the endowment of the keeper and the chaplain and their successors serving God there; that is to be done by Robert's executors as soon as possible. Executors: his brother John and John of Halwell, a chaplain. Proved on 9 May 1349 in front of John of Ware, the sequestrator general of William, the bishop of Winchester, in the archdeaconry of Winchester; the administration was entrusted to the executors. Approved at a court held in front of the bailiff, the mayor, and other citizens; the seisin of the rent was released to the legatees.
621 By his charter Nicholas Buck, a chaplain, granted to John Fifield, a chaplain, a corner tenement, with a yard and a dovecot, opposite St. Edmund's church, between a yard of late Robert of Etchilhampton's on the east side and a tenement which Nicholas Baker holds on the south side. The tenement was held by Nicholas by a feoffment of Joan, the relict of Thomas of Butterley, and, with the yard and the dovecot, is to be held for ever by John and his heirs and assigns, paying 30s. a year for ever to Joan and her heirs and assigns. Clause of warranty. Seals: Nicholas's and the common and mayoral seals of the city. Named witnesses: the bailiff, the mayor, the coroners, the reeves, a younger William Tenterer, William of Wishford, Robert of Godmanstone, Thomas of Bridgehampton, and the clerk

2 February 1362, at Salisbury
622 By his charter of John of Butterley granted to William of Wishford, a citizen of Salisbury, and Robert May, of Andover parish, all the tenements and rent which he held in Salisbury, to be held, with houses, yards, and gardens, for ever by them and their heirs and assigns. Clause of warranty and acquittance. Seals: John's and the common and mayoral seals of the city. Named witnesses: the bailiff, the mayor, the coroners, the reeves, Robert of Godmanstone, a younger William Tenterer, an elder William Tenterer, Thomas of Bridgehampton, and the clerk
623 Approval of the will of Richard Berwick, a citizen of Salisbury, made on 4 August 1361. <u>Interment</u>: in the graveyard of St. Martin's church beside the tomb in which the corpse of William of Berwick lies buried. <u>Bequests</u>: 6s. 8d. to the fabric of the cathedral church; the rest of his goods, when his debts have been paid, to be disposed of by his executors for the salvation of his soul and the souls named below. <u>Devises</u>: to Edward Cockerell the term and estate which Richard held in a tenement called Powell's Corner, opposite the high cross where fruit and other victuals are sold, in full payment of a debt in which he is bound to him. Richard devised a tenement called Hampton's Corner, standing [opposite the high cross: *cf.* **806**] where fruit and other victuals are sold, to be sold by his executors immediately after his death to discharge his debts. He devised the tenement in which he dwelt, in New Street and Brown Street, with gardens and a yard (*or* yards), and with a plot in St. Martin's Street attached to a garden of the tenement, which he held by a grant of Agnes, the relict of William of Berwick, to be sold by his executors, their executors, or subsequent executors immediately after the death of his wife Edith. The money received should be laid out, when his debts have been paid, on behalf of his soul, Edith's soul, and the souls of others. <u>Executors</u>: the lord Stephen Bodenham, a chaplain, and John Fish, a clerk; overseer, Edward Cockerell, so that they might do nothing without his help and agreement. <u>Proved</u> on 28 July 1361 in front of an officer of the subdean; the administration was entrusted to Stephen Bodenham, reserving the power to entrust it to John Fish when he might come to seek it. <u>Approved</u> at a court held in front of the bailiff, the mayor, and other citizens; the seisin of the tenements was released to the legatees.

2 March 1362, at Salisbury
624 By their charter William of Wishford, a citizen of Salisbury, and Robert May, of Andover parish, granted to John of Butterley and his wife Christine the tenements and rent which they held in Salisbury by John's grant, to be held, with houses, yards, and gardens, by John and Christine and John's heirs and assigns. Seals: those of William and Robert and the common and mayoral seals of the city. Named witnesses: the bailiff, the mayor, the coroners, the reeves, Robert of Godmanstone, Robert Bunt, George Goss, and the clerk
625 By their charter Agnes, the relict, and an executor, of John of Woodford, William of Wootton, her co-executor, John having been an executor of Robert of Woodford, of late a citizen of Salisbury, Henry Fleming, an executor of Henry

Russell, John of Woodford's co-executor, George Goss and William Buck, a chaplain, executors of John Richman, a co-executor of John of Woodford and Henry Russell, Beatrice Everard, an executor of John Everard, a co-executor of John of Woodford, Henry Russell, and John Richman, Emme, the relict, and an executor, of John Powell, a co-executor of John of Woodford, Henry Russell, John Richman, and John Everard, Walter, the provost of St. Edmund's church, and Nicholas Taylor, the mayor of Salisbury, on the strength of Robert of Woodford's will granted to John of Upton, Thomas of Britford, and Robert of Godmanstone, citizens of Salisbury, a tenement between a tenement formerly John of Sherborne's on the north side, opposite the market place where fleeces are sold, and a tenement formerly Peter Bennett's on the south side. The tenement was devised by Robert of Woodford, if his brother John were to die without issue, to be sold by his executors or their executors and by the provost and the mayor, and it is to be held for ever by John of Upton, Thomas of Britford, and Robert of Godmanstone and their heirs and assigns. Seals: those of the grantors and the common and mayoral seals of the city. Named witnesses: the bailiff, the mayor, the reeves, an elder William Tenterer, Robert Bunt, Robert of Kendal, and the clerk

16 March 1362, at Salisbury
626 The will of John, a son of Robert at the 'vuere', made on 6 November 1361. Interment: in the graveyard of the church of the Holy Cross of Binsted. Bequests: 20s. to perform his funeral rites; the rest of his goods to his wife Agnes and daughters Joan and Alice. Devises: to Agnes for life a chief tenement in Endless Street, formerly that of Walter Goss, a citizen of Salisbury. John also devised to Agnes a shop in the butchers' stalls between Stephen Spicer's shop on one side and John Holtby's shop on the other side, a shop, with a sollar, in New Street between a tenement formerly Thomas Florentine's on one side and a tenement of Kentigern of Sulham, a clerk, on the other side, and a messuage, with a yard (*or* yards), in Drake Hall Street beside John Holtby's messuage to be held for life, paying 10s. a year for the fabric of the church of Hyde [abbey], Winchester, and 10s. for the fabric of Binsted church, for 10 consecutive years from the day of John's death. After Agnes's death the chief tenement, the two shops, with the sollar, and the messuage, with the yard(s), are to be held for ever by John's daughter Alice and her issue; if Alice were to die without issue they would remain for ever to John's daughter Joan and her issue, and if Joan were to die without issue should be sold by John's executors or Agnes's executors. The money received should be laid out on masses and other alms on behalf of John's soul, Agnes's soul, and the souls of others. Executors: his wife Agnes and John at the 'vuere'. Proved on 8 January 1362 in front of the dean of Alton in the parish church there; the administration was entrusted to the executors. The will was brought forth at the court held on 16 March.
627 By his charter John Lokebet, a citizen of Salisbury, granted to Hugh of Winterbourne a tenement in Minster Street between a tenement of late Richard Frear's on the north side and John's own tenement on the south side; also a rent

of 24s. a year issuing from a tenement, which Roger Ringwood holds for life by a devise of Thomas of Hungerford, in Minster Street between a shop of late Nicholas of Breamore's on one side and John's own tenement on the other side. The tenement and the rent, with the reversion of the tenement which Roger holds when it fell due on Roger's death, were held by John by a grant of Henry Gill, the rector of Fisherton, Thomas of Britford, and the lord John of Bradwell, a chaplain, executors of Thomas of Hungerford, of late a citizen of Salisbury, and are to be held for ever by Hugh and his heirs and assigns. Clause of warranty. Seals: John Lokebet's and the common and mayoral seals of the city. Named witnesses: the bailiff, the mayor, the coroners, the reeves, a younger William Tenterer, William of Wishford, Robert of Godmanstone, and the clerk

628 By their writing Robert Fewster, a citizen of Salisbury, and his wife Alice quitclaimed to John of Upton, a citizen of Salisbury, and his heirs and assigns their right or claim to two shops in Butcher Row, formerly those of Robert Baldry, Alice's uncle, between shops formerly those of John of Langford, draper, on one side and shops formerly Walter Goss's on the other side. Seals: those of Robert and Alice and the common and mayoral seals of the city. Named witnesses: the bailiff, the mayor, the reeves, William of Wishford, Robert Bunt, George Goss, and the clerk

30 March 1362, at Salisbury
629 By his charter Nicholas Russell, a citizen of Salisbury, granted to John of Upton, a citizen of Salisbury, two conjoined cottages, with a yard (*or* yards) adjacent, in Culver Street between cottages which were Hugh Boney's on the south side and a corner tenement formerly Ingram at the brook's on the north side. The cottages were held by Nicholas by a grant of William of Wallop, butcher, and, with the yard(s), are to held for ever by John and his heirs and assigns. Clause of warranty. Seals: Nicholas's and the common and mayoral seals of the city. Named witnesses: the bailiff, the mayor, a coroner, the reeves, William Wishford, Robert of Godmanstone, William Bruton, and the clerk

630 By his charter John, a son and heir of Richard Frear, of late a citizen of Salisbury, granted to John of Heytesbury, saddler, and his wife Alice a tenement in Minster Street between a tenement of late Henry Russell's on one side and Roger Tarrant's tenement on the other side. The tenement was held by Richard by a grant of John of Heytesbury and Alice and is to be held for ever by them and their heirs and assigns. Clause of warranty. Seals: John Frear's and the common and mayoral seals of the city. Named witnesses: the bailiff, the mayor, the coroners, the reeves, George Goss, John of Oxford, and the clerk

631 By his charter Robert Play, ironmonger, of Salisbury, granted to John Chandler, a citizen of Salisbury, a rent of 6s. a year issuing from a tenement, which Robert of Boscombe, a tanner, of late held, in Gigant Street between a tenement of late John Baldry's on one side and a tenement in which Thomas Brute, a tanner, now dwells on the other side; also a rent of 8s. a year issuing from a tenement which Thomas holds for a term of 12 years by a grant of John Bunt and his wife Alice, as is contained in an indenture perfected between them; also a rent of 12s. a year issuing from a tenement which John Poulshot, a carpenter, holds for a term of 12 years by a grant of John Bunt and Alice, as is contained in an indenture perfected between them; also the reversion of the rent of 8s., and of the rent of 12s., when they fell due at the end of each term. The rents and reversions were held by Robert by a grant of Robert March, an executor of Alice, and are to be held for ever by John Chandler and his heirs and assigns. Seals: Robert's and the common and mayoral seals of the city. Named witnesses: the bailiff, the mayor, the coroners, the reeves, William of Wishford, George Goss, and the clerk

13 April 1362, at Salisbury
632 By their charter John of Upton and William Pain, citizens of Salisbury, executors of Christine, the relict of Peter Bennett, of late a citizen of Salisbury, on the strength of Christine's will granted to Agnes, the relict of John of Bodenham, of late a citizen of Salisbury, a tenement in Freren Street between a tenement formerly John of Bodenham's on the south side and a tenement of late Robert Russell's on the north side. The tenement was devised by Christine to be sold by her executors if Christine, a daughter of John of Bodenham, were to die under the age of 16 years, and it is to be held for ever by Agnes and her heirs and assigns. Seals: those of John and William and the common and mayoral seals of the city. Named witnesses: the bailiff, the mayor, a coroner, the reeves, William of Wishford, a younger William Tenterer, and the clerk. At the court held on that day John of Upton and William Pain surrendered the seisin of the tenement into the hand of the lord [bishop] to the use of Agnes.
633 By his charter of Thomas of Bridgehampton, a citizen of Salisbury, granted to Thomas Stalbridge a yard, with an adjacent wall, in Culver Street between a tenement of late Margery Leach's on the south side and a tenement of late John Richman's on the north side. The yard, with the wall, was formerly that of Simon Gillmin, of late a citizen of Salisbury, and is to be held for ever by Thomas Stalbridge and his heirs and assigns. Seals: Thomas of Bridgehampton's and the common and mayoral seals of the city. Named witnesses: the bailiff, the mayor, the coroners, the reeves, Robert of Godmanstone, Robert Bunt, George Goss, and the clerk
634 By his charter John of Wilton, the rector of St. Thomas's church, on the strength of the will of Adam of Bishopstrow, a baker, granted to Thomas Chaplin, a citizen of Salisbury, a corner tenement in New Street and Brown Street between a tenement of late Richard Salter's on the west side and a tenement of late that of a younger Robert Baldry on the south side. The tenement was devised by Adam to be sold after the death of his brother William by the rector of that church for the time being, and it is to be held for ever by Thomas and his heirs and assigns. Seals: John's and the common and mayoral seals of the city. Named witnesses: the bailiff, the mayor, the coroners, the reeves, Robert of Godmanstone, George Goss, Robert Kendal, and the clerk
635 By her charter Margery, the relict of John Pannett, of late a citizen of Salisbury, granted to George Goss, a citizen of Salisbury, a tenement in Endless

Street between a tenement of late that of John, the father of John Pannett, on one side and a tenement formerly Roger Plummer's on the other side. The tenement was held by Margery by a devise of the younger John and is to be held for ever by George and his heirs and assigns. Seals: Margery's and the common and mayoral seals of the city. Named witnesses: the bailiff, the mayor, the coroners, the reeves, Robert of Godmanstone, Robert Bunt, and the clerk

636 By his writing William of Wishford, a citizen of Salisbury, granted to John of Butterley a rent of 5s. a year issuing from a tenement in Endless Street between a tenement formerly Richard of Tidworth's on the north side and Henry Pope's tenement on the south side; also a rent of 30s. a year issuing from a corner tenement opposite the graveyard of St. Edmund's church beside Nicholas Baker's tenement on the south side; also a rent of 20s. a year issuing from a tenement in Winchester Street between a tenement of late John of Monkton's on the west side and John Cole's tenement on the east side; also a rent of 40s. a year issuing from a corner tenement in Winchester Street and Brown Street beside a tenement formerly Adam of Ludwell's on the west side; also a rent of 8s. year issuing from a tenement in Winchester Street between John Hoare's tenement on the west side and Richard Still's tenement on the east side; also a rent of 10s. a year issuing from a tenement in Minster Street between a tenement formerly Stephen Crier's on one side and a tenement of late John Richman's on the other side. Those rents were held by William by a grant of John White, the rector of Landford, John of Butterley, and Richard of Knottingley, executors of Joan Butterley, the relict of Thomas Butterley, of late a citizen of Salisbury, and are to be held for ever by John Butterley and his heirs and assigns. Seals: William's and the common and mayoral seals of the city. Named witnesses: the bailiff, the mayor, the coroners, the reeves, William of Bruton, Thomas Chaplin, and the clerk

11 May 1362, at Salisbury
637 By their charter John of Upton and William Pain, executors of Christine, the relict of Peter Bennett, of late a citizen of Salisbury, on the strength of Christine's will granted to Matthew of Fernhill a chief tenement in Carter Street and Brown Street between, in Carter Street, William Pain's tenement on the north side and a tenement of David Clark and his wife Benet on the south side and, in Brown Street, a tenement of late John Baldry's on the north side and a tenement formerly Gilbert of Wick's on the south side. The tenement was devised by Christine to be sold by her executors and is to be held for ever by Matthew and his heirs and assigns. Seals: those of John and William and the common and mayoral seals of the city. Witnesses: [*unnamed*] as above

638 By his charter Richard at the stone, tucker, of Salisbury, granted to Richard Still, a citizen of Salisbury, a tenement in Winchester Street between [a tenement] of late Jordan Mercer's on the east side and a tenement formerly John Langford's on the west side. The tenement was held by Richard at the stone by a feoffment of Richard Still and Robert Kendal, a citizen of Salisbury, and is to be held for ever by Richard Still and his heirs and assigns. Seals: Richard at the stone's and the common and mayoral seals of the city. Named witnesses: the bailiff, the mayor, the coroners, the reeves, William Wishford, Robert of Godmanstone, George Goss, and the clerk

639 By his charter William Pain, a citizen of Salisbury, granted to John Chilton, tucker, a messuage in Freren Street between a tenement of late Simon Redhead's on one side and a tenement formerly William Longbarber's on the other side. The messuage was held by William by a grant of Laurence Chandler, an executor of Stephen Basing, of late a citizen of Salisbury, and is to be held for ever by John and his heirs and assigns. Seals: William's and the common and mayoral seals of the city. Named witnesses: the bailiff, the mayor, the coroners, the reeves, Robert of Godmanstone, William of Bruton, Robert Kendal, and the clerk

640 By her charter Gillian, the relict of John of Winterbourne Ford, granted to William Knight, of Salisbury, a toft, with a yard (*or* yards), in Freren Street, towards the Franciscans' close there, between the friars' river on one side and a tenement of late William Whitehorn's on the other side. The toft was held by Gillian and John by a grant of Robert of Afton in the city of Salisbury and, with the yard(s), is to be held for ever by William Knight and his heirs and assigns. Seals: Gillian's and the common and mayoral seals of the city. Named witnesses: the bailiff, the mayor, the coroners, the reeves, William of Wishford, Robert of Godmanstone, George Goss, and the clerk

641 By their charter John of Upton, Thomas of Britford, and Robert of Godmanstone, citizens of Salisbury, granted to William of Wishford, a citizen of Salisbury, a tenement between a tenement formerly John Sherborne's on the north side, opposite the market place where fleeces are sold, and a tenement of late Peter Bennett's on the south side. The tenement was held by the grantors by a feoffment of Agnes, the relict, and an executor, of John of Woodford, and other executors [*as in* **625**], and is to be held for ever by William of Wishford and his heirs and assigns. Seals: those of the grantors and the common and mayoral seals of the city. Named witnesses: the bailiff, the mayor, William of Wishford, Robert Bunt, an elder William Tenterer, and the clerk

642 By their charter John of Upton, Thomas of Britford, and Robert of Godmanstone, citizens of Salisbury, granted to Nicholas Taylor, the mayor of Salisbury, and to the commonalty of the city, a rent of 40*s*. a year to be received from a tenement between a tenement of late John Sherborne's, opposite the market place where wool is sold, on the north side and a tenement of late Peter Bennett's on the south side. The tenement was held by the grantors by a grant of the executors of the executors of Robert of Woodford, of late a citizen of Salisbury, and the rent is to be held for ever by the mayor and commonalty of the city and their successors. Clause to permit entry on the tenement if the rent were in arrear, distraint, and the keeping of distresses until the unpaid rent was recovered. Seals: those of the grantors and the common and mayoral seals of the city. Named witnesses: the bailiff, the mayor, William Wishford, John of Oxford, Robert Bunt, an elder William Tenterer, and the clerk

25 May 1362, at Salisbury

643 By their indented charter John of Upton and John of Oxford, citizens of

Salisbury, granted to William Warmwell and his wife Agnes a tenement, in which Philip Longenough of late dwelt, in Brown Street beside a tenement which was of late John Baldry's on the north side; also 11 cottages, with yards, gardens, and a rack. Five of the cottages stand in Brown Street, opposite the tenement, between cottages of late Robert Alwin's on one side and John New's tenement on the other side; three cottages, with a yard (*or* yards) and a garden, stand in Gigant Street between cottages of late Robert Russell's on one side and cottages, with a garden, which Agnes and her son John of late held by a grant of John of Upton; three cottages, with yards and the rack, stand in Mealmonger Street between cottages of late John Powell's on one side and a cottage of late John Baldry's on the other side. The tenement and the cottages, with the yards, gardens, and rack, are to be held for ever by William and Agnes and their joint issue, and if William and Agnes were to die without such issue they would remain for ever to John, the son of John Doder and that Agnes, and his issue. Seals: those of John of Upton and John of Oxford by turns and the common and mayoral seals of the city. Named witnesses: the bailiff, the mayor, a coroner, the reeves, William of Wishford, Robert Bunt, and the clerk

644 By their charter William Buck, a chaplain, George Goss, and John Amersham, executors of John Richman, of late a citizen of Salisbury, on the strength of John's will granted to the lord Walter Cheltenham, the provost of the college of St. Edmund, and the chaplains serving God there a messuage, between Scots Lane on the north side and a tenement of late Gilbert Dubber's on the south side, in which John Richman dwelt and which he held by a feoffment of John Crichel, a vicar of the cathedral church, and Thomas of Erlestoke, a chaplain; also a messuage [?in Minster Street: *cf.* **553, 1728**], beyond the bar, beside a tenement of John of Britford, a fisherman, on the north side, which John held by a feoffment of John Powell and Henry Stapleford; also a messuage, with a yard (*or* yards) in it, in a street called Rolleston and Minster Street, beside Robert Gore's tenement on the north side, which John held by a grant of William Goldston; also a messuage, with a yard and a rack (*or* racks) built in it, beside that last messuage on the north side, which John held by a feoffment of Peter Bennett; also a messuage, with a yard and a rack (*or* racks) built in it, standing on the north side of those last two messuages, which John bought from Richard of Shrewsbury and Henry Fleming; also a messuage, with a yard (*or* yards) and a rack (*or* racks), between those three cottages [?*rectius* messuages] on the south side and George Goss's yard on the north side, which John acquired from Roger Matthew and his wife Agnes; also a yard, on a corner of the street of Rolleston, between Scots Lane on the north side and a tenement of late Thomas of Hungerford's on the south side, which John held by a grant of the lord Thomas of Erlestoke, a chaplain. Those messuages, yards, and racks were devised by John Richman to be appropriated by means of his executors, if it could be done lawfully and made permanent by a licence of the king, to the college of St. Edmund as an aid to the maintenance of a chantry of six chaplains founded by Robert of Woodford in that college. They are to be held for ever by the provost and chaplains and their successors for celebrating mass every day in the church of the college on behalf of the healthy condition of the present king, of the lord Robert, the bishop of Salisbury, and of Agnes of Woodford while they live and on behalf of their souls when they have died, on behalf of the souls of Robert of Woodford, John of Woodford, and John Richman and his wife Agace, and on behalf of the souls of all the faithful departed as is contained in the king's licence. Seals: those of the grantors and the common and mayoral seals of the city. Named witnesses: the bailiff, the mayor, the coroners, Robert of Godmanstone, John of Oxford, and the clerk

8 June 1362, at Salisbury
645 By his charter John, a son of John Richman, of late a citizen of Salisbury, granted to William of Wishford, a citizen of Salisbury, a tenement in Gigant Street between Roger of Kilmeston's tenement on the south side and a yard formerly John Coppiner's on the north side. The tenement was held by the younger John Richman by his father's devise and is to be held for ever by William and his heirs and assigns. Seals: John's and the common and mayoral seals of the city. Named witnesses: the bailiff, the mayor, the coroners, the reeves, Robert of Godmanstone, Robert Bunt, and the clerk
646 By their charter William, the vicar of Idmiston, John Upton, George Goss, and John Marshall, citizens of Salisbury, granted to William of Wishford, a citizen of Salisbury, a corner tenement, with shops, called Stint's Corner, in Wineman Street and Brown Street between Philip Aubin's tenement on one side and a tenement of late Richard Tropenel's on the other side, to be held for ever by William and his heirs and assigns. Seals: those of the grantors and the common and mayoral seals of the city. Named witnesses: the bailiff, the mayor, a coroner, the reeves, Robert of Godmanstone, Robert Bunt, and the clerk
647 By his charter John of Upton, a citizen of Salisbury, granted to William of Wishford, a citizen of Salibury, a tenement, with shops, in Wineman Street between a corner tenement called Stint's Corner on one side and Robert Rise's tenement on the other side. The tenement was of late Richard Tropenel's and, with the shops, is to be held for ever by William and his heirs and assigns. Seals: John's and the common and mayoral seals of the city. Named witnesses: the bailiff, the mayor, a coroner, the reeves, Robert of Godmanstone, Robert Bunt, and the clerk

22 June 1362, at Salisbury
648 Approval of the will of Agnes, the relict of Thomas Smith, of Amesbury, called Binsmith, made on 12 September 1361. <u>Interment</u>: in the graveyard of the church of St. Melor, Amesbury. <u>Bequests</u>: 5s. to the rector of Amesbury church, 12d. to the high altar, 12d. to the altar of the Holy Cross, 12d. to the altar of the Holy Mary, 13s. 4d. for maintaining the light of that altar (*viz.* by means of torches for the elevation of the Host), 2 bu. of barley for the communion light of that altar, 1 qr. of barley to the body of the church, and 2 bu. of barley to the light of all souls; 6d. to the high altar of the cathedral church, 6d. to the altar for matins, and 6d. to the image of the Holy Mary at the west door; 20s. for bread to be handed out to paupers on the day of her burial; 8 lb. of wax for

her funeral; 26s. 8d. for the expenses on the day of her burial; [*bequest unspecified*] to John, the parochial chaplain of Amesbury, to celebrate mass on behalf of her soul repeatedly; the rest of her goods to her brother John Hoare, his wife Gillian, and the lord Adam, a chaplain of the Blessed Mary. Devises: to her executors a tenement, in Gigant Street, which contains six cottages, to be sold at the order of her executors for 1,000 masses to be celebrated and other alms to be carried out on behalf of her soul, the soul of Thomas, formerly her husband, and the souls of others. Agnes appointed that the rest of her goods, and all the money raised from the tenement to be sold, should be received by her executors and disposed of by them on behalf of her soul. Executors: John Hoare and Adam Hoare, a chaplain of the Blessed Mary of Amesbury. Proved on 28 September 1361 in front of a commissary of the archdeacon of Salisbury; the administration was entrusted to the executors. Approved at a court held in front of the bailiff, the mayor, and other citizens; the seisin of the tenement was released to the legatee.

649 By their charter John of Beaminster, a son of William of Beaminster, of late a citizen of Salisbury, Joan of Beaminster, a sister of John, and Robert of Beechfount and his wife Agnes, a sister of John and Joan, appearing at the court held on that day granted to the lord Thomas of Erlestoke, a chaplain, and Robert Play a tenement, with shops, in Winchester Street between a tenement formerly Ingram at the brook's on the east side and a tenement formerly John of Littleton's, with a gate in Culver Street attached to it. The tenement, with the shops and the gate, was devised by William to John, Joan, and Agnes and is to be held for ever by Thomas and Robert and their heirs and assigns. Clause of warranty. Seals: those of the grantors and the common and mayoral seals of the city. Named witnesses: the bailiff, the mayor, the coroners, Robert of Godmanstone, Robert Bunt, George Goss, and the clerk

650 By her charter Emme, the relict, and an executor, of John Powell, of late a citizen of Salisbury, on the strength of John's will granted to Henry Netton a tenement in Wineman Street between William Surr's tenement on the east side and a tenement formerly John Kimble's on the west side. The tenement was devised by John Powell to be sold by his executors after the death of his son John and is to be held for ever by Henry and his heirs and assigns. Seals: Emme's and the common and mayoral seals of the city. Named witnesses: the bailiff, the mayor, the coroners, the reeves, Robert of Godmanstone, Robert Bunt, and the clerk

651 By his charter Philip, a son and heir of Philip Aubin, of late a citizen of Salisbury, granted to Matthew Fernhill a rent of 33s. 4d. a year issuing from a tenement, which Roger Fonthill and his wife Maud hold for their life, in Brown Street between a tenement which William of Wishford holds on the south side and a tenement of late John of Westbury's on the north side; also the reversion of the tenement when it fell due on the death of Roger and Maud. The tenement descended to the younger Philip by right of inheritance on the death of his father, and the rent, with the reversion, is to be held for ever by Matthew and his heirs and assigns. Clause to permit entry on the tenement if the rent were in arrear, distraint, and the keeping of distresses until the unpaid rent was recovered or, if

Matthew or his heirs or assigns preferred, to permit permanent possession of the tenement, according to the effect of an indenture perfected by Philip with Roger and Maud. Clause of warranty. Seals: Philip's and the common and mayoral seals of the city. Named witnesses: the bailiff, the mayor, John of Upton, Robert Bunt, and the clerk

6 July 1362, at Salisbury
652 By their charter William of Peakirk, the rector of Dinton, Stephen Newton, the rector of Little Langford, William Dunn, and Walter Kerry granted to Peter Clark, of Iwerne, a corner tenement, called Vellard's Corner, in Wineman Street and Endless Street between a tenement of late John Anger's on the east side and Thomas Hutchins's tenement on the north side. The tenement was held by the grantors by a grant of Thomas, a son and heir of John Tott, of Netheravon, of late a citizen of Salisbury, and is to be held for ever by Peter and his heirs and assigns. Seals: those of the grantors and the common and mayoral seals of the city. Named witnesses: the bailiff, the mayor, the coroners, the reeves, William of Wishford, Robert of Godmanstone, William of Bruton, and the clerk
653 Approval of the will of John Webb, fisher, a citizen of Salisbury, made on 3 August 1361. Interment: in the graveyard of St. Martin's church. Bequests: 12*d*. to the fabric of St. Martin's church, a black horse with all the equipment (*viz*. a saddle and a bridle), two robes, a surcoat, and a spoon capable of being ornamented to the lords Thomas of Clifton and John Chatt, chaplains, to celebrate mass on behalf of his soul, the soul of his wife Amice, and the souls of others, and 6*d*. each to the deacon and the sacristan; the rest of his goods to Amice. Devise: to Amice a tenement, beyond the bar, opposite the bishop of Salisbury's land held in villeinage, in the street leading towards St. Martin's church, between John Bunt's tenement on the north side and Joan Mayhew's tenement on the south side. The tenement was held by John by a devise of Alice, of late his wife, and is to be held for ever by Amice and her heirs and assigns. Executors: Amice and John Chatt. Proved on 7 August 1361 in front of an officer of the subdean; the administration was entrusted to the executors. Approved at a court held in front of the bailiff, the mayor, and other citizens; the seisin of the tenement was released to the legatee.
654 By their writing [*dated to the Wednesday after the feast of the translation of St. Thomas the Martyr (13 July) probably in error for the Wednesday after the feast of the translation of St. Thomas the Apostle (6 July)*] John White, the rector of Landford, John of Butterley, and Richard of Knottingley, executors of Joan Butterley, the relict of Thomas Butterley, formerly a citizen of Salisbury, quitclaimed to William of Wishford, a citizen of Salisbury, their right or claim to a rent of 22*s*. a year issuing from a tenement, opposite the market place where wool is sold, between a tenement of Thomas of Boyton, bowyer, on the north side and a tenement of an elder William Tenterer on the south side. William of Wishford now dwells in the tenement, which he holds by a grant of executors of the executors of Robert of Woodford, a citizen of Salisbury, and Joan Butterley devised the rent to be sold. Seals: those of John White, John of Butterley, and Richard of Knottingley and the common and mayoral seals of the city. Named witnesses: the bailiff, the

mayor, the coroners, the reeves, George Goss, Robert of Godmanstone, Robert Bunt, and the clerk

20 July 1362, at Salisbury
655 By his charter Henry Netton granted to Gilbert Oword, glover, and his wife Maud a tenement in Wineman Street [*as in* **650**]. The tenement was held by Henry by a grant of Emme, the relict, and an executor, of John Powell, of late a citizen of Salisbury, and is to be held for ever by Gilbert and Maud and their heirs and assigns. Seals: Henry's and the common and mayoral seals of the city. Named witnesses: the bailiff, the mayor, the coroners, the reeves, Robert of Godmanstone, William of Bruton, and the clerk.

3 August 1362, at Salisbury
656 By his writing Robert, a son of Richard Spray, of Shalbourne, quitclaimed to William Hitchcock, of Shalbourne, his right or claim to a tenement in Winchester Street between a tenement of late Henry Russell's on the west side and a tenement of late Alice Bertins's on the east side. Thomas of Shalbourne, Robert's uncle, acquired the tenement from William of Harpenden. Seals: Robert's and the common and mayoral seals of the city. Named witnesses: the bailiff, the mayor, the coroners, the reeves, William of Wishford, George Goss, and the clerk.
657 By their charter Thomas of Erlestoke, a chaplain, and Robert Play granted to Robert of Beechfount and his wife Agnes a tenement, with shops, in Winchester Street and a gate in Culver Street [*as in* **649**], which they held by a grant of John of Beaminster, a son of William of Beaminster, Joan of Beaminster, a sister of John, and Robert of Beechfount and his wife Agnes, a sister of John and Joan. The tenement, with the shops and the gate, is to be held for ever by Robert and Agnes and Robert's heirs and assigns. Seals: those of Thomas of Erlestoke and Robert Play and the common and mayoral seals of the city. Named witnesses: the bailiff, the mayor, the coroners, the reeves, William of Wishford, Robert Bunt, and the clerk.
658 By her charter Agnes, the relict of John of Bodenham, of late a citizen of Salisbury, granted to John Chandler, a citizen of Salisbury, a tenement in Freren Street between a tenement of John of Bodenham, formerly her husband, on the south side and a tenement of late Robert Russell's on the north side. The tenement was held by Agnes by a grant of John of Upton and William Pain, executors of Christine, the relict of Peter Bennett, of late a citizen of Salisbury, and is to be held for ever by John Chandler and his heirs and assigns. Seals: Agnes's and the common and mayoral seals of the city. Named witnesses: the bailiff, the mayor, the coroners, the reeves, William of Wishford, William of Bruton, and the clerk
659 By his writing Thomas, a son and heir of Stephen Glendy, of late a citizen of Salisbury, quitclaimed to Walter of Cheltenham, of Salisbury, the provost of St. Edmund's, his right or claim to a messuage, a yard (*or* yards), and a rack (*or* racks), in a street which is called Rolleston, in a croft called Martin's Croft. He

held those premises by a grant of the executors of John Richman, of late a citizen of Salisbury, on the strength of John's will. Clause of warranty. Seals: Thomas's and the common and mayoral seals of the city. Named witnesses: the bailiff, the mayor, the coroners, the reeves, William of Wishford, William of Bruton, and the clerk

660 By his writing Gilbert of Whichbury, an executor of Gilbert of Stapleford, a baker, of late a citizen of Salisbury, on the strength of Gilbert's will granted to Robert Play, ironmonger, of Salisbury, a rent of 20s. a year issuing from a tenement formerly William Stringer's beside a tenement formerly Edward of Knoyle's in Winchester Street. The rent was devised by Gilbert of Stapleford to be sold by his executors if his elder daughter Alice were to die without issue, and it is to be held for ever by Robert and his heirs and assigns. Seals: Gilbert of Whichbury's and the common and mayoral seals of the city. Named witnesses: the bailiff, the mayor, the coroners, the reeves, Robert of Godmanstone, Robert Bunt, William of Bruton, and the clerk

17 August 1362, at Salisbury
661 By his charter an elder William Tenterer, a citizen of Salisbury, by a licence of the king, granted to the dean and chapter of Salisbury two messuages which he acquired from Walter Cosham: one stands in the high street called Endless Street, opposite the Guildhall, between a tenement of late John of Woodford's on one side and John Nalder's tenement on the other side, and the other stands in Brown Street between a tenement formerly Henry Spicer's on one side and a tenement of late Henry Bold's on the other side. The two are to be held for ever by the dean and chapter and their successors to find a chaplain to celebrate mass every day for ever in the cathedral church on behalf of the healthy condition of the present king and of Robert, the bishop of Salisbury, and on behalf of the souls of all the faithful departed. Clause of warranty. Seals: William's and the common and mayoral seals of the city. Named witnesses: the bailiff, the mayor, the coroners, the reeves, Robert of Godmanstone, Robert Bunt, and the clerk

31 August 1362, at Salisbury
662 By his charter Richard Still, a citizen of Salisbury, granted to John of Butterley, a citizen of Salisbury, a tenement in Winchester Street between a tenement of late Jordan Mercer's on the east side and a tenement formerly John of Langford's on the west side. The tenement was held by Richard by a grant of Richard at the stone, a citizen of Salisbury, and is to be held for ever by John of Butterley and his heirs and assigns. Seals: Richard's and the common and mayoral seals of the city. Named witnesses: the bailiff, the mayor, the coroners, the reeves, William of Wishford, Robert of Godmanstone, and the clerk

14 September 1362
663 By his charter Henry Bunt, a burgess of Wilton, a son and heir of Peter Bunt, granted to the lord Roger of Clowne and the lord Thomas of Erlestoke a tenement, which descended to him by right of inheritance on the death of his

father, opposite the market where grains are sold, between a tenement of late John New's on the east side and a tenement formerly Thomas Drimmer's on the west side; also a tenement, which he held by a grant of Henry of Stapleford, a citizen of Salisbury, and his wife Edith opposite the market place where grains are sold, between a tenement of late Thomas Drimmer's on the west side and a tenement formerly Richard Batt's on the east side. The two tenements are to be held for ever by Roger and Thomas and their heirs and assigns. Seals: Henry's and the common and mayoral seals of the city. Named witnesses: the bailiff, the mayor, the coroners, the reeves, Robert of Godmanstone, William of Bruton, and the clerk

28 September 1362, at Salisbury
664 By their charter Agnes, the relict of John of Woodford, of late a citizen of Salisbury, she being an executor of Agnes, the relict of William Gill, of late a citizen of Salisbury, and William Wootton, John Prentice, Edward Deanbridge, John Packer, and Thomas Brute, tanner, they being her co-executors, on the strength of Agnes's will granted to John of Upton and Thomas Chaplin, citizens of Salisbury, a tenement in Endless Street. The tenement stands between a tenement of late Robert Gore's on the north side and Thomas Hutchins's tenement on the south side and extends from Endless Street as far as Brown Street. In her will Agnes devised it to be sold by her executors, and it is to be held for ever by John and Thomas and their heirs and assigns. Seals: those of the grantors and the common and mayoral seals of the city. Named witnesses: the bailiff, the mayor, a coroner, the reeves, William of Wishford, Robert of Godmanstone, Robert Bunt, George Goss, and the clerk
665 By their charter Thomas of Britford, John of Farnborough, and William Dunkerton granted to Thomas of Barford, a son and heir of John of Barford, of late a citizen of Salisbury, all the land, tenements, meadows, feeding [rights] and pasture, rent, services, and reversions in Salisbury, in the borough of Wilton, in Romsey and Landford, and in the fields of Old Sarum and Stratford near Old Sarum, which they held by a grant of Thomas of Barford, to be held for ever by Thomas of Barford and his heirs and assigns. Seals: those of the grantors and the common and mayoral seals of the city. Named witnesses: the bailiff, the mayor, a coroner, the reeves, William of Wishford, Robert ... [*other words omitted by the scribe*]

12 October 1362, at Salisbury
666 Approval of the will of Margery, the wife of Andrew Cook, of Milton *Abbatis*, dwelling in St. Thomas's parish, made on 18 November 1361. Interment: in the graveyard of St. Edmund's church. Bequests: a best gold ring to the image of the Blessed Mary of Salisbury at the west door, a gold ring and 6*d.* to the image of the altar cloth of that church, 6*d.* each to the cross above the door of the choir and the cross above the door of St. Thomas's chapel of that church, 6*d.* each to the light of the west door and the light of the Holy Cross above the door of St. Thomas's chapel; a towel to the high altar of St. Thomas's church, 6*d.* to the rector, and 4*d.*

to the parish priest; 2d. to each priest celebrating mass in St. Edmund's church to bear her corpse to that church; a red robe, a veil of best silk, and a bed to Gillian, her husband's mother; a second-best robe of her husband to Peter Needler; a tapet and a linen sheet to Thomas, her household servant; a gold ring to the wife of John Hugon; a gold ring to the lord John Ashfold; a silver brooch to Alice Costard; 15d. both to the priests celebrating mass in St. Edmund's church and the priests celebrating mass in St. Thomas's church; a furred coat and a cloak to Joan Jerrard; a 1-gallon ewer to John Ebeny, her godson; the rest of her goods to her husband Andrew. Devise: to Andrew a tenement, beyond the bar, on the way to St. Martin's church, between Roger Mutton's tenement on one side and a tenement formerly William Dogskin's on the other side, to be held for ever by him and his heirs or assigns. Executors: her husband Andrew and John Hugon. Proved on 16 September 1362 in front of an officer of the dean of Salisbury, the subdeanery being vacant; the administration was entrusted to Andrew, reserving the power to entrust it to John Hugon when he might come to seek it. Approved at a court held in front of the bailiff, the mayor, and other citizens; the seisin of the tenement was released to the legatees.

26 October 1362, at Salisbury
667 By his charter John Purbeck, weaver, of Salisbury, granted to Thomas of Britford, Gilbert of Whichbury, John Chandler, and John Basingstoke, citizens of Salisbury, the west part of a tenement in Wineman Street between the other part of that tenement, which Maud Smarts holds of Alice Sotts, of Downton, on the east side and a tenement which Richard Hosey, carder, holds on the west side. The part was held by John Purbeck and Alice, of late his wife, by a grant of William Alwin, of Downton, and his wife Isabel, the relict of John Cupping, and is to be held for ever by the grantees and their heirs and assigns. Clause of warranty. Seals: John Purbeck's and the common and mayoral seals of the city. Named witnesses: the bailiff, the mayor, a coroner, a reeve, George Goss, Robert Bunt, and the clerk

23 November 1362, at Salisbury
668 Approval of the will of Robert of Woodford, mercer, a citizen of Salisbury, made on 29 January 1362. Interment: in the graveyard of St. Edmund's church. Bequests: 13s. 4d. to the fabric of the cathedral church; 20s. to the fabric of St. Edmund's church, 13s. 4d. to the high altar for his forgotten tithes, 3s. 4d. to the parochial chaplain, 2s. to the deacon, 6d. to the sacristan, and 12d. to each chaplain of the college; 13s. 4d. both to the Franciscans of Salisbury and the Dominicans of Fisherton; 6d. to each one celebrating anniversary masses in St. Edmund's church about the time of his burial; ½ mark to the fabric of St. Margaret's church, Woodford, and 12d. to the vicar; 3s. 4d. to the church of Christ, Twineham; ½ mark to the fabric of St. Thomas's church; 2s. to the fabric of St. Martin's church; 40d. to the fraternity of the high cross in the cathedral church; ½ mark to the fraternity of the high cross in St. Edmund's church; 40d. to the fraternity of the light of the Blessed Mary at the west door of the cathedral church; 40d. each to

Ayleswade bridge and the upper bridge of Fisherton; 2s. both to the prisoners in the castle of [Old] Sarum and the prisoners in the Guildhall; ½ mark to Nicholas Newrig; 2s. to his goddaughter, a daughter of William Stanley; 40 lb. of wax, in candles alone, to be burned around his corpse at the time of his burial and, to relieve his soul, what remained after his burial to be given to the provost of the college of St. Edmund for his forgotten tithes; 100s. to be laid out in bread on the day of his burial on behalf of his soul; 40s. each for his other funeral expenses and for his obit to be celebrated on the thirtieth day after his death; 40s. to each of his executors; £20 for chaplains, to be chosen by his executors, to celebrate mass immediately after his death on behalf of his soul and the souls of others in St. Edmund's church or wherever the executors can find chaplains more quickly; 6s. 8d. [and] a best robe to Thomas, his servant; ½ mark, a coat with a hood, a tapet with a linen sheet, and a blanket to Robert, his servant; 2s. 6d. to the friar John Weston, of the order of Dominicans, to celebrate mass on behalf of his soul; 40d. to John Ingram; 6s. 8d. to Henry 'Wotthe', a chaplain, to celebrate mass on behalf of his soul; the rest of his goods to his wife Cecily if she survived him for the quarter of a year immediately following his death, or otherwise to be sold by his executors, their executors, or subsequent executors, and the money received laid out on behalf of his soul and the souls of those mentioned below. Devise: to his wife Cecily a tenement in Minster Street, between Thomas of Durrington's tenement on the south side and John Hawk's tenement on the north side, to be held for her life by her and her assigns. On Cecily's death the tenement should remain to Robert, a son of the late Philip Scriven, to be held for his life by him and his assigns; after that Robert's death it should be sold by Robert of Woodford's executors or subsequent executors. The money received should be laid out on celebrating masses and doing other charitable deeds on behalf of Robert of Woodford's soul, the souls of Isabel, of late his wife, and Cecily, and the souls of others. Executors: Cecily, Roger Ward, and Richard Lyner. Proved on 10 February 1362 in front of an officer of the dean of Salisbury, the subdeanery being vacant; the administration was entrusted to Cecily and Richard, reserving the power to entrust it to Roger when he might come to seek it. On 13 February 1362 Roger Ward appeared in front of the same officer and sought the administration, and the officer entrusted it to him. At a court held in front of the bailiff, the mayor, and other citizens the executors brought forth the will, which was approved; the seisin of the tenement was released to the legatee.

4 January 1363, at Salisbury
669 Approval of the will of John Marshall, a citizen of Salisbury, made on 20 June 1362. Interment: in the graveyard of St. Edmund's church. Bequests: 12d. to the fabric of the cathedral church, and 12d. to a lamp burning in front of the high cross in it; 12d. to the fabric of St. Edmund's church, and 12d. to the light of the fraternity there; 6s. 8d. to the Franciscans of Salisbury to celebrate mass on behalf of his soul; 12d. to Hayford bridge; 6d. to Ayleswade bridge; a coat divided into two parts, with a hood, to John, a son of Bartholomew Skinner; 6s. 8d. to John Marshall; 6 yd. of Ossett cloth to Gunhild Thoytes; 6 yd. of cloth

to William Comber and his wife Cecily; 4 lb. of wax to be burned around his corpse on the day of his burial; 20s. for all expenses on that day; a corset to Joan King, his servant; a damask gown to John Borley; cloth for a hood to Ellen Wheeler; 3s. 4d. to Robert Harding; the rest of his goods to his wife Joan to do on behalf of his soul what seemed best to her. <u>Devise</u>: to Joan a tenement in Gigant Street between John Langford's tenement on one side and a cottage of late John Cole's on the other side. The tenement was held by John Marshall by a grant of Robert Bathampton, is to be held for her life by Joan and her assigns, and after Joan's death should be sold by John's executors and Joan's or by their executors. The money received should be laid out on celebrating masses and doing other charitable deeds on behalf of John's soul, Joan's soul, and the souls of others. <u>Executors</u>: his wife Joan and Robert Harding. <u>Proved</u> on 19 November 1362 in front of an officer of the dean of Salisbury, the subdeanery being vacant; the administration was entrusted to the executors. At a court held in front of the bailiff, the mayor, and other citizens the executors brought forth the will, which was approved; the seisin of the tenement was released to the legatee.

670 By his charter William Pain, a citizen of Salisbury, granted to John Chandler, a citizen of Salisbury, two tenements, one in Carter Street between a tenement which was Edith Barber's on the north side and a tenement formerly William Ferrer's on the south side, the other in Brown Street between a tenement of late Richard Bartlet's on the north side and a tenement which was Alice Baldry's on the south side. William held the tenements by a grant of Laurence Chandler, William Whitehorn, hatter, and John of Wiltshire, executors of John Andrew, of late a citizen of Salisbury. He also granted to John a tenement, in Carter Street between a tenement of late Peter Bennett's on one side and a tenement of late John Andrew's on the other side, which he held by a grant of William Blakeney, spicer. All three tenements are to be held for ever by John Chandler and his heirs and assigns. Clause of warranty. Seals: William Pain's and the common and mayoral seals of the city. Named witnesses: the bailiff, the mayor, a coroner, the reeves, Robert Bunt, George Goss, and the clerk

1 February 1363, at Salisbury

671 Approval of the will of Richard Ryborough, a citizen of Salisbury, made on 21 January 1361. <u>Interment</u>: in the parish church of St. Thomas, or elsewhere at the will of God. <u>Bequests</u>: 5 marks to the fabric of the cathedral church; 5 marks to the fabric of St. Thomas's church, 10 marks to the high altar for his forgotten tithes and very small benefactions, 2s. to the deacon, and 12d. to the sacristan; 13s. 4d. each to the fabric of St. Edmund's church and the fabric of St. Martin's church; both to the Dominicans of Fisherton and the Franciscans of Salisbury 40s. for their pittance, a trental to each friar chaplain being in each convent on the day of his death, and 15d. to each other friar there then; a trental, to be celebrated immediately after his death, to each chaplain celebrating mass in the city on the day of his death whether friar chaplains in St. Nicholas's hospital, vicar chaplains in the cathedral church, or secular chaplains; 13s. 4d. to the lord Nicholas Hamish, a chaplain; 20s. each to John Crichel, a vicar, and the lord unimpaired estate. Clause of warranty in respect of the two tenements and of acquittance in respect of the service: John Talbot and his heirs will warrant and acquit for John of Ashley, his son Nicholas, and the male issue of John and his wife Edith and, if John were to die without male issue by Edith, for John, the son of Walter, and his male issue. Seals: those of the parties in turn and the common and mayoral seals of the city. Named witnesses: the bailiff, the mayor, a coroner, the reeves, George Goss, Robert Bunt, and the clerk

673 By her charter of Agnes of Woodford, the relict of William of Berwick, of late a citizen of Salisbury, granted to Thomas of Britford, the mayor, and to the commonalty of the city, a corner tenement, in the street [St. Martin's Street] extending from a gate of the canons' close towards St. Martin's church and in Culver Street, between a tenement formerly Thomas Vellard's on one side and a tenement formerly Reynold of Milbourne's on the other side. The tenement was held by William, Agnes, and Agnes's daughter Agnes by a grant of John Mutton, John of Clatford, and William of Evesham, executors of Roger Mutton, and is to be held for ever by the mayor the commonalty and their successors. Clause of warranty. Seals: Agnes's and the common and mayoral seals of the city. Named witnesses: the bailiff, a coroner, the reeves, Robert of Godmanstone, William of Wishford, and the clerk

674 By their charter Robert of Beechfount, and his wife Agnes, a daughter of the late William of Beaminster, a citizen of Salisbury, appearing at the court held on that day, granted to the lord Thomas of Erlestoke, a chaplain, and Robert Play a tenement in Carter Street between a tenement of late John of Bodenham's on one side and a tenement formerly Robert Fox's on the other side. The tenement was held by Agnes by a devise of Alice, who was the wife of Bertin Spicer, a citizen of Salisbury, and is to be held for ever by Thomas and Robert and their heirs and assigns. Seals: those of Robert of Beechfount and Agnes and the common and mayoral seals of the city. Named witnesses: the bailiff, the mayor, a coroner, the reeves, William of Wishford, Robert Bunt, and the clerk

675 By their charter John Hoare and Adam Hoare, a chaplain, executors of Agnes, the relict of Thomas Smith, called Binsmith, of Amesbury, on the strength of Agnes's will granted to John Cole, a citizen of Salisbury, a tenement, containing six cottages, in Gigant Street between Roger of Kilmeston's tenement on the north side and a tenement formerly Ralph Ive's on the south side. The tenement was devised by Agnes to be sold by her executors, and it is to be held, with shops and its other appurtenances, for ever by John Cole and his heirs and assigns. Seals: those of the grantors and the common and mayoral seals of the city. Named witnesses: the bailiff, the mayor, a coroner, the reeves, Robert of Godmanstone, William of Wishford, and the clerk

676 By her charter Agnes of Woodford, the relict of Edward Steward, called of Upton, of late a citizen of Salisbury, granted to the lord William Buck, a chaplain, and George Goss, a citizen of Salisbury, a corner tenement, with shops, in New Street between a tenement of Richard Hawes, tiler, on one side and Walter Calne's tenement on the other side. The tenement was held by Edward and Agnes by a grant of William of Liddington, a chaplain, and, with the shops, is to be held for ever by William and George and their heirs and assigns. [*The remainder of the charter is illegible*]

677 By their charter Thomas of Bridgehampton, Robert Bunt, and John Lea, citizens of Salisbury, granted to John Bunt and his wife Amice a tenement in Brown Street between a tenement formerly William Mohun's on the south side and a tenement of late John Baldry's on the north side; also a messuage, with a yard (*or* yards), beyond the bars, on the way to St. Martin's church, opposite the bishop of Salisbury's land held in villeinage, between a messuage of late that of John of Winterbourne, a clerk, on the south side and a messuage of late Adam of Barnwell's on the north side. The tenement and the messuage were held by Thomas, Robert, and John by Amice's grant and, with the yard(s), are to be held for ever by John Bunt and Amice and their heirs and assigns. Seals: those of the grantors and the common and mayoral seals of the city. Named witnesses: the bailiff, the mayor, a coroner, a reeve, William of Wishford, George Goss, and the clerk

678 By his charter William Goslin, a clerk, a brother and heir of John Goslin, of late a citizen of Salisbury, granted to Nicholas Bonham a messuage in Castle Street between a tenement of Thomas of Britford on either side. The messuage was held by John by a devise of Maud, the relict of John Sorrel, and is to be held for ever by Nicholas and his heirs and assigns. Clause of warranty. Seals: William's and the common and mayoral seals of the city. Named witnesses: the bailiff, the mayor, a coroner, the reeves, William of Wishford, Robert Bunt, and the clerk

15 February 1363, at Salisbury

679 By their charter William Buck, a chaplain, and George Goss, executors of John Richman, of late a citizen of Salisbury, under a licence of Edward III and of Robert, the bishop of Salisbury, granted to the lord Walter Cheltenham, the provost of the college of St. Edmund, and to the chaplains there a corner tenement, with shops, in New Street between a tenement of Richard Hawes, tiler, on one side and Walter Calne's tenement on the other side. The tenement, with the shops, is to be held for ever by the provost and chaplains and their successors as an increase in their maintenance as is contained in the king's licence, celebrating mass every day in the collegiate church on behalf of the healthy condition of the present king and of the bishop, and on behalf of the souls of Robert of Woodford, John of Woodford, and John Richman and his wife Agace, the condition of Agnes of Woodford while she lived, the souls of each of them when they have died, and the souls of all the faithful departed. Seals: those of William and George and the common and mayoral seals of the city. Named witnesses: the bailiff, the mayor and one of the coroners, the other coroner, the reeves, William of Wishford, Nicholas Taylor, Robert of Godmanstone, Robert Bunt, and the clerk

680 By their charter Gilbert of Whichbury and Thomas Chaplin, executors of Robert Alwin, of late a citizen of Salisbury, on the strength of Robert's will granted to Thomas of Britford, John of Upton, and John Chandler, citizens of Salisbury, two conjoined cottages in Drake Hall Street between a tenement of late John Hemingby's on the south side and a tenement formerly Nicholas Longborough's on the north side. The cottages were devised by Robert to be sold by his executors and are to be held for ever by the grantees and their heirs and assigns. Seals: those of the grantors and the common and mayoral seals of the city. Named witnesses: the bailiff, the mayor and one of the coroners, the reeves, William of Wishford, Robert of Godmanstone, George Goss, Robert Bunt, and the clerk

681 By their charter John of Upton and William Pain, executors of Christine, the relict of Peter Bennett, of late a citizen of Salisbury, on the strength of Christine's will granted to Thomas of Britford, Gilbert of Whichbury, and John Chandler, citizens of Salisbury, a tenement in Drake Hall Street between a tenement of late John Shalford's on one side and a tenement of late John Hemingby's on the other side. The tenement was devised by Christine to be sold by her executors and is to be held for ever by the grantees and their heirs and assigns. Seals: those of the grantors and the common and mayoral seals of the city. Named witnesses: the bailiff, the mayor and one of the coroners, the reeves, Robert of Godmanstone, William of Wishford, George Goss, and the clerk

1 March 1363, at Salisbury

682 By their charter John Polmond and his wife Alice, the relict, and an executor, of Richard Alden, of Southampton, appearing at the court held on that day, on the strength of Richard's will granted to the lord John Bailiff, a chaplain, and William Polmond a corner tenement called Florentine's Corner in New Street and Minster Street. The tenement was devised by Richard to be sold and is to be held for ever by the grantees and their heirs and assigns. Seals: those of John Polmond and Alice and the common and mayoral seals of the city. Named witnesses: the bailiff, the mayor, the reeves, William of Wishford, Robert of Godmanstone, Robert Bunt, George Goss, and the clerk

15 March 1363, at Salisbury

683 By his charter Gilbert of Whichbury, a citizen of Salisbury, granted to John Lea a cottage in Gigant Street between John's own tenement, formerly John Doder's, on the north side and Robert Fewster's cottage on the south side. Gilbert, Richard Ryborough, and Robert Alwin held the cottage for ever by a grant to them, and their heirs and assigns, of John of Bodenham, of late a citizen of Salisbury. Long before his death Richard released his right to the cottage to Gilbert and Robert and long ago Robert died; the cottage thus remained for ever to Gilbert and his heirs and assigns, and it is to be held for ever by John Lea and his heirs and assigns. Seals: Gilbert's and the common and mayoral seals of the city. Named witnesses: the bailiff, the mayor and one of the coroners, the other coroner, the reeves, Robert Bunt, George Goss, and the clerk

684 By their charter Thomas of Erlestoke, a chaplain, and Robert Play granted to Robert of Beechfount and his wife Agnes a tenement in Carter Street between a tenement of late John of Bodenham's on one side and a tenement formerly Robert Fox's on the other side. The tenement was held by Thomas and Robert by a grant of Robert and Agnes and is to be held for ever by Robert and Agnes and Robert's heirs and assigns. Seals: those of the grantors and the common and mayoral seals of the city. Named witnesses: the bailiff, the mayor and one of the coroners, the other coroner, the reeves, Robert of Godmanstone, Robert Bunt, George Goss, and the clerk

26 April 1363, at Salisbury
685 By his charter John of Upton, a citizen of Salisbury, granted to Walter Cooper, a citizen of Salisbury, two conjoined cottages, with adjacent yards, in Culver Street between cottages which were Hugh Boney's on the south side and a corner tenement formerly that of Ingram at the brook on the north side. The cottages were held by John by a grant of Nicholas Russell, a citizen of Salisbury, who held them by a grant of William of Wallop, butcher, and they are to be held, with the yards, for ever by Walter and his heirs and assigns. Seals: John's and the common and mayoral seals of the city. Named witnesses: the bailiff, the mayor and one of the coroners, the reeves, Nicholas Taylor, William of Wishford, George Goss, Robert Bunt, and the clerk
686 By his charter John of Upton, a citizen of Salisbury, granted to Thomas of Britford, Gilbert of Whichbury, John Chandler, and John Basingstoke, citizens of Salisbury, a rent of 13s. 4d. a year to be received for ever by them and their heirs and assigns from his tenement in Minster Street, beyond the bar, between a tenement of late Walter Cavenasser's on the south side and a yard of late Thomas of Hungerford's on the north side. Clause to permit entry on the tenement if the rent were in arrear, distraint, and the keeping of distresses until the unpaid rent and other losses were recovered. Clause of warranty. Seals: John of Upton's and the common and mayoral seals of the city. Named witnesses: the bailiff, the mayor and one of the coroners, the reeves, William of Wishford, Nicholas Taylor, Robert of Godmanstone, and the clerk

24 May 1363, at Salisbury
687 By their charter Richard Prior and his wife Joan a daughter and heir of John of Langford, appearing at the court held on that day, granted to John Talbot, a citizen of Salisbury, a tenement, with a yard (*or* yards), opposite the Franciscans. The tenement was John of Langford's, was held for life by John Talbot of Joan's inheritance, and was surrendered by John Talbot in that court. It is to be held, with the yard(s), for ever by John Talbot and his heirs and assigns. Clause of warranty. Seals: those of Richard and Joan and the common and mayoral seals of the city. Named witnesses: the bailiff, the mayor and one of the coroners, the other coroner, the reeves, William of Wishford, Robert of Godmanstone, and the clerk
688 By their charter John Cross and his wife Amice, the relict of John Webb, fisher, of late a citizen of Salisbury, appearing at the court held on that day, granted to Emme, the relict of Robert Gore, of late a citizen of Salisbury, a tenement, beyond the bar, opposite the bishop of Salisbury's land held in villeinage, in the street leading towards St. Martin's church, between a tenement formerly John

Bunt's on the north side and Joan Mayhew's tenement on the south side. The tenement was held by Amice by a devise of John Webb, who held it by a devise of Alice Dogskin, formerly his wife, and it is to be held for ever by Emme and her heirs and assigns. Seals: those of John Cross and Amice and the common and mayoral seals of the city. Named witnesses: the bailiff, the mayor and one of the coroners, the other coroner, the reeves, William of Wishford, Robert Bunt, George Goss, and the clerk

689 Memorandum that Henry Winslade and his wife Margery, she being examined, released to John Bailiff, a chaplain, and William Polmond their right or claim to a corner tenement called Florentine's Corner in New Street and Minster Street, with a clause of warranty. If any deed concerning the tenement kept in their possession by them or their heirs were to be found, it would be considered void. Named witnesses: the bailiff, the mayor and one of the coroners, the other coroner, and the reeves

7 June 1363, at Salisbury
690 Approval of the will of Maud of Langford, the relict of Hugh of Langford, a citizen of Salisbury, made on 8 December 1362. Interment: in the graveyard of St. Edmund's church. Bequests: a quantity of lead to the fabric of the cathedral church; 2s. to the fabric of St. Edmund's church, 2s. 6d. to the parochial chaplain, and 2s. to the high altar for her forgotten tithes; ½ mark to the Franciscans of Salisbury; 10s. to the convent of Dominicans of Fisherton; a best bowl, a piece of silver, a rosary of best amber beads, a coverlet with a best dossal, and all her pewter vessels to her son the lord Thomas, a Dominican; two silver spoons to her son Stephen, a friar; a second-best bed, a second-best brass pot, a second-best brass pan, a fork, and 6s. 8d. to Maud Baron, her maid; 20s. for all her funeral expenses on the day of her burial, and 40s. to be laid out among paupers on that day; 20s. to be laid out among paupers on the thirtieth day after her death or burial; her best robe and ½ mark to Maud, a daughter of her sister Christine; two diapered coverlets to the Dominicans of Fisherton, for use in their dormitory while the coverlets lasted; a best blue coat, with a hood, to Emme, the wife of John Baron, of Westbury; a second-best mazer to her son Stephen; 13s. 4d. to John Chandler; two best boxes, a tablecloth with a towel, and a great basin with a laver, to Maud Baron, her maid; six sheep at Somborne to the lord John Stanton, a chaplain; 10 of her sheep at Somborne to Richard Dinton; 40d. to the shepherd keeping her sheep at Somborne; the rest of her goods to her three sons to be divided equally among them; ½ mark to John Cross, of Westbury; her best belt of silk to Ellen, the wife of Thomas of Barford; 4 sheep from her flock at Little Somborne and 40d. to the fabric of Somborne church, in which the corpse of her son Andrew lies buried. Devises: to Maud Baron a tenement in Scots Lane, between Richard Ryborough's tenement on the west side and a tenement formerly William Bartlet's on the east side, to be held for ever by her and her issue for holding, once a year in St. Edmund's church, the obits of Hugh of Langford, Maud of Langford, and that Maud's son Andrew. If Maud Baron were to die without issue the tenement should be sold by Maud of Langford's

executors, their executors, or subsequent executors. The money received should be laid out on behalf of the souls of those named and the souls of others. Maud devised to John Baron, of Quidhampton, two conjoined cottages, with a yard (*or* yards), in Endless Street between William Newman's tenement on the north side and shops formerly William Bartlet's on the south side, to be held for ever by John and his issue. If John were to die without issue the cottages, with the yard(s), should be sold by Maud's executors or subsequent executors. The money received should be laid out on behalf of the souls mentioned above. It is to be understood nevertheless that Maud's will was that, first and foremost, the money should be spent on the fabric of St. Edmund's church. Maud devised to her sister Christine Stints a rent of 16*s*. a year issuing from a tenement, formerly that of John Mariner, hatter, in Minster Street between Edward Pinnock's tenement on the south side and a tenement formerly Robert Painter's on the north side. The rent is to be held for life by Christine to find a candle weighing 4 lb., *viz*. 4 lb. yearly, to burn in front of the altar called *Salve* in the monastery of Wilton, and after her death should be sold by Maud's executors or subsequent executors. The money received should be handed over to the abbess and convent of Wilton to maintain a candle of that weight yearly, to burn without fail in front of that altar, in honour of Jesus Christ and the Blessed Virgin Mary and for the salvation of the souls mentioned above. Maud devised conjoined cottages, with a barn, in Nuggeston, between a yard of late Peter Latimer's and a yard formerly John Coppiner's, to be sold by her executors immediately after her death or as soon possible by the executors or subsequent executors. From the money received she appointed £3 cash to the fabric of St. Edmund's church, £3 to her son the lord Thomas, and the remainder to be shared equally between her sons the lord Thomas, the lord John, and the lord Stephen. Executors: Richard Dinton and John Chandler; overseer, her son the lord John, a canon of St. Denis. Proved on 6 June 1363 in front of an officer of the subdean; the administration was entrusted to Richard Dinton subject to the oversight of Maud's son John, reserving the power to entrust it to John Chandler when he might come to seek it. Approved at a court held in front of the bailiff, the mayor, and other citizens; the seisin of the tenements was released to the legatees.

691 By their charter John Bailiff, a chaplain, and William Polmond granted to John Polmond a corner tenement called Florentine's Corner in New Street and Minster Street. They held it by a grant of John Polmond and his wife Alice, and it is to be held for ever by John and his heirs and assigns. Seals: those of the grantors and the common and mayoral seals of the city. Named witnesses: the bailiff, the mayor and one of the coroners, the other coroner, the reeves, William of Wishford, Nicholas Taylor, and the clerk

692 Approval of the will of John Everard, of Stratford, made on 25 August 1361. Interment: in the graveyard of the church of the Holy Cross, Stratford. Bequests: ½ mark each to the fabric of that church and the fabric of the cathedral church; 2 qr. wheat both to the Dominicans of Fisherton and the Franciscans of Salisbury; the rest of his goods to his wife Beatrice and his sons John, Jordan, and William. Devises: two rents to his wife Beatrice for life, one of 20*s*. a year which he was accustomed to receive from a tenement in Minster Street, on the west side of the street beside the north gate of the canons's close, and one of 24*s*. a year which he was accustomed to receive from a tenement of late that of John Uphill and his wife Edith, in the same street and on the east side of the street. On Beatrice's death the rents should remain for ever to John's son Jordan and Jordan's issue; if Jordan were to die without issue they would remain for ever to that John's son William and William's issue; if William were to die without issue they would remain for ever to the younger John and his issue; if that John were to die without issue they should be sold by the elder John's executors or their executors. The money received should be laid out on celebrating masses and on other pious alms on behalf of his soul, the souls of his wives Beatrice and Agnes, Robert of Woodford, and Simon Irish, and the souls of others. John appointed that half the money should be handed to his daughters Margery, Lucy, and Edith, if they were then living, to pray for the souls mentioned above. If none of them was then living, on behalf of those souls that half of the money should be handed out to paupers holding land. <u>Executors</u>: Beatrice, Thomas Drew, and Richard Farley; overseer, John Doder. <u>Proved</u> in the cathedral church on 1 September 1361 in front of an officer of the subdean; the administration was entrusted to Beatrice and Thomas, reserving the power to entrust it to Richard when he might come to seek it. <u>Approved</u> at a court held in front of the bailiff, the mayor, and other citizens; the seisin of the rents was released to the legatees.

21 June 1363, at Salisbury
693 Memorandum. At the court held on that day Richard Dinton, an executor of Maud of Langford, the relict of Hugh of Langford, on the strength of Maud's will granted to Thomas of Britford, a citizen of Salisbury, cottages in Nuggeston [*as in* **690**] to be held for ever by Thomas and his heirs and assigns.

5 July 1363, at Salisbury
694 Approval of the will of Joan, the wife of John Amesbury, made on 20 June 1363. <u>Interment</u>: in the graveyard of St. Edmund's church. <u>Bequests</u>: 2*s*. each to the fabric of that church and the fabric of the cathedral church; the rest of her goods to her executors to be disposed of by them on behalf of her soul. <u>Devises</u>: to her husband John a messuage in Endless Street, beside William Corp's tenement on the south side, to be held for his life by him and his assigns. After John's death the messuage should be held for ever by Joan's son John and his issue and, if that John were to die without issue it should be sold by her executors or their executors. The money received should be laid out on behalf of her soul, the souls of her husband and her son John, and the souls of others. Joan also devised to her husband John a messuage in Chipper Street between William Tidpit's tenement on one side and a tenement of late John Richman's on the other side. The messuage is to be held for his life by John and his assigns, after John's death is to be held for ever by Joan's son John and his issue, and if that John were to die without issue should be sold by Joan's executors or their executors. The money received should be laid out as mentioned above. Joan also devised

to her husband John a shop in Minster Street beside a corner tenement called Wimpler's Corner. The shop is to be held for life by John, after his death is to be held for ever by Joan's son John and his issue, and if that John were to die without issue should be sold by Joan's executors or their executors. The money received should be laid out as mentioned above. Joan devised to her brother John Bone a rent of 16s. a year issuing from a tenement which Alice Littles holds for life, with the reversion of the tenement when it fell due on Alice's death. The tenement stands in Minster Street near a stile of the graveyard of St. Thomas's church. The rent and the reversion are to be held for ever by John and his heirs and assigns. Executors: her husband John and Thomas Gilbert. Proved on 21 June 1363 in front of an officer of the subdean; the administration was entrusted to the executors. Approved at a court held in front of the bailiff, the mayor, and other citizens; the seisin of the tenements was released to the legatees.

30 August 1363, at Salisbury
695 By his charter Thomas of Erlestoke, a chaplain, granted to William Bleacher, of Stoke Farthing (*Stokeverdoun*), a tenement in Endless Street between a tenement of late Thomas Hungerford's on one side and a tenement of Avice Piercourt. The tenement was held by Thomas Erlestoke by a grant of Henry Teffont and his wife Maud and is to be held for ever by William and his heirs and assigns. Clause of warranty. Seals: Thomas's and the common and mayoral seals of the city. Named witnesses: the bailiff, the mayor and one of the coroners, the other coroner, the reeves, William of Wishford, Nicholas Taylor, George Goss, and the clerk

13 September 1363, at Salisbury
696 By his charter Richard Dinton, a son and an executor of Maud, who was the wife of Stephen Shearer, a citizen of Salisbury, on the strength of Maud's will granted to Robert of Beechfount a tenement in Gigant Street between John Langford's tenement on the north side and a tenement of late John Whitehorn's on the south side. The tenement was devised by Walter Goss, formerly Maud's husband, to be sold by Maud or her executors, devised by Maud to be sold by her executors for the salvation of her soul, and is to be held for ever by Robert of Beechfount and his heirs and assigns. Seals: Richard's and the common and mayoral seals of the city. Named witnesses: the bailiff, the mayor, the reeves, William of Wishford, Nicholas Taylor, George Goss, and the clerk

27 September 1363, at Salisbury
697 By his charter Thomas of Bridgehampton, a citizen of Salisbury, granted to Thomas Hindon a tenement, opposite the Guildhall, between John Nalder's tenement on the north side and a tenement formerly Robert Cheese's on the south side. The tenement was held by Thomas of Bridgehampton by a grant of the lord Thomas of Erlestoke, a chaplain, and Thomas of Britford, executors of William Costard, of late a citizen of Salisbury, and is to be held for ever by Thomas Hindon and his heirs and assigns. Clause of warranty. Seals: Thomas of Bridgehampton's and the common and mayoral seals of the city. Named witnesses:

the bailiff, the mayor and one of the coroners, the other coroner, a reeve, William of Wishford, Nicholas Taylor, Robert of Godmanstone, and the clerk

25 October 1363, at Salisbury
698 Approval of the will of Edith, the wife of Thomas Bleacher, smith, of Salisbury, made on 9 September 1361. <u>Interment</u>: in the graveyard of St. Thomas's church. <u>Bequests</u>: 6d. to the fabric of the cathedral church; 6d. to the fabric of St. Thomas's church, 6d. to the parochial chaplain, and 3d. to the deacon; a kerchief of cypress to Agnes Farthing; a kerchief of felted linen cloth to Parnel, the wife of Michael Wight; a gold brooch to Alice Stokes; a hood *de Bockehorn* [?of Bocking] to Maud Shipster; the rest of her goods to her husband Thomas. <u>Devise</u>: to Thomas a tenement which stands, opposite the cross where fruit and vegetables are sold, between a tenement formerly Edward of Warminster's and John of Marlborough's tenement on the other side. The tenement is to be held for life by Thomas and after his death should be sold by Edith's executors or their executors on behalf of her soul and the souls of others. <u>Executor</u>: her husband Thomas. <u>Witnesses</u>: Edith affixed her seal to the will with, as witnesses, Robert Play and Thomas Mackinney, the scribe. <u>Proved</u> on 12 October 1363 in front of an officer of the subdean; the administration was entrusted to the executor and to Michael Wight, sworn as a co-executor by that officer. <u>Approved</u> at a court held in front of the bailiff, the mayor, and other citizens; the seisin of the tenement was released to the legatee.

699 By his charter [*dated to the Wednesday after the feast of St. Crispin and St. Crispinian (1 November) probably in error for the Wednesday of that feast (25 October)*] Thomas of Britford granted to Walter Holbury a tenement, in the high street called End Street, between a tenement of Nicholas Taylor and his wife Ellen on the south side and a tenement of late John Pannett's on the north side. The tenement was held by Thomas by a grant of John Hoare, an executor of Thomas Smith, called the binsmith, of Amesbury, and is to be held for ever by Walter and his heirs and assigns. Seals: Thomas's and the common and mayoral seals of the city. Named witnesses: the bailiff, the mayor and one of the coroners, the other coroner, the reeves, William of Wishford, George Goss, Robert Bunt, and the clerk

25 January 1363 x 1 November 1363, at Salisbury
700 By his charter John Silvester, a son and heir of Thomas Silvester, granted to the lords Thomas of Erlestoke and John Crichel, chaplains, a tenement in New Street between a tenement formerly Richard Sealer's on one side and a tenement formerly Richard Long's on the other side. The tenement descended to John Silvester by inheritance on the death of his father and is to be held for ever by the lords Thomas and John and their heirs and assigns. Clause of warranty. Seals: John Silvester's and the common and mayoral seals of the city. Named witnesses: the bailiff, the mayor and one of the coroners, the other coroner, the reeves, Robert of Godmanstone, William Wishford, and Nicholas Taylor

22 November 1363, at Salisbury
701 By his charter Thomas Longborough, a chaplain, granted to John Chandler, a citizen of Salisbury, a messuage in New Street between a tenement which Philip Odiham of late held on the east side and Kentigern of Sulham's tenement on the west side. The messuage was acquired by Thomas from Henry Fleming, a citizen of Salisbury, and is to be held for ever by John and his heirs and assigns. Clause of warranty. Seals: Thomas's and the common and mayoral seals of the city. Named witnesses: the bailiff, the mayor, the reeves, William of Wishford, Robert of Godmanstone, Robert Bunt, and George Goss

20 December 1363, at Salisbury
702 By his charter Thomas Chaplin, a citizen of Salisbury, granted to John Bennett a corner tenement in New Street and Brown Street between a tenement of late Richard Salter's on the west side and a tenement of late that of a younger Robert Baldry on the south side. The tenement was held by Thomas by a grant of John of Wilton, the rector of St. Thomas's church, and is to be held for ever by John and his heirs and assigns. Seals: Thomas's and the common and mayoral seals of the city. Named witnesses: the bailiff, the mayor, the coroners, the reeves, William of Wishford, John Butterley, William Warmwell, and the clerk

3 January 1364, at Salisbury
703 By his charter John Lokebet, a citizen of Salisbury, granted to Thomas Sexhampcote, a dyer, a tenement in Minster Street between, on either side, a tenement of Hugh Winterbourne, butcher, which Hugh held by John's grant. The tenement was held by John by a grant of the lord Henry Gill, the rector of Fisherton, Thomas of Britford, and the lord John of Bradwell, a chaplain, executors of Thomas of Hungerford, of late a citizen of Salisbury, and is to be held for ever by Thomas and his heirs and assigns. Clause of warranty. Seals: John Lokebet's and the common and mayoral seals of the city. Named witnesses: the bailiff, the mayor, the coroners, the reeves, William of Wishford, Robert of Godmanstone, George Goss, and the clerk

8 January 1364, at Westminster
704 By his letters patent Edward III, for 16 marks paid to him by the dean and chapter of Salisbury, granted a licence, as required by the Statute of Mortmain, to Martin Mowlish, a clerk, John of Crichel, a clerk, Thomas of Erlestoke, the parson of Barford [St. Martin], and Robert Axbey, a clerk, to grant to the dean and chapter a shop, and rent of £4, in Salisbury. The shop and the rent are to be held by the dean and chapter for the maintenance of a chaplain to celebrate mass daily at the altar of St. Thomas the Martyr in the cathedral church on behalf of the healthy condition of the king, Queen Philippa, and their children, of their souls when they have died, of the souls of their forebears and successors, and of the souls of all the faithful departed. A clerk to the chaplain and to other chaplains willing to celebrate mass there is also to be maintained to serve in the celebration of masses according to the direction of the licencees. The king licensed the dean

and chapter to receive the shop and the rent, and them and their successors to hold them for ever for the maintenance of the chaplain and the clerk, the statute notwithstanding.

17 January 1364, at Salisbury
705 By his charter Thomas of Wiltshire, a son and heir of John Wiltshire, of late a citizen of Salisbury, granted to John New, tanner, a citizen of Salisbury, a tenement in St. Martin's Street between Roger Tanner's tenement on the south side and Agnes of Woodford's cottage property on the west side; also a corner tenement, with a yard next to it, beyond the bar, on the way to St. Martin's church, between a tenement of late Edward of Upton's on the west side and a tenement of late Adam of Barnwell's on the east side. The tenements descended to Thomas by right of inheritance on the death of his father and, with the yard, are to be held for ever by John New and his heirs and assigns. Clause of warranty. Seals: Thomas's and the common and mayoral seals of the city. Named witnesses: the bailiff, the mayor, a reeve, George Goss, William Warmwell, John Butterley, and the clerk

14 February 1364, at Salisbury
706 By their deed Nicholas Habgood and his wife Beatrice, the relict of John Knoyle, of Ludgershall, appearing at the court held on that day, granted to John Pack, a carpenter, a tenement, with shops, in Minster Street between a tenement of late Edward Pinnock's on either side. The tenement was held by Beatrice as dower and, with the shops, is to be held by John and his heirs and assigns of Nicholas and Beatrice for Beatrice's life, performing for them all services. Clause of warranty and acquittance. Seals: those of Nicholas and Beatrice and the common and mayoral seals of the city. Named witnesses: the bailiff, the mayor, the coroners, the reeves, William of Wishford, Robert Bunt, and the clerk
707 By his charter Nicholas Hamish, a chaplain, granted to Agnes Ferrers and Peter Cambo a tenement, opposite St. Thomas's church, between a tenement formerly Robert of Knoyle's on the east side and a tenement formerly Robert of Lavington's on the west side. The tenement was held by Nicholas by a grant of John Homington and is to be held for ever by Agnes and Peter and their heirs and assigns. Seals: Nicholas's and the common and mayoral seals of the city. Named witnesses: the bailiff, the mayor, a coroner, William of Wishford, George Goss, and the clerk
708 By his charter Thomas of Barford, a citizen of Salisbury, granted to the lord Thomas of Erlestoke, a chaplain, and Andrew of Stratford the land, tenements, meadows, feeding [rights] and pastures, rent, services, and reversions which he held in fee in Salisbury, the borough of Wilton, Romsey and Landford, the fields of Old Sarum, Stratford near Old Sarum, and elsewhere in Wiltshire, to be held for ever by Thomas and Andrew and their heirs and assigns. Clause of warranty. Seals: Thomas of Barford's and the common and mayoral seals of the city. Named witnesses: the bailiff, the mayor, the coroners, the reeves, William of Wishford, Robert of Godmanstone, and the clerk

709 By his charter Andrew Cook granted to Thomas of Britford, a citizen of Salisbury, a tenement, beyond the bar, on the way to St. Martin's church, between Roger Mutton's tenement on one side and a tenement formerly William Dogskin's on the other side. The tenement was held by Andrew by a devise of his wife Margery, the relict of Robert Osborne, a fisherman, of late a citizen of Salisbury, and is to be held for ever by Thomas and his heirs and assigns. Clause of warranty. Seals: Andrew's and the common and mayoral seals of the city. Named witnesses: the bailiff, the mayor, a coroner, the reeves, Robert Bunt, William Warmwell, and the clerk

710 By his charter Andrew Cook granted to Thomas of Britford, a citizen of Salisbury, four cottages in St. Martin's Street between Agnes of Berwick's tenement on the east side and Roger Tanner's tenement on the west side. The cottages were held by Andrew and his wife Margery by a grant of Peter Needler, an executor of Robert Osborne, a fisherman, of late a citizen of Salisbury, and are to be held for ever by Thomas and his heirs and assigns. Clause of warranty. Seals: Andrew's and the common and mayoral seals of the city. Named witnesses: the bailiff, the mayor, a coroner, the reeves, William of Wishford, Robert Bunt, and the clerk

13 March 1364, at Salisbury
711 By his charter John Hawk, a citizen of Salisbury, granted to John Justice, of Salisbury, a tenement, in the street on the way to St. Martin's church, between a tenement formerly Ralph of Coulston's on one side and a tenement of late that of John of Langford, draper, on the other side. The tenement was held by John Hawk by a grant of Richard of Hartwell, of late a citizen of Salisbury, and is to be held for ever by John Justice and his heirs and assigns. Clause of warranty. Seals: John Hawk's and the common and mayoral seals of the city. Named witnesses: the bailiff, the mayor, the coroners, the reeves, William of Wishford, Robert of Godmanstone, and the clerk

712 By his charter John Hawk, a citizen of Salisbury, granted to John Justice, of Salisbury, five conjoined cottages in Chipper Street between Henry Pope's tenement on one side and Stephen Shearer's tenement on the other side. The cottages were held by John Hawk by a grant of John Knoyle, of Ludgershall, a brother and heir of the master Henry Knoyle, and are to be held for ever by John Justice and his heirs and assigns. Clause of warranty. Seals: John Hawk's and the common and mayoral seals of the city. Named witnesses: the bailiff, the mayor, the coroners, the reeves, William of Wishford, Robert Bunt, George Goss, and the clerk

713 By his charter John Hawk, a citizen of Salisbury, granted to John Justice, of Salisbury, a tenement, in the street on the way to St. Martin's church, between John Hawk's tenement, of late that of John Passavant, a chaplain, on one side and Roger Tanner's tenement on the other side. The tenement was acquired by John Hawk from Emme Powell and is to be held for ever by John Justice and his heirs and assigns. Seals: John Hawk's and the common and mayoral seals of the city. Named witnesses: the bailiff, the mayor, the coroners, William of Wishford,

Robert Bunt, George Goss, and the clerk

714 By his charter John Hawk, a citizen of Salisbury, granted to John Justice, of Salisbury, a tenement, in the street on the way to St. Martin's church, between a tenement formerly that of John Carpenter, a baker, on the west side and a tenement formerly John of Gomeldon's on the east side. The tenement was held by John Hawk by a grant of John Passavant, a chaplain, and is to be held for ever by John Justice and his heirs and assigns. Clause of warranty. Seals: John Hawk's and the common and mayoral seals of the city. Named witnesses: the bailiff, the mayor, the coroners, the reeves, William of Wishford, Robert Bunt, George Goss, and the clerk

715 By his charter John Hawk, a citizen of Salisbury, granted to John of Upton, Thomas of Britford, John Chandler, and John Basingstoke, citizens of Salisbury, a tenement in St. Martin's Street between a tenement formerly William of Berwick's on one side and a tenement formerly Thomas Vellard's on the other side. The tenement was held by John Hawk by a grant of William of Wishford, who held it by a feoffment of John White, the rector of Landford, and it is to be held for ever by the grantees and their heirs and assigns. Seals: John Hawk's and the common and mayoral seals of the city. Named witnesses: the bailiff, the mayor, the reeves, William of Wishford, Robert Bunt, George Goss, and the clerk

716 By his charter John Hawk, a citizen of Salisbury, granted to John of Upton, a citizen of Salisbury, a rent of 40s. a year from a tenement, in which Nicholas Holtby dwells, in Minster Street between a tenement formerly John of Lyneham's on one side and a tenement of late that of Robert of Woodford, mercer, on the other side. The rent was customarily paid by Nicholas to John Hawk and is to be received for ever by John of Upton and his heirs and assigns. Clause to permit entry on the tenement if the rent were in arrear, distraint, and the keeping of distresses until the unpaid rent was recovered. Clause of warranty. So that his grant, and the confirmation of the charter, would remain valid for ever John Hawk confirmed John of Upton's seisin by paying to him 1d. by the hand of Nicholas, who holds the tenement and consents to that acknowledgement, on the day on which the charter was perfected. Seals: John Hawk's and the common and mayoral seals of the city. Named witnesses: the bailiff, the mayor, a coroner, William of Wishford, Robert of Godmanstone, Robert Bunt, George Goss, and the clerk

717 By their indented charter Robert of Beechfount and Gilbert of Whichbury, executors of Richard Ryborough, of late a citizen of Salisbury, granted to Richard's daughter Cecily, the wife of Thomas Hutchins, a tenement in Winchester Street between a tenement called the New Inn on one side and a tenement of late Thomas Long's on the other side. The tenement is to be held for ever by Cecily and her issue, and if Cecily were to die without issue it would revert to Robert and Gilbert, their executors, or subsequent executors to be sold for the salvation of Richard's soul. Seals: those of the parties and the common and mayoral seals of the city. Named witnesses: the bailiff, the mayor, the coroners, the reeves, William of Wishford, George Goss, and Robert Bunt

718 By his charter Thomas of Erlestoke, a chaplain, granted to John Fowle a tenement in Minster Street between a tenement of late that of John of Wallop, draper, on one side and a tenement of late Nicholas of Breamore's on the other side. The tenement was held by Thomas by a grant of Agnes, the relict of Laurence Chandler, a citizen of Salisbury, and is to be held for ever by John Fowle and his heirs and assigns. Seals: Thomas's and the common and mayoral seals of the city. Named witnesses: the bailiff, the mayor, the coroners, the reeves, William of Wishford, George Goss, and Robert Bunt

719 By his charter Thomas Erlestoke, a chaplain, granted to John of Upton, Gilbert of Whichbury, John Chandler, John Basingstoke, Henry Stapleford, and John Drury, citizens of Salisbury, a tenement, with shops and a gate, in New Street between a corner tenement of late Laurence Chandler's on the east side and Gilbert Baker's tenement on the west side. The tenement was held by Thomas by a grant of Agnes, the relict of Laurence, a citizen of Salisbury, and, with the shops and the gate, is to be held for ever by the grantees and their heirs and assigns. Clause of warranty. Seals: Thomas's and the common and mayoral seals of the city. Named witnesses: the bailiff, the mayor, a coroner, the reeves, William of Wishford, Robert Bunt, and George Goss

24 April 1364, at Salisbury
720 By his charter Thomas Erlestoke, a chaplain, an executor of Laurence Chandler, of late a citizen of Salisbury, on the strength of Laurence's will granted to John of Upton, Gilbert of Whichbury, John Chandler, John Basingstoke, Henry Stapleford, and John Drury, citizens of Salisbury, a corner tenement, with shops and sollars, which was Laurence's, in New Street, on a corner opposite John of Upton's tenement, between a tenement of late that of Henry Peverell, kt., on one side and five conjoined cottages, of late Laurence's, in Carter Street on the other side; also those five cottages, which stand between the corner tenement on one side and a tenement, in which of late Agnes Cooper dwelt, beside the canons' close on the other side. The tenement and the shops [?*rectius* cottages] were devised by Laurence to be sold by his executors after the death of his wife Agnes, and after the death without issue of any child being in Agnes's womb on the day of his death. They are to be held for ever by the grantees and their heirs and assigns. Seals: Thomas's and the common and mayoral seals of the city. Named witnesses: the bailiff, the mayor, a coroner, the reeves, William of Wishford, Robert of Godmanstone, and Robert Bunt

8 May 1364, at Salisbury
721 By their charter John of Upton, Gilbert of Whichbury, John Chandler, John Basingstoke, Henry of Stapleford, and John Drury, citizens of Salisbury, granted to John Fowle a corner tenement, with shops and sollars, and five cottages [*as in* 720]; also a tenement, with shops and a gate, in New Street between that corner tenement on the east side and Gilbert Baker's tenement on the west side. Those tenements, shops, and cottages were held by the grantors by a grant of Thomas Erlestoke, a chaplain, part as his own right and part as an executor of Laurence Chandler, and they are to be held for ever by John Fowle and his heirs and assigns,

paying 5 marks a year to the grantors and their heirs or assigns. Clause to permit re-entry if the rent were in arrear, distraint, and the keeping of distresses until the unpaid rent was recovered. Seals: those of the grantors and the common and mayoral seals of the city. Named witnesses: the bailiff, the mayor, a coroner, the reeves, William of Wishford, Robert Bunt, and George Goss

22 May 1364, at Salisbury
722 By his charter John of Upton, a citizen of Salisbury, granted to the lord John Wraxall, a chaplain, a tenement in Drake Hall Street between a tenement of late John Shalford's on one side and a tenement of late John Hemingby's on the other side. The tenement was held by John of Upton by a grant of Thomas of Britford, Gilbert of Whichbury, and John Chandler, citizens of Salisbury, and is to be held for ever by John Wraxall and his heirs and assigns. Seals: John of Upton's and the common and mayoral seals of the city. Named witnesses: the bailiff, the mayor, the reeves, William of Wishford, Robert of Godmanstone, George Goss, and William Warmwell

723 By their charter Thomas of Britford, John of Upton, and John Chandler, citizens of Salisbury, granted to John Wraxall, a chaplain, two conjoined cottages in Drake Hall Street between a tenement of late John Hemingby's on the south side and a tenement formerly Nicholas Longborough's on the north side. The cottages were held by the grantors by a grant of Gilbert of Whichbury and Thomas Chaplin, executors of Robert Alwin, of late a citizen of Salisbury, and are to be held for ever by John Wraxall and his heirs and assigns. Seals: those of the grantors and the common and mayoral seals of the city. Named witnesses: the bailiff, the mayor, the reeves, William of Wishford, George Goss, and Robert Bunt

5 June 1364, at Salisbury
724 By their charter Thomas Erlestoke and John Crichel, chaplains, granted to Robert Gore a tenement in New Street between a tenement formerly Richard Sealer's on one side and a tenement formerly Richard Long's on the other side. The tenement was held by Thomas and John by a grant of John Silvester, a son and heir of Thomas Silvester, and is to be held for ever by Robert and his heirs and assigns. Seals: those of Thomas and John and the common and mayoral seals of the city. Named witnesses: the bailiff, the mayor, the coroners, the reeves, Robert Bunt, George Goss, and John Hoare

725 By his charter Thomas, a son of Edith, formerly the wife of John of Wells, draper, a citizen of Salisbury, granted to Robert of Beechfount and William Warmwell, citizens of Salisbury, a tenement in Brown Street, between a tenement formerly Henry Baldry's on the south side and a tenement formerly Robert Baldry's on the north side, to be held for ever by Robert and William and their heirs and assigns. Clause of warranty. Seals: Thomas's and the common and mayoral seals of the city. Named witnesses: the bailiff, the mayor, the coroners, the reeves, William of Wishford, Robert of Godmanstone, William of Bruton, and John Chandler

19 June 1364, at Salisbury
726 Memorandum that, appearing at the court held on that day, Roger Horingham and his wife Agnes, a daughter of Edith, formerly the wife of John of Wells, Agnes being examined in the way customary in the city, released their right to the tenement [*conveyed in* **725**] to Robert of Beechfount and William Warmwell and their heirs and assigns. Clause of warranty.
727 By his charter Robert Gore granted to Margaret Redenham a tenement in New Street [*as in* **724**]. The tenement was held by Robert by a grant of Thomas Erlestoke and John Crichel, chaplains, and is to be held for ever by Margaret and her heirs and assigns. Seals: Robert's and the common and mayoral seals of the city. Named witnesses: the bailiff, the mayor, the coroners, the reeves, William Wishford, Robert Bunt, George Goss, and William Warmwell

24 July 1364, at Salisbury
728 By his charter William of Buckland, a clerk, granted to Alice, the relict of John Hemingby, of West Harnham, conjoined tenements in Drake Hall Street, between cottages of late William Mutton's on one side and cottage property of late John Holtby's on the other side, to be held for ever by Alice and her heirs and assigns. Seals: William's and the common and mayoral seals of the city. Named witnesses: the bailiff, the mayor, the coroners, the reeves, William of Wishford, Robert Bunt, George Goss, and William Warmwell

20 August 1364, at the bishop of Salisbury's manor of Woodford
729 A charter of Robert, the bishop of Salisbury. The king has licensed Martin Mowlish, John of Crichel, Thomas of Erlestoke, and Robert of Axbey to grant a shop and rent of £4 a year to the dean and chapter. The shop stands in Minster Street between a chief tenement which Mabel, the relict of Philip Montagu, holds on the south side and a shop which Richard Lyner holds on the north side. Rent, of 26s. 8d. a year in each case, issues from Stephen Shearer's tenement in Endless Street beside a corner tenement formerly Edmund of Bramshaw's, from a tenement, which John Chalke holds and dwells in, in Winchester Street between a tenement of late Ellis Homes's on the east side and a lane on the west side, and from two shops, with a sollar, in Minster Street between a tenement of late Robert Russell's on one side and a tenement of late John Uphill's on the other side. The shop and the rent are to be held by the dean and chapter and their successors for the maintenance of a chaplain and a clerk [*as in* **704**]. *The bishop added himself and his successors to the list of those on behalf of whose souls mass was to be celebrated.* By his charter the bishop granted a licence to the dean and chapter to receive the shop and the rent from Martin, John, Thomas, and Robert and for them and their successors to hold them for ever.

11 September 1364, at Salisbury
730 By his charter Peter Clark, of Iwerne, granted to Laurence de St. Martin, kt., a corner tenement called Vellard's Corner in Wineman Street and Endless Street

between a tenement of late John Anger's on the east side and Thomas Hutchins's tenement on the north side. The tenement was held by Peter by a grant of William of Peakirk, the rector of Dinton, Stephen Newton, the rector of Little Langford, William Dunn, and Walter Kerry and is to be held for ever by Laurence and his heirs and assigns. Seals: Peter's and the common and mayoral seals of the city. Named witnesses: the bailiff, the mayor, the coroners, the reeves, William of Wishford, Robert of Godmanstone, George Goss, Robert Bunt, and the clerk

731 By his charter Thomas of Erlestoke, a chaplain, an executor of Laurence Chandler, of late a citizen of Salisbury, on the strength of Laurence's will granted to John Fowle, a citizen of Salisbury, a tenement in Carter Street between shops which were Laurence's on one side and a trench of water running through the canons' close on the other side. The tenement was devised by Laurence to be sold by his executors if a child being in the womb of his wife Agnes at the time of his death were to have been born and have died without issue, and it is to be held for ever by John Fowle and his heirs and assigns. Seals: Thomas's and the common and mayoral seals of the city. Named witnesses: the bailiff, the mayor, the coroners, the reeves, William of Wishford, Robert Bunt, George Goss, and the clerk

25 September 1364, at Salisbury
732 By his charter Walter Cooper, a citizen of Salisbury, granted to the lord John Doggett, the rector of Preshute, a tenement in Winchester Street between a tenement formerly Thomas of Stratford's on one side and a tenement formerly that of Henry at the bar, a clerk, on the other side; also a cottage, with a yard, beyond the bar, opposite the bishop of Salisbury's land held in villeinage in the Old Town, between a tenement formerly Henry Dogskin's on one side and a tenement formerly Matthew Beveridge's on the other side; also two conjoined cottages, with adjacent yards, in Culver Street between cottages which were Hugh Boney's on the south side and a corner tenement formerly that of Ingram at the brook on the north side. The tenement and the cottages, with the yards, are to be held for ever by John and his heirs and assigns. Seals: Walter's and the common and mayoral seals of the city. Named witnesses: the bailiff, the mayor, the coroners, the reeves, Robert Bunt, George Goss, and William Warmwell

23 October 1364, at Salisbury
733 By his charter Nicholas Holtby, a citizen of Salisbury, granted to Walter Abbot, a citizen of Salisbury, a tenement, with shops, in Minster Street between a tenement of late John of Lyneham's on the north side and a tenement of late that of Robert of Woodford, mercer, on the south side. The tenement, with the shops, was held by Nicholas by a grant of John Hawk, a citizen of Salisbury, and is to be held for ever by Walter and his heirs and assigns. Clause of warranty. Seals: Nicholas's and the common and mayoral seals of the city. Named witnesses: the bailiff, the mayor, the coroners, the reeves, William of Wishford, Robert of Godmanstone, a younger William Tenterer, Robert Bunt, and George Goss

734 By his charter John Justice, of Salisbury, granted to John Nalder, a citizen of Salisbury, five conjoined cottages in Chipper Street between Henry Pope's tenement on one side and Stephen Shearer's tenement on the other side. The cottages were held by John Justice by a grant of John Hawk, a citizen of Salisbury, and are to be held for ever by John Nalder and his heirs and assigns. Clause of warranty. Seals: John Justice's and the common and mayoral seals of the city. Named witnesses: the bailiff, the mayor, the coroners, a reeve, William of Wishford, George Goss, Robert Bunt, and William Warmwell

735 Approval of the will of Agnes, the wife of John Camel, made on 26 August 1364. <u>Interment</u>: in the graveyard of St. Thomas's church. <u>Bequests</u>: 40*d*. each to the fabric of the cathedral church and the fraternity of the high cross in it; 10*s*. to the fabric of St. Thomas's church; the rest of her goods to her husband John. <u>Devise</u>: to John a tenement, with shops and a cellar (*or* cellars), in Minster Street between a tenement formerly Simon of Oxford's on the south side and a tenement of late Richard Wimpler's, and shops of late Stephen Buddle's, on the north side. The tenement was held by Agnes and her husband John Mariner by a grant of Nicholas Buck, a chaplain, and Robert Harnham, is to be held, with the shops, for his life by John Camel and his assigns, and on John's death it should be sold by Agnes's executors, their executors, or subsequent executors. The money received should be laid out on behalf of Agnes's soul, the souls of John Hatter and John Mariner, of late her husbands, and the souls of others. Agnes appointed, however, that John Camel might hold the reversion of the tenement for himself and his heirs and assigns for ever if he would give as much as anyone else to the executors for it. <u>Executors</u>: the lord Thomas Marden, a chaplain, John Marshall, and Richard Lyner. <u>Proved</u> on 31 August 1364 in front of an officer of the subdean; the administration was entrusted to Thomas and John, Richard, in front of the officer, expressly refusing to receive it. <u>Approved</u> at a court held in front of the bailiff, the mayor, and other citizens; the seisin of the tenement was released to the legatee.

1 January 1365, at Salisbury
736 By his charter Thomas, a son and heir of John Powell, of late a citizen of Salisbury, granted to Emme Powell, his mother, the land, tenements, shops, and cottages in Salisbury which descended to him by right of inheritance on John's death. Eight cottages stand in Mealmonger Street between John Talbot's cottage property on the south side and Richard Still's cottage property on the north side. A shop stands in Wheeler Row between John Talbot's shop on the north side and Edith Berwick's tenement called Hampton's Corner on the south side. The land, tenements, shops, and cottages are to be held for ever by Emme and her heirs and assigns. Clause of warranty. Seals: Thomas's and the common and mayoral seals of the city. Named witnesses: the bailiff, the mayor, the coroners, William of Wishford, Robert Bunt, William Warmwell, John Buddle, and Richard Still

15 January 1365, at Salisbury
737 By his charter [*known to have been perfected in 1364 or 1365, wrongly dated to the Wednesday after the feast of St. Hilary in 1366, and assumed to be of the Wednesday*

after that feast in 1365] William Candelan, a chaplain, granted to Martin Mowlish, John Crichel, Thomas of Erlestoke, and Robert Axbey, clerks, a shop in Minster Street [*as in* **729**]. The shop was of late held by William, John Purbeck, and Robert Axbey by a grant of John Knoyle, of Ludgershall, and John and Robert released their estate in it to William. It is to be held for ever by the grantees and their heirs and assigns. Seals: William's and the common and mayoral seals of the city. Named witnesses: the bailiff, the mayor, the coroners, William of Wishford, Robert Bunt, and William Warmwell

29 January 1365, at Salisbury
738 By her charter Agnes Sorrel, the relict of Roger Sorrel, in her full power and celibate, granted to Thomas Stokes and his wife Joan two cottages in Chipper Street between a tenement of late William Cofford's on the west side and George Goss's tenement on the east side. The cottages were held by Agnes by a devise of Richard Milcot, of late a citizen of Salisbury, and are to be held for ever by Thomas and Joan and their heirs and assigns. Clause of warranty. Seals: Agnes's and the common and mayoral seals of the city. Named witnesses: the bailiff, the mayor, the coroners, William of Wishford, Robert Bunt, and the clerk

739 By his charter Richard Netheravon granted to John of Stallington a tenement, opposite the market place where grains are sold, between [a tenement] of late Nicholas Skilling's on the west side and a tenement of late Richard of Tidworth's on the east side; also three conjoined shops in Scots Lane between a tenement formerly William Bartlet's on one side and a corner tenement of late Ralph of Langford's on the other side; also a rent of 20*s*. a year to be received by John and his heirs and assigns from a chief tenement, formerly John Sorrel's, opposite the market place where grains are sold, between Robert of Godmanstone's tenement on one side and a tenement of late Richard of Tidworth's on the other side. Richard Netheravon acquired the tenement, shops, and rent from Robert Hindon and his wife Edith, the relict of John Robet, of Haxton, for the life of Edith, and he acquired the reversion from William Wishford, who acquired it from William Duckman and John Wick, executors of John Robet. The tenement, shops, and rent are to be held for ever by John of Stallington and his heirs and assigns. Seals: Richard's and the common and mayoral seals of the city. Named witnesses: the bailiff, the mayor, the coroners, the reeves, Robert Bunt, William Warmwell, and the clerk

740 Approval of the will of John at the stone, made on 9 September 1361. Interment: where it pleased God. Bequests: 10*s*. each to the parson of Stratford for the common cure [of souls] and to the chaplain for forgotten tithes; 5*s*. each to the light of the Blessed Mary in Stratford church and the guild of St. James, of Stratford; 20*s*. both to the good parishioners of Stratford church to hold his anniversary mass for ever and the fabric of the cathedral church; 40*s*. both to the Franciscans of Salisbury and the Dominicans of [Fisherton]; 20*s*. among them to the college of St. Edmund to celebrate mass on behalf of his soul; 5*s*. each to the church of Christchurch and St. Nicholas's church, Salisbury [?*rectius* Wilton]; 2*s*. to the prisoners of Salisbury; 2*s*. each to St. John's hospital, Old Sarum, St.

Giles's hospital, Wilton, and St. Etheldred's church, Old Sarum; 2*d*. to each priest of Salisbury who might wish to celebrate mass on behalf of his soul on the day of his death; 1*d*. to each of them who might wish to celebrate mass at his commemoration; a russet coat with a pair of shoes to each of 12 paupers, no more than 2*s*. 6*d*. to each of them; £6 to be laid out among paupers on the day of his death; 20*s*. to be spent among his brothers and sisters on the day of his burial; 10*s*. to paupers who are blind, feeble, and unable to sustain themselves; 2*s*. to the prisoners of the castle of Old Sarum; 100*s*. to a chaplain to celebrate mass on behalf of his soul for a year in Stratford church; 2*s*. each to John 'Swengedieu', John Boss, and Simon Webb to pray for his soul; 2*s*. each to Agnes, a daughter of his goddaughter Lucy, Theobald Brownrobins, Walter Hewet, Thomas Dowden, Roger Cass, John Stickbeard, Malin Sawyer, John Dowden, John Pickard, Thomas Fish, Agnes Bacon, Henry Capp, Alice Laccombe, and Isabel Poulshot; 22*s*. to Thomas Glendy; 12*d*. each to Alice Kemps, Gillian Hart, Alice Skinner, and Alice Upton; 40*s*. to Richard Sarfy, one of his executors, for his work; 20*s*. to Roger Matthey; 40*s*. each to William Wishford and Robert Woodford whom he appointed overseers [of his executors]; the rest of his goods to his executors to be disposed of on behalf of his soul and the souls of others; a trental and 20*s*. to the lord Robert Shipton, the chaplain of Stratford, his other executor, for his work; 20*s*. to repair the king's highway when next it was necessary; 10*s*. to Ralph Webb; half a worn-out bed each to Thomas Glendy and Thomas Dowden; a worn-out tapet to Malin Sawyer so that he might work towards John's profit; half a bed to Richard Sarfy; 3*s*. to three poor widows. <u>Devises</u>: a tenement, in which he dwelt, in [Minster Street beyond the bar] between John Richman's tenement and Philip Stint's tenement should be sold. The money received should be laid out by his executors on behalf of his soul. John appointed that a messuage and a croft of arable land in Newtown ward above the castle should be sold and the money received laid out by his executors on behalf of his soul. <u>Executors</u>: Richard Sarfy, the principal, and Robert [Shipton]. <u>Proved</u> on 15 January 1365 in front of an officer of the subdean; the administration was entrusted to the executors, in such a way, however, that they should act in all matters with the advice and oversight of William of Wishford. <u>Approved</u> at a court held in front of the bailiff, the mayor, and other citizens; the seisin of the tenements was released to the legatees.

12 February 1365, at Salisbury
741 By their charter John of Upton and Thomas Chaplin, citizens of Salisbury, granted to William Boyland a tenement in Endless Street, between a tenement of late Robert Gore's on the north side and Thomas Hutchins's tenement on the south side, extending from Endless Street as far as Brown Street. The tenement was held by John and Thomas by a grant of Agnes, the relict of John of Woodford [and] an executor of Agnes, the relict of William Gill, [and] of William Wootton, John Prentice, Edward of Deanbridge, John Packer, and Thomas Brute, tanner, co-executors of Agnes, and is to be held for ever by William Boyland and his heirs and assigns. Seals: those of the grantors and the common and mayoral seals of the city. Named witnesses: the bailiff, the mayor, the reeves, a coroner, William

of Wishford, Robert Bunt, William Wootton [?*rectius* Warmwell], and the clerk

26 February 1365, at Salisbury
742 By his charter Gilbert of Whichbury, a citizen of Salisbury, granted to Agnes, the relict of John Bodenham, of late a citizen of Salisbury, two tenements in New Street, one beside Black bridge and one between a tenement formerly Roger Plummer's on the west side and a tenement formerly William of Berwick's on the east side. Both tenements were acquired by Laurence Chandler from Robert of Faringdon, Gilbert held them by a grant of Agnes, Laurence's relict, John of Bodenham, and Thomas of Erlestoke, a chaplain, executors of Laurence, and they are to be held for ever by Agnes Bodenham and her heirs and assigns. Seals: Gilbert's and the common and mayoral seals of the city. Named witnesses: the bailiff, the mayor, the coroners, the reeves, William of Wishford, John Butterley, William Warmwell, and the clerk
743 By his charter Gilbert of Whichbury, a citizen of Salisbury, granted to William Purser a tenement in Chipper Street between a tenement of late Andrew Bone's on one side and Thomas Durrington's tenement on the other side. The tenement was formerly that of John of Poulton, tucker, was acquired by Gilbert from William Tidpit, and is to be held for ever by William Purser and his heirs and assigns. Seals: Gilbert's and the common and mayoral seals of the city. Named witnesses: the bailiff, the mayor, the coroners, the reeves, William of Wishford, Robert Bunt, William Warmwell, and the clerk

12 March 1365, at Salisbury
744 By their charter George Goss, William of Wishford, and John Bosset, executors of William Cofford, of late a citizen of Salisbury, on the strength of William's will granted to William Wootton and Nicholas Baker, citizens of Salisbury, a tenement, with shops next to it, in Chipper Street and Minster Street between George Goss's tenement on one side and a tenement of late that of John Hacker and his wife Agnes on the other side. The tenement was devised by William Cofford to be sold by his executors after the death of his wife Maud and is to be held for ever by William Wootton and Nicholas Baker and their heirs and assigns. Seals: those of the grantors and the common and mayoral seals of the city. Named witnesses: the bailiff, the mayor, the coroners, the reeves, Robert of Godmanstone, Robert Bunt, William Warmwell, and the clerk
745 By their charter Martin Mowlish, a clerk, John of Crichel, a clerk, Thomas of Erlestoke, the parson of Barford [St. Martin], and Robert of Axbey, a clerk, in accordance with a licence of both the king and Robert, the bishop of Salisbury, granted to the dean and chapter of Salisbury a shop in Minster Street [*as in* **729**] and rent of £4 a year made up of three rents each of 26*s*. 8*d*. [*as in* **729**]. The shop and the rent were held by Martin, John, Thomas, and Robert by a grant, by means of various deeds, of the lord William Candelan, a chaplain. The shop is to be held, and the rent received, for ever by the dean and chapter and their successors for the maintenance of a chaplain celebrating mass [*as in* **704, 729**] and of a clerk [*as in* **704**]. Seals: those of the grantors and the common and mayoral

seals of the city. Named witnesses: the bailiff, the mayor, the coroners, the reeves, Robert of Godmanstone, William of Wishford, William Warmwell, and the clerk

746 By their charter Robert Shipton, the chaplain of Stratford, and Richard Sarfy, the executors of John at the stone, of Stratford beside the castle of Old Sarum, on the strength of John's will granted to John Fowle, a citizen of Salisbury, and his wife Rose a tenement in Minster Street, beyond the bar, between a tenement of late John Richman's on one side and Philip Stint's tenement on the other side. The tenement was devised by John at the stone to be sold by his executors and is to be held for ever by John Fowle and Rose and their heirs and assigns. Seals: those of Robert and Richard and the common and mayoral seals of the city. Named witnesses: the bailiff, the mayor, the coroners, the reeves, William of Wishford, Robert Bunt, and the clerk

747 Memorandum that Thomas, a son and heir of William at the bridge, on the day on which he granted a cottage and a tenement in the following charter was aged 16 years and more

748 By his charter Thomas, a son and heir of William at the bridge, of late a citizen of Salisbury, granted to John Lea, a citizen of Salisbury, a shop in Minster Street between a shop of late Richard Ryborough's on the north side and John Cannings's corner shop on the south side; also a tenement, with a shop attached to it, opposite the market place where linen cloth is sold, between John's own tenement on the east side and the corner shop on the west side; also a rent of 3s. a year issuing for ever from the corner shop. The shops, the tenement, and the rent descended to Thomas by right of inheritance on the death of his mother Agnes, a daughter of Henry Smith and his wife Joan, and are to be held for ever by John Lea and his heirs and assigns. Seals: Thomas's and the common and mayoral seals of the city. Named witnesses: the bailiff, the mayor, the coroners, the reeves, William of Wishford, William Warmwell, and the clerk

23 April 1365, at Salisbury
749 Approval of the will of Walter of Calne, made on 28 January 1365. Interment: in the graveyard [of the church] of the apostles Peter and Paul, Britford. Bequests: all his tools pertaining to carpentry, being in his room at the Glasshouse, to the fabric of the cathedral church; all his chattels and remaining goods, movable and immovable, to his son Henry. Devise: to Henry and his heirs and assigns a plot in St. Martin's Street which he received from Matthew Rous. Executors: his son Henry and John Lavender. Proved on 29 March 1365 in front of an officer of the jurisdiction of the farm of Britford; the administration was entrusted to Henry, John expressly declining it in front of the officer. Approved on 3 April 1365 in front of an officer of the subdean; the administration of the goods being within the subdean's jurisdiction was entrusted to Henry. Approved at a court held in front of the bailiff, the mayor, and other citizens; the seisin of the plot was released to the legatee.

7 May 1365, at Salisbury
750 By his charter Henry, a son of Walter of Calne, granted to Robert Beechfount,

a citizen of Salisbury, a plot in St. Martin's Street and Culver Street between a tenement formerly William of Berwick's on the north side and a tenement formerly Gilbert Jukes's on the west side. The plot was held by Henry by Walter's devise and is to be held for ever by Robert and his heirs and assigns. Seals: Henry's and the common and mayoral seals of the city. Named witnesses: the bailiff, the mayor, the coroners, the reeves, William of Wishford, Robert Bunt, and the clerk

751 By his charter John of Upton, a citizen of Salisbury, granted to John Bennett a tenement, with shops and a garden, in Carter Street between his own tenement on one side and a tenement of late Robert Alwin's on the other side. The tenement was held by John of Upton by a grant of Agnes, the relict of John Deanbridge, and William Pain, executors of Alice, the relict of Philip Longenough and of William Whitehorn, and, with the shops and the garden, is to be held for ever by John Bennett and his heirs and assigns. Clause of warranty. Seals: John of Upton's and the common and mayoral seals of the city. Named witnesses: the bailiff, the mayor, a coroner, the reeves, William of Wishford, Robert of Godmanstone, and the clerk

21 May 1365, at Salisbury,
752 By their writing Walter Cook and his wife Gillian, a daughter and heir of Thomas of Cirencester, appearing at the court held on that day, quitclaimed to Richard Sauter and his wife Alice, Gillian's sister, and their heirs and assigns their right or claim to a tenement in Brown Street, on the way to St. Edmund's church, between a tenement formerly Roger of Buckland's on the north side and a tenement formerly Roger of Christchurch's on the south side. The tenement descended to Gillian and Alice by right of inheritance on Thomas's death. Seals: those of Walter and Gillian and the common and mayoral seals of the city. Named witnesses: the bailiff, the mayor, a coroner, William of Wishford, Robert Bunt, William Warmwell, and the clerk

4 June 1365, at Salisbury
753 By their charter Richard Sauter and his wife Alice, a daughter of Thomas of Cirencester, appearing at the court held on that day, granted to William of Wishford, a citizen of Salisbury, a tenement in Brown Street [*as in* **752**]. The tenement descended to Alice and her sister Gillian [*as in* **752**], Gillian released her estate to Richard and Alice and their heirs, and the tenement is to be held for ever by William of Wishford and his heirs and assigns. Clause of warranty. Seals: those of Richard and Alice and the common and mayoral seals of the city. Named witnesses: the bailiff, the mayor, the coroners, the reeves, Robert Bunt, William Warmwell, and the clerk

754 By his writing Robert Blake quitclaimed to John Lea, a citizen of Salisbury, his right or claim to a tenement in New Street between a tenement of Kentigern of Sulham on the east side and John Wylye's plot of land on the west side. The tenement was of late that of Robert of Hungerford, kt., and John Lea holds it for the life of his wife Agnes by a grant of Robert Blake. Clause of warranty. Seals: Robert's and the common and mayoral seals of the city. Named witnesses: the bailiff, the mayor, the coroners, William Wishford, and the clerk

755 By his charter Edward Fountain, a son and heir of Roger Fountain, of late a citizen of Salisbury, granted to the lord John Wickham, a chaplain, and William Greenway a messuage in New Street, between Hugh of Wimborne's tenement on the west side and a tenement of Nicholas Hamish, a chaplain, on the east side, to be held for ever by John and William and their heirs and assigns. Clause of warranty. Seals: Edward's and the common and mayoral seals of the city. Named witnesses: the bailiff, the mayor, the coroners, the reeves, William of Wishford, Robert of Godmanstone, and the clerk

756 By their charter William of Bruton, a citizen of Salisbury, and his wife Agnes, appearing at the court held on that day, granted to Nicholas Russell, butcher, a shop in Butcher Row between a shop formerly Edward Knoyle's on one side and a shop which Maud, the wife of Stephen Shearer, held for a term of life on the other side. The shop was held by William and Agnes by a grant of Richard of Berwick and his wife Edith, an executor of John of Holtby, and is to be held for ever by Nicholas and his heirs and assigns. Clause of warranty. Seals: those of William and Agnes and the common and mayoral seals of the city. Named witnesses: the bailiff, the mayor, the coroners, the reeves, Robert of Godmanstone, William of Wishford, Robert Bunt, and the clerk

757 By their indented charter Nicholas Boor and Adam Gore, vicars in the cathedral church, granted at fee farm to John Justice, a citizen of Salisbury, a corner tenement in New Street between a tenement of late Thomas de Mandeville's on the east side and Culver Street on the west side. The tenement was held by Nicholas and Adam at fee farm by a grant of the dean and chapter of Salisbury and is to be held for ever by John and his heirs and assigns for the payment of a rent of 26s. 8d. a year to the dean and chapter, the payment of the charges pertaining to it to the chief lord, and the maintenance of it so that the rent of 26s. 8d. would not be lost. If the tenement was not maintained, if the charges were not paid, or if the rent was not paid for a quarter after any term the dean and chapter might immediately re-enter the tenement, take back possession, and keep it for ever, as is contained in an indented charter perfected between the dean and chapter and Nicholas and Adam. Seals: those of the parties to the parts of the charter in turn and the common and mayoral seals of the city. Named witnesses: the bailiff, the mayor, the coroners, the reeves, William of Wishford, William Warmwell, and the clerk

18 June 1365, at Salisbury

758 By his charter John Bone granted to William Thatcher, a smith, two shops in Minster Street between a shop formerly Richard of Tidworth's on one side and a stile of St. Thomas's church on the other side. The shops were held by John, by a devise of his sister Joan, who was the wife of John Amesbury, on the death of Alice Littles, who surrendered her estate to him, and they are to be held for ever by William and his heirs and assigns. Clause of warranty. Seals: John's and the common and mayoral seals of the city. Named witnesses: the bailiff, the mayor, the coroners, the reeves, William of Wishford, Robert Bunt, William Warmwell, and the clerk

759 By his letters of attorney John Bone appointed Thomas Bowyer, Thomas Mackinney, and William Dunkerton to surrender into the hand of Robert, the bishop of Salisbury, the seisin of two shops in Minster Street [*as in* **758**] to the use of William Thatcher, a smith. Seal: John's

760 By their charter John Wickham, a chaplain, and William Greenway granted to Edward, a son of Roger Fountain, and Agnes, a daughter of John Greenway, of Newton, a messuage in New Street [*as in* **755**]. The messuage was held by John and William by Edward's grant and is to be held for ever by Edward and Agnes and their heirs and assigns. Seals: those of John and William and the common and mayoral seals of the city. Named witnesses: the bailiff, the mayor, the coroners, the reeves, William of Wishford, William Warmwell, and the clerk

2 July 1365, at Salisbury

761 By her charter Margaret, the relict of William Fairwood, a baker, celibate and in her full power, granted to Robert of Beechfount, a citizen of Salisbury, a tenement in Wineman Street between a tenement of late John Kimble's on one side and a tenement of Agnes, the relict of Richard Fry, on the other side; also a messuage in Culver Street between John Talbot's tenement on one side and a tenement of Agnes on the other side. The tenement and the messuage were held by Margaret and William by Agnes's grant and are to be held for ever by Robert, and his heirs and assigns. Clause of warranty. Seals: Margaret's and the common and mayoral seals of the city. Named witnesses: the bailiff, the mayor, the reeves, William of Wishford, Robert Bunt, William Warmwell, and the clerk

762 By his writing William Warmwell, a citizen of Salisbury, quitclaimed to Robert of Beechfount, a citizen of Salisbury, his right or claim to a tenement in Brown Street between a tenement formerly Henry Baldry's on the south side and a tenement formerly Robert Baldry's on the north side. He and Robert of Beechfount acquired the tenement from Thomas, a son of Edith, formerly the wife of John of Wells, draper. Seals: William's and the common and mayoral seals of the city. Named witnesses: the bailiff, the mayor, the coroners, William of Wishford, Robert Bunt, and the clerk

763 By their charter John Lea and his wife Agnes, the relict of John Deanbridge, of late a citizen of Salisbury, appearing at the court held on that day, granted to a younger William Tenterer, a citizen of Salisbury, a tenement in New Street [*as in* **754**] of late that of Robert of Hungerford, kt. The tenement was held for her life by Agnes by a demise of Robert Blake, who released his right to John Lea and his heirs and assigns for ever, and it is to be held for ever by the younger William Tenterer, and his heirs and assigns. Seals: those of John and Agnes and the common and mayoral seals of the city. Named witnesses: the bailiff, the mayor, the coroners, the reeves, William of Wishford, Robert Bunt, and the clerk

30 July 1365, at Salisbury

764 By his charter Henry Fleming, a citizen of Salisbury, granted to a younger William Tenterer and his wife Alice a messuage in Salisbury [?in Winchester

Street: *cf.* **765**] which Henry Russell bought from Richard Tidworth, formerly a citizen of Salisbury; also an adjoining plot measuring 59 ft. in length and 38 ft. in width, with the walls appurtenant to it. The plot is part of a tenement which Henry Russell bought from Gregory Spicer, and in his will Henry devised the messuage, and the tenement of which the plot is part, to Henry Fleming. The messuage and the plot are to held for ever by William and Alice and William's heirs and assigns. Clause of warranty, except for the term which John Ball has in the messuage, excluding two rooms and a stable in it, from the date of this charter until Christmas 1365 and from then for the following six years. Seals: Henry Fleming's and the common and mayoral seals of the city. Named witnesses: the bailiff, the mayor, the coroners, the reeves, Nicholas Taylor, William Wishford, Robert of Godmanstone, Robert Bunt, and the clerk

27 August 1365, at Salisbury
765 By his charter Henry Fleming, a citizen of Salisbury, granted to Robert Play a tenement in Winchester Street between a tenement formerly Henry Russell's, now a younger William Tenterer's, on one side and a tenement formerly Stephen of Harpenden's on the other side. The tenement was formerly that of Thomas of Harpenden and his wife Christine, Henry Fleming held it by a devise of Henry Russell, of late a citizen of Salisbury, and it is to be held for ever by Robert and his heirs and assigns. Clause of warranty. Seals: Henry Fleming's and the common and mayoral seals, of the city. Named witnesses: the bailiff, the mayor, the coroners, the reeves, William of Wishford, Robert Beechfount, William Warmwell, and the clerk
766 By his letters of attorney Henry Fleming, a citizen of Salisbury, appointed William Dunkerton to surrender into the hand of Robert, the bishop of Salisbury, the seisin of a tenement in Winchester Street [*as in* **765**] to the use of Robert Play, a smith. Seals: Henry's and the mayoral seal of the city by the hand of George Goss, then the mayor
767 By his charter Henry of Stapleford, a citizen of Salisbury, granted to John Justice, a citizen of Salisbury, a yard in Culver Street beside a tenement of late John Frank's on the south side. The yard was held by Henry by a grant of Gilbert Whichbury, a citizen of Salisbury, who acquired it from John of Wallop and Roger Bleacher, executors of Henry Walsh, formerly a citizen of Salisbury, and it is to be held for ever by John Justice, and his heirs and assigns. Seals: Henry's and the common and mayoral seals of the city. Named witnesses: the bailiff, the mayor, the coroners, the reeves, William of Wishford, William Warmwell, and the clerk

22 October 1365, at Salisbury
768 By his charter John of Oxford, a skinner, a citizen of Salisbury, granted to William Purser, a citizen of Salisbury, a shop, with a sollar, in Minster Street between a tenement of late that of Robert of Lavington, a clerk, on the south side and a shop of late Edward Pinnock's, which John Wells, tailor, held, on the north side. The shop measures 35 ft. in length and 12 ft. in width. John of Oxford

held it by a demise of John Wells, his wife Alice, and their son William, and Edward Pinnock, a citizen of Salisbury, to whom the reversion belonged, released his right in it to him. It is to be held, with the sollar, for ever by William Purser and his heirs and assigns. Clause of warranty. Seals: John of Oxford's and the common and mayoral seals of the city. Named witnesses: the bailiff, the mayor, the coroners, the reeves, William of Wishford, Robert of Godmanstone, and the clerk

769 By his charter William of Wishford, a citizen of Salisbury, granted to George Goss, a citizen of Salisbury, a tenement in Gigant Street between Roger of Kilmeston's tenement on the south side and a yard formerly John Coppiner's on the north side. The tenement was acquired by William from John, a son of John Richman, and is to be held for ever by George and his heirs and assigns. Seals: William's and the common and mayoral seals of the city. Named witnesses: the bailiff, the mayor, the coroners, the reeves, Robert of Godmanstone, William Warmwell, and the clerk

770 By his indented charter [*dated to the Wednesday after the feast of St. Simon and St. Jude (29 October) probably in error for the Wednesday before that feast (22 October)*] William Tidcombe, a clerk, granted to William Morwelese and his wife Joan a tenement, opposite the market place where wheelwrights wait, between a tenement formerly Henry Bury's on the south side and a tenement formerly that of William, a son of Thomas Wheeler, on the north side. The tenement was acquired by William Tidcombe from William Grant and his wife Denise, is to be held for ever by William Morwelese and Joan and their joint issue, and if William and Joan were to die without such issue would remain for ever to the direct heirs of Joan. Clause of warranty. Seals: William Tidcombe's and the common and mayoral seals of the city. Named witnesses: the bailiff, the mayor, the coroners, the reeves, William of Wishford, William Warmwell, and the clerk

19 November 1365, at Salisbury

771 By their charter Nicholas of Astbury and his wife Emme, the relict of John Powell, of Salisbury, appearing at the court held on that day, granted to Thomas, a son and heir of John Powell, the land, tenements, shops, and cottages in Salisbury which Emme held by Thomas's grant and which descended to Thomas by right of inheritance on John's death. The premises, except a shop in Wheeler Row granted to John Talbot by Emme while she was celibate, are to be held for ever by Thomas and his heirs and assigns. Seals: those of Nicholas and Emme and the common and mayoral seals of the city. Named witnesses: the bailiff, the mayor, the coroners, the reeves, William of Wishford, John Butterley, Robert Bunt, and the clerk

772 By her charter Agnes, the relict, and an executor, of John Bodenham, who was an executor of William Stringer, of late a citizen of Salisbury, on the strength of William's will granted to John Bodenham, a citizen of Salisbury, and his wife Alice a tenement in Winchester Street between a tenement formerly Edward Knoyle's on one side and a tenement formerly John Knoyle's on the other side. The tenement was devised by William to be sold by his executors or their executors if his children Agnes and John were to die without issue and is to be held for ever by John Bodenham and Alice and their heirs and assigns. Seals: Agnes's and the common and mayoral seals of the city. Named witnesses: the bailiff, the mayor, the coroners, the reeves, William of Wishford, Robert Bunt, and the clerk

773 By her letters of attorney Agnes Bodenham [*as in* **772**] appointed William Lord to surrender into the hand of Robert, the bishop of Salisbury, the seisin of a tenement in Winchester Street [*as in* **772**] to the use of John Bodenham and his wife Alice. Seals: Agnes's and the mayoral seal of the city

1 December 1365, at Salisbury

774 By his charter Thomas, a son and heir of John Powell, of late a citizen of Salisbury, granted to the lords John Dean and John Ilberd, chaplains, a tenement (*or* tenements), shops, and cottages in Culver Street, between John Talbot's tenement on the south side and a tenement formerly Walter Cavenasser's on the north side, to be held for ever by John Dean and John Ilberd and their heirs and assigns. Clause of warranty. Seals: Thomas's and the common and mayoral seals of the city. Named witnesses: the bailiff, the mayor, the coroners, the reeves, William of Wishford, John Butterley, Robert Bunt, and the clerk

3 December 1365, at Salisbury

775 By his charter John, a son and heir of Robert Gore, of late a citizen of Salisbury, granted to John of Bodenham, a citizen of Salisbury, a yard in Freren Street, formerly that of Geoffrey Sauter, a clerk, between a tenement formerly Robert of Bodenham's on one side and a yard of late that of an elder John of Fosbury on the other side, to be held for ever by John of Bodenham and his heirs and assigns. Clause of warranty. Seals: John Gore's and the common and mayoral seals of the city. Named witnesses: the bailiff, the mayor, the coroners, the reeves, William of Wishford, Robert Bunt, and the clerk

776 By his letters of attorney Thomas Powell [*as in* **774**] appointed Nicholas of Astbury and Michael of Wight to surrender into the hand of Robert, the bishop of Salisbury, the seisin of premises in Culver Street [*as in* **774**] to the use of the lords John Dean and John Ilberd, chaplains. Seals: Thomas's and the mayoral seal of the city by the hand of John of Oxford, then the mayor

777 By his charter Thomas, a son and heir of John Powell, of late a citizen of Salisbury, granted to Thomas of Britford, a citizen of Salisbury, a tenement in Culver Street between a tenement formerly Robert Baldry's on the north side and a tenement of his father John Powell on the south side. The tenement descended to Thomas by right of inheritance on John's death, descended to John by right of inheritance on the death of his brother Robert, and is to be held for ever by Thomas of Britford and his heirs and assigns. Clause of warranty. Seals: Thomas's and the common and mayoral seals of the city. Named witnesses: the bailiff, the mayor, a coroner, the reeves, William of Wishford, Robert of Godmanstone, Robert Bunt, and the clerk

778 By his letters of attorney Thomas Powell [*as in* **777**] appointed Nicholas

Astbury and Michael Wight to surrender into the hand of Robert, the bishop of Salisbury, the seisin of a tenement in Culver Street [*as in* **777**] to the use of Thomas of Britford, a citizen of Salisbury. Seals: Thomas's and the mayoral seal of the city by the hand of John of Oxford, then the mayor

779 By his charter Thomas, a son of John Powell, of late a citizen of Salisbury, granted to Nicholas Russell, butcher, a citizen of Salisbury, two cottages, measuring 33 ft. 3 in. in length by the standard measure, in Mealmonger Street between Thomas's cottages on the south side and Richard Still's tenement on the north side. The cottages were formerly called the barn and are to be held for ever by Nicholas and his heirs and assigns. Clause of warranty. Seals: Thomas's and the common and mayoral seals of the city. Named witnesses: the bailiff, the mayor, the coroners, the reeves, William of Wishford, Robert Bunt, and the clerk

11 February 1366, at Salisbury
780 By an indenture it is testified that Adam Oxley, called Goss, of Salisbury, granted to John Fowle, a citizen of Salisbury, and his wife Rose a shop, at the butchers' stalls, between John of Upton's shop on the east side and Robert of Godmanstone's shops on the west side. The shop is to be held of Adam and his heirs and assigns by John and Rose and their assigns for the life of John and Rose and the life of the one of them living longer, without causing any waste or ruin. John and Rose are to give yearly to Adam and his heirs and assigns a rose on 24 June and to perform the services, and meet the charges, due to others in respect of the shop. Clause of warranty in respect of the shop, acquittance in respect of the rent. Seals: those of the parties to the parts of the indenture in turn and the mayoral seal of the city. Named witnesses: the bailiff, the mayor, the coroners, William Wishford, George Goss, and Robert Bunt

23 February 1366, at Fisherton Anger
781 By his writing Adam Oxley, called Goss, quitclaimed to John Fowle, a citizen of Salisbury, and his wife Rose, and to John's heirs and assigns, his right or claim to a shop at the butchers' stalls [*as in* **780**]. John and Rose held the shop for their life by his grant. Clause of warranty. Seals: that of Adam who, because his seal is unknown to many, procured the mayoral seal of the city to be likewise affixed. Witnesses: Richard Dinton, John Mercer, Nicholas Russell, John of Upton, Thomas Chaplin, and others.

25 February 1366, at Salisbury
782 By his charter Thomas Goodyear, smith, a citizen of Salisbury, granted to Robert Play, a citizen of Salisbury, a shop in Ironmonger Row between, on either side, a shop of late that of Joyce Taverner and his wife Margaret. The shop was acquired by Thomas from Maud, the relict of Richard Salter, of late a citizen of Salisbury, and is to be held for ever by Robert and his heirs and assigns. Clause of warranty. Seals: Thomas's and the common and mayoral seals of the city. Named witnesses: the mayor, the coroners, the reeves, William of Wishford, Nicholas Taylor, Robert Beechfount, and the clerk

783 By his letters of attorney Thomas Goodyear, smith, a citizen of Salisbury, appointed William Ebbesbourne to surrender into the hand of Robert, the bishop of Salisbury, the seisin of a shop in Ironmonger Row [*as in* **782**] to the use of Robert Play, a citizen of Salisbury. Seals: Thomas's and the mayoral seal of the city by the hand of John of Oxford, then the mayor

784 By an indented charter John of Oxford, a citizen, and the mayor, of Salisbury, fellow citizens, and the commonalty of the city granted to Robert of Kendal, a citizen of Salisbury, a corner tenement in St. Martin's Street and Gigant Street. The tenement was given for ever to the mayor and commonalty by Agnes, the relict of Robert of Woodford, of late a citizen of Salisbury, is to be held for ever by Robert of Kendal and his heirs and assigns paying a rent of 13s. 4d. a year for ever to the mayor and commonalty, and is to be maintained and repaired at the expense of Robert and his heirs or assigns so that the rent would not be lost. Clause to permit permanent repossession if the tenement were not maintained or the rent were in arrear for 15 days; alternatively the mayor and commonalty, if they preferred, might distrain in the tenement and keep distresses, or they might enter on Robert of Kendal's tenement, in which he dwelt, in Winchester Street between John Talbot's tenement on one side and Nicholas Baker's tenement on the other side, distrain in that, and keep distresses, until the unpaid rent was recovered. Seals: the common and mayoral seals of the city were affixed to the part of the indenture remaining in Robert of Kendal's possession, and Robert's and the common and mayoral seals were affixed [to the part] remaining in the possession of the mayor and commonalty. Named witnesses: the bailiff, the coroners, William of Wishford, Nicholas Taylor, John of Butterley, Thomas of Bridgehampton, Robert of Godmanstone, John Talbot, John Lea, William Warmwell, and the clerk

11 March 1366, at Salisbury
785 By his charter John Bennett, a citizen of Salisbury, granted to the lord John Wraxall, a chaplain, a tenement, with a shop (*or* shops) and a garden, in Carter Street, between John of Upton's tenement on one side and a tenement of late Robert Alwin's on the other side, held by John Bennett by a grant of John of Upton, a citizen of Salisbury; also a corner tenement in New Street and Brown Street, between a tenement of late Richard Salter's on the west side and a tenement of late that of a younger Robert Baldry on the south side, held by John Bennett by a grant of Thomas Chaplin, a citizen of Salisbury. Both tenements, with the shop(s) and the garden, are to be held for ever by John Wraxall and his heirs and assigns. Clause of warranty. Seals: John Bennett's and the common and mayoral seals of the city. Named witnesses: the bailiff, the mayor, the coroners, the reeves, William of Wishford, John Butterley, William Warmwell, and the clerk

786 Approval of the will of Robert Gore, a citizen of Salisbury, made on 24 August 1361. Interment: in the graveyard of St. Edmund's church beside the tomb of Clemence, formerly his wife. Bequests: 40d. to the fabric of the cathedral church; 2s. each to the high altar of St. Edmund's church for his forgotten tithes, the fabric of that church, the provost John Arnold, and the chaplain of the parish, and 6d. to each priest of the college; 5s. to the fabric of St. Thomas's [church]; 40d. both to the Franciscans of Salisbury and the Dominicans of Fisherton to celebrate mass on behalf his soul and the souls of others; 40s., a tablecloth, a towel, a second-best bed, a brass pot, and a brass pan to his son the lord Adam; after the death of his wife Emme a cup with a cover, silver gilt, to Adam; two beds with the equipment, two brass pots, two brass pans, a tablecloth, and a towel to his son Robert; 6d. to each canon present at his funeral rites; 3d. to each vicar present on the day of his burial; the rest of his goods to his wife Emme and his son Robert to support Robert while he lived. <u>Devises</u>: to Emme a tenement, in which he dwelt, in Endless Street, near the corner called Shit Lane, between a tenement formerly William Gill's on one side and a tenement of Henry Pope, dyer, near the corner called Rolleston on the other side. The tenement is to be held for life by Emme, on her death should remain to Robert's sons John, Adam, and Robert for their life or to the one of them who lives the longest, and after the death of John, Adam, and Robert should remain to the executors of the elder Robert, their executors, or subsequent executors to be sold with the oversight of the provost of St. Edmund's church for the time being and the mayor for the time being. The money received should be spent on behalf of the elder Robert's soul, the souls of Gillian, Clemence, and Emme, his wives, and the souls of others. Robert devised to Emme and his son Robert for their life [?*Robert named in error by the copyist*] two conjoined tenements, with a yard (*or* yards), in Martin's Croft between Gigant Street on the south side and a tenement formerly that of a younger John Whitefoot on the north side. The tenements should remain on Emme's death to the elder Robert's sons John, Adam, and Robert, and on their death to his executors to be sold in the way provided for above. The money received should be spent on behalf of the elder Robert's soul and the souls of others. <u>Executors</u>: Emme and his sons Adam and John. <u>Proved</u> on 30 August 1361 in the cathedral church in front of an officer of the subdean; the administration was entrusted to the executors. <u>Approved</u> at a court held in front of the bailiff, the mayor, and other citizens; the seisin of the tenements was released to the legatees.

20 May 1366, at Salisbury
787 By his charter John Bodenham, a citizen of Salisbury, and his wife Alice, appearing at the court held on that day, granted to John Fowle and John Chandler, citizens of Salisbury, a tenement in Winchester Street between a tenement formerly Edward Knoyle's on one side and a tenement formerly John Knoyle's on the other side. The tenement was held by John and Alice by a grant of Agnes, the relict, and an executor, of John Bodenham, who was an executor of William Stringer, of late a citizen of Salisbury, and it is to be held for ever by John Fowle and John Chandler and their heirs and assigns. Clause of warranty. Seals: those of John and Alice and the common and mayoral seals of the city. Named witnesses: the bailiff, the mayor, the coroners, the reeves, William of Wishford, Robert Bunt, and the clerk

788 By his charter John Bodenham, a citizen of Salisbury, granted to John Fowle and John Chandler, citizens of Salisbury, a yard in Freren Street, formerly that of

Walter Sauter, a clerk, between a tenement formerly Robert of Bodenham's on one side and a yard of late that of an elder John of Fosbury on the other side. The yard was acquired by John Bodenham from John, a son and heir of Robert Gore, of late a citizen of Salisbury, and is to be held for ever by John Fowle and John Chandler and their heirs and assigns. Clause of warranty. Seals: John Bodenham's and the common and mayoral seals of the city. Named witnesses: the bailiff, the mayor, the coroners, the reeves, William of Wishford, Robert Bunt, and the clerk

789 By their indented charter John Ashlock and his wife Margery, the relict, and an executor, of John Dyke, of late a citizen of Salisbury, and Walter Lovel, Margery's co-executor, appearing at the court held on that day, Margery being duly examined, granted to William of Wishford, a citizen of Salisbury, a house, with a plot, in Winchester Street between a tenement of late Adam Cole's on the south side and a tenement of late Henry Bold's on the north side; also a messuage, with a yard (*or* yards), in Culver Street between Stephen Shearer's tenement on one side and a messuage of late Nicholas of Breamore's on the other side. John Dyke devised those premises to Margery for life and, after her death, if his daughter Alice had died without issue, to be sold by his executors. John Ashlock, Margery, and Walter also granted to William a tenement in Scots Lane between a tenement of late Ralph of Langford's on the west side and a tenement of late Thomas Dovedale's on the east side and a messuage in Culver Street between John Powell's messuage on one side and Thomas Ive's tenement on the other side. John Dyke devised the tenement and the messuage to Margery for life and, after her death, if his daughter Joan had died without issue, to be sold by his executors. The house, tenement, and messuages, with the plot and yard(s), are to be held for ever by William of Wishford and his heirs and assigns, paying a rent of 30s. a year to John Ashlock and Margery for Margery's life. Clause to permit re-entry if the rent were in arrear for 15 days, distraint, and the keeping of distresses until the unpaid rent and other losses were recovered. Clause of warranty in respect of the premises and of acquittance in respect of the rent. Seals: those of the parties in turn and the common and mayoral seals of the city. Named witnesses: the bailiff, the mayor, the coroners, the reeves, William Warmwell, Robert Bunt, and the clerk

3 June 1366, at Salisbury
790 By his charter Robert Arnold granted to John Hill and his wife Joan, the relict of Edmund Oisel, a tenement in New Street between John of Upton's tenement on the east side and a tenement of late John of Hemingby's on the west side. The tenement was held by Robert by a grant of John Hill and Joan and is to be held for ever by John and Joan and their heirs and assigns. Seals: Robert's and the common and mayoral seals of the city. Named witnesses: the bailiff, the mayor, the coroners, the reeves, William of Wishford, Robert Bunt, and the clerk

17 June 1366, at Salisbury
791 By their writing Joyce Lutwich, taverner, a citizen of Salisbury, and his wife Margaret, appearing at the court held on that day, quitclaimed to Robert Play and

his heirs and assigns their right or claim to a shop, with a sollar, in Winchester Street, where smiths wait, between a shop of late Robert of Knoyle's on one side and a shop of late Richard Dayson's on the other side. Robert Play held the shop, with the sollar, for his life by a demise of Joyce and Margaret as is contained in an indenture perfected between them at Salisbury on 21 February 1357. Seals: those of Joyce and Margaret and the common and mayoral seals of the city. Named witnesses: the bailiff of Salisbury, the mayor, the coroners, Robert Beechfount, William Warmwell, and the clerk

9 September 1366, at Salisbury
792 By his charter George Goss, a citizen of Salisbury, granted to Thomas Chaplin, a citizen of Salisbury, a tenement in Minster Street between a tenement formerly that of John of Hagbourne, a chaplain, on one side and a tenement of late William Lord's on the other side. The tenement was held by George for ever by a grant of Thomas of Erlestoke, a chaplain, and John Richman to him and Agnes, of late his wife, and their heirs and assigns, and is to be held for ever by Thomas Chaplin and his heirs and assigns. Seals: George's and the common and mayoral seals of the city. Named witnesses: the bailiff, the mayor, the coroners, the reeves, William of Wishford, Robert Bunt, Robert Beechfount, and the clerk
793 By his letters of attorney George Goss, a citizen of Salisbury, appointed William Dunkerton to surrender into the hand of Robert, the bishop of Salisbury, the seisin of a tenement in Minster Street [*as in* **792**] to the use of Thomas Chaplin, a citizen of Salisbury. Seals: George's and the mayoral seal of the city.
794 By their deed Nicholas of Hampton and his wife Maud, appearing at the court held on that day, granted to Thomas Chaplin, a citizen of Salisbury, a tenement in Minster Street between George Goss's tenement on one side and a tenement which was Nicholas of Breamore's on the other side. The tenement was acquired by Nicholas and Maud from Richard Ryborough, of late a citizen of Salisbury, for their life or the life of the one of them living longer, and it is to be held for that term by Thomas and his heirs and assigns of Richard's heirs or assigns, according to the effect of an indenture perfected between Nicholas, Maud, and Richard, for the rent and services contained in the indenture. Nicholas and Maud gave up the indenture to Thomas in court. Seals: those of Nicholas and Maud and the common and mayoral seals of the city. Named witnesses: the bailiff, the mayor, a coroner, George Goss, Robert Bunt, William Warmwell, and the clerk
795 By their charter Agnes Ferrers and Peter Cambo granted to Thomas Chaplin, a citizen of Salisbury, a tenement, opposite St. Thomas's church, between a tenement formerly Robert of Knoyle's on the east side and a tenement formerly Robert of Lavington's on the west side. The tenement was held by Agnes and Peter by a grant of Nicholas Hamish, a chaplain, and is to be held for ever by Thomas and his heirs and assigns. Seals: those of Agnes and Peter and the common and mayoral seals of the city. Named witnesses: the bailiff, the mayor, the coroners, the reeves, William of Wishford, William Warmwell, and the clerk
796 By their charter Roger of Kilmeston, a citizen of Salisbury, and his wife Agnes, a daughter of Maud, the relict of Thomas of Netheravon, appearing at the

court held on that day, granted to Thomas Gilbert a tenement in Minster Street between George Goss's tenement on the south side and a tenement formerly Ralph of Langford's on the north side. The tenement was devised by Maud to Agnes for life and is to be held by Thomas and his heirs and assigns for Agnes's life for the services due from it. Seals: those of Roger and Agnes and the common and mayoral seals of the city. Named witnesses: the bailiff, the mayor, the coroners, William of Wishford, William Warmwell, and the clerk

22 September 1366, at Salisbury
797 By their writing Robert Beechfount and Gilbert of Whichbury, executors of Richard Ryborough, of late a citizen of Salisbury, on the strength of Richard's will quitclaimed to Thomas Chaplin, a citizen of Salisbury, their right or claim to a tenement in Minster Street [*as in* **794**]. Thomas held the tenement by a grant of Nicholas of Hampton, and his wife Maud, who held it for their life by Richard's grant [*as in* **794**]. Seals: those of Robert and Gilbert and the common and mayoral seals of the city. Named witnesses: the bailiff, the mayor, the coroners, William of Wishford, William Warmwell, and the clerk

23 September 1366, at Salisbury
798 By his charter Adam Hoare, a chaplain, an executor of Agnes, the relict of Thomas Smith, called the binsmith, of Amesbury, on the strength of Agnes's will granted to John Beeton a tenement in Gigant Street comprising six cottages between a tenement of late John of Westbury's on one side and a tenement now Roger of Kilmeston's on the other side. The tenement was devised by Agnes to be sold by her executors and is to be held for ever by John and his heirs and assigns. Seals: Adam's and the common and mayoral seals of the city. Named witnesses: the bailiff, the mayor, the coroners, the reeves, William of Wishford, Robert Bunt, William Warmwell, and the clerk
799 By his writing William, a son of Roger of Kilmeston and his wife Agnes and a brother and heir of Ellen, a sister of Joan, a sister of Agnes, a daughter of Roger and Agnes, that Agnes being a daughter of Maud, the relict of Thomas of Netheravon, quitclaimed to Thomas Gilbert and his heirs and assigns his right or claim to a tenement in Minster Street [*as in* **796**]. Thomas holds the tenement by a grant of Roger, and his wife Agnes, [*as in* **796**]. Seals: William's and the common and mayoral seals of the city. Named witnesses: the bailiff, the mayor, William of Wishford, Robert of Godmanstone, Robert Bunt, William Warmwell, John Lea, and the clerk

21 October 1366, at Salisbury
800 By his charter Richard Swooper, of Stoke Farthing (*Stoke Verdoun*), granted to John Bleacher a corner cottage in Endless Street between a cottage, in which John Amesbury dwells, on the north side and the street leading towards St. Edmund's church on the south side. The cottage was acquired by Richard from Alice Bleacher, a sister and heir of John Bleacher, formerly a citizen of Salisbury, and is to be held for ever by John Bleacher and his heirs and assigns. Seals:

Richard's and the common and mayoral seals of the city. Named witnesses: the bailiff, the mayor, the coroners, the reeves, Robert Bunt, William Warmwell, and the clerk

801 By their charter Robert Bunt and George Goss, citizens of Salisbury, granted to Thomas Chaplin, a citizen of Salisbury, two conjoined tenements in New Street between Agnes Bodenham's tenement on the west side and Richard Ryborough's tenement on the east side. Robert and George held the tenements by a grant of Peter Bouch, with all his land and other tenements in the city, in the borough and fields of Old Sarum, and in Stratford near Old Sarum. To strengthen Robert's and George's estate Peter released his right to them and their heirs for ever, as it appears in his writings and deeds. The two tenements are to be held for ever by Thomas Chaplin and his heirs and assigns. Clause of warranty. Seals: those of Robert and George and the common and mayoral seals of the city. Named witnesses: the bailiff, the mayor, the coroners, the reeves, William of Wishford, William Warmwell, and the clerk

18 November 1366, at Salisbury
802 By their charter William Wootton and Nicholas Baker, citizens of Salisbury, granted to Edmund Cofford and his wife Alice a tenement, with shops next to it, in Chipper Street and Minster Street between George Goss's tenement on one side and a tenement of late that of John Hacker and his wife Agnes on the other side. The tenement, with the shops, was held by William and Nicholas by a grant of George Goss, William of Wishford, and John Bossett, executors of William Cofford, and is to be held for ever by Edmund and Alice and their heirs and assigns. Seals: those of William and Nicholas and the common and mayoral seals of the city. Named witnesses: the bailiff, the mayor, the coroners, a reeve, William of Wishford, William Warmwell, and the clerk

803 By his charter Thomas of Britford, an executor of William Costard, of late a citizen of Salisbury, on the strength of William's will granted to the lord William Buck, a chaplain, a tenement in Wineman Street between a tenement formerly Stephen Crier's on the west side and a tenement formerly Henry Napper's on the east side. The tenement was acquired by William Costard from the lord Thomas of Erlestoke, a chaplain, was devised by him to be sold by his executors, and is to be held for ever by William Buck and his heirs and assigns. Seals: Thomas of Britford's and the common and mayoral seals of the city. Named witnesses: the bailiff, the mayor, a coroner, the reeves, William of Wishford, William Warmwell, and the clerk

804 By his charter John Snel, a citizen of Salisbury, granted to John Fowle, a citizen of Salisbury, a tenement in Endless Street between a tenement formerly Walter Goss's on one side and Stephen Shearer's tenement on the other side. The tenement was acquired by John Snel from Richard Dinton, a son of Maud, who was the wife of Stephen Shearer, and is to be held for ever by John Fowle and his heirs and assigns. Clause of warranty. Seals: John Snel's and the common and mayoral seals of the city. Named witnesses: the bailiff, the mayor, the coroners, the reeves, William of Wishford, William Warmwell, and the clerk

2 December 1366, at Salisbury
805 By his charter David, a clerk, granted to Stephen Jay and his wife Edith a tenement in Gigant Street between John Hoare's tenement, of late Richard of Knighton's, on the south side and a tenement of late Roger Ford's on the north side. The tenement was held by David by a feoffment of Richard Marwood and is to be held for ever by Stephen and Edith and Stephen's heirs and assigns. Clause of warranty. Seals: David's and the common and mayoral seals of the city. Named witnesses: the bailiff, the mayor, the reeves, a coroner, William of Wishford, Robert Godmanstone, George Goss, and William Warmwell

806 By their charter Nicholas Astbury and his wife Emme, the relict of Roger Frank, of late a citizen of Salisbury, appearing at the court held on that day, granted to the lords Thomas of Erlestoke and John Dean, chaplains, a corner tenement, with its sollars and cellars, opposite the high cross where fruit and other victuals are sold, beside the tenement called Hampton's Corner. The tenement was held by Roger and Emme by a grant of William of Hook Norton, the vicar of Britford, and Thomas of Erlestoke and, with the sollars and cellars, is to be held for ever by Thomas and John and their heirs and assigns. Seals: those of Nicholas and Emme and the common and mayoral seals of the city. Named witnesses: the bailiff, the mayor, the coroners, the reeves, William of Wishford, George Goss, William Warmwell, and the clerk

807 By their charter John Lea and his wife Agnes, the relict of John Deanbridge and a daughter and executor of Alice, the relict of Philip Longenough, of late a citizen of Salisbury, appearing at the court held on that day, on the strength of Alice's will granted to John Needler a tenement in Carter Street between a tenement in which that John now dwells on one side and John of Oxford's tenement on the other side. On the site of that tenement there were of late two tenements which Alice devised to John Deanbridge and Agnes and their joint issue if her daughter Alice had died without issue, and afterwards, if John and Agnes had died without joint issue, to be sold by her executors. Alice's daughter Alice and John Deanbridge each died without issue, and the tenement remained to Agnes for her life and, as Alice's executor, for sale. It is to be held for ever by John Needler, and his heirs and assigns, to whom John Lea and Agnes released their right to it. Seals: those of John and Agnes and the common and mayoral seals of the city. Named witnesses: the bailiff, the mayor, the coroners, the reeves, William of Wishford, John Butterley, William Warmwell, and the clerk

7 December 1366, at Salisbury
808 By his writing William Dunkerton quitclaimed to John Needler his right or claim to a tenement in Carter Street [*as in* **807**]. The two tenements on the site of that tenement were devised by Alice, the relict of Philip Longenough, [*as in* **807**]. Alice's daughter Alice and John Deanbridge having died without issue Alice's daughter Agnes held an estate in the tenement for her life which, before the present writing was perfected, John Lea and Agnes, his wife, granted to John Needler. Seals: William's and the common and mayoral seals of the city.

Named witnesses: the bailiff, the mayor, a coroner, William of Wishford, Robert Godmanstone, William Warmwell, and John Bennett

11 December 1366, at Salisbury
809 By his writing Edward, a son of Richard of Glastonbury, of late a citizen of Salisbury, quitclaimed to a younger William Tenterer his right or claim to a corner tenement called Stratford's Corner, with adjacent shops, in Winchester Street between William's tenement on the west side and a tenement of late John Baldry's on the south side. Clause of warranty. Seals: Edward's and the common and mayoral seals of the city. Named witnesses: the mayor, the coroners, the reeves, William of Wishford, Nicholas Taylor, John Oxford, George Goss, and John Butterley

16 December 1366, at Salisbury
810 By his charter David, a clerk, granted to William Guys a chief tenement, with a shop next to it, in Carter Street [Drake Hall Street in **2067**] between a shop of late John of Fosbury's on the north side and a tenement of late Thomas Callow's on the south side; also a piece of meadow lying beside that street, between a meadow formerly Robert of Ann's on the south side and a meadow of late Walter Goss's on the north side, extending from the street on the west side as far as Freren Street on the east side. Those premises were of late John of Fosbury's, and David and Benet, of late his wife, acquired them from his son John of Fosbury. Before that purchase Benet held an estate for her life by the demise of John of Fosbury the father, a feoffor of David. They are to be held for ever by William Guys and his heirs and assigns. Clause of warranty. Seals: David's and the common and mayoral seals of the city. Named witnesses: the bailiff, the mayor, the coroners, the reeves, William of Wishford, William Warmwell, and the clerk
811 By his charter David Laurence, a clerk, granted to John Justice, a citizen of Salisbury, a tenement, opposite the bishop of Salisbury's land held in villeinage, between a tenement formerly Henry Brightwin's on one side and a tenement formerly Jordan Mercer's on the other side. The tenement was acquired by David from John Sevenash, a clerk, and is to be held for ever by John Justice and his heirs and assigns. Clause of warranty. Seals: David's and the common and mayoral seals of the city. Named witnesses: the bailiff, the mayor, the coroners, William of Wishford, John Butterley, William Warmwell, and the clerk
812 By his charter John Amesbury, a citizen of Salisbury, granted to John Bleacher a cottage in Endless Street, between his own cottage on the north side and John's corner cottage on the south side, to be held for ever by John Bleacher and his heirs and assigns. Seals: John Amesbury's and the common and mayoral seals of the city. Named witnesses: the bailiff, the mayor, the coroners, the reeves, William of Wishford, William Warmwell, and the clerk
813 By his charter Nicholas Russell, butcher, granted to John Justice a tenement in Gigant Street beside a tenement formerly Robert of Faringdon's. The tenement was acquired by Nicholas from Robert Fewster, a citizen of Salisbury, and is to be held for ever by John and his heirs and assigns. Clause of warranty. Seals:

Nicholas's and the common and mayoral seals of the city. Named witnesses: the bailiff, the mayor, the coroners, a reeve, William Wishford, William Warmwell, and the clerk

30 December 1366, at Salisbury
814 By his charter John Justice granted to Thomas Chaplin, a citizen of Salisbury, a tenement in Gigant Street [*as in* **813**]. The tenement was acquired by John from Nicholas Russell, butcher, who acquired it from Robert Fewster, and it is to be held for ever by Thomas and his heirs and assigns. Clause of warranty. Seals: John's and the common and mayoral seals of the city. Named witnesses: the bailiff, the mayor, the coroners, William of Wishford, George Goss, John Butterley, William Warmwell, and the clerk
815 By his charter John Justice, a citizen of Salisbury, granted to William Guys a tenement, opposite the bishop of Salisbury's land held in villeinage, [*as in* **811**]. The tenement was acquired by John from David Laurence, a clerk, and is to be held for ever by William and his heirs and assigns. Seals: John's and the common and mayoral seals of the city. Named witnesses: the bailiff, the mayor, the coroners, William of Wishford, George Goss, William Warmwell, John Fowle, and the clerk
816 Approval of the will of Walter at the burgh, a citizen of Salisbury, made on 18 September 1366. <u>Interment</u>: in the cathedral church opposite the chapel, or altar, of St. Thomas the Martyr. <u>Bequests</u>: 20*s*. to the fabric of that church; 13*s*. 4*d*. to each rector, or vicar where there was no rector, wherever he possessed land or tenements, for his forgotten tithes and his benefactions, and where there was a rector and a vicar the 13*s*. 4*d*. should be shared equally between them; 12*d*. to each vicar of the cathedral church present at his funeral rites in the night before the day of his burial; 40*d*. to each of his tenants wherever they dwelt; 100*s*. to each of 10 chaplains, for the year after his death if they can be found and hired by his executors, to celebrate mass on behalf of his soul and the souls of others; 20 marks to his kinsman Robert, a son of Thomas at the burgh, as an aid to the repair of his corner tenement at Wilton; 20*s*. to Christine, a daughter of a younger Henry at the burgh, his brother; 100 marks for his funeral rites so that on the day of his burial 140 paupers might be clothed, each of them to have three ells of cloth of twist, and the rest of the money to be for his remaining funeral expenses with more, if necessary, at the order of his executors; 2*s*., and one of the amounts of clothing assigned above to paupers, to each of John Gardener, of South Charford, Robert Riveray, William Tosard, William Taston, Jarvis Tosard, Peter Bubble, and William Waldrich; the rest of his goods to his wife Isabel and their son John to do with them what seemed to them healthiest for the salvation of his soul; 40*d*. to each chaplain celebrating mass daily in St. Thomas's church this year; 6 marks to the prior and convent of Breamore; 20*s*. each to David Griffin and his wife and William Blyth and his wife; ½ mark each to William Coleman, Marion, of late his maidservant, and Walter, his boy; ½ mark, which he lent to him, to Nicholas, his tenant and bondman of Charford, staying at Downton; 20*s*. to William C…ssley, his household servant; 40*d*. each to Griffin, of late his servant, and Aubrey, his

maidservant; 40s. to Ellen Dunn, of late his maidservant; 10 marks to the convent of Wilton abbey. Devises: to his wife Isabel the rent which Henry at the burgh is bound to pay to him yearly and the tenement called the 'Riole' in Minster Street, which Henry holds for life, with the reversion after Henry's death; also the rent which he received from the shops attached to the tenement, with the reversion of all the shops when they fell due on the death of those holding them for life; also a cellar underneath those shops, and a shop, attached to the tenement, in which Robert Cook dwells. The rent, reversions, shop, and cellar are to be held for ever by Isabel and her heirs and assigns to complete a chantry proposed by Walter and begun at the altar of St. Thomas the Martyr in the cathedral church: a chaplain should celebrate mass there daily on behalf of Walter's soul, the souls of others, and the healthy condition of Isabel while she lived and of her soul when she died, and should ensure that Walter's yearly obit is held there for ever, although while he lived he held the obit; the estate should also be held to carry forward a chantry in the church of the Franciscans of Salisbury, which the friars promised to him, the first mass there to be celebrated by one of the friars on behalf of the souls mentioned above and on behalf of Isabel in the way described above. Walter devised to Henry at the burgh a cottage in Wilton, which John Rochelle now holds, with a garden and an adjacent meadow, standing beside Bull bridge, to be held for ever by Henry and his heirs and assigns. Walter devised to his executors his other land, tenements, rent, services, and reversions in Wilton to be sold. The money received should be laid out on behalf of his soul and the souls mentioned above. He devised to Isabel the keeping of their son John until his majority; also the keeping of Robert, the son of Thomas at the burgh, his brother, with all his goods, land, and tenements until his majority. Executors: Isabel, an elder William Tenterer, and Robert Bunt. Proved on 3 October 1366 in front of Roger of Clowne, the archdeacon of Salisbury; the administration was entrusted to Isabel, reserving the power to entrust it to the elder William Tenterer and Robert Bunt, when they might come to seek it, or to other administrators deputized by him if those co-executors refused it. Approved at a court held in front of the bailiff, the mayor, and other citizens; the seisin of the tenements, land, rent, and reversions was released to the legatees.

13 January 1367, at Salisbury
817 By his charter [*dated to the Wednesday after the feast of St. Hilary (20 January) probably in error for the Wednesday of that feast (13 January)*] John, a son of Andrew Bone, of late a citizen of Salisbury, granted to John Butterley, a citizen of Salisbury, conjoined shops, with a yard (*or* yards), in the street on the way to St. Edmund's church, between a tenement formerly that of John Banbost on one side and a yard formerly Walter Chandler's on the other side. The shops, with the yard(s), were devised by Andrew to John and his heirs and assigns for ever on condition that John would claim nothing for his reasonable portion from the goods and chattels of his father or his mother Joan, and they are to be held for ever by John Butterley and his heirs and assigns. Seals: John Bone's and the common and mayoral seals of the city. Named witnesses: the bailiff, the mayor, the coroners,

the reeves, William of Wishford Robert Godmanstone, William Warmwell, and the clerk

23 January 1367, at Salisbury
818 By his letters of attorney John, a son of Andrew Bone, of late a citizen of Salisbury, appointed Thomas Boyton, bowyer, to surrender into the hand of Robert, the bishop of Salisbury, the seisin of conjoined shops, in the street on the way to St. Edmund's church, [*as in* **817**] to the use of John Butterley. Seals: John Bone's and the mayoral seal of the city by the hand of Robert Bunt, then the mayor

27 January 1367, at Salisbury
819 By her charter Agnes, the relict of John of Bodenham, granted to Thomas Hindon, a citizen of Salisbury, three conjoined cottages in Culver Street between Thomas of Knoyle's tenement on the south side and a tenement formerly William Stringer's on the north side. The cottages were acquired by Agnes from Christine, the relict of Peter Bennett, of late a citizen of Salisbury, and are to be held for ever by Thomas and his heirs and assigns. Clause of warranty. Seals: Agnes's and the common and mayoral seals of the city. Named witnesses: the bailiff, the mayor, the coroners, the reeves, William of Wishford, John Butterley, William Warmwell, and the clerk

10 February 1367, at Salisbury
820 By her letters of attorney [*dated to the Wednesday after the feast of St. Scholastica the Virgin (17 February) probably in error for the Wednesday of that feast (10 February)*] Agnes, the relict of John of Bodenham, appointed William Dunkerton to surrender into the hand of Robert, the bishop of Salisbury, the seisin of three conjoined cottages in Culver Street [*as in* **819**] to the use of Thomas Hindon, a citizen of Salisbury. Seals: Agnes's and the mayoral seal of the city

24 February 1367, at Salisbury
821 By his charter John Amesbury, a citizen of Salisbury, an executor of Joan, of late his wife, on the strength of Joan's will granted to the master Richard Leach a shop in Minster Street, near a corner called Wimpler's Corner, between a tenement in which Thomas Scot now dwells on one side and a tenement in which John Barber now dwells on the other side. Joan devised the shop to John for life and after his death, if her son John had died without issue, to be sold by her executors for the salvation of her soul. John also released his own estate in the shop to Richard and his heirs and assigns, who are to hold the shop for ever. Seals: John's and the common and mayoral seals of the city. Named witnesses: the bailiff, the mayor, the coroners, the reeves, William of Wishford, George Goss, William Warmwell, and the clerk
822 By his charter Gilbert Whichbury, a citizen of Salisbury, granted to Thomas Hindon, a citizen of Salisbury, a tenement in Culver Street between a tenement formerly Roger of Buckland's on the south side and a tenement formerly that of

Henry Brightwin, of Christchurch, on the north side. The tenement was held by Robert Alwin and Gilbert by a grant of an elder John Bodenham together with, in general words, all his land and tenements in the city, and it is to be held for ever by Thomas and his heirs and assigns. Seals: Gilbert's and the common and mayoral seals of the city. Named witnesses: the bailiff, the mayor, the coroners, the reeves, William of Wishford, George Goss, William Warmwell, and the clerk

823 By his indented charter John Bleacher granted to William Bleacher a corner cottage, in Endless Street between a cottage now [?*rectius* formerly: *cf.* **800**] John Amesbury's on the north side and a street leading towards St. Edmund's church on the south side, which he acquired from Richard Swooper, of Stoke Farthing (*Stoke Verdoun*); also a cottage, in Endless Street between that corner cottage on the south side and John Amesbury's cottage on the north side, which he held by a feoffment of John Amesbury. The two cottages are to be held for ever by William and his heirs and assigns, paying a rent of 12*s*. cash a year to John Bleacher and his heirs or assigns. Clause to permit re-entry if the rent were in arrear for 15 days, distraint, and the keeping of distresses until the unpaid rent and other losses were recovered. Seals: those of the parties in turn and the common and mayoral seals of the city. Named witnesses: the bailiff, the mayor, the coroners, the reeves, William of Wishford, George Goss, William Warmwell, and the clerk

24 March 1367, at Salisbury
824 By his charter Thomas Hindon, a citizen of Salisbury, granted to John Justice, a citizen of Salisbury, three conjoined cottages in Culver Street [*as in* **819**]. The cottages were acquired by Thomas from Agnes, the relict of John of Bodenham, and are to be held for ever by John and his heirs and assigns. Seals: Thomas's and the common and mayoral seals of the city. Named witnesses: the bailiff, the mayor, the coroners, a reeve, William of Wishford, John Lea, William Warmwell, and the clerk

825 By his charter Thomas Hindon, a citizen of Salisbury, granted to John Justice, a citizen of Salisbury, and his wife Margery three conjoined cottages in Culver Street [*as in* **819**]; also a tenement in Culver Street [*as in* **822**], which he acquired from Gilbert of Whichbury, a citizen of Salisbury. The cottages and the tenement are to be held for ever by John and Margery and their heirs and assigns. Seals: Thomas's and the common and mayoral seals of the city. Named witnesses: the bailiff, the mayor, the coroners, a reeve, William of Wishford, John Lea, William Warmwell, and the clerk

2 June 1367, Salisbury
826 By their charter Nicholas Astbury and his wife Emme, the relict, and an executor, of John Powell, of late a citizen of Salisbury, appearing at the court held on that day, on the strength of John's will granted to John Melksham four conjoined cottages in Mealmonger Street between Thomas of Britford's cottage and … [*MS. apparently defective*] formerly John Powell's. [The four cottages] were devised by John Powell to be sold by his executors after the death of his sons Richard and William and are to be held for ever by John Melksham and his heirs

and assigns. Seals: those of Nicholas and Emme and the common and mayoral seals of the city. Named witnesses: the bailiff, the mayor, the coroners, the reeves, William of Wishford, Robert Godmanstone, John Butterley, and William Bruton

14 June 1367, at London
827 By their charter John Nott, John Aubrey, Robert Godmanstone, Robert of Hatfield, and Reynold Love granted to Thomas of Salisbury, kt., the land, rent, and tenements in the city and suburbs of Salisbury which they held by his feoffment, and the land and tenements in Bemerton, Quidhampton, and Fisherton which they held likewise. All the land, rent, and tenements are to be held for ever by Thomas and his heirs and assigns. Seals: those of the grantors. Named witnesses: John Ward, John Hatfield, Nicholas Chaucer, John Philpot, and Thomas Thorney, citizens of London, Nicholas Taylor, William Wishford, Robert Bunt, John Butterley, and Thomas of Hindon, citizens of Salisbury, Thomas Hungerford, Robert Ramsbury, and John Harnham, of Wiltshire

15 June 1367, at London
828 By his letters of attorney Thomas of Salisbury, kt., appointed William Britford to receive from John Nott, John Aubrey, Robert Godmanstone, Robert of Hatfield, and Reynold Love the seisin of the land, rent, and tenements in Salisbury, Bemerton, Quidhampton, and Fisherton [*as in* **827**] which they granted to him. Seal: Thomas's
829 By their letters of attorney John Nott, John Aubrey, Robert Godmanstone, Robert of Hatfield, and Reynold Love appointed John of Hatfield, Nicholas Huxtworth, and Thomas Garnet to release to Thomas of Salisbury, kt., or his attorney the seisin of the land, rent, and tenements in Salisbury, Bemerton, Quidhampton, and Fisherton [*as in* **827**] which they granted to him. Seals: those of the grantors

30 June 1367, at Salisbury
830 By their charter John Lea and his wife Agnes, the relict of John Deanbridge and a daughter and executor of Alice, the relict of Philip Longenough, of late a citizen of Salisbury, appearing at the court held on that day, on the strength of Alice's will granted to Thomas Chaplin, a citizen of Salisbury, a tenement in Carter Street between a tenement in which John Needler now dwells on one side and a tenement of late Richard Ryborough's on the other side. Alice devised the tenement, if her daughter Alice died without issue, to John Deanbridge and Agnes and their joint issue and afterwards, if John and Agnes died without such issue, to be sold by her executors. The younger Alice and John Deanbridge each died without issue, and the tenement remained to Agnes for her life and, as Alice's executor, for sale. It is to be held for ever by Thomas Chaplin and his heirs and assigns, to whom John and Agnes released their right or claim to it. Seals: those of John Lea and Agnes and the common and mayoral seals of the city. Named witnesses: the bailiff, the mayor, the coroners, the reeves, William of Wishford, William Warmwell, and the clerk

28 July 1367, at Salisbury
831 Approval of the will of Stephen Shearer, a citizen of Salisbury, made on 22 April 1367. Interment: in the graveyard of St. Edmund's church beside the grave in which the corpse of Joan, of late his wife, lies at rest. Bequests: 40*d*. to the fabric of the cathedral church and 12*d*. to the fraternity of the high cross in it; 40*d*. to the fabric of St. Edmund's church, 20*d*. to the fraternity of the high cross in it, 40*d*. to the provost for his forgotten tithes and lesser benefactions, 6*d*. to each collegiate chaplain, a brass pot called God's crock to those chaplains for their use, 3*d*. to each of the other chaplains celebrating mass there on the day of his burial, 6*d*. to the deacon, and 3*d*. to the sacristan; 40*d*. both to the Franciscans of Salisbury and the Dominicans of Fisherton; 16 lb. of wax to make candles to be burned around his corpse on the day of his burial; 60*s*. for all his other funeral expenses on that day; a nutshell bound with silver with a silver foot, 3 qr. of second-grade malt, six silver spoons, a coffer with a brass pot enclosed within, and a second-best pan to Amice, a daughter of his deceased son Richard; 6*d*. to each of his godchildren; 6*s*. 8*d*. to John Bright, his servant, and a bed according to the order of his executors; a pair of tongs called garland, a coat, and a second-best coat to Thomas, his apprentice; 6*s*. 8*d*. each to Joan, a daughter, and John, a son, of Richard Dinton; 13*s*. 4*d*., a best bed, and a featherbed to Alice Barnaby; 20*d*. to Eve Maynes; a best cloak to John at the New Inn; 10*s*. to Margery, a daughter of John Duke; 12*d*. each to Maud and Marion, his servants; 4 marks to Richard Shearer, a debt which Richard owed to him; a brass pot containing 7 gallons, a brass pot containing 4 gallons, two pans, one best and the other third-best, a large mazer bound with silver, a best robe, four best pairs of tongs, and all the other tools, except five pairs of tongs, pertaining to his trade, a bed, a featherbed, a best basin with a laver, and all his utensils pertaining to the trade of brewer to John Duke and his wife James; a second-best robe to an elder John Duke; the term which he has in Thomas, his apprentice, to a younger John Duke; 6*s*. 8*d*. each to the lord John Chatt and the lord John Heanor; the rest of his goods to be sold by his executors, and the money received to be laid out on behalf of his soul and the souls of those mentioned below. Devises: to Amice, the daughter of Richard, two conjoined shops in Butcher Row, between William of Bruton's shops on the east side and a tenement which Hugh of Winterbourne holds on the west side, to be held for ever by her and her heirs and assigns. Stephen devised to the younger John Duke and his wife James a tenement, with shops next to it, in Endless Street, between Edmund Bramshaw's [corner; *cf.* **729**] tenement on the north side and John Fowle's tenement on the south side, to be held for ever by them and John's heirs and assigns. Stephen bequeathed to John and James two ovens being in that tenement. He devised a tenement, and a plot of land with racks on it, to be sold by his executors as soon after his death as is convenient: the tenement stands in Mealmonger Street between cottage property of late Nicholas Breamore's on the south side and a street called Nuggeston on the north side, and the plot lies, with the racks, opposite the graveyard of St. Edmund's church, between George Goss's garden on the west side and Gigant Street on the east side. The money

received should be laid out on celebrating masses and doing other charitable deeds on behalf of Stephen's soul, the souls of Joan and Maud, of late his wives, and the souls of others. <u>Executors</u>: the younger John Duke, the lord John Chatt, a chaplain, and the lord John Heanor, a chaplain. <u>Proved</u> on 17 July 1367 in front of the subdean; the administration was entrusted to the executors. <u>Approved</u> at a court held in front of the bailiff, the mayor, and other citizens; the seisin of the tenements, shops, land, and racks was released to the legatees.

832 Approval of the will of John Hoare, a citizen of Salisbury, made on 6 June 1367. <u>Interment</u>: in the graveyard of St. Edmund's church. <u>Bequests</u>: 6d. each to the fabric of the cathedral church and the fabric of St. Martin's church; 12d. to the fabric of St. Edmund's church; 6s. 8d. to the lord John Chatt; 20s. to John Cole; a piece of silver with a cover both to his wife Gillian and his son William; a piece of silver called boar to his daughter Ellen; 6d. to each chaplain celebrating mass in St. Edmund's church on the day of his burial; 13s. 4d. to Emme, a daughter of John Cole; 2s. 6d. both to the Franciscans of Salisbury to celebrate a trental on behalf his soul and to the Dominicans of Fisherton to celebrate mass likewise; the rest of his goods to his wife Gillian, his son William, and his daughter Ellen. <u>Devises</u>: to Gillian a tenement, with shops next to it, except a shop which John Palmer, tailor, and his wife Maud hold for their life by John's demise, in Winchester Street between John Shove's tenement on the east side and a tenement of late John Ferrer's on the west side. The tenement, apart from the excepted shop, is to be held for her life by Gillian and her assigns, and after Gillian's death for ever by John's son William and his issue; if William were to die without issue it should be held for ever by John's daughter Ellen and her issue, and if Ellen were to die without issue it would remain for ever to John's direct heirs. John devised to Gillian for life a rent of 20s. a year issuing from the shop, which John Palmer and Maud hold for their life, beside the tenement in Winchester Street, with the reversion of the shop if it should fall due in her lifetime. After Gillian's death the rent and the reversion should be held for ever by William and his issue, if William were to die without issue they should be held for ever by Ellen and her issue, and if Ellen were to die without issue they would remain for ever to John's direct heirs. John devised to Ellen a corner tenement, with shops next to it, in Winchester Street between a tenement of late William Goldston's on the east side and a tenement of William Warmwell and his wife Agnes on the south side. The tenement, with the shops, is to be held for ever by Ellen and her issue, if Ellen were to die without issue it should be held for ever by William and his issue, and if William were to die without issue, it would remain for ever to John's direct heirs. John devised to Gillian for life a shop, opposite the Guildhall, between Nicholas Taylor's shops on the north side and a shop, which William Till holds, on the south side. After Gillian's death the shop should be held for ever by William and his issue, if William were to die without issue it should be held for ever by Ellen and her issue, and if Ellen were to die without issue, it would remain for ever to John's direct heirs. John devised to Gillian for life a rent of 40s. a year issuing from a tenement, which John Denis and his wife Agnes hold for Agnes's life, in Winchester Street and Gigant Street between

William of Wishford's tenement on the east side and Stephen Jay's tenement on the north side, with the reversion of the tenement on Agnes's death if it fell due in her lifetime. After Gillian's death the rent and the reversion should be held for ever by Ellen and her issue, and if Ellen were to die without issue they should be held for ever by William and his issue. If William were to die without issue, and if it could be done lawfully, the rent and the reversion should be appropriated by the provost for the time being of St. Edmund's church for the use of the chaplains of the college there as an increase of their maintenance. If the provost could not do that lawfully the rent and the reversion should be sold by him. The money received should be converted to the use of the chaplains to celebrate mass on behalf of John's soul, the soul of his wife Gillian, and the souls of others. John devised to Gillian for life two conjoined cottages in New Street beside a tenement of late Thomas Mandeville's on the west side. After Gillian's death the cottages should be held for ever by William and his issue, if William were to die without issue they should be held for ever by Ellen and her issue, and if Ellen were to die without issue they would remain for ever to John's direct heirs. John devised to Gillian for life three more properties, a tenement in Winchester Street between a corner tenement of late John Cheese's on the west side and a shop, which John Palmer and his wife Maud hold, on the east side, a shop, in which William Till dwells, opposite the Guildhall, beside a chief tenement of late John Cheese's on the south side, and a yard in Gigant Street between Nicholas Chardstock's cottages on the north side and Robert of Godmanstone's cottages on the south side. After Gillian's death the tenement, the shop, and the yard should be held for ever by William and his issue, if William were to die without issue they should be held for ever by Ellen and her issue, and if Ellen were to die without issue they would remain for ever to John's direct heirs. John devised to Thomas of Britford a garden in Brown Street between George Goss's cottage on the south side and Nicholas Chardstock's cottage property on the north side. After Thomas's death the garden should be held for ever by John's son William and his issue, if William were to die without issue it should be held for ever by Ellen and her issue, and if Ellen were to die without issue it would remain for ever to John's direct heirs. John devised to his wife Gillian the keeping of William and Ellen until their majority, she finding sufficient security to the mayor as is customary. <u>Executors</u>: Gillian and William. <u>Proved</u> on 15 June 1367 in front of the subdean; the administration was entrusted to the executors. <u>Approved</u> at a court held in front of the bailiff, the mayor, and other citizens; the seisin of the tenements, shops, and rents was released to the legatees.

11 August 1367, at Salisbury
833 By his charter William Sire, a citizen of Salisbury, granted to Thomas Sexhampcote, a citizen of Salisbury, a corner tenement in Wineman Street, between Gilbert Oword's tenement on one side and Henry Pope's tenement on the other side, to be held for ever by Thomas and his heirs and assigns. Clause of warranty. Seal: William's. Named witnesses: the bailiff, the mayor, the coroners, the reeves, William of Wishford, William Warmwell, John Lea, and the clerk. For

greater security William Sire procured the common and mayoral seals of the city to be affixed on that same day.

12 August 1367, at Salisbury
834 By his letters of attorney William Sire, a citizen of Salisbury, appointed Thomas Bourchier to surrender into the hand of the bishop of Salisbury a corner tenement in Wineman Street [*as in* **833**] to the use of Thomas Sexhampcote, a citizen of Salisbury. Seals: William's and the mayoral seal of the city

25 August 1367, at Salisbury
835 By their charter John Bodenham, a citizen of Salisbury, and his wife Alice, appearing at the court held on that day, granted to John Heanor, a chaplain, a tenement in Gigant Street between a tenement formerly Robert Russell's on one side and a tenement of an elder John Chandler on the other side. The tenement descended to Alice by right of inheritance on the death of her brother William Gore and is to be held for ever by John Heanor and his heirs and assigns. Clause of warranty. Seals: those of John and Alice and the common and mayoral seals of the city. Named witnesses: the bailiff, the mayor, the coroners, the reeves, William of Wishford, George Goss, and the clerk

22 September 1367, at Salisbury
836 By their writing Adam Ludwell and his wife Isabel, the relict of Adam Haxton, appearing at the court held on that day, granted to John Farnborough and Thomas Friday a tenement, with shops, in Minster Street, between two shops, which Adam Haxton devised to Isabel, on the south side and a tenement of late Robert New's on the north side, to be held for the life of Isabel by them and their assigns. For a sum of money paid to them in advance Adam and Isabel, an executor of Adam Haxton, also sold the reversion of the tenement, with the shops attached to it, except the two shops which Adam Haxton devised to Isabel, to be held for ever by them and their heirs or assigns. Adam and Isabel quitclaimed to John and Thomas and their heirs or assigns their right or claim to the tenement, with the shops, apart from the excepted shops. Seals: those of Adam and Isabel and the common and mayoral seals of the city. Named witnesses: the bailiff, the mayor, the coroners, the reeves, William Wishford, John Butterley, William Warmwell, and the clerk

22 October 1367, at Salisbury
837 By her charter Emme, the relict of Robert Gore, of late a citizen of Salisbury, in her chaste widowhood, granted to John of Stallington, a clerk, a tenement, with an adjacent garden, in the city, in the street called the Old Town, opposite the bishop of Salisbury's land held in villeinage, between Joan Mayhew's tenement on one side and Walter Cooper's tenement on the other side, to be held for ever by him and his heirs and assigns. Clause of warranty. Seals: Emme's and the common and mayoral seals of the city. Named witnesses: the bailiff, the mayor, the reeves, a coroner, an elder William Tenterer, William Wishford, and Robert

Godmanstone, citizens of Salisbury, and the clerk

3 November 1367, at Salisbury
838 By his charter William Buck, a chaplain, granted to Thomas Hindon, a citizen of Salisbury, a tenement in Wineman Street between a tenement formerly Stephen Crier's on the west side and a tenement formerly Henry Napper's on the east side. The tenement was acquired by William from Thomas of Britford, an executor of William Costard, of late a citizen of Salisbury, and is to be held for ever by Thomas Hindon and his heirs and assigns. Seals: William's and the common and mayoral seals of the city. Named witnesses: the bailiff, the mayor, the coroners, the reeves, William of Wishford, George Goss, William Warmwell, and the clerk

23 February 1368, at Salisbury
839 By his charter William Heal, a brother and heir of Alan Heal, granted to Richard Haxton a yard in Nuggeston beside a tenement of late Maud of Langford's on the west side and Henry Pope's tenement on the east side. The yard descended to William by right of inheritance on Alan's death and is to be held for ever by Richard and his heirs and assigns. Clause of warranty. Seals: William's and the common and mayoral seals of the city. Named witnesses: the bailiff, the mayor, the coroners, the reeves, William of Wishford, George Goss, and Thomas Hindon

23 August 1368, at Salisbury
840 By his charter John Dinton, a butcher, granted to John Sherfield two conjoined tenements, with a yard (*or* yards), in the street on the way to St. Martin's church, between the graveyard of that church on the south side and a tenement of late Jordan Mercer's on the north side. The tenements, with the yard(s), were held by John Dinton by a grant of William of Bruton, a citizen of Salisbury, and are to be held for ever by John Sherfield and his heirs and assigns. Clause of warranty. Seals: John Dinton's and the common and mayoral seals of the city. Named witnesses: the bailiff, the mayor, the coroners, the reeves, William Wishford, Robert Godmanstone, John Butterley, and William Warmwell

Here is to be seen how John of Stallington acquired from Ellen, the relict of Edward Pinnock, 40s. [rent] from a tenement, in which Alice of Homington dwelt, in Minster Street

16 December 1368, at Salisbury
841 By her writing Alice Homington, of Salisbury, in her widowhood, granted to Ellen, the relict of Edward Pinnock and a daughter of Simon of Oxford, formerly a citizen of Salisbury, a tenement, in which she dwelt, with shops, in Minster Street between a tenement of John Scammel [*otherwise* Camel: *cf.* **1642, 1943**], hatter, on the north side and a tenement formerly John Ludgershall's, now John Pack's, on the south side, stretching from the high street on the east side as far as the great river on the west side. Edward and Ellen granted the tenement, with

the shops, to John of Homington, formerly Alice's husband, now dead, to Alice, and to their son Richard, also now dead, for their life and the life of the one of them living longest. Seals: Alice's and the common and mayoral seals of the city. Named witnesses: the bailiff, the mayor, the coroners, Robert Bunt, William Wishford, an elder William Tenterer, a younger William Tenterer, Nicholas Taylor, and John of Oxford

18 December 1368, at Salisbury
842 By her charter Ellen Pinnock, of West Harnham, in her chaste widowhood, granted to John of Stallington, a clerk, a rent of 40s. a year issuing from her tenement, with shops attached to it, in Minster Street [*as in **841***]. Ellen held the tenement, with the shops, by a devise of Simon of Oxford, her father, formerly a citizen of Salisbury, and Alice of Homington, who held it for life, surrendered her estate in it to her for ever. The rent is to be held for ever by John of Stallington and his heirs and assigns. Clause to permit entry on the tenement and shops, into the hand of whomever they might have come, if the rent were in arrear, and to permit distraint and the keeping of distresses until the unpaid rent and other losses were recovered. Clause of warranty. So that her gift, and the confirmation of the charter, would remain valid for ever Ellen confirmed John's seisin by paying to him 1*d*. on the day on which the charter was perfected. Seals: Ellen's and the common and mayoral seals of the city. Named witnesses: the bailiff, the mayor, the coroners, Robert Bunt, William Wishford, an elder William Tenterer, a younger William Tenterer, Nicholas Taylor, and John of Oxford, citizens of Salisbury

26 September 1381, at Westminster
843 By his writ the king directed the sheriff of Wiltshire to order Thomas Bowyer, of Salisbury, to deliver to Ellen, the relict of Thomas of Barford, the dower which pertained to her from a freehold which her husband held in Salisbury. She had nothing of it, as is said, and it is complained that Thomas wrongfully withheld it from her. If Thomas did not deliver the dower, and if Ellen gave security to the sheriff in respect of her claim, the sheriff should summon Thomas to appear in front of the king's justices at Westminster on 12 November 1381 to show why he did not.

[12 November] in Michaelmas term 1381, at Westminster in front of Robert Belknap and his fellows, justices of the [Common] Bench
844 Ellen, the relict of Thomas of Barford, in her own person, claimed from Thomas Bowyer, of Salisbury, a third part of a messuage in Salisbury as the dower bestowed on her by her husband. Thomas Bowyer came [in front of the justices] by means of Richard Monk, his attorney. Ralph, the bishop of Salisbury, came by means of the same attorney and claimed his liberties, namely to have cognizance of the plea to be held at Salisbury in front of his bailiffs of the city. The attorney referred to a charter by means of which Henry III granted liberties to the cathedral church, to Richard, then the bishop, and the canons, and to their men; also to a charter by means of which Edward III confirmed liberties to the

bishop and canons and to the citizens of Salisbury. He explained that Edward III affirmed that, whereas the citizens brought forth pleas concerning covenants, contracts, and trespasses relating to their tenements to be determined in front of the bishop's bailiff, in future such pleas might include challenges (*calumpnia*) not before expressly included; the citizens might not be compelled to leave the city in connexion with any plea, plea of assize, or inquest unless any such plea or inquest touched the king or the commonalty of the city. The attorney brought forth a charter of Edward III, attested on 7 May 1345, to exemplify those charters, and he brought forth a charter of Richard II, dated 24 May 1378, in which the liberties of the bishop and canons, and of the citizens, were confirmed. He also brought forth the tenor of records and processes concerning pleas of land and trespasses held in front of Robert of Thorpe and his fellows, of late Edward III's justices of the [Common] Bench, in which actions the bishop had cognizance of those pleas to be held in front of his bailiffs in the city on the strength of that charter. The exemplification of which letters of exemplification was given under the Great Seal on 20 May 1366, and in Michaelmas term 1370, again in front of Robert of Thorpe and his fellows, the bishop was allowed his liberty in a plea of dower between Joan, the relict of John Peak, the demandant, and John Goodall, the defendant, concerning a third part of a messuage in Salisbury, as is shown in rot. 370 of the record for that term. The attorney further brought forth a writ of Richard II directed to the justices and attested on 26 October 1381. The king referred to the liberties granted to the bishop and canons, and to the citizens, by former kings, his confirmation of them, and the allowance made to the bishop, he acknowledged that the grantees had hitherto made use of those liberties, and he ordered the justices to allow them to continue to use them. The justices, having heard none say why the bishop should not have his liberties, and having seen the charters, letters of exemplification, allowance, and writ, confirmed them to him. The bishop should have his liberty in the current plea. Richard Monk then fixed 8 January 1382 as the day on which Ellen and Thomas should appear in front of the bishop's bailiff at Salisbury, and undertook that they would have full and speedy justice.

BOOK 4
[in the form of a list of contents taken from book 6: WSA G 23/1/214]

25 January 1369 x 24 January 1370
845 The will of John Fifield, a chaplain of the college of St. Edmund, which includes a tenement, with a cottage (*or* cottages), opposite the graveyard of St. Edmund's church devised to Walter Cheltenham, the provost, and John Chatt, a chaplain, of that college. Approved
846 A charter of Richard, a son of Richard Blick, perfected for Robert Bunt concerning a tenement in Minster Street and a tenement in Endless Street in fee, with warranty; with letters of attorney for delivering the seisin
847–8 Two writings concerning a shop in Carter Street, which John Lea held by a grant of Robert [?*rectius* Roger], of late the bishop of Salisbury: John's deed of

release perfected for John Fosbury, and a charter of John Fosbury perfected for William Guys

849 The will of Alice Holbury, the wife of Hugh Oliver, which includes a tenement in Endless Street devised to Hugh

850 A charter of Robert Beechfount, an executor of Richard Ryborough, perfected for Gilbert Whichbury concerning a corner tenement in Ironmonger Row, a corner [?shop: *cf. 434*] in Winchester Street where smiths wait, a corner shop in Butcher Row, a corner shop in Winchester Street, and a shop in the butchers' street

851–2 Two charters of Agnes, the relict, and an executor, of Gilbert Whichbury, and Nicholas Baker and William Lord, her co-executors: one perfected for John Camel, hatter, concerning two ... [shops: *cf. 882*] at the butchers' stalls, and one perfected for a younger William Tenterer concerning a rent of 13*s*. 4*d*. issuing from a tenement in Winchester Street

853 A charter of Nicholas Baker perfected for Richard Smith, tiler, concerning a messuage in Gigant Street

854 A charter of Hugh Oliver perfected for Walter Holbury concerning a tenement in Endless Street in fee simple, with warranty

855 A charter of William Dunkerton perfected for William Thatcher, a smith, concerning two ... [shops: *cf. 1674*] near a stile of the graveyard of St. Thomas's church

856 A charter of Robert Kendal perfected for Nicholas Russell and his wife Agnes concerning a corner tenement in St. Martin's Street and Gigant Street, which Robert held by a grant of the mayor and commonalty of the city, for a rent from it of 13*s*. 4*d*. a year to be paid to the mayor and commonalty, with warranty

857 The will of John Pack, of Ludgershall, which includes various tenements and burgages in Ludgershall and a tenement, with a shop (*or* shops), in Salisbury. Not approved

858 A charter of John Admot perfected for Thomas Castleton, mercer, concerning a tenement in Winchester Street, with warranty

859 A charter of Henry Pack, a chaplain, perfected for the lord Richard Boltford, a chaplain, concerning a tenement in Minster Street beside Edward Pinnock's tenement

860 A charter of Thomas Bleacher, called Play, perfected for Robert Play concerning a tenement opposite the cross where fruit and vegetables are sold, with the reversion of it

861 A charter of John Heanor, a chaplain, perfected for Thomas Redenham and his wife Agnes concerning a tenement in Gigant Street

862 A charter of Agnes, the relict, and an executor, of Gilbert Whichbury, and Nicholas Baker and William Lord, her co-executors, perfected for John Sprot, a baker, and his wife Edith concerning the reversion of a tenement in New Street

863 The will of Margery, the wife of John Ashlock, which includes various rents devised to her husband and to her son John Dyke. Approved

864 A charter of William Anger perfected for Richard Upton, a baker, concerning a tenement in Wineman Street beside Beaminster's Corner

865 The will of William of Wishford, draper, which includes several tenements devised and a rent of 30s. a year appointed to the mayor and commonalty to be received from a corner tenement in Winchester Street opposite Bull Hall. Approved

866 A charter of Richard Boltford, a chaplain, perfected for John Goodall, painter, concerning a tenement, with a shop (*or* shops), in Minster Street

867 A charter of Henry Goosebeard, of Southampton, perfected for an elder John Chandler concerning a rent of 50s. issuing from a tenement, of late Walter Idmiston's, in Endless Street in fee

868 A charter of Matthew Fernhill perfected for William Guys concerning a piece of garden land in Carter Street, measuring in length 87½ ft. and in width 12 ft., in fee simple

869 A charter of William Painter, of Salisbury, perfected for an elder John Chandler and John Basingstoke concerning a yard in Freren Street

870 A charter of Thomas Hutchins perfected for William Wilton, butcher, and his wife Joan concerning a shop in Butcher Row

871 A charter of Henry Chark and his wife Edith, the relict of William Newman, perfected for Hugh Stalbridge concerning a messuage in Endless Street

872 A charter of John Wraxall, a chaplain, perfected for John Bennett concerning a tenement, with a shop (*or* shops) and a garden (*or* gardens), in Carter Street and a corner tenement in New Street and Brown Street

873 A charter of John of Oxford, skinner, perfected for John Marshall concerning two shops in Minster Street

874 A charter of Roger Halwell, called Tanner, perfected for William Preston [?*MS. defective*] Marshall concerning a tenement, [with] a hidden yard (*or* yards), on the way to St. Martin's church

875 A charter of Robert Beechfount, an executor of Richard Ryborough, perfected for Thomas Hutchins concerning two shops in New Street

876 A charter of John Butterley, an executor of William of Wishford, perfected for Robert Godmanstone, Thomas Chaplin, and an elder William Tenterer concerning a rent of 30s. issuing from a tenement, in Winchester Street and Brown Street, opposite Bull Hall

877 The will of Thomas, a son of William at the bridge, which includes the reversion of a tenement beside the [?upper] bridge of Fisherton and the reversion of a tenement in the market place. Approved

878 An indented deed of William Anger perfected for Richard Upton concerning a tenement in Wineman Street to be held for a term of life for a rent of 5 marks a year

879 A charter of Isabel, the relict of James of Bromham, and another (*or* others), executors of James, perfected for John Portman, a furbisher, concerning the reversion of a corner tenement in Minster Street, with a release in respect of it

25 January 1370 x 24 January 1371

880 A final agreement made in the king's court between Hugh Stalbridge, plaintiff, and Henry Chark and his wife Edith, deforciants, concerning a messuage in Salisbury

881 A charter of Henry [?*rectius* Robert: *cf.* **671**] Beechfount, an executor of Richard Ryborough, perfected for Robert Play, ironmonger, concerning a rent of 12s. issuing from a tenement in Winchester Street

882 A charter of John Camel, hatter, perfected for Richard Stoke, called Carentham, concerning two shops at the butchers' stalls

883 A charter of John Chandler perfected for John Wraxall, a chaplain, concerning half a toft in Freren Street

884 A charter of Thomas Stalbridge and his wife Amice perfected for John Butterley concerning cottages in Rolleston and Brown Street

885–6 Two charters of John Mildenhall and his wife Edith perfected for Henry Stapleford: one concerning all [their] cottages, yards, and dovecots beyond the bar [of Castle Street: *cf.* **892**], and one concerning rent of 10s., with the reversion of a tenement in Culver Street, a rent of 13s. 3d. [issuing from] a tenement in Minster Street, and a tenement in St. Martin's Street

887–8 Two charters perfected for John Justice: one of Agnes Barnwell, a daughter of Adam Barnwell, concerning a tenement in New Street, and one of Nicholas Russell, butcher, concerning two cottages in Mealmonger Street

889 A charter of George Goss perfected for Robert Bunt and others concerning all his land and tenements in the city

890 A charter of Thomas Britford perfected for William Handley, tucker, concerning a yard (*or* yards) in St. Martin's Street

891 A charter of Thomas Leicester and his wife Agnes perfected for Robert Godmanstone concerning two shops in Carter Street

892 A charter of Henry Stapleford perfected for John Mildenhall, his wife Edith, and Edith's heirs and assigns concerning all [his] land, tenements, yards, and dovecots beyond the bar of Castle Street, and rent and the reversion [of a tenement] in Culver Street

25 January 1371 x 24 January 1372

893 A charter of John Butterley, an executor of William Wishford, with the assent of another (*or* other) executor(s), perfected for Richard Upton, a baker, concerning a tenement in Wineman Street

894 A charter of John Portman, a furbisher, perfected for William Dunkerton and Isabel, a daughter of John Marshall, concerning a corner tenement in Minster Street

895 A charter of Robert Beechfount perfected for Robert Play and his wife Margaret concerning a plot of land in Culver Street

896 A charter of William Hoare perfected for Nicholas Baker concerning a corner tenement at the butchers' stalls and Winchester Street

897 A charter of Maud, a daughter of Nicholas Baker, perfected for Nicholas concerning two tenements, one in Winchester Street and the other in Gigant Street

898 A charter of Thomas Salisbury, kt., perfected for Reynold Love, of London, and William Wild, a chaplain, concerning all his land and tenements in Salisbury and its suburbs, Bemerton, Quidhampton, and Fisherton; with letters of attorney

899 A charter of Thomas Erlestoke, a chaplain, and Andrew Stratford perfected for Reynold Love concerning a tenement in Minster Street

900 A charter of John Farnborough and Thomas Friday perfected for Adam Ludwell concerning a tenement in Minster Street

901 A charter of John Cousen, weaver, and his wife Alice perfected for John Stallington concerning a rent of 10s. issuing from a tenement in Minster Street

902 The will of Henry Sutton, dyer, which includes a tenement in Minster Street devised to his wife Joan and his children. Approved

903 The will of Alice Barnaby, the wife of Richard Shearer, which includes a tenement in Minster Street, and a tenement in Culver Street, to be sold by her executors. Approved

904 A charter of John Taverner, an executor of Alice Barnaby, perfected for Richard Leach concerning two tenements in Minster Street

905 A charter of Henry Pope and his wife Cecily perfected for Thomas Chaplin concerning a messuage, with a yard (*or* yards), in Freren Street

906–7 Two writings perfected for John Bennett: one of Robert Scriven concerning his estate for a term of life in a tenement in Minster Street, and one of Thomas Hindon concerning a yard (*or* yards) in Drake Hall Street

908 A deed of release of John Stallington perfected for Thomas Chaplin concerning a tenement opposite the market place, two cottages in Scots Lane, and a rent of 20s. issuing [from premises] of late John Sorrel's opposite the market place

909 A deed of William Hurn, a dyer, perfected for William Scamell and his wife Joan concerning his estate for a term of life in a tenement opposite the market place where grains are sold

910 The will of William Purser, which includes a shop (*or* shops) in Minster Street. Approved

911 A charter of William Scamell and his wife Joan perfected for William in the hurn and his wife Joan concerning a tenement opposite the market place [where grains are sold] for a term of life and a certain rent to be paid from it

912–13 Two writings of Nicholas Baker perfected for Thomas Hindon, a citizen of Salisbury: a charter concerning a rent of 10s. issuing from a tenement in Carter Street, and a deed of release concerning that rent

914–15 Two writings concerning a corner tenement in Wineman Street: the will of Joyce Lutwich, who devised it to his wife Margaret to enfeoff Richard Upton, baker, in it on a condition, and a charter of Margaret perfected for Richard

916–17 Two charters perfected for Thomas Hindon: one of Agnes, the relict of Gilbert Whichbury, and another (*or* others), executors of Gilbert, concerning a cottage (*or* cottages) in Drake Hall Street, and one of Oliver of Harnham concerning a yard (*or* yards) there

918 A charter of Thomas Gilbert, John Sexhampcote, a chaplain, and William Lord perfected for Nicholas Longstock and his wife Agnes concerning three tenements, one in Butcher Row, one towards St. Martin's church, and the other in Minster Street

919 A charter of Roger Tanner perfected for an elder John New concerning a tenement towards St. Martin's church
920 A charter of Maud, the relict of Richard Salter, perfected for Robert Play concerning two tenements in New Street
921 A charter of William Montagu perfected for a younger William Tenterer concerning a yard (*or* yards) in Winchester Street within William Montagu's tenement
922 The will of William Stanley, which includes five cottages in Gigant Street near Nuggeston. Not approved
923 The will of William at the bridge, dyer, which includes a tenement in which he dwelt
924 A charter of Thomas Hindon perfected for David Fletcher concerning a cottage (*or* cottages) in Drake Hall Street, a rent of 13*s*. 4*d*. issuing from a cottage (*or* cottages), and a piece of a yard, in Freren Street for a term of years, the reversion of the cottage(s) and the piece of a yard, and another (*or* other) cottage(s) there
925 The will of William Wootton, which includes a tenement in Minster Street and several other tenements. Approved
926 A charter of John Chatt and John Heanor, chaplains, perfected for John Palmer concerning a tenement and a cottage (*or* cottages) opposite the graveyard of St. Edmund's church
927 A charter of Robert Play perfected for Nicholas Baker concerning a tenement in Winchester Street and two shops in Ironmonger Row
928 A charter of John Butterley, an executor of William Wishford, perfected for Nicholas Woodhill concerning a corner tenement in Wineman Street and Brown Street

25 January 1373 x 24 January 1374
929–30 Two writings perfected for John of Upton concerning a messuage, with two shops, in New Street: a charter of John Somborne and his wife Edith and a deed of release of John Somborne, an executor of Richard Salter
931 A charter of William Agodeshalf perfected for Agnes Burden concerning a cottage, with a yard, in Gigant Street
932 A charter of William Bleacher perfected for Robert Play and his sons John and Thomas concerning a corner tenement in Endless Street and a cottage beside it
933 A charter of Nicholas Baker perfected for Robert Play and his wife Margaret concerning a tenement in Winchester Street and two shops in Ironmonger Row
934–5 Two charters perfected for John Bennett: one of John Upton concerning a messuage, with two shops, in New Street, and one of Nicholas Bonham, John of Upton, and others concerning a cottage (*or* cottages) beside a gate of the Franciscans and concerning another (*or* other) cottage(s) there
936 A charter of Hugh Stalbridge, butcher, perfected for Robert of Godmanstone concerning a tenement in Endless Street
937 A deed of release of George Goss, an executor of John Richman, perfected for Robert Kirtlingstoke concerning a tenement in Wineman Street

938–9 Two writings concerning a tenement towards St. Martin's church: a charter of John New, William Tenterer, Thomas Bridgehampton, and Nicholas Baker, and a deed of John Justice perfected for John Lea concerning a rent of 2s. issuing from it

940 A charter of Nicholas Baker perfected for Robert Play and his wife Margaret concerning four shops in Ironmonger Row

25 January 1374 x 24 January 1375

941 A charter of Hugh Winterbourne perfected for Robert Pope and his wife Maud concerning a tenement in Minster Street

942–3 Two charters perfected for Thomas Sexhampcote: one of John Palmer, a tailor, concerning a corner yard, with a rack (*or* racks), opposite the graveyard of St. Edmund's church, and one of John New, tanner, concerning a tenement in Scots Lane

944 A charter of Adam Ludwell perfected for John Pain, a chaplain, and John Wick concerning a tenement in Minster Street opposite the market place where grains are sold

945 A charter of Cecily, the wife of Adam Ludwell, perfected for William Godmanstone and his wife Margaret concerning a tenement in Winchester Street and conjoined shops in Brown Street and Gigant Street

946 A charter of Robert Beechfount, an executor of Richard Ryborough, perfected for Cecily, the relict of Nicholas Chardstock, concerning two conjoined tenements in St. Martin's Street

947 A charter of Nicholas Baker and William Lord, executors of Gilbert Whichbury, perfected for John Baker, grocer, concerning a tenement in Winchester Street beside Henry Bergh's corner tenement

948 A charter of Alice Farley, a daughter and heir of Richard Farley, perfected for Thomas Erlestoke and William Chanter concerning two tenements in New Street

949 A charter of John Dinton, butcher, perfected for Hugh Winterbourne concerning two cottages in Gigant Street towards St. Edmund's church

950 A charter of Henry Stapleford perfected for John Beeton, draper, concerning a tenement in Castle Street

951 A charter of Emme, the relict of Nicholas Astbury, perfected for Nicholas Woodhill concerning four cottages in Culver Street

952 A charter of John Sivier and his wife Emme, the relict of Richard Cook, perfected for an elder John Chandler concerning a yard in Freren Street

953 A charter of Henry Pope and his wife Cecily perfected for John Creed and his wife Sarah concerning a yard (*or* yards), with a rack, in Chipper Street

954 The will of Thomas Hutchins, which includes three shops in New Street and a tenement in Endless Street devised to his wife Cecily for life, and after her death to his daughters; also a rent of 10s. in Pot Row to be sold. Approved

955 A charter of Cecily, the relict, and an executor, of Thomas Hutchins, perfected for Richard Leach concerning a rent of 10s. issuing from a tenement in Pot Row

956 A charter of Robert Bunt, William Warmwell, and Robert Deverill perfected for George Goss concerning all the land and tenements in Salisbury which they held by his grant

957 A charter of Henry Pope and his wife Cecily perfected for John Pope and John Nalder concerning a corner tenement in Endless Street and a rent of 8*s.* issuing from a tenement in Wineman Street

958 A deed of release of John Doder, a son of Agnes Doder, perfected for William Warmwell concerning all John's land and tenements in Salisbury

959 A charter of John Warneford perfected for Robert Arnold concerning a rent of 13*s.* 4*d.* issuing from a tenement in Endless Street, with the reversion of the tenement

960 A charter of John Heytesbury and his wife Alice perfected for John Ball concerning a tenement in New Street

961 The will of John Wick, which includes a tenement in Castle Street devised to Adam Ludwell in fee simple

962 A charter of William Ogbourne, a clerk, perfected for William Dunkerton and William Lord concerning a tenement in Winchester Street and two cottages, with a yard (*or* yards), in Culver Street

963 A charter of William Dunkerton and William Lord perfected for John Butterley concerning a tenement in Winchester Street, a yard (*or* yards) opposite the bishop of Salisbury's land held in villeinage in the Old Town, and two cottages in Culver Street

964–5 Two writings concerning a shop in Endless Street: a deed of release of John Jarvis, a brother of Thomas Jarvis, perfected for Robert Dowding, and a charter of Robert perfected for Richard Pope, a chaplain

966 A charter of Thomas Erlestoke and John Wraxall, chaplains, perfected for Thomas Shove concerning a corner tenement in New Street and Brown Street

967 A charter of Thomas Burford perfected for John Butterley concerning a rent of 53*s.* 4*d.* issuing from Adam Gallon's tenement in Wineman Street, with the reversion of the tenement

968 The will of John Oxford, which includes a tenement opposite the market place and rent and several other tenements in the city [and] in Wells. Not approved

969 A charter of John of Wylye, a son and heir of Adam Wylye, perfected for David Fletcher concerning a tenement in St. Martin's Street

970 A charter of David Fletcher perfected for a younger William Tenterer concerning two shops in New Street

971 A charter of Thomas of Erlestoke and John Dean, chaplains, perfected for John Baron and his wife Emme concerning a corner tenement [opposite the high cross: *cf. 806*] where fruit and other victuals are sold

972 A charter of John Baron and his wife Emme perfected for Thomas Erlestoke, a chaplain, and John Buddle concerning a cottage (*or* cottages) in Mealmonger Street

973 A charter of [Thomas] of Erlestoke, a chaplain, an executor of John Essington, taverner, perfected for David Fletcher concerning a messuage in Drake Hall Street

974 A charter of Walter Ryborough and his wife Joan, an executor of William Wootton, and another (*or* other) executors of William perfected for William

Warmwell and William Lord concerning a corner tenement, with shops, in New Street and Gigant Street, a tenement in Nuggeston, and a tenement in Minster Street

975 The will of Robert of Godmanstone, which includes several tenements, as much concerning the appropriation of Lime's Corner as another appropriation. Approved

976 The will of John Marshall, which includes various tenements devised to his wife for life. After her death they should remain to his son Thomas and his issue. Approved

977 A charter of John Butterley, an executor of William Wishford, with the assent of another (*or* other) executor(s), perfected for Thomas Sexhampcote concerning a tenement in Scots Lane

978 A charter of Nicholas Russell and his wife Agnes perfected for William Woodway concerning a corner tenement in St. Martin's Street and Gigant Street

25 January 1375 x 24 January 1376
979 A charter of William Knight perfected for William Lord concerning a toft in Freren Street

980 The will of John Bennett, a canon of Wells, which includes a tenement called Cavenasser's Corner. Not approved

981 A charter of Honour, the relict of Edward Longenough, perfected for Nicholas Taylor, draper, concerning a cottage towards St. Martin's church

982 A charter of Roger of Kilmeston perfected for Thomas Sexhampcote concerning five cottages in Gigant Street

983 An indented charter of John Plummer, of Wilton, perfected for William P..., weaver, concerning a tenement in Mealmonger Street for a rent to be paid to John for ever

984 A charter of John Taverner, an executor of Alice Barnaby, perfected for Thomas Boyton, bowyer, concerning a yard (*or* yards) in Culver Street

985 A charter of Margaret Woodborough perfected for Joan Woodborough for the release of a tenement in Endless Street

986 A charter of Joan, the relict, and an executor, of Robert of Godmanstone, and other executors of Robert perfected for John Lea and others concerning two shops at the fishermen's stalls

987 A charter of Nicholas Hamish, a chaplain, perfected for Edmund Penstone concerning a tenement in New Street

988 The will of Richard Pope, a chaplain, which includes two shops in Endless Street. The seisin of them was released, as it is said, by means of Robert Arnold, as is shown there in the approval.

989 A charter of John Mildenhall and his wife Edith perfected for John Upton, John Chandler, and others concerning a tenement in St. Martin's Street

990 The will of John Chalke, a clothier, which includes all his land and tenements devised to his son John and that John's issue, with remainder in default of such issue to the elder John's daughter Emme and her issue, and in default of such issue to the elder John's executors to be sold. Approved

991 A charter of John Halliday, a skinner, an executor of John Chalke, perfected for David Fletcher concerning all [John Chalke's] land and tenements in Salisbury
992 A charter of David Stook, called Fletcher, perfected for William Warmwell concerning rent of 13s. 4d. issuing from cottages in Freren Street, with the reversion of the cottages
993 A charter of Christine Goldston, an executor of William Goldston, perfected for Thomas Boyton, bowyer, concerning a garden in Freren Street
994 A charter of Walter Abbot perfected for an elder John Chandler concerning a tenement beside the upper bridge of Fisherton
995 A charter of John Stallington, a clerk, perfected for Thomas Chaplin concerning a rent of 10s. issuing from a tenement in Minster Street

25 January 1376 x 24 January 1377
996 A charter of John Cousen, and his wife Alice, perfected for Thomas Chaplin concerning a tenement in Minster Street
997 A charter of Richard Ellis, the parson of Sherfield church, perfected for John Ettshall, cordwainer, and his wife Maud concerning a tenement in New Street
998 The will of an elder William Tenterer, which includes a tenement beside the lower bridge of Fisherton devised to his wife
999 A charter of Adam Dyer and his wife Beatrice perfected for John Bennett, John Fowle, and others concerning rent of 19s. issuing from various tenements
1000 A charter of Alice Gromville, of Battlesden, perfected for Robert Kirtlingstoke concerning a tenement in Endless Street
1001 The will of Stephen Jay, which includes a single tenement. Where it stands was not mentioned when the will was approved.
1002 A charter of John Wade, brewer, and his wife Agnes perfected for William Godmanstone and his wife Margaret concerning cottages, with a yard (*or* yards), in Endless Street and a piece of a yard there
1003–4 Two charters concerning a tenement, with three shops, in Minster Street: one of Adam Ludwell perfected for Robert Bunt, and one of Robert perfected for Thomas Deverill and his wife Agnes
1005 A charter of William Lord, a son and heir of William Lord, perfected for John Harnham, cordwainer, and his wife Agnes concerning a shop
1006–7 Two writings of Henry Pope and his wife Edith, the relict of Stephen Jay, perfected for William Puddlemill: a deed concerning a tenement in Gigant Street for a term of life, and a charter concerning the reversion of it
1008 A charter of Thomas Boyton, bowyer, perfected for John Stoke and his wife Margaret concerning a tenement in Winchester Street
1009–10 Two writings of Christine, the relict of William Goldston, perfected for Thomas Boyton: a deed concerning an estate for a term of life in a tenement in Winchester Street, and, as an executor of William, a charter concerning the reversion of that tenement
1011 The will of Agnes, the relict of John of Woodford, which includes various rents and cottages in St. Martin's Street. Approved
1012–14 Three writings concerning a yard, with a rack (*or* racks), in Freren Street:

an indenture of John Chilton perfected for William Ashley for a term of life, a deed of William perfected for Thomas Focket concerning his estate in it, and a deed of release of John perfected for Thomas

1015 A charter of John Creed and his wife Sarah perfected for Hugh Winterbourne concerning a yard (*or* yards), with a rack, in Chipper Street

1016 A deed of Christine Goldston perfected for John Stoke and his wife Margaret concerning her estate in a tenement in Winchester Street

1017 A charter of Isabel Cole, an executor of John Cole, and another (*or* other) executor(s) of John perfected for Thomas Hindon concerning a cottage (*or* cottages) in Gigant Street

1018 A charter of Walter Abbot perfected for John Farnborough and his wife Alice concerning a tenement in Minster Street

1019 A charter of Robert Beechfount, an executor of Richard Ryborough, perfected for William Godmanstone and his wife Margaret concerning a shop (*or* shops) in Minster Street near the graveyard of St. Thomas's church

1020 A deed of Dominic Uphill perfected for Roger Fakenham and others concerning a tenement in Minster Street

1021 A deed of Nicholas Baker perfected for William Lord concerning a tenement in Winchester Street and a tenement in Gigant Street

1022 A charter of Walter Skilling, a chaplain, perfected for Simon Tredinnick concerning a yard (*or* yards) in Freren Street; with letters of attorney

1023 A charter of Gillian, the relict of an elder William Tenterer, perfected for Thomas Erlestoke concerning a tenement beside the [lower] bridge of Fisherton

1024 A charter of Thomas Bridgehampton perfected for Thomas Focket concerning a tenement in St. Martin's Street, with letters of attorney for delivering the seisin, and a yard in Freren Street

1025 The will of a younger William Tenterer, which includes several tenements and rent. Approved

1026 The will of John Basingstoke, which includes a tenement in Brown Street. Approved

1027 The will of Henry Stapleford, which includes several tenements. Approved

25 January 1377 x 21 June 1377

1028 A charter of Nicholas Baker perfected for William Hoare concerning a corner tenement at the butchers' stalls in fee simple

1029 A charter of William Hoare perfected for William Lord concerning a tenement in Winchester Street and a tenement in Gigant Street

1030 The will of John Winterbourne, carpenter, which includes a tenement in Brown Street. Approved

1031 The will of Agnes, the wife of Hugh Hoare, which includes several tenements and cottages. Approved

1032 A charter of William Handley, tucker, perfected for William Puddlemill concerning a yard (*or* yards), with a rack, in Freren Street

1033 A charter of Nicholas Baker and William Lord, executors of Gilbert Whichbury, perfected for John Fowle concerning rent, with the reversion of a tenement in New Street

1034–5 Two charters of Robert Beechfount, an executor of Richard Ryborough: one perfected for John Webb, of Woodlands, concerning a tenement, with a shop (*or* shops), in Brown Street and a piece of a yard, and one perfected for John Ball concerning a corner tenement, with a yard (*or* yards), and a tenement in Winchester Street

1036–7 Two writings perfected for Robert Kirtlingstoke: a charter of Edith Richman concerning a rent of 14*s*. issuing from a tenement in Wineman Street, and a deed of release of George Goss and William Buck, executors of John Richman, concerning a tenement in Endless Street

1038 The will of William Montagu, which includes a tenement in Winchester Street to be sold immediately by his executors. Approved

1039 A charter of Margaret Coleman and Gilbert Skinner, executors of William Montagu, perfected for John Ball concerning the tenement mentioned above

1040–1 Two charters perfected for John Lea and John Buddle: one of Hugh Hoare concerning a corner tenement in Gigant Street, and one of Hugh Hoare and Adam Gore, executors of Hugh's wife Agnes, concerning the reversion of a tenement in Wineman Street

1042 The will of Robert Kendal, which includes a tenement in Winchester Street and a garden in St. Martin's Street. Approved

1043 The will of John Amesbury, which includes several tenements. Approved

22 June 1377 x 21 June 1378

1044 A charter of John Dyke perfected for John Barrett concerning a tenement in St. Martin's Street

1045–7 Three charters of John New: one perfected for William Buckland and his wife Joan concerning a tenement in Brown Street, one perfected for Joan Hunt concerning a shop in Wheeler Row, and one perfected for Adam Teffont and his wife Parnel concerning a corner tenement towards St. Martin's church

1048 A charter of Thomas Erlestoke perfected for John Mower concerning a tenement towards the lower bridge of Fisherton

1049 A final agreement reached in the king's court between John Wallop, draper, and Roger Wallop and his wife Joan concerning a tenement in Salisbury

1050–1 Two charters concerning a tenement in Castle Street: one of Nicholas Longstock and his wife Agnes perfected for John Wallop concerning the estate of Joan [?Wallop] in it, and one of John perfected for Nicholas and Agnes

1052–3 Two charters of Robert Bunt perfected for William Lord: one concerning his estate in a tenement in Minster Street, and one, as an executor of his wife Agnes, concerning the reversion of that tenement

1054 A charter of John Boor, a chaplain, and John Camel perfected for Robert Langford concerning 'all land and tenements'

1055 A charter of Thomas Boyton, bowyer, perfected for John Fowle concerning a yard (*or* yards) in Culver Street

1056 A charter of John Swift, a chaplain, perfected for Richard Cormell and his wife Agnes concerning a tenement in Carter Street

1057–8 Two charters perfected for Walter Ryborough and John Camel, hatter: one of Bartholomew Durkin, goldsmith, and his wife Edith concerning an estate in six messuages, four shops, and a dovecot, and a yearly rent in Salisbury, and one, in the name of a release, of John Butterley concerning the tenements and messuages

1059 A charter of Robert Langford perfected for Thomas Chaplin concerning a corner tenement, with a shop (*or* shops), in Castle Street; with letters for delivering the seisin

1060–2 Three writings concerning a tenement in Winchester Street which was of late William Montagu's: a charter of John Ball perfected for John Butterley, a charter of Gilbert Skinner perfected for John Butterley and his wife Alice concerning a rent of 20s. issuing from it, and a deed of release of Gilbert perfected for John and Alice concerning a rent of 13s. 4d. issuing from it

1063 The will of Thomas Newman, which includes a tenement in Brown Street and an estate in various tenements and shops. Approved

1064 A charter of William Woodway perfected for Thomas Focket concerning a corner tenement in St. Martin's Street

1065 A deed of John Ingram, of Andover, perfected for John Wansey, of Andover, concerning a tenement opposite the market place

1066 A deed of attorney of John Sand and his wife Joan perfected for Richard Monk and John Still concerning the manor of West Tytherley and messuages and rent in Southampton, Shirley, and elsewhere

1067 A deed of grant of John Butterley, an executor of William Wishford, perfected for John Admot concerning a tenement in Winchester Street

1068–9 Two writings perfected for Thomas Shove concerning a tenement in New Street: a charter of Robert Play, ironmonger, and a deed of release of William Lord

1070 The will of Robert Langford which includes a tenement in Castle Street and another (*or* other) tenement(s) in the city. Approved

1071 A charter of Agnes, the relict of Robert Langford, and John Camel, executors of Robert, perfected for John Wallop, draper, concerning a tenement in Castle Street

22 June 1378 x 21 June 1379

1072 A charter of William Lord perfected for John Cole and his wife Isabel concerning various tenements in the city

1073 A charter of Thomas Boyton, bowyer, perfected for John Butterley concerning rent, with the reversion of a tenement (*or* tenements) and a shop (*or* shops) in New Street

1074–5 Two charters perfected for William Lord: one of John Stoke, an executor of his wife Margaret, concerning a tenement in Brown Street, and one of John Cole concerning various tenements in the city

1076 A charter of William Lord perfected for John Stoke concerning a tenement in Brown Street of late John Winterbourne's

1077 An indented charter of John Stoke perfected for William Cockerell and his wife Alice concerning tenements in Winchester Street and Brown Street for a rent of 5 marks a year

1078 A charter of John Cole and his wife Isabel perfected for Simon Bunt and his wife Alice concerning a corner tenement in Winchester Street and cottages in Culver Street for a rent to be paid from them

1079 A charter of Nicholas Baker perfected for Robert Play and his wife Margaret concerning two shops, in Butcher Row and Winchester Street, and rent, with the reversion of another shop there

1080 A charter of John Cole perfected for Adam Ward, tucker, concerning a yard (*or* yards), with a rack (*or* racks), in Nuggeston for a rent to be paid to John

1081 A charter of William Ashley perfected for Robert Hindon and his wife Isabel concerning a tenement in St. Martin's Street

1082 The will of John Handley, which includes all [his] tenements in Salisbury devised to William Handley. Approved [*added*: and in Old Sarum]

1083 A charter of Nicholas Baker and William Lord, executors of Gilbert Whichbury, perfected for John Salisbury concerning a tenement in New Street

1084 A charter of John Courtman and his wife Margery perfected for John Lea concerning rent of 100s. from various tenements in Salisbury

1085 A charter of John Lea perfected for John Courtman and his wife Margery concerning a tenement in Winchester Street and a cottage in Gigant Street

1086 The will of John Cole, which includes several tenements, cottages, and yards. Approved

1087 An indented charter of William Warmwell perfected for Thomas Dunball concerning a tenement in Nuggeston for a rent from it to be paid to William

1088 An indented charter of Isabel Cole perfected for Adam White concerning a yard in Gigant Street, on a corner, for a rent to be paid to her

1089 A charter of Agnes, the relict of John Bodenham, perfected for John Newman, cardmaker, concerning a tenement in Carter Street

1090–2 Three writings of Thomas Britford and others, executors of John Oxford: a charter perfected for Thomas Shove concerning the reversion of a tenement opposite the market place, a charter perfected for John Wallop, draper, concerning the reversion of a corner tenement in Gigant Street, and a deed perfected for John Shove concerning the reversion of a tenement in Winchester Street

1093 A charter of Robert Bunt, an executor of his wife Agnes, perfected for Thomas Britford, John Upton, and others concerning a rent of 20s. issuing from a tenement opposite the cross called Powell's Corner

1094 A charter of Thomas Sexhampcote perfected for William Lord and Simon Bunt concerning a corner tenement in Wineman Street and Culver Street

1095 A charter of Thomas Hindon perfected for David Fletcher concerning a tenement in Wineman Street; with letters for delivering the seisin

1096 A charter of Agnes Bodenham perfected for William Lord concerning a tenement in Gigant Street

1097–8 Two writings of Agnes of Oxford: a deed perfected for David Fletcher and Thomas Cook, a chaplain, concerning her estate in all [her] tenements in Salisbury and elsewhere, and a charter perfected for John Butterley and Thomas

Erlestoke concerning the reversion of all [her] land, tenements, cottages, and rent in Salisbury and Wells

1099 A deed of David Fletcher and Thomas Cook, a chaplain, perfected for John Butterley and Thomas Erlestoke concerning all the land and tenements which they held by a grant of Agnes of Oxford, by means of an attornment to John and Thomas

1100 A deed of Thomas Shove perfected for John Butterley and Thomas Erlestoke concerning a tenement opposite the market place, by means of an attornment

1101 A deed of John Wallop, draper, perfected for John Butterley and Thomas Erlestoke concerning a corner tenement in Gigant Street, by means of an attornment

1102 A charter of Isabel Cole perfected for William Lord concerning rent, and the reversion of a yard (*or* yards) in Culver Street

1103–4 Two charters perfected for William Lord: one of John Chandler concerning a tenement in Gigant Street beside William Guys's tenement, and one of John Wylye concerning a tenement in New Street

1105 A charter of Hugh Gundy and his wife Alice perfected for Nicholas Purser concerning a tenement in Minster Street

1106 A charter of John Chandler perfected for William Godmanstone concerning a yard (*or* yards) in Freren Street

1107 A charter of Robert Reading and his wife Cecily perfected for Bartholomew Durkin and William Lord concerning a tenement in Minster Street

1108–9 Two charters concerning a tenement in Chipper Lane and two cottages in Endless Street: one of the lord John Heanor, a chaplain, and John Little perfected for John Mower and his wife Cecily, and one of John Amesbury perfected for John Heanor and John Little

1110 A charter of William Hoare perfected for William Godmanstone concerning [Chantrell's Corner: *cf.* *1727*], a corner tenement at the end of Butchery

1111 A charter of John Gatcombe and his wife Joan perfected for Robert Arnold and Simon Bunt concerning two cottages in Chipper Street

1112 A charter of Agnes, the relict of John Hacker, perfected for Robert Arnold and Simon Bunt concerning a yard (*or* yards) in Endless Street; with letters for delivering the seisin

1113 A charter of Simon Tredinnick perfected for Thomas Cook, a chaplain, concerning a yard (*or* yards) in Freren Street

1114 The will of William Anger, which includes a rent of 5 marks, devised to his son Walter, issuing from a tenement of Richard Upton in Wineman Street. Approved

1115–16 Two charters perfected for John Lea and others: one of Joan, the relict of Robert Godmanstone, concerning her estate in a tenement called Lime's Corner opposite the fishermens' stalls, and one of Joan and others, executors of Robert, concerning the reversion of the tenement

1117–18 Two charters of Thomas Erlestoke and Thomas Britford, executors of William Costard, perfected for Richard Leach: one concerning a shop in Minster Street, and one concerning another shop in Minster Street

1119 A charter of David Fletcher perfected for Robert Body concerning a tenement in Wineman Street

1120 A charter of William Bleacher perfected for Robert Play concerning a cottage in Endless Street

1121 The will of John Luckham, which includes a tenement, with an empty plot of land, in Brown Street. Not approved

1122 A charter of John Lea, John Jewell, and John Still, a chaplain, perfected for Joan Godmanstone concerning a tenement opposite the fishermens' stalls

1123 A charter of Agnes, the relict of John Hacker, perfected for Robert Arnold and Simon Bunt concerning a yard (*or* yards) in Endless Street

1124 The will of Nicholas Purser, which includes a tenement, with a shop, in Minster Street and a garden in Freren Street

1125–7 Three writings concerning two tenements in Minster Street near the bar: a deed of Thomas Sexhampcote and his wife Joan perfected for Robert Sexhampcote concerning the estate which they held in them, a deed of Thomas and Joan, an executor of Henry Stapleford, and of John Drury, Joan's co-executor, concerning the reversion of them, and a charter of Robert perfected for Thomas, Joan, and Thomas's heirs and assigns

1128 A charter of Robert Arnold and Simon Bunt perfected for John Gatcombe concerning two cottages in Chipper Street

22 June 1379 x 21 June 1380

1129 A deed of release of Simon Bunt perfected for Robert Arnold concerning a yard (*or* yards) in Endless Street

1130 The will of Agnes Bodenham, which includes several tenements and rent. Approved

1131 A charter of Hugh Winterbourne, butcher, perfected for Robert Woodborough concerning a yard (*or* yards), with a rack, in Chipper Street

1132 A charter of Christine Friend perfected for Thomas Focket concerning a portion of an empty plot of land in Gigant Street

1133 A charter of Thomas of Erlestoke perfected for Robert Way concerning two shops in Minster Street

1134 A deed of Thomas Erlestoke and William Dunkerton perfected for Roger Stapleford and his wife Lucy concerning a rent of 20s. issuing from a tenement in Minster Street beyond the bar, with the reversion of the tenement

1135 The will of Thomas Britford, which includes several tenements, cottages, and rent. Approved

1136 A charter of Gilbert at the brook, skinner, perfected for John Stoke concerning 13s. 4d. issuing from a tenement in Minster Street

1137 A charter of Thomas Erlestoke perfected for William at the hurn concerning a rent of 40s. issuing from a tenement opposite the market place, with the reversion of the tenement

1138 A charter of Thomas Burford perfected for John Butterley concerning a tenement in Winchester Street, a cottage, with a yard, beyond the bar [opposite the bishop of Salisbury's land held in villeinage in the Old Town: *cf. 1155*], and two cottages in Culver Street; with letters of attorney for delivering the seisin

1139 The will of Margaret, the wife of John Pilling, which includes a tenement opposite the market place. Approved

1140 The will of Joan, the relict of Robert of Godmanstone, which includes several tenements and rent. Approved

1141 The will of Roger of Kilmeston, which includes a tenement in Castle Street. Approved

1142 A charter of Agnes, the relict of Simon Tinker, perfected for William of Godmanstone concerning a yard at the end of Endless Street

22 June 1380 x 21 June 1381

1143 A charter of Thomas Erlestoke and John Chandler, executors of Joan, the wife [?relict: *cf.* **1140**] of Robert Godmanstone, perfected for Thomas Boyton concerning three shops in Butcher Row

1144 A charter of Thomas Erlestoke and Richard Jewell, executors of Robert Godmanstone, perfected for Richard Leach concerning a tenement beside Agnes Bruton's tenement in Winchester Street

1145 A charter of Robert, a son of William Godmanstone, perfected for his father concerning two cottages, with a rack (*or* racks), in Gigant Street

1146 A charter of Thomas Erlestoke and Richard Jewell, executors of Robert Godmanstone, perfected for John Lea concerning a tenement in Winchester Street and two shops in Carter Street

1147 A charter of Thomas Erlestoke and John Chandler, executors of Joan, the wife [?relict: *cf.* **1140**] of Robert Godmanstone, perfected for John Lea concerning a tenement in Carter Street

1148 A charter of Nicholas Woodhill perfected for David Fletcher concerning a cottage (*or* cottages) in Culver Street; with letters of attorney for delivering the seisin

1149 A charter of Thomas Boyton perfected for Nicholas Purser concerning a garden in Freren Street; with letters for delivering the seisin

1150 A charter of George Goss and his wife Alice perfected for William Warmwell concerning a tenement in Gigant Street

1151 A charter of Richard Leach perfected for Nicholas Taylor concerning a shop in Minster Street

1152 A charter of John Deakin, of North Widhill, and his wife Edith perfected for Robert Woodborough and his wife Alice concerning a tenement in Castle Street

1153 The will of Richard at the bridge, dyer, which includes a tenement beside [the upper] bridge of Fisherton. Approved

1154 A charter of Thomas Deverill and his wife Agnes perfected for John Chandler and Thomas Deverill concerning a tenement opposite the market place where grains are sold

1155 A deed of grant and release of Walter Cooper and his wife Alice perfected for John Butterley concerning a tenement in Winchester Street, a cottage, with a yard, beyond the bar, opposite the bishop of Salisbury's land held in villeinage in the Old Town, and two cottages, with a yard, in Culver Street

1156 A charter of John Mildenhall perfected for John Chandler, John Drury, and John Wells concerning two cottages in Castle Street beyond the bar

1157 A charter of William Buck, a chaplain, perfected for John Wallop, draper, concerning a tenement in Scots Lane

1158–9 Two writings concerning a tenement in Winchester Street: letters of attorney of William Cockerell perfected for Simon Bunt and others, to surrender it to the use of John Stoke, tailor, and a charter of William and his wife Alice perfected for John

1160 A charter of John Stoke perfected for John Wallop, draper, concerning the tenement mentioned above and rent of 53s. 4d. a year for the life of John [?Stoke]

22 June 1381 x 21 June 1382

1161–2 Two charters of William Warmwell perfected for Thomas Focket: one concerning a tenement in St. Martin's Street paying a rent of 15s. a year for ever, and one concerning a toft in Shit Lane paying a rent of 16d. a year for ever

1163–4 Two writings concerning two shops at the fishermens' stalls: letters of attorney of Thomas Erlestoke, a chaplain, an executor of Joan, the wife [?relict: *cf. 1140*] of Robert Godmanstone, to deliver the seisin to Thomas Boyton, bowyer, and a charter of Thomas Erlestoke and John Chandler, executors of Joan, perfected for that same Thomas

1165 A charter of John Board, carpenter, perfected for Thomas Focket concerning a portion of a yard lying in St. Martin's Street

1166 The will of Thomas of Bridgehampton, which includes two tenements and seven cottages. Approved

1167 A charter of John Dean and John Dean [?*rectius* Farley: *cf. 1205*], chaplains, perfected for John Iwerne, a chaplain, concerning a rent of 10s. a year issuing from a tenement of late Roger Kilmeston's in Minster Street

1168 A charter of William Bleacher, of Stoke Farthing (*Stokeverdoun*), perfected for Robert Play concerning a tenement in Endless Street

1169 A charter of Thomas Chaplin perfected for John Preston concerning a yard (*or* yards) in Freren Street

1170 A charter of John Prout and his wife Agnes perfected for John Drury concerning a tenement in Minster Street beyond the bar

1171–2 Two writings of Adam Courtier and his wife Agnes, the relict, and an executor, of Robert Langford, perfected for Richard Whiteparish: a charter concerning Agnes's estate in a tenement in Minster Street, and a deed concerning the reversion of the tenement

1173 A charter of John Drury perfected for John Prout and his wife Agnes concerning a tenement in Minster Street beyond the bar

1174–5 Two writings of John Barford, a son of Thomas Barford: a charter perfected for Thomas Burford concerning all [his] land, tenements, rent, and reversions in Salisbury, and letters of attorney perfected for William Lord and Robert Arnold for delivering the seisin to Thomas

1176 The will of John Stockton, of Wilton, which includes various little meadows in Wilton and rent in Salisbury

1177 The will of Richard Hawes, hellier, which includes various tenements in Salisbury. Approved

1178 A charter of John Bodenham perfected for John at the heath and Stephen Brown concerning a garden (*or* gardens), beyond the bar, towards St. Martin's church

1179 A charter of John Teffont perfected for Thomas Focket and his wife Margaret concerning three cottages in New Street beside a ditch

1180 The will of John Fosbury, which includes a tenement in St. Martin's Street and a cottage (*or* cottages) on a corner there. Not approved

1181 A charter of Nicholas Longstock and his wife Agnes perfected for an elder John Salisbury, grocer, concerning a toft towards St. Martin's church

1182–3 Two writings of Robert, a son of Henry Smith, perfected for Edmund Cofford: an indenture concerning two cottages in Chipper Street for a term of life, and a deed concerning a rent of a rose from the two cottages and the reversion of them

1184 A charter of John Cook, of Romsey, an executor of Richard at the bridge, perfected for John Stoke, tailor, concerning a tenement beside the upper bridge of Fisherton

22 June 1382 x 21 June 1383

1185 A charter of an elder John Chandler perfected for an elder Thomas Deverill, his wife Agnes, and their son Thomas concerning a tenement, with a shop (*or* shops), opposite the market place

1186 A deed of Richard Still, an executor of William Higdon, an executor of Hugh Boney, perfected for Bartholomew Durkin concerning two cottages in Culver Street

1187 The will of Robert Bunt, which includes various tenements in Minster Street and Castle Street and land and a croft in Old Sarum. Approved

1188 A charter of Richard Jewell, an executor of Robert Godmanstone, perfected for Nicholas Russell and his wife Agnes concerning three shops in Butcher Row

1189 A charter of John Lea perfected for John at the heath and his wife Alice concerning a messuage, with a shop (*or* shops), in Winchester Street

1190 A charter of Walter Furmage perfected for John Needler in [?*rectius* concerning] a cottage (*or* cottages) in Culver Street

1191 A charter of Robert Bride, weaver, and his wife Mabel perfected for John Iwerne, a chaplain, concerning a corner tenement in St. Martin's Street and Gigant Street

1192 A charter of Thomas Focket perfected for John Newman, cardmaker, concerning [Focket Place: *cf.* **2005**], a corner tenement, with a cottage (*or* cottages), in St. Martin's Street and Gigant Street

1193 A charter of John Upton perfected for the master John Turk, John Stratford, and other canons of the cathedral church, and for the vicars of that church, concerning three cottages in New Street; with letters of attorney for giving up the seisin

1194 A charter of William Kilmeston perfected for John Farley, a chaplain, concerning a tenement in Castle Street. There follows a release upon the feoffment.

1195 A charter of John at the 'vuere', an executor of John, a son of John at the 'vuere', perfected for Henry Popham concerning various tenements, shops, and cottages in Salisbury

1196 A charter of Robert Bunt perfected for Richard Whiteparish concerning a shop in Minster Street; with letters of attorney for delivering the seisin

1197–9 Three writings perfected for Thomas Castleton concerning a tenement in St. Martin's Street: a charter of George Goss and John Buddle, a release of Richard Still, and a release of Richard Cole, carpenter

1200 A deed of John Lewisham and his wife Agnes, an executor of Robert Bunt, perfected for John Christchurch, a chaplain, concerning a rent of 8s. issuing from a tenement, of late Walter Holbury's, in Endless Street

1201–2 Two charters concerning a shop in Wheeler Row: one of Richard Cormell and his wife Joan perfected for Adam Teffont and Thomas Cofford, and one of Adam and Thomas perfected for Richard and Joan

1203–4 Two charters perfected for Thomas Castleton and John Newman: one of Thomas Focket concerning several tenements and cottages in Salisbury, and one of John Bailiff, a chaplain, concerning a messuage in Freren Street

1205 A charter of John Dean and John Farley, chaplains, perfected for William Kilmeston concerning various tenements which they held by his gift

1206 The will of Walter Holbury, which includes rent and various tenements and cottages in Salisbury. Approved

1207 A charter of John Creed, called Melksham, perfected for Walter Ryborough concerning a cottage (*or* cottages) in Mealmonger Street and a tenement in Culver Street

1208 The will of the lord John Iwerne, a vicar of Salisbury, which includes a rent of 10s., from a tenement in Castle Street, and a tenement in St. Martin's Street. Approved

22 June 1383 × 21 June 1384

1209 A deed of George Goss perfected for John Twyford concerning the reversion of a tenement in Endless Street

1210 A charter of John Love perfected for John Polmond and William Lord concerning two shops in Pot Row

1211 A charter of John of Upton perfected for John Boor and John Homes concerning a yard (*or* yards) in Drake Hall Street, a cottage (*or* cottages) in Brown Street, and two shops in Butcher Row

1212 A charter of John Boor and John Homes perfected for John Upton, his wife Margaret, and their joint issue concerning a tenement, a toft, and the shops mentioned above; if John and Margaret were to die without such issue the premises would remain to John Upton's son John and his assigns for ever

1213 A charter of Thomas Castleton perfected for John Newman concerning a tenement opposite the market place where grains are sold

1214 The will of William Dunkerton, which includes several tenements in the city. Approved

1215 The will of Joan, who was the wife of Richard Jewell, which includes a tenement in New Street. Approved

1216 A charter of Robert Beechfount, an executor of Richard Ryborough, perfected for John Ball concerning two tenements in Wineman Street

1217 A charter of John Chandler and Thomas Hindon, executors of Agnes Bodenham, perfected for Thomas Eyre and his wife Alice concerning a tenement in New Street

1218 The will of Ellen, the wife of John Canning, which includes a shop opposite the market place. Approved

1219 A charter of Walter Rodway and his wife Alice perfected for John Brute, of Swindon, concerning [Grandon's Corner: *cf.* **2015, 2017**], a corner tenement opposite the market place; with letters of attorney for delivering the seisin

1220 A charter of Richard Leach perfected for Thomas Deverill concerning two shops in Minster Street

1221 A charter of John Polmond perfected for Robert Deverill concerning a shop in Wineman Street

1222 A charter of Robert Deverill perfected for William Warmwell and George Goss concerning two tenements in Winchester Street

1223 A charter of Joan Woodborough perfected for John Maddington concerning a messuage, with a yard (*or* yards), in Endless Street

1224 A charter of Oliver of Harnham perfected for Thomas Play concerning 26s. 8d. from a shop opposite St. Thomas's church, with the reversion of the shop

1225 A charter of John Heath and Stephen Brown perfected for John Salisbury concerning a cottage (*or* cottages) towards St. Martin's church

1226 A deed of John Ringwood perfected for Edmund Cofford concerning a cottage (*or* cottages) in Chipper Street

1227 A release of John Dyke perfected for John Barrett concerning a tenement in St. Martin's Street

1228 A charter of William at the hurn perfected for Henry Berwick concerning a tenement opposite the market place

1229 The record of an assize which John Brond and his wife Joan brought against William Warmwell and others concerning a tenement in Salisbury

1230 A charter of Isabel Laurence perfected for John Dinton and his daughter Joan concerning a messuage opposite the bishop of Salisbury's land held in villeinage; with letters of attorney

1231 A charter of Thomas Honeyland perfected for William Godmanstone concerning an empty plot of land in Winchester Street

1232 A charter of John Bosset, an executor of William Cofford, perfected for Edmund Cofford concerning a yard in Martin's Croft

22 June 1384 x 21 June 1385

1233 A charter of Thomas Focket perfected for John Newman concerning a

portion of land opposite John Tavente's cottage property in New Street
1234 The will of Robert Woodborough, which includes a tenement in Castle Street and a tenement in Rolleston near Mealmonger Street
1235 A charter of Thomas Burford perfected for Henry Southwick concerning a cottage (*or* cottages) in New Street
1236–7 Two charters of Thomas Chaplin: one perfected for his son Thomas concerning a corner tenement in Carter Street and New Street, and one perfected for his son Thomas, John Chandler, and William Lord concerning all his other tenements
1238 A charter of William Lord perfected for Thomas Chaplin, a clerk, concerning a tenement in Castle Street beside John Farley's tenement
1239 A charter of John Christchurch, a chaplain, perfected for John Drury and others concerning a tenement, of late Walter Holbury's, in Endless Street
1240 The will of Henry at the burgh, which includes rent from various tenements in the city, and various tenements and rent in Wilton. Approved
1241 A charter of John Chandler, an executor of Maud of Langford, perfected for John Camel, hatter, concerning a rent of 16s. from a tenement which John Camel himself holds in Minster Street
1242 A charter of Nicholas Taylor, draper, perfected for Thomas Castleton concerning a tenement opposite the market place where fleeces are sold
1243 A charter of William Warmwell perfected for John Needler concerning a cottage (*or* cottages) in Mealmonger Street for a rent of 16s. a year for ever
1244 A charter of John of Upton perfected for John Salisbury, grocer, concerning a tenement in New Street
1245 A charter of George Goss perfected for John Collier, tucker, concerning a piece of land on the east side of Castle Street
1246 A general discharge of George Goss and his wife Alice, a daughter of William Wishford, perfected for John Butterley, an executor of William
1247 The will of Richard Upton, called Baker, which includes all his tenements, rent, and cottages in the city [devised] to his wife Joan. Approved
1248 A charter of George Goss and his wife Alice perfected for John Butterley concerning 33s. 4d. issuing from a tenement in Nuggeston, with the reversion of the tenement
1249–50 Two writings of Edmund Tetsworth perfected for John Knottingley and his wife Elizabeth: a charter concerning a tenement in Wineman Street, a shop in Pot Row, and a rent of 30s. issuing from another shop in Pot Row, with the reversion of that shop when it fell due, and a release concerning the same tenement, shops, and reversion
1251 The will of Alice, of late the wife of Hugh Gundy, which includes two tenements and rent of 5s. devised for ever to Hugh. Not approved
1252 The will of John Sprot, which includes a tenement in New Street. Approved
1253 A charter of Thomas at the mere, of Chilmark, perfected for Thomas Cook, a chaplain, concerning a tenement in Culver Street
1254 A charter of Peter of Upton and John Coulston, of Upton Scudamore, perfected for John of Upton concerning various tenements in New Street

22 June 1385 x 21 June 1386
1255 A charter of Joan, the relict of John Luckham, perfected for Henry Swain and Stephen Edington concerning the reversion of a tenement in Brown Street, with a piece of land
1256 A charter of Robert Pope, draper, perfected for John Guyon, of Shaftesbury, and Robert Body concerning a tenement in Minster Street
1257 A charter of Nicholas Russell, butcher, perfected for Thomas Sexton, ironmonger, concerning a shop in Butcher Row
1258 A charter of Richard Haxton perfected for Richard Cormell and his wife Joan concerning a yard in Nuggeston
1259–60 Two charters concerning a tenement in Carter Street: one of John Bennett perfected for Edward Elion, a chaplain, and William Lord, and one of Edward and William perfected for John and his wife Edith
1261 A charter of John Justice perfected for John King, roper, and his wife Edith concerning two cottages in Mealmonger Street
1262–3 Two deeds of Barnabas Kendal perfected for John Forest, weaver: one concerning the title of a garden towards St. Martin's church, and one concerning the reversion of the garden
1264 A charter of John Bennett and his wife Edith perfected for John Baker, draper, concerning a tenement in Carter Street
1265 A charter of Hugh Gundy perfected for Robert Play concerning rent, with the reversion of a tenement in Carter Street
1266 A charter of Edmund Bramshaw perfected for Thomas Friday concerning a corner tenement in Endless Street; with letters of attorney for delivering the seisin
1267 A charter of Robert Rise perfected for John Needler concerning a tenement in Wineman Street
1268 A charter of William Dunkerton and William Lord perfected for Joan, the relict of William Polmond, concerning rent, with the reversion of a tenement in Endless Street
1269 A charter of Thomas Focket perfected for John Lea and William Ashton concerning all his land and tenements in Salisbury and Stratford
1270 The will of Richard Still, which includes the tenement in Winchester Street in which he dwelt and an empty plot of land. Approved
1271 A charter of John Knight perfected for William Whaddon and John Chandler concerning a tenement in Carter Street
1272 A charter of John Guyon, of Shaftesbury, and Robert Body perfected for Robert Pope and his wife Joan concerning a tenement in Winchester Street
1273 A charter of Walter Orme, and his wife Agnes, an executor of Nicholas Purser, perfected for Roger Farnborough, a chaplain, and John Franklin concerning the reversion of a tenement in Minster Street
1274 A charter of Alice, the relict of Thomas of Britford, perfected for William Buck, a chaplain, concerning a tenement in New Street
1275 A charter of William Buck, a chaplain, perfected for the lord William

Herring and John Crass concerning a shop in Minster Street and seven cottages in Nuggeston, and concerning a rent issuing from Edmund Bramshaw's [corner] tenement [in Endless Street: cf. *1266*]

1276 A charter of William Herring, a chaplain, and John Crass perfected for Alice Britford concerning a shop in Minster Street

1277 A charter of an elder John Chandler perfected for John Sewin concerning a tenement beside the upper bridge of Fisherton

1278–80 Three charters perfected for William River and his wife Joan: one of John Butterley concerning a rent of 22s. issuing from Henry Southwick's corner tenement, one of Thomas Stalbridge concerning a rent of 18s. issuing from that tenement, and one of Henry Southwick and his wife Isabel concerning the tenement

1281 A charter of William River and his wife Joan perfected for Henry Southwick and his wife Isabel concerning the corner tenement mentioned above for a rent of 52s. for ever

1282 A release of Thomas Burford perfected for William River and his wife Joan concerning the same tenement

22 June 1386 x 21 June 1387

1283 A release of John Butterley and Thomas Stalbridge perfected for William River and his wife Joan concerning two cottages in Brown Street

1284 A release of William River and his wife Joan perfected for John Butterley and Thomas Stalbridge concerning a tenement opposite the Franciscans, and concerning a tenement in Carter Street

1285 A deed of Roger Farnborough and John Franklin perfected for Walter Orme and his wife Agnes concerning their estate and right in a tenement in Minster Street

1286 A charter of John Baron, of Quidhampton, perfected for John Lymington, mercer, concerning a tenement in Endless Street

1287 A charter of John Odiham perfected for William Wilton, a citizen of London, concerning all his tenements

1288–9 Two charters of William Warmwell and Robert Arnold perfected for Joan, the relict of John Wickham: one concerning a corner tenement in Endless Street, and one concerning a tenement in Castle Street and a tenement in Brown Street

1290 A charter of John Taylor, draper, and John Parson perfected for John Yate and his wife Joan concerning a corner tenement in Scots Lane and Endless Street

1291 A charter of Joan, the relict of John Wickham, perfected for John Taylor, draper, and John Parson concerning the tenements mentioned above

1292 A charter of Adam Gill, tanner, and his wife Maud perfected for John Chandler concerning a tenement in Endless Street

1293 A charter of Robert Pope and his wife Joan perfected for John Camel, hatter, concerning a tenement in Minster Street

1294 A charter of Henry London perfected for John Butterley concerning a tenement in Wineman Street; with letters of attorney for delivering the seisin

1295 A charter of Walter Ryborough and John Camel perfected for John Ettshall concerning two shops in New Street and a rent of 16*d*. from that tenement

1296 A release of Henry Selwood perfected for John Butterley concerning a tenement in Wineman Street

1297 A release of Bartholomew Durkin perfected for John Ettshall concerning two shops in New Street

1298 The will of John Beeton, which includes a tenement in Castle Street. Approved

1299 The will of John Ball, which includes a corner tenement in Wineman Street and Brown Street. Approved

1300 A charter of John Needler, John Chandler, and others perfected for William Guys concerning [Buckland's Place; *cf. 1964*], a messuage in Freren Street

1301 A charter of John Bennett perfected for William Warmwell, John Needler, and others concerning all the ground where the gate of the Franciscans stands. Mention is made to heed the immunities of the feoffment in the possession of the chief lord concerning all the charges.

1302 The will of John Abingdon, which includes a tenement in Minster Street. Approved

1303 The will of John Justice, which includes various tenements and cottages in the city. Approved

1304 A charter of Alice, the relict of Thomas of Britford, concerning a shop in Castle Street

1305 A defeasance perfected upon a statute merchant by means of which John Gowan is bound to Thomas Wroughton and John Mildenhall

1306 A charter of John Mildenhall perfected for an elder John Gowan concerning a cottage (*or* cottages), with a yard (*or* yards), in Castle Street beyond the bar

1307 A release of John Gowan perfected for John Starr and his wife Edith concerning three cottages in Minster Street

1308 A release of John Starr and his wife Edith perfected for an elder John Gowan concerning a cottage (*or* cottages), with a yard (*or* yards), in Castle Street beyond the bar and another (*or* other) tenement(s) in the city

1309 A charter of John Gowan perfected for Richard Ryde concerning a tenement in Culver Street

1310 A deed of Richard Whiteparish perfected for John Newman concerning a rent of 20*s*. to be received from a tenement in Castle Street

1311 A deed of Henry Tucker, of Avon, and his wife Ellen perfected for John Gowan concerning a cottage (*or* cottages), with a yard (*or* yards), in the city

1312 A charter of William Herring, a chaplain, and John Crass perfected for William Buck, a chaplain, concerning a rent of 12*s*. issuing from a tenement in Pot Row and a rent of 8*s*. issuing from Edmund Bramshaw's corner tenement [in Endless Street: *cf. 1266*]

1313 The will of John Dogskin, which includes a tenement towards St. Martin's church. Approved

1314 The record [of a cause], by means of a writ *ex gravi querela*, between Thomas Knoyle, plaintiff, and Thomas Warlond, his wife Maud, and other named persons, defandants, concerning a tenement in the city

1315–16 Two charters concerning various tenements and rent in the city: one of Thomas Knoyle perfected for Thomas Hindon, William Warmwell, and John Butterley, and one of re-enfeoffment of Thomas, William, and John perfected for Thomas Knoyle, his wife Joan, and their joint issue. If Thomas and Joan were to die without such issue all the land, tenements, and rent would remain to the mayor and commonalty of Salisbury.

1317 A charter of John New, tanner, perfected on a condition for Adam Teffont and his wife Parnel concerning a tenement in Brown Street

1318 A charter of William Moore, tailor, and his wife Denise perfected for John Fox, a chaplain, and Thomas Shipton concerning a tenement opposite the Guildhall

1319 The will of John Buddle, which includes a corner tenement, with a shop and cottages, in Wineman Street. Mention is made of a cottage (*or* cottages) to remain, for the want of an heir, to the mayor and commonalty. Approved

1320 A charter of William Kilmeston, a vicar of Salisbury, perfected for John Waite, hosier, concerning a piece of land in Minster Street

1321 A charter of Robert Fewster and his wife Alice perfected for William Warmwell concerning three cottages in Gigant Street and three shops there

1322 A deed of John Yate and his wife Joan perfected for John Dinton concerning the title of their tenement in Endless Street

1323–4 Two releases of John Polmond: one perfected for John Yate and his wife Joan concerning a rent of 10*s.* issuing from a tenement in Endless Street, and one perfected for John Dinton and Thomas Pasker concerning a rent of 20*s.* from a tenement in Endless Street

1325–6 Two writings perfected for John Barrett concerning cottages in Culver Street: a charter of William Boyland and John Salisbury, executors of John Justice, and a release of Margery Justice

1327 A charter of John Dinton perfected for John Yate and his wife Joan concerning a rent of 26*s.* 8*d.* issuing from a tenement in Endless Street

1328 An extent of the land and tenements of Thomas Focket perfected for John Lea and Thomas Butlingsey, of Southampton

1329 The will of Maud, the wife of John Wallop, which includes a tenement in Chipper Lane. Without approval

1330 A charter of John King, roper, and his wife Edith perfected for Thomas Sexton concerning a cottage (*or* cottages) in Mealmonger Street

1331 The will of William Heal, which includes a tenement and shops near the graveyard of St. Thomas's [church]. Approved

22 June 1387 x 21 June 1388

1332 A charter of John Wraxall, a chaplain, perfected for Richard Hellier, barber, concerning cottages in Drake Hall Street

1333 A charter of John Polmond perfected for William Godmanstone concerning [Florentine's Corner: *cf.* **512, 682**], a corner tenement in New Street and Minster Street

1334 The will of John Shove, kt., which includes several tenements and rent. Approved

1335 A charter of John Bennett perfected for William Warmwell concerning a rent of 16s. issuing from a tenement in New Street, with the reversion of the tenement

1336 A charter of John Newman perfected for Richard Clark, of Pensford, concerning [Clark's Place: *cf.* **2005**], a tenement in St. Martin's Street and Gigant Street

1337–9 Three writings perfected for Robert Play and Thomas Marshall: a charter of Cecily Marshall, an executor of William Dunkerton, concerning a corner tenement, with the reversion of a shop in Brown Street, a charter of Robert Newport and his wife Agnes concerning a tenement in Winchester Street, and a release of Robert and Agnes concerning the corner tenement

1340 A charter of John Bennett perfected for Robert Play concerning a rent of 1 mark from a tenement in Drake Hall Street

1341–3 Three writings concerning a corner tenement in Endless Street and Scots Lane: a release of William Warmwell and Robert Deverill perfected for George Goss, a deed of William Clark, weaver, and his wife Beatrice perfected for George and his wife Alice, and a charter of George and Alice perfected for William and Beatrice

1344 The will of William Puddlemill, which includes a tenement in Gigant Street and a rent of 4s. from a tenement in Wineman Street. Approved

1345 A charter of John Pope, Thomas Butterley, and Philip Lea, executors of Barnabas Kendal, a chaplain, perfected for Richard Spencer and his wife Agnes concerning a tenement in Winchester Street

1346 A charter of Walter Ryborough and John Camel, hatter, perfected for Bartholomew Durkin and his wife Agnes concerning three messuages

1347 A deed of William Boyland perfected for Margery Justice concerning a rent of 20s. to be received from a tenement in Endless Street

1348–9 Two charters concerning a tenement in Castle Street: one of Richard Ludd perfected for John Forest and Edward Breamore, and one of John and Edward perfected for Richard and his wife Margaret

1350–9 Ten writings concerning a corner tenement, with a shop (*or* shops), in Winchester Street and Brown Street: a charter of John Butterley, an executor of William Wishford, perfected for Thomas Shove, his wife Agace, and their son John, a charter of Thomas and Agace perfected for John Thorburn and his wife Joan, a deed of John Toogood, the parson of Fifield, and another (*or* others), executors of John Shove, perfected for John Thorburn and Joan, a deed of Gillian, the wife [?relict] of John Shove, perfected for John Thorburn and Joan, a deed of Agnes, the relict of John Oxford, and another (*or* others), executors of John, perfected for John Shove concerning the reversion, a deed of Thomas Shove and Agace perfected for John Thorburn concerning their estate in the tenement, a deed of John Toogood and another (*or* others), executors of John Shove, kt., perfected for John Thorburn and Joan concerning the reversion, a release of Gillian, the relict of John Shove, kt., perfected for John Thorburn and Joan, a release of John Frome and Robert Bower, a son, perfected for John Thorburn and Joan, and a release of Edmund Spearcock perfected for John Thorburn and Joan

22 June 1388 x 21 June 1389
1360–3 Four charters of William Boyland and John Salisbury, executors of John Justice, perfected for Edmund Enfield, a clerk, concerning premises in St. Martin's Street: one concerning three messuages, one concerning a tenement, one concerning three shops, and one concerning three tenements
1364 An indented charter of John Butterley perfected for Thomas Burford and his wife Agnes concerning a tenement opposite the market place where grains are sold
1365 A charter of Thomas Burford perfected for David Fletcher and Thomas Cook, a chaplain, concerning a rent of a rose, with the reversion of a tenement in Castle Street, and concerning two tenements there
1366 A charter of David Fletcher and Thomas Cook, a chaplain, perfected for Thomas Burford and his wife Agnes concerning the rent and tenements mentioned above
1367 A charter of Robert Play and Thomas Marshall perfected for John Ettshall concerning a corner tenement in Winchester Street and Brown Street
1368 The will of Richard Ryde, which includes a tenement in Culver Street. Approved
1369 The will of Robert Beechfount, which includes several tenements and rent. Approved
1370 A charter of John Farley, a chaplain, perfected for an elder John Chandler concerning a tenement in Castle Street
1371 A charter of Adam Keynes perfected for John at the ash, mason, concerning a cottage in St. Martin's Street
1372 A charter of Emme of Gloucester perfected for an elder John Chandler concerning three shops in St. Martin's Street
1373 A charter of Nicholas Taylor, draper, perfected for Edward Elion, a chaplain, and Thomas Wallington concerning all his land and tenements in the city
1374 A charter of John Chandler perfected for John Gilbert, called Sumner, concerning a tenement in New Street
1375 The will of John Pinnock, which includes several tenements and rent in the city. Approved
1376 The will of David Stook, called Fletcher, which includes tenements and rent in the city. Approved
1377 A deed of John Fox, a chaplain, perfected for William Moore and William Lord concerning rent, with the reversion of a tenement in Cordwainer Row
1378 A charter of John Still, a chaplain, perfected for William Buck, a chaplain, concerning a tenement in Winchester Street
1379–81 Three writings concerning a tenement in New Street of late that of Clarice Baker and John Salisbury: a charter of the king perfected for John Boor, a clerk, letters of attorney of John Boor perfected for Richard West for receiving

an attornment concerning Clarice's tenement in New Street, and letters patent of William Warmwell, the mayor of the city, on the attornment perfected for Richard, Clarice's attorney in the present will

1382–3 Two deeds of John Twyford perfected for John Hogman, weaver: one concerning the reversion of a tenement in Endless Street, and one concerning his title to that tenement

1384–6 Three writings perfected for John Forest: a deed of Nicholas Taylor, draper, concerning his whole estate in a tenement in Endless Street, a deed of Nicholas concerning the reversion of that tenement, and a release of Edward Elion and Thomas Wallington concerning the same tenement

1387 The will of John Sewin, ironmonger, which includes a tenement towards the upper bridge of Fisherton for a term of life. The reversion should be sold by means of the mayor of the city. Approved

1388–92 Five writings concerning a tenement in New Street and Gigant Street: a charter of Thomas Shove perfected for John Chandler and William Lord, letters of attorney of Thomas perfected for Robert Arnold and John Gatcombe for delivering the seisin, a charter of John and William perfected for Thomas and his wife Agace, letters of attorney of Thomas and Agace perfected for Robert and John for receiving the seisin, and an indented charter of Thomas and Agace perfected for William Walter and his wife Parnel

1393 A deed of Thomas Marshall perfected for John Shipton concerning a tenement beyond the bar of Castle Street

1394 A deed of William Moore, Robert Body, and others

1395 A deed of release of William Moore and others perfected for Bartholomew Durkin concerning rent, with the reversion of a shop in Minster Street

1396 A deed of Robert Bowyer and his wife Christine perfected for Richard Spencer concerning a rent of 20s. to be received from a tenement in Wineman Street

1397–8 Two writings concerning a tenement in Wineman Street: an indenture of William Sall and his wife Joan perfected for John Osborne for a term of life, and a deed of release of John perfected for William and Joan concerning that tenement and another tenement in the city

1399 A charter of John Manning, a chaplain, and Thomas Manning perfected for John Walbourne, a chaplain, and William Moore concerning all the tenements etc.

1400 A charter of John Walbourne and William Moore perfected for William Sall and his wife Joan concerning all the land and tenements of late Richard Upton's

1401 A deed of William Sall and his wife Joan perfected for John Walbourne, a chaplain, and William Moore concerning Joan's title to a tenement in the city

1402–3 Two writings concerning a corner tenement in Brown Street and Chipper Street: a charter of William Lord perfected for Richard Spencer, and a deed of release of John Butterley and William Warmwell perfected for William Lord

1404–7 Four deeds concerning various tenements: one of Alice, the relict of David Stook, called Fletcher, perfected for Edmund Enfield concerning her estate in them, one of that Alice and of Robert Kirtlingstoke, executors of David, perfected for Edmund concerning the reversion of them, one of Robert Play and Richard Leach of confirmation perfected on a grant of Alice and Robert, and one of release of Robert and Richard perfected for Edmund

1408–9 Two deeds of John Boor, a clerk, perfected for Walter Nalder and his wife Isabel: one concerning a tenement in New Street, and one concerning rent of 2*d*. a year, with the reversion of that tenement

1410–11 Two charters concerning a cottage (*or* cottages) in Brown Street: one of William Lord, an executor of Gilbert Whichbury, perfected for William Warmwell, and one of William Warmwell perfected for Henry Southwick

22 June 1389 x 21 June 1390

1412 The will of Walter Ryborough, which includes several tenements. Approved

1413 The will of Robert Arnold, which includes a tenement and two shops. Approved

1414 A final agreement in front of the king's justices between William Guys and Richard Lichfield concerning a tenement in the city

1415 The will of Robert Harass, which includes a tenement towards St. Martin's church

1416–17 Two charters of John Coulston perfected for John Stallington, a clerk: one concerning three cottages in Culver Street, with letters of attorney, and one concerning rent, with the reversion of a tenement in Culver Street

1418 A charter of Margery Justice perfected for William Reynold concerning a tenement (*or* tenements) in New Street and Culver Street, and concerning a piece of a yard

1419–20 Two writings of George Goss and his wife Alice perfected for William Clark, weaver, and his wife Beatrice: a charter concerning four shops in Scots Lane, and a release concerning that tenement

1421 A deed of William Higdon perfected for the master William Ferrer and his wife Isabel concerning two cottages, with a plot of land, in Endless Street

1422 An indented charter of John Gillingham perfected for an elder John Chandler concerning a corner tenement in Brown Street

1423–4 Two releases of John, a son of John Cole, perfected for Isabel Cole and Nicholas Harding: one concerning three tenements in Wineman Street and Winchester Street, and one concerning a tenement formerly his father's

1425–6 Two deeds perfected for Thomas Hindon and John Chandler: one of Isabel Cole concerning her estate in a tenement in Winchester Street, and one of Isabel, John Stoke, and Nicholas Harding, executors of John Cole, concerning the reversion of that tenement

1427 A charter of Thomas Hindon and John Chandler perfected for Nicholas Harding concerning a tenement in Winchester Street of late John Cole's

1428 A charter of William Buck, a chaplain, an executor of Thomas Britford, perfected for John Butterley and others concerning a rent of 1 mark from a tenement in Minster Street

1429 The will of Nicholas Russell, butcher, which includes three shops in Pot Row. Not approved

1430 The will of John Baker, a clothier, which includes a tenement in Carter Street. Approved

1431 A charter of Robert Harass perfected for John Butterley and William Godmanstone concerning cottages, with a dovecot, towards St. Martin's church

1432–3 Two charters of John Maddington perfected for John Waite, hosier, and his wife Maud: one concerning rent, with the reversion of a shop in Endless Street, and one concerning rent, with the reversion of a messuage in Endless Street

1434 An indenture of 'G of D' perfected for 'P of A' concerning a licence to place a gutter on his timber of a tenement in Minster Street

22 June 1390 x 21 June 1391

1435 The will of Alice Rushall, which includes a corner tenement in Brown Street and New Street

1436 A charter of George Goss and his wife Alice perfected for John Collier and his wife Alice concerning a cottage (*or* cottages), with a yard (*or* yards), in Brown Street

1437–8 Two charters of William Warmwell: one perfected for Matthew Fernhill and his wife Isabel concerning a tenement, with a yard (*or* yards), in Brown Street and Carter Street, and one perfected for Robert Play and John Chandler concerning rent, with the reversion of a kitchen attached to a gate in Brown Street

1439 The will of John Lea, which includes various tenements and rent in the city. Approved

1440–1 Two charters perfected for the master Edmund Enfield and his wife Alice: one of John Bennett concerning a tenement in Brown Street, and one of John Chandler concerning a tenement in Freren Street

1442 A charter of Christine Dowding perfected for John Belter [*?otherwise* Barber] and his wife Alice concerning a messuage in Winchester Street

1443 A charter of Richard Hilary and Gilbert at the brook perfected for Robert Way, skinner, concerning two shops in Minster Street

1444–5 Two charters concerning a tenement opposite the Guildhall: one of John Fox, a chaplain, perfected for William Moore and his wife Denise, and one of William and Denise perfected for John Stoke, tailor, concerning a rent of 2 marks from it

22 June 1391 x 21 June 1392

1446 A charter of Thomas Harnham, the rector of Odstock, perfected for Gilbert at the brook, skinner, concerning land and tenements in the city

1447 A charter of Gilbert at the brook perfected for Reynold Glover and his wife Agnes concerning a tenement in Minster Street

1448 A charter of Mabel Puddlemill, an executor of William Puddlemill, perfected for John Clement, weaver, and his wife Alice concerning the reversion of a tenement in Gigant Street

1449–51 Three writings concerning a tenement opposite the market place:

a charter of John Gatcombe and his wife Joan perfected for Simon Bunt and Reynold Glover concerning their estate in it, a deed of Richard Quarrendon, a chaplain, an executor of Thomas Stoke, perfected for Simon and Reynold concerning the reversion of it, and a charter of Simon and Reynold perfected for John and Joan

1452 A charter of William Moore perfected for John Wishford concerning a tenement in Cordwainer Row

1453 The will of William Knoyle, painter, which includes a tenement in St. Martin's Street. Approved

1454–5 Two charters concerning a tenement opposite the Guildhall: one of Thomas Hindon perfected for William Lord and Nicholas Harding, and one of William and Nicholas perfected for Thomas and his wife Alice

1456 A charter of William Godmanstone perfected for William Bailiff, taverner, concerning two shops in Castle Street

1457 The will of Christine Friend, which includes a tenement in New Street devised to her son William and his assigns for ever. Approved

1458 The will of John Upton, which includes several tenements and rent

1459 A charter of William Warmwell perfected by means of an indenture for William Lord concerning an empty plot of land in Gigant Street

1460 A charter of John Dinton perfected for Thomas Sexton concerning two cottages in Castle Street

1461–2 Two charters concerning shops near the graveyard of St. Thomas's [church]: one of John Swift and his wife Christine, and another (*or* other), executor(s) of William Heal, perfected for Thomas Sexton and James Brock, and one of Thomas and James perfected for John and Christine

1463–5 Three writings concerning a corner tenement called Florentine's Corner: a charter of William Godmanstone perfected for Richard Enterbush, a charter of Richard perfected for William Hill and others, and a release of Edward Elion and John Chandler perfected for William Hill and others

1466 A charter of John Wells, weaver, perfected for Robert Play and others concerning a tenement in New Street

1467 The will of John Duke, which includes a tenement in Endless Street. Approved

1468–70 Three writings concerning two cottages in Chipper Lane: a charter of Thomas Farrant and his wife *Jac'* [?Jacquemine *or* Jackett] perfected for Richard Spencer, a release of William Duke perfected for Richard, and a charter of Richard perfected for Thomas

1471 A charter of John Butterley and William Godmanstone perfected for Robert Harass concerning two cottages, with a yard (*or* yards), near St. Martin's church

1472–3 Two writings of John Chandler perfected for the master William Ferrer: a charter concerning a tenement, above a ditch in Winchester Street, of late John Bodenham's, and a deed concerning rent, with the reversion of two rooms above a ditch

1474 A deed of William Boyland perfected for Geoffrey Justice concerning a rent of 6*s*. 8*d*. to be received from a tenement in Endless Street

1475–6 Two writings concerning a shop beside the Rose: a charter of John Polmond, of Southampton, perfected for Walter Clopton, kt., with letters of attorney for delivering the seisin, and letters of attorney of Walter perfected for Oliver Harnham and others for receiving the seisin

1477 A charter of John Florentine perfected for Richard Alden, of Southampton, concerning [Florentine's Corner: *cf.* **512, 682**], a corner tenement in Minster Street, and rent, with the reversion of a shop in Minster Street and New Street

1478 The will of Richard Alden, of Southampton, which includes [Florentine's Corner: *cf.* **512, 682**], a corner tenement, and a shop, in New Street and Minster Street

1479–80 Two writings concerning a corner tenement in Endless Street and Chipper Street: a deed of an elder John Chandler perfected for John Drury concerning a rent of 10*s.* to be received from it, and an indented charter perfected between John Chandler and John Little and his wife Maud

1481 A charter of John Waite, tailor, and his wife Maud perfected for John Needler concerning a tenement in Minster Street

1482 The will of Alice, the wife of John Churchhay, which includes *cout'* [?a yard] in St. Martin's Street. Approved

1483–4 Two deeds perfected for Thomas Bowyer, Edmund Enfield, and Thomas Cook, a chaplain, concerning a tenement in Winchester Street: one of John Butterley and his wife Alice concerning the tenement, with a piece of a yard, and one of William Warmwell and William Lord, executors of William Tenterer, concerning the tenement

1485 A deed of John Butterley and his wife Alice, and others, executors of William Tenterer, perfected for William Bailey concerning the reversion of a tenement in New Street

1486 A charter of Margaret, the relict of John Upton, and of Thomas Upton and Hugh Upton, [all three being] executors of John, perfected for Edmund Enfield concerning a tenement in Minster Street beyond the bar

1487 A charter of John Stallington, a clerk, perfected for Walter Bradley concerning cottages in Culver Street; with letters of attorney for delivering the seisin

1488 A charter of Thomas Hindon perfected for Geoffrey Sunbury and his wife Margery concerning rent of 18*s.*, with the reversion of a shop in Drake Hall Street; with letters of attorney for delivering the seisin

22 June 1392 x 21 June 1393

1489 A charter of John Chandler perfected for Edmund Enfield concerning a rent of 13*s.* 4*d.* issuing from a tenement beyond the bar of Castle Street

1490 A charter of John Wallop, draper, perfected for Richard Leach concerning a rent of 40*s.* issuing from a tenement in Winchester Street above a ditch

1491 A charter of John Wallop, draper, the mayor of Salisbury, perfected for Edmund Enfield concerning a rent of 40*s.* issuing from a tenement opposite the market place where fleeces are sold

1492 A charter of Thomas Cutting, a son of Agnes Burden, perfected for John

Wishford concerning a cottage, of late that of William Agodeshalf, in Gigant Street

1493–4 Two deeds of John Clement and his wife Alice perfected for John Baker, grocer: one concerning a tenement in Gigant Street, whatever [pertained] to his estate, and one concerning the reversion of it

1495 A charter of John Drury and others perfected for John Ettshall concerning a rent of 8s. issuing from a tenement in Endless Street of late W[alter] Holbury's

1496 A release of John Chandler and John Wells perfected for John Drury concerning cottages in Castle Street beyond the bar

1497 A deed of John Chandler and John Drury perfected for Robert Play concerning a rent of 5 marks from a tenement (*or* tenements) in Carter Street and New Street

1498–9 Two charters of John Chandler: one perfected for Robert Play concerning a tenement in St. Martin's Street, and one perfected for John Ettshall concerning a rent of 13s. 4d. issuing from the west part of Henry Selwood's tenement in Wineman Street

1500 A charter of John Chandler and John Drury perfected for John Ettshall concerning a tenement in St. Martin's Street

1501 A charter of Thomas Hindon perfected for Richard Jewell concerning a tenement in Gigant Street beside John Ball's garden

1502 A charter of Thomas Hindon and John Needler perfected for John Wallop concerning a rent of 10s. issuing from a tenement in Scots Lane

1503–4 Two writings concerning a tenement in New Street where Thomas Biston dwells: a charter of Robert Play, Richard Jewell, and others perfected for the lord Peter Burton and others, and a release of John Wells, weaver, perfected for Peter and others

1505 The will of Nicholas Baker, which includes several tenements. Approved

1506 A charter of John Hackwell [?*rectius* Halwell], the rector of the church of Berwick [St. John], and Nicholas Thurman perfected for John Street, a chaplain, and others concerning a corner tenement called Cheese Corner; with letters of attorney for delivering the seisin

1507 A charter of Thomas Hindon and his wife Alice perfected for Adam Teffont and his wife Parnel concerning a cottage (*or* cottages) in Gigant Street

1508 A charter of Adam Countwell perfected for John Dicker, a chaplain, concerning a messuage, with a shop (*or* shops), in Minster Street

1509 A charter of John Dicker, a chaplain, perfected for Adam Countwell, his wife Agnes, and their joint issue

1510 A charter of John Ellis, limeburner, perfected for William Buck and John Walbourne, chaplains, concerning the reversion of a tenement in St. Martin's Street of late William Knoyle's

1511 A charter of John Polmond perfected for an elder Nicholas Baynton concerning various tenements in the city; with letters of attorney for delivering the seisin

1512 The will of Agnes, the wife of Bartholomew Durkin, goldsmith, which includes several tenements. Not approved

1513 A charter of Thomas Deverill, his wife Agnes, and their son Thomas perfected for Richard Spencer concerning a tenement in Castle Street; with letters for delivering up the seisin

1514–15 Two charters concerning a tenement in Minster Street: one of Thomas Deverill perfected for the master Walter Bradley and John Drury, and one of Walter and John perfected for a younger Thomas Deverill and his issue

1516 A charter of Simon Bunt and John Drury perfected for William Warmwell and William Lord concerning meadows beside the Avon

1517 A charter of John Wishford perfected for Thomas Ham, tailor, and his wife Alice concerning a tenement in Gigant Street

1518 A charter of Roger Farnborough perfected for Richard Oword and his wife Margery concerning a tenement near the graveyard of St. Thomas's [church]

1519–21 Three releases of Geoffrey Crier: one perfected for John Butterley concerning a corner tenement opposite the Rose and a tenement in Fisherton, one perfected for John concerning a shop at the butchers' stalls, and one perfected for Thomas Boyton concerning two shops in Butcher Row

1522 A charter of Walter Seymour perfected for Edward Cheese and his wife Agnes concerning a corner tenement called Cheese Corner

1523 A deed of Agnes, the relict of Nicholas Russell, perfected for Walter Nalder concerning an estate in three shops in Pot Row, and concerning that fee

1524–5 Two charters concerning two tenements in Winchester Street: one of Isabel Cole perfected for William Lord, and one of William perfected for Isabel and her son William

1526–9 Four writings concerning a tenement, on the way to a bridge of Fisherton, near the graveyard of St. Thomas's [church]: a charter of George Goss and his wife Alice, a kinswoman of Richard Ryborough, perfected for John Butterley and others, a charter of John Butterley, William Warmwell, and John Collier perfected for Richard Pitts, a canon of Salisbury, William Holyman, a clerk, and John Gowan, a release of George Goss perfected for the master Richard Pitts and the others as above, and a release of Agnes, a daughter of George, perfected for Richard and the others

1530 A deed of Richard Leach and William Lord perfected for John Purdy concerning a rent of a rose, with the reversion of the same tenement in Endless Street

1531 A charter of Richard Spencer perfected for Thomas Hart concerning a tenement in Castle Street

1532 An indenture of Nicholas Wilcock and his wife Christine perfected for Roger Fadder concerning a tenement beside John Ball's tenement in Brown Street

1533 A charter of Thomas Hart, draper, perfected for John Dyer, of Longbridge Deverill, concerning a tenement in Castle Street

1534 A charter of John Butterley perfected for Thomas Boyton concerning a shop at the butchers' stalls

1535 A charter of Edmund Enfield and his wife Alice perfected for William West, baker, and his wife Agnes concerning a corner tenement in New Street and

Brown Street

1536–8 Three writings concerning three shops: a licence of King Richard granted to John Turk, John Boor, and others for appropriating them, a licence of John, the bishop of Salisbury, perfected for the same men for the same purpose, and a charter of those men perfected for the dean and chapter of Salisbury; with letters of attorney for delivering the seisin

22 June 1393 x 21 June 1394
1539 A charter of Hugh Gundy perfected for John Staggard, weaver, concerning a tenement in Scots Lane
1540 The will of Gillian Harass, which includes a tenement near the graveyard of St. Martin's [church]. Approved
1541 A charter of John Salisbury and Richard Leach perfected for William Lord and Richard Harlwin concerning all the land and tenements of late Bartholomew Durkin's
1542 A charter of Henry Southwick perfected for Edmund Enfield and John Chandler concerning various tenements and cottages in the city
1543–5 Three writings concerning a corner tenement in New Street and Shit Lane: the will of Thomas Shove, approved, the will of Thomas's relict Agace, approved, and a charter of John Wallop, an executor of Agace, perfected for John Wishford
1546 A deed of William Lord and William Algar perfected for Edmund Enfield and his wife Alice concerning a tenement of late John Bennett's in St. Martin's Street
1547 The will of John Bourton, a chaplain, which includes a tenement in St. Martin's Street
1548 A charter of a younger John Chandler perfected for John Newman and Nicholas Harding concerning two tenements
1549 A charter of Thomas Bartlet, a chaplain, perfected for William Lord, John Wilmington, and Walter Foyle, a chaplain, concerning three cottages in Brown Street
1550 A charter of William Buck, a chaplain, perfected for John Chandler and William Lord concerning a corner tenement in Endless Street
1551 A deed of Thomas Sexhampcote, an executor of William Wootton, an executor of William Gill, perfected for William Bartlet concerning a tenement in Minster Street
1552 A charter of John Stanley perfected for John Newman concerning three shops in Carter Street
1553 The will of Robert Play, which includes several tenements, cottages, and shops. Not approved
1554 A release of Thomas Burford perfected for John Butterley concerning a corner tenement in New Street
1555 A charter of Richard at the row perfected for Robert Deverill concerning a tenement in Winchester Street
1556 A charter of William Lord and Richard Harlwin perfected for John Barrett,

weaver, concerning two shops at the butchers' stalls

1557 The will of Robert Russell, kt., which includes several tenements, cottages, and rent in the city. Not approved

1558 The will of John Yate, of Mere, which includes various tenements. Not approved

1559 A charter of George Goss perfected for Nicholas Baynton concerning rent, with the reversion of a tenement in Endless Street

1560 A release of Richard Upavon, a vicar of Salisbury, perfected for Richard Leach concerning a corner tenement in Wineman Street and Gigant Street

1561–2 Two charters concerning a corner tenement in St. Martin's Street: one of Walter Bown and his wife Margaret perfected for Edmund Enfield and Roger Farnborough, and one of Edmund and Roger perfected for Walter and Margaret

1563 A charter of William Lord and Richard Harlwin perfected for William Reynold, weaver, concerning cottages in Culver Street

1564 A charter of William Lord and others, executors of Robert Play, perfected for Walter Bown and his wife Margaret concerning various tenements, cottages, and rent in the city

22 June 1394 x 21 June 1395

1565 A charter of Alice, the wife [*rectius* relict: *cf.* ***1722***] of Thomas Durrington, perfected for Thomas Chaplin and Thomas Cofford concerning a tenement in Minster Street

1566 A charter of Richard Upavon, a chaplain, Nicholas Woodhill, and Hugh Garnon perfected for Richard Leach concerning a corner tenement in Wineman Street and Gigant Street

1567 A charter of William Lord perfected for William Upavon, a chaplain, and John Salisbury concerning a tenement in Gigant Street

1568 A charter of John Wallop, draper, perfected for William Buck, a chaplain, and John Chandler concerning various tenements, shops, cottages, and rent in the city

1569 A release of Alice, the wife [?relict] of Thomas Hindon, perfected for Adam Teffont and his wife Parnel concerning a cottage (*or* cottages) in Gigant Street

1570 The will of John Fowle, which includes several tenements. Approved

1571–2 Two wills which include rent, with the reversion of a tenement in Castle Street: that of Rose, the wife of John Fowle, approved, and that of John Fowle, a chaplain, approved

1573–5 Three writings perfected for Thomas Coombe and Ralph Hampstead, chaplains: a charter of John Mower concerning a tenement in New Street beside a trench, a charter of John Little and Richard Spencer, executors of John Amesbury, concerning a corner tenement in Endless Street and Chipper Street, and a deed of John Mower and his wife Cecily concerning the [corner] tenement mentioned above

1576 A charter of John Knottingley perfected for his son John concerning a tenement in Winchester Street and another tenement; with letters of attorney for delivering the seisin

1577 The will of William Ashton, which includes several tenements. Approved
1578 A charter of William Buck, a chaplain, perfected for Thomas Hart concerning a tenement in Winchester Street
1579 A charter of John Man, a kinsman of John Iwerne, a vicar of Salisbury, perfected for Walter Bradley concerning a [corner: *cf.* ***1729, 1750***] tenement in St. Martin's Street and Culver Street
1580 A charter of John Hurst and his wife Joan perfected for Edmund Enfield and William Irish, of Andover, concerning a tenement in Castle Street
1581 A charter of William Boyland perfected for John Thorburn concerning a cottage (*or* cottages) in Chipper Street; with letters for delivering the seisin
1582 A charter of Robert Newport and his wife Agnes perfected for John Hill concerning a rent of 20*s.* to be received from a tenement in the city
1583 A deed of Joan, a daughter of Thomas Hutchins, perfected for Hugh Adam and others concerning her estate in a tenement in Endless Street; with letters for receiving the seisin
1584 A charter of William Bailiff, taverner, perfected for John Newman concerning two shops in Castle Street
1585–6 Two charters concerning a tenement opposite the market place: one of Henry Berwick perfected for John Forest and Thomas Eyre, and one of an elder John Forest and Thomas Eyre perfected for Henry Berwick, weaver, and his wife Agnes
1587 The will of William Boyland, which includes a tenement in Endless Street. Approved
1588 A charter of Thomas Sexton, ironmonger, perfected for Henry Winpenny, butcher, concerning a shop in Butcher Row
1589–90 Two charters perfected for Edith, the relict of William Boyland, concerning a tenement in Endless Street: one of John Thorburn and John Grandon, executors of William, and one of the same substance
1591 A charter of William Guys perfected for Henry Pentridge, a chaplain, and others concerning a tenement in Carter Street
1592 A charter of Richard Whiteparish perfected for John Horningsham, a chaplain, and William Lord concerning a tenement in Castle Street; with letters of attorney for delivering the seisin
1593–4 Two charters concerning all Nicholas Taylor's land and tenements in the city: one of Nicholas perfected for Edward Elion and Thomas Wallington, and one of Edward and Thomas perfected for Nicholas and his wife Lucy; with letters of attorney in Thomas's name for delivering the seisin, other letters of attorney for receiving the seisin, and letters for admittance under the necessary seal
1595 A charter of Edith, the relict of William Boyland, perfected for Thomas Bleacher concerning a tenement in Endless Street

22 June 1395 x 21 June 1396
1596–8 Three writings concerning a tenement in Winchester Street: the will of Thomas Hart, approved, which includes it, a deed of Alice, Thomas's relict, perfected for Edmund Enfield and Richard Spencer concerning her estate in it,

and a deed of Alice, an executor of Thomas, perfected for Edmund and Richard concerning the reversion of it

1599 A deed of release of John Chandler perfected for John, a son of William Knight, concerning a tenement in Carter Street

1600 A charter of John Hill, carpenter, perfected for Robert Salter, of Sarson, concerning rent of 20s. issuing from a tenement (*or* tenements) in Carter Street and Brown Street

1601 The will of John Harnham, which includes a shop near the graveyard of St. Thomas's [church]. Approved

1602 The will of Thomas Sexhampcote, which includes several tenements, shops, and cottages and rent. Approved

1603–4 Two deeds perfected for William Stout concerning two cottages in Gigant Street: one of Joan, the relict of Thomas Sexhampcote, concerning her estate in them, and one of Joan and another (*or* others), executors of Thomas

1605 A charter of Robert Deverill perfected for John Forest and William Lord concerning all his land and tenements in the city

1606 The will of an elder John Needler, which includes a tenement in Carter Street. Approved

1607–10 Four writings concerning a tenement in Castle Street: the will of Richard Whiteparish, approved, which includes it, a charter of William Lord perfected for Edward Elion, a chaplain, a charter of Alice, Richard's relict, perfected for Edward, as concerning her whole estate, and a deed of Alice perfected for Edward concerning the reversion of it

1611 The will of Thomas Stalbridge, which includes various tenements and cottages in the city. Approved

1612 A charter of William Warmwell perfected for John Sydenham and William Huggin concerning a tenement, with a cottage (*or* cottages), in New Street for a rent to be paid from it

1613–14 Two writings perfected for Nicholas Harding concerning a tenement in Carter Street of late that of an elder John Needler: a charter of John Needler, and a deed of release of a younger John Needler

1615 A charter of Robert Newport and his wife Agnes perfected for John Chandler and William Moore concerning two shops in Carter Street

1616 A charter of John Chandler perfected for John Ettshall concerning a tenement in Carter Street

1617–19 Three charters of Thomas Bleacher and others, executors of Robert Play: one perfected for William Dowding and his wife Christine concerning a tenement in Winchester Street, one perfected for John Salisbury, grocer, concerning a shop (*or* shops) at the end of Butcher Row, and one perfected for William and Christine concerning a tenement in Winchester Street

1620 A deed of release of Thomas Bleacher, a kinsman of Robert Play, perfected for William Dowding concerning the tenement mentioned above

1621 A charter of John Chandler perfected for Edmund Enfield and his wife Edith concerning three shops in Freren Street

1622–4 Three writings concerning a corner tenement, with shops, in Wineman

Street and Culver Street: a charter of William Surr perfected for William Lord, William Spencer, and Reynold Cook, a deed of release of William Lord perfected for William Spencer and Reynold, and a charter of William Spencer and Reynold perfected for William Surr and his wife Tamsin

1625 A charter of John Ettshall perfected for an elder John Chandler concerning a tenement in Carter Street

1626–7 Two charters of William Stourton, William River, and others: one perfected for John Justice concerning a tenement in Winchester Street, and one perfected for Richard Spencer and Robert Hazelbury concerning cottages, shops, and a yard (*or* yards) in Rolleston

1628 A charter of Walter Butterley perfected for John Mower and his wife Cecily concerning a rent of 40*s.* from Thomas Britford's tenement in Carter Street

1629 A charter of Christine, the relict, and an executor, of Robert Beechfount perfected for William Buck, a chaplain, concerning a tenement in Carter Street

1630–5 Six charters of William Stourton, William River, Edmund Enfield, John Blickling, William Buck, and William Winslow: one perfected for John Camel, grocer, concerning rent of 13*s.* 4*d.*, with the reversion of a tenement in New Street, and a chief tenement in New Street and Minster Street, one perfected for that John concerning a tenement in Brown Street, one perfected for that John concerning two shops in Brown Street called Bakehouse, one perfected for John Mower and his wife Cecily concerning a corner tenement [?in Endless Street and Chipper Street: *cf.* ***1108–9***, ***1575***, ***1865***], with a shop (*or* shops), called Bedred Row, one perfected for Richard Spencer concerning a corner tenement in New Street and Gigant Street, and one perfected for Richard concerning a tenement in Winchester Street now John Pope's

1636 A charter of Thomas Bleacher and others, executors of Robert Play, perfected for Nicholas Harding concerning a tenement in Endless Street

1637 A charter of John Chandler and William Moore perfected for Henry Prettyjohn and his wife Agnes concerning two shops in Carter Street

1638 A charter of Richard Spencer perfected for John Bosham and his wife Christine concerning a tenement in Winchester Street

1639 A charter of Thomas Bleacher and others, executors of Robert Play, perfected for John Camel, grocer, concerning a corner tenement in Endless Street

1640 A charter of John Ettshall perfected for Robert Netton, a chaplain, concerning a tenement in St. Martin's Street

1641 The will of John at the heath, which includes a tenement, with a shop (*or* shops), in Winchester Street. Approved

1642–4 Three writings concerning tenements in Minster Street and Castle Street: the will of John Camel, hatter, approved, which includes them, a deed of John's relict Isabel perfected for Henry Berwick concerning her estate in them, and a deed of Isabel, John Stoke, and Simon Bunt, executors of John, perfected for Henry concerning the reversion of them

1645 A charter of William Stourton, William River, and others, as [*in* ***1630–5***] above, perfected for John Camel, grocer, concerning a tenement called Bull Hall and a corner tenement in Carter Street and Winchester Street called Dyne's

Corner; with letters of attorney for receiving the seisin

1646 The will of Margaret Bown, the relict of Robert Play, which includes several tenements, cottages, and rent in the city. Approved

1647 The will of Nicholas Taylor, draper, which includes all his rent [?*rectius* tenements], cottages, and rent in the cities of London and Salisbury. Approved

1648 The will of John Thorburn, which includes a rent of 2 marks from cottages in Chipper Lane. Approved

1649–52 Four deeds perfected for Richard Jewell and Robert Play concerning the reversion of a tenement in Wineman Street: one of Reynold Drury and his wife Alice, an executor of Walter Leacher, an executor of Mary, the wife of Ralph Ive, one of John Brewer and his wife Alice by means of trustees and attorneys, one of James Goldsmith, called Ive, and another of James concerning the reversion on the death of George Merriott

1653–4 Two charters of John Mildenhall perfected for Walter Nalder: one concerning all his land and tenements in the city, with letters of attorney for surrendering the seisin, and one concerning a rent of 13*s*. 4*d*. from a tenement in Castle Street and a rent of 6*s*. 8*d*. issuing from a tenement in Culver Street

1655 A charter of John Stoke and Nicholas Harding, executors of John Cole, perfected for William Warmwell concerning three cottages, with a yard (*or* yards) and a dovecot, in Castle Street beyond the bar

BOOK FIVE

WSA G 23/1/213

There begins a volume in the time of a younger William Lord, [the clerk]

28 April 1361, at Salisbury

1656 By her deed Alice, the relict of Philip Longenough, of late a citizen of Salisbury, granted to Philip Aubin, of Winchester, a citizen of that city [?Salisbury: *cf.* **1657**], a rent of 20*s*. a year to be received for ever by him and his heirs and assigns from her two shops, with sollars, and a lower shop which stand conjoined in Carter Street in front of a tenement of hers. The two shops, with the sollars, stand beside a tenement formerly that of a younger Robert Baldry on the south [?*rectius* north] side, and the lower shop stands between the two shops on the north side and the chief entrance of Alice's tenement on the south side. Philip of late claimed from Alice that rent, which he, his ancestors, and the others who held his estate were accustomed to receive from a time from which no memory exists, as is supposed, and he quitclaimed to her and her heirs the rent and his right or claim to the shops. Clause to permit distraint in the three shops, into the hand of whomever they might have come, if the rent were in arrear, and to permit the keeping of distresses until the unpaid rent was recovered. So that her grant, and the confirmation of the charter, would remain valid for ever Alice confirmed Philip's seisin by paying to him 1*d*. on the day on which the charter was perfected. Clause of warranty perfected. Seals: Alice's and the common and mayoral seals of the city. Named witnesses: the bailiff, the mayor, the coroners, the reeves, John of Upton, William Wishford, Robert of Godmanstone, Thomas of Britford, Henry at the burgh, John of Deanbridge, and the clerk

1 September 1361, at Salisbury
1657 By his charter Philip Aubin, a citizen of Salisbury, granted to Stephen Haim, a citizen of Winchester, rent of 20s. a year issuing from two shops, with sollars, and a lower shop in Carter Street [*as in* **1656**], to be held for ever by him and his heirs and assigns. Clause to permit entry on the shops if the rent were in arrear for a quindene, distraint, and the keeping of distresses until the unpaid rent was recovered. Clause of warranty. Seals: Philip's and the common and mayoral seals of the city. Named witnesses: the bailiff, the mayor, the reeves, John of Upton, Robert of Godmanstone, William of Wishford, Thomas of Bridgehampton, George Goss, and Thomas of Britford

13 March 1387, at Salisbury
1658 A deed of William, a son and heir of William Sire, of late a citizen of Salisbury. The younger William had brought a writ of novel disseisin against Bartholomew Durkin, goldsmith, Walter Ryborough, and John Camel, hatter, concerning two cottages and two tofts, pretending to have a right in them when he had no such right. The cottages and tofts lie conjoined in Wineman Street between Robert Deverill's cottages on the east side and a corner tenement of late Hugh Boney's on the west side. William now quitclaimed to Bartholomew, Walter, and John and their heirs and assigns his right or claim to them; also his right or claim to a rent of 12s. a year, which his father acquired from Peter of Wimborne, the provost of St. Edmund's church, and Adam Ludwell, executors of Henry Bury, a citizen of Salisbury, issuing from that corner tenement, in Wineman Street and Culver Street, between the tofts on the east side and a tenement of late Robert Baldry's on the south side; also his right or claim to all the land and tenements which Bartholomew, Walter, and John hold in the city. Clause of warranty. Seals: William's and the common and mayoral seals of the city. Named witnesses: the bailiff, the mayor, the reeves, Nicholas Taylor, William Warmwell, and William Lord

18 August 1395, at Salisbury
1659 By his tripartite charter John, a son and heir of William Knight, granted to Richard Fulham and William Saunder a tenement, with shops, in Carter Street between William Guys's tenement on the north side and Thomas Burford's shop property on the south side. The tenement is to be held for ever by Richard and William and their heirs and assigns for a rent of 40s. cash a year to be paid for ever to John and his issue and for a slop worth 5s. to be given to John yearly at Christmas while he lived. It is to be maintained and repaired at their own expense by Richard and William and their heirs and assigns so that the rent would not be lost. Clause to permit re-entry if that were not done or if for 15 days the rent were overdue or the slop not given, and to permit distraint and the keeping of distresses until the unpaid rent and other losses were recovered; also, if the rent of 40s. were

in arrear for a quarter during John's life, to permit repossession for his life, saving to Richard and William and their heirs and assigns the reversion on his death. If while he lived John were to grant the rent to anyone for a term of years, lose it by the judgement of a court, or forfeit it in any way the payment of it would cease and the tenement be exonerated from it, there being no fraud, deceipt, or collusion on the part of Richard and William and their heirs and assigns. If John were to die without issue the payment of the 40s. would cease and the tenement be quit of it. Clause of warranty. Seals: those of the parties to the parts of the charter in turn and the common and mayoral seals of the city. Named witnesses: the bailiff, the mayor, a coroner, the reeves, John Butterley, William Warmwell, Thomas Bowyer, John Mower, Richard Leach, and the clerk

26 April 1396, at Salisbury
1660 By his charter an elder William Lord granted to Robert Reading a tenement, with shops, in Minster Street between Thomas Chaplin's shop property on the north side and a shop which John Kimpton, weaver, holds on the south side. The tenement was of late held by William with Bartholomew Durkin, a goldsmith, and John Camel, hatter, citizens of Salisbury, now dead, by a feoffment of Robert and his wife Cecily, and it is to be held for ever by Robert and his heirs and assigns. Seals: William's and the common and mayoral seals of the city. Named witnesses: the bailiff, the mayor, the reeves, William Warmwell, John Mower, John Salisbury, grocer, Richard Leach, and Richard Spencer

13 September 1396, at Salisbury
1661 By his charter Richard Leach, of Salisbury, granted to Margaret, the relict of William Godmanstone, of late a citizen of Salisbury, the land, tenements, rent, services, and reversions in Salisbury which he and an elder William Lord of late held by William's grant, to be held for ever by Margaret and her heirs and assigns. Seals: Richard's and the common and mayoral seals of the city. Named witnesses: the bailiff, the mayor, the coroners, the reeves, William Warmwell, John Mower, John Salisbury, grocer, John Camel, and John Needler

29 September 1396, at Salisbury
1662 By his deed an elder William Lord quitclaimed to Margaret, the relict of William Godmanstone, a citizen of Salisbury, his right or claim to the land and tenements in Salisbury which he held by William's grant. Seals: William's and the common and mayoral seals of the city. Named witnesses: the bailiff, the mayor, the coroners, the reeves, William Warmwell, John Mower, and the others as above [*in* **1661**]

22 November 1396, at Salisbury
1663 A charter of Hugh Winterbourne, an executor of Christine, of late his wife and an executor of Thomas 'Grauntpe', formerly an executor of Joan Pechin, who devised to her daughters Agnes and Christine and their issue for ever a tenement standing in Pot Row between a tenement of William Wilton,

butcher, on the west side and John Barnaby's tenement on the east side. If Agnes and Christine were to die without issue the tenement should be sold by Joan's executors or subsequent executors. The money received should be laid out on behalf of Joan's soul, the soul of Adam Pechin, formerly her husband, and the souls of others. Agnes and Christine died without living issue so that the sale of the tenement pertained to Hugh, and on the strength of Joan's will Hugh now granted the tenement to Richard Leach to be held for ever by him and his heirs and assigns. Seals: Hugh's and the common and mayoral seals of the city. Named witnesses: the mayor, a coroner, the reeves, William Warmwell, John Mower, John Salisbury, grocer, Thomas Bowyer, John Wallop, and Robert Deverill

6 December 1396, at Salisbury
1664 Approval of the will of Robert Sexhampcote, made on 29 May 1396. Interment: in the graveyard of St. Edmund's church. Bequests: 40*d*. each to the fabric of that church, the fabric of the cathedral church, and the fabric of the church of the Blessed Michael, at Figheldean, where he was born; 2*s*. 6*d*. both to the Franciscans of Salisbury and the Dominicans of Fisherton; 12*d*. to each of his two godsons; 40*d*. to Alice King; a silver bowl marked by his own hands to each of his brother the lord John Sexhampcote, a chaplain, and Alice, a daughter of his brother Roger; a small silver bowl to Henry Durnford; the rest of his goods to his wife Pauline. Devise: to Pauline for her dower a cottage in Scots Lane, which he held by a gift and devise of his deceased brother Thomas, to be held for ever by Pauline and her heirs and assigns. Executor: Pauline. Proved on 13 August 1396 in front of Thomas Montagu, the dean of Salisbury, the subdeanery being vacant; the administration was entrusted to Pauline. Approved at a court held in front of the bailiff, the mayor, and other citizens; the seisin of the cottage was released to the legatee.
1665 By their release William Stourton, William River, and Edmund Enfield, and John Blickling, William Buck, and William Winslow, chaplains, quitclaimed to Alice, the relict of John Butterley, of late a citizen of Salisbury, and her heirs and assigns their right or claim to a messuage, with an adjoining plot of land, measuring 59 ft. in length and 38 ft. in width including the walls appurtenant to the messuage and plot. The messuage, formerly that of Henry Russell, a citizen of Salisbury, stands, with the plot, in Winchester Street, above the common trench, between a tenement of late William Montagu's on the west side and a tenement of late Robert Play's, now William Dowding's, on the east side. William Stourton and the others also quitclaimed to Alice and her heirs and assigns their right or claim to a tenement, with two shops and two sollars, in Winchester Street, above the common trench, between a tenement of John Baker, grocer, on the west side and the messuage, in which Alice now dwells, with the plot of land, on the east side; also to a tenement, with a garden, in New Street between John Wishford's tenement on the east side and William Bailey's tenement on the west side; also to a tenement, with shops and a garden next to it, in Winchester Street, near Milford bars, between a tenement of late John Butterley's, now Margery Justice's, on the west side and the city's ditch on the east side. Seals: those of the six who

quitclaimed and the common and mayoral seals of the city. Named witnesses: the bailiff, the mayor, a coroner, the reeves, John Mower, John Camel, John Baker, grocer, Thomas Boyton, the master Richard Leach, Robert Deverill, and the clerk

8 December 1396, at Salisbury
1666 A deed of Thomas Bowyer, a citizen of Salisbury, and Thomas Cook, a chaplain, who of late granted to Alice, the relict of John Butterley, of late a citizen of Salisbury, a messuage, with an adjoining plot of land [*as in* **1665**], to be held by her for her life paying a rent of a rose a year to them. Thomas and Thomas now quitclaimed to Alice and her heirs and assigns their right or claim to the messuage, with the plot. Seals: those of Thomas and Thomas and the common and mayoral seals of the city. Named witnesses: the bailiff, the mayor, a coroner, the reeves, John Mower, John Camel, John Baker, grocer, the master Richard Leach, Robert Deverill, William Hill, and the clerk

11 December 1396, at London
1667–9 By their letters of attorney Thomas Wallington, John Werring, and Thomas Jarvis, executors of Nicholas Taylor, formerly a citizen and clothier of London, appointed William Lord to surrender, together with Edward Elion, a chaplain, a co-executor, into the hand of Richard, the bishop of Salisbury, the seisin of several premises to the use of William Bailey [*as in* **1671**], Simon Tredinnick [*as in* **1672**], and William Bishop [*as in* **1673**]. Seals: in each case those of Thomas Wallington, John Werring, and Thomas Jarvis

3 January 1397, at Salisbury
1670 By her charter Margery, the relict of Geoffrey Sunbury, in her widowhood and full power, granted to Edmund Enfield, a clerk, and his wife Edith a shop, with a sollar, in Drake Hall Street between Henry Southwick's tenement on the north side and a schoolhouse on the south side. The shop was held by Margery and Geoffrey by a grant of Thomas Hindon, a citizen of Salisbury, and is to be held for ever by Edmund and Edith and Edmund's heirs and assigns. Clause of warranty. Seals: Margery's and the common and mayoral seals of the city. Named witnesses: the mayor, a coroner, the reeves, William Warmwell, John Mower, John Salisbury, grocer, Richard Leach, John Needler, Adam Teffont, and the clerk
1671 A charter of Edward Elion, a chaplain, Thomas Wallington, John Werring, and Thomas Jarvis, executors of Nicholas Taylor, of late a citizen and clothier of London and Salisbury. By his will, proved in the husting court of London concerning pleas of land held on 31 January 1396, approved at a court held at Salisbury on 13 September 1396 and sealed with the mayoral seal, Nicholas devised the land, rent, and tenements which he held in the cities and suburbs of London and Salisbury to his son John to be held for ever by John and his heirs. If John were to die without issue Nicholas devised the land, rent, and tenements for ever to his own son Roger and his issue, and if Roger were to die without

issue to his own executors to be sold. John died without issue, afterwards Roger died likewise, and as a result the right in the land, rent, and tenements has accrued to the executors. On the strength of Nicholas's will Edward, Thomas, John, and Thomas granted to William Bailey, draper, of Salisbury, and his wife Alice a messuage in Minster Street, otherwise called Castle Street, between a tenement of Thomas Boyton, bowyer, on the south side and John Newman's shops on the north side, to be held for ever by William and Alice and their heirs and assigns of the chief lord of the renowned city of Salisbury. Seals: those of the grantors and the common and mayoral seals of the city. Named witnesses: the mayor, a coroner, the reeves, William Warmwell, John Mower, John Salisbury, grocer, John Wallop, John Needler, Richard Leach, Adam Teffont, and the clerk

1672 A charter of Edward Elion, a chaplain, Thomas Wallington, John Werring, and Thomas Jarvis, executors of Nicholas Taylor, of late a citizen and clothier of London and Salisbury. *Details and relevant provisions of Nicholas's will, and of later events, were recounted* [*as in* **1671**]. On the strength of that will those executors granted to Simon Tredinnick, draper, of Salisbury, a tenement in Pot Row between a tenement of William Wilton, butcher, on the east side and Thomas Knoyle's tenement on the west side, to be held for ever by Simon and his heirs and assigns; also a tenement in Wheeler Row between John Bonham's tenement on the north side and a tenement of John Franklin, wheeler, on the south side, to be held for ever by Simon and his heirs and assigns. Seals: those of the grantors and the common and mayoral seals of the city. Named witnesses: the mayor, a coroner, the reeves, John Mower, William Warmwell, John Salisbury, grocer, Richard Leach, John Needler, and the clerk

1673 A charter of Edward Elion, a chaplain, Thomas Wallington, John Werring, and Thomas Jarvis, executors of Nicholas Taylor, of late a citizen and clothier of London and Salisbury. *Details and relevant provisions of Nicholas's will, and of later events, were recounted* [*as in* **1671**]. Under that will the money from the sale of Nicholas's land, rent, and tenements should be laid out on the salvation of his soul and the soul of Lucy, of late his wife, and on various charitable deeds. On the strength of it those executors granted to William Bishop, of Salisbury, a messuage in Winchester Street, opposite the common trench of running water, between a tenement of late William Ashton's on the west side and Thomas Knoyle's tenement on the east side, extending from the street on the north side as far as Thomas Chaplin's tenement [?in New Street: *cf.* **1701**] on the south side. The messuage is to be held for ever by William Bishop and his heirs and assigns as that which he bought from the executors for a sum of money reaching its true value. Seals: those of the grantors and the common and mayoral seals of the city. Named witnesses: the mayor, a coroner, the reeves, William Warmwell, John Mower, Richard Leach, John Needler, Adam Teffont, John Newman, and the clerk

17 January 1397, at Salisbury
1674 A charter of John Swift, ironmonger, and his wife Christine, the relict, and an executor, of William Heal, smith, called Thatcher, who devised to Christine for life a tenement in Minster Street between a tenement of late Bartholomew

Durkin's on the south side and shops formerly William Dunkerton's, now those of John and Christine, on the north side. The tenement should remain on Christine's death to William Smith, William Thatcher's brother, for his life, and on the death of William Heal and Christine should be sold by William Thatcher's executors or subsequent executors. The money received should be laid out on celebrating masses, giving alms, and doing other charitable deeds on behalf of William's soul, Christine's soul, and the souls of others. William Heal has died, Thomas Sexton has paid to John and Christine a sum of money reaching the true value of the reversion of the tenement, and John and Christine, appearing at the court held on that day, on the strength of William Thatcher's will granted the reversion to Thomas. On Christine's death the tenement is to be held for ever by Thomas and his heirs and assigns. Seals: those of John and Christine and the common and mayoral seals of the city. Named witnesses: the mayor, a coroner, the reeves, William Warmwell, John Mower, John Baker, grocer, Richard Leach, John Needler, Adam Teffont, and the clerk

1675 By his charter Richard Harlwin granted to John Swift, ironmonger, a tenement in Minster Street between John's tenement on the north side and a tenement of late that of an elder John Harnham, a cordwainer, of Salisbury, on the south side. The tenement was held by Richard and an elder William Lord, now dead, by a grant of John Salisbury, grocer, and Richard Leach, and is to be held for ever by John Swift and his heirs and assigns. Seals: Richard's and the common and mayoral seals of the city. Named witnesses: the mayor, a coroner, the reeves, William Warmwell, John Mower, John Needler, John Wallop, Adam Teffont, and the clerk

1676 By his charter Simon Treddinick, of Salisbury, granted two tenements to Edward Elion, a chaplain, and William Wareham. One tenement stands in Pot Row [*as in* **1672**] and the other in Wheeler Row [*as in* **1672**]. They were both of late held by Simon by a grant of Edward Elion, Thomas Wallington, and John Werring, executors of Nicholas Taylor, of late a citizen and clothier of London and Salisbury, and are to be held for ever by Edward and William and their heirs and assigns. Clause of warranty. Seals: Simon's and the common and mayoral seals of the city. Named witnesses: the mayor, a coroner, the reeves, William Warmwell, John Mower, John Salisbury, grocer, Richard Leach, John Needler, and the clerk

18 January 1397, at Salisbury
1677 A writing of John Swift, ironmonger, and his wife Christine, the relict of William Heal, smith, called Thatcher, who devised to Christine for her life a tenement in Minster Street [*as in* **1674**]. John and Christine now quitclaimed their right or claim to it to Thomas Sexton and his heirs and assigns. Seals: those of John and Christine and the common and mayoral seals of the city. Named witnesses: the mayor, a coroner, John Needler, Adam Teffont, and the clerk

19 January 1397, at Salisbury
1678 By his charter Thomas Sexton granted to John Swift, ironmonger, and his

wife Christine a tenement in Minster Street [*as in* **1674**], to be held for ever by John and Christine and their heirs and assigns. Seals: Thomas's and the common and mayoral seals of the city. Named witnesses: the mayor, a coroner, the reeves, William Warmwell, John Mower, John Baker, grocer, Richard Leach, John Needler, Adam Teffont, and the clerk

31 January 1397, at Salisbury
1679 A deed of William Saunder, weaver, of Salisbury. By his tripartite charter John, a son and heir of William Knight, of late granted to William Saunder and Richard Fulham a tenement, with shops, in Carter Street between William Guys's tenement on the north side and a shop which Margery Whaddon holds on the south side, to be held for ever by William and Richard and their heirs and assigns. William now quitclaimed to Richard and his heirs and assigns his right or claim to it. Seals: William Saunder's and the common and mayoral seals of the city. Named witnesses: the mayor, a coroner, the reeves, William Warmwell, Thomas Bowyer, John Mower, Richard Leach, John Needler, Adam Teffont, and the clerk

14 February 1397, at Salisbury
1680 Approval of the will of John Yate, of Mere, a burgess of Salisbury [?*rectius* Old Sarum], made at Mere on 25 February 1393. Interment: in Mere church. Bequests: 20*s*. to the fabric of Mere church; 2*s*. 6*d*. each to the vicar of that church, the lord William Wymont, the lord William, the parish priest, the lord John Stock, and the lord Robert Horningsham; 3*s*. 4*d*. to the cathedral church; 12*d*. each to Richard Man and Anselm Cowage, clerks; 6*s*. 8*d*. each to the convents of Maiden Bradley, Longleat, and Stavordale; 3*s*. 4*d*. to the friar John Bartlet; 20*s*. to Henry Rochelle; 40*s*. each to John Gardener and Benet Little; 12*d*. to each of his godsons; 12*d*. to each extraneous priest present at his funeral rites and at a mass on the morrow; 2 marks and a coverlet with a green tapet to Walter, his household servant; 3*s*. 4*d*. to Maud, the wife of Henry Plebs; on the day of his burial 100*s*. for interring his corpse; 20*s*. to Sandhurst church; the rest of his goods to his wife Joan. Devises: John appointed that a corner tenement and a rent of 26*s*. 8*d*. should be sold by his executors after the death of his wife Joan. The tenement stands in Scots Lane between John Lymington's tenement on the north side and Adam Morris's tenement on the west side, in St. Edmund's parish; the rent issues from a tenement, which Thomas Redenham, a tanner, holds, in Endless Street between a tenement of John Taylor, called Hosier, on the north side and St. Edmund's chantry on the south side, in St. Edmund's parish. In both cases the money received should be laid out on behalf of his soul. Executors: his wife Joan, John Gardener, and Benet Little. John Yate affixed his seal to the will. Witnesses: the lord John Dunn, the vicar of Mere, William Wymont, Robert Horningsham, John Gardener, Benet Little, and others. Proved on 21 June 1393 in front of an officer of the dean of Salisbury; the administration was entrusted to Joan, reserving the power of entrusting it to John Gardener and Benet Little when they might come to seek it. Approved at a court held in front of the bailiff,

the mayor, and other citizens; the seisin of the tenement was released to the legatees.

1681 A deed of Christine, the relict, and an executor, of Robert Beechfount, of late a citizen of Salisbury, who devised to his son Robert a tenement, with shops, and a gate. The tenement, with the shops, stands on the north side of Winchester Street between Robert Deverill's tenement on the east side and Thomas Castleton's tenement on the west side. The gate stands in Culver Street between Robert Deverill's shops on the south side and John Mower's cottages on the north side. The tenement, shops, and gate were to be held for ever by the younger Robert and his issue, if that Robert were to die without issue would remain for life to the elder Robert's daughter Margaret, and after Margaret's death should be sold by the elder Robert's executors or subsequent executors. The money received should be laid out on behalf of the elder Robert's soul and the souls of his wives and others. Margaret died long before the younger Robert, the younger Robert died without issue, and as a result the right in the tenement, shops, and gate accrued to Christine, as an executor, to be sold. On the strength of the elder Robert's will Christine now granted the tenement, with the shops, and the gate to John Barrett, weaver, of Salisbury, and his wife Amice, to be held for ever by them and John's heirs and assigns, as that which John and Amice bought from her for a sum of money reaching their full value. Seals: Christine's and the common and mayoral seals of the city. Named witnesses: the mayor, a coroner, the reeves, William Warmwell, John Mower, Richard Leach, John Needler, Adam Teffont, and the clerk

15 February 1397, at Salisbury
1682 By their writing John Beechfount, a chaplain, and an elder John Chandler, executors of Robert Beechfount, of late a citizen of Salisbury, quitclaimed to John Barrett, weaver, of Salisbury, his wife Amice, and to John's heirs and assigns, their right or claim to a tenement, with shops, and a gate [*as in* **1681**]. John and Amice of late acquired the tenement, shops, and gate from Christine, the relict, and an executor, of Robert Beechfount. Seals: those of John Beechfount and John Chandler and the common and mayoral seals of the city. Named witnesses: the mayor, a coroner, the reeves, William Warmwell, John Mower, John Needler, Adam Teffont, and the clerk

28 February 1397, at Salisbury
1683 A deed of Christine, the relict, and an executor, of Robert Beechfount, of late a citizen of Salisbury. Robert acquired a messuage in Carter Street, between a tenement then John Baker's, now Thomas Field's, on the south side and John Preston's tenement on the north side, and by his will, approved according to the custom of the city and sealed with the mayoral seal on 3 March 1389, devised it to Christine for life as dower. On Christine's death the messuage should remain for ever to Robert's son Robert and his issue, if that Robert were to die without issue would remain for life to Margaret, a daughter of the elder Robert, and after Margaret's death should be sold by the elder Robert's executors. The money

received should be laid out on behalf of souls [*as in* **1681**]. The younger Robert and Margaret have died, with no issue of Robert living. On the strength of the will Christine, who took upon herself the burden of it, all the other executors having renounced, granted to William Warin, of Salisbury, the reversion of the messuage when it fell due on her death. From then the messuage is to be held for ever by William and his heirs and assigns as that which he bought from Christine for a sum of money reaching the full value of the reversion. To acknowledge his lordship of the messuage Christine attorned to William by paying to him 4*d*. on the day on which the deed was perfected. Seals: Christine's and the common and mayoral seals of the city. Named witnesses: the mayor, the coroners, the reeves, William Warmwell, John Mower, John Needler, and the clerk

11 March 1397, at Salisbury
1684 By their writing William Stourton, William River, and Edmund Enfield, and John Blickling, William Buck, and William Winslow, chaplains, granted to William Alker and Edward Russell, chaplains, of Salisbury, a rent of 10*s*. a year issuing from a tenement in Minster Street between a tenement formerly Stephen Crier's on one side and a tenement of late John Richman's on the south side. The rent was held by them by a grant of John Butterley, a citizen of Salisbury, and is to be held for ever by William and Edward and their heirs and assigns on condition that the grantors might not be called to warrant the rent to the grantees. Seals: those of the grantors and the common and mayoral seals of the city. Named witnesses: the bailiff, the mayor, the coroners, the reeves, William Warmwell, John Mower, John Camel, Richard Leach, William Hill, and the clerk

14 March 1397, at Salisbury
1685 Approval of the will of Joan, the wife of William Warmwell, a citizen of Salisbury, made on 7 September 1396. <u>Interment</u>: in St. Thomas's church. <u>Devises</u>: to her husband William a tenement, in which she dwelt, in Minster Street, which is called Castle Street, between John Wallop's tenement on the south side and a tenement which of late Richard Rowde held, to be held for his life by William and his assigns, and after William's death to be sold by her executors. The reversion should be sold in William's lifetime if that can be done advantageously by the executors. The money received should be laid out on celebrating masses and doing other charitable deeds on behalf of Joan's soul and the souls of William Wootton, Walter Ryborough, her husband William, and others. Joan devised to her executors a corner tenement, with shops and cottages, in New Street and Gigant Street between Thomas Eyre's tenement on the west side and Christine Handley's tenement on the north side; also tenements, yards, and gardens standing and lying as much in the street called Nuggeston as in the street on the way to the pits opposite the graveyard of St. Edmund's church. She devised [all] those premises, with a purparty of all the goods pertaining to her, to be sold. From the money received the legacies of Walter Ryborough, of late her husband, should be paid in full. If anything remains it should be laid out by the executors in the way, and on behalf of the souls, mentioned above. If the executors

had died or gone away before the sales had been made, or the distribution of the money completed, Joan wished that they had arranged for others to sell the premises and lay out the money as they would have done. Executors: Edward Elion, Thomas Marlborough, and an elder William Lord. Proved on 18 October 1396 in front of the subdean of Salisbury; the administration was entrusted to Edward and Thomas, William Lord being dead. Approved at a court held in front of the bailiff, the mayor, and other citizens; the seisin of the tenements was released to the legatees.

26 March 1397, at Salisbury
1686 By his writing William, a son of William Lord, of late a citizen of Salisbury, quitclaimed to Simon Treddinick and his heirs and assigns all the right or claim which, by virtue of a deed of attornment given at London on 11 December 1396, he could have in two tenements, one in Pot Row [*as in* **1672**] and one in Wheeler Row [*as in* **1672**]. Seals: William's and the common and mayoral seals of the city. Named witnesses: the bailiff, the mayor, the coroners, the reeves, William Warmwell, John Mower, Richard Leach, John Needler, and the clerk

28 March 1397, at Salisbury
1687 By his deed Edward Elion, a chaplain, an executor of Nicholas Taylor, of late a citizen and clothier of London and Salisbury, quitclaimed to Simon Tredinnick, draper, of Salisbury, and his heirs and assigns his right or claim to two tenements, one in Pot Row [*as in* **1672**] and one in Wheeler Row [*as in* **1672**]. Seals: Edward's and the common and mayoral seals of the city. Named witnesses: the bailiff, the mayor, the coroners, the reeves, William Warmwell, John Mower, Richard Leach, John Needler, and the clerk
1688 A deed of Edward Elion, a chaplain, Thomas Wallington, John Werring, and Thomas Jarvis, executors of Nicholas Taylor, of late a citizen and clothier of London and Salisbury. *Details and relevant provisions of Nicholas's will, and of later events, were recounted* [*as in* **1671**]. On the strength of the will those executors granted to the lord Roger Walden, a clerk, William of Waltham, Richard Pitts and George of 'Lenthorp', clerks, and John Gowan a corner tenement called Wimpler's Corner, with shops attached to it, in Minster Street, opposite Robert Deverill's tenement, on the south side of the king's highway which leads towards the Dominicans of Fisherton, between Richard Leach's shop property on the south side and Philip Goldsmith's tenement on the west side. The tenement, with the shops, was acquired by Nicholas from Richard Berwick, formerly a citizen of Salisbury, and is to be held for ever by the grantees and their heirs and assigns. Seals: those of the grantors and the common and mayoral seals of the city. Named witnesses: the bailiff, the coroners, the mayor, the reeves, William Warmwell, John Mower, John Wallop, and William Guys
1689 A charter of Edward Elion, a chaplain, Thomas Wallington, John Werring, and Thomas Jarvis, executors of Nicholas Taylor, of late a citizen and clothier of London and Salisbury. *Details of relevant provisions of Nicholas's will, and of later events, were recounted* [*as in* **1671**]. On the strength of the will those executors

granted to John Camel, grocer, a citizen of Salisbury, a shop, with a small adjacent sollar built above a small shop formerly Stephen Cheese's which John Long, tailor, holds. Maud Till holds the shop, with the sollar, opposite the fishermens' stalls, between William Hoare's shop on the south side and a shop of late Nicholas Taylor's on the north side. The shop measures 39 ft. beside William's shop, 15 ft. beside the shop of late Nicholas's, 15 ft. on the east side beside William's tenement, and 10 ft. on the west side beside the street. Its north part extends from William's tenement on the east side as far as the small shop of late Stephen Cheese's on the west side. Nicholas Taylor acquired the shop from John Fish. Also on the strength of the will the executors granted to John Camel a shop, which John Long holds, in Endless Street, opposite the market place where pelts and fleeces are sold, between a tenement of late Thomas Hindon's on the north side and the shop which Maud Till holds on the south side. The south part of the shop extends from William Hoare's tenement on the east side as far as the small shop of late Stephen Cheese's on the west side. Nicholas acquired the shop from Thomas Long. The two shops are to be held for ever by John Camel and his heirs and assigns. Seals: those of the grantors and the common and mayoral seals of the city. Named witnesses: the bailiff, the mayor, the coroners, the reeves, William Warmwell, John Mower, John Wallop, John Salisbury, grocer, Richard Leach, John Needler, William Hill, and the clerk

1690 By his charter Simon Tredinnick, of Salisbury, granted to Edmund Enfield, a clerk, and his wife Edith six cottages, with a yard (*or* yards) and two racks, in Freren Street between a yard of late Thomas Focket's on the south side and a yard of St. Nicholas's hospital on the north side, to be held for ever by Edmund and Edith and Edmund's heirs and assigns. Seals: Simon's and the common and mayoral seals of the city. Named witnesses: the bailiff, the mayor, the coroners, the reeves, William Warmwell, John Mower, Richard Leach, John Wallop, John Salisbury, grocer, William Hill, John Needler, Robert Deverill, William Guys, and the clerk

1691 A charter of Edward Elion, a chaplain, Thomas Wallington, John Werring, and Thomas Jarvis, executors of Nicholas Taylor, of late a citizen and clothier of London and Salisbury. *Details of relevant provisions of Nicholas's will, and of later events, were recounted [as in 1671]*. On the strength of the will those executors granted to Richard Spencer and John Mower, citizens of Salisbury, a tenement in Minster Street, between the graveyard of St. Thomas's church on the south side and Thomas Bowyer's tenement on the north side, extending from the street on the east side all the way to the river which is called Avon on the west side. Nicholas acquired the tenement from William of Bruton, formerly a citizen of Salisbury. The executors licensed Richard and John and their heirs and assigns to build above a stile of the graveyard as, by his charter, William licensed Nicholas. The tenement, with the building as promised, is to be held for ever by Richard and John and their heirs and assigns. Seals: those of the grantors and the common and mayoral seals of the city. Named witnesses: the bailiff, the mayor, the coroners, the reeves, William Warmwell, Richard Leach, John Wallop, John Salisbury, grocer, William Hill, John Needler, John Newman, and the clerk

1692 A deed of Edward Elion, a chaplain, and Thomas Marlborough, executors of Joan, the relict, and an executor, of William Wootton, of late a citizen of Salisbury. William devised tenements, yards, and gardens standing and lying as much in the street called Nuggeston as in the street on the way to the pits opposite the graveyard of St. Edmund's church, to his children Nicholas and Agnes, to be held for ever by them and their issue. If Nicholas and Agnes were to die without issue the tenements, yards, and gardens should be sold by William's executors or subsequent executors. The money received should be laid out on behalf of William's soul and the souls of his wives and others. Nicholas and Agnes have died without issue, John Wishford has paid to Edward Elion and Thomas Marlborough a sum of money reaching the true value of the tenements, yards, and gardens, and on the strength of William's will Edward and Thomas granted the premises to John to be held for ever by him and his heirs and assigns. Seals: those of Edward and Thomas and the common and mayoral seals of the city. Named witnesses: the bailiff, the mayor, the coroners, the reeves, John Mower, Richard Leach, John Wallop, William Hill, John Needler, and the clerk

1693 A charter of Edward Elion, a chaplain, Thomas Wallington, John Werring, and Thomas Jarvis, executors of Nicholas Taylor, of late a citizen and clothier of London and Salisbury. *Details of relevant provisions of Nicholas's will, and of later events, were recounted* [*as in* **1671**]. On the strength of the will those executors granted to John Camel, grocer, a citizen of Salisbury, a corner tenement, with shops and cottages, in Wineman Street and Brown Street, opposite a tenement of late John Ball's in which Agnes of Woodford formerly dwelt, between John Camel's tenement, which he acquired from William Stourton, William River, and Edmund Enfield, and John Blickling, William Buck, and William Winslow, chaplains, on the south side and John Needler's tenement on the east side. The tenement, with the shops and cottages, was acquired by Nicholas Taylor from Nicholas Woodhill, a citizen of Salisbury, and is to be held for ever by John Camel, and his heirs and assigns. Seals: those of the grantors and the common and mayoral seals of the city. Named witnesses: the bailiff, the mayor, the coroners, the reeves, William Warmwell, John Mower, John Wallop, John Salisbury, grocer, Richard Leach, Robert Deverill, William Hill, and the clerk

29 March 1397, at Salisbury
1694 By their deed Edward Elion, a chaplain, Thomas Wallington, John Werring, and Thomas Jarvis, executors of Nicholas Taylor, of late a citizen and clothier of London and Salisbury, quitclaimed to the lord Roger Walden, William of Waltham, Richard Pitts, and George of 'Lenthorp', clerks, and John Gowan or their heirs and assigns their right or claim to a corner tenement called Wimpler's Corner [*as in* **1688**]. Seals: those of the executors and the common and mayoral seals of the city. Named witnesses: the bailiff, the mayor, the coroners, the reeves, William Warmwell, John Mower, John Wallop, John Needler, and William Hill

1695 By his letters of attorney John Camel, a citizen of Salisbury, appointed Edmund Enfield to receive from Edward Elion, a chaplain, Thomas Wallington, John Werring, and Thomas Jarvis, executors of Nicholas Taylor, of late a citizen and clothier of London and Salisbury, the seisin of a shop, with a small adjacent sollar, [*as in* **1689**], a shop which John Long holds [*as in* **1689**], and a corner tenement, with shops and cottages, [*as in* **1693**]. Seals: John Camel's and the common and mayoral seals of the city

1696 A deed of Edward Elion, a chaplain, and Thomas Marlborough, executors of Joan, the relict, and an executor, of William Wootton, of late a citizen of Salisbury, who devised a corner tenement, with shops and cottages next to it, in New Street [and Gigant Street] between Thomas Eyre's tenement on the west side and a tenement of late that of William Handley, tucker, on the south [?*rectius* north: cf. **1685**, **2101**] side, to be held for ever by his children Nicholas and Agnes and their issue. *Relevant provisions of William's will were recounted, and the death of Nicholas and Agnes recorded,* [*as in* **1692**]. John Newman has paid to Edward and Thomas a sum of money reaching the true value of the tenement, with the shops and cottages, and on the strength of William's will they granted the tenement to John to be held for ever by him and his heirs and assigns. Seals: those of Edward and Thomas and the common and mayoral seals of the city. Named witnesses: the bailiff, the mayor, the coroners, the reeves, William Warmwell, John Mower, John Wallop, Richard Leach, Robert Deverill, and the clerk

25 April 1397, at Salisbury

1697 By their charter Edward Elion and Thomas Marlborough, executors of Joan, who was the wife of William Warmwell, a citizen of Salisbury, on the strength of Joan's will granted to William River and his wife Joan the reversion of a messuage, with a shop (*or* shops), when it fell due on William Warmwell's death. The messuage, with the shop(s), stands in Castle Street, on the west side of the street, between John Wallop's tenement on the south side and Richard Rowde's tenement on the north side. Joan devised the reversion to be sold by her executors in William's lifetime, and on his death the messuage, with the shop(s), is to be held for ever by William and Joan and their heirs and assigns. Seals: those of Edward and Thomas and the common and mayoral seals of the city. Named witnesses: the bailiff, the mayor, a coroner, the reeves, John Mower, John Salisbury, grocer, John Camel, Richard Leach, William Hill, and John Needler

1698 By his charter Hugh Gundy, a citizen of Salisbury, granted to Thomas Play and his wife Alice a tenement, with two shops next to it, and a garden, in Carter Street between a tenement of late David Clark's on the north side and a tenement of late William Knight's on the south side. The tenement, with the shops and the garden, was devised by Alice, of late Hugh's wife, a daughter and heir of Thomas Callow, to Hugh and his heirs and assigns on the death of John Bristow, now dead, the tenant for life, and it is to be held for ever by Thomas and Alice and their heirs and assigns. Seals: Hugh's and the common and mayoral seals of the city. Named witnesses: the bailiff, the mayor, a coroner, the reeves, John Mower, Richard Leach, John Needler, John Newman, and the clerk

1 May 1397, at Salisbury

1699 A writing of William Warmwell, a citizen of Salisbury, who has examined the charter, given on 25 April 1397, which Edward Elion, a chaplain, and Thomas Marlborough, executors of Joan, formerly William's wife, perfected for William River and his wife Joan. *The words of the charter were rehearsed* [*as in* **1697**]. William confirmed the grant made to William River and Joan and, to acknowledge their lordship, attorned to them by paying to them 4*d.* on the day on which the writing was perfected. Seals: William's and the common and mayoral seals of the city. Named witnesses: the bailiff, the mayor, a coroner, the reeves, John Mower, John Salisbury, grocer, John Needler, and William Hill

23 May 1397, at Salisbury
1700 By her charter Isabel Cole, in her chaste widowhood and full power, granted to Nicholas Harding, of Salisbury, and his wife Agnes a tenement in Winchester Street between Richard Spencer's tenement on the east side and the tenement in which Isabel dwells on the west side; also a tenement in Gigant Street between John Ashley's tenement on the south side and Nicholas's tenement on the north side. The two tenements were held by Isabel and her son William Cole, a chaplain, now dead, by a grant of an elder William Lord, and are to be held for ever by Nicholas and Agnes and their heirs and assigns. Clause of warranty. Seals: Isabel's and the common and mayoral seals of the city. Named witnesses: the bailiff, the mayor, the coroners, the reeves, William Warmwell, John Mower, John Salisbury, grocer, John Camel, John Needler, an elder John Forest, and the clerk

6 June 1397, at Salisbury
1701 By their charter William River, and his wife Joan, appearing at the court held on that day, granted two tenements to Edmund Enfield, a clerk, and Ralph Hampstead, a chaplain, one in New Street between Thomas Chaplin's tenement on the east side and John Poxwell's tenement on the west side, and one in Culver Street between a corner tenement of late that of Bartholomew Durkin, a goldsmith, on the north side and Nicholas Baynton's cottages on the south side, to be held for ever by Edmund and Ralph and their heirs and assigns. Clause of warranty. Seals: those of William and Joan and the common and mayoral seals of the city. Named witnesses: the bailiff, the mayor, the coroners, the reeves, William Warmwell, John Mower, John Camel, John Forest, William Hill, John Needler, and the clerk

7 June 1397, at Salisbury
1702 By his letters of attorney Hugh Gundy, a citizen of Salisbury, appointed William Lord to deliver to Thomas Play and his wife Alice and their heirs and assigns the seisin of a tenement, with two shops and a yard, in Carter Street between William Knight's tenement on the south side and William Guys's tenement on the north side. Seal: Hugh's

20 June 1397, at Salisbury
1703 By their charter Robert Deverill and Robert Body, citizens of Salisbury, granted to John Mildenhall and William Pomfret, a citizen of London, cottages,

with conjoined racks and yards, in Castle Street, beyond the bars, between a tenement of late Roger Wallop's on the south side and a tenement now John Starr's on the north side; also shops, with conjoined yards, gardens, and a dovecote, in the same street, between a tenement of late Philip Bristow's on the north side and a tenement of the keepers of the light of the fraternity of the high cross in the cathedral church on the south side. The cottages and shops, with the racks, yards, gardens, and dovecote, were held by Robert Deverill and Robert Body by a grant of an elder John Gowan, and are to be held for ever by John and William and their heirs and assigns. Seals: those of the grantors and the common and mayoral seals of the city. Named witnesses: the bailiff, the mayor, the coroners, the reeves, William Warmwell, John Mower, John Camel, Richard Leach, John Salisbury, grocer, John Needler, John Forest, and the clerk

1704 By their writing, given 'on the day and in the year contained in the charter', Robert Deverill and Robert Body, citizens of Salisbury, granted to John Mildenhall and William Pomfret, a citizen of London, two rents, each of which they held for John's life by a grant of an elder John Gowan. One, of 13s. 4d. a year, was to be received from a tenement in Castle Street between a tenement of late John Beeton's on one side and a tenement of late Robert Pope's on the other side. The other, of 6s. 8d. a year, was to be received from a tenement in Culver Street between a tenement of late Richard Ryde's on the south side and cottage property of late that of John Starr and his wife Edith on the north side. The two are to be received by John and William and their assigns on the strength, in the form, and with the effect of Robert Deverill's and Robert Body's acquisition of them perfected by John Gowan. Seals: those of the grantors and the common and mayoral seals of the city. Named witnesses: the bailiff and the mayor

18 July 1397, at Salisbury
1705 By their charter William Bailey, draper, and John Brown, tucker, granted to Edward Fountain and his wife Joan a messuage, in New Street between a tenement of late that of Nicholas Hamish, a chaplain, on the east side and Hugh of Wimborne's tenement on the west side, to be held for ever by Edward and Joan and their heirs and assigns. Seals: those of William and John and the common and mayoral seals of the city. Named witnesses: the bailiff, the mayor, the coroners, the reeves, John Mower, John Camel, John Baker, grocer, William Hill, and the clerk

1706 By her charter Margaret, the relict of William Godmanstone, of late a citizen of Salisbury, in her chaste widowhood and full power, granted to Edmund Enfield, a clerk, and his wife Edith a yard, with two racks built in it, in Freren Street between a yard of John Salisbury, grocer, on the south side and Walter Orme's yard on the north side. The yard, with the racks, measures in width at its frontage on the street 80 ft. and 20 in. It is to be held for ever by Edmund and Edith and Edmund's heirs and assigns. Clause of warranty. Seals: Margaret's and the common and mayoral seals of the city. Named witnesses: the bailiff, the mayor, the coroners, the reeves, William Warmwell, John Mower, John Camel, Richard Leach, John Forest, John Needler, and the clerk

19 July 1397, at Salisbury
1707 By her letters of attorney Margaret, the relict of William Godmanstone, of late a citizen of Salisbury, in her chaste widowhood and full power, appointed Nicholas Mason, a chaplain, to surrender into the hand of Richard, the bishop of Salisbury, the seisin of a yard, with two racks built in it, [*as in* **1706**], to the use of Edmund Enfield, a clerk, and his wife Edith. Seals: Margaret's and the mayoral seal of the city.

1 August 1397, at Salisbury
1708 By her charter Alice, the relict of John Butterley, of late a citizen of Salisbury, in her chaste widowhood and full power, granted to William Isaac, baker, of Salisbury, a tenement, with shops and a garden next to it, in Winchester Street, near Milford's bars, between a tenement of late John Butterley's, now Margery Justice's, on the west side and the city's ditch on the east side. The tenement, with the shops, measures 42 ft. 2 in. in width at its frontage on the street. It is to be held, with the shops and the garden, for ever by William and his heirs and assigns. Clause of warranty. Seals: Alice's and the common and mayoral seals of the city. Named witnesses: the bailiff, the mayor, the coroners, the reeves, William Warmwell, John Mower, John Camel, John Needler, and an elder John Forest

12 September 1397, at Salisbury
1709 Approval [*dated to the Wednesday before the feast of the nativity of the Blessed Virgin Mary (5 September) probably in error for the Wednesday after that feast (12 September)*] of the will of Maud, the wife of George Merriott, made at Lopen on 26 June 1389. Interment: in the church of All Saints, Merriott. Bequests: 2s. 6d. to John Love, a chaplain, of Lopen, to celebrate mass on behalf of her soul; the rest of her goods, her debts having been paid and her funeral expenses deducted, to her husband George. Devise: to George, to be held for ever by him and his heirs and assigns, a tenement, with shops, cottages, a rack (*or* racks), and a yard (*or* yards), in Winchester Street and Culver Street between John Creed's cottages on the north side and John Cole's tenement on the west side. Executor: George. Proved on 26 January 1391 in front of Thomas Poulton, a clerk, the commissary general of Ralph, the bishop of Bath and Wells, in the parish church of Crewkerne; the administration was entrusted to George. Approved at a court held in front of the bailiff, the mayor, and other citizens; the seisin of the tenement, with the shops, cottages, rack(s), and yard(s), was released to the legatee.
1710 By their indented charter Simon Bunt and his wife Alice, appearing at the court held on that day, granted to John Wootton, of Salisbury, a corner messuage [Holy Ghost Corner: *cf.* **2078**], with shops and cottages next to it, in Winchester Street and Culver Street between a tenement of John Pope, tailor, in Winchester Street on the west side and a garden of late an elder William …'s [*surname omitted*: ?Sall (*cf.* **2078**)] on the south side. The messuage, with the shops and cottages, was held by John Camel, hatter, now dead, and Simon and Alice by a grant of John

Cole, a citizen of Salisbury, and his wife Isabel, is to be held for ever by John Wootton and his heirs and assigns for a rent of 5 marks a year to be paid to Simon and Alice while they lived and a payment of 74s. cash to Isabel, the relict of John Cole, and is to be repaired and maintained at the expense of John and his heirs and assigns so that the rent would not be lost. Clause to permit re-entry if the rent were in arrear for 15 days, distraint, and the keeping of distresses until the unpaid rent and other losses were recovered; also, if distresses sufficient for the rent could not be found, to permit repossession for the life of Simon and Alice and the life of the one of them living longer, saving to John Wootton and his heirs and assigns the reversion of the messuage, with the shops and cottages, on the death of Simon and Alice. Clause of warranty and of acquittance. Seals: those of the parties to the parts of the charter in turn and the common and mayoral seals of the city. Named witnesses: the bailiff, the mayor, the reeves, William Warmwell, John Mower, John Camel, Richard Leach, William Hill, and the clerk

26 September 1397, at Salisbury
1711 By his writing John Hill, carpenter, quitclaimed to Robert Salter, of Sarson, in Amport parish, and his heirs and assigns his right or claim to rent of 20s. a year issuing from two tenements, one in Carter Street between a tenement of late that of an elder John Needler on the north side and Thomas Chaplin's shops on the south side, and one in Brown Street between William Warmwell's tenement on the north side and an empty plot of late William Moyne's on the south side. Clause of warranty. Seals: John's and the common and mayoral seals of the city. Named witnesses: the bailiff, the mayor, a coroner, the reeves, John Mower, John Camel, John Baker, grocer, Thomas Boyton, the master Richard Leach, Robert Deverill, and the clerk.

4 October 1397
1712 A charter of William Sire, perfected on 13 March 1387 [*given in full as* **1658**], was recorded as a copy under the seal of the mayor

24 October 1397, at Salisbury
1713 By his charter Richard Harlwin, goldsmith, of Salisbury, granted to an elder John Chandler and Thomas Middleton a corner tenement in Wineman Street and Culver Street between William River's cottage in Culver Street on the south side and cottages of late Bartholomew Durkin's on the east side; also six conjoined cottages, with gardens next to them, in Wineman Street between that corner tenement on the west side and Robert Deverill's cottage on the east side. The cottages and the corner tenement, all of late Bartholomew's, are to be held, with the gardens, for ever by John and Thomas and their heirs and assigns. Seals: Richard's and the common and mayoral seals of the city. Named witnesses: the bailiff, the mayor, the coroners, the reeves, William Warmwell, John Mower, John Salisbury, grocer, John Camel, John Forest, John Needler, and the clerk
1714 By his charter Stephen Edington, of Salisbury, granted to John Coffer, tanner, the reversion of three premises when each fell due on the death of Joan, the relict

of John Luckham: that of a tenement in Brown Street between a tenement of late Nicholas Baker's on the south side and Jarvis Worthy's garden on the north side, that of a garden lying behind the tenement, on the far side of the common trench of running water, measuring 40 ft. in length, and that of a small empty plot lying on the north side of the tenement, measuring in width 2 ft. 2½ in. and in length extending from the east corner of the hall of the tenement as far as the east corner of a house called Workhouse, with free ingress and egress through the house to the plot. Stephen Edington and Henry Swain, now dead, jointly acquired the reversion of the tenement, and of the garden under the name of an empty plot, from Joan as an executor of John Luckham. The tenement, the garden, and the empty plot with the free ingress and egress, when they fall due, are to be held for ever by John Coffer and his heirs and assigns, provided that Stephen may be held to warrant the reversions only against himself and his heirs and not against John or his heirs or assigns. Seals: Stephen's and the common and mayoral seals of the city. Named witnesses: the bailiff, the mayor, the coroners, the reeves, William Warmwell, John Mower, John Camel, John Forest, and the clerk

29 October 1397, at Salisbury
1715 A deed of Joan, the relict of John Luckham. Stephen Edington granted to John Coffer the reversion on Joan's death of a tenement in Brown Street [*as in* **1714**], of a garden [*as in* **1714**], and of a small empty plot [*as in* **1714**], in all of which Joan holds an estate for life. Joan attorned to John by means of her fealty and paying to him 4*d*. on the day on which her deed was perfected. Seals: Joan's and the common and mayoral seals of the city. Named witnesses: the bailiff, the mayor, the coroners, the reeves, William Warmwell, John Mower, John Camel, John Forest, and clerk

2 November 1396 x 1 November 1397, at Salisbury
1716 An indented deed of Thomas, a son and heir of Thomas Chaplin, who had examined a charter of Alice, the relict of Philip Longenough, formerly a citizen of Salisbury, given on 28 April 1361 [**1656**], and a charter of Philip Aubin given on 1 September 1361 [**1657**]. Thomas ratified the charters and confirmed the estate which Stephen Haim held in rent by virtue of them. Clause to permit Stephen and his heirs and assigns to distrain in the shops if the rent were in arrear and to keep distresses until the unpaid rent was recovered. Seals: those of the parties to the parts of the charter in turn and the common and mayoral seals of the city. Named witnesses: the bailiff, the mayor, a coroner, the reeves, William Warmwell, John Mower, Richard Leach, John Needler, and the clerk

7 November 1397, at Salisbury
1717 A charter of William Warmwell, an executor of a younger William Tenterer, of late a citizen of Salisbury, who devised a corner tenement in Winchester Street and Gigant Street, between a tenement of late his own, now Thomas Postle's, on the east side and William Warmwell's tenement on the south side, to his wife Alice for life. On Alice's death the tenement should remain for ever to William

Tenterer's son John and his issue, if John were to die without issue it would remain for ever to William's daughter Isabel and her issue, and if Isabel were to die without issue it should be sold by William's executors. The money received should be laid out on celebrating masses, giving alms, and doing other charitable deeds on behalf of William's soul and the souls of his wives and others. John and Isabel are now dead with no living issue, Alice survives, and the reversion of the tenement pertains to William's executors to be sold. As to which Alice, one of the executors, often required by William Warmwell, her co-executor, to allow a sale, in manifest deceipt of William Tenterer's soul altogether refused to perfect one. William Hill, who holds an estate in the tenement for Alice's life by her grant paying to her a rent of 6 marks a year, has paid to William Warmwell in advance a sum of money which reaches the true value of the reversion, and William, as an executor of William Tenterer, confirming William Hill's estate, without any fraud, and on the strength of William Tenterer's will granted to William and his heirs and assigns the reversion of the tenement on Alice's death. The tenement, when it fell due, is to be held for ever by William Hill and his heirs and assigns as that which he bought in good faith for that sum of money, which with the oversight of the mayor should be laid out on behalf of the souls mentioned above. Seals: William Warmwell's and the common and mayoral seals of the city. Named witnesses: the bailiff, the mayor, the coroners, the reeves, Richard Spencer, John Camel, John Salisbury, grocer, Richard Leach, John Needler, John Forest, and the clerk

5 December 1397, at Salisbury
1718 By his charter Robert Kirtlingstoke, a citizen of Salisbury, granted to an elder John Forest a tenement, in which John Jakes, tucker, dwells, in Wineman Street between John Needler's tenement on the west side and Isabel Cole's tenement on the east side, to be held for ever by John Forest and his heirs and assigns. Clause of warranty. Seals: Robert's and the common and mayoral seals of the city. Named witnesses: the mayor, the coroners, the reeves, William Warmwell, John Camel, John Baker, William Hill, Robert Deverill, and the clerk

10 October 1396 x c. 1397
1719 The will of John Courtman, a citizen of Salisbury, made on 10 October 1396. Interment: in the graveyard of St. Martin's church beside the tomb of Margery, of late his wife. Bequests: 20s. to the fabric of that church, 40d. to the parochial chaplain, 2s. 6d. to each other chaplain, 12d. to the deacon, and 12d. to the sacristan; 6s. 8d. both to the Franciscans of Salisbury and the Dominicans of Fisherton; 40d. to the fabric of the cathedral church; 20s. to the hospital called Almshouse; 6s. 8d. to Thomas Cooper; 2s. to each of his godsons and goddaughters; 3s. to each of his servants; 100s. each to his son John and daughter Joan; 6s. 8d. each to John Withes and William Saunders; £3 for loaves to be bought and handed out to paupers on the day of his burial; 13s. 4d. to John Lake; the rest of his goods to his wife Cecily. Devises: to Cecily for life a tenement, in which he dwelt, in Winchester Street between Edmund Cofford's tenement

on the east side and Thomas Knoyle's cottage property on the west side. On Cecily's death a house called Gatehouse, a house and a sollar on the north side of it, half an empty plot between Gatehouse and a garden, and half the garden should remain for ever to John's son John and that John's issue, and if that John were to die without issue those premises would remain for ever to the elder John's daughter Joan and her issue. Also on Cecily's death the tenement, with the other half of the empty plot and of the garden, should remain for ever to Joan and her issue, and if Joan were to die without issue those premises would remain for ever to the younger John and his issue. If John and Joan were both to die without issue the tenement, with all its appurtenances, should be sold by the elder John's executors or subsequent executors. The money received should be laid out on celebrating masses, giving alms, and doing other charitable deeds on behalf of the elder John's soul, Cecily's soul, and the souls of others. Executors: his wife Cecily and John Lake

after 6 June 1397
1720 The will of Hugh Gundy, a citizen of Salisbury, made on 1 June 1397. Interment: in the graveyard of St. Thomas's church. Bequests: 10s. to the fabric of that church, 5s. to the rector, and 4d. to each chaplain; 2s. to the fabric of the cathedral church; 10s. to the paupers of the almshouses beside Black bridge; 10s. both to the Franciscans of Salisbury and the Dominicans near Salisbury, to be distributed equally among [those of] the convent; 2s. each to the fabric of St. Edmund's church and of St. Martin's church; 20s. to his sister Alice; 20s. and a second-best slop to his kinsman Robert; 20s. to Robert's sister Alice; 12d. to each of his godsons; 2s. each to the son of John Chirstoke and Agnes Harass; 40d. to his godson Hugh, a son of a younger George Goss; 4d. to each ailing person lying bedridden in the city and to each vicar of the cathedral church; 5s. each to Edward Elion, a chaplain, Nicholas Mason, a chaplain, and Stephen Botwell, a vicar of the cathedral church; £10 to be spent by his executors on the day of his burial, and he wished that 100 masses should be celebrated on that day; 2s. 6d. each to the chaplain of Harnham and John Baynard, a chaplain; 40d. each to Henry and Matthew, his servants; 20s. to his kinswoman Maud; 12d. each to small Maud and Agnes, his servants, and to Agnes Latners; ½ mark to Reynold Glover; 40d. to John 'Chirstoke'; 3s. 4d. each to Evette Barbours, John Staggard, and William Steer; 5s. to the fabric of the monastery of Wimborne Minster; a best slop and 6s. 8d. to John Kimpton; the rest of his goods to his wife Parnel. Devises: to Parnel a tenement, with a garden, in New Street, between Cecily Mussel's tenement on the west side and Edward Fountain's tenement on the east side, to be held for ever by her and her heirs and assigns. Executors: Parnel, his principal executor, and Reynold Glover. Proved on 6 June 1397 in front of the subdean; the administration was entrusted to the executors.

2 January 1398, at Salisbury
1721 By her charter Alice, the relict of John Butterley, of late a citizen of Salisbury, in her widowhood and full power, granted to Thomas Merriott and John Deakin

two messuages, with an empty plot of land measuring 59 ft. in length and 38 ft. in width and with a garden and walls appurtenant to the messuages and plot. The messuages, with the plot, garden, and walls, stand conjoined in Winchester Street, opposite the common trench of running water, between William Dowding's tenement on the east side and a tenement of John Salisbury, grocer, on the west side. William Stourton, Edmund Enfield, William River, John Blickling, William Buck, and William Winslow released their right or claim to them to Alice and her heirs and assigns, and they are to be held for ever by Thomas Merriott and John Deakin and their heirs and assigns. Clause of warranty. Seals: Alice's and the common and mayoral seals of the city. Named witnesses: the mayor, the coroners, the reeves, Richard Spencer, Richard Leach, John Camel, William Hill, John Forest, and the clerk

30 January 1398, at Salisbury
1722 By their charter Thomas Chaplin and Thomas Cofford granted to William Warin, a citizen of Salisbury, a tenement, with an adjacent yard, in Minster Street, which is called Castle Street, between a tenement of late that of Robert of Woodford, mercer, on one side and a tenement formerly that of Nicholas Glover, of Ford, on the other side. The tenement, with the yard, was held by the grantors by a grant of Alice, the relict of Thomas of Durrington, was held by Alice and Thomas by a grant of John of Ely and Edmund Fisher, of late citizens of Salisbury, and is to be held for ever by William and his heirs and assigns. Seals: those of the grantors and the common and mayoral seals of the city. Named witnesses: the mayor, the under-bailiff, the coroners, the reeves, William Warmwell, Thomas Bowyer, George Goss, John Dogton, and the clerk

13 March 1398, at Salisbury
1723 By his charter Robert Salter, of Sarson, granted to the master Robert Ragenhill, a clerk, and John Chippenham rent of 20s. a year issuing from two tenements, one in Carter Street and one in Brown Street [*as in* **1711**]. The rent was held by Robert Salter by a grant of John Hill, carpenter, who acquired it from Robert Newport and his wife Agnes, and it is to be held for ever by Robert and John and their heirs and assigns, to whom Robert Salter released his right or claim to it. Seals: Robert Salter's and the common and mayoral seals of the city. Named witnesses: the mayor, the under-bailiff, the coroners, the reeves, William Warmwell, Richard Spencer, Edmund Enfield, Richard Leach, and the clerk
1724 By his charter Nicholas Brown, a chaplain, granted to the master Robert Ragenhill, a clerk, and John Chippenham rent of 20s. a year issuing from two tenements, one in Carter Street and one in Brown Street [*as in* **1711**], to be held for ever by Robert and John and their heirs and assigns. Clause of warranty. Seals: Nicholas's and the common and mayoral seals of the city. Named witnesses: the mayor, the under-bailiff, the coroners, the reeves, William Warmwell, Richard Spencer, Richard Leach, Edmund Enfield, and the clerk

25 March 1398

1725 By his charter John Baron, of Salisbury, granted to Richard Falconer, otherwise called Leach, of Salisbury, all his tenements opposite the cross where hay is sold, between a tenement formerly John Fool's on the west side and a tenement formerly John Lea's on the east side, with the market place on the north side, and the butchers' shambles on the south side. The tenements are to be held for ever by Richard and his heirs and assigns. Clause of warranty. Seal: John Baron's. Witnesses: the master John Francis, the rector of Saltwood, the lord William Grisley, the rector of Kelsale, the lord Thomas Needham, the rector of Stratford, of the counties of Kent and Norfolk (*rectius* Suffolk), and John Arnold and Thomas Mund, citizens of London

1726 By his letters of attorney John Baron, of Salisbury, appointed the lord Robert Newton, a chaplain, and the master John Raby, a public notary, to deliver to Richard Falconer, otherwise called Leach, of Salisbury, and his heirs and assigns the seisin of all his tenements in Salisbury. Seal: John Baron's

10 April 1398, at Salisbury

1727 By her charter Margaret, the relict of William Godmanstone, of late a citizen of Salisbury, in her widowhood and full power, granted to George Merriott, Edward Elion, a chaplain, and William Bishop a corner tenement called Chantrell's Corner, with shops, sollars, and cellars, in Winchester Street at the east end of Butchery, between Richard Carentham's shop property on the west side and the king's highway on the east side. The tenement, with the shops, sollars, and cellars, was held by Margaret by a feoffment of Richard Leach and is to be held for ever by George, Edward, and William. Seals: Margaret's and the common and mayoral seals of the city. Named witnesses: the mayor, the coroners, the reeves, Richard Spencer, William Warmwell, William Hill, John Needler, and the clerk

1728 By his writing Thomas Boyton, bowyer, a citizen of Salisbury, granted to John Gilbert, of Salisbury, the reversion of a tenement when it fell due on the death of John Paxhill, who holds an estate in it for life by Thomas's grant. The tenement stands in Castle Street, beyond the bar, between a tenement, in which John Paxhill dwells, on the south side and a tenement of the provost of St. Edmund's church on the north side. Thomas also granted to John Gilbert the reversion of the tenement in which John Paxhill and his wife Joan dwell when it fell due on the death of John and Joan. The tenement stands in Castle Street, beyond the bar, between the tenement mentioned above on the north side and a tenement of late Richard Breamore's on the south side. The two tenements, when they fell due, are to be held for ever by John Gilbert and his heirs and assigns. Seals: Thomas Boyton's and the common and mayoral seals of the city. Named witnesses: the mayor, a coroner, the reeves, William Warmwell, Richard Spencer, Richard Leach, Edmund Enfield, William Hill, John Needler, and the clerk

5 June 1398, at Salisbury

1729 Approval of the will of Walter Hoare, a clerk, of Bradley, made on 18 May

1398. Interment: in the holy burial place in front of the west door of the cathedral church if he died in Salisbury, otherwise in the church or graveyard of the parish in which he died. Bequests: 20*s*. and a rosary of amber beads coloured white to his fellow John Stallington; 26*s*. 8*d*. each to the lord Roger Davitt, a chaplain, and William Conning; 6*s*. 8*d*. each to the lord John Martin, the lord William Priest, the master Thomas Upton, and the lord William Hussey; 1 mark to be distributed to paupers for the business in which he was a supporter and not well expedited; his whole practice, which he knows not [how] to value, and 6*s*. 8*d*. to John Draper; 20*s*. to his brothers of the Carthusian house in Selwood; 6*s*. 8*d*. to an elder John Coulston, staying with the monks and friars of that house; 40*d*. to Magote Chapmans, of Britford; 20*s*. to the fabric of St. Nicholas's church, Bradley, and 6*s*. 8*d*. to Richard [Budden], the vicar; 2*s*. 6*d*. to that same Richard, the chaplain of Southwick; 6*s*. 8*d*. for improving the way between St. Nicholas's hospital and a meadow of de Vaux college; 6*s*. 8*d*. each to William Sever and Simon Unwin; 20 marks to his father and mother; the rest of his goods to his executors so that they might spend from them, especially on celebrating masses, giving alms, and doing other charitable deeds, on the salvation of his soul; 6*s*. 8*d*., moreover, to William Sever. Devises: two newly built tenements in Culver Street, which he acquired from John Stallington, to his executors to be held for ever by them and their heirs and assigns to be sold. The money received should be held in full by Walter's father and mother. In the purchase John Stallington should be preferred to others and should have the tenements for the best market price. Walter devised a corner tenement in St. Martin's Street [and Culver Street: *cf.* **1579**], which he acquired from John Man, to his executors to be held for ever by them and their heirs and assigns to be sold. The money received should be divided into four parts. One part should be released to the chaplain of the chapel of de Vaux college to hire a scribe for a new porteous to be written there and to fulfill the needs of the chapel. Another part should be released to the fellows of de Vaux college to celebrate his obit every year in the chapel of the college, in such a way that 40*d*. should be handed out each year among the chaplains and the fellows of the college present at the funeral rites and masses as long as that part lasts. Walter devised the third part to the treasury of the cathedral church to buy a vestment or cope at the choice of the lord Roger Netton, the under-treasurer. He devised the fourth part to the fabric of the cathedral church. Executors: the lord Roger Davitt and William Conning. Proved on 24 May 1398 at Cirencester in front of John of Maidenhead, a canon and residentiary of the cathedral church of Salisbury and the keeper of de Vaux college; the administration was entrusted to the executors. Approved at a court held in front of the bailiff, the mayor, and other citizens; the seisin of the tenements was released to the legatees.

1730 Approval of the will of Thomas Play, a citizen of Salisbury, made on 18 March 1398. Interment: in the graveyard of St. Thomas's church. Bequests: 12*d*. to the fabric of the cathedral church; 3*s*. 4*d*. to the high altar of St. Thomas's church for his forgotten tithes, 12*d*. to the fabric of that church, and 4*d*. to each chaplain celebrating mass in it; 3*s*. 4*d*. both to the Dominican friars of Fisherton and to Thomas Randolph; 12*d*. to each of his six servants; the rest of his goods to his wife Alice and his children. Devise: to Alice for life a tenement, opposite the cross where fruit and vegetables are sold, between a tenement of the cathedral on the west side and a tenement of John Baker, grocer, on the east side, and after Alice's death to his sons Edmund, John, and Robert and their issue. If those sons were to die without issue the tenement would remain to Thomas's daughter Isoude and her issue, and if Isoude were to die without issue it would remain for ever to his nearest kinsmen and their issue. Executors: Alice, the principal executor, and her brother John. Proved on 23 March 1398 in front of the subdean; the administration was entrusted to Alice, reserving the power to entrust it to John when he might come to seek it. Approved at a court held in front of the bailiff, the mayor, and other citizens; the seisin of the tenement was released to the legatee.

19 June 1398, at Salisbury
1731 By their charter William Buck, a chaplain, and an elder John Chandler granted to Walter Nalder, draper, a tenement in Castle Street between a lane where horses are watered near Scots Lane on the south side and a tenement of William and John, which they acquired from John Wallop and in which he dwells, on the north side. The tenement was held by William and John by a grant of John Wallop, who acquired it from William Buck and William Dunkerton, executors of Thomas Britford, a citizen of Salisbury, and it is to be held for ever by Walter and his heirs and assigns. Seals: those of the grantors and the common and mayoral seals of the city. Named witnesses: the mayor, the bailiff, the coroners, the reeves, William Warmwell, Richard Spencer, Thomas Bowyer, Richard Leach, John Dogton, and the clerk

1732 By his deed [*dated to the Wednesday after the feast of the nativity of St. John the Baptist (26 June) probably in error for the Wednesday before that feast (19 June)*] John Wallop, draper, quitclaimed to Walter Nalder, draper, and his heirs and assigns his right or claim to a tenement in Castle Street between a lane [*as in **1731***] and a tenement in which he dwells. John acquired the tenement [*as in **1731***] and granted it [*as in **1731***]. Clause of warranty. Seals: John's and the common and mayoral seals of the city. Named witnesses: the mayor, the bailiff, the coroners, the reeves, William Warmwell, Richard Spencer, Thomas Bowyer, George Goss, William Hill, John Lewisham, and the clerk

3 July 1398, at Salisbury
1733 By their charter William Buck, a chaplain, and an elder John Chandler, a citizen of Salisbury, granted to Robert Hazelbury rent of 10s. a year issuing from two tenements in Scots Lane, one William's and John's and formerly Maud Dovedale's, and one formerly held by John Nunton, tanner, and now by Roger Woodford. The tenements stand conjoined between a tenement of late Thomas Sexhampcote's, formerly John Dyke's, on the west side and a tenement of late Stephen Hooper's, now John Staggard's, on the east side. The rent was held, with land and tenements in Salisbury, by William and John by a grant of John Wallop, draper, and is to be held for ever by Robert and his heirs and assigns. Clause

to permit entry on William's and John's tenement if the rent were in arrear, distraint, and the keeping of distresses until half the unpaid rent was recovered. Seals: those of the grantors and the common and mayoral seals of the city. Named witnesses: the mayor, the bailiff, the coroners, the reeves, William Warmwell, Richard Spencer, Thomas Bowyer, George Goss, John Lewisham, and the clerk

1734 By their charter William Buck, a chaplain, and an elder John Chandler, a citizen of Salisbury, granted to William Herring, a chaplain, and Stephen Edington a rent of 26s. 8d. a year to be received for ever by them and their heirs and assigns from a chief tenement, with a gate and a yard, in Castle Street. The tenement stands between a tenement which, of late acquired by Walter Nalder, draper, from William and John, stands, beside a lane where horses are watered, on the east [rectius south: cf. **1731**; correct in **1737**] side and Roger Wallop's cottage on the north side. John Wallop, draper, now dwells in the tenement, which William Buck and John Chandler held by his grant. Clause to permit entry on the tenement if the rent were in arrear and, if a sufficient distress could not be found, on all the other land and tenements in Salisbury which William and John held by a grant of John Wallop; also to permit distraint and the keeping of distresses until the unpaid rent was recovered. So that their grant, and the confirmation of the charter, would remain valid for ever William and John confirmed the seisin of William and Stephen by paying to them 4d. on the day on which the charter was perfected. Seals: those of the grantors and the common and mayoral seals of the city. Named witnesses: the mayor, the bailiff, the coroners, the reeves, William Warmwell, Richard Spencer, George Goss, Edmund Enfield, John Needler, and the clerk

17 July 1398, at Salisbury
1735 By their writing John Starr, of Salisbury, and his wife Edith, appearing at the court held on that day, quitclaimed to John Drury, of Salisbury, and his heirs and assigns their right or claim to a rent of 6d. a year issuing from a tenement, in which he dwells, beyond the bar of Castle Street, between John Shipton's tenement on the north side and John Starr's cottage property on the south side; also their right or claim to two conjoined cottages, with a yard (*or* yards), in Castle Street, beyond the bar, between Isabel Cole's cottage property on the south side and John Mildenhall's cottage property on the north side. Seals: those of John Starr and Edith and the common and mayoral seals of the city. Named witnesses: the bailiff, the mayor, the coroners, the reeves, William Warmwell, Richard Spencer, Richard Leach, William Walter, John Needler, an elder John Forest, and the clerk

1736 By his deed John Wallop, draper, a citizen of Salisbury, quitclaimed to Robert Hazelbury and his heirs and assigns his right or claim to rent of 10s. a year issuing from two tenements in Scots Lane, one formerly Maud Dovedale's and one formerly held by John Nunton, tanner, and now by Roger Woodford [*as in* **1733**]. William Buck, a chaplain, and an elder John Chandler of late held that rent, with land and tenements in Salisbury, by John Wallop's grant, and they granted it to Robert Hazelbury. Clause of warranty. Seals: John Wallop's and the common and mayoral seals of the city. Named witnesses: the mayor, the bailiff, the coroners, the reeves, William Warmwell, Richard Spencer, Richard Leach, Richard Jewell, and the clerk

1737 By his deed John Wallop, draper, a citizen of Salisbury, quitclaimed to William Herring, a chaplain, and Stephen Edington, and their heirs and assigns his right or claim to a rent of 26s. 8d. a year which they held by a grant of William Buck, a chaplain, and an elder John Chandler, a citizen of Salisbury. The rent issues from a chief tenement in Castle Street in which John Wallop dwells [*as in 1734*]. Clause of warranty. Seals: John Wallop's and the common and mayoral seals of the city. Named witnesses: the mayor, the bailiff, the coroners, the reeves, William Warmwell, Thomas Bowyer, George Goss, John Forest, and the clerk

31 July 1398, at Salisbury

1738 By his charter of Edmund Enfield, a clerk, granted to John Camel, a citizen of Salisbury, a tenement in Winchester Street, opposite the common trench of running water, between John Homes's tenement on the east side and Shit Lane on the west side. The tenement is to be held for ever by John and his heirs and assigns. Clause of warranty. Seals: Edmund's and the common and mayoral seals of the city. Named witnesses: the bailiff, the mayor, the coroners, the reeves, William Warmwell, Richard Spencer, Richard Leach, Richard Jewell, William Hill, William Walter, John Needler, an elder John Forest, and the clerk

1739 By his letters of attorney John Camel, a citizen of Salisbury, appointed his son John to receive the seisin of a tenement [*as in 1738*] according to a charter perfected for him by Edmund Enfield, a clerk, and to do fealty for him to the chief lord of the city. Seals: the elder John Camel's and the mayoral seal of the city

9 October 1398, at Salisbury

1740 Approval [*dated to the Wednesday after the feast of St. Denis (16 October) probably in error for the Wednesday of that feast (9 October)*] of the will of Richard Stoke, a burgess of Wilton, made on 2 September 1398. <u>Interment</u>: in the graveyard of St. Nicholas in Atrio, Wilton. <u>Bequests</u>: 20d. to the fabric of the cathedral church, Salisbury; 40d. each to the fabric of St. Edith's church, Wilton, and of the church of the Holy Trinity, Wilton; 6d. each to the fabric of Christ's church, of St. Thomas's church, Canterbury, of St. Mary's church in West Street, Wilton, and of St. Michael's church, Kingsbury; 6s. 8d. each to the lord William Bloxworth, the lord John Hatter, and Henry Sireman, chaplains; 40d. both to the Dominicans of Salisbury [*rectius* Fisherton] and the Franciscans of Salisbury; 6s. 8d. to his brother Robert; 6d. to each of his godsons; £40 which John Cole owes to him, as is contained in a bond, to his wife Joan and his son John; a piece of best silver with a cover, a piece of silver without a cover, a maple-wood bowl bound with silver [and] with a silver gilt foot, two brass pots, a pan and a basin with a best laver, and four best silver spoons to his son John; a furnace and an item of lead called a yeting lid to his son John; 4 bu. of wheat to John Cabbel; 10 marks for his funeral expenses; the rest of his goods to his wife Joan and his son John. <u>Devises</u>: to Joan for life two shops [?at the butchers' stalls: *cf.* **882, 1588**] in Salisbury which Henry Winpenny holds of him. Immediately on Joan's death the shops should remain to Richard's son John and his issue, and if John were to die without issue they should be sold by Richard's executors or their executors. The money received should be laid out on the celebration of masses and the giving of other alms on behalf of their souls and [the souls] of others. Richard devised to Joan for life a tenement, with a garden, in Kingsbury Street in the borough of Wilton, opposite the Guildhall at the south end and formerly William Sireman's; also a corner tenement in the borough of Wilton at the crossroads which is called Carentham's Corner; also a meadow called Scriven's mead in Wilton. On Joan's death the tenements and the meadow should remain to Richard's son John and his issue, and if John were to die without issue they should be sold by Richard's executors or their executors. The money received should be laid out on behalf of their souls and the souls of Roger Carentham and his wives Margaret and Agnes. Richard devised to Joan for life a toft, with an adjacent yard, as it lies in a suburb of Wilton in the street of Little marsh. On Joan's death the toft, and the yard, should remain to his son John and his issue, and if John were to die without issue it should be sold by Richard's executors or their executors. The money received should be laid out as mentioned above. Richard devised to Christine, a daughter of his brother John, a cottage, with an adjacent yard, in Bullbridge Street between John Bodenham's cottage on the south side and a garden of the convent of Wilton on the north side, to be held for ever by Christine and her heirs and assigns. Executors: his wife Joan and his son John. Proved on 20 September 1398 in front of an officer of the archdeacon of Salisbury; the administration was entrusted to Joan, reserving the power to entrust it to John when he might come to seek it. Approved at a court held in front of the bailiff, the mayor, and other citizens; the seisin of the shops was released to the legatees.

6 November 1398, at Salisbury
1741 By his charter Robert Gundy, a kinsman and heir of Hugh Gundy, of late a citizen of Salisbury, granted to Walter Warwick, a chaplain, a rent of 6*d.* a year issuing from a shop, now two newly built shops with a sollar (*or* sollars), in Minster Street between a tenement formerly that of Hugh and his wife Alice, now Walter Orme's, on the south side and a tenement formerly William Porter's, which Robert Reading holds, on the north side. The rent descended to Robert Gundy by right of inheritance on Hugh's death and is to be held for ever by Walter and his heirs and assigns. Clause of warranty. Seals: Robert's and the common and mayoral seals of the city. Named witnesses: the mayor, the bailiff, the coroners, the reeves, William Warmwell, Thomas Bowyer, Richard Leach, Richard Jewell, and the clerk

20 November 1398, at Salisbury
1742 By their charter of Edmund Enfield, a clerk, a citizen of Salisbury, and William Irish, of Andover, granted to John Hurst and his wife Joan a tenement in Minster Street, which is called Castle Street, between a gate of a tenement of late John Wallop's on the south side and a tenement of late Richard Ludd's on the north side; also a shop in Pot Row between a shop of Nicholas Longstock

and his wife Agnes on the west side and shops of Walter Clopton, kt., on the east side. The tenement and the shop were held by Edmund and William by a grant of John and Joan and are to be held for ever by John and Joan and their heirs and assigns, provided that Edmund and William may be held to warrant them only against themselves and their heirs and not against John and Joan or their heirs or assigns. John and Joan are excluded from every action of warranty against Edmund and William. Seals: those of the grantors and the common and mayoral seals of the city. Named witnesses: the bailiff, the coroners, the reeves, William Warmwell, John Mower, Richard Spencer, Richard Leach, William Hill, John Needler, an elder John Forest, and the clerk

1743 By her charter Parnel, the relict of Hugh Gundy, of late a citizen of Salisbury, in her widow's right and full power, granted to Walter Warwick, a chaplain, a tenement, with a garden, in New Street between a tenement of late Thomas Mussel's on the west side and Edward Fountain's tenement on the east side. The tenement, with the garden, was held by Parnel by Hugh's devise to her and her heirs and assigns for ever and is to be held for ever by Walter and his heirs and assigns. Seals: Parnel's and the common and mayoral seals of the city. Named witnesses: the mayor, the bailiff, the coroners, the reeves, John Mower, Richard Spencer, William Warmwell, Thomas Bowyer, and the clerk

4 December 1398, at Salisbury
1744 A deed of Edmund Enfield, Thomas Bleacher, ironmonger, and a younger William Lord, executors of Robert Play, of late a citizen of Salisbury. Robert devised to Christine, the relict of Edward Herring, and her son John a rent of 13*s*. 4*d*. a year issuing from a tenement, which Maud Marions holds for life, in Drake Hall Street with the reversion of the tenement when it fell due on Maud's death. The rent and the reversion are to be held for ever by Christine and John and John's issue, and if John were to die without issue they, or the tenement when it fell due, should be sold by Robert's executors. The money received should be laid out on behalf of Robert's soul and the souls of others. Maud Marions is alive, so that the rent and the reversion, if John were to die without issue and on the death of Christine, pertain to the executors for sale. The executors, on the strength of Robert's will and if John were to die without issue, granted the rent, when it fell due after Christine's death, and the reversion, when it fell due, to John Canning, of Salisbury, to be held for ever by him and his heirs and assigns. Seals: those of the grantors and the common and mayoral seals of the city. Named witnesses: the bailiff, the coroners, the reeves, William Warmwell, John Mower, Richard Spencer, William Hill, William Walter, John Needler, an elder John Forest, and the clerk

1745 By his charter Richard Jewell, of Salisbury, granted to Richard Weston, weaver, of Salisbury, a tenement in Gigant Street between a tenement of late Robert of Godmanstone's on the north side and a garden of late John Ball's on the south side. The tenement was held by Richard Jewell a grant of Thomas Hindon, formerly a citizen of Salisbury, and is to be held for ever by Richard Weston and his heirs and assigns. Seals: Richard Jewell's and the common and mayoral seals of the city. Named witnesses: the mayor, the bailiff, the coroners, the reeves, William Warmwell, John Mower, Richard Spencer, William Walter, and the clerk

1746 By his charter Richard Jewell, a citizen of Salisbury, granted to William Dyke the reversion of [Ive's Corner: *cf.* **533, 1959–60**], a chief tenement in Wineman Street, formerly Ralph Ive's, opposite Gilbert Oword's tenement, between a tenement of late Robert Sexhampcote's on the west side and William Warmwell's cottage property on the south side, when it fell due on the death of George Merriott. Robert Play, now dead, and Richard Jewell acquired the reversion from Reynold Drury and his wife Alice, an executor of Walter Leacher, an executor of Mary, the relict, and an executor, of Ralph Ive. The tenement, when it fell due, is to be held for ever by William Dyke and his heirs and assigns. Seals: Richard Jewell's and the common and mayoral seals of the city. Named witnesses: the mayor, the bailiff, the coroners, the reeves, William Warmwell, John Mower, Richard Spencer, Richard Leach, William Hill, John Needler, William Walter, and the clerk

5 December 1398, at Salisbury
1747 By his letters of attorney Richard Jewell, of Salisbury, appointed John Gatcombe and William Lord to surrender into the hand of Richard, the bishop of Salisbury, the seisin of a tenement in Gigant Street [*as in* **1745**] to the use of Richard Weston, weaver, of Salisbury. Seals: Richard Jewell's and the mayoral seal of the city

c. 1396 x c. 1398
1748 By his charter Robert Kirtlingstoke, a citizen of Salisbury, granted to an elder John Forest a tenement in which ... [*entry aborted*]

29 January 1399, at Salisbury
1749 By his charter John Wishford granted to John Needler, of Salisbury, a cottage, with a skilling and a piece of land, of late held by Agnes, a daughter of William Kilmeston. The cottage stands in Minster Street, between a chief tenement of late that of Roger Kilmeston, William's father, on the north side and a tenement of late William's on the south side, and, with the skilling and the piece of land, measures 39 ft. in length eastwards from the street. It is to be held for ever by John Needler and his heirs and assigns. Clause of warranty. Seals: John Wishford's and the common and mayoral seals of the city. Named witnesses: the mayor, the bailiff, the coroners, the reeves, John Mower, Richard Spencer, William Walter, and the clerk

12 February 1399, at Salisbury
1750 By his charter Roger Davitt, a chaplain, an executor of Walter Hoare, a clerk, of Bradley, on the strength of Walter's will granted to John Whitmore a corner tenement in St. Martin's Street [and Culver Street: *cf.* **1579**] between William Warmwell's cottages on the north side and William's tenement on the

west side. Walter acquired the tenement from John Man, a kinsman of John Iwerne, of late a vicar of the cathedral church, and devised it to his executors to be sold. It is to be held for ever by John Whitmore and his heirs and assigns as that which John bought from Roger for a sum of money reaching its full value. Seals: Roger's and the common and mayoral seals of the city. Named witnesses: the mayor, the bailiff, the coroners, the reeves, William Warmwell, John Mower, Richard Spencer, Richard Leach, Richard Jewell, William Hill, William Walter, and the clerk

26 February 1399, at Salisbury
1751 By their charter Edmund Enfield and Richard Spencer granted to Alice, the relict of John Camel, of late a citizen of Salisbury, a tenement in Winchester Street between John Wallop's tenement on the west side and a tenement of John Baker, grocer, on the east side. The tenement is to be held for life by Alice, and on her death is to remain for ever to John Camel's executors for sale. Seals: those of Edmund and Richard and the common and mayoral seals of the city. Named witnesses: the bailiff, a coroner, the reeves, William Warmwell, John Mower, Richard Leach, Richard Jewell, William Hill, William Walter, and the clerk

23 March 1399, at Salisbury
1752 By his charter John Stoke, of Salisbury, granted to an elder John Chandler, a citizen of Salisbury, a corner tenement, with a shop, in Minster Street between shops of late Adam Inways on the east side and a shop of late John Oxford's on the north side, to be held for ever by John Chandler and his heirs and assigns. Clause of warranty. Seals: John Stoke's and the common and mayoral seals of the city. Named witnesses: the mayor, the bailiff, a coroner, the reeves, William Warwell, John Mower, Richard Spencer, Richard Leach, an elder John Forest, and the clerk

26 March 1399, at Salisbury
1753 Approval of the will of William Kilmeston, a vicar of the church of Salisbury, made on 1 March 1399. <u>Interment</u>: in the graveyard of the collegiate church of St. Edmund, where his father, mother, and godparents are interred. <u>Bequests</u>: 40*d.* to the fabric of the cathedral church; 2*s.* 6*d.* to the fabric of St. Edmund's church; 12*d.* each to the dean, the precentor, the chancellor, and the treasurer of the cathedral provided that he was present at his funeral rites on the day of his burial, 8*d.* to each of the other canons, and to each vicar of the cathedral, present at his funeral rites, and 6*d.* to each priest holding a chantry in the cathedral likewise present; 6*d.* each to the two sacristans, 4*d.* to each chorister, 40*d.* for ringing the bells at his obit, 4*d.* to each acolyte in the cathedral, and 4*d.* each to both boys of the sacristans there; at his funeral rites there should be arranged, according to his executors' order, six torches to be burned; afterwards three of the torches should remain in the chapel of the Blessed Mary of the cathedral, three in the chapel of the Blessed Mary of St. Edmund's church, there to be burned at masses celebrating the Blessed Mary; two candles each weighing 6 lb. should be burned at the head

and feet of his corpse while it was in the cathedral, and two each weighing 4 lb. while it was in St. Edmund's church; 6d. each to the four vicars of the cathedral, to be chosen by his executors, bearing his corpse from the cathedral to St. Edmund's church; 3d. each to eight other vicars of the cathedral, to be chosen by his executors, going across with his corpse in the bearing of it from the cathedral to that church; 8d. to the provost of St. Edmund's church in addition to the legacy mentioned above, 6d. to each priest of the college, 3s. to each stipendiary priest celebrating mass, and 6d. to each deacon and sacristan and for ringing the bells and making his grave; a gown of black cloth, to be bought according to his executors's order, to each of six paupers for carrying six candles at his funeral rites; the rest of his goods to his executors so that they might spend from them on behalf of his soul. <u>Devises</u>: two tenements to William Brawt and his present wife Cecily, one in Castle Street between a tenement, in which Richard Priddy now dwells, on the north side and John Hosier's tenement on the south side, and one in 'the endless street of Salisbury' between John Cheyne's tenement on the north side and John Line's tenement, in which John Love dwells, on the south side. The tenements are to be held by William and Cecily for their life and the life of the one of them living longer, and after their death should be sold by their executors or the executors of the longer liver. The money received should be laid out, according to the pious order of those executors, among the Franciscans of Salisbury, the Dominicans of Fisherton, and other paupers of Salisbury on behalf of William's soul and the souls of others. <u>Executors</u>: William Brawt, skinner, of Salisbury, and William of Dunham, a clerk, etc., etc. <u>Proved</u> on 17 March 1399 in front of Thomas Montagu, the dean of Salisbury; the administration was entrusted to the executors. <u>Approved</u> at a court held in front of the bailiff, the mayor, and other citizens; the seisin of the tenements was released to the legatees.

9 April 1399, at Salisbury
1754 By his charter Thomas Sexton, ironmonger, granted to John Barber, brazier, and John Swift, ironmonger, two conjoined cottages, with a yard (*or* yards), which he acquired from John Dinton, in Castle Street, beyond the bars, between a tenement formerly John Upton's on one side and a tenement of late Ellis Homes's on the other side; also two conjoined cottages, which he acquired from John King, roper, and his wife Edith, in Mealmonger Street between cottages of late John Justice's on the south side and a tenement of late Richard Still's on the north side. All four cottages, with the yard(s), are to be held for ever by John Barber and John Swift and their heirs and assigns. Clause of warranty. Seals: Thomas's and the common and mayoral seals of the city. Named witnesses: the mayor, the bailiff, a coroner, the reeves, John Mower, Richard Spencer, and the clerk

10 September 1399, at Salisbury
1755 By her charter Ebote, the relict, and an executor, of Richard Fulham, in her widowhood and full power, on the strength of Richard's will granted to Richard at the mill, tucker, of Salisbury, a tenement, with shops and a garden, in Carter Street between a tenement of late Thomas Play's, now Robert Fovant's,

on the north side and John Wishford's tenement on the south side. The tenement measures 61½ ft. in length at its frontage on the street. Richard devised it to be sold by his executors, and it is to be held for ever, with the shops and garden, by Richard at the mill and his heirs and assigns as that which he bought from Ebote for a sum of money which reached its true value. The money should be laid out according to Richard Fulham's will. Seals: Ebote's and the common and mayoral seals of the city. Named witnesses: the mayor, the bailiff, the coroners, the reeves, William Warmwell, John Mower, Richard Spencer, William Walter, William Hill, John Needler, and the clerk

24 September 1399, at Salisbury
1756 By his charter John Sexhampcote, a chaplain, granted to John Judd, of Salisbury, a garden, with a yard (*or* yards), and racks built in it (*or* them), in Martin's Croft opposite the graveyard of St. Edmund's church. Those premises were devised by Thomas Sexhampcote, of late a citizen of Salisbury, on the death of his wife Joan, for ever to John Sexhampcote and his heirs, to whom Joan released her right to them. They are to be held for ever by John Judd, and his heirs and assigns. Clause of warranty. Seals: John Sexhampcote's and the common and mayoral seals of the city. Named witnesses: the mayor, the bailiff, the coroners, the reeves, William Warmwell, John Mower, Richard Spencer, William Walter, William Hill, John Needler, and the clerk
1757 By her writing Joan, the relict of Thomas Sexhampcote, of late a citizen of Salisbury, quitclaimed to the lord John Sexhampcote, a chaplain, and his heirs and assigns her right or claim to a garden [*as in* **1756**]. Seals: Joan's and the common and mayoral seals of the city. Named witnesses: the mayor of Salisbury, the bailiff, the coroners, the reeves, William Warmwell, John Mower, Richard Spencer, William Walter, William Hill, John Needler, and the clerk
1758 By their deed John Salisbury, weaver, and his wife Christine, the relict of Peter Butterley, called Upton, appearing at the court held on that day, she, being examined according to the custom prevailing in the city, not coerced but voluntarily, quitclaimed to John Bosham, called Pope and his heirs and assigns their right or claim to a tenement in which that John dwells. The tenement stands in Winchester Street between John Wootton's tenement on the east side and Nicholas Monkton's tenement, of late Edmund Cofford's, on the west side. John Butterley, of late a citizen of Salisbury, gave it, with other tenements, to William Stourton, Edmund Enfield, William River, John Blickling, William Buck, and William Winslow, they gave it to Richard Spencer, a citizen of Salisbury, and he gave it to John Bosham. Seals: those of John and Christine and the common and mayoral seals of the city. Named witnesses: the mayor, the bailiff, the coroners, the reeves, William Warmwell, John Mower, Richard Spencer, Richard Leach, John Needler, an elder John Forest, and the clerk

22 October 1399, at Salisbury
1759 By their charter John Waite, hosier, and his wife Maud, appearing at the court held on that day, granted to Stephen Edington, of Salisbury, a tenement in

Endless Street between John Mower's shops on the north side and a tenement, which Thomas Redenham, tanner, holds, on the south side. The tenement extends from that street as far as the street of Rolleston. It is to be held for ever by Stephen and his heirs and assigns. Clause of warranty. Seals: those of John and Maud and the mayoral and common seals of the city. Named witnesses: the mayor, the bailiff, the coroners, the reeves, William Warmwell, John Mower, Richard Spencer, Richard Leach, Richard Jewell, William Walter, William Hill, John Needler, and the clerk

5 November 1399, at Salisbury
1760 A writing of William Bailey, draper, a citizen of Salisbury. Of late John Butterley and his wife Alice, the relict, and an executor, of William Tenterer, of late a citizen of Salisbury, and William Warmwell and William Lord, Alice's co-executors, on the strength of William's will granted for ever to William Bailey and his heirs the reversion of a tenement, with three shops next to it, in New Street between shops of late William Tenterer's on the west side and the abbot of Stanley's shops on the east side, when it fell due on the death of Christine, the relict of William Tenterer's son John. Christine is living and holds an estate for life as dower. William Bailey now granted the reversion to Walter Warwick, John Medmenham, and Roger Ferrer, chaplains, to be held for ever by them and their heirs and assigns. Clause of warranty. Seals: William Bailey's and the common and mayoral seals of the city. Named witnesses: the mayor, the bailiff, a coroner, a reeve, John Mower, William Warmwell, Richard Spencer, Richard Jewell, and the clerk
1761 By an indenture Stephen Edington, of Salisbury, granted to John Waite, hosier, and his wife Maud a tenement in Endless Street [*as in* **1759**]. The tenement was held by Stephen by a grant of John and Maud, and it is to be held by John and Maud for their life, and the life of the one of them living longer, of Stephen and his heirs and assigns without causing any waste or ruin. John and Maud are to pay a rent of 20s. a year to Stephen and his heirs and assigns and the rent and services due from the tenement to the chief lord of the city and all others. They are to maintain and repair the tenement at their own expense. Clause to permit permanent repossession if the tenement were not maintained or the rent were in arrear for a month, and to permit distraint and the keeping of distresses until the unpaid rent was recovered. On the death of John and Maud the tenement should remain for ever to Stephen and his wife Catherine and their joint issue, and if Stephen and Catherine were to die without such issue it would remain for ever to the direct heirs of John and Maud, reserving to Stephen and his heirs and assigns the rent of 20s. to be received from the tenement. Clause of warranty. Seals: those of the parties to the parts of the indenture in turn and the common and mayoral seals of the city. Named witnesses: the mayor, the bailiff, a coroner, the reeves, John Mower, and Richard Spencer

17 December 1399, at Salisbury
1762 By his charter Thomas Bash, tucker, granted to John Lake a cottage, with

a garden, in Martin's Croft, on the way to St. Edmund's church, between Hugh Winterbourne's cottage on the north side and a cottage of the provost of St. Edmund's church on the south side. The cottage, with the garden, measures in length 48 ft. at its frontage on the street. It is to be held for ever by John and his heirs and assigns. Clause of warranty. Seals: Thomas's and the common and mayoral seals of the city. Named witnesses: the mayor, the bailiff, the reeves, William Warmwell, John Mower, Richard Spencer, Edmund Enfield, Richard Leach, William Walter, John Needler, and the clerk

1763 By his charter an elder John Chandler granted to Edmund Enfield, a citizen of Salisbury, a garden, with a rack, in Freren Street, between Edmund's cottage property on the south side and a garden of St. Nicholas's hospital on the north side, to be held for ever by Edmund and his heirs and assigns. Clause of warranty. Seals: John's and the common and mayoral seals of the city. Named witnesses: the mayor, the bailiff, a coroner, the reeves, William Warmwell, John Mower, Richard Spencer, Richard Leach, Richard Jewell, William Walter, John Needler, and the clerk

1764 By their charter an elder John Chandler and John Drury granted to Edmund Enfield a small plot of land in Bug moor between a meadow of St. Nicholas's hospital on the south side and a new ditch of the city on the north side. The plot was held by them by a grant of William Ashton and is to be held for ever by Edmund and his heirs and assigns. Clause of warranty. Seals: those of the grantors and the common and mayoral seals of the city. Named witnesses: the mayor, the bailiff, a coroner, the reeves, William Warmwell, John Mower, Richard Spencer, Richard Leach, William Walter, John Needler, William Hill, and the clerk

1765 By his writing Richard, a son of John Focket, an uncle of Thomas Focket, of late a citizen of Salisbury, quitclaimed to Edmund Enfield, a citizen of Salisbury, and his heirs and assigns his right or claim to a garden, with two old racks built in it, lying on the east side of Freren Street between Edmund's cottage property on the north side and the great ditch of the city on the south side. Seals: Richard's and the common and mayoral seals of the city. Named witnesses: the mayor, the bailiff, a coroner, the reeves, William Warmwell, John Mower, Richard Spencer, Richard Leach, William Walter, and the clerk

24 December 1399, at Westminster
1766 By his letters patent Henry IV granted to Adam Teffont, the mayor of Salisbury, the master of the hospital of the Holy Trinity in the city, that to support the hospital and the feeble and sick paupers dwelling in it he might acquire land and tenements to the value of £20 a year which are not held of the king in chief. The land and tenements may be held for ever by the mayor and master and his successors, the Statute of Mortmain notwithstanding, provided that, inquests having been taken and recorded in Chancery, it could be done without loss to the king.

14 January 1400, at Salisbury
1767 By his writing Thomas Boyton, called Bowyer, a citizen of Salisbury,

granted to Robert Deverill, a citizen of Salisbury, the reversion of a tenement, which John Paxhill holds for life by Thomas's grant, in the street on the way to the upper bridge of Fisherton between a shop of John Butt, a cordwainer, on one side and the Avon on the other side; also the reversion of three conjoined shops, which John Paxhill holds of him for life, in the same street between John Butt's shop property on the west side and Robert's own tenement on the east side. The tenement and the shops, with other tenements in the city, were held by Thomas by a grant of William Lord, of late a citizen of Salisbury, and they are to be held, when they fell due on the death of John Paxhill, for ever by Robert and his heirs and assigns. Seals: Thomas's and the common and mayoral seals of the city. Named witnesses: the mayor, the bailiff, a coroner, the reeves, William Warmwell, John Mower, Richard Spencer, Richard Jewell, John Needler, and the clerk

25 February 1400, at Salisbury
1768 A deed of John Lewisham, an executor of Agnes, the relict, and an executor, of Robert Bunt, of late a citizen of Salisbury. Robert devised to Agnes for life a messuage, with yards and gardens, in Minster Street opposite a field; also a tenement, with a yard (*or* yards), in the same street, beyond the bar, between cottage property of late John Mildenhall's on the south side and the field on the north side; also 23 acres of arable land, which was Peter Bouch's, lying in the field of Old Sarum; also a croft, inclosed by hedges and ditches, lying in Old Sarum between the king's highway on the east side and land of late Robert's own on the west side. On Agnes's death those premises should remain for life to her son Edward, and on Edward's death should be sold by Robert's executors or their executors. Agnes has died, Edward has granted his estate in the premises to Richard Leach, a citizen of Salisbury, and on the strength of Robert's will John Lewisham now granted the premises to Richard to be held for ever by him and his heirs and assigns. Seals: John's and the common and mayoral seals of the city. Named witnesses: the mayor, the bailiff, a coroner, the reeves, John Avery, then the mayor of the borough [of Old Sarum], William Warmwell, George Goss, Robert Kirtlingstoke, John Staggard, John Collier, John Warminster, and the clerk

1769 By his charter [*dated to the Wednesday after the feast of St. Mathias (3 March) probably in error for the Wednesday of that feast (25 February)*] Richard Harlwin, goldsmith, of Salisbury, granted to Walter Nalder, of Salisbury, a tenement in Minster Street between William Coventry's messuage on the south side and the tavern of a tenement of late that of John Camel, hatter, on the north side. The tenement, with other tenements in Salisbury, was held by an elder William Lord, now dead, and Richard by a grant of John Salisbury, grocer, and Richard Leach, and it is to be held for ever by Walter and his heirs and assigns. Clause of warranty. Seals: Richard's and the common and mayoral seals of the city. Named witnesses: the mayor, the bailiff, a coroner, the reeves, John Mower, Richard Spencer, Richard Jewell, William Hill, John Needler, and the clerk

10 March 1400, at Salisbury

1770 By his writing Simon Bunt, of Salisbury, quitclaimed to Richard Leach, a citizen of Salisbury, and his heirs and assigns his right or claim to a messuage in Minster Street, a tenement in the same street, 23 acres, and a croft [*all as in* **1768**]. Seals: Simon's, the common and mayoral seals of the city, and the mayoral seal of the borough [of Old Sarum]. Named witnesses: the mayor, the bailiff, a coroner, the reeves, John Avery, then the mayor of the borough [of Old Sarum], William Warmwell, an elder George Goss, John Staggard, John Collier, tucker, Robert Kirtlingstoke, and the clerk

1771 By his writing John Drury, of Salisbury, quitclaimed to Richard Leach, a citizen of Salisbury, his right or claim to a messuage in Minster Street, a tenement in the same street, 23 acres, and a croft [*all as in* **1768**]. Seals: John's, the common and mayoral seals of the city, and the mayoral seal of the borough [of Old Sarum]. Named witnesses: the mayor, the bailiff, a coroner, the reeves, John Avery, then the mayor of Old Sarum, William Warmwell, George Goss, John Staggard, John Collier, Robert Kirtlingstoke, Thomas Manning, and the clerk

24 March 1400, at Salisbury

1772 By his deed [*dated to the Wednesday after the feast of the annunciation of the Blessed Virgin Mary (31 March) probably in error for the Wednesday before that feast (24 March)*] an elder John Chandler, of Salisbury, an executor of Agnes, the relict of John of Bodenham, of late a citizen of Salisbury, quitclaimed to John Wishford and his heirs and assigns his right or claim to a rent of 20s. a year issuing from that John's tenement in Castle Street between a tenement of late William Steercock's on the south side and a tenement of late John Bennett's on the north side. Agnes devised the rent to be sold by her executors after the death of Nicholas Odiham, now dead. Seals: John Chandler's and the common and mayoral seals of the city. Named witnesses: the mayor, the bailiff, a coroner, the reeves, William Warmwell, John Mower, Richard Spencer, William Hill, an elder John Forest, and the clerk. Clause of warranty

1773 By his charter Thomas Fyport, dyer, of Salisbury, granted to Edward Elion, a chaplain, a tenement in Castle Street between Richard Leach's tenement on the south side and John Dogton's tenement on the north side. The tenement was held by Thomas by a grant of Robert Bunt and is to be held for ever by Edward and his heirs and assigns, rendering to Richard Jewell, of Salisbury, and to all others the rent and charges in any way applicable to it. Clause of warranty. Seals: Thomas's and the common and mayoral seals of the city. Named witnesses: the mayor, the bailiff, a coroner, the reeves, William Warmwell, John Mower, Richard Spencer, William Hill, an elder John Forest, and the clerk

1774 By his letters of attorney Thomas Fyport, dyer, of Salisbury, appointed William Lord to surrender into the hand of Richard, the bishop of Salisbury, the seisin of a tenement in Castle Street [*as in* **1773**] to the use of Edward Elion, a chaplain. Seals: Thomas's and the mayoral seal of the city

7 April 1400, at Salisbury

1775 By his charter Henry Pope, a citizen of Salisbury, granted to John Pope, a chaplain, two conjoined tenements, with a shop (*or* shops), in Endless Street and Chipper Street, between a tenement of late Robert Arnold's on the north side and a trench of running water on the east side, to be held for ever by John and his heirs and assigns. Clause of warranty. Seals: Henry's and the common and mayoral seals of the city. Named witnesses: the mayor, the bailiff, a coroner, the reeves, John Mower, Richard Spencer, John Salisbury, grocer, William Walter, and the clerk

1776 By his letters of attorney Henry Pope, a citizen of Salisbury, appointed John Gatcombe and Stephen Edington to surrender into the hand of Richard, the bishop of Salisbury, the seisin of two conjoined tenements [*as in* **1775**] to the use of John Pope, a chaplain. Seals: Henry's and the mayoral seal of the city

21 April 1400, at Salisbury
1777 By his charter an elder George Goss, a citizen of Salisbury, granted to Richard Spencer, an elder John Forest, William Walter, Nicholas Harding, Walter Nalder, Richard Weston, Robert Hazelbury, and John Barrett a tenement, with two shops, in Minster Street between a tenement of late Thomas Dovedale's, now that of John Gilbert, a vicar of the cathedral church, on the north side and a tenement formerly that of Alice, who was the wife of William Allen, of late Edmund Cofford's, on the south side. The tenement extends from the street on the west side as far as a tenement [?in Endless Street: *cf.* **610**] of a younger John Pannett, now John Noble's, on the east side, beside Thomas Dovedale's tenement on the north side, and on the south side as far as a tenement formerly Henry Smith's. It was held, with the shops, by George by a grant of John Powell, Henry of Stapleford, and William Lord, executors of Roger at the well, an executor of John Burgess, mercer, formerly a citizen of Salisbury, and is to be held for ever by the grantees and their heirs and assigns. Clause of warranty. Seals: George's and the common and mayoral seals of the city. Named witnesses: the mayor, the bailiff, a coroner, the reeves, William Warmwell, John Mower, John Salisbury, grocer, Richard Leach, Richard Jewell, William Hill, John Needler, and the clerk

5 May 1400, at Salisbury
1778 Approval of the will of John Caundle, of late a matins clerk in the cathedral church, made on 16 April 1400. <u>Interment</u>: in the graveyard of the cathedral in front of the image of the Blessed Mary at the south door. <u>Bequests</u>: 20*s*. to the fabric of that church; 6*s*. 8*d*. to the fabric of St. Thomas's church, and 40*d*. to the rector for his forgotten tithes and oblations; 6*s*. 8*d*. both to the Franciscans of Salisbury and the Dominicans of Fisherton; 40*d*. both to the prisoners at the Guildhall and to those of Old Sarum; 40*d*. to the paupers of the hospital of the Holy Trinity; 1*d*. to each pauper ill in bed in Salisbury; a bed woven with scallop shells to Edith, a daughter of his sister; 20*s*. and a basin with a laver to John Hargreave, his servant, to be released to him according to the order of his executors; a bed to little Agnes, his servant, to be released to her likewise; a basin with a third-best laver to William Hillmay, a servant of Thomas Biston; a bed

with a tester, blue in colour, woven with lilies, to the lord William Caundle, a chaplain in the cathedral; 12*d*. to his godson John, a son of William West; 6*d*. to each of his other godsons; 6*s*. 8*d*. to his kinsman Simon Carmerdin; 20*s*. to John Farthing, of late his servant; 40*d*. to Edith, his servant; 6*d*. to the vicar celebrating mass on behalf of his soul on the day of his burial, and 4*d*. to each of 12 vicars, and to each acolyte of the cathedral church, being present at the mass and burial; 6*d*. to both sacristans at the cathedral church for ringing the bells on the day of his burial, and 2*d*. to the boy of each one; the rest of his goods to his executors so that they might spend as they wished on behalf of his soul. <u>Devises</u>: a toft, with ½ acre of arable land, at Old Sarum, which he acquired from Agnes Young and John 'Glondy', should be sold by his executors to pay his debts. John devised a tenement, in which he dwelt, in New Street, with all the necessary vessels and utensils in it, to Margaret Denman, his servant, to be held by her for life if she keeps herself celibate, respected, and without a husband. After Margaret's death the tenement, with the vessels and utensils, should be sold by John's executors or their executors. The money received should be laid out on masses, paupers, and other good deeds on behalf of John's soul, the souls of John Deverill and Alice Rushall, formerly his wife, and the souls of others. If Margaret should take a husband, or not keep herself respected and without the consortship of a man, and thereupon became united, she would lose and leave the tenement, with the vessels and the utensils, for the agreed repair of which she is bound and which should be sold immediately by John's executors or their executors. The money received should be laid out in the way mentioned above on behalf of John's soul and the souls of others. Margaret, while she lived and held the tenement, should hold John's obit, and Alice Rushall's, yearly wherever she wished. <u>Executors</u>: Margaret Denman, the principal executor, and the lord William Caundle, a priest, and Robert Denman as executors jointly with her. William and Robert might do nothing about the sale and disposition of John's goods or the execution of his will without Margaret's agreement. <u>Proved</u> on 6 April 1400 in front of the subdean; the administration was entrusted to the executors. <u>Approved</u> at a court held in front of the bailiff, the mayor, and other citizens; the seisin of the tenement was released to the legatees.

19 May 1400, at Salisbury
1779 By his charter Richard Hellier, barber, granted to Hugh Braban, tailor, of Salisbury, three conjoined cottages, with gardens, in Drake Hall Street between cottages of the master Thomas Southam, a canon in the cathedral church, on the south side and cottages of the vicars of that church on the north side; also four conjoined cottages, with gardens, in the same street between cottages of Simon Belch, tucker, on the south side and cottages of late Robert Play's, which John Ferrer, carter, and his wife Maud hold on the north side. Richard held the three cottages, with the gardens, under the name of two cottages, and the four cottages, with the gardens, under the name of a tenement, by a grant of John Wraxall, a chaplain, and all seven are to be held for ever by Hugh and his heirs and assigns. Clause of warranty. Seals: Richard's and the common and mayoral

seals of the city. Named witnesses: the mayor, the bailiff, a coroner, the reeves, William Warmwell, John Mower, Richard Spencer, William Walter, William Hill, and the clerk

1780 By their deed William Herring, a chaplain, and Stephen Edington, granted to William Buck, a chaplain, a rent of 26s. 8d. a year issuing both from a chief tenement, with a yard and a gate, in which John Wallop, draper, dwells, in Castle Street between Walter Nalder's tenement on the south side and a tenement of late Roger Wallop's on the north side, and from all the other land and tenements in Salisbury which were of late John Wallop's and in which William Buck and an elder John Chandler were enfeoffed. The rent is to be held for ever by William Buck and his heirs and assigns according to the effect of the acquisition of it by William Herring and Stephen Edington. Seals: those of the grantors and the common and mayoral seals of the city. Named witnesses: the bailiff, the mayor, a coroner, the reeves, John Mower, William Warmwell, Richard Spencer, Richard Jewell, and the clerk

2 June 1400, at Salisbury
1781 Approval of the will of John Wise, made on 12 June 1341. <u>Interment</u>: in the graveyard of St. Edmund's church. <u>Bequests</u>: 4d. to the fabric of the cathedral church; 6d. each to the fabric of the church of the Blessed Edmund and to the parochial chaplain there, 4d. to the deacon, and 2d. to the sacristan; the rest of his goods to his wife Alice. <u>Devise</u>: to Alice a rent of 5s. a year from a tenement in Minster Street between a tenement formerly Ralph of Langford's on the north side and Thomas Dovedale's tenement on the south side, to be held for life by Alice and after her death for ever by John's daughter Ellen and her heirs and assigns. <u>Executors</u>: his wife Alice and Peter Topp, weaver. <u>Proved</u> on 23 June 1341 in front of an officer of the subdean; the administration was entrusted to the executors. <u>Approved</u> at a court held in front of the bailiff, the mayor, and other citizens; the seisin of the rent was released to the legatees.

2 July 1400, at Westminster
1782 By his letters patent Henry IV of late licensed Adam Teffont, the mayor of Salisbury, the master of the hospital of the Holy Trinity, to acquire land and tenements to the value of £20 a year [*as in* **1766**]. The king now licensed an elder John Chandler, of Salisbury, to give to the mayor, the master of the hospital, 2 messuages, 15 cottages, and rent of 4s., in Salisbury, not held of the king in chief, and worth 67s. 4d. a year. The true value was found by means of an inquest taken by John Bernard, the king's escheator in Wiltshire, and recorded in the king's Chancery. The messuages, cottages, and rent are to be held for ever by the mayor and master and his successors to support the hospital and the feeble and sick paupers dwelling in it, to the value of 100s. in part fulfilment of the £20. The king likewise granted a licence to the mayor and master to receive the messuages, cottages, and rent from John Chandler and to him and his successors to hold them for ever, the Statute of Mortmain notwithstanding.

28 July 1400, at Salisbury
1783 Approval of the will of William Handley, tucker, made on 4 February 1393. Interment: in St. Martin's church in front of the altar of the Blessed Mary. Bequests: 12*d.* to the fabric of the cathedral church; 2*s.* to the fabric of St. Martin's church, 6*d.* to each chaplain, 12*d.* to the parochial chaplain, 6*d.* to the deacon, and 4*d.* to the sacristan; 6*s.* 8*d.* to the Franciscans of Salisbury; 5*s.* to the Dominicans of Fisherton; a press, a pair of shears, and 12 pairs of handles to William Shergold; a tunic with a hood both to William Bond and John Handley; 12*d.* to the hospital called Almshouse; 4*d.* to each of his godchildren; a red cloak to Roger Howe; 10*s.* to be handed out to paupers in bread or cash on the day of his burial; a coverlet and a linen sheet to his sister according to the order of his wife Christine; his best tunic, with a hood, and a cloak to his brother Adam; a mazer and, after Chistine's death, a large mazer to his daughter Margery; the rest of his goods, his debts having been paid and the expenses connected with his funeral having been met, to Christine. Devises: to Christine a tenement, in which he dwells, in Gigant Street between a cottage of William Warmwell on either side, to be held for her life by Christine and her assigns. On Christine's death the tenement should remain for ever to Nicholas Hayward and his wife Margery, William's daughter, and their heirs and assigns. William devised to Nicholas and Margery a tenement in New Street, between John Chandler's tenement on one side and Thomas Burford's tenement on the other side, to be held for ever by them and their heirs and assigns. He devised to Christine a tenement in the township of Old Sarum, which was of late John Handley's, to be held for ever by her and her heirs and assigns. He charged Nicholas and Margery with holding the obit of William Handley and John Handley. Executors: his wife Christine and Nicholas Hayward. Proved on 17 July 1393 in front of the subdean; the administration was entrusted to the executors. Approved at a court held in front of the bailiff, the mayor, and other citizens; the seisin of the tenements was released to the legatees.
1784 By his charter Richard Spencer, a citizen of Salisbury, granted to John Parch, weaver, conjoined cottages and shops, with a yard (*or* yards), in Rolleston [*margin*: Rolleston Lane] between a yard of John Waite, hosier, on the north side and Thomas Farrant's cottage on the west side. The premises were acquired by Richard Spencer and Robert Hazelbury from William Stourton, William River, and Edmund Enfield, and John Blickling, William Buck, and William Winslow, chaplains, Robert released his right or claim to them to Richard, and they are to be held for ever by John Parch and his heirs and assigns. Seals: Richard's and the common and mayoral seals of the city. Named witnesses: the bailiff, the mayor, a coroner, the reeves, William Warmwell, John Salisbury, grocer, Richard Leach, an elder John Forest, William Hill, John Needler, and the clerk
1785 By his charter John Lake granted to the master Robert Ragenhill, a clerk, and John Mower and Richard Spencer, citizens of Salisbury, a cottage, with a yard (*or* yards) and an empty plot of land, in Martin's Croft, near the graveyard of St. Edmund's church, between Hugh Winterbourne's cottage on the north side and a cottage of the provost of St. Edmund's church on the south side. The cottage was acquired by John from Thomas Bash and is to be held, with the yard(s)

and the empty plot, for ever by the grantees and their heirs and assigns. Clause of warranty. Seals: John Lake's and the common and mayoral seals of the city. Named witnesses the bailiff, the mayor, a coroner, the reeves, William Warmwell, Richard Leach, John Forest, John Needler, and the clerk

11 August 1400, at Salisbury
1786 Approval of the will of Thomas Boyton, bowyer, a citizen of Salisbury, made on 25 July 1400. Interment: in the parish church of St. Thomas beside the tomb in which the corpse of Agnes, of late his wife, lies buried. Bequests: 13*s*. 4*d*. to the fabric of the cathedral church; 20 marks, from the debt which John Gilbert owes to him, for the new fabric of the south aisle in St. Thomas's church for the salvation of the souls of John Fisher, his wife Christine, and others (and if John Gilbert should be tardy or remiss in paying the 20 marks the wardens and parishioners of that church should claim it from him and, with their own expenses, procure it from him); 12*d*. to the parochial chaplain of St. Thomas's church, 4*d*. to each chaplain of that church present at his funeral rites, 4*d*. to the deacon, and 4*d*. to the sacristan; 4*d*. to each chaplain of St. Edmund's church and of St. Martin's church to pray for his soul and the souls of others; 8*d*. to each Dominican friar in the conventual church of Fisherton, whom his executors should consider poor and in need, to pray for his soul, the soul of Agnes, of late his wife, and the souls of others, and 6*s*. 8*d*. to have a pittance for the convent there; ½ mark to the convent of the Franciscans of Salisbury, and 4*d*. to each friar there considered poor and in need; 4*d*. to each vicar of the cathedral church to pray for his soul and the souls of others; 4*d*. to each person ailing and bedridden in the city; a silver bowl with a cover, of late that of Henry Gill, the rector of Fisherton, a silk belt furnished with silver, which Thomas received from Thomas Erlestoke, his best sword, and two bows to his kinsman William Boyton; a breastplate, a basinet, a 'b' pallet, and a pair of plated gloves also to William; the rest of his body armour to Robert, a son of his wife Gunnore; a mazer bound with silver, with a small badge, and six silver spoons marked inside with roses to James, a Dominican friar; a small piece of silver with a cover, and a mazer bound with silver, to Margaret, a nun of Amesbury and a daughter of his wife Gunnore; a gown with a hood, at the discretion of his executors, to John Baynton; a gown with a hood, at the same discretion, to Thomas, a brother of William Boyton; a brass pot, at the same discretion, and a gown to Edith, the wife of Richard Peutherer, of Bristol; a second-best sword and two bows to Thomas Marlborough; a gown to John, the husband of his kinswoman Margery, and a coat to Margery; a coat to Margery's son John and, at the discretion of his executors, to each of his servants; a slop to Thomas, a son of William Boyton; a small piece, to be chosen by his executors, to the lord Ralph Hampstead, a chaplain, and a slop of russet at the petition of his [Thomas's] wife; to the parish church of Boyton a chalice with a cover, silver gilt, to carry the body of Christ to the sick and feeble of the parish in their last days, to be in service there for ever; a porteous covered in red, and a temporal covered in white, to the lord Nicholas Tucker, a chaplain; 40*s*. to Richard Leach and 20*s*. to his wife Alice; a pair of chequer-work vestments to

Wilsford church; another pair of vestments, with a missal, to remain, and be of use, to the chaplains celebrating mass on behalf of his soul in St. Thomas's church, and, the celebration finished, to remain for ever to the parish church of Boyton; a black psalter and [a book of] matins to Thomas, a son of William Boyton, to be held when he reached the age of 8 years, remaining in the meantime in the keeping of the elder Thomas's executors; a psalter, covered in red, to William Oakden, to be held when he reached that same age and, if he were to die under the age of 7 years, to be sold and the money raised from it laid out by those executors on behalf of his soul and the souls of others; the rest of his goods to Gunnore; all his books and statutes of the law to William Boyton. Devises: to his wife Gunnore for life two conjoined shops, opposite Poultry, between John at the burgh's empty plot on the east side and John Wishford's tenement on the west side. After Gunnore's death the shops should be held for life by her son Robert, and after Robert's death should be sold by Thomas's executors, their executors, or subsequent executors. Of the money received half should be released for the fabric of St. Thomas's church and half for the fabric of the cathedral church. Thomas appointed two conjoined shops opposite the fishermen's stalls to be sold immediately after his death. With the money raised from the sale a chaplain to be chosen by his executors should celebrate mass on behalf of his soul, the soul of Agnes, of late his wife, and the souls of others. Thomas devised to Gunnore a chief tenement, in which he dwelt, in Minster Street, which is called Castle Street, between a tenement of late Nicholas Taylor's on the south side and a tenement of William Bailey, draper, on the north side, to be held for life as dower and by her executor for the year following her death. After Gunnore's death and that year the tenement should remain to William Boyton for life, and, after his death should be sold by Thomas's executors or subsequent executors. The money raised from the sale should be divided into four parts, one for the fabric of the cathedral church, one for the fabric of St. Thomas's church, one for the pavement of the market, and one for the improvement of the upper bridge of Fisherton. Thomas devised to Gunnore for life six conjoined shops in Butcher Row between John Camel's shop on the east side and Henry Popham's shop on the west side. After Gunnore's death the shops should be sold by Thomas's executors or subsequent executors. Of the money received Thomas appointed part, at the discretion of the mayor for the time being, for the improvement and maintenance of Drake Hall Street, of the way leading to Ayleswade bridge, and of the bridge itself; he appointed part for the fabric of the cathedral church, part for the fabric of Boyton church, and part for the improvement of the way opposite the Dominicans of Fisherton and of the upper bridge there. Thomas devised to William Boyton a tenement, with three shops, opposite the market place where yarn, linen cloth, and woollen cloths are sold, between John Grandon's tenement on the north side and Thomas Castleton's tenement on the south side, to be held for ever by him and his issue. If William were to die without issue the tenement, and the shops, would remain to Thomas's executors or subsequent executors to be sold. Of the money received part should remain to William to discharge his debts, if he should be indebted; otherwise it should remain for the fabric of the church of the Dominicans of Fisherton. Thomas appointed part for the fabric of the church of the Franciscans of Salisbury, and a third part to poor scholars of de Vaux college studying at Oxford, having it for their own uses, to pray for his soul and the souls of others. The fourth part should be laid out, through the oversight of the mayor for the time being, on the improvement of Drake Hall Street, of the way leading to Ayleswade bridge, and of the bridge itself. Thomas appointed that William Boyton should have the reversion of the chief tenement, in which Thomas dwelt, before anyone else; without perpetrating fraud or collusion he might have it for the best market price and for less by £25 than anyone else might. He appointed that none of his tenements or shops should be sold in demesne or reversion except at the true value, avoiding fraud, deceipt, and collusion. If any of his executors, their executors, or subsequent executors should alienate any tenement or shop in demesne or reversion contrary to that order a co-executor, notwithstanding any such alienation, might enter on, take possession of, and sell such tenement or shop at the true value, saving the estate in the tenement and shops devised to Gunnore. Executors: Gunnore, Ralph Hampstead, a chaplain, and William Lord. Witnesses: the lords William Upavon and Edward Elion, chaplains. Proved on 2 August 1400 in front of the subdean; the administration was entrusted to the executors, they appearing in person. Approved at a court held in front of the bailiff, the mayor, and other citizens; the seisin of the tenements was released to the legatees.

8 September 1400, at Salisbury
1787 By their charter Walter Dyne and his wife Christine appearing at the court held on that day, granted to John Mower and William Pickard, citizens of Salisbury, a tenement, in which they dwelt, in Endless Street between John Wishford's tenement on the south side and a tenement of John Newman, hatter, on the north side, to be held for ever by them and their heirs and assigns. Clause of warranty. Seals: those of Walter and Christine and the common and mayoral seals of the city. Named witnesses: the mayor, the bailiff, a coroner, the reeves, William Warmwell, Richard Spencer, William Walter, an elder John Chandler, and Nicholas Harding
1788 By his letters of attorney Walter Dyne appointed Thomas Biston and Edmund Bower to surrender, together with his wife Christine, into the hand of Richard, the bishop of Salisbury, the seisin of a tenement in Endless Street [*as in* **1787**] to the use of John Mower and William Pickard, citizens of Salisbury. Seals: Walter's and the mayoral seal of the city

22 September 1400, at Salisbury
1789 By his charter John Baker, a citizen of Salisbury, granted to William Clement, a chaplain, a son of John Clement and his wife Alice, a tenement in Gigant Street between a corner tenement of late John Ashley's on the south side and a tenement of Thomas Ham, tailor, on the north side. The tenement was acquired by John Baker from John and Alice and is to be held for ever by William and his heirs and assigns. Seals: John Baker's and the common and mayoral seals

of the city. Named witnesses: the bailiff, the mayor, a coroner, the reeves, William Warmwell, John Mower, Richard Spencer, Richard Leach, John Forest, and the clerk

1790 By his charter an elder John Chandler granted to an elder John Sampson, of Salisbury, and his wife Edith six conjoined cottages, with gardens, in Brown Street between a gate of a chief tenement, in which Nicholas Comme dwells, on the north side and Henry Southwick's cottage on the south side. The cottages, with the gardens, and with other tenements and shops in the city, were held by John Chandler and Robert Play, now dead, by a grant of Matthew Fernhill and his wife Isabel, and are to be held for ever by John and Edith and their heirs and assigns. Seals: John Chandler's and the common and mayoral seals of the city. Named witnesses: the bailiff, the mayor, the reeves, William Warmwell, John Mower, Richard Spencer, Richard Leach, an elder John Forest, and the clerk

1791 By his charter an elder John Chandler, a citizen of Salisbury, granted to Adam Teffont, the mayor, the master of the hospital of the Holy Trinity in the city, to support the hospital and the feeble and sick paupers dwelling in it, a messuage, with two shops adjoining it, in New Street towards Barnwell cross between Nicholas Hayward's tenement on the west side and Margaret Godmanstone's tenement on the east side; also a corner messuage, with five shops adjoining it, in Wineman Street between Robert Deverill's tenement on the east side and William River's tenement on the south side, six shops in New Street between the hospital's trench on the east side and John's shops on the west side, a shop in Culver Street between William Reynold's tenement on the south side and Nicholas Mansfield's tenement on the north side, a shop in Endless Street between Robert Kirtlingstoke's tenement on the south side and Margaret Godmanstone's tenement on the north side, and a rent of 4*s*. a year issuing from William Chapman's tenement in Wineman Street between a tenement in which John Brewer dwells on the east side and a tenement in which John Butler, mercer, dwells on the west side. The messuages, shops, and rent are to be held for ever by the mayor, the master of the hospital, and his successors as mayor and master. Clause of warranty. Seals: John Chandler's and the common and mayoral seals of the city. Named witnesses: the bailiff, the mayor, the reeves, John Mower, John Baker, Richard Spencer, Richard Jewell, William Warmwell, and the clerk

20 October 1400, at Salisbury

1792 By their charter Gunnore, the relict, and an executor, of Thomas Boyton, bowyer, of late a citizen of Salisbury, and Ralph Hampstead and William Lord, her co-executors, on the strength of Thomas's will granted to Adam Teffont, a citizen of Salisbury, two conjoined shops, opposite the fishermen's stalls, between Robert Kirtlingstoke's tenement on the west side and Thomas Knoyle's tenement on the east side. Thomas devised those shops to be sold and the money received to be laid out on celebrating masses on behalf of his soul, the soul of Agnes, formerly his wife, and the souls of others. The shops are to be held for ever by Adam and his heirs and assigns. Seals: those of the grantors and the common and mayoral seals of the city. Named witnesses: the bailiff, the reeves, William

Warmwell, John Mower, Richard Spencer, Richard Leach, an elder John Forest, William Hill, John Needler, and the clerk

3 November 1400, at Salisbury
1793 By his charter [*dated to the Wednesday after the feast of St. Simon and St. Jude in the 4th year of the reign of Henry IV (1 November 1402), witnessed by reeves chosen on 2 November 1400 and replaced on 2 November 1401, possibly of 2 November 1401, but here assumed to be of the Wednesday after that feast in the 2nd year of the reign of Henry IV (3 November 1400)*] Richard Leach, a citizen of Salisbury, granted to William Coventry, William Mercer, and John Purvis a tenement in Pot Row between John Barnaby's tenement on the east side and a tenement in which William Wilton dwells on the west side, to be held for ever by them and their heirs and assigns. Clause of warranty. Seals: Richard's and the common and mayoral seals of the city. Named witnesses: the bailiff, the coroners, the reeves, John Mower, Richard Spencer, Edmund Enfield, Adam Teffont, William Walter, John Needler, Nicholas Harding, and the clerk

12 January 1401, at Salisbury
1794 By his charter Adam Teffont, a citizen of Salisbury, granted to William Slegge, of Salisbury, two conjoined shops, opposite the fishermen's stalls, [*as in* **1792**]. The shops were acquired by Adam from the executors of Thomas Boyton, bowyer, [*as in* **1792**] and are to be held for ever by William and his heirs and assigns. Seals: Adam's and the common and mayoral seals of the city. Named witnesses: the mayor, the bailiff, the coroners, the reeves, William Warmwell, John Mower, Richard Spencer, William Walter, John Forest, Nicholas Harding, and the clerk
1795 By his charter John Kingbridge, a citizen of Salisbury, granted to Richard Jewell, a citizen of Salisbury, and Gunnore, the relict of Thomas Boyton, bowyer, two tenements in New Street. One stands between a tenement of late that of Gilbert Whichbury, baker, on the west side and a tenement of late Thomas Mussel's on the east side, and the other between a tenement of late John Upton's on the east side and a tenement which John Wells, weaver, of late held, now Thomas Biston's, on the west side. They are to be held for ever by Richard and Gunnore and their heirs and assigns. Clause of warranty. Seals: John Kingbridge's and the common and mayoral seal, of the city. Named witnesses: the mayor, the bailiff, the reeves, John Mower, William Warmwell, John Baker, grocer, Richard Spencer, John Newman, Walter Nalder, and the clerk

26 January 1401, at Salisbury
1796 By his charter an elder George Goss, a citizen of Salisbury, granted to Richard Spencer, William Walter, an elder John Forest, and Nicholas Harding a messuage, with a yard, in Chipper Street between a tenement of William Purchase, tucker, on the west side and a tenement of late Roger Stapleford's on the east side. The messuage, with the yard, was acquired by George from Walter of Cosham and his wife Joan and is to be held by the grantees and their heirs

and assigns. Clause of warranty. Seals: George's and the common and mayoral seals of the city. Named witnesses: the mayor, the bailiff, the coroners, the reeves, William Warmwell, John Mower, John Needler, William Hill, William Guys, an elder John Chandler, and the clerk

9 February 1401, at Salisbury
1797 By their charter Richard Jewell, a citizen of Salisbury, and Gunnore, the relict of Thomas Boyton, bowyer, she in her celibate widowhood, granted to John Kingbridge and his wife Alice two tenements in New Street, one between a tenement of late that of Gilbert Whichbury, baker, now Walter Nalder's, on the west side and a tenement of late Thomas Mussel's on the east side, and one between a tenement of late John Upton's on the east side and a tenement which John Wells of late held, now Thomas Biston's, on the west side. Both tenements were held by Richard and Gunnore by a grant of John Kingbridge and are to be held for ever by John and Alice and John's heirs and assigns. Seals: those of Richard and Gunnore and the common and mayoral seals of the city. Named witnesses: the bailiff, the mayor, the coroners, the reeves, John Mower, Edmund Enfield, John Baker, grocer, William Walter, and the clerk

23 March 1401, at Salisbury
1798 By his charter Nicholas Monkton granted to the master Robert Ragenhill, a clerk, and Stephen Edington a tenement, with conjoined shops, in Minster Street, which is called Castle Street, and Chipper Street, on a corner and opposite the corner tenement of late Thomas Britford's, between a tenement of late that of an elder George Goss on the north side and shops of late John Hacker's, now John Gatcombe's, on the east side. The tenement, with the shops, was held by Nicholas by a grant of Edmund Cofford, some time ago a citizen of Salisbury, and is to be held for ever by Robert and Stephen and their heirs and assigns. Clause of warranty. Seals: Nicholas's and the common and mayoral seals of the city. Named witnesses: the bailiff, the mayor, the coroners, the reeves, John Mower, Richard Spencer, William Warmwell, William Walter, an elder John Forest, William Hill, and the clerk

24 March 1401, at Salisbury
1799 By his writing Nicholas Monkton, a son and heir of Alice, who was the wife of Edmund Cofford, quitclaimed to the master Robert Ragenhill, a clerk, and Stephen Edington and their heirs and assigns his right or claim to a tenement, with conjoined shops, in Minster Street [*as in* **1798**]. Clause of warranty. Seals: Nicholas's and the common and mayoral seals of the city. Named witnesses: the bailiff, the mayor, the coroners, the reeves, John Mower, William Warmwell, Richard Spencer, an elder John Forest, William Walter, Nicholas Harding, and the clerk

6 April 1401, at Salisbury
1800 By his charter John Collier, tucker, of Salisbury, granted to Richard Spencer,

a citizen of Salisbury, his estate in a rent of 11s. a year. George Goss is accustomed to receive that rent for his life from a yard, with a rack built in it, which Robert Gollan and his wife Agnes hold for their life by George's grant. The yard lies in Martin's Croft, on the way to St. Edmund's church, between a yard of the provost of that church on the south side and John Judd's yard on the north side. John also granted to Richard the reversion of the yard, with the rack, when it fell due on the death of Robert and Agnes. The rent, to be received after George's death, and the reversion were granted to John by George and are to be held for ever by Richard and his heirs and assigns. Clause of warranty. Seals: John's and the common and mayoral seals of the city. Named witnesses: the bailiff, the mayor, the coroners, the reeves, William Warmwell, John Mower, William Walter, John Needler, an elder John Forest, Nicholas Harding, and the clerk

1 June 1401, at Salisbury
1801 By his charter William Buck, a chaplain, granted to William Tull, of Bedwyn, a tenement, with a shop (*or* shops) fronting on the street, in Carter Street between John Newman's tenement on the north side and a tenement of John Preston, grocer, of late Agnes Bodenham's, on the south side. The tenement was held by William Buck by a grant of Christine, the relict, and an executor, of Robert Beechfount, of late a citizen of Salisbury, and, with the shop(s), is to be held for ever by William Tull and his heirs and assigns. Seals: William Buck's and the common and mayoral seals of the city. Named witnesses: the bailiff, the mayor, the coroners, the reeves, John Mower, William Warmwell, Richard Spencer, Adam Teffont, Thomas Castleton, William Sall, and the clerk
1802 By his charter John Coffer, tanner, granted to William Slegge, weaver, of Salisbury, the reversion of three premises when each fell due on the death of his own wife Joan, the relict of John Luckham, tanner: that of a tenement in Brown Street between a tenement of late Nicholas Baker's on the south side and Thomas Manning's garden on the north side, that of a garden lying behind the tenement, on the far side of the common trench of running water, measuring 40 ft. in length, and that of a small empty plot lying on the north side of the tenement, measuring in width 2 ft. 2½ in. and in length extending from a corner of the hall of the tenement as far as the east corner of a house called Workhouse, with free ingress and egress through the house to the plot. The reversions were acquired by John Coffer from Stephen Edington, and the tenement, the garden, and the empty plot, with the ingress and egress, when they fell due, are to be held for ever by William Slegge and his heirs and assigns. Clause of warranty. Seals: John's and the common and mayoral seals of the city. Named witnesses: the bailiff, the mayor, the coroners, the reeves, William Warmwell, John Mower, Richard Spencer, Edmund Enfield, Adam Teffont, William Walter, John Needler, Nicholas Harding, and the clerk

15 June 1401, at Salisbury
1803 By their deed John Coffer, tanner, and his wife Joan, the relict of John Luckham, tanner, of late a citizen of Salisbury, granted to William Slegge, weaver,

of Salisbury, their estate in a tenement in Brown Street [*as in 1802*] and in a garden lying behind it [*as in 1802*]. The tenement and the garden were devised by John Luckham to Joan for her life, and they are to be held for her life by William and his heirs and assigns. Clause of warranty. Seals: those of John and Joan and the common and mayoral seals of the city. Named witnesses: the bailiff, the mayor, the coroners, the reeves, John Mower, William Warmwell, Richard Spencer, Adam Teffont, Thomas Castleton, William Sall, and the clerk

29 June 1401, at Salisbury
1804 By their charter Walter Warwick and John Medmenham, chaplains, granted to John Lippiatt and his wife Alice a tenement, with shops, in New Street between shops of late William Tenterer's on the west side and shops of the abbot of Stanley on the east side. The tenement, with the shops, was held by Walter and John by a grant of William Bailey, draper, is to be held for ever by John and Alice and the issue begotten between them, and if John and Alice were to die without such issue it would remain for ever to that John's direct heirs. Seals: those of the grantors and the common and mayoral seals of the city. Named witnesses: the bailiff, the mayor, the coroners, the reeves, John Mower, William Warmwell, Richard Spencer, John Baker, grocer, Adam Teffont, and the clerk

1805 By his charter Thomas Postle granted to John Newman, grocer, a tenement in Winchester Street between a corner tenement of late William Tenterer's, which William Hill holds, on the east side and a tenement of John Baker, grocer, on the west side; also a tenement, with shops fronting on the street, and with a garden, in New Street between a tenement of late William Tenterer's, now that of John Lippiatt and his wife Alice, on the west side and a tenement of late William Tenterer's, which William Merriott and his wife Alice hold, on the east side; also two shops in New Street between shops of late John Butterley's, now Laurence Gowan's, on the west side and shops of John Lippiatt and Alice on the east side; also a cottage in Drake Hall Street between a shop of the dean and chapter of Salisbury, which William Pickard holds, on the north side and shop property of Robert Russell, kt., on the south side. The tenements, shops, and cottage are to be held for ever by John Newman and his heirs and assigns. Clause of warranty. Seals: Thomas's and the common and mayoral seals of the city. Named witnesses: the bailiff, the mayor, the coroners, the reeves, John Mower, William Warmwell, Richard Spencer, John Salisbury, grocer, Edmund Enfield, and the clerk

13 July 1401, at Salisbury
1806 By his charter an elder John Chandler, a citizen of Salisbury, granted to an elder John Sampson and his wife Edith a tenement, with shops, cottages, and gardens, as much in Carter Street as in Brown Street. He and Robert Play, dead, held it by a feoffment of Matthew Fernhill and his wife Isabel, who together held it by a feoffment of William Warmwell. In Carter Street the tenement stands between Richard Knolle's tenement on the north side and William Guys's tenement on the south side, and in Brown Street between William Warmwell's tenement on the north side and Henry Southwick's tenement on the south side.

John also granted to John and Edith a rent of a rose a year issuing from a gate with rooms built above it, from a kitchen joined to that gate, from an empty plot, and from a house called Cowhouse, all which premises Matthew holds for his life by a grant of William Warmwell, together with the reversion of the premises when it fell due on Matthew's death. John also granted to John and Edith free ingress and egress through the gate, with the easement to be had in the plot. The rent, the premises, the ingress and egress, and the easement were held by John and Robert by a grant of William Warmwell, and, with the tenement, shops, cottages, and gardens, are to be held for ever by John and Edith and John's heirs and assigns. Seals: John Chandler's and the common and mayoral seals of the city. Named witnesses: the bailiff, the mayor, the coroners, the reeves, John Mower, Richard Spencer, Edmund Enfield, Adam Teffont, John Needler, William Walter, Nicholas Harding, an elder John Forest, and the clerk

19 October 1401, at Salisbury
1807 By their charter William Surr and his wife Tamsin, appearing at the court held on that day, granted to Thomas Slegge, weaver, of Salisbury, four cottages, with part of a garden measuring 16 ft. in length and 7 ft. in width, in Culver Street between Gilbert Oword's tenement on the south side and William's corner tenement [Bert's Corner: *cf.* **2072**] on the north side. The cottages, with the part of the garden, are to be held for ever by Thomas and his heirs and assigns, paying 4*d*. a year to the chief lord as William and Tamsin were accustomed to pay. Clause of warranty. Seals: those of William and Tamsin and the common and mayoral seals of the city. Named witnesses: the bailiff, the mayor, the coroners, the reeves, John Mower, William Warmwell, Richard Spencer, Richard Jewell, William Hill, and the clerk

16 November 1401, at Salisbury
1808 By his charter an elder Thomas Castleton, mercer, a citizen of Salisbury, granted to Stephen Brown, grocer, a tenement in Winchester Street, opposite a tenement of late John Lea's, between a tenement of late Robert Beechfount's on the east side and a tenement which William Mower of late held of John Hoare on the west side, to be held for ever by Stephen and his heirs and assigns. Clause of warranty. Seals: Thomas's and the common and mayoral seals of the city. Named witnesses: the bailiff, the mayor, the reeves, John Mower, Richard Spencer, William Warmwell, an elder John Forest, William Walter, and John Needler
1809 By her charter Margery, the relict of John Justice, granted to Thomas Biston three conjoined cottages in Culver Street between the gate of William Reynold's tenement on the south side and John Camel's cottages on the north side. The cottages were acquired by John and Margery from Henry Stapleford and are to be held for ever by Thomas and his heirs and assigns. Clause of warranty. Seals: Margery's and the common and mayoral seals of the city. Named witnesses: the bailiff, the mayor, the coroners, the reeves, William Warmwell, John Mower, Richard Spencer, William Walter, and the clerk
1810 By her letters of attorney Margery, the relict of John Justice, appointed John

Aynel, a chaplain, to surrender into the hand of Richard, the bishop of Salisbury, the seisin of three conjoined cottages in Culver Street [*as in 1809*] to the use of Thomas Biston. Seals: Margery's and the mayoral seal of the city

25 January 1402, at Salisbury
1811 By his charter Hugh Braban, tailor, of Salisbury, granted to a younger Nicholas Baynton, William Bishop, the master Thomas Turk, the vicar of Downton, John Humphrey, the vicar of Romsey, and William Handley, a tailor, three conjoined cottages, with gardens, in Drake Hall Street between cottages of the master Thomas Southam, a canon in the cathedral church, on the south side and cottages of the vicars of that church on the north side; also four conjoined cottages, with gardens, in the same street between cottages of Simon Belch, tucker, on the south side and cottages of late Robert Play's, which John Ferrer, carter, and his wife Maud hold, on the north side. The three cottages, with the gardens, under the name of two cottages, and the four cottages, with the gardens, under the name of a tenement, were held by Hugh by a grant of Richard Hellier, barber, and are to be held for ever by the grantees and their heirs and assigns. Clause of warranty. Seals: Hugh's and the common and mayoral seals of the city. Named witnesses: the bailiff, the mayor, the coroners, the reeves, William Warmwell, John Mower, Richard Spencer, John Forest, William Walter, Nicholas Harding, and the clerk
1812 By his letters of attorney Hugh Braban, tailor, of Salisbury, appointed John Griffith, a tailor, to surrender into the hand of Richard, the bishop of Salisbury, the seisin of three conjoined cottages, with gardens, in Drake Hall Street [*as in 1811*], and of four conjoined cottages in the same street [*as in 1811*], to the use of a younger Nicholas Baynton and others [*as in 1811*]. Seals: Hugh's and the common and mayoral seals of the city

22 March 1402, at Salisbury
1813 By his charter William Coventry granted to William Mercer, John Judd, John Purvis, and Nicholas Stoke, a chaplain, two tenements which Adam Daubeney, fisher, holds at the east end of Pot Row and which were of late those of Walter Clopton, kt. The tenements are to be held for ever by the grantees and their heirs and assigns. Clause of warranty. Seals: William Coventry's and the common and mayoral seals of the city. Named witnesses: the mayor, the bailiff, the coroners, a reeve, William Warmwell, John Mower, Richard Spencer, Edmund Enfield, William Walter, John Needler, an elder John Forest, and the clerk

3 May 1402, at Salisbury
1814 Approval of the will of Hugh Winterbourne, a citizen of Salisbury, made on 21 December 1401. <u>Interment</u>: in the graveyard of St. Edmund's church. <u>Bequests</u>: 6*s*. 8*d*. to the fabric of that church, 40*d*. to the rector for his forgotten tithes, and 4*d*. to each chaplain to pray for his soul; 12*d*. each to the fabric of St. Thomas's church and the fabric of the cathedral church; 6*d*. to the fabric of St. Martin's church; 12*d*. to John Pope, a chaplain, to pray for his soul; 2*s*. 6*d*. both to the Dominicans of Fisherton and the Franciscans of Salisbury to pray for his

soul; his best tunic, with its hood, to Hain Dedman; 12 lb. of wax to be burned around his corpse, and 100 masses to be celebrated on behalf of his soul, on the day of his burial; the rest of his goods to his wife Alice. Devises: to Alice for life a tenement in Castle Street, between Edward Breamore's tenement on the south side and a tenement of late Thomas Sexhampcote's on the north side, and after her death to be sold by his executors, their executors, or subsequent executors. The money received should be laid out on masses and other charitable deeds on behalf of Hugh's soul and the souls of others. Hugh devised to William Shipton a cottage, in Gigant Street, on the west side of the street, between cottage property of the provost of St. Edmund's church on the south side and a garden of Robert Gollan, tucker, on the north side, to be held for ever by him and his heirs and assigns. Executors: his wife Alice and William Shipton; overseer, the lord John Jakes, a chaplain. Proved on 23 December 1401 by an officer of the subdean; the administration was entrusted to the executors. Approved at a court held in front of the bailiff, the mayor, and other citizens; the seisin of the tenement and of the cottage was released to the legatees.

17 May 1402, at Salisbury
1815 By their charter Ralph Hampstead, a chaplain, William Lord, and Gunnore, the relict of Thomas Boyton, bowyer, of late a citizen of Salisbury, Thomas's executors, on the strength of Thomas's will granted to Richard Leach, a citizen of Salisbury, the reversion of six conjoined shops, which Gunnore holds for her life by Thomas's devise, in Butcher Row between John Camel's shop on the east side and Henry Popham's shop on the west side. The shops are to be held for ever, when they fell due, by Richard and his heirs and assigns. Seals: those of the grantors and the common and mayoral seals of the city. Named witnesses: the mayor, the bailiff, the coroners, the reeves, William Warmwell, John Mower, Richard Spencer, John Forest, William Walter, Nicholas Harding, and John Needler

28 June 1402, at Salisbury
1816 By his charter Stephen Thorburn granted to Thomas Stabber five conjoined cottages in Chipper Lane, between a tenement of late Henry Pope's on the west side and Thomas Farrant's cottages on the east side, to be held for ever by Thomas and his heirs and assigns. Clause of warranty. Seals: Stephen's and the common and mayoral seals of the city. Named witnesses: the bailiff, the mayor, the coroners, the reeves, William Warmwell, John Mower, Richard Spencer, John Forest, William Walter, John Needler, and the clerk

12 July 1402, at Salisbury
1817 By their charter Robert Ragenhill, a clerk, and John Mower and Richard Spencer, citizens of Salisbury, granted to William Warmwell, a citizen of Salisbury, a tenement in St. Martin's Street, between a tenement of the provost of St. Edmund's church on the east side and a tenement of the vicars of the cathedral church on the west side, to be held for ever by William and his heirs and assigns.

Seals: those of the grantors and the common and mayoral seals of the city. Named witnesses: the bailiff, the mayor, the coroners, the reeves, William Walter, an elder John Forest, William Hill, John Needler, and William Warin

1818 By his letters of attorney Robert Ragenhill, a clerk, appointed Robert Netton, a chaplain, and Stephen Edington, together with John Mower and Richard Spencer, citizens of Salisbury, to surrender into the hand of Richard, the bishop of Salisbury, the seisin of a tenement in St. Martin's Street [*as in 1817*] to the use of William Warmwell, a citizen of Salisbury. Seals: Robert Ragenhill's and the mayoral seal of the city

23 August 1402, at Salisbury
1819 By his charter John Ettshall, a citizen of Salisbury, granted to an elder Thomas Castleton, mercer, a citizen of Salisbury, a tenement, which is now built as two cottages, with gardens, in a street called Rolleston, on a corner, opposite cottages of the provost and chaplains of St. Edmund's church on the way to that church, and between Stephen Edington's yard, which John Waite, hosier, holds, on the south side and John Mower's yard, through a trench of running water, on the west side. [*The location of the tenement is described slightly differently in 1821*] The tenement was held by John by a grant of John Newman and Nicholas Harding, citizens of Salisbury, who held it by a feoffment of a younger John Chandler, and, with the gardens, is to be held for ever by Thomas and his heirs and assigns. Clause of warranty. Seals: John Ettshall's and the common and mayoral seals of the city. Named witnesses: the bailiff, the mayor, the coroners, the reeves, John Mower, Richard Spencer, William Warmwell, Richard Leach, and the clerk

1820 By their charter Agnes Ball and Roger Grateley, baker, granted to Gilbert at the brook, skinner, and his wife Maud a tenement, with a garden, in Gigant Street, between Thomas Chaplin's tenement on the south side and a tenement of late Hugh Hoare's, now John Lewisham's on the north side, to be held for ever by them and the issue begotten between them. If Gilbert and Maud were to die without such issue the tenement, with the garden, would remain for ever to their heirs or assigns. Seals: those of Agnes and Roger and the common and mayoral seals of the city. Named witnesses: the bailiff, the mayor, the coroners, the reeves, John Mower, Richard Spencer, Richard Leach, William Hill, and the clerk

6 September 1402, at Salisbury
1821 By his deed an elder John Chandler, a citizen of Salisbury, quitclaimed to Thomas Castleton, mercer, a citizen of Salisbury, and his heirs and assigns his right or claim to a tenement, which is now built as two cottages, with a yard, in a street called Rolleston, on a corner, opposite cottages of the provost of St. Edmund's church, standing beside Stephen Edington's yard, which John Waite, hosier, holds, on the south side and, with its yard, extending as far as a trench of running water. Clause of warranty. Seals: John's and the common and mayoral seals of the city. Named witnesses: the bailiff, the mayor, the coroners, the reeves, John Mower, William Warmwell, John Forest, William Walter, and the clerk

1822 By his deed a younger John Chandler, a son of Walter Chandler, of late a citizen of Salisbury, quitclaimed to an elder Thomas Castleton, mercer, a citizen of Salisbury, and his heirs and assigns his right or claim to a tenement, which is now built as two cottages, with gardens, in a street called Rolleston [*as in the first part of both* **1819** *and* **1821**]. Thomas held the tenement by a grant of John Ettshall, a citizen of Salisbury. Clause of warranty. Seals: John's and the common and mayoral seals of the city. Named witnesses: the bailiff, the mayor, the coroners, the reeves, John Mower, Richard Leach, William Walter, William Sall, and the clerk

1823 By his charter William Guys, a citizen of Salisbury, granted to Thomas Castleton, mercer, a citizen of Salisbury, and his wife Maud [Guys's Place: *cf.* **2005**], a tenement, with shops, cellars, and a garden, in which William of late dwelt, in Carter Street between a tenement of late Matthew Fernhill's, now that of Nicholas Comme and John Sampson, on the north side and a tenement formerly Thomas Callow's, which Roger Pentridge now holds and John Bristow of late held, on the south side. A shop, which William acquired from John Fosbury, is comprised and built in the tenement. William acquired the tenement in part from David, a clerk, and acquired the garden now appurtenant to the tenement from Matthew. The tenement, with the shops, cellars, and garden, is to be held for their life by Thomas Castleton and Maud, after their death should remain for ever to their son John and his heirs and assigns, and if John were to die without issue while Thomas was living would remain for ever to Thomas and his heirs and assigns. Clause of warranty. Seals: William's and the common and mayoral seals of the city. Named witnesses: the bailiff, the mayor, the coroners, the reeves, John Mower, William Warmwell, William Walter, an elder John Forest, and the clerk

13 September 1402, at Salisbury
1824 By his deed William Guys, a citizen of Salisbury, quitclaimed to Thomas Castleton, mercer, a citizen of Salisbury, his wife Maud, their son John, and the heirs and assigns of Thomas and John his right or claim to a tenement, with shops, cellars, and a garden, which Thomas, Maud, and John acquired from him, in Carter Street [*as in* **1823**]. The tenement was of late that of David, a clerk. Clause of warranty. Seals: William's and the common and mayoral seals of the city. Named witnesses: the bailiff, the mayor, the coroners, the reeves, John Mower, William Warmwell, William Hill, William Sall, and the clerk

1825 By his deed an elder John Chandler, a citizen of Salisbury, quitclaimed to Thomas Castleton, mercer, a citizen of Salisbury, his wife Maud, their son John, and the heirs and assigns of Thomas and John his right or claim to a rent of 10 marks a year which he acquired from Richard Spencer, a citizen of Salisbury, who acquired it from William Guys, a citizen of Salisbury. The rent issues from a tenement, with shops, cellars, and a garden, in which William of late dwelt, in Carter Street [*as in* **1823**]. John also quitclaimed to them his right or claim to the tenement. Clause of warranty. Seals: John's and the common and mayoral seals of the city. Named witnesses: the bailiff, the mayor, the coroners, the reeves, John Mower, Richard Leach, John Lewisham, William Sall, and the clerk

4 October 1402, at Salisbury
1826 By their charter an elder John Chandler, John Ettshall, and Nicholas Brown, a chaplain, appearing at the court held on that day, granted to William Lord all the land and tenements in Salisbury, with the rent, services, and reversions, which they held by a grant of John Salisbury, grocer, a citizen of Salisbury, to be held for ever by William and his heirs and assigns. Seals: those of the grantors and the common and mayoral seals of the city. Named witnesses: the bailiff, the mayor, the coroners, the reeves, William Warmwell, John Mower, William Walter, John Needler, and John Wallop

18 October 1402, at Salisbury
1827 By his charter William Lord granted to an elder John Chandler and John Ettshall, citizens of Salisbury, all the land and tenements in Salisbury, with the rent, services, and reversions, which he held by their grant, to be held for ever by them, and their heirs and assigns. Clause of warranty, but only against William himself. Seals: William's and the common and mayoral seals of the city. Named witnesses: the bailiff, the mayor, the coroners, the reeves, John Mower, William Warmwell, an elder John Forest, William Walter, and John Needler

1 November 1402, at Salisbury
1828 Approval of the will of Lucy, the wife of John Noble, of Salisbury, made on 18 September 1402. Interment: in the graveyard of St. Edmund's church. Bequests: 6s. 8d. to the fabric of that church, 3s. 4d. to the provost for her forgotten tithes, 6d. to each collegiate chaplain to pray for her soul, and 2d. to each other chaplain celebrating mass there; 5s. both to the Dominicans of Fisherton and the Franciscans of Salisbury to pray for her soul; a tunic of russet and a small brass pot to Edith Tanner; a cloak of red and blue, a furred tunic with a blood-red hood, a veil of cypress, and a rosary of amber beads to Margaret Davy; a cloak of red and blue to John Pierce; a furred gown of sendal, a green kirtle with a hood of the same cloth, and a veil to Joan Pierce; a blue kirtle, furred, to Alice Pierce; a red bed, a pair of blankets, and a pair of linen sheets to a younger John Pierce; a veil to Maud Shipton; a cloak and a veil to William (*Willelma*) Latticemaker; a veil to Joan Freaks; a blue coat worth 8s. and a kerchief of cypress to Joan Noble; a kerchief *de Pynchard* each to Edith Tanner and Joan Kings; a furred tunic to Gillian Simmonds; a blood-red kirtle to Agnes Knights; 26s. 8d. to be handed out to paupers on the day of her burial; 3s. 4d. to Richard, a chaplain, to pray for her soul; the rest of her goods to her husband John. Devise: to John a tenement, in which she dwelt, in Castle Street, beyond the bar, between John Camel's tenement on the south side and John Starr's tenement on the north side, to be held for ever by him and his heirs and assigns. Executors: her husband John and John Durnford. Proved on 16 October 1402 in front of an officer of the subdean; the administration was entrusted to the executors, they having voluntarily accepted it. Approved at a court held in front of the bailiff, the mayor, and other citizens; the seisin of the tenement was released to the legatee.
1829 By their charter an elder John Bosham, called Pope, and his wife Christine,

appearing at the court held on that day, granted to John Gatcombe, of Salisbury, a tenement in Winchester Street between John Wootton's tenement on the east side and Adam Dummer's tenement on the west side, to be held for ever by him and his heirs and assigns. Clause of warranty. Seals: those of John and Christine and the common and mayoral seals of the city. Named witnesses: the bailiff, the mayor, the coroners, the reeves, William Warmwell, John Mower, William Walter, an elder John Forest, and the clerk

1830 By his charter Richard Spencer, a citizen of Salisbury, granted to a younger John Bosham, called Pope, and his wife Alice a messuage between Nicholas Hayward's tenement in New Street on the east side and Robert Durrant's cottage in Gigant Street on the north side, to be held for ever by them and their heirs and assigns. Clause of warranty. Seals: Richard's and the common and mayoral seals of the city. Named witnesses: the bailiff, the coroners, the reeves, John Mower, William Warmwell, William Walter, an elder John Forest, John Needler, and the clerk

15 November 1402, at Salisbury
1831 By his indented charter John Gatcombe granted to an elder John Bosham, called Pope, and his wife Christine a tenement in Winchester Street [*as in* **1829**], to be held by them for their life and the life of the one of them living longer. On the death of John and Christine the tenement should remain for ever to a younger John Bosham, called Pope, and his wife Alice and their joint issue, if John and Alice were to die without such issue it would remain for ever to Joan, a daughter of John and Christine, and her issue, and if Joan were to die without issue it would remain for ever to the elder John's direct heirs. Seals: John Gatcombe's and the common and mayoral seals of the city. Named witnesses: the bailiff, the mayor, the coroners, the reeves, John Mower, William Warmwell, William Walter, an elder John Forest, John Needler, and the clerk

29 November 1402, at Salisbury
1832 By his charter Edmund Enfield, a citizen of Salisbury, granted to Walter Dean, a chaplain, a tenement in Castle Street, beyond the bars, between a tenement of late that of Thomas Sexton, ironmonger, on the north side and a tenement of John Shipton, dubber, on the south side. The tenement was acquired by Edmund and his wife Alice, now dead, from an executor (*or* executors) of John of Upton, of late a citizen of Salisbury, and is to be held for ever by Walter and his heirs and assigns. Clause of warranty. Seals: Edmund's and the common and mayoral seals of the city. Named witnesses: the bailiff, the mayor, the coroners, the reeves, John Mower, Richard Spencer, William Warmwell, Adam Teffont, and the clerk

27 December 1402, at Salisbury
1833 By their charter an elder John Forest and Nicholas Harding, citizens of Salisbury, granted to Thomas Eyre, a citizen of Salisbury, a corner tenement, with shops and cottages next to it, in New Street between Thomas's tenement

on the west side and a tenement of late that of William Handley, tucker, [in Gigant Street: cf. *1685, 2101*] on the north side. The tenement, with the shops and cottages, and with other land and tenements in the city, was held by John and Nicholas by a grant of John Newman, a citizen of Salisbury, and is to be held for ever by Thomas and his heirs and assigns. Seals: those of John and Nicholas and the common and mayoral seals of the city. Named witnesses: the bailiff, the mayor, the coroners, the reeves, John Mower, Richard Spencer, William Warmwell, John Needler, and the clerk

1834 By their deed an elder John Forest and Nicholas Harding, citizens of Salisbury, quitclaimed to George Goss, tucker, of Salisbury, and his heirs and assigns their right or claim to a messuage in Castle Street, between Thomas Chaplin's tenement on the north side and John Wallop's tenement on the south side, and to a rent of 20s. a year issuing from it. Seals: those of John and Nicholas and the common and mayoral seals of the city. Named witnesses: the bailiff, the mayor, the coroners, the reeves, John Mower, Richard Spencer, William Warmwell, John Needler, and the clerk

10 January 1403, at Salisbury

1835 By their charter William Coventry, William Mercer, and John Purvis granted to John Brown, butcher, and his wife Joan a tenement in Pot Row between John Barnaby's tenement on the east side and a tenement in which William Wilton dwells on the west side. The tenement was held by them by a grant of Richard Leach, a citizen of Salisbury, and is to be held for ever by John and Joan and their heirs and assigns. Clause of warranty. Seals: those of the grantors and the common and mayoral seals of the city. Named witnesses: the bailiff, the mayor, the coroners, the reeves, John Mower, William Warmwell, Richard Spencer, an elder John Forest, John Needler, and the clerk

7 February 1403, at Salisbury

1836 Approval of the will of Thomas Sexton, a citizen of Salisbury, made on 13 October 1401. Interment: Thomas appointed his corpse to the Holy Sepulchre, to be interred in the conventual church of the Dominicans of Fisherton. Bequests: 6s. 8d. to the fabric of the cathedral church; 20s. each to the fabric of St. Thomas's church and to the rector for his forgotten tithes and lesser payments, 20d. to each chaplain of that church present at his funeral rites and mass on the day of his burial, 6d. to the deacon, and 4d. to the sacristan; 6s. 8d. each to the fabric of St. Edmund's church and the fabric of St. Martin's church; 6s. 8d. to the fabric and repair of the de Vaux college; 3s. 4d. for the repair of St. Nicholas's hospital; 20s. to the convent of the Franciscans of Salisbury; £10 for a window in the choir in the conventual church of the Dominicans of Fisherton to be glazed, a silver gilt piece for the high altar of that church, 2s. to each Dominican in that church, being in the order of a priest, to celebrate mass on behalf of his soul, and 12d. to each other friar of that convent to pray for his soul; 6s. 8d. each to the friars John Montagu, John Till, and William Coombe; 10 marks and a piece of silver to the friar Henry Wallis to celebrate the trental of St. George on behalf of his soul; £50 of gold coinage, a basin with a laver, a tablecloth with a towel, 12 silver spoons, two silver bowls, a gold ring, a coverlet with a tester, a pair of linen sheets, two blankets, a cistern, a great brass pot, a brass pan, and a belt furnished with silver in which letters are engraved in the mother tongue uttering 'God help' to his daughter Gunnore. If Gunnore were to die before she reached her majority all the movable goods bequeathed to her should be sold by Thomas's executors immediately after her death except the belt which, after her death, Thomas wished should remain in the possession of her mother Maud. The money raised from the sale, with the £50, should be laid out by those executors on pious uses for the salvation of his soul, the souls of his wives Gillian and Maud, and the souls of others, especially in the church in which their corpses lie buried. Thomas bequeathed £50 of gold coinage, a tablecloth with a towel, two silver bowls, six silver spoons, a coverlet with a tester, a pair of linen sheets, two blankets, and a 'cavenas' to his child being in the womb of his wife Maud and, if the child should be male, all his armour. If the child were to die before reaching his or her majority all the movable goods bequeathed to him or her should be sold by Thomas's executors with all speed after his or her death. The money raised from the sale, with the £50, should be laid out immediately by those executors on pious uses, namely on celebrating masses and doing other charitable deeds, on behalf of Thomas's soul, the souls of Gillian and Maud, and the souls of others. If the child should be a girl the armour should be sold by the executors and [the proceeds] laid out in the way described above on behalf of Thomas's soul and the souls of others. Thomas appointed that all the goods bequeathed to his children should be in the keeping of John Swift and John Barber, brazier, two of his executors, so that the children, when they reach their majority, might receive from his executors all the goods bequeathed to them entirely and without diminution. They should meanwhile be supported with the goods and profit from the rent of cottages devised to them, together with the interest on the money and goods bequeathed to them. Thomas bequeathed £100 of gold coinage, five silver bowls, two coverlets with testers, two pairs of linen sheets, four blankets, two 'cavenas', all his basins and lavers and his brass pots and pans except those bequeathed to his children, a mazer, 12 silver spoons, and all his pewter vessels to his wife Maud. She and his children should have all the movable and immovable goods bequeathed to them for their shares from his contingent goods, should each be satisfied with his or her legacy, and none of them should implead or trouble the executors on account of his or her portion. If they, or any of them, should thus implead, question, or trouble the executors, or demand or claim more than was bequeathed to them, they should lose all the goods bequeathed to them. The executors should immediately take charge of such goods and dispose of them for the salvation of Thomas's soul, the soul of Gillian, of late his wife, and the souls of others, especially in the place in which the corpses lie buried. Thomas bequeathed £3 and a piece of silver to his sister Maud; 40s. and a piece of silver to his sister Alice; a pipe of oil to Evelotte Souter; 13s. 4d. to Ralph Butcher; a dagger furnished with silver to John Noble beyond the bar; a dagger to Stephen Cole; 20d. to each of his godsons and goddaughters; his best silver belt to John Trumper; 20s. to the mother of his wife Maud; 13s. 4d.

to Maud's sister; 20s. to Edward, of late his apprentice; 40s. each to William, his apprentice, and Alice, his servant; 20s. and a piece of silver to Edith, his servant; 4d. to each ailing and bedridden pauper in Salisbury, Fisherton, and St. Nicholas's hospital to pray for his soul; a piece of silver each to Martin Ironmonger and Robert Poole; 100s. to be handed out among paupers on the day of his burial; £20 to find six friars in the conventual church of the Dominicans of Fisherton, and £10 to find two chaplains in St. Thomas's church, in each case to celebrate mass for a year after his death on behalf of his soul and the soul of Gillian, formerly his wife; a round silver goblet to Henry Pay; a gold ring and 40s. each to John Swift and John Barber; the rest of his goods to his executors to be laid out on pious uses, such as celebrating masses, giving alms, and doing other charitable deeds, for the salvation of his soul, the souls of his wives Gillian and Maud, and the souls of others, especially in the place and church in which their corpses lie buried. Devises: to his children two cottages, in Mealmonger Street between cottages of late John Justice's on the south side and a tenement of late Richard Still's on the north side, in which John Swift and John Barber are enfeoffed. The cottages are to be held by the children for their life and the life of the one of them living longer and, immediately after their death, should be sold by Thomas's executors, their executors, or subsequent executors. The money raised from the sale should be laid out with all speed by the executors on pious uses [*as above*]. Thomas devised to his wife Maud two cottages, in Castle Street, beyond the bars, between a tenement of late John Upton's on one side and a tenement of late Ellis Homes's on the other side, in which John Swift and John Barber are enfeoffed. The cottages are to be held for life by Maud, on Maud's death should remain to Thomas's children equally for their life and the life of the one of them living longer, and immediately after their death should be sold by Thomas's executors or subsequent executors. The money raised from them should be laid out without delay by the executors on pious uses [*as above*]. Executors: the friar Henry Wallis, John Swift, and John Barber. Proved on 17 January 1403 in front of an officer of the subdean; the administration was entrusted to the executors. Approved at a court held in front of the bailiff, the mayor, and other citizens; the seisin of the cottages was released to the legatees.

21 March 1403, at Salisbury
1837 Approval of the will of Edmund Cofford, of Marlow, of late a citizen of Salisbury, made on 2 February 1399. Interment: in the parish church of All Saints, Marlow. Bequests: £10 to the fabric of Marlow church; a cloak to John Cofford, of Marlow; a gown, with a hood, each to Hugh Carter and William Carter; 2s. each to John Clark, of Marlow, and William Barrett; 12d. to William Hartell; 6d. each to Geoffrey Plowman and Simon Carter; the rest of his goods to his executors for them to dispose of as seemed best to them. Devise: to his wife Alice two racks, with garden ground, situated conjointly in [Martin's Croft: *cf.* **552, 1232**], which he acquired from John Snel, called Bosset, an executor of William Cofford, to be held for ever by her and her heirs and assigns. Executors: his wife Alice and Nicholas Monkton, of Marlow. Proved on 30 September …

[*year not given*] in front of Stephen of Marston, bachelor in law, a commissary general of the archdeacon of Buckingham, in the parish church of Wycombe; the administration was entrusted to the executors. Approved on 27 March 1402 in front of the subdean of Salisbury; the administration was entrusted to the executors. Approved at a court held in front of the bailiff, the mayor, and other citizens; the seisin of the racks and the garden was released [to the legatees].

4 April 1403, at Salisbury
1838 By his charter John Clark, a chaplain, granted to William Tull and Walter Shirley a tenement, with two shops next to it, in Carter Street between Thomas Castleton's tenement, of late William Guys's, on the north side and Richard at the mill's tenement on the south side. The tenement, with the shops, was held by John, together with Nicholas Spurgeon, a clerk, by a grant of Alice, the relict of Thomas Play, while she was celibate, and was granted for ever to Thomas and Alice and their heirs by Hugh Gundy, of late a citizen of Salisbury. Thomas and Alice recovered it by an assize of novel disseisin held at Salisbury on 10 October 1397 in front of Thomas Hungerford, then the bailiff of Salisbury, against William Guys. It is to be held, with the shops, for ever by William Tull and Walter Shirley and their heirs and assigns. Seals: John Clark's and the common and mayoral seals of the city. Named witnesses: the bailiff, the mayor, the coroners, the reeves, John Mower, William Warmwell, Richard Spencer, an elder John Forest, and the clerk

2 May 1403, at Salisbury
1839 Approval of the will of Robert Way, a skinner, a citizen of Salisbury, made on 3 April 1403. Interment in the graveyard of St. Thomas's church. Bequests: 40*d.* to the rector there for his forgotten tithes; 12*d.* to the fabric of the cathedral church; 2*s.* 6*d.* both to the Franciscans of Salisbury and the Dominicans of Fisherton, in each case to celebrate a trental on behalf of his soul; 20*s.* in merchandize or money to Richard Hilary, skinner; 20*s.* to his daughter Joan; 10*s.* to Gilbert Oword; 12*d.* to the parochial chaplain; 20*s.* in merchandize or money and a tunic of best ray to William Stangman; a best tunic to John Cheekwell; 2*s.* to his godson Robert, a son of William Blyth; 6*d.* to each of his godsons and goddaughters. Devise: to his wife Christine for life two conjoined shops, with sollars, in Minster Street between a tenement of late Robert Russell's on one side and Dominic Uphill's tenement on the other side. On Chistine's death the shops, with the sollars, should remain for life to Robert's son John, on John's death they should be divided between Robert's daughters Edith and Margery and remain to them for their life, if either Edith or Margery were to die they would remain to the other for life, and on the death of the longer liver they would remain to John's issue. If John were to die without issue the shops, with the sollars, should be sold by Robert's executors, their executors, or subsequent executors. The money received should be laid out on celebrating masses, giving alms, repairing ways, and doing other charitable deeds on behalf of his soul and the souls of others. Executors: his wife Christine and Richard Hilary; overseer, Gilbert Oword. Proved on 20 April 1403 in front of an officer of the subdean; the administration

was entrusted to the executors. Approved at a court held in front of the bailiff, the mayor, and other citizens; the seisin of the shops, with the sollars, was released to the legatees.

13 June 1403, at Salisbury
1840 By his charter Richard Spencer, a citizen of Salisbury, granted to William Fewster and his wife Edith two conjoined tenements in Minster Street, near the bars, between William Lord's tenement on the south side and a ditch of running water on the north side. The tenements were bought by Richard from Joan Sexhampcote, John Sexhampcote, the vicar of Whiteparish (*albi menesterii*), and Roger Woodford, executors of Thomas Sexhampcote, a citizen of Salisbury, were devised by Thomas to be sold by his executors, and are to be held for ever by William and Edith and William's heirs. Clause of warranty. Seals: Richard's and the common and mayoral seals of the city. Named witnesses: the bailiff, the mayor, the coroners, the reeves, William Warmwell, John Mower, Adam Teffont, Richard Jewell, John Needler, an elder John Forest, Nicholas Harding, John Lewisham, and the clerk
1841 By his charter Thomas Castleton, mercer, a citizen of Salisbury, granted to William Walter, a citizen of Salisbury, a tenement, which is now built as two cottages, with gardens, in a street called Rolleston, [*as in 1819*]. The tenement was held by Thomas by a grant of John Ettshall, a citizen of Salisbury, and, with the gardens, is to be held for ever by William, and his heirs and assigns. Clause of warranty. Seals: Thomas's and the common and mayoral seals of the city. Named witnesses: the bailiff, the coroners, the reeves, William Warmwell, Richard Spencer, an elder John Forest, William Hill, John Needler, and the clerk

3 October 1403, at Salisbury
1842 By her charter Margaret, the relict of William Godmanstone, in her chaste widowhood and full power, granted to John Montagu two conjoined tenements in Winchester Street, between a tenement of late John Butterley's on the west side and John Ettshall's tenement on the east side, to be held for ever by John and his heirs and assigns. Clause of warranty. Seals: Margaret's and the common and mayoral seals of the city. Named witnesses: the bailiff, the mayor, the coroners, the reeves, John Mower, Richard Spencer, William Warmwell, an elder John Forest, John Needler, and the clerk

9 January 1404, at Salisbury
1843 By their charter Nicholas Harding and an elder John Forest, citizens of Salisbury, granted to Nicholas Melbury, draper, of Salisbury, three shops, with their appurtenances except a garden and a sollar above the kitchen of the shop standing on the south side of a chief tenement, of late John Newman's, in which Nicholas Bell dwells; the garden and the sollar are newly attached to that tenement. The three shops stand conjoined in Carter Street between that tenement on the north side and William Tull's tenement on the south side, were formerly devised for ever by Hugh Fox to his son Robert and Robert's heirs, were some time ago

devised by Robert for ever to his wife Joan and her heirs, were granted by John [Newman], with other land and tenements which he held in the city, to Nicholas Harding and John Forest, as is contained in writings and wills perfected in the matter, and, with their appurtenances except the garden and the sollar, are to held for ever by Nicholas Melbury and his heirs and assigns. Nicholas Harding and John Forest debarred themselves and their heirs and assigns from the shops but did not warrant them to Nicholas Melbury or his heirs or assigns. Seals: those of Nicholas and John and the common and mayoral seals of the city. Named witnesses: the bailiff, the mayor, the coroners, the reeves, William Warmwell, John Mower, Richard Spencer, Adam Teffont, Richard Leach, John Needler, William Sall, Walter Nalder, and the clerk

6 February 1404, at Salisbury
1844 By his indented charter William Clement, a chaplain, granted to Thomas Messenger and his wife Edith a tenement in Gigant Street between a corner tenement of late John Ashley's on the south side and a tenement of Thomas Ham, tailor, on the north side. The tenement was held by William by a feoffment of John Salisbury, called Baker, a citizen of Salisbury, who held it by a grant of John Clement, William's father, and his wife Alice. It is to be held for ever by Thomas and Edith and their joint issue, and if Thomas and Edith were to die without such issue it would revert, and remain for ever, to William and his heirs and assigns. Clause of warranty. Seals: William's and the common and mayoral seals of the city. Named witnesses: the bailiff, the mayor, the coroners, the reeves, John Mower, Richard Spencer, William Walter, Richard Leach, William Hill, and the clerk
1845 By his letters of attorney William Clement, a chaplain, appointed George Goss and Stephen Edington to surrender into the hand of Richard, the bishop of Salisbury, the seisin of a tenement in Gigant Street [*as in* **1844**] to the use of Thomas Messenger and his wife Edith. Seals: William's and the mayoral seal of the city
1846 By his charter Robert Reading granted to Thomas Castleton, mercer, a citizen of Salisbury, a tenement, with shops, in Minster Street between a tenement of late Thomas Chaplin's on the north side and a shop of late John Kimpton's, now William Pickard's, on the south side. The tenement was held by Robert by a grant of an elder William Lord who, with Bartholomew Durkin, a goldsmith, and John Camel, hatter, held it by a grant of Robert and his wife Cecily, and, with the shops, it is to be held for ever by Thomas Castleton and his heirs and assigns. Clause of warranty. Seals: Robert's and the common and the mayoral seals of the city. Named witnesses: the bailiff, the mayor, the coroners, the reeves, John Mower, William Warmwell, Richard Spencer, Richard Leach, John Forest, and the clerk

20 February 1404, at Salisbury
1847 By his charter John Staggard, weaver, of Salisbury, granted to Simon Bradley, baker, of Salisbury, and his wife Edith a tenement in Scots Lane between William Woodroff's shop property, of late George Goss's, on the east side and a tenement

of Alice, a daughter of Roger Woodford, of late Thomas Sexhampcote's, on the west side. The tenement was held by John by a grant of Hugh Gundy, of Salisbury, and is to be held for ever by Simon and Edith and Simon's heirs and assigns. Clause of warranty. Seals: John's and the common and mayoral seals of the city. Named witnesses: the bailiff, the mayor, the coroners, the reeves, John Mower, Richard Spencer, William Warmwell, John Forest, John Needler, and the clerk

28 February 1404, at Salisbury
1848 By his letters of attorney James Ive, otherwise called Goldsmith, a kinsman and heir of Ralph Ive, of late a citizen of Salisbury, appointed William Lord to enter on, and take possession of [Ive's Corner: *cf.* **1959–60**], a messuage in which John Hampton, brewer, dwells, in Wineman Street. John acquired the messuage for himself and his heirs for ever from George Merriott, the tenant of it for life by the curtesy with reversion to James and his heirs. James gave to William the power to expel John and George and any other claiming the estate of them or either of them. Seal: James's

5 March 1404, at Salisbury
1849 By their charter an elder John Chandler and John Drury, citizens of Salisbury, granted to John Drury, a clerk, a third part of a messuage in Castle Street between Henry Berwick's tenement on the south side and a tenement of Thomas, a son and heir of John Beeton, on the north side. The third part was entered on by the grantors by a demise of Reynold Drury, to whom John Starr and his wife Edith, one of the daughters, and an heir, of Richard Frear, demised it for a term of years not yet complete. It is to be held by John Drury, the clerk, and his executors and assigns according to the effect of the demise of John and Edith. John Chandler and John Drury also granted to John Drury, the clerk, the other two parts of the messuage, which they held by Reynold Drury's grant, to be held for ever by him and his heirs and assigns. Seals: those of the grantors and the common and mayoral seals of the city. Named witnesses: the bailiff, the mayor, the coroners, the reeves, John Mower, Richard Spencer, William Warmwell, an elder John Forest, John Needler, and the clerk
1850 By their charter an elder John Forest and Nicholas Harding, of Salisbury, granted to John Needler a tenement, with shops fronting on the street, and with a garden, in New Street between the abbot of Stanley's shop on the west side and a tenement which George Merriott holds on the east side; also two shops in New Street between Laurence Gowan's shops on the west side and shops of late John Lippiatt's on the east side; also a cottage in Drake Hall Street between a shop of the dean and chapter of Salisbury, which William Pickard holds, on the north side and shop property of late that of Robert Russell, kt., on the south side. The tenement, shops, and cottage, with the garden, were held by John and Nicholas by a grant of John Newman, together with his other land and tenements in Salisbury, and they are to be held for ever by John Needler and his heirs and assigns. John and Nicholas debarred themselves and their heirs from the premises

but did not warrant them to John Needler or his heirs. Seals: those of the grantors and the common and mayoral seals of the city. Named witnesses: the bailiff, the mayor, the coroners, the reeves, John Mower, William Warmwell, Richard Spencer, William Walter, William Hill, Adam Teffont, and the clerk

1851 By his charter James Ive, otherwise called Goldsmith, a kinsman and heir of Ralph Ive, of late a citizen of Salisbury, granted to William Dyke and his wife Edith, Thomas Mason, John Dyke, and Peter Dyke [Ive's Corner: *cf.* **1959–60**], a messuage in which John Hampton, brewer, dwells, in Wineman Street. The messuage, formerly Ralph's, is to be held for ever by the grantees and William's heirs and assigns. Seals: James's and those of Andrew Pill, Stephen Clark, Thomas Westsby, John Tanner, the bailiff of Axbridge, and Henry Anglesey; James also procured the common and mayoral seals of the city to be likewise affixed. Named witnesses: the bailiff, the mayor, the coroners, the reeves, John Mower, Richard Spencer, Adam Teffont, Nicholas Harding, William Hill, Robert Body, Thomas Field, John Parch, and the clerk

6 March 1404, at Salisbury
1852 By his letters of attorney John Drury, a citizen of Salisbury, appointed John Gatcombe and Roger Enterbush to surrender, with an elder John Chandler, a citizen of Salisbury, into the hand of Richard, the bishop of Salisbury, the seisin of two parts of a messuage in Castle Street [*as in* **1849**] to the use of John Drury, a clerk. Seals: that of John Drury, the citizen, and the mayoral seal of the city

12 March 1404, at Westminster
1853 By his writ the king directed the sheriff of Wiltshire to order George Merriott and his wife Alice to uphold for John Mower, Richard Spencer, William Walter, and Nicholas Harding the agreement made between them concerning two messuages in Salisbury. If they did not, and if John, Richard, William, and Nicholas provided security to him for their claim, the sheriff should distrain George and Alice to appear in front of the king's justices at Westminster three weeks from Easter to show why not.

18 March 1404, at Westminster
1854 By his writ the king gave to William Hankford, a justice of the [Common] Bench, the power to receive recognizances from John Mower, Richard Spencer, William Walter, and Nicholas Harding and from George Merriott and his wife Alice. A plea of covenant between John, Richard, William, and Nicholas on the one side, and George and Alice on the other side, was pending and the king ordered William to receive the recognizances, and to inform his fellow justices, so that a fine concerning two messuages in Salisbury might be levied in front of him and his fellows between those parties.

19 March 1404, at Salisbury
1855 By his charter John Drury, a clerk, granted to Edward Dubber [*cf.* **1857**] and his wife Joan a third part of a messuage in Castle Street [*as in* **1849**] which he held

by a grant of an elder John Chandler and John Drury, citizens of Salisbury, to be held by Edward and Joan and their executors and assigns according to the effect of a demise of John Starr and his wife Edith, a daughter, and an heir, of Richard Frear, made to Reynold Drury for a term of years not yet complete; also the other two parts of the messuage, which he held by a feoffment of John Chandler and John Drury, to be held for ever by Edward and Joan and Edward's heirs and assigns. Clause of warranty in respect of the two parts. Seals: the grantor's and the common and mayoral seals of the city. Named witnesses: the bailiff, the mayor, the coroners, the reeves, John Mower, William Warmwell, Richard Spencer, William Walter, an elder John Forest, John Needler, and the clerk

1856 By his indented charter Thomas Burford, a citizen of Salisbury, granted in frankmarriage to William Tull and Joan, his daughter, a tenement, in which he dwells, with shops, a cottage (*or* cottages), and a garden next to it, in a street called Chipping Place, opposite the market place where grains are sold, between John Gatcombe's tenement on the east side and a tenement of late Thomas Chaplin's on the west side. The tenement, with the shops, cottage(s), and garden, extends from Chipping Place as far as Chipper Street. It is to be held for ever by William and Joan and their issue and the issue of either of them, if William and Joan were to die without issue it would remain for ever to Thomas 'Prestempde' and his wife Margaret, Thomas's sister, and the issue begotted between them, and if Thomas and Margaret were to die without such issue it would remain for ever to the direct heirs of William Tull. Clause of warranty. Seals: Thomas Burford's to the parts of the charter and the common and mayoral seals of the city. Named witnesses: the bailiff, the mayor, the coroners, the reeves, John Mower, William Warmwell, Richard Spencer, Richard Leach, William Walter, and the clerk

20 March 1404, at Salisbury
1857 By his letters of attorney John Drury, a clerk, appointed John Gatcombe and Roger Enterbush to surrender into the hand of Richard, the bishop of Salisbury, the seisin of two parts of a messuage in Castle Street [*as in* **1849**] to the use of Edward Gilbert, dubber, and his wife Joan. Seals: John Drury's and the mayoral seal of the city

Easter 1404, at Westminster
1858 In a final agreement reached in the king's court three weeks from Easter 1404 in front of William Thirning, William Rickhill, John Markham, William Hankford, and William Brenchesley, justices, between John Mower, Richard Spencer, William Walter, and Nicholas Harding, plaintiffs, and George Merriott and his wife Alice, defendants, concerning two messuages in Salisbury, George and Alice acknowledged the messuages to be the right of Richard, as that which the four plaintiffs held by their gift. For that acknowledgement the plaintiffs granted the messuages to George and Alice and rendered them to them in court. The messuages are to be held for their life by George and Alice of the plaintiffs and the heirs of Richard, paying to them a rent of a grain of wheat a year at Michaelmas for all the services pertaining to them. George and Alice, on behalf

of the plaintiffs and the heirs of Richard, are also to render to the chief lord all the services appurtenant to the messuages. On the death of George and Alice the messuages should revert to John, Richard, William, and Nicholas and the heirs of Richard quit of the heirs of George and Alice, to be held by them for ever.

16 April 1404, at Salisbury
1859 Approval of the will of John Drury, a citizen of Salisbury, made on 26 March 1404. Interment: in the graveyard of St. Edmund's church. Bequests: 13s. 4d. and a leaden vessel called saltinglead to the fabric of that church, 40d. to the provost for his forgotten tithes, 40d. to the parochial chaplain, 2s. 6d. to Robert Spreed, a chaplain, to pray for his soul, 18d. to each chaplain of the college, by whom Robert might be envied, 8d. to each other annual chaplain, 12d. to the deacon, and 8d. to the sacristan; 40d. to the fabric of the cathedral church; 5s. to the fabric of St. Thomas's church; 40d. to the fabric of St. Martin's church; 10s. to the hospital of the Holy Trinity called Almshouse, and 40d. to Agnes, the overseer of it; 40d. to the fabric of the church of the Dominicans of Fisherton; 5s. to the fabric of the church of the Franciscans of Salisbury; 40d. to the fabric of St. Peter's church, Marlborough; 30s. to his sister Alice; ½ each mark to Stephen, his servant, William, his household servant, Agnes Bonham, his servant, and John Knight, of late his servant; 40s. to Joan, a daughter of John Knight, which should be kept according to the order of his executor until Agnes's [?*rectius* Joan's] legal discretion; 6d. to each of his godchildren, male and female; 40d. and a slop, with a hood, to Janus, of late a household servant of Robert Bunt; 13s. 4d. to Alice, a daughter of John Lewisham; 4d. to each destitute, ailing, bedridded person in Salisbury, and to each prisoner in the Guildhall; 12d. to the prisoners in [Old] Sarum castle, to be divided among them in common; 13s. 4d. to John Lewisham, his executor; 6s. 8d. to John Barnes, his overseer; the rest of his goods to be disposed of on behalf of his soul and the souls of others as provided for below. Devises: a tenement in which he dwelt, [in Castle Street] beyond the bar, between John Shipton's tenement on the north side and John Starr's tenement on the south side, to be be sold immediately after his death, when it could be done advantageously, by his executor or his executor's executors. The money received should be laid out by the executor or executors on celebrating masses, giving alms, repairing ways and bridges, and doing other charitable deeds on behalf of his soul and the souls of others. John devised to John Lewisham, his executor, two cottages in the same street [Castle Street], on the other side from the tenement in which he dwelt, between John Newman's tenement on the north side and William Warmwell's tenement on the south side, to be sold immediately after his death by John, if then living, or by John's executors. The money received should be laid out in the way stated above. Executor: John Lewisham; overseer John Barnes, a chaplain. Proved on 5 April 1404 in front of an officer of the subdean; the administration was entrusted to the executor. Approved at a court held in front of the bailiff, the mayor, and other citizens; the seisin of the tenement and the cottages was released to the executor.

9 July 1404, at Salisbury

1860 Approval of the will of John Canning, of Salisbury, made on 24 June 1404. <u>Interment</u>: in the graveyard of St. Thomas's church. <u>Bequests</u>: 12*d*. each to the fabric of the cathedral church, the fabric of St. Edmund's church, and the fabric of St. Thomas's church; 2*d*. to each Dominican friar present at his mass and funeral rites on the day of his burial; 6*s*. 8*d*. each to William Sivier, John Ferrer, his sister Christine Herring, and Thomas Bleacher; 16*s*. to be laid out by his executors, on the day of his burial, on loaves for paupers of Salisbury; a mazer, with a foot, bound with silver to John Herring, a canon of Mottisfont; 12*d*. each to his goddaughter Margaret and Margaret, his servant; the rest of his goods to his wife Joan. <u>Devises</u>: to Joan a corner tenement, in which he dwelt, opposite the market place where grains are sold, between a tenement of Agnes Lea on either side, to be held by her for life, and after her death to be sold by his executors. The money received should be laid out on celebrating masses, giving alms, and doing other charitable deeds on behalf of John's soul, Joan's soul, and the souls of others. John devised to Joan a rent of 7*s*. a year issuing from a tenement, in which John Ferrer dwells, beside his corner tenement opposite the market place where grains are sold, between the corner tenement on the west side and Agnes Lea's shop on the east side. The rent is to be held by Joan and her assigns for her life, and after her death should be sold by John's executors, their executors, or subsequent executors. The money issuing from the sale should be laid out by the executors in the way, and on behalf of the souls, mentioned above. John devised to his executors a cottage in Drake Hall Street, between Edmund Enfield's cottage property on the north side and John Deakin's cottage property on the south side, to be sold. John Ferrer, carter, now dwells in the cottage, and Christine Herring holds an estate in it for her life by a grant of Robert Play. From the money received John Canning's obit and rites should be held yearly, and celebrated for ever, for the salvation of his soul and the souls of others in a way in which his rites might have value. <u>Executors</u>: Thomas Bleacher, John Ferrer, and William Sivier. <u>Proved</u> on 4 July 1404 in front of an officer of the subdean; the administration was entrusted to the executors. <u>Approved</u> at a court held in front of the bailiff, the mayor, and other citizens; the seisin of the tenement and the cottage was released to the legatees.

1861 Approval of the will of Gilbert Oword, a citizen of Salisbury, made on 11 April 1404. <u>Interment</u>: in the graveyard of St. Edmund's church. <u>Bequests</u>: 6*s*. 8*d*. to the fabric of that church, 40*d*. to the provost, 12*d*. to the parochial chaplain, and 4*d*. to each other chaplain; 40*d*. to the fabric of the cathedral church; a leaden vessel for making malt to the fabric of St. Thomas's church; 4*d*. to each Franciscan friar of Salisbury, and each Dominican friar of Fisherton, present at his funeral rites and mass; 6*d*. to each of his godsons and goddaughters; 6*s*. 8*d*. to his son Richard; 2*s*. to each of the sons and daughters of his daughter Christine; 12*d*. each to St. Giles's hospital near Wilton and to the hospital of the Holy Trinity; 10*s*. to an elder John Chandler; 40*d*. to Margery, the wife of his son Richard; half his malt to his wife Alice and the other half to his executors to be disposed of on behalf of his soul; half of the rest of his goods to Alice and the other half to his executors to be disposed of on behalf of his soul. <u>Devises</u>: to Alice a tenement, in which he dwelt, in Wineman Street, between Robert Bowyer's tenement on the west side and a tenement of late William Surr's on the east side, to be held by her for life, and after her death to be sold by his executors or their executors. Of the money received Gilbert appointed 40s. to his son John and the remainder to be laid out by his own executors or their executors on celebrating masses, giving alms, repairing ways, and doing other charitable deeds on behalf of his soul and the souls of others. He devised three cottages in Culver Street, between Robert Bowyer's cottages on the south side and Thomas Slegge's cottage property on the north side, to be sold. The money received should be divided equally by his executors or their executors between his son Richard and daughter Christine. <u>Executors</u>: his son Richard and an elder John Chandler. <u>Proved</u> on 22 June 1404 in front of an officer of the subdean; the administration was entrusted to Richard, reserving the power to entrust it to John when he might come to seek it. <u>Approved</u> at a court held in front of the bailiff, the mayor, and other citizens; the seisin of the tenement and the cottages was released to the legatees.

6 August 1404, at Salisbury
1862 By his writing Richard Leach, a citizen of Salisbury, quitclaimed to Gunnore Bowyer his right or claim to six conjoined shops in Butcher Row, between Thomas Camel's shop on the east side and Henry Popham's shop on the west side, which Gunnore holds for her life with reversion to him and his heirs. Seals: Richard's and the common and mayoral seals of the city. Named witnesses: the bailiff, the mayor, the coroners, the reeves, William Warmwell, John Mower, Richard Spencer, Adam Teffont, William Walter, Nicholas Harding, and the clerk

20 August 1404, at Salisbury
1863 By his charter John Wells, butcher, granted to Gunnore Bowyer a shop in Pot Row between Simon Tredinnick's tenement on the west side and a tenement of John Brown, butcher, on the east side. The shop was held by John by a grant of Joan, the relict of William Wilton, butcher, and is to be held for ever by Gunnore and her heirs and assigns. Clause of warranty. Seals: John's and the common and mayoral seals of the city. Named witnesses: the bailiff, the mayor, the coroners, the reeves, William Warmwell, John Mower, Richard Spencer, Adam Teffont, Nicholas Harding, an elder John Forest, and the clerk

1 October 1404, at Salisbury
1864 By his charter William Shipton, of Salisbury, an executor of Hugh Winterbourne, of late a citizen of Salisbury, on the strength of Hugh's will granted to Robert Hazelbury a tenement in Castle Street between Edward Breamore's tenement on the south side and a tenement of John Sexhampcote, the vicar of Whiteparish, on the north side. Hugh devised the tenement to be sold by his executors after the death of his wife Alice, now dead. The money received should be laid out on masses and other charitable deeds on behalf of Hugh's soul and the souls of others. The tenement was bought by Hugh and his wife Isabel,

buried before him, from William Bailiff and [?forename omitted] Wincanton for themselves and their heirs for ever, and it is to be held for ever by Robert and his heirs and assigns. Seals: William's and the common and mayoral seals of the city. Named witnesses: the bailiff, the mayor, the coroners, the reeves, William Warmwell, John Mower, Richard Spencer, Adam Teffont, William Walter, Nicholas Harding, John Needler, an elder John Forest, and the clerk

1865 By his writing Thomas Hampstead, a brother and heir of Ralph Hampstead, a chaplain, quitclaimed to John Mower, a citizen of Salisbury, and his wife Cecily, and to John's heirs and assigns his right or claim to a tenement in Endless Street, on a corner, between a tenement of late William Boyland's on the south side and Chipper Lane on the north side. The tenement was held for her life by Cecily by a devise of John Amesbury, and the reversion was bought by Ralph Hampstead and Thomas Coombe, chaplains, both now dead, from Richard Spencer and John Little, John's executors. Seals: Thomas's and the common and mayoral seals of the city. Named witnesses: the bailiff, the mayor, the coroners, the reeves, William Warmwell, Richard Spencer, Adam Teffont, William Walter, an elder John Forest, Nicholas Harding, and the clerk

1866 By his charter Thomas Hampstead, a brother and heir of Ralph Hampstead, a chaplain, granted to John Mower, a citizen of Salisbury, a tenement, with shops, a cottage (*or* cottages), and a yard (*or* yards), in New Street between a trench of running water on the west side and a tenement of the de Vaux scholars on the east side. The tenement, with the shops, cottage(s), and yard(s), was held by Ralph Hampstead and Thomas Coombe, chaplains, both now dead, by John's grant and is to be held for ever by John and his heirs and assigns. Seals: Thomas's and the common and mayoral seals of the city. Named witnesses: the bailiff, the mayor, the coroners, the reeves, William Warmwell, Richard Spencer, Adam Teffont, William Walter, an elder John Forest, Nicholas Harding, and the clerk

12 November 1404, at Salisbury
1867 By their charter William Spicer, a chaplain, and John Stephens, weaver, granted to William Walter, a citizen of Salisbury, six conjoined cottages, with gardens and a dovecot, of late those of Bartholomew Durkin, goldsmith, in Culver Street between Thomas Knoyle's cottage property on the south side and cottage property of late Batholomew's on the north side. The cottages, with the dovecot and the other appurtenances, and with other land and tenements in Salisbury, were held by William Spicer and John Stephens by a grant of William Reynold, weaver, of Salisbury, and are to be held for ever by William Walter and his heirs and assigns. Seals: those of the grantors and the common and mayoral seals of the city. Named witnesses: the bailiff, the mayor, the coroners, the reeves, John Mower, Richard Spencer, William Warmwell, Adam Teffont, William Bishop, and the clerk

26 November 1404, at Salisbury
1868 By his deed William Reynold, weaver, of Salisbury, quitclaimed to William Walter, a citizen of Salisbury, and his heirs and assigns his right or claim to six

cottages, with gardens and a dovecote, [*as in 1867*]. The cottages, with their appurtenances, were held by William Walter by a feoffment of the lord William Spicer, a chaplain, and John Stephens, weaver, who held them, with other land and tenements in Salisbury, by William Reynold's grant, and they were formerly those of Bartholomew Durkin, goldsmith. Clause of warranty. Seals: William Reynold's and the common and mayoral seals of the city. Named witnesses: the bailiff, the mayor, the coroners, the reeves, John Mower, William Warmwell, Nicholas Harding, William Hill, William Sall, and the clerk

1869 By their charter John Hurst, and his wife Joan a daughter and heir of Roger Wallop, of late a citizen of Salisbury, and his wife Christine, appearing at the court held on that day, granted to Robert Hazelbury a toft, or plot of land, which was of late built on and that of Roger and Christine. The toft lies in Castle Street between a gate of a tenement, in which John Wallop dwells, on the south side and a tenement of late Richard Ludd's, in which William Bower now dwells, on the north side, and extends in length from the street as far as the Avon. It is to be held for ever by Robert and his heirs and assigns to whom John and Joan released their right or claim to it. Clause of warranty. Seals: those of John and Joan and the common and mayoral seals of the city. Named witnesses: the bailiff, the mayor, the coroners, the reeves, John Mower, William Warmwell, Richard Spencer, Nicholas Harding, William Sall, and the clerk

10 December 1404, at Salisbury

1870 By their writing Richard Bristow and his wife Tamsin, the relict of William Surr, of Salisbury, appearing at the court held on that day, she, being examined there in accordance with the custom of the city, not coerced by fear or force but by her own free will, quitclaimed to Henry Berwick and his heirs and assigns their or Tamsin's right or claim to three shops in Pot Row, opposite the butchers' stalls, between Thomas Knoyle's tenement on the west side and Thomas Child's tenement on the east side. Clause of warranty. Seals: those of Richard and Tamsin and the common and mayoral seals of the city. Named witnesses: the bailiff, the mayor, the coroners, John Mower, William Warmwell, William Walter, William Bishop, William Dowding, and the clerk

1871 Approval of the will of the lord John Pope, a collegiate chaplain of St. Edmund's church, made on 2 November 1404. <u>Interment</u>: in the chapel of the Blessed Mary in front of her image. <u>Bequests</u>: 40*s*. to the fabric of that church, and 40*s*. and his best furnished bowl, that is the one of note, to Robert Ragenhill, the provost, a book called *The Golden Legends* to Richard Oxford, 6*s*. 8*d*. to each chaplain of the college, 40*d*. to each of the other chaplains celebrating mass in the church, 40*d*. each to the deacon and the sacristan, 4*d*. to each boy wearing a surplice, a large maple-wood bowl to the college, a doublet and 40*d*. to John Brown, their household servant, and a lined coat and 6*d*. to his boy; 6*s*. 8*d*. both to the Franciscans and the Dominicans; a second-best fur gown and 10*s*. to Edith, his father's relict; 40*s*., six silver spoons, a pair of maple-wood bowls, a best robe, a pair of linen sheets, a best bed, a basin with a laver, and a tablecloth with a towel to his sister Sarah, and he remits to her all the debts by right due to him; a silver bowl and a maple-wood bowl with a cover to his kinsman Thomas Read; 20*s*. to the lady Catherine Weymouth, a nun of Amesbury; a third-best robe, a book called children's manual, a green bed, a mattress, two old blankets, a pair of linen sheets, and 20*s*. to Richard, his household servant; 6*s*. 8*d*. to Isabel Cooper; a new forcer, a silk purse, and a mirror, to Alice, the wife of the master Leach; 10*s*. to his kinsman John Pope; a large silver gilt ring, with a red and excellent stone, to that John's wife Edith; 40*d*., a *circum de perreye* with a *counterfilet* to Alice, a daughter of Thomas Read; 40*d*. to John Doll; a *copaginat'* spoon and a small belt furnished with silver to the lord Henry Warin; a silver spoon and a harp to Robert Mason, a chaplain; a silver spoon and a book called *Pars Oculi* to the lord John Wells; a silver spoon and a small porteous to the lord Nicholas Brown; 12*d*. to each of his four fellow priests bearing his corpse to the church; a red gilded belt to Agnes Ball; the rest of his goods to be laid out by the lord Henry Warin and Robert Mason, chaplains of the college of St. Edmund, on behalf of his soul, of the souls of others, and of paupers, and for other things eleemosynary, at the disposition of his fellow priests. <u>Devises</u>: to his kinsman Thomas Read all his tenements, rent, and reversions in Salisbury to be held for ever by Thomas and his heirs and assigns on condition that he would give adequate security to John's sister Sarah for giving to her for her life 40*s*. a year, her clothing or 3*s*. 4*d*. once a year, and the easement of a room assigned to her; Thomas should create for Edith, the relict of John's father, an estate for her life in a chief tenement which John Pope now holds. <u>Executors</u>: Henry Warin and the lord Robert Mason. <u>Proved</u> on 16 November 1404 in front of the master Robert Ragenhill, the provost of the church and college of St. Edmund, the ordinary in that matter; the administration was entrusted to the executors. <u>Approved</u> at a court held in front of the bailiff, the mayor, and other citizens; the seisin of the tenements and rent was released to the legatees.

1872 By his charter William Shipton, weaver, granted to John Judd, draper, two conjoined cottages in Gigant Street between a cottage of the master Robert Ragenhill and John Mower on the south side and a garden of late that of Robert Gollan, tucker, on the north side. The two cottages, by the name of one cottage, were held by William by a devise of Hugh Winterbourne, a citizen of Salisbury, who acquired them from John Dinton, butcher, and they are to be held for ever by John Judd and his heirs and assigns. Clause of warranty. Seals: William's and the common and mayoral seals of the city. Named witnesses: the bailiff, the mayor, the coroners, the reeves, John Mower, Richard Spencer, William Warmwell, Richard Leach, William Walter, and the clerk

18 February 1405, at Salisbury
1873 By their charter William Bishop and William Handley, a tailor, granted to Nicholas Bell, Thomas Child, and Stephen Edington three cottages, with gardens, in Drake Hall Street between cottages of late those of the master Thomas Southam on the south side and cottages of the vicars of the cathedral church on the north side; also four conjoined cottages, with gardens, in that street between Simon Belch's cottages on the south side and cottages of late Robert Play's, which John Ferrer, carter, and his wife Maud hold, on the north side. The seven cottages

were formerly those of John Wraxall, a chaplain, were held, with other things named in their charter of feoffment, by William Bishop and William Handley by a grant of Hugh Braban, tailor, of Salisbury, and are to be held for ever by Nicholas, Thomas, and Stephen and their heirs and assigns. Seals: those of the grantors and the common and mayoral seals of the city. Named witnesses: the bailiff, the mayor, the coroners, the reeves, William Warmwell, John Mower, Richard Spencer, William Walter, Adam Teffont, and William Sall

25 February 1405, at Salisbury
1874 By their charter John Brute, of Hindon, and William Langport, executors of John Deakin, of Downton, quitclaimed to Nicholas Bell, Thomas Child, and Stephen Edington and their heirs and assigns their right or claim to three cottages, with gardens, in Drake Hall Street [*as in* **1873**]; also their right or claim to four conjoined cottages, with gardens, in that street [*as in* **1873**]. The seven cottages, with the gardens, were formerly those of John Wraxall, a chaplain, and were held by Nicholas, Thomas, and Stephen by a grant of William Bishop and William Handley, a tailor. Seals: those of the grantors and the common and mayoral seals of the city. Named witnesses: the bailiff, the mayor, the coroners, the reeves, William Warmwell, John Mower, Richard Spencer, William Walter, Adam Teffont, and William Dowding
1875 By their deed a younger Nicholas Baynton, Thomas Turk, the vicar of Downton, and John Humphrey, the vicar of Romsey, quitclaimed to Nicholas Bell, Thomas Child, and Stephen Edington their right or claim to three cottages, with gardens, in Drake Hall Street [*as in* **1873**]; also their right or claim to four conjoined cottages, with gardens, in that street [*as in* **1873**]. The seven cottages, with the gardens, were formerly those of John Wraxall, a chaplain, of Winterbourne, and were held by Nicholas, Thomas, and Stephen by a grant of William Bishop and William Handley, a tailor. Seals: those of the grantors and the common and mayoral seals of the city. Named witnesses: the mayor, the bailiff, the coroners, the reeves, William Warmwell, John Mower, Richard Spencer, William Walter, William Sall, and William Dowding

1 April 1405, at Salisbury
1876 By her charter Agnes Langton, a daughter and heir of Roger Fowle, of late a citizen of Salisbury, granted to Thomas Farrant, mercer, and his wife Christine a tenement in Castle Street between a tenement of late John Beeton's, which his son Thomas now holds, on the south side and a tenement of late William Lord's, which Edmund Purdy now holds, on the north side, to be held for ever by Thomas and Christine and their heirs and assigns. Clause of warranty. Seals: Agnes's and the common and mayoral seals of the city. Named witnesses: the bailiff, the mayor, the coroners, the reeves, William Warmwell, John Mower, Richard Spencer, William Walter, William Bishop, and the clerk
1877 By their charter John Swift and Thomas Farrant, mercer, quitclaimed to Thomas Bleacher, ironmonger, and his heirs and assigns their right or claim to the land, tenements, reversions, and rent in Salisbury and elsewhere in Wiltshire

which they held by Thomas's grant. Seals: those of the grantors and the common and mayoral seals of the city. Named witnesses: the bailiff, the mayor, the coroners, the reeves, John Mower, William Warmwell, Richard Spencer, William Walter, William Sall, and the clerk

15 April 1405, at Salisbury
1878 By his charter John Wansey, of late of Andover, now of Fisherton Anger, granted to William Walter, a citizen of Salisbury, a tenement, opposite the market place where grains are sold, between a tenement formerly Roger Sorrel's, which John Shad, draper, now holds, on the west side and a tenement formerly John Nugg's, which Andrew Plummer now holds, on the east side, to be held for ever by William and his heirs and assigns. Clause of warranty. Seals: John's and the common and mayoral seals of the city. Named witnesses: the mayor, the bailiff, the coroners, the reeves, William Warmwell, John Mower, Richard Spencer, Richard Leach, Adam Teffont, and the clerk

29 April 1405, at Salisbury
1879 By his deed William Buck, a chaplain, granted to Stephen Edington and Nicholas Brown, a chaplain, a tenement, in which Stephen dwells, in St. Martin's Street between a tenement of the vicars of the cathedral church on the west side and a tenement of the scholars of de Vaux college on the east side, to be held for ever by them and their heirs and assigns. Seals: William's and the common and mayoral seals of the city. Named witnesses: the bailiff, the mayor, the coroners, the reeves, William Warmwell, John Mower, Richard Spencer, Richard Leach, William Sall, and William Moore

27 May 1405, at Salisbury
1880 A charter [*dated to the Wednesday after the festival of the Ascension (3 June) probably in error for the Wednesday before that festival (27 May)*] of William Buck, a chaplain, an executor of Thomas Britford, of late a citizen of Salisbury. Thomas devised a corner tenement, with shops and a bakehouse, in which he dwelt, which he held by a feoffment of William Cripps and his wife Denise, which stands in Castle Street and Chipper Street, and in which Nicholas Buckland now dwells, to be sold after the death of his wife Alice by William Buck and William Dunkerton, his executors, or by the one of them surviving. The money raised from the sale should be laid out on pious uses on behalf of Thomas's soul, Alice's soul, and the souls of others. William Dunkerton has died and for the sale of the tenement William Buck has received in advance from John Mower, a citizen of Salisbury, and his wife Cecily a large sum of money from which he has partly, and will fully, carry out Thomas's will. On the strength of the will William granted the tenement, with the shops and the bakehouse, to John and Cecily, to be held for ever by them and their heirs and assigns as that which they have bought from him in good faith and have paid for in full. Seals: William's and the common and mayoral seals of the city. Named witnesses: the bailiff, the mayor, the coroners, the reeves, William Warmwell, Richard Spencer, William Walter, Richard Leach,

William Sall, and the clerk

10 June 1405, at Salisbury
1881 By his charter William Buck, a chaplain, granted to Walter Shirley, grocer, a rent of 26s. 8d. a year which he was accustomed to receive from a tenement, with a gate and a yard, of late that of John Wallop, draper, and dwelt in by him, in Castle Street between Walter Nalder's tenement on the south side and William's own tenement on the north side. The gate, with the yard, stands beside a toft of late Roger Wallop's, now Robert Hazelbury's, which of late was also built over, on the north side. The rent was held by William by a grant of William Herring, a chaplain, and Stephen Edington and is to be held for ever by Walter and his heirs and assigns. Seals: William's and the common and mayoral seals of the city. Named witnesses: the bailiff, the mayor, the coroners, the reeves, John Mower, William Warmwell, Richard Spencer, William Walter, William Sall, and the clerk

24 June 1405, at Salisbury
1882 Approval of the will of William Buck, a chaplain, a vicar of the cathedral church, made on 14 June 1405. Interment: in the graveyard of the cathedral church in front of the west door. Bequests: 6s. 8d. each to the fabric of the cathedral church and the fabric of St. Edmund's church; 40d. each to the fabric of St. Thomas's church and the fabric of St. Martin's church; 12d. to each canon, and each vicar, of the cathedral church present at his funeral rites; 6d. to each annual chaplain celebrating mass in the cathedral church to pray for his soul, and 4d. to each sacristan, each chorister, each acolyte, and each of the two servants of the sacristy; 6d. to each Dominican friar of Fisherton and each Franciscan friar of Salisbury; 24 paupers should be clothed from new cloth of russet or white; 24 lb. of wax should be burned around his corpse on the day of his burial; 1d. to each pauper present on the day of his obit; 6 yd. of sendal and a gold ring to Joan, the relict of William Goodall; three silver spoons and a tulle belt furnished with silver to Edith of Wickham, weaver; a porteous without notation, a set of six short silver spoons, a basin with a laver, a tablecloth with a towel, and a bed with a tester to Laurence Groom, a chaplain; 2s. each to Thomas Stalbridge, carpenter, John Moulton, porter, and William, a workman of the cathedral church; a short cloak, blue and lined with red, to Adam Buck, of Wallop; 5s. to his goddaughter, the wife of Sanger of Britford; a large psalter with a hymn book, a book of collects, placebo, and dirge, and his best cope with a surplice to the lord Robert Everard, a vicar; a leather belt furnished with silver to John Oword; a bowl called Nhote furnished with silver gilt, with a cover, [and] 10 ells of linen to an elder John Chandler; a porteous with notation to Richard James, a vicar; 2s. 6d. to the vicar of Britford; 2s. to Thomas Allen, a chaplain; all the firewood lying in a house of his dwelling house to the hospital called Almshouse; 40d. in victuals to the prisoners of each of the two serjeants of the city, *viz.* 40d. to each serjeant; 5 marks to John Mitchell, a chaplain, to celebrate mass on behalf of, and to pray for, his soul; the rest of his goods to his executors to be disposed of, one part on celebrating masses, a second part on the needy and poor, a third part on improving

ways and on other charitable deeds, on behalf of his soul and the souls of others; 100*s.* of English money, which William Winslow, a chaplain, an executor of John Butterley, owes to him from a bequest of John, to the fabric of the cathedral church. Immediately after William's death his executors should hand out 1*d.* each week to each paralytic pauper in the city, except those in the hospital called Almshouse and St. Nicholas's hospital, and such payments should be continued by his executors or their executors by the week for the 20 years next following his death. <u>Devises</u>: to his executors, in each case to be sold, a tenement in Castle Street between a tenement of late that of John Wallop, deceased, on the south side and John's gate on the north side, seven conjoined cottages, with a yard (*or* yards), in Nuggeston between William Sall's shops on the south side and Richard Knolle's tenement on the east side, a rent of 12*s.* a year to be received from Gillian Bold's tenement in Pot Row, and a rent of 8*s.* a year to be received from a corner tenement [in Endless Street: *cf.* **1266**] of Eleanor, the relict of Edmund Bramshaw. William devised to John Hathaway, a cordwainer, a tenement in New Street between a tenement of John Baker, grocer, on the east side and a tenement of the de Vaux scholars on the west side. The tenement was held by William by a grant of Alice, the relict of Thomas of Britford, formerly a citizen of Salisbury, in her celibate widowhood and is to be held for ever by John and his heirs and assigns according to the effect of the charter perfected for him by William. William devised to his executors, in each case for sale, a shop, in which Richard Chesham now dwells, in Castle Street, opposite William Warmwell's tenement, between William's own two shops, in which Thomas Boughton, a cordwainer, now dwells, on the north side and a shop of late John Ashley's on the south side, and the two shops, in which Thomas Boughton dwells, in Castle Street between a shop of a corner tenement of John Mower on the north side and William's own shop, in which Richard Chesham dwells, on the south side. The money received from the sale of the two shops should be laid out by William's executors to celebrate mass on behalf of his soul, and the souls of others, in St. Edmund's chapel in the cathedral church. William devised to Laurence Groom, a chaplain, a vicar of the cathedral church, a house, with a garden next to it, in which William himself lives, in the Close between the house called Common Hall on the west side and the master William Frank's house on the east side, to be held for ever by Laurence and his assigns, except for a low room with a sollar and with free ingress and egress. William granted the room, with the sollar, to John Mitchell, a chaplain, for life, together with the easement of a hall, a kitchen, a garden, a well, and a latrine, as is contained in a deed perfected in the matter. William devised the room, with the sollar, to Laurence and his assigns for ever on John's death. From the money received from the sale of the tenement, cottages, shops, and rents four chaplains, annual and stipendiary, chosen by William's executors as quickly as can be done with consideration, should be found to celebrate mass in St. Edmund's chapel in the cathedral church on behalf of his soul and the souls of others for one year or two years at least if it cannot be done otherwise; £20 should be spent by his executors for six virtuous girls of good character and behaviour to be married, that is 5 marks to each; the rest should be laid out by his executors on paupers, improving ways, shoes, and other charitable deeds on behalf of his soul. Executors: Laurence Groom and John Mitchell. Proved on 20 June 1405 in front of John Chandler, the dean of Salisbury; the administration was entrusted to the executors. Approved at a court held in front of the bailiff, the mayor, and other citizens; the seisin of the tenements, cottages, shops, and rents was released to the executors and legatees.

1883 By his charter an elder John Chandler, a citizen of Salisbury, granted to William Walter, a citizen of Salisbury, a tenement in Winchester Street between a tenement of late Richard Still's, now Thomas Bonham's, on the east side and a corner tenement of late John Hoare's on the west side [*described slightly differently in **1886***]. The tenement, with other land and tenements in the city, was held by William Buck, a chaplain, now dead, and John Chandler by a grant of John Wallop, a citizen of Salisbury, who held it by a grant of John Stoke, tailor, and it is to be held for ever by William and his heirs and assigns. Seals: John Chandler's and the common and mayoral seals of the city. Named witnesses: the bailiff, the mayor, the coroners, the reeves, John Mower, Richard Spencer, Adam Teffont, Richard Leach, Nicholas Harding, and the clerk

1884 By his charter an elder John Chandler, a citizen of Salisbury, granted to John Mower, a citizen of Salisbury, a tenement in Chipper Street between a tenement of late Andrew Bone's, now John Mower's, on the east side and a tenement of late Thomas Durrington's, now John Noble's, on the west side. The tenement, with other land and tenements in the city, was held by William Buck, a chaplain, now dead, and John Chandler by a grant of John Wallop, of late a citizen of Salisbury. It was formerly held by that John by a devise of his wife Maud, who was enfeoffed in it jointly with her husband Thomas Gilbert by a grant of William Purser, a citizen of Salisbury, and it is to be held for ever by John Mower and his heirs and assigns. Seals: John Chandler's and the common and mayoral seals of the city. Named witnesses: the bailiff, the mayor, the coroners, the reeves, William Wamwell, Richard Spencer, William Walter, Richard Leach, William Sall, and the clerk

1885 By his charter an elder John Chandler, a citizen of Salisbury, granted to William Warmwell, a citizen of Salisbury, a tenement in Scots Lane between a tenement of late Thomas Sexhampcote's on either side. The tenement, with other land and tenements in the city, was held by William Buck, a chaplain, now dead, and John Chandler by a grant of John Wallop, a citizen of Salisbury, who held it by a feoffment of William Buck. It is to be held for ever by William Warmwell and his heirs and assigns. Seals: John Chandler's and the common and mayoral seals of the city. Named witnesses: the bailiff, the mayor, the coroners, the reeves, John Mower, Richard Spencer, William Walter, Adam Teffont, William Bishop, and the clerk

8 July 1405, at Salisbury
1886 By his deed John Stoke quitclaimed to William Walter, a citizen of Salisbury, and his heirs and assigns his right or claim to a tenement, which William held by a feoffment of John Chandler, and which John Wallop, draper, a citizen of

Salisbury, previously held by John's own grant, in Winchester Street between a tenement of late Richard Still's, now John Montagu's, on the east side and a corner tenement of late John Hoare's opposite Bull Hall on the west side [*described slightly differently in 1883*]. Seals: John Stoke's and the common and mayoral seals of the city. Named witnesses: the bailiff, the mayor, the coroners, the reeves, John Mower, Richard Spencer, William Warmwell, Nicholas Harding, and the clerk

1887 By her deed Maud, the relict of Gilbert at the brook, skinner, granted to her mother Alice, the wife of Thomas Hammond, the reversion of a tenement, in which she dwells, when it fell due on her death. The tenement, of late held jointly by Gilbert and Maud by a feoffment of Agnes Ball and Roger Grateley, baker, stands in Gigant Street between a tenement of late Hugh Hoare's, now John Lewisham's, on the north side and a tenement of late Thomas Chaplin's, in which John Dyer, weaver, dwells, on the south side. The reversion, when it fell due, is to be held for ever by Alice and her heirs and assigns. Clause of warranty. Seals: Maud's and the common and mayoral seals of the city. Named witnesses: the bailiff, the mayor, the coroners, the reeves, William Warmwell, John Mower, Richard Spencer, William Walter, William Sall, and the clerk

5 August 1405, at Salisbury
1888 Approval of the will of William Woodrow, weaver, a citizen of Salisbury, made on 3 May 1405. <u>Interment</u>: in the graveyard of St. Edmund's church, in front of the west door and under the marble tomb there. <u>Bequests</u>: 100*s*. and his biggest brass pot for the fabric of that church, 2*s*. to the provost to celebrate his sepulchral mass, 12*d*. to each collegiate chaplain present at his funeral rites and burial mass, and 4*d*. to each other chaplain being likewise present; 40*d*. to the fabric of the cathedral church; 12*d*. each to the fabric of St. Thomas's church and the fabric of St. Martin's church; 6*s*. 8*d*. both to the Franciscans of Salisbury and the Dominicans of Fisherton to be present at his funeral rites and mass and to pray for his soul; 6*d*. each to the fabric of St. Clement's church, Fisherton, and to the hospital called Almshouse; 40*d*. to the fabric of the church of Sturminster Newton (*Newton Castle*); 6*s*. 8*d*. to his godson John Hunt; a striped gown with a green champ to his godson Simon Little; 40*d*. to his godson William Gilbert; 6*s*. 8*d*. to a younger John Forest; 25 lb. of wax to be burned around his corpse on the day of his burial; 33*s*. 4*d*. for 400 masses to be celebrated on behalf of his soul on the day of his obit as soon as possible; a round basin to John Gould, a chaplain; a pot (*cacobum*) containing 16 gallons, a movable table, a black gown with white fur, and 20*s*. to Edith Knights; 6*s*. 8*d*. to his sister Agnes; a winnowing sheet, three sacks for putting malt in, and a best vat to Margery, a daughter of Agnes; a brass pot and 40*d*. to 'Elisett', his servant; a ewer, with a star, and 40*d*. to Alice White, formerly his servant; all his tools pertaining to his art of weaving to William Perrin; a gown, and a blanket for a bed, to John Curtis, his servant; a blanket for a bed to each of his tenants; his best gown to Thomas Kent; the rest of his goods to be disposed of by his executors on behalf of his soul and the souls of others; his belt and 20*s*. to Thomas Eyre. <u>Devises</u>: to Edith Knights, called Shipster, of Salisbury, for life a shop, with a sollar, in Scots Lane between Simon Baker's tenement on

the west side and William's own shops on the east side, and after Edith's death to be sold by his executors, their executors, or subsequent executors. The money received should be laid out by the executors on celebrating masses, [giving] alms, repairing ways, and doing other charitable deeds on behalf of William's soul and the souls of others. William devised to his wife Gillian for life a corner tenement, in which he dwelt, in Endless Street between Nicholas Baynton's tenement on the south side, a street called Scots Lane on the north side, and his own shops in that street on the west side, and after Gillian's death to be sold by his executors or subsequent executors. The money received should be laid out by the executors in the manner described above, and especially in St. Edmund's church, on behalf of William's soul, the soul of Beatrice, of late his wife, Gillian's soul, and the souls of others. William devised to his executors three conjoined shops in Scots Lane between a tenement, in which he dwelt, on the east side and the shop devised to Edith Knights on the west side, to be sold immediately after his death. The money raised should be laid out in the same way as that from the reversion of the shop devised above. <u>Executors</u>: Thomas Eyre, John Lewisham, and Edith Knights, shipster. <u>Proved</u> on 20 July 1405 in front of an officer of the subdean; the administration was entrusted to the executors. <u>Approved</u> at a court held in front of the bailiff, the mayor, and other citizens; the seisin of the tenement and the shops was released to the legatees.

1889 By their charter Richard Jacob, a chaplain, and an elder John Chandler granted to Laurence Groom and John Mitchell, chaplains, executors of William Buck, a chaplain, two shops which Thomas Boughton, a cordwainer, holds, which were of late Thomas Britford's, and which stand conjoined in Castle Street between John Mower's tenement, which John Saddler, baker, holds, on the north side and a shop which Richard Chesham now holds on the south side. The shops are to be held for ever by Laurence and John and their heirs and assigns. Seals: those of the grantors and the common and mayoral seals of the city. Named witnesses: the bailiff, the mayor, the coroners, the reeves, William Warmwell, John Mower, Richard Spencer, William Walter, William Sall, and the clerk

1890 By their charter Laurence Groom, a chaplain, and John Mitchell, a chaplain, executors of William Buck, a chaplain, granted to Richard Chesham, tucker, and his wife Joan a shop, with a sollar, in Castle Street, opposite William Warmwell's tenement, between shops which Thomas Boughton, a cordwainer, holds of them on the north side and a shop of late John Ashley's on the south side. The shop [was devised] by William Buck to his executors to be sold and is to be held for ever by Richard and Joan and their heirs and assigns. Richard and Joan bought it in good faith for a sum of money which Laurence and John will spend on the salvation of William Buck's soul. Seals: those of the grantors and the common and mayoral seals of the city. Named witnesses: the bailiff, the mayor, the coroners, the reeves, John Mower, William Warmwell, Richard Spencer, William Walter, Thomas Mason, and the clerk

1891 By their charter Laurence Groom, a chaplain, and John Mitchell, a chaplain, executors of William Buck, a chaplain, granted to Walter Shirley, grocer, and William Sall, citizens of Salisbury, a tenement in Castle Street between a chief tenement of late that of John Wallop, draper, which Walter now holds, on the south side and a gate of that chief tenement on the north side. The tenement, of late that of William Bartlet, a citizen of Salisbury, was devised by William Buck to his executors to be sold and is to be held for ever by Walter and William and their heirs and assigns. Seals: those of the grantors and the common and mayoral seals of the city. Named witnesses: the bailiff, the mayor, the coroners, the reeves, John Mower, William Warmwell, Richard Spencer, William Walter, Nicholas Harding, and the clerk

19 August 1405, at Salisbury
1892 By their charter Thomas Eyre and John Lewisham, executors of William Woodrow, weaver, and Edith Knights, shipster, their co-executor, on the strength of William's will granted to William Dunning, weaver, and his wife Maud three conjoined shops in Scots Lane between a corner tenement [in Endless Street: *cf. **1888***], in which William Woodrow of late dwelt, on the east side and a shop, with a sollar, devised by that William to Edith, on the west side. The shops were devised by William to his executors to be sold immediately after his death and are to be held for ever by William Dunning and his heirs and assigns. William and Maud bought them in good faith for a sum of money with which Thomas, John, and Edith are satisfied and which they will spend according to William Woodrow's intention. Seals: those of the grantors and the common and mayoral seals of the city. Named witnesses: the bailiff, the mayor, the coroners, the reeves, John Mower, William Warmwell, Richard Spencer, William Walter, William Sall, and the clerk

1893 A charter of Thomas Eyre and John Lewisham, executors of William Woodrow, weaver, of late a citizen of Salisbury, and of Edith Knights, their co-executor. William devised to his wife Gillian for life a [corner] tenement, in which he then dwelt, in Endless Street [*as in **1888***], and to Edith Knights, shipster, for life a shop, with a sollar, in Scots Lane [*as in **1888***]. He appointed that the tenement, after Gillian's death, and the shop, with the sollar, after Edith's death, should be sold by his executors. The money received should be laid out by them on the salvation of his soul and the souls of others. William Dunning, weaver, has come to an agreement with Thomas, John, and Edith for him and his wife Maud to acquire the reversion of the tenement and of the shop for a sum of money in part paid to them in advance, on the strength of the will Thomas, John, and Edith granted to them the reversion of both on the death of Gillian and of Edith, and the tenement and the shop, when they fell due, are to be held for ever by William and Maud and their heirs and assigns. William and Maud bought the reversions in good faith for that sum of money which Thomas, John, and Edith will spend according to William Woodrow's intention. Seals: those of the grantors and the common and mayoral seals of the city. Named witnesses: the bailiff, the mayor, the coroners, the reeves, John Mower, William Warmwell, Richard Spencer, William Walter, William Sall, and the clerk

1894 By his charter an elder John Chandler, a citizen of Salisbury, granted to John Mower and Richard Spencer, citizens of Salisbury, a tenement in Castle Street, in which Thomas Steer now dwells, between a tenement of George Goss, tucker, on the north side and a tenement of late Thomas Gilbert's on the south side. The tenement, with other land, tenements, shops, and cottages in the city, was held by John Chandler and William Buck, now dead, by a grant of John Wallop, draper, of late a citizen of Salisbury, and is to be held for ever by John Mower and Richard Spencer and their heirs and assigns. Seals: John Chandler's and the common and mayoral seals of the city. Named witnesses: the bailiff, the mayor, the coroners, the reeves, William Warmwell, William Walter, Richard Leach, Adam Teffont, William Bishop, and the clerk

1895 By their indented charter an elder John Chandler and John Ettshall, citizens of Salisbury, granted to John Salisbury, grocer, of Salisbury, and his wife Alice a chief tenement, in which John and Alice now dwell, in New Street between a tenement of late John Upton's, which John Nash, mason, now holds, on the east side and a tenement of late that of William Buck, a chaplain, now John Hathaway's, on the west side; also a tenement [in Minster Street: *cf.* **816**], with shops, which Simon Tredinnick holds, above a ditch, between a tenement called the 'Riole' on the west side and a tenement of George Merriott, and his wife Alice, which William Isaac of late held, on the east side; also conjoined shops, which Thomas Bleacher, ironmonger, and John Manning, butcher, hold, at the west end of Butchery between a street there called Ironmonger Corner on the west side and Thomas Knoyle's shop on the east side. The tenements and the shops, with other land and tenements in the city, were held by John Chandler and John Ettshall by a grant of William Lord, are to be held by John Salisbury and Alice and their assigns for the life of John and Alice and the life of the one of them living longer, and on the death of John and Alice should remain to Joan, the wife of Henry Delves, a daughter of the late John Salisbury, kt., a brother of John Salisbury, grocer, and her heirs. Seals: those of John Chandler and John Ettshall and the common and mayoral seals of the city. Named witnesses: the bailiff, the mayor, the coroners, the reeves, John Mower, William Warmwell, Richard Spencer, William Walter, Richard Jewell, and the clerk

1896 By their charter an elder John Chandler and John Ettshall, citizens of Salisbury, granted to John Salisbury, grocer, of Salisbury, two conjoined tenements in Winchester Street, of late those of Nicholas Baker, his father, between Thomas Bonham's tenement, which John Montagu holds, on the west side and a tenement of late Thomas Postle's, now William Hill's, on the east side; also conjoined cottages in Nuggeston and Gigant Street, on the way to St. Edmund's church, between cottages which were of late John Butterley's, afterwards William Coventry's, on the north side and John Needler's tenement in Nuggeston on the east side; also conjoined cottages, in the street on the way to St. Martin's church, between cottages of an elder John Forest on the south side and a gate of a meadow called Bug moor on the north side; also a corner tenement in St. Martin's Street, opposite the gate of the Franciscans, between Margaret Godmanstone's cottage property on the west side in that street and William Warmwell's cottage property in Freren Street on the south side; also a garden in Freren Street, of late Nicholas Baker's, between a garden [with] racks, which John Pinch holds, on the north side and a garden with racks, which John Tidworth holds, on the south side; also four conjoined shops, at the east end of Poultry, between a tenement of late Thomas Play's, now that of John Lippiatt and his wife Alice, on the west side and shops of late John Ashley's on the south side. The tenements, shops, and cottages, and the garden, with other land and tenements in the city, were held by John Chandler and John Ettshall by a grant of William Lord and are to be held for his life by John Salisbury, grocer, and his assigns. On John's death the cottages in Nuggeston and Gigant Street should remain for life to a younger John Scot, and on that John's death should remain for ever to William Warin, John Mower, Richard Spencer, William Walter, William Bishop, and William Sall, citizens of Salisbury, and their heirs and assigns to the use of the mayor and commonalty of the city. Also on John Salisbury's death the tenements, the shops, the other cottages, and the garden should remain for ever to Joan, the wife of Henry Delves, a daughter of John Salisbury, kt., a brother of John Salisbury, and to her heirs. Seals: those of John Chandler and John Ettshall and the common and mayoral seals of the city. Named witnesses: the bailiff, the coroners, the reeves, Edmund Enfield, Adam Teffont, Richard Leach, Nicholas Harding, John Forest, William Dowding, and the clerk

2 September 1405, at Salisbury
1897 By his deed John Lewisham, the executor of John Drury, of late a citizen of Salisbury, on the strength of John's will granted to Edmund Purdy, weaver, and Walter Nalder a tenement, in which that John of late dwelt, in Castle Street, beyond the bars, between John Shipton's tenement on the north side and John Starr's tenement on the south side. The tenement was devised by John Drury to be sold by his executor immediately after his death, as soon as it could be done advantageously, and it is to be held for ever by Edmund and Walter and their heirs and assigns. It was bought from John Lewisham by Edmund and Walter in good faith for a sum of money paid in part to John, which whole sum he would spend on the salvation of John Drury's soul and the souls of others and on giving to God. Seals: John Lewisham's and the common and mayoral seals of the city. Named witnesses: the bailiff, the mayor, the coroners, the reeves, William Warmwell, Richard Spencer, William Walter, William Sall, Thomas Mason, draper, and the clerk
1898 By his charter an elder John Chandler, a citizen of Salisbury, granted to William Warin, William Bishop, and Simon Tredinnick, citizens of Salisbury, and to Thomas Ringwood a rent of 8 marks a year issuing from a tenement which William Horn and his wife Amice hold for their life, and the life of the one of them living longer, and which their executors or assigns [will] hold for a year after their death; also the reversion of the tenement when it fell due on the death of William and Amice. The tenement stands in Castle Street between a tenement of Nicholas Longstock and his wife Agnes on the south side and William Warmwell's tenement, which was of late Walter Ryborough's, on the north side. The rent, and the reversion when it fell due on the death of William and Amice and after the year, are to be held for ever by the grantees and their heirs and assings. Seals:

John's and the common and mayoral seals of the city. Named witnesses: the bailiff, the coroners, the reeves, John Mower, William Warmwell, Richard Spencer, William Walter, William Sall, and the clerk

1899 By his charter an elder John Chandler, a citizen of Salisbury, granted to William Warin, William Bishop, and Simon Tredinnick, citizens of Salisbury, and to Thomas Ringwood a tenement in Castle Street [*as in **1898***], in which William Horn and his wife Amice dwell. The tenement, with other land, tenements, shops, cottages, rent, and reversions in Salisbury, was held jointly by William Buck, a chaplain, now dead, and John Chandler by a grant of John Wallop, draper, a citizen of Salisbury, and is to be held for ever by the grantees and their heirs and assigns. Seals: John Chandler's and the common and mayoral seals of the city. Named witnesses: the bailiff, the coroners, the reeves, William Warmwell, John Mower, Richard Spencer, William Walter, William Sall, and the clerk

16 September 1405, at Salisbury
1900 By her charter Margaret Godmanstone, the relict of William Buckland, of late a citizen of Salisbury, granted to an elder John Chandler, a citizen of Salisbury, a cottage, with a yard, in New Street, of late William's and of late held by John Grinder, between a tenement of late Henry Stapleford's, now appropriated to the hospital of the Holy Trinity, on the west side and cottage property of late that of Simon Gillmin, a citizen of Salisbury, now that of Thomas Jarvis and his wife Agnes, on the east side. The cottage was of late Simon Gillmin's and, with the yard, is to be held for ever by John Chandler and his heirs and assigns. Seals: Margaret's and the common and mayoral seals of the city. Named witnesses: the bailiff, the mayor, the coroners, the reeves, John Mower, William Warmwell, Richard Spencer, Adam Teffont, William Walter, Nicholas Harding, and the clerk

1901 By her letters of attorney Margaret Godmanstone, the relict of William Buckland, of late a citizen of Salisbury, appointed Nicholas Mason, a clerk, and John Gatcombe to surrender into the hand of Richard, the bishop of Salisbury, the seisin of a cottage, with a yard, in New Street [*as in **1900***] to the use of John Chandler, a citizen of Salisbury. Seals: Margaret's and the mayoral seal of the city

1902 By his charter William Bishop, a citizen of Salisbury, granted to William Warin, a citizen of Salisbury, a tenement, of late that of John Franklin, wheeler, and his wife Alice, which he held by a grant of William Woodrow, draper, and that same Alice, then William's wife. The tenement stands in Wheeler Row, opposite the market place, between a tenement of late Nicholas Taylor's, now Simon Tredinnick's, on the north side and a tenement of late John New's, now Richard Knolle's, on the south side, and is to be held for ever by William Warin and his heirs and assigns. Seals: William Bishop's and the common and mayoral seals of the city. Named witnesses: the bailiff, the coroners, the reeves, John Mower, William Warmwell, Richard Spencer, William Walter, an elder John Chandler, William Sall, and the clerk

30 September 1405, at Salisbury
1903 By his charter an elder John Chandler, a citizen of Salisbury, granted to

Walter Nalder, a citizen of Salisbury, a toft, which is now held as a garden, in Castle Street, beyond the bars, between [a tenement] of John Homes, of late that of his father Ellis Homes, on the south side and cottage property of late Walter Chippenham's on the north side. The toft or garden was of late that of John Wallop, draper, a citizen of Salisbury, and with other land and tenements in the city was held jointly by William Buck, a chaplain, now dead, and John Chandler by his grant. It is to be held for ever by Walter and his heirs and assigns, to whom John quitclaimed his right or claim to it. Seals: John Chandler's and the common and mayoral seals of the city. Named witnesses: the bailiff, the mayor, the coroners, the reeves, John Mower, William Warmwell, Richard Spencer, William Walter, Walter Shirley, Thomas Mason, draper, and the clerk

1904 By his charter William Lord granted to William Sall, a citizen of Salisbury, a yard in Culver Street between a cottage of late John Justice's, now William Sall's, on the south side and a cottage of late Simon Bunt's, now John Wootton's, on the north side. The yard is to be held for ever by William Sall and his heirs and assigns, to whom William Lord quitclaimed his right or claim to it. Seals: William Lord's and the common and mayoral seals of the city. Named witnesses: the bailiff, the mayor, the coroners, the reeves, John Mower, Richard Spencer, William Walter, Richard Leach, Adam Teffont, John Lewisham, and the clerk

14 October 1405, at Salisbury

1905 By their deed an elder John Chandler, a citizen of Salisbury, and Thomas Steer quitclaimed to William Sall, a citizen of Salisbury, and his heirs and assigns their right or claim to a yard in Culver Street [*as in* **1904**], which William held by a grant of William Lord. Thomas warranted the yard to William Sall. Seals: those of John and Thomas and the common and mayoral seals of the city. Named witnesses: the mayor, the bailiff, the coroners, the reeves, John Mower, Richard Spencer, William Walter, Adam Teffont, Nicholas Harding, William Hill, and the clerk

1906 By his charter Walter Nalder granted to Henry Berwick three shops, which he acquired from Agnes, the relict of Nicholas Russell, in Pot Row between a tenement of late John Talbot's on one side and a tenement of late Catherine Bold's, now Thomas Child's, on the other side. The shops are to be held for ever by Henry and his heirs and assigns. Seals: Walter's and the common and mayoral seals of the city. Named witnesses: the bailiff, the mayor, the coroners, the reeves, John Mower, William Warmwell, Richard Spencer, William Walter, John Forest, and the clerk

1907 By their charter John Brown, butcher, and his wife Joan, appearing at the court held on that day, granted to Henry Berwick a tenement, which they held by a grant of William Coventry, William Mercer, and John Purvis, in Pot Row between John Barnaby's tenement on the east side and a tenement of late William Wilton's on the west side. The tenement was held by William Coventry, William Mercer, and John Purvis by a grant of Richard Leach, a citizen of Salisbury, and is to be held for ever by Henry and his heirs and assigns. Clause of warranty. Seals: those of John and Joan and the common and mayoral seals of the city. Named witnesses: the bailiff, the mayor, the coroners, the reeves, John Mower, William Warmwell, William Walter, Richard Leach, John Forest, and the clerk

1908 By their deed Robert Alexander, of Aldington, and his sons John and William quitclaimed to William Bishop, a citizen of Salisbury, and his heirs and assigns their right or claim to a tenement, of late that of John Franklin, wheeler, and his wife Alice in Wheeler Row [*as in* **1902**]. Seals: those of Robert, John, and William and the common and mayoral seals of the city. Named witnesses: the bailiff, the mayor, the coroners, the reeves, John Mower, William Warmwell, Richard Spencer, William Walter, William Sall, and the clerk

28 October 1405, at Salisbury

1909 Approval of the will of Alice, the wife of Robert Durrant, draper, a citizen of Salisbury, made on 23 May 1405. <u>Interment</u>: in St. Martin's church by the tomb of Richard Hellier, of late her husband, near the baptismal font. <u>Bequests</u>: 10*s*. for the fabric of that church, 8*d*. for the maintenance of the light of the Blessed Mary, 2*s*. 6*d*. to the parochial chaplain to pray for her soul, 40*d*. to the high altar for her forgotten tithes and lesser benefactions, 12*d*. to each of the other chaplains to pray for her soul and be present at her funeral rites, 4*d*. to the deacon, and 6*d*. to the sacristan; 40*d*. for the fabric of the cathedral church and 12*d*. to the light of the high cross in that church; 6*d*. to each of her godchildren; 12*d*. each to each of her *hockiatr'*, each of her tenants, the fabric of the church of St. Peter, Tidpit, and the fabric of the church of Martin; 5*s*. both to the Franciscans of Salisbury and the Dominicans of Fisherton to pray for her soul and be present at her funeral rites; a hood of sendal and a kerchief to Joan Sifray; 12*d*. each to Richard Sifray and Edith Keyford; 6*d*. to Edith's husband John; a silk kerchief to William, the wife of Robert Latticemaker; 12*d*. each to Alice Gitting and Agnes Reaps; a silk kerchief to Lucy Woodcock; 40*d*. each to Roger Wormell and John, her servant; a blanket, a linen sheet, and 40*d*. to William, her servant; a rosary of amber beads, a silk kerchief, two spoons, a brass pot, a pan, a belt furnished with silver, and 6*s*. 8*d*. to Joan, a daughter of her husband Robert; a rosary, a kerchief, two silver spoons, a brass pot, a pan, and 6*s*. 8*d*. to Robert's son James; a piece of silver, a small mazer, a best tablecloth with a towel, four best silver spoons, a basin with a laver, and 20*s*. cash to her son Thomas Hellier, a chaplain; 20*s*. to be handed out in bread or cash among paupers on the day of her burial on behalf of her soul; the rest of her goods to her husband Robert. <u>Devises</u>: to Robert a tenement, with shops and a cottage (*or* cottages), in which she dwelt, in New Street between cottage property of the provost of St. Edmund's church on one side and John Wishford's cottage property on the other side, to be held for his life by him and his assigns, and after his death to be sold by Alice's executors or their executors. If it seemed better the reversion should be sold in Robert's lifetime by him and Alice's son Thomas at the will, and with the assent, of both. The money received should be laid out on celebrating masses, giving alms, repairing ways and bridges, and doing other charitable deeds on behalf of Alice's soul, the souls of Richard, of late her husband, Robert, and Thomas, and the souls of others. Alice devised to Thomas a tenement, with four conjoined cottages, in St.

Martin's Street between [Clark's Place: cf. **2005**], a corner tenement of Richard Clark, of Pensford, on the west side and William Warin's cottage property on the east side, to be held for ever by him and his heirs and assigns. She appointed that immediately after her death, as soon as it could be done advantageously, her executors should sell the reversion of the cottage which Roger Wormell holds for his life; also conjoined cottages in Gigant Street between a corner tenement of a younger John Pope, of late Thomas Burford's, on the south side and cottage property of the provost of St. Edmund's church on the north side. The money received should be laid out, in the same way as that received from the other sales, on behalf of her soul and the souls of those named above according to the sound conscience of her executors acting as one. <u>Executors</u>: her husband Robert and her son Thomas. <u>Proved</u> on 11 October 1405 in front of an officer of the subdean; the administration was entrusted to the executors, appearing in person and sworn to act jointly. <u>Approved</u> at a court held in front of the bailiff, the mayor, and other citizens; the seisin of the tenements and cottages was released to the legatees.

11 November 1405, at Salisbury
1910 By her indented charter Margaret Godmanstone, the relict of William Godmanstone, of late a citizen of Salisbury, in her widow's right and full power, granted to Henry Chubb, baker, and his wife Agnes three conjoined tenements in New Street, on the way to the lower bridge of Fisherton, between a tenement of late Richard at the cellar's on the east side and Reynold Glover's tenement beside the river on the west side. The tenements were of late those of Margaret's father William Ellis, a citizen of Salisbury, and afterwards of William's wife Emme, Margaret's mother, and they are to be held for ever by Henry and Agnes and Henry's heirs and assigns, paying rent of £8 cash a year to Margaret and her assigns for Margaret's life. The rent will cease on Margaret's death. Clause to permit re-entry if the rent were in arrear for a quarter, repossession, and the retention by Margaret of her former estate in fee simple. Seals: Margaret's and the common and mayoral seals of the city. Named witnesses: the bailiff, the mayor, the coroners, the reeves, John Mower, William Warmwell, Richard Spencer, William Walter, William Bishop, and the clerk

1911 By her letters of attorney Margaret Godmanstone, the relict of William Godmanstone, of late a citizen of Salisbury, appointed Nicholas Mason, a clerk, John Gatcombe, and Stephen Edington to surrender into the hand of Richard, the bishop of Salisbury, the seisin of three conjoined tenements in New Street [*as in* **1910**] to the use of Henry Chubb, baker, and his wife Agnes. Seals: Margaret's and the mayoral seal of the city

9 December 1405, at Salisbury
1912 By his charter William Warin, a citizen of Salisbury, granted to Richard Cormell, called Knolle, and his wife Joan a tenement, of late that of John Franklin, wheeler, and his wife Alice, which he held by a feoffment of William Bishop, a citizen of Salisbury. The tenement stands opposite the market place, in Wheeler Row, [*as in* **1902**] and is to be held for ever by Richard and Joan and Richard's

heirs and assigns. Clause of warranty. Seals: William Warin's and the common and mayoral seals of the city. Named witnesses: the bailiff, the mayor, the coroners, the reeves, John Mower, William Warmwell, Richard Spencer, William Walter, William Bishop, William Dowding, and the clerk

1913 By their indented charter the master John Chandler and John Aynel, clerks, granted to William Bayford and his wife Joan a tenement in Castle Street between John Gowan's tenement, of late Richard Priddy's, on the south side and Joan Cheyne's cottage property on the north side. The tenement, with other land and tenements in the city, was held by John Chandler and John Aynel by a grant of Thomas Chaplin, is to be held for ever by William and Joan and the issue begotten between them, and if William and Joan were to die without such issue would remain for ever to Thomas Chaplin and his heirs. Seals: those of John Chandler and John Aynel and the common and mayoral seals of the city. Named witnesses: the bailiff, the mayor, the coroners, the reeves, John Mower, William Warmwell, Richard Spencer, William Warin, William Walter, and the clerk

1914 By their letters of attorney the master John Chandler and John Aynel, clerks, appointed Thomas Chaplin, John Grateley, and John Gatcombe to surrender into the hand of Richard, the bishop of Salisbury, the seisin of a tenement in Castle Street [*as in* **1913**] to the use of William Bayford and his wife Joan. Seals: those of John Chandler and John Aynel and the mayoral seal of the city

23 December 1405, at Salisbury

1915 By her charter Margaret Godmanstone, the relict of William Godmanstone, of late a citizen of Salisbury, in her widow's right and full power, granted to John Mower, William Sall, John Gatcombe, and Nicholas Mason, a chaplain, a tenement, which John Fish, weaver, holds, with the two racks and other appurtenances built within it. The tenement stands in Gigant Street, on the way to St. Edmund's church, between Richard Weston's tenement, standing beside a garden of late John Ball's, on the south side and William Hoare's yard, with racks, which Nicholas Buckland holds, on the north side and, with the racks and other appurtenances, is to be held for ever by the grantees and their heirs and assigns. Seals: Margaret's and the common and mayoral seals of the city. Named witnesses: the bailiff, the mayor, the coroners, the reeves, William Warmwell, Richard Spencer, Willliam Warin, William Walter, Adam Teffont, Richard Leach, and the clerk

1916 By her letters of attorney Margaret Godmanstone, the relict of William Godmanstone, appointed William Bowyer and Stephen Edington to surrender into the hand of Richard, the bishop of Salisbury, the seisin of a tenement in Gigant Street [*as in* **1915**] to the use of John Mower, William Sall, John Gatcombe, and Nicholas Mason, a chaplain. Seals: Margaret's and the mayoral seal of the city

6 January 1406, at Salisbury

1917 By his charter an elder John Chandler, granted to Richard Prentice, a clerk, John Mower, grocer, a citizen of Salisbury, and Walter Shirley, grocer, a citizen of Saisbury, a tenement, with a gate next to it, in Castle Street between Walter

Nalder's tenement on the south side and Robert Hazelbury's empty plot, of late Roger Wallop's, on the north side. The tenement, with the gate, was of late held by Richard, John, and Walter for a term of years by John's grant and is to be held for ever by them and their heirs and assigns. Seals: John Chandler's and the common and mayoral seals of the city. Named witnesses: the bailiff, the mayor, the coroners, the reeves, Richard Spencer, William Warin, Edmund Enfield, William Sall, William Bishop, William Dowding, and the clerk

20 January 1406, at Salisbury
1918 By his deed John Cosser, of London, quitclaimed to Stephen Edington and his heirs and assigns his right or claim to a tenement, with shops, or to a rent of 20s. a year issuing from it which he claimed, received, or was accustomed to receive. The tenement, of late Edmund Cofford's, stands in Castle Street and Chipper Street on a corner between Thomas Mason's tenement, of late an elder George Goss's, on the north side and John Gatcombe's cottages in Chipper Street, of late John Sorrel's, on the east side. John also released to Stephen all actions, real and personal, which he has, had, or could have against him. Seals: John's and the common and mayoral seals of the city. Named witnesses: the mayor, the bailiff, the coroners, the reeves, John Mower, William Warmwell, Richard Spencer, William Warin, William Sall, and Thomas Child

1919 By his deed John Rothwell, of Sarson (*Savage*), quitclaimed to Stephen Edington and his heirs and assigns his right or claim to a tenement, with shops, or to a rent of 20s. a year issuing from it. The tenement, of late Edmund Cofford's, stands, on a corner in Castle Street and Chipper Street [*as in 1918*]. Clause of warranty in respect of the rent. Seals: John's and the common and mayoral seals of the city. Named witnesses: the mayor, the bailiff, the coroners, the reeves, John Mower, William Warmwell, Richard Spencer, William Warin, William Sall, and Thomas Child

1920 By their charter William Warin, William Bishop, and Simon Tredinnick, citizens of Salisbury, granted to a younger John Bodenham, of Wilton, a tenement in which William Horn and his wife Amice dwell, which was of late that of John Wallop, draper, and which they held by a grant of an elder John Chandler, a citizen of Salisbury. The tenement stands in Castle Street, between a tenement of Nicholas Longstock and his wife Agnes on the south side and William Warmwell's tenement, of late Walter Ryborough's, on the north side, and is to be held for ever by John Bodenham and his heirs and assigns. Seals: those of the grantors and the common and mayoral seals of the city. Named witnesses: the bailiff, the mayor, the coroners, the reeves, John Mower, William Warmwell, Richard Spencer, William Walter, and the clerk

1921 By their charter William Warin, William Bishop, and Simon Tredinnick, citizens of Salisbury, granted to John Bodenham, of Wilton, a rent of 8 marks a year issuing from a tenement which William Horn and his wife Amice hold for their life, which was of late that of John Wallop, draper, and which stands in Castle Street [*as in 1920*]; also the reversion of the tenement when it fell due on the death of William and Alice. The rent and the reversion were held by the grantors by a grant of an elder John Chandler, a citizen of Salisbury, and are to be held for ever by John Bodenham and his heirs and assigns. Seals: those of the grantors and the common and mayoral seals of the city. Named witnesses: the bailiff, the mayor, the coroners, the reeves, John Mower, William Warmwell, Richard Spencer, William Walter, and the clerk

1922 By his deed an elder John Chandler quitclaimed to Richard Prentice, a clerk, John Mower, grocer, a citizen of Salisbury, and Walter Shirley, grocer, a citizen of Salisbury, his right or claim to a tenement, with a gate next to it, in Castle Street [*as in* **1917**]. Seals: John Chandler's and the common and mayoral seals of the city. Named witnesses: the bailiff, the mayor, the coroners, the reeves, Richard Spencer, William Warin, William Walter, Edmund Enfield, William Sall, and the clerk

3 February 1406, at Salisbury

1923 By his charter John Rothwell, of Sarson (*Annesavage, Upsavage*), quitclaimed to Richard Spencer, William Walter, Nicholas Harding, and an elder John Forest, citizens of Salisbury, and their heirs and assigns his right or claim to a tenement, with adjacent shops, or to a rent of 13*s*. 4*d*. a year issuing from it. The tenement, of late that of an elder George Goss, now Thomas Mason's, stands in Minster Street, which is called Castle Street, between a tenement of late Edmund Cofford's, now Stephen Edington's, on the south side and a tenement of late Thomas Gilbert's on the north side. Clause of warranty. Seals: John's and the common and mayoral seals of the city. Named witnesses: the bailiff, the mayor, the coroners, a reeve, John Mower, William Warmwell, William Warin, Walter Nalder, William Boyton, and the clerk

17 March 1406, at Salisbury

1924 By his deed Robert Hazelbury granted to William Warmwell, a citizen of Salisbury, a rent of 10*s*. a year, which Robert was accustomed to receive, issuing from two conjoined tenements in Scots Lane between a tenement of late Thomas Sexhampcote's on the west side and a tenement of late John Staggard's, now that of Simon Bradley, baker, on the east side. One tenement is now William's and was formerly that of John Wallop, draper; Roger Woodford now holds the other, and John Nunton formerly held it. The rent was held by Robert by a grant of William Buck, a chaplain, and an elder John Chandler and is to be held for ever by William and his heirs and assigns. Seals: Robert's and the common and mayoral seals of the city. Named witnesses: the bailiff, the mayor, the coroners, the reeves, John Mower, Richard Spencer, William Warin, Walter Shirley, and the clerk

1925 By his deed John Wilmington quitclaimed to Thomas Manning and his heirs and assigns his right or claim to a garden or yard in which, with Thomas, he was enfeoffed by a grant of Richard Mawardine and his wife Edith. The garden or yard lies in two parts. One part lies in Brown Street, between William Slegge's tenement, of late John Luckham's, on the south side and a tenement of Robert Newport and his wife Agnes on the north side, and extends in length from the street on the west side as far as a trench of running water on the east side. The other part, in Gigant Street behind the garden of a tenement which Christine Fox holds of William Guys, measures in length 103½ ft. from Christine's garden on the east side as far as the trench of water on the west side and in width 44 ft. from the stone wall of William Warmwell's garden on the north side as far as another little garden of William Guys on the south side. Seals: John's and the common and mayoral seals of the city. Named witnesses: the bailiff, the mayor, the coroners, the reeves, John Mower, William Warmwell, Richard Spencer, Adam Teffont, Nicholas Harding, William Sall, and the clerk

31 March 1406, at Salisbury
1926 By his charter Thomas Manning granted to William Slegge, weaver, a yard, which he acquired from Richard Mawardine and his wife Edith, in Gigant Street behind the garden of a tenement of William Guys, which Christine Fox holds, and measuring [*as in* **1925**]; also land 75 ft. in length and 1½ ft. in width, for the gutters of William Slegge's house falling on the ground of a garden there, in Brown Street. The yard and the land are to be held for ever by William Slegge and his heirs and assigns. Clause of warranty. Seals: Thomas's and the common and mayoral seals of the city. Named witnesses: the bailiff, the mayor, the coroners, the reeves, John Mower, Richard Spencer, William Walter, Adam Teffont, Nicholas Harding, and the clerk

14 April 1406, at Salisbury
1927 By his indented charter Thomas Manning granted to Philip Wanstrow, carpenter, a part of a garden which he acquired from Richard Marwardine and his wife Edith. The part lies in Brown Street [*as in* **1925**] and, except for a gutter called Onesfall of William Slegge's house previously granted to William, is to be held for ever by Philip and his heirs and assigns. Philip is to pay a rent of 22*d.* cash a year to the chief lord and, for Thomas and his heirs, a rent of 6*s.* cash a year to Richard and Edith for their life and the life of the one of them living longer. Clause of warranty. Seals: Thomas's to one part of the indented charter, Philip's to the other part, and the common and mayoral seals of the city. Named witnesses: the bailiff, the mayor, the coroners, the reeves, John Mower, William Warmwell, Richard Spencer, William Warin, Adam Teffont, and the clerk

28 April 1406, at Salisbury
1928 By his indented charter Henry Berwick, granted to Richard Gage, weaver, a tenement in Castle Street between a tenement of John Sexhampcote, a chaplain, which John Durnford holds, on the south side and Edward Gilbert's tenement, of late Reynold Drury's, on the north side, to be held for ever by Richard and his heirs and assigns. Richard is to pay a rent of 26*s.* 8*d.* cash a year to Henry and his wife Agnes and their assigns for the life of Henry and Agnes and the life of the one of them living longer, and after the death of Henry and Agnes a rent of 13*s.* 4*d.* cash a year to Henry's heirs and assigns for ever. Clause to permit re-entry if the rent of 26*s.* 8*d.* or 13*s.* 4*d.* were in arrear for a year, distraint, and the

keeping of distresses until the unpaid rent was recovered; also, if the distresses were not sufficient for the rent, to permit permanent repossession and the retention of Henry's former estate. Clause of warranty in respect of the tenement, of acquittance in respect of the rent. Seals: Henry's to the part of the charter in Richard's possession, Richard's to the part in Henry's; present together in the Guildhall they procured the common and mayoral seals of the city to be likewise affixed. Named witnesses: the bailiff, the mayor, the coroners, the reeves, John Mower, William Warmwell, Richard Spencer, William Warin, William Walter, and the clerk

1929 By his indented charter Henry Berwick granted to Thomas Stabber, draper, and his wife Alice, his own daughter, three shops in Pot Row between Thomas Child's tenement, of late Catherine Bold's, on the east side and John Knottingley's tenement on the west side, to be held for ever by them and the issue begotten between them. Thomas and Alice are to pay a rent of 40s. cash a year to Henry and his wife Agnes for their life and the life of the one of them living longer. If Thomas and Alice were to die without such issue the shops would remain for ever to Henry's direct heirs. Thomas and Alice and their heirs should maintain and repair the shops in all things necessary at their own expense so that the rent would not be lost. Clause to permit re-entry if the shops were not maintained or the rent were in arrear for half a year, distraint, and the keeping of distresses until the unpaid rent was recovered; also, if the distresses were not sufficient for the rent, to permit permanent repossession by Henry and his assigns and the retention of Henry's former estate. Clause of warranty in respect of the shops, of acquittance in respect of the rent. Seals: Henry's to the part of the charter in Thomas's and Alice's possession, those of Thomas and Alice to the part in Henry's possession; present together they procured the common and mayoral seals of the city to be likewise affixed. Named witnesses: the bailiff, the mayor, the coroners, the reeves, John Mower, William Warmwell, Richard Spencer, William Warin, John Judd, and the clerk

26 May 1406, at Salisbury

1930 Approval of the will of William Upton, made on 24 June 1405. <u>Interment</u>: in the church of Durnford according to the order of his executors. <u>Bequests</u>: a small mazer, which he held by a gift of Agnes Baker, to the vicar of Durnford to celebrate mass on behalf of his soul and Agnes's soul; a large coffer standing in his room at Salisbury to his brother the master Thomas Upton; 20s. to each of his executors; the rest of his goods to his wife Mary; a trental to the vicar of Durnford to celebrate mass on behalf of his soul and the souls of others. <u>Devises</u>: to Richard Wells and his wife Agnes the room which they held within his tenement in New Street, on the way to the bridge, between a tenement of John Baker, grocer, on the west side and William Orme's tenement on the east side, to be held for their life and the life of the one of them living longer. William devised the tenement to his wife Mary for life and appointed that, after her death, there should be spent from it what seemed best to the master Thomas Upton. He also appointed that there should be spent from his tenement, land, meadows, feeding, pastures, reversions, and rents in Amesbury or Little Amesbury, Fugglestone near Wilton, Upton Scudamore, Norridge, Warminster, Leigh, and Coulston what seemed best to Thomas. <u>Executors</u>: Thomas, his kinsman John Warminster, Roger [Maidenhead], the vicar of Durnford, and Thomas Newman, to all of whom William gave full power to do with his goods what seemed best to them, providing that it was done at the order and discretion of Thomas, whom he nominated his principal executor. <u>Proved</u> on 30 June 1405 in front of an officer of the prebendal jurisdiction of Durnford; the administration was entrusted to Thomas Upton, Roger, the vicar of Durnford, and Thomas Newman, reserving the power to entrust it to John Warminster when he might come to seek it. Afterwards the executors appeared, accounted with the officer, and were dismissed. <u>Approved</u> at a court held in front of the bailiff, the mayor, and other citizens; the seisin of the room was released to the legatee.

1 June 1406, at Westminster
1931 Letters patent of Henry IV. Considering that two thirds of the city lies in the hands of clerics and outsiders and scarcely a third in the hands of citizens, so that the citizens cannot support the burdens of taxes and subsidies without serious harm, the king has granted to the mayor and commonalty of Salisbury, for 100 marks paid to him by them, that they and their successors might acquire land, tenements, and rent in the city to the value of 100 marks a year and, to mitigate those burdens, keep them for ever notwithstanding the Statute of Mortmain or that the land, tenements, and rent are held in chief, provided that it was ascertained by inquests held, and returned to Chancery, that no harm would be done to the king.

21 July 1406, at Salisbury
1932 By his deed John Cary granted to Richard Spencer, William Walter, William Warin, and William Bishop, citizens of Salisbury, his estate in a corner tenement, with shops and a gate, in Winchester Street and Brown Street, opposite Bull Hall, between a tenement, in which John Thorburn of late dwelt, in Winchester Street on the west side and a gate of that tenement in Brown Street on the north side. The tenement was held by John Cary and Margery, of late his wife, a daughter of John Thorburn and his wife Joan, by a grant of John and Joan, as is declared in a charter perfected for them, and the estate in it is to be held for ever by the grantees and their heirs and assigns. Seals: John Cary's and the common and mayoral seals of the city. Named witnesses: the bailiff, the mayor, a coroner, the reeves, William Warmwell, Adam Teffont, Richard Leach, William Sall, John Forest, and the clerk

28 July 1406, at Salisbury
1933 A deed of John Cary. Joan, the relict of John Thorburn, called Taylor, of late a citizen of Salisbury, holds for her life a tenement, with adjacent shops and a gate, in which she now dwells, in Winchester Street and Brown Street. The tenement, with the shops, stands in Winchester Street between William Hoare's tenement,

in which Henry Chubb, baker, now dwells, on the west side and a tenement of late John Cary's, now that of Richard Spencer, William Walter, William Warin, and William Bishop, on the east side. The gate stands in Brown Street. The reversion of the tenement, with the shops and the gate, pertains to John and his heirs, and John now granted it to Richard Spencer, William Walter, William Warin, and William Bishop so that on Joan's death the tenement should remain not to him and his heirs but to them and their heirs and assigns. John quitclaimed his right or claim to the tenement, with the shops and the gate, to the grantees and their heirs and assigns. Clause of warranty. Seals: John's and the common and mayoral seals of the city. Named witnesses: the mayor, the bailiff, a coroner, the reeves, William Warmwell, John Mower, Adam Teffont, Richard Leach, Edmund Enfield, William Sall, and the clerk

1934 A deed of John Cary. John Thorburn, called Taylor, and his wife Joan granted to John Cary and his wife Margery, now dead, a daughter of John and Joan, a corner tenement, with shops and a gate, in Winchester Street and Brown Street [*as in* **1932**], to be held for ever by John and Margery and their joint issue, as is declared in the charter perfected for them. Margery died without issue, John of late granted his estate in the tenement, with the shops and the gate, to Richard Spencer, William Walter, William Warin, and William Bishop, citizens of Salisbury, and now quitclaimed his right or claim to it to them and their heirs and assigns. Clause of warranty. Seals: John Cary's and the common and mayoral seals of the city. Named witnesses: the mayor, the bailiff, a coroner, the reeves, John Mower, William Warmwell, Adam Teffont, Richard Leach, William Sall, and the clerk

4 August 1406, at Salisbury
1935 By his charter John Montagu granted to Thomas Child, mercer, a citizen of Salisbury, a rent of a rose a year issuing from two tenements, which Margaret Godmanstone holds for life by John's grant, with the reversion of the tenements when it fell due on Margaret's death. The tenements stand conjoined in Winchester Street between a tenement of late John Butterley's, now Laurence Gowan's, on the west side and John Ettshall's tenement on the east side. John Montagu held them in fee simple by Margaret's grant. The rent and the reversion are to be held for ever by Thomas Child and his heirs and assigns. Clause of warranty. Seals: John's and the common and mayoral seals of the city. Named witnesses: the bailiff, the mayor, a coroner, the reeves, William Warmwell, John Mower, Richard Spencer, William Warin, William Walter, William Bishop, and the clerk

18 August 1406, at Salisbury
1936 Approval of the will of Agnes, the wife of Thomas Glover, a citizen of Salisbury, made on 10 July 1406. <u>Interment</u>: in the graveyard of St. Martin's church. <u>Bequests</u>: in each case in respect of that church 12*d.* to the fabric, 6*d.* to the vicar, the provost of St. Edmund's church, 6*d.* to Thomas Bennett, a chaplain, her confessor, 4*d.* each to John Aynel, a chaplain, and to the parochial chaplain,

and 2d. to each other chaplain; 20d. both to the Franciscans of Salisbury and the Dominicans of Fisherton to pray for her soul; 6d. each to the fabric of the cathedral church and the fabric of St. Edmund's church; a blue gown with rabbit fur to her daughter Agnes; a gown with rabbit fur to Alice Millward; a half piece of a silk veil and a blue kirtle to Maud, a veil of Paris to Alice, and a blue kirtle to Edith, each a maid of William Warin; a best blue hood to Alice Skinpain; 2s. 6d. to the lord John Wimborne, a canon of Christchurch, to celebrate a trental on behalf of her soul; 2s. 6d. to her kinsman the lord Alexander, a chaplain of Shaftesbury; 12d. to William, her household servant, and a green hood to his mother; the rest of her goods to her husband Thomas. <u>Devises</u>: to Thomas for life cottages, with a dovecot (*or* dovecots) and a garden (*or* gardens), on the way to St. Martin's church, between a tenement of late John Dogskin's on one side and the graveyard of St. Martin's church on the other side. The cottages, with their appurtenances, should be divided after Thomas's death among Agnes's children Agnes, William, John, and Richard to be held for ever by them and their issue, if the children were to die without issue they should remain to the elder Agnes's sister Maud and her issue, and if Maud were to die without issue they should be sold by Agnes's executors, if they were then surviving, or by their executors or subsequent executors. The money received should be laid out on behalf of Agnes's soul, the soul of Robert Harass, of late her husband, and the souls of others. Agnes begged William Warin and his wife Maud, her sister, to help her daughter Agnes in her advancement. <u>Executors</u>: her husband Thomas and William Warin. <u>Proved</u> on 28 July 1406 in front of an officer of the subdean; the administration was entrusted to the executors, appearing in person. <u>Approved</u> at a court held in front of the bailiff, the mayor, and other citizens; the seisin of the cottages, with the dovecot(s) and the garden(s), was released to the legatees.

15 September 1406, at Salisbury
1937 By their charter Robert Bowyer, weaver, and his wife Christine, appearing at the court held on that day, granted to a younger John Brown, of St. Edmund's college, and his wife Agnes, their daughter, two conjoined cottages, with small gardens extending as far as the garden of their own tenement, in Culver Street between John Mower's cottage property on the south side and cottages of late Gilbert Oword's on the north side. The cottages, with other tenements in the city, were of late held by Robert and Christine by a grant of Thomas Hill, carpenter, and are to be held for ever by John and Agnes and their heirs and assigns. Clause of warranty. Seals: those of Robert and Christine and the common and mayoral seals of the city. Named witnesses: the bailiff, the mayor, the coroners, the reeves, John Mower, Richard Spencer, William Walter, an elder John Forest, William Sall, and the clerk

1938 Approval of the will of Edmund Enfield, a citizen of Salisbury, made on 2 March 1404. <u>Interment</u>: in the chancel of St. Martin's church, on the right side of the monument to Alice, formerly his wife, in the tomb intended for his corpse, and beside his children interred there. <u>Bequests</u>: £4 3s. 4d. for celebrating 1,000 masses immediately after his death; £4 3s. 4d. to be handed out among feeble old people and sick paupers immediately after his death, before the day of his burial and nothing on that day; a silver bowl with a silver gilt cover, called Belle, to the lord John Chitterne, a canon of Salisbury; 20s. to the fabric of the cathedral church, 20s. to the high altar and the communion of canons, and 8s. 4d. to the communion of vicars on the day of his burial so that they might pray for his soul, to be divided among them if they wished; 6s. 8d. to the fabric of St. Martin's church; 3s. 4d. to the fabric of St. Edmund's church; 6s. 8d. to the parish church of Enfield, and his vestments of muslin, of a grey and red colour, with their tablecloths and corporal, to the altar of St. Nicholas in that church, to be there, as long as they might last, in the keeping of the proctors of that altar to celebrate mass in them on St. Nicholas's day and at the obits of him and his kinsmen if they were to be celebrated; 20s. to those proctors and to their successor proctors to buy for those obits two cows to be kept, the location of them according to the advice of the rector, and for holding the obit the rector will depute a chaplain or minister of that church; a banquet should be held on the day of his burial, both for his executors and for eight paupers carrying the torches and 20 other paupers; 6s. 8d. to the fabric of the church of Christ, Twineham; 6s. 8d. to two scholars of de Vaux college to be divided equally between them, a book of decretals to the library of the college to be chained there for ever, and a large oak mazer, to be carried to the graces after the early meal, to that college; a piece of silver *de secunda nova forma*, and a rosary of amber beads, with a necklace hanging with them, to a younger Edith Camel; six pieces of silver with a covering, *de nova forma*, to his wife Edith, and she shall have her portion without deception; two bundles of schedules relating to the office of the registrar of the archdeaconry and the office of notary, with a third-best gown, to Richard Willesden; a mazer, with a cover, called Goblet to John Whitmore; his best gown, with its hood, all the provincial and synodal regulations, and a book concerning the practice of bound paper, to William Algar, one of his executors; his second-best gown, with its hood, with his missal, to Edward Russell, one of his executors; 6s. 8d. to the lord William Spicer, the chaplain of St. Martin's; a gold ring with a sapphire to Margery Brewer; the rest of his goods to his executors to be disposed of on behalf of his soul and the souls of others. Edmund wished that his executors should enjoy the use of what was bequeathed to them provided that they carried out the administration, otherwise not. He wished that there should be delivered, each at his own expense, the host on high to St. John's hospital, Ludlow, a book called *Passipon* to the abbot of Hailes, and a book of the Trinities to the prior of Cricklade. <u>Devises</u>: to William Algar and Edward Russell, two of his executors, tenements in St. Martin's Street, which he bought from an executor (*or* executors) of John Justice, and a tenement called 'Stapult' Hall to be held for ever by them and their heirs and assigns so that they might be sold to him offering the most and paying immediately. The money received should be laid out by them among debtors, in part, and on behalf of his soul, the souls of his wife Edith, Robert Play, John Butterley, John at the pit, David Fletcher, and the souls of others. Edmund devised all his other tenements in Salisbury, except the principal tenement devised as follows to his wife Edith for her dower and the other tenements in which Edith is jointly enfeoffed with him, with the reversion of those excepted tenements, for ever to his children, if there should be any at the time of his death, and to their issue, to be divided equally among them. If any of the children were to die prematurely his or her portion should be added to that of the survivor or to those of the survivors. If all were to die all the tenements, with the reversions, would remain to Edmund's executors, or to their executors if his executors had died, to be held for ever by them and their heirs, so that they might be sold by the executors and the money laid out on the pious uses mentioned above. Edmund devised to Edith his principal tenement in St. Martin's Street for her dower, with the keeping of his children, heeding the mayor, as is customary, with the oversight of the executors, so that the children might be kept and governed well; otherwise the executors should take the keeping of the children together with their goods and rent. <u>Executors</u>: Edith and the lord William Algar and the lord Edward Russell, chaplains. <u>Proved</u> on 11 September 1406 in front of an officer of the subdean; the administration was entrusted to Edith and William, reserving the power to entrust it to Edward when he might come to seek it. On 15 September 1406 Edward appeared in front of the officer and the administration was entrusted to him as a co-executor. <u>Approved</u> at a court held in front of the bailiff, the mayor, and other citizens; the seisin of the tenements, with the reversion, was released to the legatees.

27 September 1406
1939 By his charter Richard Clark, of Pensford, granted to Thomas Castleton, of Salisbury, his son John, and their heirs and assigns the land, tenements, rent, reversions, and services which he held in the township of Salisbury, to be held by them for ever. Seals: that of Richard who, because his seal is unknown to many, procured the seal of the office of the mayor of Bristol to be likewise affixed. Witnesses: Thomas Bonham, a steward, John Gowan, the bailiff of the bishop of Salisbury, John Mower, Richard Spencer, William Warin, William Bailey, and many others.
1940 By his letters of attorney Richard Clark, of Pensford, appointed Gilbert Wick and John Gardener to place Thomas Castleton, of Salisbury, and his son John in full seisin of the land, tenements, rent, reversions, and services [*as in **1939***]. Seals: [*as in **1939***]

11 October 1406
1941 By his deed [*dated to 11 October in the 7th year of the reign of Henry IV (1405) evidently in error for that day in the 8th year of that reign (1406)*] Richard Clark, of Pensford, quitclaimed to Thomas Castleton, of Salisbury, his son John, and their heirs and assigns his right or claim to land, tenements, rent, reversions, and services [*as in **1939***]. Seals: [*as in **1939***]. Witnesses: [*as in **1939***]

8 December 1406, at Salisbury
1942 By their charter Thomas Bleacher, John Ferrer, and William Sivier, executors of John Canning, of late a citizen of Salisbury, on the strength of John's

will granted to Thomas Manning a corner tenement, in which John of late dwelt, opposite the market place where grains are sold, between a tenement of Agnes Lea on either side. The tenement was devised by John to be sold by his executors after the death of his wife Joan, who is now dead, and is to be held for ever by Thomas Manning and his heirs and assigns as that which Thomas acquired from the executors for a sum of money paid to them to fulfil John's will. Seals: those of the grantors and the common and mayoral seals of the city. Named witnesses: the bailiff, the mayor, the coroners, the reeves, William Warmwell, John Mower, Richard Spencer, William Walter, Thomas Child, and the clerk

22 December 1406, at Salisbury
1943 Approval of the will of Henry Berwick, a citizen of Salisbury, made on 25 October 1406. <u>Interment</u>: in the graveyard of the parish church of St. John the Baptist, Bishopstone. <u>Bequests</u>: 6s. 8d. to the fabric of the cathedral church; in each case to pray for his soul 2s. 6d. both to the Franciscans of Salisbury and the Dominicans of Fisherton, 20s. to the vicar of Bishopstone, 15d. to each chaplain in Bishopstone parish except the vicar, 6d. to each parochial clerk in Bishopstone church, 6d. to each of the other chaplains being present at his funeral rites and mass on the day of his burial, and 4d. to the beadsman there; two sheep to the light beside the image of St. John in the chancel of Bishopstone church, to keep it after his death into the hand of whomever it might have come; two sheep for St. Stephen's light likewise; 6d. to each of his godchildren; 12d. to the vicar of Bishopstone on condition that he would say six sequences of the gospel at the six crosses in Bishopstone and 'Bolebergh' or a psalter in the graveyard of Bishopstone; 5 marks to his brother John Smith; 20 marks to the fabric of a tower above Bishopstone church when the parishioners have begun to build it from new, to be paid within the four years from the start of the work at 5 marks a year; 20s. each to Dominic Uphill, his wife Alice, Robert Poole's wife Agnes, and Joan, the wife of John Crablane, [of] Salisbury; sufficient food and drink to all coming to his obit; a halfpenny loaf to each pauper coming to his burial; 2d. to the vicar of Bishopstone for the time being to celebrate two masses each week, on the Wednesday and the Friday, for the 38 years following his death on behalf of his soul and the souls of others, the 2d. to be received from his executors from a cottage of his in Throope; 2s. and two sheep to the fabric of Faulston church; 40d. to the light of the holy cross of Bishopstone; a best silver bowl and what is called a cup, with a best brass pot, to Thomas Stabber; 20d. to the light of St. Anne of Flamston; 2s. to Robert, a household servant of Dominic Uphill; a bell worth 22 marks to Bishopstone church; 6s. 8d. to John, a son of Dominic Uphill; 13s. 4d. to the lord John Oliver; the rest of his goods to his wife Agnes on condition that she would sell nothing of them except with the oversight of Thomas Stabber, and if she did otherwise half of the goods to Thomas and his wife Alice. His goods should be administered by none but his executors. <u>Devises</u>: to Thomas Stabber and his wife Alice a tenement, with shops, in which Robert Poole dwells, in Minster Street between a tenement of late Bartholomew Durkin's on the south side and Richard Leach's shops on the north side. The tenement was acquired

by Henry from an executor (*or* executors) of John Scammel [*otherwise* Camel: *cf.* ***1642***], hatter, and, with the shops, is to be held for ever by Thomas and Alice and their joint issue to find a chaplain to celebrate mass in Bishopstone church on behalf of Henry's soul for the seven years following his death. If Thomas and Alice were to die without such issue the tenement, with the shops, should be sold by Henry's executors, their executors, or subsequent executors. The money received should be laid out on pious uses on behalf of Henry's soul and the souls of others. Henry appointed that, if his movable goods were not sufficient to pay his debts and bequests, a tenement in Butcher Row, between John Barnaby's tenement on the west side and Gunnore Bowyer's tenement on the east side, should be sold by his executors or their executors and his will carried out with the money received. If his movable goods should be sufficient the tenement should be held for ever by Thomas Stabber and his wife Alice and their joint issue, and if Thomas and Alice were to die without such issue it should be sold by the executors. The money received should be laid out in the way described above. <u>Executors</u>: his wife Agnes, Dominic Uphill, and Thomas Stabber. <u>Proved</u> on 25 November 1406 in front of an officer of the archdeacon of Salisbury; the administration was entrusted to the executors. <u>Approved</u> at a court held in front of the bailiff, the mayor, and other citizens; the seisin of the tenements was released to the executors, then present and avowing the movable goods to be sufficient to carry out the will.

2 February 1407, at Salisbury
1944 By their charter William Algar and Edward Russell, chaplains, executors of Edmund Enfield, of late a citizen of Salisbury, on the strength of Edmund's will granted to Richard Spencer, a citizen of Salisbury, and his wife Edith tenements, with gardens, of late those of John Justice, a citizen of Salisbury, which Edmund acquired from John's executor (*or* executors), or of late William Upton's, which Edmund acquired from William Dunn, John Cole, and John Warminster. The tenements stand conjoined in St. Martin's Street, between a tenement of late John Lea's, which Roger Berwick holds, on the west side and a tenement of late John New's, which Thomas Cofford, tanner, of late held, on the east side, and, with the gardens, were devised by Edmund to his executors for sale. They are to be held for ever by Richard and Edith and Richard's heirs and assigns as that which Richard and Edith bought in good faith for a sum of money which William and Edward will lay out according to the tenor of the will. Seals: those of William and Edward and the common and mayoral seals of the city. Named witnesses: the bailiff, the mayor, a coroner, the reeves, William Warmwell, John Mower, William Walter, William Warin, Adam Teffont, William Sall, and the clerk

16 February 1407, at Salisbury
1945 By their deed John Starr and his wife Edith, a daughter and heir of Richard Frear, of late a citizen of Salisbury, and his wife Edith, appearing at the court held on that day, and especially Edith, who was examined in front of the mayor and the bailiff according to the custom of the city, not in fear, not coerced, but of her own volition, together, for themselves and their heirs and at all events for

Edith's, quitclaimed to Thomas Ryde, a son of the late Richard Ryde, a citizen of Salisbury, and William Walter, a citizen of Salisbury, and their heirs and assigns their right or claim, or Edith's right or claim, to a tenement in Culver Street between a tenement of late Richard Ryde's, in which Thomas Cook, a chaplain, was enfeoffed, on the south side and a tenement now Richard Butler's on the north side. Richard [?Frear or Ryde] built the tenement from new. Clause of warranty. Seals: those of John and Edith and the common and mayoral seals of the city. Named witnesses: the bailiff, the mayor, a coroner, the reeves, William Warmwell, John Mower, Richard Spencer, William Warin, Adam Teffont, William Sall, and the clerk

1946 By his charter an elder John Chandler, a citizen of Salisbury, granted to Nicholas Hayward, a merchant, a cottage and a house, with a sollar and a building called a skilling newly consructed within the cottage, and with the walls and fences constructed on the east side of them and attached or adjacent to them. The cottage measures in width 11 ft. at its frontage on the street and 12 ft. at the back, and in length with those other buildings 109 ft. from the street as far as a yard appurtenant to a cottage of the provost of St. Edmund's [?in New Street: *cf.* **1909**]. It stands in New Street on the way to Barnwell's cross, between Nicholas's own tenement, of late William Handley's, on the west side and a tenement which John Fry, weaver, holds, appropriated to the hospital of the Holy Trinity, called Almshouse, on the east side, and, with the buildings, walls, and fences, is to be held for ever by Nicholas and his heirs and assigns. Clause of warranty. Seals: John's and the common and mayoral seals of the city. Named witnesses: the bailiff, the mayor, a coroner, the reeves, William Warmwell, John Mower, Richard Spencer, Adam Teffont, Thomas Eyre, and the clerk

2 March 1407, at Salisbury

1947 By his charter John Gatcombe, called Sergeant, a citizen of Salisbury, granted to William Ashley, a chaplain, a son of William Ashley, of late a citizen of Salisbury, and John Smith, a chaplain, a tenement which he held by a grant of John Ashley, a brother of the younger William. The tenement stands in St. Martin's Street, between John at the marsh's tenement on the west side and a corner shop of late that of the elder William Ashley, which William Assendon and his wife Christine now hold, on the east side, and is to be held for ever by William and John and their heirs and assigns. Seals: John Gatcombe's and the common and mayoral seals of the city. Named witnesses: the bailiff, the mayor, a coroner, the reeves, William Warmwell, John Mower, Richard Spencer, John Needler, William Sall, an elder John Forest, and the clerk

1948 By his letters of attorney John Gatcombe, called Sergeant, of Salisbury, appointed Walter Short and Stephen Edington to surrender into the hand of Richard, the bishop of Salisbury, the seisin of a tenement in St. Martin's Street [*as in* **1947**], which he held by a grant of John, a son of William Ashley, of late a citizen of Salisbury, to the use of William, a chaplain, also a son of William Ashley, and John Smith, a chaplain. Seals: John Gatcombe's and the mayoral seal of the city

1949 By his charter Robert Deverill, a citizen of Salisbury, granted to an elder Nicholas Baynton and Stephen Edington a cottage, with a yard, and with a toft or portion of ground which he held by a devise of John Buddle, called Prentice, beside the city's ditch. The cottage, by the name of a shop, was held by Robert by a grant of John Polmond, of Southampton, who held it by a feoffment of Richard Marwood, called Callis. It stands in Wineman Street, between a cottage which Nicholas holds of the hospital of the Holy Trinity on the west side and an empty plot leading from Laverstock on the east side, and, with the ground, is to be held for ever by Nicholas and Stephen and their heirs and assigns. Clause of warranty. Seals: Robert's and the common and mayoral seals of the city. Named witnesses: the bailiff, the mayor, a coroner, the reeves, William Warmwell, John Mower, Richard Spencer, William Walter, William Warin, and Richard Jewell

1950 By her deed Alice, a daughter of Richard Thorburn, a brother of John Thorburn, called Taylor, of late a citizen of Salisbury, in her free and celibate power, quitclaimed to Richard Spencer, William Walter, William Warin, and William Bishop, citizens of Salisbury, and their heirs and assigns her right or claim to all the tenements, with shops and gates, which were of late John Thorburn's in Winchester Street and Brown Street between William Hoare's tenement, which Henry Chubb, baker, [holds], on the west side in Winchester Street and the common trench of running [water] in Brown Street on the north side. Seals: Alice's and the common and mayoral seals of the city. Named witnesses: the mayor, the bailiff, a coroner, the reeves, William Warmwell, John Mower, Adam Teffont, John Needler, William Sall, Thomas Child, and the clerk

1951 By his deed Robert Deverill, a citizen of Salisbury, granted to an elder Nicholas Baynton and Stephen Edington the estate which he held by a grant of Joan, the relict of Thomas Blunt, kt., in a yard or portion of ground in Wineman Street beside the city's ditch on the east side and a cottage of late his own, which John Smith holds, on the west side. The yard or portion of ground extends in length from the street as far as a wall appurtenant to a yard [?in Winchester Street] of John Barber, brazier, of late a citizen of Salisbury, and is to be held for ever by Nicholas and Stephen and their heirs and assigns according to the effect of Robert's acquisition of it. Seals: Robert's and the common and mayoral seals of the city. Named witnesses: the mayor, the bailiff, a coroner, the reeves, William Warmwell, John Mower, Richard Spencer, Adam Teffont, John Needler, John Forest, William Sall, and John Lewisham

1952 By their indented deed Nicholas Harding, the mayor of Salisbury and the master and keeper of the hospital of the Holy Trinity and St. Thomas of Canterbury, and an elder John Chandler, a citizen of Salisbury, the under-keeper, proctor, and principal overseer of the hospital, by a licence of the king and of a chaplain of the lord of the city granted to an elder Nicholas Baynton a cottage measuring 18 ft. at its frontage on the street, with a yard next to it, extending in length as far as a yard of Richard Butler's tenement beside Nicholas's tenement, in Culver Street; also a small cottage beside that cottage, and a small portion of ground behind it, measuring 13 ft. on the street. The two cottages stand in Wineman Street between cottages appropriated to the hospital, which were of late Bartholomew Durkin's, on the west side and Robert Deverill's tenement, of late John Polmond's, on the east side, were of late held by John Mayo, called Wilkin, and were surrendered by him to Nicholas Harding and John Chandler. They are to be held, with the yard and the other appurtenances, by Nicholas Baynton and his heirs and assigns of the mayor, his successors as mayor, and the masters and keepers of the hospital, from the day of the perfecting of this charter for 160 years, paying to them and their proctors and assigns a rent of 14s. cash a year for all other secular services owed to the chief lord. Nicholas Baynton and his heirs and assigns should repair and maintain the cottages in all things necessary at their own expense so that the rent would not be lost. Clause to permit re-entry if the rent were in arrear for a month, distraint, and the keeping of distresses until the unpaid rent was recovered; also, if distresses sufficient for the rent could not be found, to permit the mayor, his successors as mayor, and the masters and keepers to enter on Nicholas's tenements in Culver Street, beside the yard, distrain, and keep distresses until the unpaid rent was recovered. Clause of warranty in respect of the cottages until the end of the term, of acquittance in respect of the rent. Seals: John Chandler's, the common seal of the hospital, and the mayoral seal of the city to one part of the charter, Nicholas Baynton's to the part remaining in the possession of Nicholas Harding and John Chandler. Named witnesses: the bailiff, a coroner, the reeves, William Warmwell, John Mower, Richard Spencer, Adam Teffont, William Walter, William Warin, William Sall, and the clerk

16 March 1407, at Salisbury
1953 By his charter Thomas Biston, a citizen of Salisbury, granted to John Ruddock, weaver, and his wife Joan three cottages, with gardens, which he held by a grant of Margery, the relict of John Justice. The cottages stand in Culver Street between a gate of William Reynold's tenement on the south side and cottages of late John Camel's on the north side and, with the gardens, are to be held for ever by John and Joan and John's heirs and assigns. Clause of warranty. Seals: Thomas's and the common and mayoral seals of the city. Named witnesses: the bailiff, the mayor, a coroner, the reeves, William Warmwell, John Mower, Richard Spencer, Adam Teffont, John Needler, William Sall, and the clerk
1954 Approval of the will of Margery, the relict of John Justice, formerly a citizen of Salisbury, celibate in her widowhood, made on 22 February 1406. <u>Interment</u>: in the graveyard of St. Martin's church beside her husband's tomb. <u>Bequests</u>: in each case in respect of St. Martin's church, 40d. to the fabric, 20d. to the parochial chaplain, 12d. to each other chaplain celebrating mass on behalf of her soul, 6d. to the deacon, 6d. to the sacristan, 4d. to each fraternity of it, and 8d. in each year, for the seven years following her death, to the fraternity of the Holy Sepulchre in it; 12d. to Nicholas Brown, a chaplain; ½d. to be handed out on the day of her burial to each pauper present at her funeral rites; on the day of her burial 13 paupers should be clothed in white cloth; 30 lb. of wax made into candles and torches to be burned around her corpse; a missal to John Aynel, a chaplain, during his life, wherever he might be; after his death John should restore the missal to divine use in St. Martin's church, to be in service for ever for praying for

her soul, the souls of John Justice, John Dean, a chaplain, John Aynel, a priest, and the souls of others, and for restoring that book John should be bound by nothing but his own good faith; an iron pan for coals and a black box to John Aynel; a red box and a chest to Thomas Biston; a best coverlet to Agnes, the wife of Thomas Biston; 6d. each to Robert and John, servants of Peter Brazier; 12d. to Joan, who was a servant at Dean; a silver spoon each to Alice Barber and Maud Witts; 20d. to her goddaughter Margery Deverill; 20d. or her best kerchief to Christine Handley; her best cloak to Cecily Buffing, of Hill Deverill; her best tunic to Margery Reynold; her second-best tunic to Maud Berwick; her third-best tunic and an old brass paten to Joan Woodborough; 12d. to Alice, her servant; the rest of her goods to her executors to be sold and disposed of on behalf of her soul and the souls of those mentioned above; 20s. each to her executors for their work. Devises: to Thomas Biston a tenement, in which she dwelt, in Winchester Street between a tenement of late William Isaac's on the east side and cottage property of late John Upton's on the west side, to be held for ever by Thomas and his heirs and assigns. Margery charged Thomas, his heirs, or his executors to pay John Aynel, a chaplain, to celebrate mass in St. Martin's church for two years after her death, at the usual times until £10 had been paid, on behalf of her soul and the souls of those mentioned above, or an alternative chaplain if John should give up the celebration. Margery also devised to Thomas an empty piece of land, lying beside a ditch at the end of New Street on the east side and cottages of late Thomas Focket's on the west side, to be held for ever by him and his heirs and assigns. Executors: the lord John Aynel, a chaplain, and Thomas Biston, a citizen of Salisbury. Proved on 9 December 1406 in front of an officer of the subdean; the administration was entrusted to Thomas Biston, John Aynel appearing in person and expressly refusing it. Approved at a court held in front of the bailiff, the mayor, and other citizens; the seisin of the tenement was released to the legatees; the seisin of the empty piece of land was respited.

1955 By his charter Thomas Bleacher, ironmonger, a citizen of Salisbury, an executor of Robert Play, of late a citizen of Salisbury, on the strength of Robert's will granted to Nicholas Melbury, a citizen of Salisbury, a tenement in Endless Street between a tenement of late John Amesbury's, now John Mower's, on the south side and a tenement of late William Bleacher's, now Nicholas Harding's, on the north side. The tenement was devised by Robert to his executors to be sold, and it is to be held for ever by Nicholas and his heirs and assigns as that which Nicholas bought from Thomas in good faith for a sum of money paid to him in advance for Robert's will to be fulfilled. Seals: Thomas's and the common and mayoral seals of the city. Named witnesses: the bailiff, the mayor, a coroner, a reeve, William Warmwell, John Mower, Richard Spencer, John Needler, Walter Nalder, William Sall, and the clerk

1956 By his charter William Hill, a merchant, of Salisbury, granted to William Bishop and to William Dowding, a merchant, of Salisbury, the land, tenements, shops, cottages, rent, and reversions which he held in Salisbury on the day on which the charter was perfected. He also granted and released to them all his other goods and chattels, movable and immovable, which he had in the city or elsewhere. Everything granted is to be held for ever by William Bishop and William Dowding and their heirs and assigns. Clause of warranty in respect of the land, tenements, shops, and cottages. Seals: William Hill's and the common and mayoral seals of the city. Named witnesses: the bailiff, the mayor, a coroner, the reeves, William Warmwell, John Mower, Richard Spencer, William Warin, William Sall, and the clerk

1957 By his letters of attorney William Hill, a merchant, appointed Roger Enterbush and Henry Blackmoor to surrender into the hand of Richard, the bishop of Salisbury, the seisin of the land, tenements, shops, cottages, rent, and reversions, which he held in Salisbury, to the use of William Bishop and William Dowding, of Salisbury. Seals: William Hill's and the mayoral seal of the city

1958 An indented deed of Thomas Chaplin and his wife Joan. By means of a fine levied in the king's court on 12 November 1402 Thomas and Joan acknowledged three conjoined shops, by the name of a messuage, to be the right of John Judd as that which he had by their grant, and for that acknowledgement John granted the messuage to Thomas and Joan and the issue begotten between them. The messuage stands in Poultry, opposite Cordwainer Row, between Thomas Knoyle's tenement, which John Chamberlain, tailor, holds, beside a little lane there on the east side and a tenement of late Thomas Play's, which William Ripley, shearman, formerly held, on the west side. In default of such issue the reversion of it was reserved to John Judd and his heirs. Appearing at the court held on 16 March 1407 Thomas and Joan granted their estate in the messuage to Thomas Yeovil, tailor, and his wife Joan, and the estate and the messuage are to be held for ever by them and Thomas's heirs and assigns, paying to Thomas Chaplin and Joan and their heirs a rent of 52s. cash a year. In return for the rent Thomas Chaplin and Joan are obliged for their life to acquit Thomas Yeovil and Joan, and that Thomas's heirs and assigns, against the chief lord of the city for the rent due to him from the messuage. Clause to permit re-entry if the rent of 52s. were in arrear for a month, distraint, and the keeping of distresses until the unpaid rent was recovered; also, if the rent were in arrear for two months and sufficient distresses could not be found, to permit repossession by Thomas Chaplin and Joan and the issue begotten between them and the retention of their former estate. Clause of warranty in respect of the messuage and the estate, of acquittance in respect of the rent. Seals: those of Thomas Yeovil and Joan and those of Thomas Chaplin and Joan to the parts of indented deed in turn and the common and mayoral seals of the city. Named witnesses: the bailiff, the mayor, a coroner, the reeves, William Warmwell, John Mower, Richard Spencer, William Walter, William Warin, William Sall, and the clerk

1959 By his deed George Merriott, a citizen of Salisbury, quitclaimed to John Hampton, brewer, and his heirs and assigns his right or claim to a messuage or tenement, with shops, which John now holds and in which he dwells, [called Ive's Corner: *cf. 1960*], in Wineman Street and Mealmonger Street, opposite a corner tenement of late William Surr's, between a tenement of William Chapman, weaver, of late John Poulton's, on the west side and William Warmwell's cottage property in Mealmonger Street on the north side. The tenement, with the shops, was of late Ralph Ive's. Clause of warranty. George also released to John all personal actions against him on account of anything contracted between them. Seals: George's and the common and mayoral seals of the city. Named witnesses: the bailiff, the mayor, a coroner, the reeves, John Mower, William Warmwell, Richard Spencer, William Warin, John Lewisham, and the clerk

1960 By their writing William Dyke, of Winterbourne Ford, Peter Dyke, Richard Jewell, William Lord, and Thomas Felix, a clerk, quitclaimed to John Hampton, brewer, and his heirs and assigns their right or claim to a tenement or messuage, with shops, in which John now dwells, called Ive's Corner, in Wineman Street and Mealmonger Street [*as in 1959*]. Clause of warranty, provided that, although in the future the tenement or messuage might be recovered against John Hampton or his heirs, neither those who quitclaimed nor their heirs will pay anything towards its value by reason of the warranty. Those who quitclaimed also released to John all actions, pleas, and demands, real and personal, which they have, had, or could have against him. Seals: those of William, Peter, Richard, William, and Thomas and the common and mayoral seals of the city. Named witnesses: the bailiff, the mayor, a coroner, the reeves, John Mower, Richard Spencer, William Walter, William Warin, Adam Teffont, John Needler, and the clerk

1961 A deed of Robert Durrant, draper, an executor of Alice, of late his wife, the relict of Richard Hawes, hellier. Alice devised to Robert for life a tenement, with shops and a cottage (*or* cottages), in which he now dwells, in New Street between cottage property of the provost of St. Edmund's church on one side and John Wishford's cottage property on the other side. She appointed that after Robert's death the tenement should be sold by her executors or their executors, or that the executors might sell the reversion in his lifetime, with his assent, if it could be done advantageously. Robert, as an executor, because it was his fixed resolve to carry out Alice's will in his lifetime, on the strength of the will now granted to William Sall, a citizen of Salisbury, the reversion of the tenement, with the shops and other appurtenances, when it fell due on his death. The reversion, and the tenement when it fell due, are to be held for ever by William and his heirs and assigns as that which he bought from Robert in good faith for a sum of money which will be laid out on the salvation of Alice's soul according to her intention. Seals: Robert's and the common and mayoral seals of the city. Named witnesses: the bailiff, the mayor, a coroner, the reeves, John Mower, Richard Spencer, Adam Teffont, William Walter, William Bishop, and the clerk

30 March 1407, at Salisbury

1962 By his indented charter an elder John Chandler, a citizen of Salisbury, granted to Richard Jewell, a citizen of Salisbury, a tenement, in which Richard Sherman dwells, in Carter Street extending into Brown Street between, in Carter Street, a tenement formerly Edith Barber's, which Robert Wolf now holds, on the north side and a tenement formerly William Ferrer's, now that of Richard Cormell, called Knolle, on the south side and, in Brown Street, a tenement of late Richard Bartlet's on the north side and a tenement of late Alice Baldry's, now William Warmwell's, on the south side. The tenement is to be held for ever by Richard and his heirs and assigns, paying a rent of 5 marks cash a year to John, his executors, or his assigns at Easter for the following six years beginning at Easter next [1408]. Clause to permit re-entry if the rent were not paid in any year, distraint, and the keeping of distresses until the unpaid rent was recovered. Clause of warranty in respect of the tenement, of acquittance [in respect of the rent]. Seals: John's to one part of the charter, Richard's to the other part, and the common and mayoral seals of the city. Named witnesses: the bailiff, the mayor, a coroner, the reeves, John Mower, Richard Spencer, Adam Teffont, William Warin, William Bishop, Thomas Child, and the clerk

1963 By his letters of attorney an elder John Chandler, a citizen of Salisbury, appointed his son John and Stephen Edington to surrender into the hand of Richard, the bishop of Salisbury, the seisin of a tenement, in which Richard Sherman dwells, in Carter Street extending into Brown Street [*as in* **1962**] to the use of Richard Jewell, a citizen of Salisbury. Seals: the elder John's and the mayoral seal of the city

1964 By his charter William Guys, a citizen of Salisbury, granted to John Mabley, tucker, and his wife Edith cottages, with a yard [and] racks built in them, which, by the name of a messuage with its appurtenances, he held by a grant of John Needler, an elder John Chandler, and William Lord, citizens of Salisbury. The messuage, called Buckland's Place, stands in Freren Street between a stone wall of the Franciscans of Salisbury on the north side and a yard of St. Nicholas's hospital on the south side, and the racks built in the yard extend in length from the street as far as a little trench at the east end of those racks near the meadow called Bug moor; except a portion of ground beside the wall, with free ingress and egress, for roofing the wall when it might be necessary, as is contained in William's charter of acquisition. The cottages, with the yard and racks, except the portion of ground, are to be held for ever by John Mabley and Edith and their heirs and assigns. Clause of warranty. Seals: William's and the common and mayoral seals of the city. Named witnesses: the bailiff, the mayor, a coroner, the reeves, William Warmwell, John Mower, Richard Spencer, William Walter, William Warin, William Bishop, and the clerk

31 March 1407, at Salisbury

1965 A deed of William, a son of John Bleacher. Robert Play, of late a citizen of Salisbury, devised to William, his kinsman, a tenement in Endless Street between a tenement of late John Amesbury's, now John Mower's, on the south side and a tenement of late that of William Bleacher, William's uncle, now Nicholas Harding's, on the north side. In his will there was a condition which Robert wished William to observe and, if William refused to observe it, Robert devised the tenement to be sold by his executors. William refused to observe the condition, it is agreeable to him that to fulfill Robert's will the executors have sold the tenement to Nicholas Melbury and his heirs and assigns, and he quitclaimed to Nicholas and his heirs and assigns his right or claim to it. Seals: William's and the common and mayoral seals of the city. Named witnesses: the bailiff, the mayor, a coroner, a reeve, William Warmwell, John Mower, Richard

Spencer, William Walter, and William Sall

27 April 1407, at Salisbury
1966 By his deed John Judd quitclaimed to Thomas Yeovil, tailor, and his wife Joan and to Thomas's heirs and assigns his right or claim to three conjoined shops, by the name of a messuage, which Thomas and Joan hold by a grant of Thomas Chaplin and his wife Joan. The messuage stands in Poultry [*as in* **1958**]. Clause of warranty. Seals: John's and the common and mayoral seals of the city. Named witnesses: the bailiff, the mayor, a coroner, the reeves, John Mower, Richard Spencer, William Warin, William Sall, Thomas Child, William Tull, and the clerk

22 June 1407, at Salisbury
1967 By his deed John Chitterne, a clerk, granted to Stephen Edington, of Salisbury, a portion of land or a yard, which Stephen now holds and which Robert Deverill of late held by a grant of Joan, the relict of Thomas Blunt, kt., in Wineman Street between the city's ditch on the east side and a tenement of late Robert's, now Stephen's, on the west side. The land is to be held for ever by Stephen and his assigns, to whom John quitclaimed his right or claim to it. Seals: John's and the common and mayoral seals of the city. Named witnesses: the mayor, John Mower, Richard Spencer, William Walter, William Warin, Richard Jewell, William Sall, and William Lord

29 June 1407, at Salisbury
1968 By his charter an elder John Chandler, a citizen of Salisbury, granted to a younger John Bodenham, of Wilton, a rent of a rose a year issuing from a corner tenement, with shops, which John Stoke, of Salisbury, holds for life of John Chandler in Minster Street and Winchester Street between shops of late Adam Inways's above a ditch on the east side and shops of late John Oxford's, beside Thomas Marshall's tenement in Minster Street, on the north side; also the reversion of the tenement, with the shops, when it fell due on the death of John Stoke. The rent and the reversion are to be held for ever by John Bodenham and his heirs and assigns. Clause of warranty. Seals: John Chandler's and the common and mayoral seals of the city. Named witnesses: the bailiff, the mayor, a coroner, the reeves, William Warmwell, John Mower, Richard Spencer, William Warin, Richard Jewell, William Bishop, and the clerk
1969 By his deed an elder John Chandler, a citizen of Salisbury, granted to William Bishop, a citizen of Salisbury, and Thomas Bellidge two messuages or tenements which he held by a grant of an elder William Lord. One, of late that of Robert Bunt, a citizen of Salisbury, in which John Duckton has for long dwelt, stands in Castle Street between John Fosbury's tenement on the north side and Thomas Viport's tenement on the south side. The other stands in Freren Street between a cottage of late Edmund Enfield's on either side. They are to be held for ever by William and Thomas and their heirs and assigns. Seals: John's and the common and mayoral seals of the city. Named witnesses: the bailiff, the mayor, a coroner, the reeves, William Warmwell, John Mower, Richard Spencer, William

Warin, Richard Jewell, William Dowding, and the clerk

1970 By his letters of attorney an elder John Chandler, a citizen of Salisbury, appointed his son John and Stephen Edington to surrender into the hand of Richard, the bishop of Salisbury, the seisin of two messuages, one in Castle Street and one in Freren Street [*as in **1969***], to the use of William Bishop, a citizen of Salisbury, and Thomas Bellidge. Seals: John's and the mayoral seal of the city

31 August 1407, at Salisbury
1971 Approval of the will of Nicholas Brown, a chaplain, made on 29 June 1407. Interment: in St. Edmund's church in front of St. Nicholas's altar. Bequests: 20s. to the fabric of that church but 6s. 8d. if he were to be interred outside it, 6s. 8d. to the provost, and 20d. to each collegiate chaplain; 40d. to the fabric of the cathedral church; 6s. 8d. to the fabric of St. Thomas's church; 6s. 8d. to the fabric of St. Martin's church, and 7s. to the fraternity of the Holy Sepulchre to have him and the soul of Joan Ringwood in its prayers for the following seven years; 12d. to each annual chaplain of St. Edmund's church to be present at his funeral rites and to bear his corpse to his grave; 6d. to each chaplain of St. Martin's church to do likewise; 6d. to each chaplain of St. Thomas's church to do likewise if he should happen to die in the house which is now a hospital; he of the chaplains who absented himself from those matters should have 4d.; 6s. 8d. to the fabric of St. Nicholas's church, Fyfield, and 3s. 4d. to the light of St. Nicholas in it; 20d. to the fabric of the church of Andover, and 20d. each to the lights of the Blessed Mary, the Holy Cross, and St. Nicholas of that church; 3s. 4d. each to the fabric of the chapel of [East] Cholderton and the fabric of the church of Weyhill; 3s. 4d. both to the Franciscans of Salisbury and the Dominicans of Fisherton to be present at his funeral rites and to bear his corpse to his grave; 3s. 4d. to the community in the hospital of the Holy Trinity called Almshouse; 6s. 8d. to his kinswoman Maud, the wife of John Shipton, and her two children, and 3s. 4d. to her daughter Agnes; 6s. 8d. each to an elder John Bosham, called Pope, and his son John; 20d. each to Joan Wither, Agnes Lord, and one Alice, staying with Richard Coof; 6s. 8d. to Alice, the relict of John Baker, with whom he was housed, 3s. 4d. to her son John Cann, 20d. to her son Robert, 12d. to John Scot, staying with them, 2s. to Maud, Alice's servant, and 6d. to each of her other servants; 20s. to be handed out among paupers on the day of his burial; 6s. 8d. each to his kinswoman Joan, the wife of John Hayward, and Felice, the wife of Roger Taylor, of Amport, and her children; 13s. 4d. to the wife of John Pewsey, of Penton, and her sister, to be received between them; six silver spoons, being in his keeping, to Robert Salter; 6s. 8d. each to Stephen Edington, John Brown, of Chute, and John's wife; a tunic of russet, with a hood, to John Calf, and Nicholas remits the debt which John owes to him; 100s. to his kinsman Nicholas Brown, one of his executors; the rest of his goods to be disposed of by Nicholas on behalf his soul. Devise: to Nicholas two cottages, which John Harnham, weaver, now holds [and] dwells in, in New Street between William Warmwell's corner tenement, in which William Ildsley dwells, on the west side and Thomas Bleacher's tenement, of late Robert Play's, on the east side, to be held for ever by Nicholas and his heirs and assigns.

Executors: Nicholas Brown, and Stephen Edington as an assistant to him. Proved on 2 August 1407 in front of William Spaldwick, a canon of Salisbury, deputed to carry out episcopal jurisdiction in certain places and causes, the seat of the bishop being vacant; the administration was entrusted to the executor. Approved at a court held in front of the mayor, the bailiff, and other citizens; the seisin of the cottages was released to the legatees.

14 September 1407, at Salisbury
1972 By his deed John Judd granted to Thomas Yeovil, tailor, and his wife Joan, the reversion of three conjoined shops, by the name of a messuage, in Poultry, opposite Cordwainer Row, [*as in 1958*], which John held by a grant of Thomas Chaplin and his wife Joan by means of a fine levied in the king's court. The reversion, and the messuage when it fell due on the death of Thomas Chaplin and Joan, are to be held for ever by Thomas Yeovil and Joan and Thomas's heirs and assigns. Clause of warranty. Seals: John's and the common and mayoral seals of the city. Named witnesses: the mayor, a coroner, the reeves, William Warmwell, John Mower, Richard Spencer, Richard Jewell, Thomas Child, and the clerk
1973 By his indented charter William Warmwell, a citizen of Salisbury, granted to Robert Warmwell, of Salisbury, a tenement, of late John Wallop's, which William acquired from an elder John Chandler, a citizen of Salisbury, in Scots Lane between a tenement of late Thomas Sexhampcote's on either side; also a rent of 5s. a year, which William acquired from Robert Hazelbury, a citizen of Salisbury, issuing from another tenement there, now Robert Linden's and of late Thomas Sexhampcote's, between the tenement mentioned above on the east side and a tenement now that of John Butler, mercer, on the west side. The tenement and the rent are to be held for ever by Robert Warmwell and his [heirs and] assigns, paying to William and his assigns for William's life 31s. 8d. cash a year. Robert and his heirs should maintain the tenement in all things necessary at their own expense so that the rent of 31s. 8d. would not be lost. Clause to permit repossession of the tenement and the rent of 5s. for William's life if the rent of 31s. 8d. were in arrear for 15 days; alternatively, if William and his assigns preferred, to permit re-entry on the tenement, distraint, and the keeping of distresses until the unpaid rent was recovered. The rent of 31s. 8d. is not to be extinguished on William's death, and the tenement is to descend for ever to Robert and his heirs. Clause of warranty in respect of the tenement and the rent of 5s., of acquittance in respect of the rent [of 31s. 8d.]. Seals: those of William and Robert to the parts of the indented charter in turn and the common and mayoral seals of the city. Named witnesses: the mayor, a coroner, the reeves, John Mower, Richard Spencer, William Warin, William Walter, William Sall, and the clerk

28 September 1407, at Salisbury
1974 By his charter William Lord granted to Peter Dyke a garden, which John Coombe, weaver, now holds, in Culver Street, between Thomas Biston's garden on the north side and a garden of late Thomas Focket's on the south side, to be held for ever by Peter and his heirs and assigns. Clause of warranty. Seals:

William's and the common and mayoral seals of the city. Named witnesses: the mayor, a coroner, the reeves, John Mower, William Warmwell, Richard Spencer, Walter Nalder, Thomas Mason, draper, and the clerk

1975 By his letters of attorney William Lord appointed Thomas Dereham and George Goss to surrender into the hand of ... [*MS. blank*], the bishop of Salisbury, the seisin of a garden in Culver Street [*as in* **1974**] to the use of Peter Dyke. Seals: William's and the mayoral seal of the city

12 October 1407, at Salisbury
1976 By his charter Thomas, a son and heir of John Beeton, of late a citizen of Salisbury, granted to Thomas Bleacher, ironmonger, and Severin at the oak a tenement in Castle Street, between a tenement of late Reynold Drury's, now that of Edward Gilbert, dubber, on the south side and a tenement of late Roger Fowle's, now Thomas Farrant's, on the north side, to be held for ever by Thomas and 'Severinus' and their heirs and assigns. Clause of warranty. Seals: Thomas Beeton's and the common and mayoral seals of the city. Named witnesses: the mayor, a coroner, the reeves, William Warmwell, Adam Teffont, John Needler, William Bishop, Thomas Mason, draper, and the clerk

26 October 1407, at Salisbury
1977 By their charter John Mabley, tucker, and his wife Edith, appearing at the court held on that day, granted to Stephen Leonard ('Lythenard'), tucker, and his wife Emme cottages, with a yard, and [with] racks built in them, which they held by a grant of William Guys, a citizen of Salisbury. The cottages stand in Freren Street between a portion of land, small in width, beside a stone wall of the Franciscans on the north side and a yard of St. Nicholas's hospital, the possessors of the wall to have free ingress and egress through the yard and cottages to repair the wall when necessary. The racks built in the yard extend from Freren Street as far as a little trench, at the east end of the racks, near the meadow called Bug moor. The cottages, with the yard and racks, except the free ingress and egress, are to be held for ever by Stephen and Emme and their heirs and assigns. Clause of warranty. Seals: those of John and Edith and the common and mayoral seals of the city. Named witnesses: the bailiff, the mayor, a coroner, the reeves, John Mower, Richard Spencer, William Walter, Adam Teffont, William Sall, Thomas Eyre, and the clerk

9 November 1407, at Salisbury
1978 Approval of the will of Robert Kirtlingstoke, a citizen of Salisbury, made on 14 November 1406. Interment: in St. Thomas's church in front of the altar of St. Michael, for which he appointed 6s. 8d. to the fabric of that church. Bequests: ½ mark to the rector of St. Thomas's church for his forgotten tithes, and 6s. 8d. to William Upavon, a chaplain of that church; a gown, with a hood, to John Richman, of Avon; 5s. to provide a candle to burn in front of the images of St. John the Baptist and St. John the Evangelist in the church of Little Woodford, to pray for his soul and the souls of others, and, thus provided, for the candle to

burn there henceforward if his executors should have the wherewithal to bring that about; the rest of his goods to his executors to be disposed of; ½ mark cash to John Judd, one of his executors, for his work; from the rest of his goods all his debts should be paid in full. Devises: to his daughters Margaret and Agnes the reversion of a corner tenement, with shops and a tavern, opposite the fishermen's stalls, beside shops formerly Thomas Bowyer's, now those of William Slegge, weaver, and of a tenement in Endless Street which John Parch of late held of him for a term of years. The reversion of the two tenements, with the shops and the tavern, when it fell due on the death of his wife Joan, is to be held for ever by Margaret and Agnes and their issue, and if Margaret and Agnes were to die without issue the tenements, with the tavern and the shops, should be sold by his executors, their executors, or subsequent executors. The money received should be laid out by the executors on celebrating masses and other divine services and on alms and other charitable deeds by whom and when seemed best to the executors, as they would be willing to answer for before God and all his saints, on behalf of Robert's soul, the souls of his wife Joan, their parents and their children, William Ashton, and Robert Godmanstone, and the souls of others. Robert devised to Margaret and Agnes a tenement, with a yard (*or* yards), in Endless Street, between a tenement formerly Alice Hungerford's on the south side and a tenement formerly John Ellis's on the north side, which John Richman, formerly a citizen of Salisbury, devised to him and his issue. The tenement, with the yard(s), is to be held for ever by Margaret and Agnes and their issue, and if Margaret and Agnes were to die without issue, which God forbid, should be sold by the executors. The money received should be laid out on celebrating masses and other alms on behalf of Robert's soul, the souls of his wife Joan, his children, and John Richman, and the souls of others. Executors: the lord William Upavon, a chaplain, John Judd, a merchant, who should give effect to the will consensually. Proved on 8 November 1407 in front of John Chandler, the dean of Salisbury, who, the subdeanery being vacant, had jurisdiction in the city and its suburbs; the administration was entrusted to the executors. Approved at a court held in front of the mayor, the bailiff, and other citizens; the seisin of the tenements was released to the legatees.

23 November 1407, at Salisbury
1979 Approval of the will of William Mercer, a citizen of Salisbury, made on 10 July 1407. Interment: in St. Edmund's church near the altar of the Holy Trinity beside the tomb of his daughter Joan. Bequests: 10s. to the fabric of the cathedral church; 100s. to the fabric of a new building of St. Edmund's church, 20s. to the provost for his forgotten tithes and lesser benefactions, 12d. to each chaplain of the college, 6s. 8d. to Nicholas Stoke, a chaplain, 12d. to the deacon, and 6d. to the sacristan; 40d. to the fabric of St. Martin's church; 6s. 8d. to the fabric of St. Thomas's church; 40s. to the fabric of Pentridge church; 20s. to the fabric of East Garston church; 6s. 8d. to the fabric of Ashampstead church; 12d. to each bedridden pauper in the hopital called Almshouse, 6d. to each other pauper wandering into it, and 12d. to each chaplain of it to pray for his soul; 6d. to each

prisoner in the Guildhall, the houses of the serjeants-at-mace, and the castle of Old Sarum; 2*d*. to each prisoner at Newgate, 4*d*. to each prisoner at Ludgate, and 6*s*. 8*d*. in each case to the prisoners in the King's Bench, the King's Marshalsea, and the Fleet; 20*s*. for its maintenance to the bridge which was to be built anew near St. Nicholas's hospital at the end of Drake Hall Street, 20*s*. to three other bridges in the market place, and 6*s*. 8*d*. to Ayleswade bridge; 20*s*. to the maintenance of the way beneath Clarendon called Hamptons way; 6*s*. 8*d*. each to the way from Wantage called Townsherd, the way from Walhampton at the bridge, the way between Colebrooke and Langford, the way between Langford and 'Smalmalet', and the way leading towards Newnham hill; 40*d*. to the bridge of 'Grauniford'; 20*s*. to the way from Hook; £20 to each bedridden pauper in Salisbury, except the paupers of the Almshouse, and for all his other funeral expenses on the day of his burial; £10 to each needy and destitute pauper now living, from whom he bought cloth, in Wiltshire and Somerset in mitigation of their poverty, to be handed out in equal portions by his executors; £20 to needy masters, and to paupers, with whom he traded in London, to be handed out by his executors in equal portions; 13*s*. 4*d*., his second-best tunic, a second-best coat, and 20 sheep to John Cripps, of East Garston; £10 to his kinswoman Christine for her marriage, and 50 sheep just as they come out of the flock; 40*s*. each to John Neale and Catherine, his servants; 40*d*. to Richard, his servant; 10*s*. each to Alice and Gifford, his servants; 40*s*., a plain tunic, and 20 sheep to a younger John Cripps; 40*s*. to an elder John Hain, loader; 20 sheep to a younger John Hain; 40 sheep to John at the mill, of Gomeldon; £20 to John Purvis, of London, so that he might attend to the fulfilling of his will and the levying of his debts; 100*s*. to John Judd; 400 sheep in Henry Chasey's flock, and £200 of the debts in the hand of John Purvis, to his wife Edith; any sheep which remain beyond those bequeathed above are to be sold by his executors for the salvation of his soul; the rest of his goods to his executors to be disposed of on behalf of his soul. <u>Devises</u>: to Edith for life a tenement, in which he dwells, in Wineman Street between Robert Bowyer's tenement on the east side and John Lewisham's tenement on the west side, and two tenements, which Adam Daubeney of late held and which were of late those of Walter Clopton, kt., at the east end of Pot Row. On Edith's death the tenement in Wineman Street should remain to his kinswoman Christine to be held for ever by her and her issue, and if Christine were to die without issue it should be sold by William's executors, their executors, or subsequent executors. The money received should be laid out on celebrating masses, giving alms to paupers, repairing ways and bridges, and doing other charitable deeds for the salvation of William's soul and the souls of others. After Edith's death the other two tenements should be sold by the executors, and the money received should be laid out in the way described above. William devised to Edith for life a mediety of the manor of Salterton, with the liberties and franchises appurtenant to it, and a mediety of land, tenements, rent, services, reversions, meadow, pasture, and feedings in Salterton, Newton, Netton, and Durnford. After Edith's death the mediety of the manor should be sold by the executors, and the money raised should be laid out on the salvation of William's soul and the souls of others.

John Judd is to be preferred before all others in the purchase of the mediety. Executors: John Judd and John Purvis; overseer, William's wife Edith. Proved on 16 July 1407 in front of John Perch, a clerk, a registrar of the court of Canterbury, a commissary general of the archbishop of Canterbury; the administration was entrusted to the executors. Approved at a court held in front of the bailiff, the mayor, and other citizens; the seisin of the tenements was released to the legatees.

7 December 1407, at Salisbury
1980 Approval of the will of William Higdon, baker, of Wilton, made on 16 June 1398. Interment: in the graveyard of the Dominicans of Wilton. Bequests: 40d. to the fabric of the cathedral church; 20d. to the fabric of the church of the Blessed Michael, South Street, Wilton; 40d. to Robert Stonard, baker, of Salisbury; 20s. each to a younger John Bodenham, of Wilton, and John Staggard, of Salisbury; the rest of his goods to his wife Agnes. Devise: to Agnes for life two tenements, with a yard (*or* yards) adjacent, in Minster Street [*cf.* ***1982–3***] between Robert Body's tenement on the south side and a tenement of an elder John Needler on the north side. On Agnes's death the tenements, with the yard(s), should remain for ever to William's son John and John's issue, and if John were to die without issue they should be sold by William's executors or their executors. The money raised should be laid out by the executors on behalf of William's soul. Executors: his wife Agnes, the younger John Bodenham, and John Staggard. Proved on 30 July 1398 in front of an officer of the archdeacon of Salisbury; the administration was entrusted to the executors. Approved at a court held in front of the mayor, the bailiff, and other citizens; the seisin of the tenements was released to the legatee.

4 January 1408, at Salisbury
1981 By his charter John Ettshall, a citizen of Salisbury, granted to John, a son of Walter Chandler, and his wife Tamsin a tenement, in which that John now dwells and which he himself held by a grant of John Newman and Nicholas Harding, citizens of Salisbury, in Carter Street between a tenement of late that of an elder John Chandler, now his son John's, on the north side and Thomas Knoyle's tenement, which Robert Wolf holds, on the south side, to be held for ever by John Chandler and Tamsin and John's issue. Seals: John Ettshall's and the common and mayoral seals of the city. Named witnesses: the mayor, the bailiff, a coroner, the reeves, John Mower, Richard Spencer, William Warin, Thomas Child, William Dowding, and the clerk
1982 By their indented deed John Cole, baker, and his wife Agnes, the relict of William Higdon, of late a citizen of Salisbury, appearing at the court held on that day, granted to Robert Stonard and his wife Gillian the estate which Agnes held for her life by a devise of William in two conjoined tenements, with a yard (*or* yards) adjacent, in Castle Street [*cf.* ***1980, 1983***] between a tenement of late Robert Body's on the south side and John Needler's tenement on the north side. That estate is to be held by Robert and Gillian and their assigns for a yearly rent of 58s. 8d. cash to be paid to Agnes and her assigns for Agnes's life, and Robert

and Gillian and their assigns are to maintain the tenement in all things necessary at their own expense so that the rent would not be lost. Clause to permit re-entry if the rent were in arrear for a month, distraint, and the keeping of distresses until the unpaid rent was recovered. Clause of warranty in respect of the tenements, of acquittance in respect of the rent. Seals: those of the parties to the parts of the deed in turn and the mayoral seal of the city. Named witnesses: the bailiff, the mayor, a coroner, the reeves, John Mower, William Warmwell, Richard Spencer, Nicholas Harding, Walter Shirley, and the clerk

1983 A deed of John Cole, baker, and his wife Agnes, the relict, and an executor, of William Higdon, baker, of late a citizen of Salisbury. William devised to Agnes for life two tenements, with a yard (*or* yards) adjacent, in Minster Street, which is called Castle Street, [*as in* ***1980, 1982***]. He appointed that on Agnes's death the tenements, with the yard(s), should remain for ever to his son John and John's issue, and if John were to die without issue they should be sold by his own executors. The money received should be laid out on the salvation of William's soul. Robert Stonard, baker, who held Agnes's estate in the tenements, in the presence of the mayor and other citizens gave a sum of money to Agnes, as William's executor, reaching the true value of the reversion of the tenements, with the yard(s), for the reversion on Agnes's death, and by their deed John Cole and Agnes, she as an executor, in court and on the strength of William's will granted the reversion to Robert and his wife Gillian. The reversion, and the tenements, with the yard(s), when they fell due on Agnes's death, are to be held for ever by Robert and Gillian and Robert's heirs and assigns as that which Robert bought in good faith from Agnes, the executor, for that sum of money to be spent on the salvation of William's soul. Seals: those of John Cole and Agnes and the common and mayoral seals of the city. Named witnesses: the bailiff, the mayor, a coroner, the reeves, John Mower, William Warmwell, Richard Spencer, Nicholas Harding, Walter Shirley, William Sall, and the clerk

1984 By his charter Edmund, a son and heir of Thomas Friday and his wife Joan, granted to Roger Enterbush, of Salisbury, two cottages, with a yard (*or* yards), which Edmund Enfield, a clerk, built from new and which Roger held of Edmund Friday. The cottages stand in Mealmonger Street between a tenement of William Mead, weaver, on the south side and cottage property of Adam Dummer on the north side. They are to be held, with the yard(s), for ever by Roger and his heirs and assigns, to whom Edmund Friday quitclaimed his right or claim to them. Clause of warranty. Seals: Edmund's and the common and mayoral seals of the city. Named witnesses: the bailiff, the mayor, a coroner, the reeves, John Mower, William Warmwell, Richard Spencer, John Needler, John Lewisham, and the clerk

18 January 1408, at Salisbury

1985 Approval of the will of Alice, the wife of George Merriott, esq., a citizen of Salisbury, and the relict of a younger William Tenterer, made on 13 November 1406. <u>Interment</u>: in the chapel, of late that of the younger William Tenterer, a citizen of Salisbury, in St. Thomas's church. <u>Bequests</u>: 20*s*. to the high altar of that church for her neglected tithes and oblations, 20s. to the fabric, and 12d. to each chaplain to pray for her soul; 6d. to each friar of the Dominican order at Fisherton and of the Franciscan order at Salisbury, to pray for her soul; a rosary of silver beads with a gilded crucifix to the fabric of the cathedral church; 4d. to each man and woman being in the Almshouse to pray for her soul; 2d. to each prisoner in the castle of Old Sarum, the Guildhall, and the keeping of the serjeants to pray for her soul; a blue gown, furred with grey, to Gunnore Bowyer; 6s. 8d. each to William Upavon, a chaplain, and Nicholas Tucker, a chaplain, to pray for her soul; 12d. to each of her godsons; a crimson kerchief of six pleats to Joan, the wife of John Brute, of Hindon; a russet gown furred with rabbit to Catherine Rider; 6s. 8d. to Richard Brewer, her servant; all her old vestments (*viz.* coats, kirtles, smocks, cloaks, and hoods) to the order of her husband George Merriott; a tan cloak to John Hemingby, and a red and blue cloak to his wife Isabel; the rest of her goods to her husband; a broad mazer to the house and convent of St. Thomas of Acre, London, a bell[- metal] mazer to the house and convent of the Franciscans of Salisbury, and a bowl mazer to the house and convent of the Dominicans of Fisherton, in each case to be kept and drunk from, to pray for her soul, and not to be sold; two harnessed girdles, gilded, to be sold, and the money received to be laid out on behalf of her soul; a pair of beryl beads to be sold, and the money received to be laid out on masses and other charitable deeds on behalf of her soul and the souls of others. [*There follows a passage of about 460 words written in English to the following effect*] Alice charged William Warmwell, of Salisbury, an executor of the younger William Tenterer, of late her husband, to lay out the gold and money which he had received, and would receive, from Cold Corner and the place in which she wove, in Salisbury, on alms to poor men and women, on broken bridges and staples, and on making feeble ways about the city on behalf of William's soul, the souls of his mother and father, and the soul of Alice herself according to William's will. William Warmwell had received, or would receive, 200 marks of gold, and more of money, from the sale of those tenements, and Alice asked the bishop of Salisbury to order him to spend it as he was required to. Alice bequeathed £100 to the commonalty of the city, which was to be applied by the arbitrament of John Mower, Richard Spencer, John Wallop, and others to discharge the tallages imposed on it, and she enjoined that the £100 from the sale of George's Inn should be applied on behalf of William Tenterer's soul at the arbitrament of John Mower, Richard Spencer, William Walter, and Nicholas Harding according to indentures perfected between them, the mayor for the time being, and Alice. [*Whereafter the text of the will is again in Latin*] <u>Devises</u>: to her husband George a tenement in New Street, between John Needler's tenement on the west side and John Gilbert's tenement on the east side, opposite Walter Nalder's tenement and a tenement of late John Kingsbridge's on the south side, to be held by him for ever so that he might find a chaplain to celebrate mass for four years in St. Thomas's church. Alice also devised to George a corner tenement in Southampton, in St. John's parish, between a tenement formerly John Fivemark's on the east side and French Street on the west side, opposite a bridge called Wool bridge, to be held for ever by George and his heirs and assigns. <u>Executor</u>: her

husband George. Proved on 7 January 1408 in front of an officer of the subdean; the administration was entrusted to the executor in the presence of the discreet men Thomas Randolph and John Hemingby. Approved at a court held in front of the mayor, the bailiff, and other citizens; the seisin of the tenement in Salisbury was released to the legatee.
1986 By their deed William Upavon, a chaplain, and John Judd, a merchant, executors of Robert Kirtlingstoke, of late a citizen of Salisbury, on the strength of Robert's will, for a sum of money paid to them in advance, granted and quitclaimed to John Stone, of Wilton, and his wife Joan, a daughter and heir of John Ashley, their right or claim to all Robert's land and tenements in Salisbury. The land and tenements are to be held for ever by John and Joan and John's heirs. Seals: those of William Upavon and John Judd and the common and mayoral seals of the city. Named witnesses: the bailiff, the mayor, a coroner, the reeves, William Warmwell, John Mower, Richard Spencer, William Warin, William Dowding, and the clerk
1987 By his charter William, a son and heir of Walter Chippenham and his wife Alice, granted to his kinsman John Chippenham, of Salisbury, and Nicholas Sutton all his land, tenements, meadow, feeding and pasture, rent, and reversions in Salisbury, or in the vill or fields of Newton Tony, to be held for ever by John and Nicholas and their heirs and assigns. Clause of warranty. Seals: William's and the common and mayoral seals of the city. Named witnesses: the bailiff, the mayor, a coroner, the reeves, John Mower, William Warmwell, Richard Spencer, William Warin, William Walter, Walter Shirley, and the clerk
1988 By his letters of attorney William, a son and heir of Walter Chippenham and his wife Alice, appointed Stephen Edington and Walter Short to surrender into the hand of Robert, the bishop of Salisbury, the seisin of all the land and tenements, which he held in Salisbury, to the use of his kinsman John Chippenham, of Salisbury, and Nicholas Sutton; also to release to them the seisin of all the land, tenements, meadow, feeding and pasture, rent, and reversions which he held in the vill or fields of Newton Tony. Seals: William's and the mayoral seal of the city
1989 By his indenture Roger Enterbush, of Salisbury, granted to Edmund, a son of the late Thomas Friday, two cottages, with a yard (*or* yards), which Roger held by Edmund's grant and which Edmund Enfield, a clerk, built and held. The cottages stand in Mealmonger Street [*as in* **1984**] and, with the yard(s), are to be held by Edmund and his assigns of Roger and his heirs and assigns for the life of Edmund for a rent of a rose a year, for discharging the rents and services owed to the chief lord of the city, and for maintaining and repairing the cottages in all things necessary at their own expense. Clause of warranty. Seals: those of the parties to the parts of the indenture in turn and the mayoral seal of the city. Named witnesses: the bailiff, the mayor, a coroner, the reeves, John Mower, Richard Spencer, William Walter, John Lewisham, and the clerk
1990 By his charter John Swift, ironmonger, a citizen of Salisbury, granted to William Warin, grocer, a citizen of Salisbury, two cottages, by the name of a tenement, with a yard (*or* yards), which he and John Barber, brazier, now deceased, held by a grant of Thomas Sexton, a citizen of Salisbury. The cottages,

in Castle Street, beyond the bar, between a tenement of late John Upton's on one side and John Homes's tenement on the other side, were held by Thomas by a grant of John Dinton, a butcher, and, with the yard(s), are to be held for ever by William and his heirs and assigns. Seals: John's and the common and mayoral seals of the city. Named witnesses: the bailiff, the mayor, a coroner, the reeves, John Mower, Richard Spencer, William Warmwell, William Walter, Thomas Child, Walter Shirley, and the clerk

12 March 1408, at Salisbury
1991 By his deed of Nicholas, a son of John Newman, grocer, of late a citizen of Salisbury, acknowledged that he had received from an elder John Forest and Nicholas Harding, executors of his father, £53 cash, and various bonds, securities, and evidences by means of which Henry Clark and Henry Pay were bound to his father in the sum of £200, in full satisfaction of everything that he could claim from his father's goods and chattels, and quitclaimed to John and Nicholas personal actions of every sort against them. Seals: that of Nicholas who, because his seal is unknown to many, procured the mayoral seal of the city to be affixed. Named witnesses: Richard Spencer, John Mower, William Warin, William Walter, Walter Shirley, Henry Summer, and Mark the fair

14 March 1408, at Salisbury
1992 Approval of the will of Adam Wardour, a citizen of Salisbury, made on 17 January 1396. Interment: in the graveyard of St. Edmund's church. Bequests: 12*d*. to the fabric of that church; all his implements appurtenant to the art of fulling to his son Thomas; the rest of his goods to his wife Margaret. Devise: a tenement in Nuggeston, in which he dwelt, with the adjacent cottage property, racks, and garden ground, should be sold, to John Needler as a principal if he wished to have it. The money received should be divided into three parts, one for his wife Margaret, one for his son Thomas and his daughter Agnes, and one to pay his debts. Adam appointed to Margaret anything which remained [of the third portion]. Executors: Margaret, and the lord John Jakes, a chaplain, Adam's confessor, as overseer. Proved on 29 January 1396 in front of an officer of the subdean; the administration was entrusted to the executor. Approved at a court held in front of the bailiff, the mayor, and other citizens; the sale of the tenement, with the seisin of it, was entrusted to Margaret.
1993 By his charter Robert Hazelbury, of Salisbury, granted to John Durnford, dyer, of Salisbury, a tenement in Castle Street between Edward Breamore's tenement on the south side and a tenement of John Sexhampcote, the vicar of Whiteparish, on the north side. The tenement was acquired by Robert from William Shipton, of Salisbury, an executor of Hugh Winterbourne, of late a citizen of Salisbury, and is to be held for ever by John and his heirs and assigns. Seals: Robert's and the common and mayoral seals of the city. Named witnesses: the bailiff, the mayor, a coroner, the reeves, William Warmwell, John Mower, Richard Spencer, William Warin, William Walter, John Needler, Nicholas Harding, John Forest, Walter Shirley, William Sall, William Dowding, and the

clerk

1994 A deed of Joan, the relict, and an executor, of Robert Arnold, of late a citizen of Salisbury. Robert devised to Joan for life two tenements, with adjacent shops, in Endless Street, one between a tenement of late Henry Pope's on the south side and a tenement of late that of John Christchurch, a chaplain, on the north side, and one between a tenement of late William Godmanstone's on the south side and cottages of late William Higdon's on the north side. On Joan's death the tenements should remain for ever to Robert's son Edmund and his issue, and if Edmund were to die without issue they should be sold by Robert's executors or their executors. The money received should be laid out by the executors on behalf of Robert's soul and the souls of others. Edmund has entered into holy orders without living issue whereupon he seems to have no estate in the tenements unless for his life, the reversion of the tenements on Joan's death pertains to her as executor to be sold, and Richard Weston, weaver, now holding the tenements, has advanced a sum of money for the reversion [and] to acquire the tenements on the death of Edmund and Joan. Joan has in part disposed of that money to the commonalty of the city to pray for Robert's soul, and as an executor of Robert on the strength of his will now granted the reversion to Richard and his wife Alice. The reversion, and the tenements, with the shops, when they fell due, are to be held for ever by Richard and Alice and Richard's heirs and assigns as that which Richard bought from Joan in good faith for that sum of money to be spent in accordance with Robert's will. Seals: Joan's and the common and mayoral seals of the city. Named witnesses: the bailiff, the mayor, a coroner, the reeves, John Mower, Richard Spencer, William Warmwell, William Walter, Walter Shirley, and the clerk

28 March 1408, at Salisbury
1995 By his writing William Shipton, of Salisbury, an executor of Hugh Winterbourne, quitclaimed to John Durnford, dyer, of Salisbury, and his heirs and assigns his right or claim to a tenement in Castle Street [*as in **1993***]. Clause of warranty. Seals: William's and the common and mayoral seals of the city. Named witnesses: the bailiff, the mayor, a coroner, the reeves, William Warmwell, John Mower, Richard Spencer, William Warin, William Walter, John Needler, Nicholas Harding, William Sall, John Forest, Walter Shirley, William Dowding, and the clerk

1996 By their charter Richard Harlwin, goldsmith, and his wife Margery, appearing at the court held on that day, granted to John Chitterne, a clerk, a messuage or tenement, with adjacent shops, which was of late that of John Gilbert, a chaplain, a son of Thomas Gilbert, of late a citizen of Salisbury. The messuage or tenement, with the shops, stands in Minster Street, which is called Castle Street, between a tenement of late that of John Wallop, draper, which Thomas Steer now holds, on the north side and a tenement of late that of an elder George Goss, now that of Thomas Mason, draper, on the south side, and is to be held for ever by John Chitterne and his heirs and assigns. Clause of warranty. Seals: those of Richard and Margery and the common and mayoral seals of the city. Named witnesses:

the bailiff, the mayor, a coroner, the reeves, William Warmwell, Richard Spencer, Adam Teffont, Richard Jewell, and the clerk

1997 By his deed Thomas, a son and heir of Adam Wardour, called Ward, sealer, of Salisbury, quitclaimed to John Needler, draper, a citizen of Salisbury, and his heirs and assigns his right or claim to a messuage or tenement, with a yard (*or* yards) and racks, which was of late Adam's, in Nuggeston between a tenement formerly John Stalbridge's, now John Lake's, on the east side and a tenement formerly Peter Bennett's, now John Needler's, on the west side. Clause of warranty, provided that, although the messuage might have been recovered from John or his heirs or assigns, neither Thomas nor his heirs would contribute to the value. Seals: Thomas's and the common and mayoral seals of the city. Named witnesses: the bailiff, the mayor, a coroner, the reeves, John Mower, Richard Spencer, William Warin, Richard Leach, John Forest, and the clerk

11 April 1408, at Salisbury
1998 By his deed [*dated to the Wednesday of the feast of St. Ambrose (4 April) probably in error for the Wednesday after that feast (11 April)*] John Needler, a citizen of Salisbury, an executor of an elder John Needler, of late a citizen of Salisbury, quitclaimed to John Chitterne, a clerk, and his heirs and assigns his right or claim to a tenement, with adjacent shops, in Minster Street, which is called Castle Street, [*as in 1996*]. The tenement, with the shops, was of late that of Thomas Gilbert, a citizen of Salisbury, and afterwards that of his son John, a chaplain. Seals: John Needler's and the common and mayoral seals of the city. Named witnesses: the bailiff, the mayor, a coroner, the reeves, John Mower, Richard Spencer, William Warmwell, William Warin, William Dowding, and the clerk

1999 By her deed Margaret, the relict of Adam Wardour, called Ward, sealer, for a sum of money paid to her in advance quitclaimed to John Needler, a citizen of Salisbury, and his heirs and assigns her right or claim under Adam's will or otherwise to a messuage, with a yard (*or* yards) and racks, which was of late Adam's, in Nuggeston [*as in 1997*]. Clause of warranty, provided that, although the messuage might have been recovered from John or his heirs or assigns, neither Margaret nor her heirs would contribute to the value. Seals: Margaret's and the common and mayoral seals of the city. Named witnesses: the bailiff, the mayor, a coroner, the reeves, John Mower, William Warmwell, Richard Spencer, William Warin, William Lord, and the clerk

2000 By their deed Thomas Collins, weaver, and his wife Agnes, a daughter of the late Adam Wardour, called Ward, sealer, appearing at the court held on that day, and upon an examination of Agnes in front of the mayor and the bailiff, quitclaimed to John Needler, a citizen of Salisbury, and his heirs and assigns their right or claim, or Agnes's right or claim, to a messuage, with a yard (*or* yards) and racks, which was of late Adam's, in Nuggeston [*as in 1997*]. Clause of warranty, provided that, although the messuage might have been recovered from John or his heirs or assigns, neither Thomas nor Agnes nor their heirs would contribute to the value. Seals: those of Thomas and Agnes and the common and mayoral seals of the city. Named witnesses: the bailiff, the mayor, a coroner, the reeves, John

Mower, Richard Spencer, William Warmwell, William Warin, and William Lord

2001 By his deed an elder John Forest, a citizen of Salisbury, quitclaimed to Thomas Castleton, a citizen of Salisbury, and his heirs and assigns his right or claim to all the land, tenements, shops, cottages, rent, and reversions which he held by Thomas's grant in Salisbury, Devizes, Marlborough, or elsewhere. He also released to Thomas and his heirs and executors all actions, real and personal, against him which he had, or could have, by reason of any grant of Thomas's goods or chattels, movable or immovable, made to him by Thomas before the date of the deed or by reason of any other cause. Seals: John's and the common and mayoral seals of the city. Named witnesses: the bailiff, the mayor, a coroner, the reeves, John Mower, Richard Spencer, John Needler, Nicholas Harding, William Sall, and the clerk

2002 A charter of a younger William Lord, an executor of Robert Play, of late a citizen of Salisbury. In his will Robert appointed that two conjoined shops in Ironmonger Row, between shops of late John Talbot's on one side and shops which Robert held by a feoffment of Nicholas Baker on the other side, should remain on the death of his wife Margaret, now dead, to Robert and Edmund, sons of Thomas Play, and their issue, and if Robert and Edmund were to die without issue that they should be sold by the first Robert's executors or their executors. The money received should be laid out on behalf of the first Robert's soul and the souls of others. Robert and Edmund have died without living issue, so that the shops pertain to the executors of the first Robert to be sold. Because Thomas Bleacher, one of the executors, often asked by William Lord, has refused to do that, on the strength of the will William granted the shops to Gunnore, the relict of Thomas Boyton, and her son Robert Ogbourne to be held for ever by them and their heirs and assigns as that which Gunnore and Robert bought from him in good faith for a sum of money, reaching the true value of the shops, to be laid out on behalf of Robert's soul and the souls of others. Seals: William's and the common and mayoral seals of the city. Named witnesses: the bailiff, the mayor, a coroner, the reeves, William Warmwell, John Mower, Richard Spencer, Adam Teffont, Richard Leach, John Needler, William Walter, William Warin, Nicholas Harding, John Forest, William Sall, and the clerk

25 April 1408, at Salisbury
2003 By their writing John Codford, a chaplain, and Thomas Bleacher, an executor of Robert Play, of late a citizen of Salisbury, quitclaimed to Gunnore, the relict of Thomas Boyton, and her son Robert Ogbourne and their heirs their right or claim to two conjoined shops in Ironmonger Row [*as in* **2002**], which a younger William Lord, an executor of Robert Play, on the strength of Robert's will sold to Gunnore and Robert. Seals: those of John and Thomas and the common and mayoral seals of the city. Named witnesses: the bailiff, the mayor, a coroner, the reeves, William Warmwell, John Mower, Richard Spencer, William Warin, William Walter, Adam Teffont, John Needler, Nicholas Harding, William Sall, and the clerk

2004 By his deed Thomas Felix, a clerk, quitclaimed to John Hampton, brewer, and his heirs and assigns his right or claim to a corner messuage or tenement, with shops and a cottage (*or* cottages), which John now holds, was of late Ralph Ive's, and is called Ive's Corner, in Wineman Street and Mealmonger Street between a tenement of William Chapman, weaver, which was of late John Poulton's, on the west side and William Warmwell's cottage property in Mealmonger Street on the north side. Seals: Thomas's and the common and mayoral seals of the city. Named witnesses: the bailiff, the mayor, a coroner, the reeves, John Mower, William Warmwell, Richard Spencer, John Needler, William Sall, and the clerk

9 May 1408, at Salisbury
2005 By his deed John, a son of Thomas Castleton, a citizen of Salisbury, quitclaimed to Thomas and his heirs and assigns his right or claim to a tenement, with shops, in which Thomas dwells, opposite the market where fleeces and the yarns of wool are sold, between a tenement of the dean and chapter of Salisbury on the south side and a tenement of William Boyton, called Bowyer, on the north side; also to a tenement in St. Martin's Street between a tenement of the provost and college of St. Edmund's on the west side and a tenement which Robert Tawell holds of the choristers of the cathedral church on the east side; also to the reversion of a tenement, with shops, which Robert Reading holds, in the high street, which is called Minster Street, between William Pickard's tenement on the south side and a tenement of late Thomas Chaplin's, beside Pinnock's Inn, on the north side; also to the land, tenements, rents, and reversions which, with an elder John Forest, a citizen of Salisbury, he held by Thomas's grant in Devizes, Marlborough, or elsewhere. John also released to Thomas all actions against him which he had, or could have, by reason of any grant of Thomas's goods or chattels, movable or immovable, made to him by Thomas before the date of the deed, except the grant to him of three tenements, with shops and a cottage (*or* cottages), called Guys's Place, in Carter Street, [and] Focket Place and Clark's Place, in St. Martin's Street and Gigant Street. Seals: John Castleton's and the common and mayoral seals of the city. Named witnesses: the mayor, a coroner, the reeves, John Mower, Richard Spencer, William Walter, John Forest, William Sall, and the clerk

4 July 1408, at Salisbury
2006 By his charter Robert Hazelbury, of Salisbury, granted to Walter Shirley, a merchant, a newly built tenement, in which he dwelt and which, by the name of a toft, he acquired from John Hurst and his wife Joan, a daughter and heir of Roger Wallop, of late a citizen of Salisbury. The tenement stands in Castle Street, between a gate of Walter's tenement, which was of late John Wallop's, on the south side and a tenement of late Richard Ludd's, now William Bower's, on the north side, and is to be held for ever by Walter and his heirs and assigns. Clause of warranty. Seals: Robert's and the common and mayoral seals of the city. Named witnesses: the bailiff, the mayor, a coroner, the reeves, John Mower, William Warmwell, Richard Spencer, William Warin, William Walter, William Sall, and the clerk

2007 By his letters of attorney Robert Hazelbury, of Salisbury, appointed Roger Enterbush, Walter Short, and John Sibley to surrender into the hand of Robert, the bishop of Salisbury, the seisin of a newly built tenement, which he acquired [*as in* **2006**] in Castle Street [*as in* **2006**] to the use of Walter Shirley. Seals: Robert Hazelbury's and the mayoral seal of the city

18 July 1408, at Salisbury
2008 By his indented deed Walter Shirley, a merchant, a citizen of Salisbury, granted to Robert Hazelbury, of Salisbury, and his wife Margaret a tenement, in which Robert and Margaret now dwell and which Walter held by Robert's grant, in Castle Street [*as in* **2006**]. The tenement is to be held by Robert and Margaret and their assigns for the life of Robert and Margaret and the life of the one of them living longer, paying to Walter and his assigns a rent of a rose a year and maintaining and repairing the tenement in all things necessary at their own expense. Clause of warranty, the reversion after the death of Robert and Margaret always belonging to Walter and his heirs and assigns. Seals: those of the parties to the parts of the indented charter in turn and the mayoral seal of the city. Named witnesses: the bailiff, the mayor, a coroner, the reeves, John Mower, William Warmwell, Richard Spencer, Nicholas Harding, Thomas Mason, and the clerk

26 September 1408, at Salisbury
2009 By his charter John Wishford granted to Richard Gage a corner tenement, with shops, a cottage (*or* cottages), and a garden, in New Street and Shit Lane, between a tenement and cottage property of late Thomas Focket's, now John Castleton's, on the south side and a tenement of late Richard Hawes's, which Robert Durrant now holds, on the east side. The tenement, with the shops and cottage(s), was held by John Wishford by a feoffment of John Wallop, an executor of Agace, the relict of Thomas Shove, a citizen of Salisbury, and is to be held for ever by Richard and his heirs and assigns. Clause of warranty. Seals: John Wishford's and the common and mayoral seals of the city. Named witnesses: the mayor, the bailiff, the reeves, William Warmwell, John Mower, Richard Spencer, William Warin, Nicholas Harding, Thomas Eyre, and the clerk

7 November 1408, at Salisbury
2010 By their deed Thomas Stabber and his wife Alice, a daughter and heir of Henry Berwick, at the court held on that day, quitclaimed to Richard Gage and his heirs and assigns their right or claim, or Alice's right or claim, to a rent of 13*s.* 4*d.* a year when it fell due on the death of Alice's mother Agnes. The rent issues from a tenement, in which Richard now dwells and which he held by Henry's grant, in Castle Street between a tenement of John Sexhampcote, a chaplain, which John Durnford holds, on the south side and a tenement of Edward Gilbert, dubber, of late Reynold Drury's, on the north side. Clause of warranty. Seals: those of Thomas and Alice and the common and mayoral seals of the city. Named witnesses: the bailiff, the mayor, the reeves, John Mower, William Warmwell, Richard Spencer, William Walter, Nicholas Harding, and the clerk

21 November 1408, at Salisbury
2011 Approval of the will of Alice, the relict of John Barber, brazier, made on 5 January 1408. <u>Interment</u>: in St. Edmund's church beside John's tomb. <u>Bequests</u>: 3s. 4d. to the fabric of the cathedral church; 20s. to the fabric of St. Edmund's church, 3s. 4d. to the high altar for her forgotten tithes, 2s. to the parochial chaplain, 6d. to each member of the college, 6d. to the deacon, 4d. to the sacristan, and 6d. to each other chaplain; 6s. 8d. to the fabric of St. Martin's church; 2s. to the fabric of St. Thomas's church; 6s. 8d. both to the Franciscans of Salisbury and the Dominicans of Fisherton; 12d. to the hospital of the Holy Trinity; a brass pot worth 6s. 8d. to the fabric of St. John's church, Alderbury; 40s., a belt furnished with silver, a silver seal, and six silver spoons to her son Peter, a ring of gold from Paris and a gown, with a hood and furred, to his wife Christine, and 6s. 8d. to his daughter Alice; 40s., a fifth gold ring, a green belt furnished with silver, with bells, and six silver spoons to her son John, a plain gold ring and a gown of medley with fur of grey to his wife Agnes, and 40d. to William, a servant dwelling with him; another gold ring and 20s. to John Patcham; a fourth gold ring to Christine, the wife of John Pope; 3s. 4d. to Maud, the wife of Adam White; a noble or a noble's worth, and 3s. 4d. or the value, to Joan, a daughter of John Pope; 6s. 8d. to her goddaughter Alice Pipards; 12d. to each of her other godchildren; a pan worth 2s., or 2s., to each of Thomas Tonner, Richard Staggard, Thomas Durrington, John Fry, Richard Spindler, an elder John Palmer, William Sivier, Edmund Durley, David, Edmund Pinkbridge, Adam Doley, John Palmer, Agnes Whitehead, and William Preston; 3s. 4d. to Thomas Farnborough; 12d. to Thomas, her servant; 6s. 8d. each to Thomas Wheeler and Alice, her servant; 10s., or chattels worth 10s., to John Avon, her servant; 40d., and the debt which he owes to her, to John Goslin; 40d. to Agnes, the wife of William Reynold; 6d. to Robert Milton; a blood-red gown with fur to Joan Pope; 12d. to William Diggon; 6s. 8d. to improve the way under Clarendon opposite Sharp gore; 26s. 8d. to an elder John Pope on condition that he would take on the administration of her will; the rest of her goods to her sons Peter and John so that they might find a chaplain to celebrate mass on behalf of her soul for a year in St. Edmund's church if there was sufficient, and they should dispose of freely whatever might be left over; £4 3s. 4d. to be handed out among paupers on the day of her burial, ½d. to each pauper. <u>Devises</u>: to her son Peter a chief tenement, in which she dwells, with a gate and a way next to it on the west side, together with a vacant plot and all the other houses called workhouses, with the adjacent garden at the back, in Winchester Street between Thomas Knoyle's tenement, which Adam White now holds, on the east side and another tenement of Alice, newly built, and part of a garden of Thomas Knoyle, on the west side, to be held for ever by Peter and his heirs and assigns, paying a rent of 5s. cash a year for ever to her son John and his heirs and assigns. If the rent were in arrear for 15 days John and his heirs and assigns might enter on the tenement, distrain, and keep distresses until the unpaid rent was recovered. Alice devised to John the newly built tenement, with a sollar above the gate devised to Peter, in

Winchester Street between the gate and the way of the chief tenement on the east side and Thomas Knoyle's garden on the west side. The tenement measures in length 65½ ft. westwards from the way as far as the vacant plot, in length 63½ ft. along the east side, and in width at the back 25½ ft., and, with the sollar, is to be held for ever by John and his heirs and assigns. That tenement, with the sollar, and the chief tenement were held jointly by John Barber and Alice by a grant of Christine Dowding, as appears in a charter perfected for them. Alice wished that Peter should hold an obit for John and her in St. Edmund's church for the 16 years following her death. Executors: her son John and John Pope. Witnesses: John Wootton, Adam White, Thomas Tonner, Adam Doley, and others. Proved at London on 20 September 1408 in front of John Perch, a registrar of the court of Canterbury; the administration was entrusted to Alice's son John, reserving the power to entrust it to John Pope when he might come to be admitted. Approved at a court held in front of the mayor, the bailiff, and other citizens; the seisin of the tenements was released to the legatees.

2012 By his deed Thomas Wheeler, an executor of John Barber, brazier, of late a citizen of Salisbury, released to John Goslin, bell-founder, a son of Alice, of late John's wife, his right or claim by reason of John Barber's will or otherwise to a tenement which Alice's son John held by Alice's devise. The tenement stands in Winchester Street beside a tenement, in which John Barber and Alice lived, between that chief tenement on the east side and Thomas Knoyle's garden on the west side. Seals: Thomas Wheeler's and the common and mayoral seals of the city. Named witnesses: the mayor, the bailiff, a coroner, the reeves, John Mower, Richard Spencer, Nicholas Harding, John Lewisham, Thomas Ryde, and the clerk

19 December 1408, at Salisbury
2013 By their deed Thomas of Tyldesley, Hugh of Tyldesley, and Richard Enterbush, a chaplain, quitclaimed to John Riggs, a chaplain, and his heirs and assigns their right or claim to a tenement, of late that of John Stoke, tailor, which John Crablane, dyer, of late held and dwelt in. The tenement stands in Salisbury, at the east end of the upper bridge of Fisherton, on the way to the Dominicans, between a tenement of late Philip Goldsmith's on the east side and the Avon on the west side. Seals: those of Thomas, Hugh, and Richard and the common and the mayoral seals of the city. Named witnesses: the mayor, the bailiff, the reeves, William Warmwell, Richard Spencer, William Walter, William Lord, and the clerk

16 January 1409, at Salisbury
2014 By his charter John Riggs, a chaplain, granted to John Mower, a citizen of Salisbury, a tenement, which John Crablane, dyer, of late held and dwelt in, at the east end of the upper bridge of Fisherton [*as in* **2013**], to be held for ever by John Mower and his heirs and assigns. Seals: John Riggs's and the common and mayoral seals of the city. Named witnesses: the mayor, the bailiff, a coroner, the reeves, William Warmwell, Richard Spencer, William Warin, William Bishop,

William Sall, and the clerk

13 February 1409, at Salisbury
2015 By his indented charter John Brute, of High Swindon, granted to Thomas Bernard, called Bower, draper, a corner tenement, which he acquired from Walter Rodway and his wife Alice, a daughter and heir of John Scot, of late a citizen of Salisbury. The tenement [Grandon's Corner: *cf. 2017*] stands, opposite the market place and in Wineman Street, between a tenement of William Boyton, called Bowyer, which was formerly Roger Buckland's, on one side and a small trench of running water beside William Sall's tenement in Wineman Street on the other side, extends from the vicinity of the market place as far as the trench, and is to be held for ever by Thomas and his heirs and assigns. Clause of warranty. The grant was made, and the seisin given, on condition that Thomas, or any other on his behalf, would pay for the tenement to John or his assigns £60 cash at Salisbury at the following times: £20 at Easter 1409 or within 15 days after it, £10 on 2 February 1410 or within 15 days, and £10 on 2 February or within 15 days for each of the following three years. If Thomas makes such payments the charter and the seisin shall keep their force and effect. Clause to permit repossession, and the retention of John's former estate, if Thomas were to default in any payment. Seals: those of the parties to the parts of the indented charter in turn and the common and mayoral seals of the city. Named witnesses: the bailiff, the mayor, a coroner, the reeves, John Mower, Richard Spencer, William Warin, William Sall, Nicholas Melbury, and the clerk

2016 By her deed Joan, the relict of John Gatcombe, called Sergeant, in her widow's right and power, quitclaimed to William Sall and Nicholas Melbury, citizens of Salisbury, and their heirs and assigns her right or claim to a tenement, with shops and rooms, in which John dwelt. The tenement stands, opposite the market place where grains are sold, between William Tull's tenement, of late Thomas Burford's, on the west side and Nicholas Melbury's tenement, which John Shad, draper, holds, on the east side. Clause of warranty. Seals: Joan's and the common and mayoral seals of the city. Named witnesses: the mayor, the bailiff, a coroner, the reeves, John Mower, William Warmwell, Richard Spencer, William Bishop, Nicholas Harding, and the clerk

20 February 1409, at Salisbury
2017 By their deed an elder John Grandon, of Salisbury, and a younger John Grandon, the rector of Kislingbury, quitclaimed to Thomas Bernard, called Bower, draper, and his heirs and assigns their right or claim to a corner tenement, called Grandon's Corner, opposite the market place and in Wineman Street, [*as in 2015*]. Clause of warranty. Seals: those of the elder John and the younger John and the common and mayoral seals of the city. Named witnesses: the mayor, the bailiff, a coroner, the reeves, John Mower, William Warmwell, Richard Spencer, William Warin, William Sall, and the clerk

27 February 1409, at Salisbury

2018 By his writing William, a son of John Staggard, quitclaimed to Simon Bradley, baker, and his heirs and assigns his right or claim to a tenement, in which Simon dwells and which he held by a grant of William's father John, in Scots Lane between shops of late William Woodrow's, now William Dunning's, on the east side and a tenement of late Thomas Sexhampcote's on the west side. Seals: William Staggard's and the common and mayoral seals of the city. Named witnesses: the mayor, the bailiff, a coroner, the reeves, John Mower, Richard Spencer, William Warin, William Sall, Thomas Mason, draper, and the clerk

13 March 1409, at Salisbury
2019 By their charter William Sall and Nicholas Melbury, citizens of Salisbury, granted to a younger John Bodenham, of Wilton, a tenement, with shops and rooms, in which John Gatcombe, called Sergeant, of late dwelt, opposite the market place where grains are sold [*as in* **2016**]. The tenement, with other land and tenements in Salisbury, was held by William and Nicholas by a grant of John Gatcombe, and, with the shops and rooms, is to be held for ever by John Bodenham and his heirs and assigns. Seals: those of William and Nicholas and the common and mayoral seals of the city. Named witnesses: the bailiff, the mayor, a coroner, a reeve, William Warmwell, John Mower, Richard Spencer, William Warin, William Bishop, and the clerk

27 March 1409, at Salisbury
2020 By his indented deed a younger John Bodenham, of Wilton, granted to Joan, the relict of John Gatcombe, called Sergeant, a tenement, with shops and rooms, in which that John of late dwelt, opposite the market place where grains are sold [*as in* **2016**]. The tenement, with the shops and rooms, is to be held for her life by Joan and her assigns of John and his heirs and assigns, paying a rent of a rose a year to John and his heirs and assigns, performing all services due to the chief lord of the city, and maintaining and repairing the tenement in all things necessary at their own expense. If they failed to do that, or caused waste, loss, or ruin, the parties agree to submit themselves to the arbitrament of four honourable men, to be chosen on both sides, so that neither John nor his heirs would trouble or implead Joan for any kind of waste or loss, while yet she would, at the discretion of the four men, make good any waste, loss, or defect or make amends for it. If the four men could not agree John and his heirs might value the waste, ruin, or loss and seek to recover the value from Joan. Clause of warranty for the life of Joan, the reversion of the tenement always pertaining to John and his heirs and assigns on Joan's death. Seals: those of John and Joan to the parts of the indented deed in turn and the mayoral seal of the city. Named witnesses: the bailiff, the mayor, a coroner, a reeve, John Mower, William Warmwell, Richard Spencer, William Walter, Nicholas Harding, and the clerk
2021 By his charter John Thorburn, the father, and an executor, of the late Stephen Thorburn, for a sum of money paid to him in advance sold and quitclaimed to William Packing and his wife Alice and to William's heirs and assigns his right or claim to two tenements, with a yard (*or* yards) adjacent, in Chipper Street as

demarcated by the metes and bounds, which William and Alice hold for Alice's life. Clause of warranty. Seals: John's and the common and mayoral seals of the city. Named witnesses: the bailiff, the mayor, a coroner, the reeves, John Mower, Richard Spencer, William Warin, William Walter, William Bishop, and the clerk

2022 By his charter John Wootton, a citizen of Salisbury, granted to Richard Spencer, a citizen of Salisbury, a rent of 30s. a year to be received for ever by Richard and his heirs and assigns from a corner tenement or messuage [Holy Ghost Corner: cf. *2078*], with conjoined shops and cottages, in Winchester Street and Culver Street between a tenement of an elder John Pope in Winchester Street on the west side and William Sall's yard in Culver Street on the south side. Clause to permit entry on the messuage, with the shops and cottages, if the rent were in arrear for 15 days, distraint, and the keeping of distresses until the unpaid rent and other losses were recovered. So that his grant, and the confirmation of the charter, would remain valid for ever John attorned to Richard, and so confirmed his seisin, by paying to him 4d. in the presence of the mayor, and of the other witnesses named below, on the day on which the charter was perfected. Clause of warranty. Seals: John's and the common and mayoral seals of the city. Named witnesses: the bailiff, the mayor, a coroner, the reeves, John Mower, William Warmwell, William Warin, William Walter, William Sall, and the clerk

10 April 1409, at Salisbury
2023 By his indented charter Richard Leach, a citizen of Salisbury, granted to Walter Intborough a messuage called Bunt's Place, with a yard (*or* yards) and gardens, in Minster Street, which is called Castle Street, on the west side of the street, opposite a field; also a tenement, with a yard, in the same street, beyond the bars, on the east side of the street, between Henry Summer's cottages, of late John Mildenhall's, on the south side and a field on the north side. The messuage and the tenement, with the yards and gardens, were acquired by Richard from John Lewisham, an executor of Agnes, the relict, and an executor, of Robert Bunt, of late a citizen of Salisbury, who devised them, after the death of Agnes and her son Edward, who have died, to be sold by his executors or their executors, and they are to be held for ever by Walter and his heirs and assigns. The grant was made on condition that if Walter or his heirs would pay to Richard or his executors £70 on 24 June 1409 it would maintain its force. Clause to permit permanent repossession if the £70 were not then paid. Clause of warranty. Seals: those of the parties to the parts of the indented charter in turn and the common and mayoral seals of the city. Named witnesses: the mayor, the bailiff, a coroner, the reeves, William Warmwell, John Mower, Richard Spencer, William Warin, William Walter, William Bishop, John Needler, and the clerk

24 April 1409, at Salisbury
2024 By his charter John Gilbert, called Sumner, granted to John Chitterne, a clerk, John Frank, a clerk, and Thomas Merriott a messuage or tenement in New Street between John Wishford's tenement on the east side and a tenement of late Kentigern of Sulham's, now George Merriott's, on the west side. The

messuage was held by John Gilbert by a grant of John Chandler, of late a citizen of Salisbury, who held it by a feoffment of Thomas Longborough, a chaplain, and it is to be held for ever by John Chitterne, John Frank, and Thomas Merriott and their heirs and assigns. Clause of warranty. Seals: John Gilbert's and the common and mayoral seals of the city. Named witnesses: the bailiff, the mayor, a coroner, the reeves, John Mower, William Warmwell, Richard Spencer, William Warin, William Dowding, and the clerk

2025 By his charter James Hemingby, a son and heir of Alice Hemingby, granted to his son John and John's wife Alice conjoined cottages, with a garden (*or* gardens) adjacent, of late those of James's mother Alice, in Drake Hall Street between Nicholas Bell's cottages, of late those of John Wraxall, a chaplain, on the north side and a cottage of late David Fletcher's, now William Coventry's, on the south side. The cottages, with the garden(s), are to be held for ever by John and Alice and John's issue, and if John were to die without issue they would remain for ever to his direct heirs. Clause of warranty. Seals: James's and the common and mayoral seals of the city. Named witnesses: the bailiff, the mayor, a coroner, the reeves, John Mower, William Warmwell, Richard Spencer, Nicholas Harding, Thomas Child, and the clerk

2026 By his deed Richard Enterbush, a clerk, granted to Richard Holhurst, Roger Enterbush, and William Cook, of Salisbury, the estate which he held by virtue of a writ of the king on account of a valuation perfected for him or by any right or title whatsoever in a tenement, with shops, of late that of John Preston, a merchant, of Salisbury, in Carter Street between William Tull's tenement on the north side and a tenement of William Warin, a citizen of Salisbury, on the south side; also all other land and tenements, and his estate in them, which he held in the city for the reason previously stated. The land and tenements, and Richard Enterbush's estate in them, are to be held by the grantees and their heirs and assigns according to the form and effect of the valuation or other acquisition by that Richard. Seals: Richard Enterbush's and the mayoral seal of the city. Named witnesses: the mayor, the bailiff, the reeves, John Mower, Richard Spencer, William Warin, William Sall, Thomas Child, and the clerk

22 May 1409, at Salisbury
2027 By her indented charter Margaret, the relict of William Godmanstone, of late a citizen of Salisbury, granted to John Clive, tanner, and his wife Joan two conjoined cottages, in which John and Joan now dwell, in Endless Street, extending in length from the street as far as a little trench of water running behind the cottages through a yard of the provost of St. Edmund's, fronting on the street, and between a tenement of late that of an elder John Chandler, now appropriated to the hospital of the Holy Trinity, called Almshouse, on the south side and James Caundle's tenement, which Thomas Seager, tanner, holds, on the north side. The cottages are to be held for ever by John and Joan and John's heirs and assigns, paying a rent of 26s. 8d. a year to Margaret and her assigns for Margaret's life and for 2 cwt. of tan-turf a year likewise. Clause to permit re-entry if the rent or the tan-turf were in arrear for a month, distraint, and the keeping of

distresses until the unpaid rent and other losses were recovered; also, if distresses sufficient for the rent could not be found, to permit permanent repossession and the retention of Margaret's former estate in fee simple. Clause of warranty in respect of the cottages, of acquittance in respect of the rent. Seals: those of the parties to the parts of the indented charter in turn and the common and mayoral seals of the city. Named witnesses: the bailiff, the mayor, a coroner, the reeves, John Mower, William Warmwell, Richard Spencer, William Warin, Nicholas Harding, William Sall, and the clerk

2028 By her letters of attorney Margaret, the relict of William Godmanstone, of late a citizen of Salisbury, appointed Nicholas Mason, a clerk, and William Boyton to surrender into the hand of Robert, the bishop of Salisbury, the seisin of two conjoined cottages in Endless Street [*as in* **2027**] to the use of John Clive, tanner, and his wife Joan. Seals: Margaret's and the mayoral seal of the city

2029 Approval of the will of an elder John Forest, a citizen of Salisbury, made on 8 April 1409. Interment: in the graveyard of St. Edmund's church beside the tomb of his son Thomas, a canon, near a stile. Bequests: 12*d.* to the fabric of the cathedral church, and 20*d.* to the high altar; 20*s.* to his parish church, St. Edmund's, 12*d.* to each chaplain, both collegiate and annual, being present at his funeral rites, mass, and burial, to pray for his soul; five candles each weighing 5 lb., and six torches of one kind, to be burned around his corpse during his funeral rites, the bearing of it to its burial, and the whole mass while it was interred; all that wax to the provost of St. Edmund's church to satisfy his other debts there and lesser benefactions; 2*s.* each to the fabric of St. Thomas's church and the fabric of St. Martin's church; 5*s.* both to the Dominicans of Fisherton and the Franciscans of Salisbury, in each case to pray for his soul; 10*s.* to John Jakes, a chaplain, to pray for his soul; 1*d.* to each pauper coming to the distribution on the day of his burial; 2*s.* to his godson John Wickham; 12*d.* to each of his other godchildren; 12*d.* to each of his successive stepchildren; a new slop to each of the two beadsmen in the city; 100*s.* to the master and overseer of his art of weaving in the city to make continuous a priest among them for that art, to pray for his soul; 40*s.* to the commonalty of the city in aid of their tallage, to pray for his soul; 10*s.* to his younger son John; 40*d.* to Christine, his servant; 3*s.* 4*d.* to John Ballingdon, his servant; 20*d.* to Walter, his household servant; the rest of his goods to his wife Christine to be disposed of on behalf of his soul. Devises: to his wife Christine for life a tenement, in which he dwelt, and two conjoined tenements beside it, in Wineman Street between Agnes Ball's tenement on the west side and cottages of late John Prentice's on the east side; also a tenement, in the same street, opposite his tenement, between John Needler's tenement on the west side and Richard Leach's cottage property on the east side; also a shop in Endless Street between his chief tenement, which his [younger] son John holds, on the south side and Roger Enterbush's tenement on the north side; also a cottage, with the garden of two cottages, on the way towards St. Martin's church, between his own cottage on the south side and cottage property of late that of John Baker, grocer, on the north side. After Christine's death the tenements, the shop, and the cottage should be sold by John's executors or, if it could be done advantageously, sold by those executors in Christine's lifetime with her assent. All sales should be effected with the individual consent of all the executors, none of whom might act against the will of the other surviving executors, and nothing might be done secretly. If any of the executors did anything by himself, without the consent of the others then living, the sales would be invalid and quashed, but if they were effected with the unanimous consent of the executors they would be valid. The money received should be laid out on celebrating masses, giving alms, and doing charitable deeds on behalf of John's soul and the souls of others. John devised to his elder son John for life one of the two cottages on the way to St. Martin's church, between the cottage devised to his wife Christine on the north side and Maud Palmer's tenement on the south side. After that John's death the cottage should be sold by his father's executors with their individual consent, as is described above. The money received should be laid out in the way described above on behalf of John's soul and the souls of others. John devised to his younger son John for life that single tenement or dwelling house, in which that John now dwells, in Endless Street between the shop devised to Christine on the north side and John Little's cottage property on the south side. After that John's death the tenement, except the shop, should be sold by his father's executors by their unanimous consent, as is described above. The money received should be laid out in the way described above on behalf of John's soul and the souls of others. If all John's executors were to die before effecting the sale of the tenements, the shop, and the cottages, which God forbid, the sales should be made in the same way by their executors. <u>Executors</u>: his wife Christine, Nicholas Harding, and Robert Forest; overseer, the lord John Jakes. <u>Proved</u> on 27 April 1409 in front of William Summerhill, the subdean; the administration was entrusted to the executors, and the seal of the office of the subdean was affixed in the presence of John Jakes, John Forest, the elder son, Stephen Edington, the clerk, and others. <u>Approved</u> at a court held in front of the bailiff, the mayor, and other citizens; the seisin of the tenements, the shop, and the cottages was released to those named above, the elder son John Forest then being dead.

5 June 1409, at Salisbury
2030 By his writing Richard Leach, a citizen of Salisbury, quitclaimed to Walter Intborough and his heirs and assigns his right or claim to a messuage called Bunt's Place, with a yard (*or* yards) and gardens, in Minster Street, which is called Castle Street, [*as in* **2023**]; also to a tenement, with a yard, in the same street, beyond the bars, on the east side of the street, [*as in* **2023**]. Clause of warranty. Seals: Richard's and the common and mayoral seals of the city. Named witnesses: the bailiff, the mayor, a coroner, the reeves, William Warmwell, John Mower, Richard Spencer, William Warin, William Walter, William Bishop, John Needler, and the clerk

3 July 1409, at Salisbury
2031 By their deed Richard Holhurst, a clerk, Roger Enterbush, and William Cook, of Salisbury, granted to James Day and John, a son of the late John Preston, the estate which they held in a tenement, of late the elder John Preston's, in

Carter Street [*as in* **2026**], and in the other land or tenements, rent, and reversions, which were John Preston's in Salisbury and which they held by a grant of Richard Enterbush, a clerk. The land and tenements are to be held by James and John and their heirs and assigns according to the form and effect of the acquisition of them by the grantors, who release to them their whole right or claim. Seals: those of the grantors and the mayoral seal of the city. Named witnesses: the bailiff, the mayor, a coroner, the reeves, John Mower, Richard Spencer, William Bishop, Richard Jewell, William Dowding, and the clerk

2032 By her deed Christine, the relict of an elder John Forest, of late a citizen of Salisbury, granted to William Harnhill, barber, the estate which she held for her life by John's devise in a cottage, with a garden, on the way towards St. Martin's church, between a cottage of late John's on the south side and cottage property of late John Bodenham's, afterwards that of John Baker, grocer, on the north side. The cottage, with the garden, is to be held by William and his heirs and assigns according to the form and effect of that devise. Seals: Christine's and the mayoral seal of the city. Named witnesses: the mayor, the bailiff, the reeves, John Mower, Richard Spencer, William Walter, Nicholas Harding, William Sall, and the clerk

31 July 1409, at Salisbury

2033 A deed of Christine, the relict, and an executor, of an elder John Forest, a citizen of Salisbury, and of Nicholas Harding and Robert Forest, her co-executors. John devised to Christine for her life a cottage, with the conjoined gardens of two cottages, in the street on the way towards St. Martin's church, and he devised the other cottage to his elder son John for that John's life. The cottages stand between a cottage of late John Dogskin's, now Maud Palmer's, on the south side and cottage property of late John Bodenham's, afterwards that of John Baker, grocer, on the north side. John appointed that after the death of Christine and John the two cottages, or before then the reversion if it could be done advantageously in their lifetime with their consent, should be sold by the executors. The money received should be laid out on the salvation of his soul and the souls of others. The son John, who held an estate in one of the cottages, has died, Christine of late granted her estate in the other cottage to William Harnhill, barber, and declares that the cottages, and the reversion of them, pertain to the executors for sale, and William Harnhill has reached agreement with the executors for a sum of money, part paid and to be paid in full, for the cottages and the reversion to be held by him. On the strength of the elder John Forest's will the executors, with a unanimous assent and will, granted to William the two cottages, with the gardens, and the reversion to be held for ever by him and his heirs and assigns as that which he bought from them in good faith for that sum of money to be laid out according to the will. Seals: those of the grantors and the common and mayoral seals of the city. Named witnesses: the mayor, the bailiff, reeves, John Mower, Richard Spencer, William Walter, Richard Leach, William Sall, and the clerk

25 September 1409, at Salisbury

2034 By his charter John, a son of Joan, who was the wife of John Mildenhall, of late a citizen of Salisbury, granted to Richard Harlwin, goldsmith, a tenement in Minster Street between William Coventry's tenement on the south side and a tenement of late that of John Scammel [*otherwise* Camel: *cf.* **1642, 1943**], hatter, now Thomas Stabber's, on the north side. The tenement was held by John, the son of Joan, by a feoffment of Walter Nalder and is to be held for ever by Richard and his heirs and assigns. Clause of warranty. Seals: John's and the common and mayoral seals of the city. Named witnesses: the bailiff, the mayor, the reeves, John Mower, Richard Spencer, William Warmwell, William Dowding, and the clerk
2035 By his letters of attorney John, a son of Joan, who was the wife of John Mildenhall, of late a citizen of Salisbury, appointed Thomas Biston and Walter Short, citizens of Salisbury, to surrender into the hand of Robert, the bishop of Salisbury, the seisin of a tenement in Minster Street [*as in* **2034**] to the use of Richard Harlwin. Seals: John's and the mayoral seal of the city

20 November 1409, at Salisbury
2036 By his deed John Gowan, of Norrington, granted to William Penton, dyer, and his wife Christine, a corner tenement, with a garden next to it, in which John Buddle, called Prentice, of late a citizen of Salisbury, dwelt, in Wineman Street and Gigant Street, between cottages, with gardens and buildings, which were of late that John Prentice's, in Wineman Street on the west side and Agnes Ball's garden in Gigant Street on the north side. The tenement was held by John Gowan by a grant of an elder John Forest and Stephen Edington, that John Prentice's executors, and, with the garden, is to be held for ever by William and Christine and William's heirs and assigns, to whom John Gowan quitclaimed his right or claim to it. Seals: John's and the common and mayoral seals of the city. Named witnesses: the bailiff, the mayor, the reeves, John Mower, Richard Spencer, Richard Leach, William Walter, John Needler, and the clerk
2037 By his letters of attorney John Gowan, of Norrington, appointed Walter Short, Roger Enterbush, and Henry Blackmoor to surrender into the hand of Robert, the bishop of Salisbury, the seisin of a corner tenement, of late that of John Buddle, called Prentice, a citizen of Salisbury, in Wineman Street and Gigant Street [*as in* **2036**] to the use of William Penton, dyer, and his wife Christine. Seals: John's and the mayoral seal of the city

4 December 1409, at Salisbury
2038 Approval of the will of John Cross, saddler, of Salisbury, made on 11 September 1409. Interment: in the graveyard of St. Thomas's church. Bequests: 6*d.* to the fabric of the cathedral church; 12*d.* to the fabric of St. Thomas's church; 12*d.* each to the fabric of St. Edmund's church, the high altar for his forgotten tithes, and the parochial chaplain; a russet tunic to Richard Ireland, tailor; the rest of his goods to his son Thomas. Devise: to Thomas and Thomas's issue a yard, with a rack, in Mealmonger Street, and if Thomas were to die without issue the yard should be sold by John's executors or their executors. The money received should be laid out on behalf of John's soul and the souls

of others. Executor: his son Thomas. Proved on 27 September 1409 in front of the subdean; the administration was entrusted to the executor, who afterwards appeared, accounted with an officer, and was dismissed. Approved at a court held in front of the bailiff, the mayor, and other citizens; the seisin of the yard and the rack was released to the legatee.

18 December 1409, at Salisbury
2039 By their writing Richard Brice and his wife Alice, appearing at the court held on that day, she not coerced by fear or force, granted to William Walter, a citizen of Salisbury, the estate which they held for their life in a messuage in Gigant Street between William's cottage, beside a gate of his tenement, of late that of Thomas Shove and his wife Agace, on the north side and cottage property of late Thomas Focket's on the south side. The estate is to be held by William and his heirs and assigns according to the effect of a grant to Richard and Alice, who release to William and his heirs and assigns their right or claim to the estate. Seals: those of Richard and Alice and the mayoral seal of the city. Named witnesses: the bailiff, the mayor, the reeves, John Mower, William Warmwell, Richard Spencer, William Warin, William Bishop, William Dowding, and the clerk

15 January 1410, at Salisbury
2040 By their charter John Nash, mason, and his wife Joan, appearing at the court held on that day, granted to Margaret Godmanstone, Nicholas Mason, a chaplain, and William Bailiff a cottage in St. Martin's Street, on the way from the east gate of the canons' close towards St. Martin's church, between a cottage of Margaret on either side. The cottage was held by John and Joan by a grant of Adam Keynes, who held it by a devise of Bertin Spicer, and it is to be held for ever by Margaret, Nicholas, and William and their heirs and assigns. Clause of warranty. Seals: those of John and Joan and the common and mayoral seals of the city. Named witnesses: the bailiff, the mayor, the reeves, John Mower, Richard Spencer, William Warin, Thomas Child, William Dowding, and the clerk

29 January 1410, at Salisbury
2041 By his writing Stephen Edington, an executor of John Buddle, called Prentice, of late a citizen of Salisbury, quitclaimed to William Penton, dyer, and his heirs and assigns his right or claim by reason of John's will or otherwise to a corner tenement, in which William now dwells and which he held by a grant of John Gowan, in Wineman Street and Gigant Street [*as in 2036*]. Seals: Stephen's and the common and mayoral seals of the city. Named witnesses: the mayor, the bailiff, the reeves, John Mower, Richard Spencer, William Walter, John Needler, Richard Leach, and John Lewisham

12 February 1410, at Salisbury
2042 Approval of the will of Thomas Dunball, carpenter, of Salisbury, made on 8 January 1409. Interment: in the graveyard of St. Edmund's church. Bequests: 6*d*. to the fabric of the cathedral church; 6*d*. to the fabric of St. Edmund's church, 6*d*.

to the parochial chaplain, and 6*d*. to the high altar for his forgotten and detained tithes; a gown to his brother John Pierce; the rest of his goods to his wife Maud. Devise: to Maud a tenement, in which he lived, in Nuggeston between Thomas Bonham's cottages, of late those of John Stallington, a clerk, on the east side and a tenement of a younger John Forest on the west side, to be held for ever by her and her heirs and assigns, paying the yearly rent to be paid by right to William Warmwell. Executor: his wife Maud. Proved on 3 February 1410 in front of the subdean; the administration was entrusted to Maud, who at length appeared, accounted with an officer, and was dismissed. Approved at a court held in front of the bailiff, the mayor, and other citizens; the seisin of the tenement was released to Maud.

2043 By her charter Maud, the relict of Thomas Dunball, carpenter, of Salisbury, granted to Thomas Ferring, weaver, and his wife Edith, Maud's daughter, a tenement, in which she lives and which she held by Thomas's devise, in Nuggeston [*as in* **2042**], to be held for ever by them and the issue begotten between them. If Thomas and Edith were to die without such issue the tenement should remain to Maud's executors to be sold. The money received should be laid out by the executors or their executors on behalf of Maud's soul, her husband's soul, and the souls of others. Clause of warranty. Seals: Maud's and the common and mayoral seals of the city. Named witnesses: the bailiff, the mayor, the reeves, John Mower, William Warmwell, Richard Spencer, Richard Leach, Richard Jewell, and the clerk

2044 By her letters of attorney Maud, the relict of Thomas Dunball, carpenter, of Salisbury, appointed a younger John Shute and Thomas Clark to surrender into the hand of Robert, the bishop of Salisbury, the seisin of a tenement, in which she lives and which she held by Thomas's devise, in Nuggeston [*as in* **2042**] to the use of Thomas Ferring, weaver, and his wife Edith, Maud's daughter. Seals: Maud's and the mayoral seal of the city

2045 By his charter Nicholas Harding, a citizen of Salisbury, granted to John Mower, Richard Spencer, Walter Shirley, and William Dowding, citizens of Salisbury, a tenement in Winchester Street between a corner tenement of late that of a younger William Tenterer, in which William Hill dwelt, on the east side and a tenement of late Nicholas Baker's, now Henry Delves's, on the west side. The tenement, with other land and tenements in Salisbury, was held by Nicholas and an elder John Forest, now dead, by a grant of John Newman, a merchant, a citizen of Salisbury, and is to be held for ever by the grantees and their heirs and assigns. Seals: Nicholas's and the common and mayoral seals of the city. Named witnesses: the bailiff, the mayor, the reeves, William Warmwell, William Warin, William Walter, William Bishop, and the clerk

12 March 1410, at Salisbury

2046 By his indented charter William Warmwell, a citizen of Salisbury, granted to Thomas Ferring and his wife Edith, a daughter of Thomas Dunball, carpenter, two cottages, with small adjacent gardens, extending as far as a yard of Thomas and Edith. The cottages were built by Thomas Dunball, and William acquired them from John Butterley, of late a citizen of Salisbury. They stand in Mealmonger Street between Thomas Bonham's cottages, of late those of John Stallington, a clerk, on the north side and cottage property of John Breamore, weaver, on the south side and, with the gardens, are to be held for ever by Thomas and Edith and their heirs and assigns, paying a rent of 10s. cash a year for ever to William and his heirs and assigns. Thomas and Edith and their heirs and assigns should maintain and repair the cottages in all things necessary at their own expense so that the rent would not be lost. Clause to permit re-entry if the rent were in arrear for six weeks, distraint, and the keeping of distresses until the unpaid rent was recovered; also, if sufficient distresses for the rent could not be found, or if Thomas and Edith or their heirs were not to maintain and repair the cottages so that the rent would be lost, to permit repossession and the retention of William's former estate. Clause of warranty in respect of the cottages, of acquittance in respect of the rent. Seals: those of the parties to the parts of the indented charter in turn and the common and mayoral seals of the city. Named witnesses: the bailiff, the mayor, the reeves, John Mower, Richard Spencer, Walter Shirley, William Walter, John Lewisham, and the clerk

2047 By his letters of attorney William Warmwell, a citizen of Salisbury, appointed Roger Enterbush, Walter Short, and Stephen Edington to surrender into the hand of Robert, the bishop of Salisbury, the seisin of two cottages, with small adjacent gardens, [*as in* **2046**] to the use of Thomas Ferring and his wife Edith, a daughter of Thomas Dunball. Seals: William's and the mayoral seal of the city

26 March 1410, at Salisbury

2048 By his charter Roger, a son of John Upton and his wife Margaret, granted to Walter Intborough, esq., a corner tenement [*margin*: Warr's Corner], with a shop (*or* shops), in Winchester Street and Culver Street between Thomas Biston's tenement, of late Margery Justice's, on the east side and a tenement appropriated to the hospital of the Holy Trinity, called Almshouse, on the south side; also cottages, with a yard (*or* yards), in Brown Street between William West's tenement on the north side and a tenement of late Thomas Chaplin's, which Laurence Lane holds, on the south side; also two shops in Butcher Row between William Sall's shop property on the east side and Richard Spencer's shop property on the west side; also a yard, with a meadow, in Drake Hall Street between Richard Spencer's yard on the south side and a yard of late William Guys's on the north side. The tenement, the shops, the cottages, and the yards were of late his father's and are to be held for ever by Walter and his heirs and assigns. Clause of warranty. Seals: Roger's and the common and mayoral seals of the city. Named witnesses: the bailiff, the mayor, the reeves, William Warmwell, Walter Shirley, William Walter, John Needler, William Dowding, and the clerk

2049 By their charter John Kilham and his wife Joan, the relict of William at the hurn, dyer, appearing at the court held on that day, granted to Simon Sydenham, a clerk, and John Sydenham, of Salisbury, a tenement, opposite the market place where grains are sold, between a tenement formerly Hugh of Langford's, which was of late Robert Charles's, on the west side and a tenement of late that of the lord Thomas of Erlestoke, a chaplain, now Thomas Stabber's, which John Downton, draper, holds, on the east side. The tenement was held by William and Joan in fee simple by a grant of William Scammel and his wife Joan and is to be held for ever by Simon and John and their heirs and assigns. Clause of warranty. Seals: those of John and Joan and the common and mayoral seals of the city. Named witnesses: the bailiff, the mayor, the reeves, John Mower, Richard Spencer, William Warmwell, Walter Shirley, William Warin, and the clerk

23 April 1410, at Salisbury
2050 By their indented deed Simon Sydenham, a clerk, and John Sydenham, of Salisbury, granted to Thomas Yeovil, tailor, and his wife Joan, a daughter of Joan, the wife of John Kilham, a rent of 20s. a year to be received for ever, after the death of the elder Joan, by Thomas and Joan and the issue of that Joan from a tenement, of late that of William at the hurn, dyer, which Simon and John held by a grant of John Kilham and his wife Joan. The tenement stands, opposite the market place where grains are sold, [*as in* **2049**]. Clause to permit entry on the tenement if the rent, after it fell due on the death of Joan, the wife of John Kilham, were in arrear for a month, and to permit distraint in the tenement and the keeping of distresses until the unpaid rent was recovered. If Joan, the wife of Thomas Yeovil, were to die without issue the rent would cease and be extinguished. Seals: those of Simon and John to the parts of the deed and the common and mayoral seals of the city. Named witnesses: the bailiff, the mayor, a coroner, the reeves, John Mower, Richard Spencer, William Warmwell, William Warin, Thomas Mason, draper, and the clerk

7 May 1410, at Salisbury
2051 By their indented charter Simon Sydenham, a clerk, and John Sydenham, of Salisbury, granted to Robert Watercombe and his wife Agnes, a daughter of the late William at the hurn, dyer, a rent of 20s. a year issuing from a shop, which John Bodenham holds for the life of Joan, the wife of John Kilham, with the reversion of the shop when it fell due on Joan's death. The shop stands, fronting on the street, [in] a tenement which was of late William at the hurn's and which Simon and John held by a grant of John Kilham and Joan, between a tenement formerly Hugh of Langford's [*as in* **2049**]. Simon and John also granted to Robert and Agnes that same tenement, except a room, with a sollar, within the tenement formerly reserved to Joan under a condition of a grant. The rent, with the reversion, and the tenement are to be held for ever by Robert and Agnes and Agnes's issue, paying a rent to John Kilham and Joan for Joan's life and, after Joan's death, to Thomas Yeovil and his wife Joan, a sister of Agnes and an heir of Joan, as due and formerly granted to them. The tenement is to be maintained and repaired in all things necessary at the expense of Robert and Agnes and their heirs so that the rent would not be lost. If Agnes were to die without issue the rent from the shop, with the reversion, and the tenement would remain for ever on the death of her husband Robert to Thomas Yeovil and his wife Joan and Joan's issue for the rent to be paid to Joan, the wife of John Kilham. If Joan, the

wife of Thomas Yeovil, were to die without issue the rent from the shop, with the reversion, and the tenement would remain for ever to Agnes's brother John and his issue, and if John were to die without issue they would remain for ever to John Sydenham and his issue. If John Sydenham were to die without issue they would revert and remain to Joan, the wife of John Kilham, if she was then alive, and to her heirs; otherwise they should remain to the mayor for the time being to be sold and disposed of, according to the discretion of him and four honourable men, to fulfill the will of William at the hurn. Seals: those of Simon and John to the parts of the indented charter and the common and mayoral seals of the city. Named witnesses: the bailiff, the mayor, a coroner, the reeves, John Mower, Richard Spencer, William Warmwell, William Warin, and the clerk

21 May 1410, at Salisbury
2052 A deed of Nicholas Harding, a citizen of Salisbury, and Robert Forest, executors of an elder John Forest, of late a citizen of Salisbury. John devised to his wife Christine for life two tenements, which he acquired under the name of one tenement from John Butterley, in Wineman Street beside a tenement, in which he dwelt, and between that tenement on the east side and Agnes Ball's tenement on the west side. He appointed that after Christine's death the tenements should be sold by his executors, with their unanimous consent, if they outlived Christine and if the tenements had not been sold in her lifetime. The money received should be laid out on the salvation of John's soul and the souls of others. Christine has died, the tenements remain unsold and John Bodenham, a citizen of Salisbury, and John Hain have agreed with Nicholas and Robert to acquire and hold them for a sum of money, reaching the value of them, in part paid and with security held for the payment of the larger part, and on the strength of John Forest's will, and with their unanimous consent, Nicholas and Robert granted the tenements to John Bodenham and John Hain to be held for ever by them and their heirs and assigns as that which they bought in good faith from Nicholas and Robert to fulfil that will. Seals: those of Nicholas and Robert and the common and mayoral seals of the city. Named witnesses: the bailiff, the mayor, a coroner, the reeves, John Mower, William Warmwell, Richard Spencer, Richard Leach, John Needler, John Lewisham, and the clerk

4 June 1410, at Salisbury
2053 By his deed John, a son of an elder John Forest, of late a citizen of Salisbury, quitclaimed to John Bodenham, a citizen of Salisbury, and John Hain and their heirs and assigns his right or claim to two tenements which they held by a sale of Nicholas Harding, a citizen of Salisbury, and Robert Forest, executors of the elder John Forest. The elder John devised the tenements to be sold by his executors after the death of Christine, his wife, the younger John's mother, who is now dead. The tenements stand in Wineman Street [*as in* **2052**]. Seals: the younger John Forest's and the common and mayoral seals of the city. Named witnesses: the bailiff, the mayor, a coroner, the reeves, John Mower, Richard Spencer, Walter Shirley, Richard Leach, John Needler, and the clerk

18 June 1410, at Salisbury
2054 A deed of Richard Weston, weaver, and his wife Alice, who jointly acquired from Joan, the relict, and an executor, of Robert Arnold, of late a citizen of Salisbury, the reversions of two tenements in Endless Street in which Joan and her son Edmund Arnold, a chaplain, held estates for their life and the life of the one of them living longer. One of the tenements stands between a tenement of late Henry Pope's on the south side and a tenement, of late John Christchurch's, appropriated to a [?St. Edmund's] chantry, on the north side, and one stands between William Godmanstone's tenement on the south side and cottages of late William Higdon's on the north side. The reversions, when they fell due on the death of Joan and Edmund, were to be held for ever by Richard and Alice and Richard's heirs and assigns. William Stout, Peter Daw, mercer, and Robert Warmwell have paid a sum of money to Richard and Alice for the reversions and, appearing at the court held on that day, Richard and Alice, she being examined according to the custom of the court, acknowledging of her own will that she was not coerced by fear or force but was acting by her own free will and with her husband assisting, granted them, when they fell due, to William, Peter, and Robert to be held for ever by them and their heirs and assigns according to the form and effect of Richard's and Alice's acquisition. Richard and Alice quitclaimed to William, Peter, and Robert and their heirs and assigns their right or claim to them. Seals: those of Richard and Alice and the common and mayoral seals of the city. Named witnesses: the bailiff, the mayor, a coroner, the reeves, John Mower, William Warmwell, Richard Spencer, Walter Shirley, Nicholas Melbury, and the clerk

2 July 1410, at Salisbury
2055 Approval of the will of John Hurst made on 1 June 1410. <u>Interment</u>: in the graveyard of St. Leonard's, Andover. <u>Bequests</u>: 6*d.* to the relics of St. Swithun, Winchester; 3*s.* 4*d.* to the fabric of Andover church, and 8*d.* to the vicar; 6*d.* to each chaplain present on the day of his burial, and 4*d.* to each clerk present; a coverlet, a pair of linen sheets, a furred gown, a pot, and a pan to Isabel, his servant; a gown of russet to John 'Fetbien'. <u>Devises</u>: to his wife Joan, the lord William Salisbury, the perpetual vicar of the parish church of Ashley, and John Robbs, tailor, of Andover, a tenement in Pot Row, Salisbury, and all his tenements in Andover, with all the land, meadows, pasture, and feeding lying near those tenements in the vill and fields of Andover, on condition that they would sell them in the best way possible and pay all his debts with the money received. Whatever remained after the payment of the debts should be laid out by Joan, William, and John for the use of the poor and on other pious uses for the salvation of John's soul, his wife's soul, and the souls of others. John appointed that John Robbs should have the tenement in Andover in which that John dwelt at a price lighter by 40*s.* than any other might have it, if he wished to buy it. <u>Executors</u>: his wife Joan, the lord William Salisbury, and John Robbs. <u>Proved</u> at Winchester on 11 June 1410 in front of John Pain, an officer of the

lord of Winchester deputed a commissary in his absence; the administration was entrusted to the executors. Seals: the one used in the office, together with John Pain's private seal. <u>Approved</u> at a court held in front of the bailiff, the mayor, and other citizens; the seisin of the tenement in Salisbury was released to the legatees.

16 July 1410, at Salisbury
2056 By their deed William Salisbury, the vicar of Ashley, and John Robbs, tailor, of Andover, granted to Edward Gilbert, dubber, of Salisbury, a tenement, with a cellar, which they held by a devise of John Hurst, of Andover. The tenement stands in Pot Row, extending towards the market place on the north side, between a tenement of late that of Walter Clopton, kt., on the east side and a tenement, with a cellar, of Agnes Longstock, of Southampton, on the west side. It is to be held, with the cellar, for ever by Edward and his heirs and assigns, to whom William and John quitclaimed their right or claim to it. Seals: those of William and John and the common and mayoral seals of the city. Named witnesses: the bailiff, the mayor, a coroner, the reeves, John Mower, Richard Spencer, Walter Shirley, William Dowding, Thomas Child, and the clerk

30 July 1410, at Salisbury
2057 By his writing John Wishford quitclaimed to Richard Ferrer, of Salisbury, and his wife Cecily and their heirs and assigns his right or claim to a rent of 20s. a year which he was accustomed to receive from a corner tenement, opposite the market place where grains and linen cloth are sold, between a tenement formerly that of Henry Hussey and his wife Joan on the east side and Minster Street on the west side; also his right or claim to the tenement. Clause of warranty. Seals: John's and the common and mayoral seals of the city. Named witnesses: the bailiff, the mayor, a coroner, the reeves, William Warmwell, John Mower, Richard Spencer, Adam Teffont, John Needler, and the clerk

13 August 1410, at Salisbury
2058 By his charter Walter Intborough granted to Nicholas Latimer and John Jakes, a chaplain, a messuage called Bunt's Place, with a yard (*or* yards) and gardens, in Minster Street, which is called Castle Street, beyond the bar, on the west side of the street opposite a field; also a tenement, with a yard, in the same street, on the east side of the street, between Henry Summer's cottages, of late John Mildenhall's, on the south side and a field on the north side. The messuage and the tenement, with the yards and gardens, were held by Walter by a grant of Richard Leach, a citizen of Salisbury, and are to be held for ever by Nicholas and John and their heirs and assigns. Seals: Walter's and the common and mayoral seals of the city. Named witnesses: the bailiff, the mayor, a coroner, the reeves, John Mower, Richard Spencer, Walter Shirley, William Walter, John Lewisham, and the clerk

10 September 1410, at Salisbury
2059 By their charter Nicholas Latimer and John Jakes, a chaplain, granted to

Walter Intborough and his wife Joan a messuage called Bunt's Place, with a yard (*or* yards) and gardens, in Minster Street, which is called Castle Street, [*as in* **2058**]; also a tenement, with a yard, in the same street, [*as in* **2058**]. The messuage and the tenement, with the yards and gardens, were held by Nicholas and John by Walter's grant and are to be held for ever by Walter and Joan and Walter's heirs and assigns. Seals: those of Nicholas and John and the common and mayoral seals of the city. Named witnesses: the mayor, the bailiff, a coroner, the reeves, John Mower, Richard Spencer, William Warmwell, William Warin, William Bishop, and the clerk

24 September 1410, at Salisbury
2060 A deed of Dominic Uphill and Thomas Stabber, executors of Henry Berwick. By his will Henry appointed that a tenement in Butcher Row, called Pot Row, extending towards the market place on the north side, between John Barnaby's tenement on the east side and Gunnore Bowyer's tenement on the west side, should be sold by his executors or their executors to make up the difference if his movable goods were not sufficient to pay his debts and satisfy his legacies. Because the will could not be executed, the goods not being sufficient to satisfy the legacies, on the strength of it Dominic and Thomas granted the tenement to Richard Gage, a citizen of Salisbury, to be held for ever by him and his heirs and assigns as that which he bought from them in good faith to fulfill Henry's will. Seals: those of Dominic and Thomas and the common and mayoral seals of the city. Named witnesses: the bailiff, the mayor, a coroner, a reeve, John Mower, Richard Spencer, William Warin, Walter Shirley, John Becket, and the clerk

8 October 1410, at Salisbury
2061 Approval of the will of Richard Jewell, a citizen of Salisbury, made on 23 July 1410. Interment: in St. Thomas's church in front of St. Bartholomew's altar. Bequests: 13s. 4d. to the fabric of that church, 6s. 8d. to the high altar for his forgotten tithes, 12d. to the parochial chaplain, and 6d. to each other chaplain of that church present at his funeral rites and mass; 10s. to the fabric of the cathedral church; a sword to John Ellis; a silver belt furnished with roses to John Moore; a belt furnished with silver and gilded to Richard Titling, a vicar of the cathedral church; a dagger to John Trippon; a belt with a dagger to John Besil; a gown with the fur of squirrel to Thomas Martin, of Homington, and a plain piece [?of silver *or* cloth] to his wife; a plain piece [?of silver *or* cloth] to John Warminster; 20s. to John Smith, a chaplain; a horn for drinking to remain in the chantry for two chaplains founded in St. Thomas's church, to be held by the ordained chaplains now there and by their successors for ever; the rest of his goods to his wife Gillian to be disposed of on behalf of his soul. Devises: to Gillian for life a tenement, in which he dwelt, in New Street between his own tenement, of late Thomas Chaplin's, on the east side and John Wishford's tenement on the west side. After Gillian's death the tenement should be sold by Richard's executors or, with her assent and if it seemed better to the executors, the reversion might be sold in Gillian's lifetime. The money received should be laid out by the executors on

celebrating masses, bestowing alms, and doing other charitable deeds on behalf of Richard's soul, the souls of Joan, of late his wife, and Gillian, and the souls of others. Richard devised to Gillian a tenement, which he acquired from an elder John Chandler and which Richard Sherman holds, in Carter Street between Thomas Knoyle's tenement, which Robert Wolf holds, on the north side and Richard Knolle's tenement on the south side. The tenement should be held by Gillian for her life on condition that she would pay all Richard's debts with his movable goods, if they are valuable enough; if not she, and Richard's other executor, when the time seemed right to them, should sell the tenement with their unanimous assent. From the money received they should pay Richard's debts, and if anything remained it should be laid out in the way described above on behalf of the souls of those named above. Richard devised to his executors a tenement, which is now held as two dwelling houses, in New Street between his own tenement, in which he dwelt, on the west side and cottages, which John Lake holds of William Ferrer, on the east side, to be sold immediately after his death when it seemed best to them. He appointed that from the money received his legacies should be given effect, his debts paid, and other charitable deeds done for the salvation of his soul and the souls of those named above. <u>Executors</u>: his wife Gillian and the lord John Smith, a chaplain. <u>Proved</u> in the cathedral church on 10 August 1410 in front of the subdean; the administration was granted to the executors. <u>Approved</u> at a court held in front of the mayor, the bailiff, and other citizens; the seisin of the tenements was released to the legatees.

2062 By their deed Thomas Stabber and his wife Alice, a daughter of Henry Berwick, appearing at the court held on that day, quitclaimed to Richard Gage, a citizen of Salisbury, and his heirs and assigns their right or claim, or Alice's right or claim, to a tenement in Butcher Row, called Pot Row, [*as in* **2060**], which Richard held from a sale of Henry's executors. Seals: those of Thomas and Alice and the common and mayoral seals of the city. Named witnesses: the bailiff, the mayor, a coroner, a reeve, William Warmwell, Richard Spencer, William Walter, Nicholas Harding, and the clerk

22 October 1410, at Salisbury

2063 Approval of the will of George Merriott, esq., made on 28 August 1410. <u>Interment</u>: in the church of the Dominicans of Fisherton Anger, between two columns on the south side of the church, immediately behind the grave of Roger Beauchamp, kt. <u>Bequests</u>: 20s. each to the fabric of the cathedral church, the fabric of St. Thomas's church, the fabric of St. Edmund's church, and the fabric of St. Martin's church; 20s. both to the Franciscans of Salisbury and the Dominicans of Fisherton, in each case to be divided among them equally by the hand of his executors; 13s. 4d. both to the paupers of the hospital of the Holy Trinity called Almshouse and the paupers of St. Nicholas's hospital, in each case to be divided among them likewise; 20s. to the rector of St. Thomas's church for his forgotten tithes and lesser benefactions, 6s. 8d. to the lord James Green, the parochial chaplain, to pray for his soul, 6d. to each other chaplain of that church present at his funeral rites and mass on the day of his burial, 6d. to the deacon, and 6*d*. to the sacristan; there should be provided by his executors five candles, each weighing 5 lb., with 12 torches, to be burned around his corpse on the day of his burial; 10 paupers, and two men chanting, carrying candles [and] wearing white cloth on the day of his burial, to pray for his soul; 10 marks to be handed out on the day of his burial to bedridden paupers and other paupers; a scarlet gown with the fur of pullen to Thomas Curl, a chaplain; a long gown, particoloured with blue, with the fur of lamb, to Thomas Randolph; a blue gown with the fur of *scarche* to Catherine Rider, his servant, and 20*s*. to her daughter Christine, to pray for his soul; 20*s*. and a doublet to John Mund, his servant; 40*d*. to each of his other servants who were then with him, if they remained until the day of his anniversary; there should be provided two pairs of ecclesiastical vestments from a gown, one part scarlet and the other part silken, one pair for the altar of St. Stephen in St. Thomas's church to pray for his soul and the soul of his late wife Alice, and the other pair for Downton church to pray for his soul and the soul of his mother Maud; a fur of beaver and a fur of foin, with his whole body armour, to his brother Thomas Merriott; he charged Thomas to dispose of a fur of miniver on behalf of the soul of his mother Maud, in the best way in which with speed after his death his soul can be acquitted, according to Maud's will; two furs, one of squirrel and one of grey, to his executors to be sold and, immediately after his death, disposed of on behalf of his soul and the soul of his late wife Alice; two belts, furnished with silver, which were Alice's, to be sold by his executors immediately after his death and the money raised laid out on pious uses on behalf of his soul and Alice's soul; an ouch of gold, with a retort, for the ornamentation of the chief image of St. Kyneburg the Virgin, at Gloucester; all his gold and silver gilt jewells (*viz.* ouches, necklaces, rings, [prayer] beads, with stones of pearl and other precious stones), all his gold and silver gilt vessels (*viz.* silver pottles with covers, spoons, mazers, silver salt-cellars), and all his utensils and movable goods and chattels to be sold by his executors or their executors and the money raised, over and above the amounts bequeathed above and below, laid out by them on the pious uses which were the most necessary, such as on bridges, ways, paupers, chapels, poor places, and in other ways where the need was greatest and where the benefit to the souls of those mentioned above would be greatest; £10 to the fabric of St. Stephen's chapel on the south side of St. Thomas's church, in the event that the chapel was begun and fully built from new within three years after his death; 16*s*. 8*d*. to be laid out by his executors on behalf of the soul of Richard Brewer, formerly his household servant; 40*s*. to the fabric of St. Catherine's chapel, Merriott, where his late wife Maud lies; 40*s*. to the fabric of the parish church of St. Peter, South Petherton, to prepare and adorn in turn the place where his mother Maud is buried; 10 marks to each of his executors to carry out his will; £10 for carrying out the repair and improvement of Ayleswade bridge; his goods and utensils in his inn, George's Inn, (*viz.* coverlets, blankets, linen sheets, mattresses, testers, painted cloths and cloths called shalloons, tablecloths, towells, basins, lavers, candlesticks [of] brass, enamel, and pewter, brass pots and pans, 12 silver spoons, spits, bars, and trivets of iron, a pewter vessel, leaden vessels for ale to be placed in, pewter cellars, three boxes, hay, fuel, charcoal, trestle tables with the trestles), and all his movable goods therein to his executors to be sold immediately after his death, [and the money raised] to be laid out by the executors on behalf of his soul, the soul of his late wife Alice, and the souls of others; 10 marks to improve and repair the street behind Butcher Row; 20s. to Thomas Randolph; 26s. 8d. to remit the debt which John Hemby owed to him. <u>Devises</u>: to Catherine Rider, his servant, for her good service, a middle tenement in New Street, between a tenement of his on either side, to be held by her for life, and on her death the tenement should remain for ever to George's brother Thomas and his issue. George devised to Thomas the tenements, on either side of that devised to Catherine, in New Street between John Wishford's tenement on the east side and John Needler's tenement on the west side, with the reversion of the middle tenement when it fell due on Catherine's death, to be held for ever by him and his issue. If Thomas were to die without issue the three tenements should be sold by George's executors, their executors, or subsequent executors and the money raised laid out by the executors on celebrating masses, repairing ways, giving alms to paupers, and doing other charitable deeds on behalf of George's soul, the souls of his father and mother, his wife Alice, and William Tenterer, and the souls of others. George devised to William Alexander two tenements, in which George dwelt, in Winchester Street, with the two shops which William Dowding and John Taylor hold severally, [and] with a garden lying between those tenements on the north side and George's tenement, which he devised to his brother Thomas, and a tenement formerly Richard Jewell's on the south side; also a tenement, in which William Lilley now dwells, standing, with those shops, between William Dowding's tenement on the east side and a tenement, in which Simon Tredinnick now dwells, on the west side, for 200 marks to be paid to William Fry, John Kirkby, and Thomas Merriott, executors of George, to provide sufficient security between them and William, a fourth executor. The tenements, with the shops and the garden, are to be held for ever by William Alexander and his heirs and assigns. By a charter George granted to Henry Popham, William Fry, John Kirkby, Thomas Merriott, and William Alexander and their heirs a meadow called Scammel's mead in Fisherton Anger and all his land, tenements, rent, and reversions in Berwick St. James: he now appointed that, if William Alexander were to pay the 200 marks to his co-executors, Henry, William Fry, John, and Thomas should quitclaim their right or claim to the meadow, land, tenements, rent, and reversions. The payment of that sum should be made as follows: William should pay to his co-executors £100 on the day of George's death, 100 marks within the following 6 months, and 50 marks within the following 6 months, and this to provide sufficient security to the co-executors. Those sums should be laid out by the co-executors on pious uses on behalf of the souls of those mentioned above. If William Alexander declined to pay those sums, defaulted in any payment, or would not provide sufficient security to his co-executors George devised the land, tenements, meadow, garden, rent, and reversions to his executors to be sold by them, their executors, or subsequent executors. The money received should be laid out by the executors on pious uses on behalf of George's soul, the souls of his wife Alice and his mother Maud, and the souls of others. Executors: Thomas Merriott, William Fry, John Kirkby, and William Alexander, who should be of common assent in executing the will. The other three might do nothing without the will and assent of Thomas in acquitting George's debtors, or those against whom George or his executors could have any action in his name which could turn into the impairment or delay of the will. Proved in London on 23 September 1410 in front of John Perch, a clerk, a registrar of the court of Canterbury, deputed a commissary of Thomas, the archbishop of Canterbury; the administration was granted to Thomas Merriott. Approved at a court held in front of the mayor, the bailiff, and other citizens; the seisin of the tenements in the city of Salisbury was released to the legatees.

2064 Approval of the will of Thomas Eyre, a citizen of Salisbury, made on 25 May 1410. Interment: in St. Martin's church in front of the image of the glorified Virgin. Bequests: 40*d*. each to the fabric of the cathedral church and to the light of the fraternity of the Holy Cross in that church; 20*s*. to the fabric of St. Martin's church, 6*s*. 8*d*. to the parochial chaplain, 12*d*. each to the other two chaplains, and 40*d*. to the fraternity of the Holy Sepulchre; 6*s*. 8*d*. to the fabric of St. Thomas's church, 40*d*. to the parochial chaplain for publicly pronouncing to his parishioners on each Sunday for the year following Thomas's death to pray for Thomas's soul, and 6*d*. to each chaplain of that church present at his funeral rites; 40*d*. to the fabric of St. Edmund's church, 2*s*. to the fraternity of the Holy Cross, 20*s*. to the light of the art of the weavers of Salisbury, and a brass pot containing 30 gallons, to be had on the death of his wife Alice, to the fraternity of that light; 40*d*. to the fabric of Thruxton church; a tunic of blood-red ray, of the style of the citizens, to William Cormell, tailor; a tunic, of the style of the citizens of the present year, to Richard Gage; a quarter's rent was pardoned to each of John Dorset, John Parson, John London, to whom Thomas also bequeathed a white bow, and Abbot Pyle; 5*s*. was remitted to Simon Canon; an old gown of motley and 6*s*. 8*d*. to John Cale so that he might apply his diligence about the instruction of Thomas's apprentices; two blankets and a coverlet to John Snow, his apprentice; 20*s*. and a painted bow to Robert, his apprentice, if he should serve Thomas's wife well and faithfully until the end of his term; a tunic, of Thomas's own style, to Peter, his servant; a hood to John Richman; his strongest bow to John Daniel; 40*d*. each to Edith and Alice, his household servants; 6*s*. 8*d*. which she should have paid for medicines was pardoned to a younger Alice, his household servant; a riding tunic and 40*s*. to Walter Cox for his work; 40*s*., which he owed to him with security, was remitted to Peter Forster; 11*s*., which he owed to him, was remitted to Richard Forster; a tunic of green ray to John Bulmer; 13 wax candles, each weighing 1 lb., to be burned around his corpse ...[*MS. damaged*]; 12*d*. to each of his godchildren; a ring of pure gold to Agnes, a daughter of Nicholas Hayward, of Salisbury; enough new cloth for a new coat to be made for her to Alice, a daughter of John Kill; 100*s*. to be laid out after the death of him and his wife Alice, or in Alice's lifetime if it could be done advantageously, among paupers and the feeble in the hospital of the Holy Trinity to pray for his soul; a mazer furnished with silver, called Christmas, to the priory of Easton;

100 masses should be celebrated, immediately after his death if that could be done advantageously, on behalf of his soul and the souls of others; 10s. both to the Dominicans of Fisherton and the Franciscans of Salisbury, [in each case] to pray for his soul and the souls of others; all [his] clothes and their accoutrements without any kind of condition to his wife Alice; 40s. and a piece of silver, with a cover, called the great bowl to Nicholas Harding; the rest of his goods to Alice if she kept herself celibate and without a husband; if Alice married, half of the rest of the goods to Nicholas, one of Thomas's executors, to be sold and disposed of on behalf of Thomas's soul and the souls of others; 20s. to the mayor for the time being who outlived Thomas's will concerning the tenements, so that it might be faithfully carried out. Devises: Thomas wished that his wife Alice would relieve his brother William for his life in all things necessary for him, such as food and clothing, according to the demands of his condition, that William would have for life the room in Thomas's tenement in which he dwells, and that after William's death the room would remain to Alice for her life. If Alice failed to maintain William, Thomas devised to him for his life a rent of 60s. a year to be received from a corner tenement [in New Street and Gigant Street: cf. **2101**] of late John Newman's and from Thomas's tenement except the room devised to him. If the rent were in arrear for 15 days William might enter on the tenements, distrain, and keep distresses until the unpaid rent and other losses were recovered. Thomas devised to Alice for life all his land and tenements in Salisbury [in New Street and Gigant Street: cf. **2101**], with shops and cottages, except the room mentioned above. After Alice's death those premises should remain to Thomas's executors or their executors to be sold, the sale to be made with the oversight of the mayor for the time being. Otherwise the reversion of the premises might be sold by the executors in Alice's lifetime. The money received should be laid out on celebrating masses, giving alms, repairing ways, and doing other charitable deeds on behalf of Thomas's soul and the souls of others. Executors: his wife Alice and Nicholas Harding; overseer, Walter Cox. Proved on 29 May 1410 in front of William Summerhill, the subdean; the administration was entrusted to Alice, Nicholas Harding utterley refusing it. Approved at a court held in front of the mayor, the bailiff, and other citizens; the seisin of the tenements was released to the legatees.

19 November 1410, at Salisbury
2065 Approval [*dated to the Wednesday after the feast of St. Edmund the King (26 November) probably in error for the Wednesday before that feast (19 November)*] of the will of William Surr, of Salisbury, made on 30 March 1404. Interment in the graveyard of St. Edmund's church. Bequests: 6d. each to the fabric of the cathedral church and to the light of the Holy Cross in that church; 2s. to the fabric of St. Edmund's church, and 2s. 6d. to six priests of that church; the rest of his goods to his wife Tamsin to pay his debts and lay out on behalf of his soul. Devises: to Tamsin for life [Bert's Corner: cf. **2072**], the tenement in which he lived; also to Tamsin for life cottages and shops in Wineman Street and Culver Street between a tenement of Gilbert Oword on either side [cf. **1807, 2071**]. After Tamsin's

death the tenement, shops, and cottages should be sold by her executors, or the reversion of them when it fell due might be sold by Tamsin, as William's executor, and Roger Capon, the overseer of his will. The money received should be laid out on behalf of William's soul, Tamsin's soul, and the souls of others. Executor: Tamsin; overseer, Roger Capon. Witnesses: William Chapman, William Spencer, and others. Proved on 11 April 1404 in front of an officer of the subdean; the administration was entrusted to the executor. Approved at a court held in front of the bailiff, the mayor, and other citizens; the seisin of the tenement, shops, and cottages was released to the legatee.

17 December 1410, at Salisbury
2066 A deed of Richard Spencer and John Little, executors of John Amesbury, of late a citizen of Salisbury. John Amesbury devised to his wife Cecily for life a tenement in Culver Street, which is called Mealmonger Street, between a tenement of late Walter Furmage's, now John Needler's, on the south side and a tenement of late Richard Meager's, now John Breamore's, on the north side. On Cecily's death the tenement should remain for ever to his son John and his issue, if that John were to die without issue it would remain for ever to the elder John's daughter Agnes and her issue, and if Agnes were to die without issue it should be sold by the elder John's executors or their executors. The money received should be laid out by the executors on behalf of the elder John's soul and the souls of others. Cecily has died, the younger John and Agnes have died without living issue, the tenement pertains to the executors to be sold, and on the strength of the will Richard Spencer and John Little granted it to John Huish, weaver, and his wife Agnes, to be held for ever by them and John's heirs and assigns as that which John bought for a sum of money paid to the executors to fulfill John Amesbury's will. Seals: those of Richard Spencer and John Little and the common and mayoral seals of the city. Named witnesses: the bailiff, the mayor, a coroner, the reeves, William Warmwell, William Warin, Walter Shirley, William Bishop, Nicholas Harding, and the clerk

2067 By her charter Maud, the relict of William Guys, granted to James Green, a chaplain, four cottages, with a portion of meadow land, which, under the name of a piece of meadow land, she and William jointly acquired from David, a clerk. The cottages, with little gardens appurtenant to them, stand in Drake Hall Street [Carter Street in **810**], the portion of meadow land lies beside them, and a large portion of the meadow land was taken up in the common ditch of the city there. The cottages, with the portion of meadow land, are bounded by a meadow formerly Robert of Ann's on the south side and a meadow of late Walter Goss's on the north side, and the portion of meadow land extends from Drake Hall Street to Freren Street. They are to be held for ever by James and his heirs and assigns. Clause of warranty. Seals: Maud's and the common and mayoral seals of the city. Named witnesses: the bailiff, the mayor, a coroner, a reeve, William Warmwell, William Warin, Richard Leach, Nicholas Bell, John Becket, and the clerk

2068 By her letters of attorney Maud, the relict of William Guys, appointed

William Boyton, called Bowyer, to surrender into the hand of Robert, the bishop of Salisbury, the seisin of four cottages and a portion of meadow land [*as in* **2067**] to the use of James Green, a chaplain. Seals: Maud's and the mayoral seal of the city

2069 By their charter Margaret Denman, an executor of John Caundle, a matins clerk in the cathedral church, and William Caundle, a chaplain, and Robert Denman, her co-executors, on the strength of John's will granted to the master Henry Harborough, a clerk, and William Boyton, called Bowyer, a corner tenement, in which John dwelt and which was previously Alice Rushall's, in New Street and Brown Street between a tenement of William Warmwell on either side. The tenement is to be held for ever by Henry and William and Henry's heirs and assigns. Seals: those of the grantors and the common and mayoral seals of the city. Named witnesses: the bailiff, the mayor, a coroner, a reeve, William Warmwell, John Mower, Richard Spencer, William Sall, William Warin, and the clerk

2070 An indenture perfected between the master Henry Harborough, a clerk, and William Boyton, called Bowyer, on one side and Margaret Denman, William Caundle, a priest, and Robert Denman on the other side. Margaret, William, and Robert, as executors of John Caundle, of late a matins clerk in the cathedral church, granted to Henry and William a corner tenement, in which John dwelt, in New Street and Brown Street [*as in* **2069**], to be held for ever by Henry and William and Henry's heirs and assigns. Henry and William, however, now grant that, if Margaret, William, and Robert, or anyone on their behalf, should pay to Henry or his assigns at Salisbury for the following five years after next Christmas £4 cash a year by equal portions at the four usual terms, or within a month after each of the terms, beginning next Easter, the charter of feoffment perfected for them would be annulled. If Margaret, Robert, and William defaulted in any payment the charter and the feoffment perfected by it would hold their force. Seals: those of the parties to the parts of the indenture in turn and the mayoral seal of the city

2071 By their deed Richard Bristow and his wife Tamsin, the relict of William Surr, appearing at the court held on that day, granted to John Self and John Brock, chaplains, John Stone, of Wilton, and Stephen Edington their estate, or Tamsin's estate, in [Bert's Corner: *cf.* **2072**], a corner tenement, with cottages, which was of late William's. The tenement stands in Wineman Street and Culver Street, opposite [Ive's Corner: *cf.* **2004**], a tenement of John Hampton, brewer, between a tenement of late Gilbert Oword's in Wineman Street on the west side and Thomas Slegge's cottages, of late appurtenant to the corner tenement [*cf.* **1807, 2065**], in Culver Street on the south side, and, with the cottages, is to be held by the grantees and their heirs and assigns. Seals: those of Richard and Tamsin and the mayoral seal of the city. Named witnesses: the bailiff, the mayor, a coroner, the reeves, John Mower, Richard Spencer, William Sall, William Dowding, and John Lewisham

31 December 1410, at Salisbury

2072 A deed of Richard Bristow and his wife Tamsin, the relict, and an executor, of William Surr, and of Roger Capon. William devised to Tamsin for life a tenement, with shops and cottages, in Wineman Street and Culver Street on a corner [*as in* **2071**] [*margin*: Bert's Corner]. After Tamsin's death the tenement should be sold by her executors, or the reversion might be sold by Tamsin and Roger in Tamsin's lifetime. The money received should be laid out on behalf of William's soul and the souls of others. John Self and John Brock, chaplains, John Stone, of Wilton, and Stephen Edington hold Tamsin's estate in the tenement and have paid a sum of money to Tamsin to have the reversion to fulfill William's will. Richard and Tamsin, she as William's executor, and Roger, appearing at the court held on that day, on the strength of William's will now granted to John Self, John Brock, John Stone, and Stephen Edington the reversion of the tenement, with the shops and the cottages, to be held for ever by them and their heirs and assigns as that which they bought from Richard, Tamsin, and Roger, who released to them and their heirs and assigns their right or claim to the tenement. Seals: those of Richard, Tamsin, and Roger and the common and mayoral seals of the city. Named witnesses: the bailiff, the mayor, a coroner, the reeves, John Mower, Richard Spencer, Walter Shirley, William Sall, and William Dowding

14 January 1411, at Salisbury
2073 By his deed Nicholas Harding, a citizen of Salisbury, quitclaimed to William Sall, a citizen of Salisbury, and his heirs and assigns his right or claim to a corner tenement, with a yard (*or* yards) and a shop (*or* shops), of late Robert Body's, which Nicholas and William of late held jointly by Robert's grant. The tenement stands, in Wineman Street and Brown Street, between John Wishford's tenement in Wineman Street on the west side and Henry Popham's cottage property, appurtenant to a tenement which Martin Dyer holds, in Brown Street on the north side. Seals: Nicholas's and the common and mayoral seals of the city. Named witnesses: the bailiff, the mayor, a coroner, the reeves, John Mower, Richard Spencer, Walter Shirley, William Walter, William Bishop, and the clerk
2074 By his deed William Sall, a citizen of Salisbury, granted to William Stout and a younger John Pope the reversion of a tenement, with a yard (*or* yards), when it fell due on the death of Robert Durrant, draper. The tenement, of late that of Richard Hawes, hellier, in which Robert now dwells, stands in New Street, towards Barnwell's cross, between cottage property of the provost of St. Edmund's church on the east side and a tenement of late John Wishford's, now Richard Gage's, on the west side. The reversion, and the tenement when it fell due, are to be held for ever by William Stout and John Pope and their heirs and assigns. Seals: William Sall's and the common and mayoral seals of the city. Named witnesses: the bailiff, the mayor, a coroner, the reeves, John Mower, Richard Spencer, William Walter, Adam Teffont, William Dowding, and the clerk

28 January 1411, at Salisbury
2075 A deed of Gillian, the relict, and an executor, of Richard Jewell, of late a citizen of Salisbury, and of John Smith, a chaplain, her co-executor. Richard devised two tenements to Gillian for life, one, in which Richard dwelt, in New

Street [*as in* **2061**], and the other, in which Richard Sherman dwells, in Carter Street [*as in* **2061**]. Richard appointed that after Gillian's death the tenements should be sold by his executors, or if it seemed best the reversion of them might be sold in her lifetime. The money received should be laid out on behalf of Richard's soul and the souls of others. Richard devised to his executors a tenement, which is now held as two dwelling houses, in New Street [*as in* **2061**] to be sold immediately after his death. The money received was to pay his debts and fulfil his legacies. William Besil, esq., has paid to the executors a sum of money, the true value both of the reversion of the two tenements when they fall due on Gillian's death and of the tenement to be held by him immediately, to fulfil the intention of Richard's will and Gillian, and John Smith, on the strength of the will granted to him the reversion of the two tenements and the third tenement. The reversion and the tenement are to be held for ever by William and his heirs and assigns as that which he bought from Gillian and John in good faith, saving to Gillian her estate for life in the two tenements. Seals: those of Gillian and John and the common and mayoral seals of the city. Named witnesses: the bailiff, the mayor, a coroner, the reeves, John Mower, Richard Spencer, Walter Shirley, William Sall, and the clerk

11 February 1411, at Salisbury
2076 A deed of John at the hurn, a son of William at the hurn, dyer, of late a citizen of Salisbury, and his wife Joan. By their indented charter the master Simon Sydenham, a clerk, and John Sydenham, of Salisbury, granted to Robert Watercombe and his wife Agnes a sister of John at the hurn, a rent of 20*s.* a year issuing from a shop in Salisbury which John Bodenham holds for the life of Joan, John at the hurn's mother, and a tenement of late William's opposite the market place where grains are sold, [*as in* **2049–50**]. The rent and the tenement are to be held by Robert and Agnes and Agnes's issue. John at the hurn now confirmed those grants to Robert and Agnes, saving to himself and his heirs a right to the reversion of the tenement if it fell due according to the terms of the indented charter. Seals: John's and the mayoral seal of the city. Named witnesses: the mayor, the bailiff, a coroner, the reeves, John Mower, Walter Shirley, William Warin, Thomas Mason, draper, Nicholas Melbury, and the clerk

25 March 1411, at Salisbury
2077 By his deed Thomas Castleton, mercer, a citizen of Salisbury, granted to Thomas Chaffin, cardmaker, of Warminster, a rent of a rose a year issuing from a tenement, which Robert Reading holds for life, and the reversion of the tenement when it falls due on Robert's death, to be held for ever by Thomas Chaffin and his heirs and assigns. The tenement, of late that of William Purser and his wife Cecily, stands in Minster Street between the tenement of Pinnock's Inn on the north side and a tenement of late Roger Tarrant's on the south side. Seals: Thomas Castleton's and the common and mayoral seals of the city. Named witnesses: the bailiff, the mayor, a coroner, the reeves, John Mower, Richard Spencer, Walter Shirley, William Bishop, Thomas Child, and the clerk.

Endorsement: Robert Reading, the tenant for life, present in the court, by the reading aloud of the deed in full court in front of the mayor, the bailiff, and many others, manifestly attorned to Thomas Chaffin.
2078 By his charter John Wootton, a citizen of Salisbury, granted to Richard Spencer, a citizen of Salisbury, a corner tenement or messuage, with conjoined shops and cottages, in Winchester Street and Culver Street between an elder John Pope's tenement in Winchester Street on the west side and William Sall's yard in Culver Street on the south side [*margin*: Holy Ghost Corner], to be held for ever by Richard, and his heirs and assigns. Clause of warranty. Seals: John's and the common and mayoral seals of the city. Named witnesses: the bailiff, the mayor, a coroner, the reeves, John Mower, William Warmwell, William Walter, Walter Shirley, and the clerk

8 April 1411, at Salisbury
2079 By his charter William Duke, ironmonger, granted to John Swift, ironmonger, and John Hellier, ironmonger, a tenement in Endless Street between a tenement of late Edmund Bramshaw's, now Thomas Farrant's, on the north side and a tenement of late John Fowle's on the south side. The tenement was of late Stephen Shearer's, descended to William by right of inheritance on the death of his father John Duke, and is to be held for ever by John Swift and John Hellier and their heirs and assigns. Clause of warranty. Seals: William's and the common and mayoral seals of the city. Named witnesses: the bailiff, the mayor, a coroner, the reeves, John Mower, Richard Spencer, Walter Shirley, Nicholas Melbury, and the clerk
2080 By his charter John, a son of Nicholas Breamore, of late a citizen of Salisbury, granted to John Hogman and John Butler, citizens of Salisbury, a messuage, in which he dwelt, in Culver Street, which is called Mealmonger Street, on the south side of a tenement, of late William Warmwell's, which Thomas Ferring now holds. The messuage descended to John Breamore by right of inheritance on the death of his sister Denise and is to be held for ever by John Hogman and John Butler and their heirs and assigns. Clause of warranty. Seals: John Breamore's and the common and mayoral seals of the city. Named witnesses: the bailiff, the mayor, a coroner, the reeves, John Needler, Richard Leach, John Lewisham, Nicholas Melbury, William Slegge, and the clerk
2081 By his indented deed Richard Spencer, a citizen of Salisbury, granted to William Walter and William Warin, citizens of Salisbury, a corner tenement or messuage, with conjoined shops and cottages, in Winchester Street and Culver Street [*as in* **2078**] [*margin*: Holy Ghost Corner], to be held for ever by them and their heirs and assigns for a rent of 30s. a year to be paid to Richard and his heirs and assigns. The grantees and their heirs and assigns should maintain and repair the premises in all things necessary at their own expense so that the rent would not be lost. Clause to permit re-entry if the rent were in arrear for 15 days, distraint, and the keeping of distresses until the unpaid rent and other losses were recovered; also, if the rent were in arrear for a month, to permit repossession until the unpaid rent and other losses were recovered. Seals: those of the parties to

the parts of the indented deed in turn and the common and mayoral seals of the city. Named witnesses: the bailiff, the mayor, a coroner, the reeves, John Mower, William Warmwell, William Bishop, Nicholas Harding, and the clerk

22 April 1411, at Salisbury
2082 By his charter John Needler, a citizen of Salisbury, granted to William Sall, a citizen of Salisbury, and Peter Daw, mercer, a tenement, with a yard and a garden, in Mealmonger Street, between William Warmwell's cottage property on the south side and cottage property of late John Mower's, now John Huish's, on the north side, to be held for ever by them and their heirs and assigns. Clause of warranty. Seals: John Needler's and the common and mayoral seals of the city. Named witnesses: the bailiff, the mayor, a coroner, the reeves, Richard Spencer, Walter Shirley, William Walter, Richard Leach, John Lewisham, and the clerk

6 May 1411, at Salisbury
2083 By their charter John Hogman and John Butler, citizens of Salisbury, granted to John Breamore, weaver, and his wife Alice a messuage, in which that John dwells and which they held by his grant, in Culver Street, which is called Mealmonger Street, [*as in* **2080**]. The messuage is to be held for ever by John and Alice and the issue begotten between them, and if John and Alice were to die without such issue it would remain for ever to the direct heirs of John's blood. Seals: those of John Hogman and John Butler and the common and mayoral seals of the city. Named witnesses: the bailiff, the mayor, a coroner, the reeves, William Sall, William Walter, Richard Leach, John Needler, John Lewisham, and the clerk

30 September 1410 x 29 September 1411
2084 The will of Edmund Penstone, which includes a tenement in New Street. Approved
2085–6 Two writings concerning a tenement in New Street: charter of William Warmwell and William River perfected for Thomas Biston and his wife Agnes, and letters of attorney for delivering the seisin
2087 A ratification of Joan, the wife of John Kilham, perfected for Robert Watercombe and his wife Agnes concerning a tenement opposite the market place [where grains are sold: *cf.* **2076**]
2088–90 Three writings perfected for the commonalty of the vicars of the cathedral church: two licences, one of the king and one of the bishop of Salisbury, to appropriate a tenement (*or* tenements), and a charter of John Gowan concerning a tenement (*or* tenements) in the city
2091–2 Two deeds concerning a tenement towards St. Martin's church: one of Maud, the wife [?relict: *cf.* **1313**, **2111**] of John Dogskin, perfected for John Levenoth and his wife Isabel, with letters for delivering the seisin, and one of 'the same John perfected for the same John and Maud'
2093–4 Two writings perfected for Edward Frith concerning a tenement in Endless Street: a charter of Stephen Edington, and a release of John Waite, hosier,

and his wife Maud

2095 A charter of James Green, a chaplain, perfected for John 'Shorberd' concerning cottages in Drake Hall Street

2096 A deed of a younger John Forest perfected for Nicholas Harding and Robert Forest, executors of an elder John Forest, concerning a tenement in Endless Street

2097–8 Two writings of Nicholas Harding and Robert Forest, executors of an elder John Forest: a deed perfected for a younger John Forest, and a charter perfected for Nicholas Melbury concerning a tenement in Wineman Street

16 December 1411, at Salisbury

2099 A deed of Nicholas Harding, a citizen of Salisbury, and Robert Forest, executors of an elder John Forest, of late a citizen of Salisbury. John devised to a younger John Forest, his [younger] son, for his life a tenement, in which the younger John then dwelt, except an attached shop, appurtenant to the tenement, devised to the elder John's wife Christine for her life. The shop stands in Endless Street between the tenement on the south side and Roger Enterbush's tenement on the north side, and the tenement stands between the shop on the north side and a cottage then that of John Little, mercer, on the south side. After the death of Christine and the younger John the tenement and the shop should be sold by the executors. Christine is dead, and the younger John has released his estate in the tenement to the executors for ever, so that the whole tenement, with the shop, belongs to the executors to be sold. On the strength of the John Forest's will Nicholas and Robert granted the tenement, with the shop, to a younger John Shute, weaver, to be held for ever by him and his heirs and assigns as that which he bought from them in good faith for a sum of money, reaching the value of the tenement, to be laid out by them according to the will of the elder John Forest. Seals: those of Nicholas and Robert and the common and mayoral seals of the city. Named witnesses: the bailiff, the mayor, a coroner, the reeves, William Warmwell, Richard Spencer, William Sall, William Bishop, John Becket, and the clerk

5 April 1412, at Salisbury

2100 A licence of Robert, the bishop of Salisbury, the lord of the city of Salisbury, and of the dean and chapter [*the licence is wrongly dated to the Tuesday after Easter day in the 14th year of the reign of Henry IV, an impossible date, and is assumed to be of that day in the 13th year of that reign*]. On 1 June 1406 the king granted that the mayor and commonalty of the city might acquire land, tenements, and rent in the city to the value of 100 marks a year [*as in **1931***]. By their writing the bishop and the dean and chapter, to enhance the status of the mayor and to ease the burdens of the city, for themselves and their successors licensed the mayor and commonalty and their successors to acquire land, tenements, and rent in the city to the value of £40 a year, notwithstanding the Statute of Mortmain or that the land, tenements, and rent might be held of the bishop as of his church and bishopric, provided that the mayor and commonalty might enter on nothing under colour of this licence before they had certified the true value of it in front of the bishop's officers. Seals:

those of the bishop and the dean and chapter

6 April 1412, at Salisbury
2101 A deed of John Bromley and his wife Alice, the relict, and an executor, of Thomas Eyre, of late a citizen of Salisbury, and of Nicholas Harding, also an executor of Thomas. Thomas devised to Alice for her life all his land and tenements, with shops and cottages, in the city except a room in a tenement of his, in which his brother William dwelt, and a rent of 60s. a year, which he devised to William for his life. The rent is to be received from that tenement and from a tenement and a cottage (*or* cottages) of late John Newman's on a condition contained in the will. The land, tenements, shops, and cottages on Alice's death, and the room and rent on William's death, should remain to Thomas's executors to be sold; alternatively, they might be sold by the executors in Alice's lifetime. The money received should be laid out on behalf of Thomas's soul and the souls of others. The land, tenements, shops, and cottages stand conjointly in New Street and Gigant Street between a tenement, the hospital of the Holy Trinity, on the west side and Christine Handley's tenement in Gigant Street on the north side. Richard Fitton, John Hurle, and William Mottram, clerks, have agreed with the executors, for 100 marks to be paid to the executors at agreed terms, for the premises to be held by them and, because it would be more certain and advantageous to fulfill Thomas's will in the lifetime of his executors rather than to rely on their executors, on the strength of the will John and Alice, and Nicholas, at the court held on that day granted to Richard, John, and William all the land, tenements, shops, and cottages, except what was devised for life to William Eyre, to be held for ever by them and their heirs and assigns. Seals: those of the grantors and the common and mayoral seals of the city. Named witnesses: the bailiff, the mayor, a coroner, the reeves, John Mower, Richard Spencer, Walter Shirley, William Warin, Walter Nalder, and the clerk

2102 By his charter Richard Oword, a citizen of Salisbury, granted to John Smith, a chaplain, and Stephen Edington a tenement, in which he dwelt, near the graveyard of St. Thomas's church, between a tenement of late William Godmanstone's on the south side and a corner tenement of late Thomas Burford's, now that of the master John Chitterne, on the north side, to be held for ever by them and their heirs and assigns. Clause of warranty. Seals: Richard's and the common and mayoral seals of the city. Named witnesses: the bailiff, the mayor, a coroner, the reeves, John Mower, Richard Spencer, Walter Shirley, William Sall, and Thomas Mason

2103 By her charter Alice, the relict of William Bailey, draper, of Salisbury, granted to John Smith, a chaplain, and Stephen Edington a tenement, with a shop (*or* shops) and a cellar (*or* cellars), in Minster Street, which is called Castle Street, between a tenement of late Thomas Bowyer's on the south side and a tenement, with a shop (*or* shops), of John Dyer, of Longbridge Deverill, on the north side, to be held for ever by them and their heirs and assigns. Clause of warranty. Seals: Alice's and the common and mayoral seals of the city. Named witnesses: the bailiff, the mayor, a coroner, the reeves, John Mower, Richard

Spencer, Walter Shirley, William Sall, and Thomas Mason

20 April 1412, at Salisbury
2104 Approval of the will of an elder John Bodenham, a citizen of Salisbury, made on 28 March 1412. Interment: at Wilton at the head of the tomb of his late wife Isabel. Bequests: 6s. 8d. to the fabric of the cathedral church; 40s. to the fabric of St. Thomas's church; 20s. to the fabric of St. Edmund's church; 13s. 4d. both to the Dominicans of Fisherton and the Franciscans of Salisbury, in each case to pray for his soul; 6s. 8d. for the maintenance of the hospital called Almshouse; 20s. to the fabric of St. Edith's church, Wilton; 40s. each to the fabric of St. Michael's church in South Street, Wilton, and in aid of the rector's dwelling when he began to build it; 3s. 4d. to the fabric of each of the other parish churches of Wilton; 20s. to the fabric of St. Giles's church near Wilton; 13s. 4d. to the fabric of the church of the Dominicans there, and 2s. 6d. to each of the two friars to pray for his soul; £20 to his son the lord William, a chaplain, to pray for his soul; £10 each to Edward Frith and John Parch, his executors; £10 to his daughter Olive, John Parch's wife; £100 to his wife Alice for the share of his goods appurtenant to her, besides the stock of his house which is called household appurtenant to her share, on condition that she would hold herself content with the tenement devised to her below as her dower and with the bequests to her, that she would not implead or trouble John's executors for more of his goods, and that, if she did, she would go without everything appointed to her; 20s. a year to the lord John Hatter to pray for, and celebrate mass on behalf of, his soul, the soul of his late wife Isabel, and the souls of others, for the six years following his death; 6d. to each nun properly in Wilton abbey; his executors should appoint a chaplain to celebrate mass at Wilton for the seven years following his death on behalf of his soul, Isabel's soul, and the souls of others; his executors should also appoint a chaplain to celebrate mass in St. Thomas's church in a similar way, for the same time, and on behalf of the same souls; the rest of his goods to his executors to be disposed of on behalf of his soul and other souls. Devises: to his brother William for life three conjoined cottages in Kingsbury Street, Wilton, and after his death for ever to John's son Henry and his heirs and assigns. John devised to his son John two conjoined meadows in the borough of Wilton, one called Castle mead and one called Middle mead, to be held for ever by him and his heirs and assigns. He devised to that John for life a croft lying in Little moor near Wilton, with the reversion of a messuage and a yard which John Chamber holds there for his life, and on the death of the younger John Bodenham the croft and the reversion, when it fell due on the death of John Chamber, should remain for ever to Olive, a daughter of the elder John Bodenham's son Henry, and her heirs and assigns. John devised to John Netton, of Wilton, a messuage, in which that John dwells, in Minster Street, Wilton, near the abbey, to be held for ever by him and his heirs and assigns. He devised to Hugh Mack, of Wilton, a tenement, of which Hugh is possessed, in West Street, Wilton, to be held for ever by him and his heirs and assigns. He devised to his son John a rent of a rose a year issuing from a tenement of late John Gatcombe's, which that John's relict Joan holds for her life,

in Salisbury, opposite the market place where grains are sold, between William Tull's tenement on the west side and Nicholas Melbury's tenement, which John Shad holds, on the east side, with the reversion of the tenement when it fell due on Joan's death; also shops in Salisbury, which the elder John acquired from an elder John Chandler and which were of late those of John Ferrer, a citizen of Salisbury, on a corner in Minster Street and Winchester Street; also a tenement, built for a dwelling house, in Castle Street, Salisbury, between a tenement of late Nicholas Longstock's on the south side and a tenement, in which the elder John Bodenham lived, on the north side. The rent, the reversion, the shops, and the tenement are to be held for ever by the younger John and his heirs and assigns. The elder John appointed that the feoffees in two cottages, which he acquired from William Sall and Joan Gatcombe, in Chipper Street should enfeoff his daughter Olive, and her heirs and assigns, in them for ever. He devised to his son Henry all the land, tenements, mills, meadows, pasture, and feeding which he held in Wilton, and which is not specified above nor outside the borough, to be held for ever by him and his heirs and assigns on condition that he would pay 7 marks cash a year for the following 27 years to John's executors, and give sufficient security to the executors, to hold yearly at Wilton for his life the obit of Henry Bunt and his wives, as he was wont to. John devised to his wife Alice the tenement, with the easements appointed to it, in which he dwelt, in Castle Street, between William Warmwell's tenement on the north side and the tenement devised to his son John on the south side, to be held by her for life as dower. If Alice were to go without everything appointed to her, or on her death, death the tenement would descend and remain to the younger John Bodenham to be held for ever by him and his heirs and assigns. John devised to Alice for her life a rent of 7 marks a year to be paid to her by his executors or their assigns. <u>Executors</u>: his son John, Edward Frith, and John Parch. <u>Proved</u> on 3 April 1412 in front of an officer of the subdean; the administration was entrusted to the executors. <u>Approved</u> at a court held in front of the mayor, the bailiff, and other citizens; the relict Alice and the son John, the legatees, being present, the seisin of the tenements, rent, and shops in Salisbury was released to them.

2105 By his charter James Caundle granted to John Clive, tanner, a tenement, with a yard and its other appurtenances in length as in breadth, in Endless Street between John's tenement, of late Margaret Godmanstone's, on the south side and John Hogman's tenement on the north side. The tenement was of late that of James's grandfather Thomas Caundle, was afterwards that of James's father William, on William's death descended to James by right of inheritance, and, with the yard and other appurtenances, is to be held for ever by John Clive and his heirs and assigns. Clause of warranty. Seals: James's and the common and mayoral seals of the city. Named witnesses: the bailiff, the mayor, a coroner, the reeves, William Warmwell, Richard Spencer, William Walter, Thomas Child, John Becket, and the clerk

4 May 1412, at Salisbury
2106 By his charter John Needler, a citizen of Salisbury, granted to Robert

Stonard, baker, a tenement, which he acquired from John Waite, tailor, and his wife Maud, in Minster Street, which is called Castle Street, between his own cottage on the north side and Robert's tenement, of late William Higdon's, on the south side; also 1 ft. of ground, touching the tenement on the north side of it, which from long ago was appurtenant to the tenement for a gutter falling from it, called in English waterfall, 71 ft. in length from the hall of the tenement eastwards and 1 ft. in width everywhere. The tenement measures in width 13½ ft. at its frontage on the street and 17 ft., with the waterfall, at the back. It is to be held, with the ground, for ever by Robert and his heirs and assigns. Clause of warranty. Seals: John's and the common and mayoral seals of the city. Named witnesses: the bailiff, the mayor, a coroner, the reeves, John Mower, Richard Spencer, Walter Shirley, William Sall, Thomas Mason, and the clerk

18 May 1412, at Salisbury
2107 By their deed William Needler and Richard Needler, sons of John Needler, a citizen of Salisbury, quitclaimed to Robert Stonard, baker, and his heirs and assigns their right or claim to a tenement, which Robert held by John's grant, in Minster Street, which is called Castle Street, [*as in* **2106**]; also to 1 ft. of ground [*as in* **2106**]. Seals: those of William and Richard and the common and mayoral seals of the city. Named witnesses: the bailiff, the mayor, a coroner, the reeves, Richard Spencer, William Sall, William Walter, John Lewisham, William Fewster, and the clerk

15 June 1412, at Salisbury
2108 By their charter Robert Bowyer, weaver, and his wife Christine, appearing at the court held on that day, granted to John Brown, a household servant of the college of St. Edmund, and his wife Agnes a tenement in Wineman Street between a tenement of late William Mercer's, formerly Thomas Chaplin's, on the west side and a tenement of late Gilbert Oword's on the east side, to be held for ever by them and their heirs and assigns. Clause of warranty. Seals: those of Robert and Christine and the common and mayoral seals of the city. Named witnesses: the bailiff, the mayor, the coroners, the reeves, William Warmwell, Richard Spencer, William Sall, William Walter, John Lewisham, and the clerk

29 June 1412, at Salisbury
2109 By his deed John Thorburn, of Amersham, a brother of John Thorburn, of late a citizen of Salisbury, quitclaimed to John Mower, Richard Spencer, William Warin, William Walter, William Bishop, and John Judd, citizens of Salisbury, and their heirs and assigns his right or claim to all the land, tenements, shops, cottages, rent, and reversions in Salisbury of late those of John Shove, kt., and afterwards of John Thorburn [of Salisbury]. Seals: John Thorburn's and the common and mayoral seals of the city. Named witnesses: the mayor, the bailiff, a coroner, the reeves, William Warmwell, Walter Shirley, William Sall, Walter Nalder, and the clerk
2110 By his charter John Prentice, a clerk, of Salisbury, granted to Thomas Ryde,

a merchant, a citizen of Salisbury, a cottage, with a garden next to it, in Culver Street, on the east side of the street, between Thomas Knoyle's cottage property on the north side and John's own cottages on the south side. The cottage, with the garden, measures 29 ft. in width at its frontage on the street and extends in length from the street as far as the city's ditch. It is to be held for ever by Thomas and his heirs and assigns. Clause of warranty. Seals: John's and the common and mayoral seals of the city. Named witnesses: the bailiff, the mayor, the coroners, the reeves, John Mower, Richard Spencer, William Warin, William Sall, and the clerk

13 July 1412, at Salisbury
2111 By their charter John 'Levenoth' and his wife Isabel, appearing at the court held on that day, granted to Walter Nalder, a citizen of Salisbury, and Thomas Hellier, a chaplain, a tenement, with a cottage and a yard, in the street on the way towards St. Martin's church, between cottage property of late Robert Boyce's, now Thomas Glover's, on one side and cottage property of late John Forest's, now that of William Harnhill, barber, on the other side. The tenement, with the cottage and its other appurtenances, was of late John Dogskin's and was acquired by John and Isabel from Maud, the relict of John Dogskin, as his executor. It is to be held, with the cottage and the yard, for ever by Walter and Thomas and their heirs and assigns. Clause of warranty. Seals: those of John and Isabel and the common and mayoral seals of the city. Named witnesses: the bailiff, the mayor, the coroners, the reeves, William Warmwell, William Warin, William Walter, Thomas Child, John Becket, and the clerk

10 August 1412, at Salisbury
2112 By her charter Margaret, the relict of William Godmanstone, of late a citizen of Salisbury, granted to John Swift, ironmonger, a citizen of Salisbury, and his wife Christine a messuage, with a room (*or* rooms) and a sollar (*or* sollars) above it, which, by the name of shops, William and Margaret acquired from Robert Beechfount, an executor of Richard Ryborough, of late a citizen of Salisbury. The messuage stands in Minster Street, near the graveyard of St. Thomas's church, between a tenement of late John Farnborough's, afterwards Richard Oword's, on the north side and shop property of the vicars of the cathedral church on the south side. It is to be held for ever, with the room(s) and the sollar(s), by John and Christine and their heirs and assigns. Clause of warranty. Seals: Margaret's and the common and mayoral seals of the city. Named witnesses: the bailiff, the mayor, the coroners, the reeves, John Mower, Richard Spencer, Walter Shirley, William Sall, Walter Nalder, and the clerk
2113 By her letters of attorney Margaret, the relict of William Godmanstone, of late a citizen of Salisbury, appointed William Bowyer, Walter Short, and Roger Enterbush to surrender into the hand of Robert, the bishop of Salisbury, the seisin of a messuage, with a room (*or* rooms) and a sollar (*or* sollars), in Minster Street, near the graveyard of St. Thomas's church, [*as in* **2112**], to the use of John Swift, ironmonger, and his wife Christine. Seals: Margaret's and the mayoral seal

of the city

2114 By their writing John Mower and Richard Spencer, grocer, citizens of Salisbury, demised to William Dowding, a citizen of Salisbury, a tenement, which they held by a grant of William Hyde, grocer, and William Pickard, in Minster Street between Walter Orme's tenement on the south side and a tenement of late Robert Reading's on the north side. The tenement is to be held for ever by William Dowding and his heirs and assigns. Seals: those of John and Richard and the common and mayoral seals of the city. Named witnesses: the bailiff, the coroners, the reeves, William Warmwell, Walter Shirley, William Walter, Walter Nalder, Thomas Mason, draper, and the clerk

24 August 1412, at Salisbury

2115 By his deed William Pickard, grocer, quitclaimed to William Dowding, a citizen of Salisbury, and his heirs and assigns his right or claim to a tenement, which William Dowding held by a demise of John Mower and Richard Spencer, citizens of Salisbury, in Minster Street [*as in* **2114**]. Clause of warranty. Seals: William Pickard's and the common and mayoral seals of the city. Named witnesses: the bailiff, the coroners, the reeves, William Warmwell, Walter Shirley, William Walter, Walter Nalder, Thomas Mason, and the clerk

2116 By her indented deed Alice, the relict of John Sewin, of late a citizen of Salisbury, granted to John Swift, ironmonger, a citizen of Salisbury, and his wife Christine her estate for life in a tenement, with shops, in which John Sewin dwelt, in the street on the way towards the upper bridge of Fisherton, between a tenement of late Nicholas Taylor's on the east side and a tenement of late Richard at the bridge's, which John Crablane of late held, on the west side. There are excepted from the grant, and reserved to Alice for her life, two rooms fronting on the street, one above a shop appurtenant to the tenement and the other above a gate of the tenement, with free ingress to, and egress from, those rooms by means of an ascent, called stair, within the tenement. The estate and the tenement, with the shops and except the rooms, are to be held for Alice's life by John and Christine and John's heirs and assigns, paying a rent of 26s. 8d. cash a year to Alice or her assigns for Alice's life. John and Christine should repair and maintain the tenement, with the shops, in all things necessary at their own expense so that the rent would not be lost. Clause to permit re-entry if the rent were in arrear for 15 days, distraint, and the keeping of distresses until the unpaid rent was recovered; also, if sufficient distresses could not be found, to permit repossession and the retention of Alice's former estate. Seals: those of the parties to the parts of the indented charter in turn and the mayoral seal of the city. Named witnesses: the bailiff, the mayor, the coroners, the reeves, John Mower, Richard Spencer, Walter Shirley, William Sall, and the clerk

7 September 1412, at Salisbury

2117 By his charter William Dowding, a citizen of Salisbury, granted to Thomas Chaffin, called Cardmaker, of Warminster, a tenement in Minster Street [*as in* **2114**], to be held for ever by him and his heirs and assigns. Clause of warranty.

Seals: William's and the common and mayoral seals of the city. Named witnesses: the bailiff, the coroners, the reeves, William Warmwell, John Mower, Richard Spencer, Walter Shirley, John Becket, and the clerk

2118 By her writing Agnes, the relict of John Green, cooper, and a sister of John Sewin, of late a citizen of Salisbury, in her celibate widowhood, quitclaimed to John Swift, ironmonger, a citizen of Salisbury, and his wife Christine and to John's heirs and assigns her right or claim, or her right or claim after the death of Alice, the relict of John Sewin, to a tenement, with a shop, of late John Sewin's. The tenement stands in a street on the way towards the upper bridge of Fisherton, [*as in* **2116**]. Seals: Agnes's and the common and mayoral seals of the city. Named witnesses: the bailiff, the mayor, the coroners, the reeves, John Mower, Richard Spencer, William Warin, William Sall, and the clerk

2119 By their charter Walter Shirley and William Dowding, citizens of Salisbury, quitclaimed to John Mower and Richard Spencer, citizens of Salisbury, and their heirs and assigns their right or claim to a tenement which they held with John and Richard by a grant of Nicholas Harding, a citizen of Salisbury. The tenement stands in Winchester Street, between a tenement of late that of a younger William Tenterer, in which William Hill dwelt, on the east side and a tenement of late Nicholas Baker's on the west side, and was of late that of John Newman, a merchant, a citizen of Salisbury. Seals: those of Walter and William and the common and mayoral seals of the city. Named witnesses: the bailiff, the coroners, the reeves, William Warmwell, William Warin, William Sall, Walter Nalder, and the clerk

2120 By his deed William Sall, a citizen of Salisbury, quitclaimed to John Mower [and Richard Spencer *deleted*], citizens of Salisbury, and their heirs and assigns his right or claim to a tenement, with racks and a yard (*or* yards), or to a rent of 26*s*. 8*d*. a year issuing from it, which was of late Margaret Godmanstone's. The tenement stands in Gigant Street, on the way towards St. Edmund's church, between Richard Weston's cottage property, beside a garden of late John Ball's, on the south side and William Hoare's yard, which Nicholas Buckland holds, on the north side. Seals: William's and the common and mayoral seals of the city. Named witnesses: the mayor, the bailiff, the coroners, the reeves, William Warmwell, Walter Nalder, Nicholas Bell, Thomas Mason, Thomas Child, and the clerk

21 September 1412, at Salisbury
2121 A deed of William Dowding, a citizen of Salisbury, and of Richard Oword and Robert Warmwell, the keepers of the fabric and goods of St. Thomas's church. John Sewin, a citizen of Salisbury, devised to his wife Alice for life a tenement in a street on the way towards the upper bridge of Fisherton, [*as in* **2116**]. On Alice's death the tenement should remain for ever to the direct heirs begotten between John and her and to the issue of those heirs, if those heirs were to die without issue it would remain for life to John's sister Agnes, and after Agnes's death it should be sold by the mayor for the time being and by the keepers of the fabric and goods of St. Thomas's church for the time being. The money received should be laid out on behalf of John's soul and the souls of others. Because it is well

known to the current mayor and the current keepers that all the issue of John and Alice have died in their minority without issue, because Alice granted the estate which she had in the tenement for her life to John Swift, ironmonger, a citizen of Salisbury, and his wife Christine, because Agnes released her right or claim to the tenement which would fall due to her on Alice's death to John and Christine and John's heirs and assigns, and because that John has paid to the mayor and keepers a sum of money for the tenement and the reversion of it, on the strength of John Sewin's will the mayor and the keepers granted the tenement, and the reversion of it when it fell due, to John and Christine to be held for ever by them and John's heirs and assigns. The mayor and the keepers release for themselves and their successors to John and Christine and John's heirs and assigns their right or claim to the tenement. Seals: those of the grantors and the common and mayoral seals of the city. Named witnesses: the bailiff, the coroners, the reeves, John Mower, Richard Spencer, Walter Shirley, William Warin, and the clerk

2122 By his charter William Warmwell, a citizen of Salisbury, granted to William Slegge, a citizen of Salisbury, a rent of 6s. a year issuing, and which he was accustomed to receive, from a tenement, now William Slegges's, of late Robert Boscombe's, afterwards that of William Guys, of late a citizen of Salisbury, in Gigant Street between a tenement formerly John Baldry's on one side and a tenement of late William Lord's, which Thomas Brute formerly held, on the other side. The rent was acquired by William Warmwell from John Chandler, a citizen of Salisbury, who acquired it from Robert Play, ironmonger, a citizen of Salisbury, and it is to be held for ever by William Slegge and his heirs and assigns. William Warmwell released to William Slegge and his heirs and assigns his right or claim to the tenement or rent. Clause of warranty. Seals: William Warmwell's and the common and mayoral seals of the city. Named witnesses: the bailiff, the mayor, the coroners, the reeves, John Mower, Richard Spencer, Walter Shirley, William Sall, Walter Nalder, and the clerk

2123 By their deed Walter Shirley, William Warin, William Bishop, and William Sall, citizens of Salisbury, quitclaimed to John Mower and Richard Spencer, citizens of Salisbury, and their heirs and assigns their right or claim to three cottages, with houses, gardens, and an empty plot, of late those of John Buddle, called Prentice, or to rent of 53s. 4d. a year issuing from them. The cottages stand in Wineman Street between a corner tenement of late that John Prentice's, now William Penton's, on the east side and a tenement of late that of an elder John Forest on the west side. Seals: those of the four who quitclaimed and the common and mayoral seals of the city. Named witnesses: the mayor, the bailiff, the coroners, the reeves, William Warmwell, Walter Nalder, John Becket, Thomas Mason, and the clerk

2124 By their deed William Warin, William Walter, William Bishop, and William Sall, citizens of Salisbury, quitclaimed to John Mower and Richard Spencer, citizens of Salisbury, and their heirs and assigns their right or claim, when it fell due on the death of a younger John Scot, to conjoined cottages of late those of John Salisbury, grocer. The cottages stand in Nuggeston and Gigant Street, on the way towards St. Edmund's church, between cottages of late John Butterley's, afterwards William Coventry's, on the north side and John Needler's tenement in Nuggeston on the east side. Seals: those of the four who quitclaimed and the common and mayoral seals of the city. Named witnesses: the mayor, the bailiff, the coroners, the reeves, William Warmwell, Walter Nalder, John Becket, Nicholas Bell, and the clerk

30 September 1411 x 29 September 1412
2125 A release of Edmund Dauntsey perfected for Thomas Linford concerning a tenement in Poultry
2126 A charter of Thomas Child and Edmund Purdy perfected for Walter Nalder concerning a tenement [?in Castle Street: *cf. 1897*] beyond the bar
2127 A charter of Thomas Ailward, a clerk, and others perfected for John Mower and William Walter concerning a tenement called Glastonbury's Corner
2128 A charter of Walter Dean, a chaplain, perfected for Gunnore Bowyer concerning a tenement [?in Castle Street: *cf. 1832*] beyond the bar; with letters of attorney for delivering the seisin
2129 A charter of Maud, the wife [?relict: *cf. 2067*] of William Guys, perfected for William Slegge concerning a tenement in Gigant Street
2130 A release of Robert Linden and his wife Alice perfected for John Sexhampcote, a chaplain, concerning a tenement in Castle Street
2131 A charter of John Fleming, of Snoddington, and his wife Agnes perfected for William Slegge concerning a tenement in Gigant Street
2132 A charter of John Sexhampcote, a chaplain, perfected for Robert Gilbert, a tanner, concerning a tenement in Castle Street
2133–5 Three writings perfected for Thomas Cardmaker, of Warminster: a charter of Edward Gilbert, dubber, concerning a tenement in Pot Row, a charter of William Warin concerning another tenement in Pot Row, and a release of William Warin and William Dowding concerning the second tenement
2136 A charter of Henry Delves and his wife Joan perfected for John Becket concerning various tenements in the city; with letters for delivering the seisin
2137 A charter of John Little perfected for Richard Spencer concerning a corner tenement in Endless Street
2138–9 Two writings perfected for John Cornish concerning a tenement in Castle Street: a charter of Thomas Fyport, and a release of Simon Blackhall
2140–2 Three charters concerning a tenement in New Street beside the bridge: one of John Mower perfected for William Fewster, one of William Fewster perfected for William Sall, and one of William Sall perfected for William Fewster and his wife Edith
2143 A release of Richard Spencer, William Sall, and others perfected for John Mower concerning a tenement in New Street
2144–5 Two charters concerning a tenement in Castle Street: one of Thomas Burford, dyer, perfected for Thomas Dereham and others, and one of re-feoffment perfected for 'the same John' [?*rectius* Thomas Burford] and his wife Joan
2146 A charter of Richard Leach perfected for William at the lea and his wife Christine concerning a tenement above a ditch

2147 A charter of Richard Spencer perfected for John Little and his wife Joan concerning a corner tenement in Endless Street
2148 A charter of Richard Leach perfected for Richard Spencer and John Jakes concerning all [his] land and tenements in the city
2149 A charter of William Sall and Peter Daw perfected for William Needler and his wife Agnes concerning a tenement in Mealmonger Street
2150 A charter of Reynold Glover perfected for Thomas Cardmaker concerning a tenement in Minster Street
2151 A charter of John Castleton perfected for Thomas Castleton and his wife Goude concerning a tenement and a cottage (*or* cottages) in St. Martin's Street and Shit Lane
2152 The will of an elder John Chandler, which includes various tenements and rent. Approved

16 November 1412, at Salisbury
2153 By his charter Richard Spencer, a citizen of Salisbury, granted to Thomas Ryde, a merchant, a citizen of Salisbury, a tenement in New Street between a messuage of late that of an elder John Chandler on the east side and a tenement of late Richard's, now that of a younger John Pope, on the west side; also the reversion, when it fell due on the death of Christine, the relict of William Handley, tucker, of a messuage in Gigant Street between William Warmwell's tenement on the north side and cottage property of late John Newman's, afterwards Thomas Eyre's, on the south side. The tenement and the reversion were held in fee simple by Richard by a grant of Nicholas Hayward, of Salisbury, and his wife Margery on a condition, as is declared in a charter of feoffment, of the payment to Richard of a sum of money in the matter, not paid. They are to be held for ever by Thomas and his heirs and assigns. Seals: Richard's and the common and mayoral seals of the city. Named witnesses: the bailiff, the mayor, the coroners, the reeves, John Mower, Walter Shirley, William Warin, Walter Nalder, Thomas Child, and the clerk

25 January 1413, at Salisbury
2154 Approval of the will of John Newman, hatter, a citizen of Salisbury, made on 7 January 1413. <u>Interment</u>: in the graveyard of St. Edmund's church. <u>Bequests</u>: 12*d*. to the fabric of the cathedral church; 3*s*. 4*d*. to the fabric of St. Thomas's church, 6*d*. to the high altar for his forgotten tithes and oblations, 6*d*. to the lord James, the parochial chaplain, and 2*d*. to each chaplain of that church present at his funeral rites; 2*d*. to each chaplain of St. Edmund's church present at his funeral rites, and 4*d*. to each of them crossing with his corpse from St. Thomas's church to St. Edmund's church on the day of his burial; 12*d*. each to the fabric of St. Edmund's church and the hospital of the Holy Trinity; 6*s*. 8*d*. and a saving board with a caldron and a plate attached to it to John Jennway, his servant; 13*s*. 4*d*. each to Nicholas Lord, a clerk, and William Chandler; the rest of his goods to Nicholas and William to be laid out on the salvation of his soul. <u>Devise</u>: all his land and tenements in Salisbury, in Endless Street, to Nicholas and William to be sold.

The money received should be laid out on giving alms, repairing ways, and doing other charitable deeds on behalf of his soul and the souls of others, except only 40s. of that money which he appointed to his wife Emme (*Emmotte*). Executors: Nicholas Lord and William Chandler. Seal: John's. Witnesses: Thomas Ferring, John Catthorpe, a barber, John Jennway, William Hatter, and others. Proved on 18 January 1413 in front of the subdean; the administration was entrusted to the executors. Approved at a court held in front of the bailiff, the mayor, and other citizens. Emme, the relict of John Newman, came to that court and claimed a tenement, which Reynold Wishford holds, in Endless Street for her dower from John's land and tenements, to be held for life according to the custom of the city. Because in the city there has hitherto been observed a custom that a wife, on the death of her husband, can claim and hold for her life the best tenement in the city of which her husband died seised, Emme should be allowed to hold the tenement which she claimed. The seisin of the other land and tenements, with the reversion of the tenement allowed to Emme, was released to the legatees.

2155 Approval of the will of Richard Cormell, called Knolle, mercer, of Netheravon, a citizen of Salisbury, made on 1 April 1408. Interment: where his saviour pleased. Bequests: 40s. to the fabric of Netheravon church, 10s. to the vicar, and 3s. 4d. to the clerk; 1d. to each pauper coming to his burial, and ½d. to each pauper coming to his obit; 20 pairs of linen sheets, 10 pairs of smocks with breeches, and 10 smocks for pregnant wives to be handed out among paupers where need was greatest; from his goods and chattels his executors should find a chaplain to celebrate mass on behalf of his soul and the souls of others in Netheravon church for three years, and another chaplain to celebrate mass on behalf of the same souls in St. Thomas's church for two years; 6s. 8d. each to the fabric of the cathedral church, the fabric of St. Thomas's church, and the fabric of St. Edmund's church; 3s. 4d. each to the fabric of St. Martin's church, the Franciscans of Salisbury, the Dominicans of Fisherton Anger, and the hospital called Almshouse; 4d. to each prisoner of Salisbury [?*rectius* Old Sarum] castle; immediately after his death 1,000 masses should be celebrated on behalf of his soul; 3s. 4d. each to the fabric of St. John's church, Devizes, the fabric of Upavon church, a bridge called Cart bridge in that village, the fabric of Enford church, the fabric of Fittleton church, the fabric of Figheldean church, and the parish church of Amesbury; 3s. 4d. for the improvement of the way called Newport; 20s. for the improvement of the ways in Lude marsh; 4d. to each nun of Amesbury [abbey] and each chaplain there; 6d. to each chaplain being at his funeral rites, and 2d. to each clerk being there; 20d. to the four men bearing his corpse before his burial; 12d. to the making of his tomb; 6d. for the bells to be rung on behalf of his soul; 40s. to his sister Christine, the wife of William Dowding, and 20s. to her daughter Alice; 20 pairs of shoes to be handed out among paupers where need was greatest; all his corn, sheep, wool, and brass pots and pans, with all his household stock, except the merchandise fully pertaining to his shop which is to be disposed of by his executors on behalf of his soul, to his wife Joan and his children; two parts of the debt of all his debtors to Joan and his children; the third part of such debt to his executors to be spent on alms for the needy and poor and on other charitable deeds on behalf of his soul and the souls of others; 40s. each to William Dowding and Adam Teffont for their work as executors. Devise: to his wife Joan a tenement in Wheeler Row between his other tenement on the south side and Simon Tredinnick's tenement on the north side. The tenement was held by Richard by a grant of William Warin, a citizen of Salisbury, is to be held by Joan for life, and immediately after Joan's death should remain for ever to his son John and his issue. If John were to die without issue the tenement would remain for ever to Richard's younger son William and his issue, if William were to die without issue it would remain for ever to Richard's elder son William and his issue, and if that William were to die without issue it would remain for ever to Richard's sister Christine and her heirs. Executors: his wife Joan as the principal executor and William Dowding and Adam Teffont, citizens of Salisbury, as her co-executors. Proved on 25 February 1412 in front of the subdean; the administration was entrusted to the executor, and she was admitted to it of her free will. Approved at a court held in front of the bailiff, the mayor, and other citizens; the seisin of the tenement was released to Joan, the legatee.

8 February 1413, at Salisbury
2156 Approval of the will of Walter Orme made on 13 November 1411. Interment: in St. Thomas's church opposite the image of the Blessed Mary on the south side of the church. Bequests: 40d. to the fabric of the cathedral church; 6s. 8d. to the fabric of St. Thomas's church, 6d. each to the parochial chaplain and Nicholas Stafford, a chaplain, 12d. to the lord Nicholas Gifford, and 4d. to each other chaplain present at his funeral rites and mass on the day of his burial to pray for his soul; 2s. 6d. both to the Franciscans of Salisbury and the Dominicans of Fisherton if they were present at his funeral rites and mass on the day of his burial; 20d. to John Sprot, a Dominican friar in the convent of Fisherton, to pray for his soul, and 20d. which Robert Taylor owes to him; 12d. to his godson, a son of William Debden; 6d. to his goddaughter, a daughter of John Hurlbatt; 12d. of the debt which John Round owes to him to John's son Walter; 12 lb. of wax for torches to be made and to be burned around his corpse on the day of his burial; 13s. 4d. for bread to be handed out among paupers on the day of his burial; 100 masses to be celebrated on the day of his obit; a green gown, furred, with black skins to his godson at Bonham, a son of Henry Mack; a red hood to the son Nicholas Breton; a cloak, coloured blue and russet, to Nicholas Millward; half a gown of motley to Richard Merriott; a striped gown to John Friday, at the discretion of his own wife Agnes; his harnessed dagger to John Kingsbury; 6s. 8d. to Richard Oword; the rest of his goods, movable and immovable, to his wife Agnes to intercede on behalf of his soul. Devises: to Agnes a tenement, in which he lived, in Minster Street, between William Pickard's tenement on the north side and Reynold Glover's tenement on the south side, to be held for ever by her and her heirs and assigns; also a garden in Freren Street, beside cottage property of late Edmund Enfield's, now Richard Spencer's, to be held for ever by her and her heirs and assigns. Executors: his wife Agnes and Richard Oword. Proved on 7 January 1413 in front of the subdean; the administration was entrusted to the executors.

Approved at a court held in front of the bailiff, the mayor, and other citizens; the seisin of the tenement and the garden was released to Agnes, the legatee.

21 February 1413, at Westminster
2157 Letters patent of Henry IV. By his letters patent of 1 June 1406 the king granted to the mayor and commonalty of Salisbury that they might acquire land, tenements, and rent to the value of 100 marks a year in the city [*as in **1931***]. By these present letters he granted a licence to John Mower and Richard Spencer to assign to the mayor and commonalty four messuages, and 4 marks worth of rent, in the city and not held of the king. The messuages are worth 100*s*. a year according to a valuation computed by an inquest held in front of William Warblington, the king's escheator in Wiltshire, and returned in Chancery. The messuages and rent, to the value of £10 a year, are to be held by the mayor and commonalty and their successors in part satisfaction of the 100 marks of land, tenements, and rent. The king also granted a licence to the mayor and commonalty to receive the messuages and rent from John and Richard, and to them and their successors to hold them for ever notwithstanding the Statute of Mortmain and saving to the chief lord all services owed and customary.

7 March 1413, at Salisbury
2158 By their charter John Mower and Richard Spencer, citizens of Salisbury, on the strength of a licence of Henry IV and a licence of Robert, the bishop of Salisbury, and the dean and chapter of Salisbury granted to John Becket, the mayor, and the commonalty four messuages in the city. One, called George's Inn, with a laundry, houses, rooms, sollars, cellars, and shops, stands in Minster Street between shops, which Walter Cook holds of Nicholas Harding, on the north side and a shop, which John Ettshall holds of de Vaux college, on the south side. Another, with shops, rooms, and houses, of late that of Nicholas Taylor, draper, stands at the south end of Castle Street between a tenement, in which Gunnore Bowyer dwells, on the north side and the graveyard of St. Thomas's church on the south side; it extends from Castle Street as far as the Avon, and there is a room appurtenant to it, on its east side, above a stile at the entrance of the graveyard [*margin*: Adam Haxton, Tott, Bruton, Taylor, Spencer and Mower. *Cf.* ***466, 476, 549, 1691***]. A third, with houses and a yard (*or* yards), in which Thomas Steer now dwells, stands on the east side of Castle Street between a tenement of late Thomas Gilbert's, now that of John Chitterne, a clerk, on the south side and a tenement of George Goss, tucker, on the north side. The fourth, with houses, stands on the south side of Winchester Street between a corner tenement of late William Hill's, in which William Cox now dwells, on the east side and a tenement of late that of John Baker, grocer, now John Becket's, on the west side. The mayor and the commonalty and their successors are to hold all four messuages, with the laundry, houses, rooms, sollars, cellars, and shops, for ever in mitigation of all taxes and subsidies falling on them, and John Mower and Richard Spencer quitclaimed their right or claim to the premises to them. Seals: those of John and Richard and those of the office of the sheriff of Wiltshire and

the office of the bailiff of Salisbury. Witnesses: Walter Charlton, then the sheriff of Wiltshire, William Westbury, then the bailiff of Salisbury, William Stourton, John Gowan, Thomas Bonham, Henry Thorpe, Thomas Manning, and others.

2159 A deed of John Mower and Richard Spencer, citizens of Salisbury. John and Richard were seised in their demesne as of fee of three cottages, with houses, gardens, and an empty site, of late those of John Buddle, called Prentice, and of late held by Richard Pate and his wife Joan, now dead, a daughter of John Prentice, on the north side of Wineman Street between a corner tenement of late John Prentice's, now William Penton's, on the east side and John Forest's tenement on the west side. By their deed John and Richard, on the strength of a licence of Henry IV and a licence of Robert, the bishop of Salisbury, and the dean and chapter of Salisbury now granted to John Becket, the mayor, and the commonalty and their successors a rent of 26s. 8d. a year to be received for ever by them from the cottages, houses, gardens, and empty site. John and Richard also granted to the mayor and commonalty and their successors a rent of 26s. 8d. a year to be received by them for ever from a newly built messuage, with a yard (*or* yards) and gardens, of late Margaret Godmanstone's. The messuage stands in Gigant Street, on the way towards St. Edmund's church, between Richard Weston's cottage property, standing beside a garden of late John Ball's, on the south side and a yard of late held by Nicholas Buckland of William Hoare on the north side. Clause to permit entry on the cottages, messuage, houses, gardens, yard(s), and empty site if the rent were in arrear, distraint, and the keeping of distresses until the unpaid rent was recovered. So that the grants of the rents would remain for ever firm for the mayor and the commonalty and their successors John and Richard attorned to the mayor and commonalty by the payment to them of 4d. on the day of the perfection of the deed in the presence of the witnesses named below. Seals: those of John and Richard and those of the office of the sheriff of Wiltshire and the office of the bailiff of Salisbury. Witnesses: Walter Charlton, then the sheriff of Wiltshire, William Westbury, then the bailiff of Salisbury, William Stourton, John Gowan, Thomas Bonham, Henry Thorpe, Thomas Manning, and others.

8 March 1413, at Salisbury
2160 Approval of the will of Christine Salisbury, the wife of John Salisbury, weaver, of Salisbury, made on 25 April 1409. Interment: in the graveyard of St. Martin's church. Bequests: 6d. each to the fabric of St. Martin's church and the fabric of the cathedral church; 4d. each to the lord William Spicer and the lord Thomas Bennett; the rest of her goods to her husband John for him to dispose of on behalf of her soul as he might wish. Devise: to John a tenement in St. Martin's Street, between Walter Burton's tenement on the east side and cottage property of the provost of St. Edmund's church on the north side, to be held for ever by him and his heirs and assigns. Executor: her husband John; overseer, Thomas Bennett. Proved on 10 May 1409 in front of William Summerhill, the subdean; the administration was entrusted to the executor, who at length appeared, was heard, accounted with the officer, and was dismissed. Approved at a court held in front of the bailiff, the mayor, and other citizens; the seisin of the tenement was

released to the legatee.

2161 A deed of William Sall and Nicholas Harding, citizens of Salisbury. [*The deed, known to have been perfected between 2 November 1412 and 1 November 1413, is dated to the Wednesday after the feast of St. Perpetua and St. Felicity in the first year of the reign of Henry V (14 March 1414), probably in error for the Wednesday after that feast in the last year of Henry IV (8 March 1413): cf.* **2167**]. Robert Body and his wife Alice, the relict, and an executor, of Robert Woodborough, of late a citizen of Salisbury, granted to William and Nicholas the reversion of a tenement in Minster Street, which is called Castle Street, between a tenement of Robert Woodborough on the south side and a tenement of late William Higdon's on the north side, to be held for ever by them when it fell due on Alice's death. By their deed William and Nicholas now granted the reversion to Walter Shirley, a citizen of Salisbury, to be held for ever by him and his heirs and assigns. Seals: those of William and Nicholas and the common and mayoral seals of the city. Named witnesses: the bailiff, the mayor, the reeves, John Mower, Richard Spencer, William Warin, William Dowding, and the clerk

22 March 1413, at Salisbury
2162 By his deed John Chancellor, a son and heir of Thomas Hutchins, called Chancellor, of late a citizen of Salisbury, and his wife Cecily, granted to John Hain, loader, John Lewisham, and Richard Curtis, a clerk, his estate, right, or claim to conjoined tenements on the north side of Scots Lane. The tenements, of late those of Thomas and Cecily, descended to John on the death of Cecily and are to be held for ever by the grantees and their heirs and assigns. Clause of warranty in respect of the two of the tenements which stand between Adam Morris's tenement on the east side and a tenement which Robert Blake claims on the west side. Seals: John Chancellor's and the common and mayoral seals of the city. Named witnesses: the bailiff, the mayor, the reeves, John Mower, Richard Spencer, Walter Shirley, William Sall, Nicholas Bell, and the clerk

2163 A deed of Thomas Durnford, of Salisbury, and his wife Margaret, the relict of Robert Hazelbury, of Salisbury. By an indenture Walter Shirley, a citizen of Salisbury, granted to Robert and Margaret, then Robert's wife, for their life and the life of the one of them living longer a tenement, in which they then dwelt, in Castle Street between a gate of Walter's tenement, of late that of John Wallop, draper, on the south side and a tenement of late Richard Ludd's on the north side. By their deed Thomas and Margaret, at the court held on that day, for a sum of money paid to Margaret now surrendered to Walter the estate which Margaret held in the tenement, to be held by him and his assigns. Thomas and Margaret, for themselves and their heirs and at least for the heirs of Margaret, released to Walter and his heirs and assigns their right or claim to the tenement. Seals: those of Thomas and Margaret and the mayoral seal of the city. Named witnesses: the bailiff, the mayor, the reeves, John Mower, Richard Spencer, William Warin, William Sall, and the clerk

5 April 1413, at Salisbury

2164 By his deed John Chancellor, a son and heir of Thomas Hutchins, called Chancellor, of late a citizen of Salisbury, and his wife Cecily, quitclaimed to John Hain, loader, John Lewisham, and Richard Curtis his right or claim to tenements, of late those of Thomas and Cecily, which John Hain, John Lewisham, and Richard Curtis held by his gift. The tenements stand on the north side of Scots Lane. Clause of warranty in respect of the two of the tenements which stand conjoined [*as in* **2162**]. Seals: John Chancellor's and the common and mayoral seals of the city. Named witnesses: the bailiff, the mayor, the reeves, John Mower, Richard Spencer, Walter Shirley, William Sall, Thomas Mason, and the clerk

2165 By his charter John Needler, a citizen of Salisbury, granted to his son William a tenement, with shops fronting on the street, in New Street between the abbot of Stanley's shop on the west side and a tenement of late George Merriott's on the east side; also two shops in New Street between Laurence Gowan's shops on the west side and shops of late John Lippiatt's on the east side; also a cottage in Drake Hall Street between a shop which William Pickard holds of the dean and chapter of Salisbury on the north side and cottage property of late that of Henry Russell, kt., on the south side. The tenement, garden ground, shops, and cottage are to be held for ever by William and his heirs and assigns. Clause of warranty. Seals: John's and the common and mayoral seals of the city. Named witnesses: the bailiff, the mayor, the reeves, Richard Spencer, Walter Shirley, William Sall, Walter Nalder, Thomas Mason, draper, and the clerk

2166 By her charter Alice, the relict of Robert Woodborough, of late a citizen of Salisbury, granted to Walter Shirley, a citizen of Salisbury, a tenement in Minster Street, which is called Castle Street, between a tenement of late that of John Camel, grocer, formerly John Fowle's, on the south side and a tenement of late Christine Matthew's, afterwards Robert's, on the north side, to be held for ever by Walter and his heirs and assigns. Clause of warranty. Seals: Alice's and the common and mayoral seals of the city. Named witnesses: the bailiff, the mayor, the reeves, John Mower, Richard Spencer, William Warin, William Sall, William Dowding, and the clerk

2167 A deed of Alice, the relict of Robert Woodborough, of late a citizen of Salisbury. Walter Shirley, a citizen of Salisbury, held by a grant of William Sall and Nicholas Harding, citizens of Salisbury, the reversion of a tenement when it fell due on Alice's death. The tenement stands in Minster Street, which is called Castle Street, [*as in* **2161**]. William and Nicholas held the reversion by a grant of Alice's husband Robert Body and of Alice herself. By her deed Alice, in her celibate widowhood and power, now granted to Walter her estate in the tenement, to be held by him and his heirs and assigns, and released to him and his heirs and assigns her right or claim to the tenement. Clause of warranty. Seals: Alice's and the common and mayoral seals of the city. Named witnesses: the bailiff, the mayor, the reeves, John Mower, Richard Spencer, William Warin, William Dowding, and the clerk

3 May 1413, at Salisbury
2168 By his charter Robert Deverill, a citizen of Salisbury, granted to Edward

Gilbert, dubber, a tenement, with an adjacent shop, beside the upper bridge of Fisherton, near the bishop of Salisbury's mill there, between a shop of John Butt, a cordwainer, on the east side and the Avon on the west side. The tenement was of late that of John Paxhill, now dead, whose estate for his life was acquired from him by Robert, the reversion of it then pertaining to Robert by a grant of Thomas Bowyer, of late a citizen of Salisbury. It is to be held, with the shop, for ever by Edward and his heirs and assigns, to whom Robert quitclaimed his right or claim to it. Clause of warranty. Seals: Robert's and the common and mayoral seals of the city. Named witnesses: the bailiff, the mayor, the reeves, John Mower, Richard Spencer, Walter Shirley, William Warin, Walter Nalder, and the clerk

14 June 1413, at Salisbury
2169 Approval of the will of John Stone, of Wilton, made on 6 December 1412. Interment: wherever it pleased God. Bequests: 6s. 8d. each to the fabric of the cathedral church and the fabric of St. Michael's church, South Street, Wilton; 20s. each to the fabric of the conventual church of St. Edith, Wilton, and the fabric of the church of the Blessed Peter, of Bull bridge; 40 sheep, two brass pots formerly Nicholas Stone's, and 13s. 4d. which he received from the sale of a ... [omitted in MS.] in the vill of Tarrant called Souter's Place to the fabric of the church of Tarrant Gunville; a silver gilt chalice and two silver ewers to the lady Joan Beauchamp, the abbess of Wilton; 12d. to each nun there of the monastic habit; 13s. 4d. to his rector for his forgotten tithes and to pray for his soul; an embroidered blue bed, with two blankets, two pairs of linen sheets, and all its equipment, a harnessed silver belt engraved with the letters 'in god is all', a silver bowl with a cover of middling quality, a maple-wood bowl called 'Goblet', and six silver spoons of middling quality to his daughter Felice; a silver belt, a small mazer with a cover, a piece of silver with a cover, and six silver spoons of middling quality to his daughter Margaret, a nun of Wilton; a silver belt engraved with a vine to Alice Lambard; a silver belt and a best dagger to John Whitehorn; a silver belt and a harnessed dagger to Thomas Knight; a silver gilt cup, a gilded bowl with its cover, and a silver bowl with a cover to the lady Margaret of Romsey, a nun of Wilton abbey, to be disposed of on behalf of his mother's soul; a sword and a harnessed silver dagger to Robert Ashley; a harnessed silver horn to John Lambard; a mazer without a cover to his daughter Olive; the rest of his goods to his wife Joan for the support of his children, to be disposed of on behalf of them and of his soul. Devises: Thomas Manning and his fellows, feoffees in four shops in Corn Street, in the borough of Wilton, formerly Henry Bunt's, under the name of all the land and tenements which John held in that borough, should enfeoff his daughter Felice so that the four shops are to be held by her and her issue. If Felice were to die without issue the shops would remain for life to John's wife Joan, on Joan's death they would remain to his son John and his issue, if that John were to die without issue they would remain to the elder John's son Thomas and his issue, if Thomas were to die without issue they would remain to the elder John's daughter Joan and her issue, and if Joan were to die without issue they should be sold by the elder John's executors or their executors. The money

raised should be laid out on the salvation of John's soul and the souls of others. John devised to his wife Joan for life a tenement, in which he then lived, in South Street, in the borough of Wilton; on Joan's death the tenement should remain to John's daughter Olive and her issue, and if Olive were to die without issue it would remain for ever to John's direct heirs. John appointed that John Lambard, the feoffee in a messuage in New Street, Salisbury, formerly Bartholomew Durkin's, should enfeoff his daughter Felice so that the messuage is to be held by her and her issue. If Felice were to die without issue the messuage would remain to an elder John Lambard, of Dinton, to be held for ever by him and his heirs and assigns. John devised to John Whitehorn, of Wilton, and his wife Olive the reversion of a place called the Barns, with a garden and a little meadow called Long ham appurtenant to it, when it fell due on the death of Olive Haversham, to be held for ever by them and that John's heirs and assigns. John devised to his wife Joan for life all his other land and tenements in Salisbury; he appointed them on Joan's death to his son Thomas and Thomas's issue, if Thomas were to die without issue they would remain to John's son John and his issue, if that John were to die without issue they would remain to the elder John's daughter Joan and her issue, and if Joan were to die without issue they should remain to the elder John's executors or their executors, who should sell them at the best price possible. The money raised should be laid out on the salvation of John's soul and the souls of others. John appointed that Richard Taunton and Thomas Bonham, clerks, the feoffees in a tenement called Boggle's Place, in West Street in the borough of Wilton, should enfeoff his wife Joan so that the tenement is to be held by her for life; on Joan's death the tenement should remain to John's son John and his issue, if that John were to die without issue it would remain to his brother Thomas and his issue, if Thomas were to die without issue it would remain to his sister Joan and her issue, and if Joan were to die without issue it should remain to the elder John's executors or their executors, who should sell it in the way described above. The money raised should be laid out on the salvation of John's soul and the souls of others. John devised to his wife Joan all his other land and tenements in the borough of Wilton and its suburbs, except those which he held of the prior of Breamore, and of the prior of St. John's hospital, near Wilton, for a fixed term of years; also the reversion of a messuage, formerly John Merchant's, in that borough, when it fell due on the death of Christine, that John's relict. The land and tenements in the borough and its suburbs, and the reversion, are to be held by Joan for life; on Joan's death they should remain to John's son John and his issue, if that John were to die without issue they would remain to his brother Thomas and his issue, if Thomas were to die without issue they would remain to his sister Joan and her issue, and if Joan were to die without issue they should remain to the elder John's executors or their executors to be sold. The money raised should be laid out on behalf of the elder John's soul and the souls of others. <u>Executors</u>: the master John Tisbury, the master John Pedwell, the rector of West Dean, and an elder John Lambard, of Dinton. <u>Proved</u> on 12 April 1413 in front of the archdeacon of Salisbury; the administration was entrusted to John Pedwell and John Lambard, reserving the power to entrust it to John Tisbury when he might come to seek it. <u>Approved</u> on 20 June 1413 in front of John Hardy, the mayor of the borough of Wilton; in respect of the tenements in that borough, a proclamation having been made according to the custom of the borough, it was considered that the seisin of the tenements should be released according to the will. <u>Approved</u> at a court held in front of the bailiff of Salisbury, the mayor, and other citizens. Because Joan, John Stone's relict, was not present in court the seisin of the tenements in Salisbury, to be released on the strength of the will, was respited until she, according to the custom, might come to claim and accept it.

WITNESSES TO DOCUMENTS

As the bailiff of Salisbury (the bishop's bailiff)
William Boyton, bowyer, 1971
Walter at the burgh, 550–3, 555–77, 582, 585–98, 601–25, 627–36, 638–75, 677–92, 694–703, 705–25, 727–8, 730–46, 748–58, 760–5, 767–72, 774–5, 777, 779–80, 784–92, 794–7, 1656–7
Laurence Drew, 1659
elder John Gowan, 1778–81, 1783–7, 1789–1809, 1811, 1813–17, 1819–44, 1846–7, 1849–51, 1855–6, 1859–1900, 1902–10, 1912–13, 1915, 1917–30, 1932–9, 1941–7, 1949–56, 1958–66, 1968–9, 1977–87, 1989–90, 1992–2004
Oliver (of) Harnham, 1722–4 (*as* under-bailiff), 1729–38, 1740–6, 1749–65, 1767–73, 1775, 1777
Thomas Hungerford, 824–6, 830–3, 835–42
Thomas Hungerford, kt., 1658, 1660–2, 1664–6, 1680, 1684–94, 1696–1701, 1703–6, 1708–11, 1713–17
Michael at the mead, 798–808, 810–17, 819, 821–3
William Randolph, 543–4
William Westbury, 2006, 2008–34, 2036, 2038–43, 2045–6, 2048–67, 2069, 2071–83, 2099, 2101–12, 2114–24, 2153–6, 2158–69

As the mayor of the city
John Becket, grocer, 2153–6, 2160–9
William Bishop, grocer, 1978–87, 1989–90, 1992–2006, 2008–9
Thomas (of) Britford, 668–72, 674–5, 677–92, 694–700
Robert Bunt, 802–17, 819, 821–7, 830–3, 835–40
Thomas Burford, 1659–62
John (of) Butterley, 1658
Thomas Chaplin (d. by 1397), 841–2
William Dowding, merchant, 2099, 2101–12, 2116, 2118, 2120, 2122–4
Edmund Enfield, clerk, 1741, 1743, 1745–6, 1749–50, 1752–9
Robert of Faringdon, 544
elder George Goss, 736–46, 748–58, 760–5, 767–70
Nicholas Harding, 1942–7, 1949–51, 1953–6, 1958–62, 1964–9, 1971–4, 1976–7
Richard Leach, 1794–1807

Adam (of) Ludwell, 543
John Mower, grocer, 1717–18, 1721–4, 1727–38, 1740
Walter Nalder, draper, 2065–7, 2069, 2071–83
younger John Needler, draper, 1910, 1912–13, 1915, 1917–30, 1932–8
John Newman, cardmaker, 1808–9, 1811, 1813–17, 1819–20
John of Oxford, skinner, 771–2, 774–5, 777, 779–80, 782, 785–92, 794–801
John Salisbury, grocer, 1843–4, 1846–7, 1849–51, 1855–6, 1859–66
William Sall, 2036, 2038–43, 2045–6, 2048–64
Walter Shirley, grocer, merchant, 2010–34
Richard Spencer, grocer, 1663–6, 1670–94, 1696–1701, 1703–6, 1708–16, 1821–9, 1831
Nicholas Taylor, draper, clothier, 596–8, 601–25, 627–36, 638–67 (*in 609 the younger William Tenterer was named as mayor evidently in error for Nicholas Taylor*)
Adam Teffont, 1760–5, 1767–73, 1775, 1777–81, 1783–7, 1789–91
elder William Tenterer, 701–3, 705–25, 727–8, 730–5
younger William Tenterer, 546, 550–3, 555–77, 582, 585–95, 609, 1656–7 (*in 609 the younger William Tenterer was named as mayor evidently in error for Nicholas Taylor*)
William Walter, 1832–40, 1842
William Warin, grocer, 1867–95, 1897, 1900, 1903–9

As a coroner of the city
Robert Alwin, 1656
William Bailey, draper, 1793–4, 1796–1807, 1809, 1811, 1813, 1815–17, 1819–27, 1829–35, 1838, 1840–4, 1846–7, 1849–51, 1855–6, 1862–70, 1872–81, 1883–7, 1889–1900, 1902–8, 1910, 1912–13, 1915, 1917–29, 1937, 1942, 1944–7, 1949–53, 1955–6, 1958–62, 1964–6, 1968–9, 1972–4, 1976–7, 1981–4, 1986–7, 1989–90, 1993–2006, 2008, 2012, 2014–25, 2027, 2030–1
John Baker, grocer, *see* John Salisbury
Thomas (of) Britford, 597–8, 601–2, 604–5, 607–8, 610–11, 613–18, 621–2, 624, 627, 629–36, 638–40, 643–7, 649–50, 652, 654–64, 679–81, 683–9, 691, 695, 697, 699–700, 702–3, 706, 708, 711–14, 716–21, 724–5, 727–8, 730–4, 736–9, 741–6, 748, 750–8, 760, 762–5, 767–72, 774–5, 779–80, 782, 784–5, 787–92, 794–8, 800–2, 804, 806–7, 809–15, 817, 819, 821–6, 830, 833, 835–6, 838–42
Robert Deverill, 2050–4, 2056–60, 2062, 2066–7, 2069, 2071–83, 2099, 2101–3, 2105–7
John of Ely, 544
Richard Jewell, 1659, 1661–3, 1665–6, 1670–9, 1681–4, 1686–94, 1696–1701, 1703, 1705–6, 1708, 1711, 1713–18, 1721–2
John Judd, draper, merchant, 2108, 2110–12, 2114–24, 2153
Robert Kirtlingstoke, 1793–4, 1796–1807, 1809, 1811, 1813, 1815–17, 1819–27, 1829–35, 1838, 1840–4, 1846–7, 1849–51, 1855–6, 1862–70, 1872–81, 1883–7, 1889–1900, 1902–8, 1910, 1912–13, 1915, 1917–29, 1934–5, 1937, 1942
Nicholas Melbury, draper, 2108–12, 2114–24, 2153
John Powell, 544

John Richman, 1656

John Salisbury, grocer, 1723–4, 1727–8, 1731–8, 1741–6, 1749–50 (*John Baker, grocer, named as a coroner in nos. 1731–4 and 1737, is assumed to have been John Salisbury: cf. 1844, 1896*)

Thomas Sexton, ironmonger, 1752, 1755–61, 1763–5, 1767–73, 1775, 1777, 1779–80, 1784–5, 1787, 1789

Richard Spencer, grocer, 1661–2

Adam Teffont, 1683–4, 1686–94, 1696, 1700–1, 1703, 1705–6, 1708, 1713–15, 1717–18, 1721–4, 1727, 1731–8, 1741–6, 1749–51, 1754–9

John (of) Upton, 597–8, 601–2, 604–5, 607–8, 610–11, 613–16, 618, 621–2, 624, 627, 630–1, 633–6, 638–40, 644–5, 649–52, 654–63, 665, 667, 670, 672–5, 677–9, 683–4, 687–9, 691, 695, 697, 699–700, 702–3, 706–14, 717–18, 724–5, 727–8, 730–4, 736–9, 742–6, 748, 750, 753–8, 760, 762–5, 767–72, 774–5, 777, 779–80, 782, 784–5, 787–92, 795–8, 800–15, 817, 819, 821–6, 830, 833, 835–42

As a reeve of the city

Walter Abbott, 670, 672–5, 677–89, 691, 695–7, 699–700

William Bailey, draper, 1761–5, 1767–73, 1775, 1777, 1779–80, 1784–5, 1787, 1789–92

John Barber, brazier, 1717–18, 1721–4, 1727–8, 1731–8

John Becket, grocer, 2010, 2012–27, 2029–34

Nicholas Bell, 1981–4, 1986–7, 1989–90, 1993–2006, 2008–9

William Bishop, grocer, 1793–1807

Thomas Bleacher, ironmonger, 1741–6, 1749–52, 1754–9

John Bodenham, 2010, 2012–18, 2021–7, 2029–34

William Boyton, bowyer, 2066, 2071–83

Thomas (of) Bridgehampton, 670, 672–5, 678–89, 691, 695–6, 699–700

John Camel, (?hatter), 838–40

John (of) Chalke, clothier, 552, 555, 561–3, 572, 574–6, 585–94, 1656–7

John Chandler (fl. c. 1360), 739, 741–6, 748, 750–1, 753, 755–8, 760–1, 763–5, 767–70

Thomas Child, mercer, 1843–4, 1846–7, 1849–51, 1855–6, 1862–6

Pleasant Day, 2099, 2101–3, 2105–12, 2114–24

William Dowding, merchant, 1793–1807

Edmund Enfield, clerk, 1659

Thomas Eyre, 1741–6, 1749–52, 1754–9

William Fewster, 2066–7, 2069, 2071–83

William Friend, 552, 1656–7

Richard Gage, weaver, 2153, 2161–8

Nicholas Harding, 1660–2

William Hill, merchant, 1660–2

Walter Holbury, 803–7, 809–10, 812–13, 817, 819, 821–6, 830, 833, 835–7

Thomas Hutchins, 838–40

Richard Jewell, 1658

John Judd, draper, merchant, 1808–9, 1811, 1815–17, 1819–27, 1829–31

John Justice, 802–7, 809–10, 812, 817, 819, 821–3, 826, 830, 833, 835–7
Robert (of) Kendal, 561–3, 572, 574–6, 584–94
John Lake, 2099, 2101–3, 2105–12, 2114–24
John Lewisham, 1663, 1665–6, 1670–6, 1678–9, 1681–4, 1686–94, 1696–1701, 1703, 1705–6, 1708, 1710–11, 1713–16
Edward Longenough, 544
John Marshall, 739, 741–6, 748, 750–1, 753, 755–8, 760–1, 763–5, 767–70
Thomas Mason, draper, 1910, 1912–13, 1915, 1917–22, 1924–9, 1932–5, 1937
Nicholas Melbury, draper, 1942, 1944–7, 1949–53, 1956, 1958–62, 1964, 1966, 1968–9, 1972–4, 1976–7
William Mercer, 1910, 1912–13, 1915, 1917–29, 1932–5, 1937
George Merriott, esq., 2036, 2039–41, 2043, 2045–6, 2048–54, 2056–9
John Nalder, 701–3, 705–6, 708–12, 714–15, 717–25, 727–8, 730–3
Walter Nalder, draper, 1663, 1665–6, 1670–6, 1678–9, 1681–4, 1686–94, 1696–1701, 1703, 1705–6, 1708, 1710–11, 1713–16
elder John New, tanner, 701–3, 706, 708–12, 714–15, 717–25, 727–8, 730–4
John Newman, cardmaker, 1658
Richard Oword, 2153, 2161–8
John of Oxford, skinner, 544
John Parch, weaver, 2036, 2039–41, 2043, 2045–6, 2048–54, 2056–60, 2062
William Pickard, grocer, 1808–9, 1811, 1813, 1815–17, 1819–27, 1829–31
William Purser, 771–2, 774–5, 777, 779, 782, 785, 787–90, 792, 795, 798, 800–1
Thomas Ryde, merchant, 1867–9, 1872–81, 1883–7, 1889–1900, 1902–8
William Sall, 1832–5, 1838, 1840–2
Thomas Sexton, ironmonger, 1717–18, 1721–4, 1727–8, 1731–8
Walter Shirley, grocer, merchant, 1942, 1944–7, 1949–53, 1955–6, 1958–62, 1964–6, 1968–9, 1972–4, 1976–7
William Slegge, weaver, 1867–9, 1872–81, 1883–7, 1889–1900, 1902–8
William Stanley, 771–2, 774–5, 777, 779, 782, 785, 787–90, 792, 795, 798, 800–1
Henry (of) Stapleford, 596–8, 601–2, 604–5, 607–8, 610–18, 621–2, 624–5, 627–36, 638–40, 643, 645–7, 650, 652, 654–65, 667
John Swift, ironmonger, 1832–5, 1838, 1840–2
Simon Tredinnick, draper, 1843–4, 1846–7, 1849–51, 1855–6, 1862–6
William Tull, 1981–4, 1986–7, 1989–90, 1993–2006, 2008–9
William Walter, 1659
William Warin, grocer, 1760–5, 1767–73, 1775, 1777, 1779–80, 1784–5, 1787, 1789–92
Gilbert (of) Whichbury, baker, 596–8, 601–2, 604–5, 607–8, 610–18, 621–2, 624–5, 627–36, 638–40, 643, 645–7, 650, 652, 654–65

As the clerk of the city
William Dunkerton, 561, 572, 589–90, 592, 594, 596–8, 601–2, 604–5, 607–17, 621–2, 624–5, 627–36, 638–47, 649–52, 654–64, 667, 670, 672–5, 677–88, 691, 695–7, 699, 702–3, 705–16, 730–1, 738–9, 741–6, 748, 750–8, 760–5, 767–72, 774–5, 777, 779, 782, 784–5, 787–92, 794–804, 806–7, 810–15, 817, 819, 821–5,

830, 833, 835–8
Edmund Dyer, 547, 1656
Stephen Edington, 1869–70, 1872, 1876–8, 1883–7, 1889–1900, 1902–8, 1910, 1912–13, 1915, 1917, 1920–9, 1932–5, 1937, 1942, 1944–7, 1950, 1952–3, 1955–6, 1958–62, 1964, 1966, 1968–9, 1972–4, 1976–7, 1981–4, 1986–7, 1989–90, 1993–9, 2001–6, 2008–10, 2012–27, 2029–34, 2036, 2039–40, 2043, 2045–6, 2048–54, 2056–60, 2062, 2066–7, 2069, 2073–83, 2099, 2101, 2105–12, 2114–24, 2153, 2161–8
younger William Lord, 1659, 1665–6, 1670–9, 1681–4, 1686–7, 1689–93, 1696, 1698, 1700–1, 1703, 1705–6, 1710–11, 1713–18, 1721–4, 1727–8, 1731–8, 1741–6, 1749–52, 1754–60, 1762–5, 1767–73, 1775, 1777, 1779–80, 1784–5, 1789–1807, 1809, 1811, 1813, 1816, 1819–25, 1829–35, 1838, 1840–4, 1846–7, 1849–51, 1855–6, 1862–8
John Richman, 544

As a citizen
William Bailey, draper, 1939, 1941
John Baker, grocer, *see* John Salisbury
John Becket, grocer, 2060, 2067, 2099, 2105, 2111, 2117, 2123–4
Robert (of) Beechfount, 765, 782, 791–2
Nicholas Bell, 2067, 2120, 2124, 2162
John Bennett, 808
Peter Bennett, 544
William Bishop, grocer, 1867, 1870, 1876, 1885, 1894, 1910, 1912, 1935, 1961–2, 1964, 1968, 1976, 2014, 2016, 2019, 2021, 2023, 2030–1, 2039, 2045, 2059, 2066, 2073, 2077, 2081, 2099
Robert Body, 1851
Thomas Boyton, bowyer, 1659, 1663, 1665, 1679, 1711, 1722, 1731–3, 1737, 1741, 1743
William Boyton, bowyer, 1923
Thomas (of) Bridgehampton, 552, 575–6, 585–6, 611, 621–2, 784, 1657
Thomas (of) Britford, 547, 552, 555, 561, 572–4, 585–8, 590–4, 596, 1656–7
William of Bruton, 555, 572, 613, 618, 629, 636, 639, 652, 655, 658–60, 663, 725, 826
John Buddle, 736
Robert Bunt, 555, 561, 575–6, 587, 597–8, 601–2, 604, 608, 614, 624–5, 628, 633, 641–3, 645–7, 649–51, 654, 657, 660–1, 664, 667, 670, 672, 674, 678–80, 682–5, 688, 699, 701, 706, 709–10, 712–21, 723–4, 727–8, 730–4, 736–9, 741, 743–4, 746, 750, 752–3, 756, 758, 761–4, 771–2, 774–5, 777, 779–80, 787–90, 792, 794, 798–800, 827, 841–2
John Butterley, 702, 705, 742, 771, 774, 784–5, 807, 809, 811, 814, 819, 826–7, 836, 840, 1659
Thomas (of) Butterley, 544
John Camel, (?grocer), 1661–2, 1665–6, 1684, 1697, 1700–1, 1703, 1705–6, 1708, 1710–11, 1713–15, 1717–18, 1721

Thomas Castleton, mercer, 1801, 1803
John Chandler (fl. c. 1360), 613, 725, 1787, 1796, 1902
Thomas Chaplin (d. by 1397), 636, 781
Thomas Child, mercer, 1918–19, 1942, 1950, 1962, 1966, 1972, 1981, 1990, 2025–6, 2040, 2056, 2077, 2105, 2111, 2120, 2153
John Cole, 544
John Collier, tucker, 1768, 1770–1
John of Deanbridge, 1656
Robert Deverill, 1663, 1665–6, 1690, 1693, 1696, 1711, 1718
Richard Dinton, 781
John Dogton, 1722, 1731
William Dowding, merchant, 1870, 1874–5, 1896, 1912, 1917, 1969, 1981, 1986, 1993, 1995, 1998, 2024, 2031, 2034, 2039–40, 2048, 2056, 2071–2, 2074, 2161, 2166–7
Edmund Enfield, clerk, 1723–4, 1728, 1734, 1762, 1793, 1797, 1802, 1805–6, 1813, 1896, 1917, 1922, 1933
Thomas Eyre, 1946, 1977, 2009
John of Farnborough, 555
William Fewster, 2107
Thomas Field, 1851
John Forest, weaver, 1700–1, 1703, 1706, 1708, 1713–15, 1717, 1721, 1735, 1737–8, 1742, 1744, 1752, 1758, 1772–3, 1784–5, 1789–90, 1792, 1794, 1798–1800, 1806, 1808, 1811, 1813, 1815–17, 1821, 1823, 1827, 1829–31, 1835, 1838, 1840–2, 1846–7, 1849, 1855, 1863–6, 1896, 1906–7, 1932, 1937, 1947, 1951, 1993, 1995, 1997, 2002, 2005
John Fosbury, 544
John Fowle, 815
Robert (of) Godmanstone, 547, 552, 561–3, 572–6, 588–91, 594, 598, 601–2, 604–5, 607–8, 610–18, 621–2, 624, 627, 629, 633–5, 638–40, 644–7, 649–50, 652, 654–5, 660–4, 673, 675, 679–82, 684, 686–7, 697, 700–1, 703, 708, 711, 716, 720, 722, 725, 730, 733, 744–5, 751, 755–6, 764, 768–9, 777, 784, 799, 805, 808, 817, 826, 837, 840, 1656–7
elder George Goss, 547, 555, 573, 575, 593, 597–8, 601–2, 604, 611, 614, 617, 624, 628, 630–1, 633–4, 638, 640, 649, 654, 656, 664, 667, 670, 672, 677, 680–5, 688, 695–6, 699, 701, 703, 705, 707, 712–19, 721–4, 727–8, 730–4, 780, 794, 805–6, 809, 814–15, 821–3, 835, 838–9, 1657, 1722, 1732–4, 1737, 1768, 1770–1
William Guys, 1688, 1690, 1796
Nicholas Harding, 1787, 1793–4, 1799–1800, 1802, 1806, 1811, 1815, 1840, 1851, 1862–6, 1868–9, 1883, 1886, 1891, 1896, 1900, 1905, 1925–6, 1982–3, 1993, 1995, 2001–3, 2008–10, 2012, 2016, 2020, 2025, 2027, 2032, 2045, 2052–3, 2062, 2066, 2073, 2081, 2096–9, 2119
Henry at the burgh, 1656
William Hill, merchant, 1666, 1684, 1689–94, 1697, 1699, 1701, 1705, 1710, 1718, 1721, 1727–8, 1732, 1738, 1742, 1744, 1746, 1750–1, 1755–7, 1759, 1764, 1769, 1772–3, 1777, 1779, 1784, 1792, 1796, 1798, 1807, 1817, 1820,

1824, 1841, 1844, 1850–1, 1868, 1905
Thomas Hindon, 827, 839
John Hoare, 724
Richard Jewell, 1736, 1738, 1741, 1750–1, 1759–60, 1763, 1767, 1769, 1777, 1780, 1791, 1807, 1840, 1895, 1949, 1967–9, 1972, 1996, 2031, 2043
John Judd, draper, merchant, 1929
Robert (of) Kendal, 625, 634, 639
Robert Kirtlingstoke, 1768, 1770–1
John Lea, 784, 799, 824–5, 833
Richard Leach, 1659–60, 1665–6, 1670–4, 1676, 1678–9, 1681, 1684, 1686–7, 1689–93, 1696–8, 1703, 1706, 1710–11, 1716–17, 1721, 1723–4, 1728, 1731, 1735–6, 1738, 1741–2, 1746, 1750–2, 1758–9, 1762–5, 1777, 1784–5, 1789–90, 1792, 1819–20, 1822, 1825, 1843–4, 1846, 1856, 1872, 1878–80, 1883–4, 1894, 1896, 1904, 1907, 1915, 1932–4, 1997, 2002, 2033, 2036, 2041, 2043, 2052–3, 2067, 2080, 2082–3
John Lewisham, 1732–3, 1825, 1840, 1904, 1951, 1959, 1984, 1989, 2012, 2041, 2046, 2052, 2058, 2071, 2080, 2082–3, 2107–8
Philip Longenough, 544
elder William Lord, ?1658
younger William Lord, 1967, 1999–2000, 2013
Adam (of) Ludwell, 544
Thomas Manning, 1771
Mark the fair, 1991
Thomas Mason, draper, 1890, 1897, 1903, 1974, 1976, 2008, 2018, 2050, 2076, 2102–3, 2106, 2114–15, 2120, 2123, 2164–5
Nicholas Melbury, draper, 2015, 2054, 2076, 2079–80
John Mercer, 781
William Moore, tailor, 1879
John Mower, grocer, 1659–63, 1665–6, 1670–6, 1678–9, 1681–4, 1686–90, 1692–4, 1696–1701, 1703, 1705–6, 1708, 1710–11, 1713–16, 1742–6, 1749–52, 1754–65, 1767, 1769, 1772–3, 1775, 1777, 1779–80, 1789–1809, 1811, 1813, 1815–16, 1819–27, 1829–35, 1838, 1840, 1842–4, 1846–7, 1849–51, 1855–6, 1862–4, 1867–70, 1872–9, 1881, 1883, 1885–7, 1889–93, 1895, 1898–1900, 1902–8, 1910, 1912–13, 1918–21, 1923–9, 1933–5, 1937, 1939, 1941–2, 1944–7, 1949–53, 1955–6, 1958–62, 1964–9, 1972–4, 1977, 1981–4, 1986–7, 1989–91, 1993–5, 1997–2006, 2008–10, 2012, 2015–27, 2030–4, 2036, 2039–41, 2043, 2046, 2049–54, 2056–60, 2069, 2071–9, 2081, 2101–3, 2106, 2110, 2112, 2116–18, 2121–2, 2153, 2161–4, 2166–8
Walter Nalder, draper, 1795, 1843, 1923, 1955, 1974, 2101, 2109, 2112, 2114–15, 2119–20, 2122–4, 2153, 2165, 2168
younger John Needler, draper, 1661–2, 1670–9, 1681–3, 1686–7, 1689–92, 1694, 1697–1701, 1703, 1706, 1708, 1713, 1716–17, 1727–8, 1734–5, 1738, 1742, 1744, 1746, 1755–9, 1762–4, 1767, 1769, 1777, 1784–5, 1792–3, 1796, 1800, 1802, 1806, 1808, 1813, 1815–17, 1826–7, 1830–1, 1833–5, 1840–3, 1847, 1849, 1855, 1864, 1947, 1950–1, 1953, 1955, 1960, 1976, 1984, 1993, 1995,

2001–4, 2023, 2030, 2036, 2041, 2048, 2052–3, 2057, 2080, 2083
John Newman, 1673, 1691, 1698, 1795
John of Oxford, skinner, 546, 612, 630, 642, 644, 809, 841–2
John Parch, weaver, 1851
John Richman, 546
Henry Russell, 544
Nicholas Russell, butcher, 781
Thomas Ryde, merchant, 2012
John Salisbury, grocer, 1660–3, 1665–6, 1670–2, 1674, 1676, 1678, 1689–91, 1693, 1697, 1699–1700, 1703, 1705, 1711, 1713, 1717–18, 1775, 1777, 1784, 1791, 1795, 1797, 1804–5
(*John Baker, grocer, named as a witness in several writings, is assumed to have been John Salisbury: cf. 1844, 1896*)
William Sall, 1801, 1803, 1822, 1824–5, 1843, 1868–9, 1873, 1875, 1877, 1879–81, 1884, 1887, 1889, 1892–3, 1897–9, 1902, 1908, 1917–19, 1922, 1925, 1932–4, 1937, 1944–5, 1947, 1950–3, 1955–6, 1958, 1965–7, 1973, 1977, 1983, 1993, 1995, 2001–6, 2014–15, 2017–18, 2022, 2026–7, 2032–3, 2069, 2071–2, 2075, 2083, 2099, 2102–3, 2106–10, 2112, 2116, 2118–19, 2122, 2162–6
Walter Shirley, grocer, merchant, 1903, 1924, 1982–3, 1987, 1990–1, 1993–5, 2046, 2048–9, 2053–4, 2056, 2058, 2060, 2066, 2072–3, 2075–9, 2082, 2101–3, 2106, 2109, 2112, 2114–17, 2121–2, 2153, 2162, 2164–5, 2168
Thomas Slegge, merchant, 2080
Richard Spencer, grocer, 1660, 1717, 1721, 1723–4, 1727–8, 1731–6, 1738, 1742–6, 1749–50, 1752, 1754–65, 1767, 1769, 1772–3, 1775, 1779–80, 1787, 1789–95, 1798–9, 1801–9, 1811, 1813, 1815–16, 1819–20, 1832–5, 1838, 1841–4, 1846–7, 1849–51, 1855–6, 1862–7, 1869, 1872–81, 1883–7, 1889–93, 1895, 1897–1900, 1902–6, 1908, 1910, 1912–13, 1915, 1917–22, 1924–9, 1935, 1937, 1939, 1941–2, 1945–7, 1949, 1951–3, 1955–6, 1958–62, 1964–9, 1972–4, 1977, 1981–4, 1986–7, 1989–91, 1993–2006, 2008–10, 2012–21, 2023–7, 2030–4, 2036, 2039–41, 2043, 2046, 2049–54, 2056–60, 2062, 2069, 2071–5, 2077, 2079, 2082, 2099, 2101–3, 2105–8, 2110, 2112, 2116–18, 2121–2, 2161–8
John Staggard, weaver, 1768, 1770–1
Edmund Steercock, 546
Richard Still, 736
Henry Summer, 1991
John Talbot, 784
Nicholas Taylor, draper, clothier, 555, 572, 586, 590–1, 679, 685–6, 691, 695–7, 700, 764, 782, 784, 809, 827, 841–2, 1658
Adam Teffont, 1670–1, 1673–5, 1677–9, 1681–2, 1793, 1801–4, 1806, 1832, 1840, 1843, 1850–1, 1862–7, 1873–4, 1878, 1883, 1885, 1894, 1896, 1900, 1904–5, 1915, 1925–7, 1932–4, 1944–6, 1950–3, 1960–2, 1976–7, 1996, 2002–3, 2057, 2074
elder William Tenterer, 622, 625, 641–2, 837, 841–2
younger William Tenterer, 604, 607–8, 610–11, 614–16, 618, 621–2, 627, 632, 733, 841–2

William Tull, 1966
John (of) Upton, 544, 546, ?547, 552, 555, 562–3, 573–6, 585, 588–9, 591–4, 596, 609, 651, 781, 1656–7
William of Upton, 609
John Wallop, draper, 1663, 1671, 1675, 1688–94, 1696, 1826
William Walter, 1735, 1738, 1744–6, 1749–51, 1755–7, 1759, 1762–5, 1775, 1779, 1787, 1793–4, 1797–1800, 1802, 1806, 1808–9, 1811, 1813, 1815–17, 1821–3, 1826–7, 1829–31, 1844, 1850, 1855–6, 1862, 1864–6, 1870, 1872–7, 1880–1, 1884–5, 1887, 1889–95, 1897–1900, 1902–8, 1910, 1912–13, 1915, 1920–2, 1926, 1928, 1935, 1937, 1942, 1944, 1949, 1952, 1958, 1960–1, 1964–5, 1967, 1973, 1977, 1987, 1989–91, 1993–5, 2002–3, 2005–6, 2010, 2013, 2020–3, 2030, 2032–3, 2036, 2041, 2045–6, 2048, 2058, 2062, 2073–4, 2078, 2082–3, 2105, 2107–8, 2111, 2114–15
William Warin, grocer, 1817, 1913, 1915, 1917–19, 1922–4, 1927–9, 1935, 1939, 1941, 1944–5, 1949, 1952, 1956, 1958–60, 1962, 1964, 1966–9, 1973, 1981, 1986–7, 1991, 1993, 1995, 1997–2000, 2002–3, 2006, 2009, 2014–15, 2017–19, 2021–4, 2026–7, 2030, 2039–40, 2045, 2049–51, 2059–60, 2066–7, 2069, 2076, 2101, 2110–11, 2118–19, 2121, 2153, 2161, 2163, 2166–8
John Warminster, 1768
William Warmwell, 702, 705, 722, 727–8, 732, 734, 736–7, 739, ?741, 742–5, 748, 752–3, 757–8, 760–1, 765, 767, 769–70, 784–5, 789, 791, 794–808, 810–15, 817, 819, 821–5, 830, 833, 836, 838, 840, 1658–63, 1670–6, 1678–9, 1681–4, 1686–91, 1693–4, 1696, 1700–1, 1703, 1706, 1708, 1710, 1713–16, 1718, 1722–4, 1727–8, 1731–8, 1741–6, 1750–2, 1755–60, 1762–5, 1767–8, 1770–3, 1777, 1779–80, 1784–5, 1787, 1789–92, 1794–6, 1798–1805, 1807–9, 1811, 1813, 1815–16, 1819, 1821, 1823–4, 1826–7, 1829–35, 1838, 1840–3, 1846–7, 1849–50, 1855–6, 1862–70, 1872–81, 1884, 1886–7, 1889–95, 1897–1900, 1902–3, 1906–8, 1910, 1912–13, 1915, 1918–21, 1923, 1925, 1927–9, 1932–5, 1942, 1944–7, 1949–53, 1955–6, 1958–9, 1964–5, 1968–9, 1972, 1974, 1976, 1982–4, 1986–7, 1990, 1993–6, 1998–2000, 2002–4, 2006, 2008–10, 2013–14, 2016–17, 2019–20, 2022–5, 2027, 2030, 2034, 2039, 2043, 2045, 2048–52, 2054, 2057, 2059, 2062, 2066–7, 2069, 2078, 2081, 2099, 2105, 2108–9, 2111, 2114–15, 2117, 2119–20, 2123–4
William (of) Wishford, draper, 547, 552, 555, 561–3, 572–6, 585, 587–92, 596–8, 601–2, 604, 607–12, 614–18, 621, 627–9, 631–2, 638, 640–3, 652, 656–9, 662, 664–5, 673–5, 677–82, 685–8, 691, 695–7, 699–703, 706–8, 710–23, 725, 727–8, 730–1, 733–4, 736–8, 741–3, 745–6, 748, 750–2, 754–8, 760–5, 767–8, 770–2, 774–5, 777, 779–80, 782, 784–5, 787–8, 790, 792, 795–9, 801–15, 817, 819, 821–7, 830, 833, 835–42, 1656–7
William (of) Wootton, dyer, ?741

INDEX ONE

General index: persons, places, and subjects

Abbott, Wal., 733, 994, 1018; *and see* witnesses: reeve
Abbotsbury
  Alice, w. of Wm. of, 261, 263
  Wm. of, 261, 263–4
Abingdon, John, 1302
Ackerman
  Guy, s. of Hen., 10
  Isabel, relict of Hen., 9
Adam, Hugh, 1583
Admot, John, 858, 1067
Affpuddle, the master
  Wm., clerk, 619
Afton, Rob. of, 640
Agnes, nun of Amesbury, 671
Agnes, overseer of Holy Trinity hospital, 1859
Agnes, servant, 1720
Agnes, little, servant, 1778
Agodeshalf, Wm., tailor, 602, 931, 1492
Ailward, Thos., clerk, 2127
Alden
  Alice, relict of Ric., *see* Polmond
  Ric., 512, 682, 1477–8
Alderbury, Ric. of, 591
Alderbury, 461
  church of St. John, 2011
Aldington, 1908
Alexander, chaplain, of Shaftesbury, 1936
Alexander
  Rob., and his sons John and Wm., 1908
  Wm., 2063
Algar, Wm., chaplain, 1546, 1938, 1944
Alice, a maid, 1936
Alice, household servants of the name, 2064
Alice, servants of the name, 1836, 1954, 1979, 2011
Alker, Wm., chaplain, 1684
Allen
  Alice, w. of Wm., 1777
  Thos., chaplain, 1882
  Wm., 1777
Alton
  John of, 139
  John, 567
Alton (Hants)
  dean, 626
  parish church, 626
Alvediston
  Norrington, *q.v.*
Alwin
  Isabel, w. of Wm., relict of John Cupping, 667
  Parnel, w. of Rob., 612
  Rob., 390–1, 393, 405–7, 431, 434, 479, 482, 541, 570, 587, 604, 607, 612, 614, 617, 643, 680, 683, 723, 751, 785, 822; *and see* witnesses: coroner
  Wm., 667
Amersham, John, 644
Amersham (Bucks.), 2109
Amesbury
  Agnes, 2066
  Cecily, w. of John, 2066
  Joan, w. of John, sis. of John Bone, 758, 821; will, 694
  her s. John, 694, 821
  John, 694, 758, 800, 812, 821, 823, 1043, 1109, 1574, 1865, 1955, 1965, 2066
  John, s. of John, 2066
Amesbury, 489, 520, 592–3, 648, 675, 699, 798
  abbey
    chaplains, 2155
    nuns, 2155; *and see* Agnes; Boyton; Haw; Weymouth
  church of St. Melor, 648, 2155
    altars, graveyard, lights, 648
    parochial chaplain, *see* John
    rector, 648
Amesbury, Little (in Amesbury), 1930
Amport (Hants), 1971
  Cholderton, East, *q.v.*
  Sarson, *q.v.*
Andover (Hants), 622, 624, 1065, 1580, 1742, 1878, 2055–6
  church, 1971
  lights, 1971
  church of St. Leonard, 2055
    chaplains, clerks, 2055
    graveyard, 2055
    vicar, 2055
Andrew the hatter, and his w. Alice, 80
Andrew, John, 670
Anger
  John, 557, 574–6, 600, 652, 730; will, 595
  Rob., 595
  Wal., 1114
  Wm., 595, 600, 864, 878, 1114
Anglesey, Hen., 1851
Ann
  Christine, w. of Rob. of, 88, 107

Christine of, *see* Bennett
Gillian, dau. of Rob. of, 88
Gillian of, 254
Rob. of, 88, 106–7, 222, 810, 2067–8
apprentices, 2064; *and see* Barfleet; Edward; John; Robert; Thomas; William; Woodhill
armour, 1786, 1836, 2063
Arnold
  Edm., chaplain, 1994, 2054
  Joan, relict of Rob., 1994, 2054
  John, citizen of London, 1725
  John, provost of the college of St. Edmund's church, 786
  Rob., 790, 959, 988, 1111–12, 1123, 1128–9, 1175, 1288–9, 1389, 1391, 1413, 1775–6, 1994, 2054
ash, at the, *see* Nash
Ashampstead (Berks.), church, 1979
Ashfold, the lord John, 666
Ashley
  Edith, w. of John, 672
  Joan, *see* Stone
  John (of), 672, 1700, 1789, 1844–5, 1882, 1890, 1896, 1986
  John (?same), s. of Wm., 1947–8
  Nic., 672
  Rob., 2169
  Wm., 549, 556, 570, 608, 1012–13, 1081, 1947–8
  Wm., chaplain, s. of Wm., 1947–8
Ashley (Hants), vicar of, *see* Salisbury
Ashlock
  John, 789, 863
  Margery, w. of John, relict of John Dyke, 789, 863
Ashton, Wm., 1269, 1577, 1673, 1764, 1978
Aslin, Nic., 17, 308
Assendon, Wm., and his w. Christine, 1947–8
assize (*unspecified*), 1229; *and see* novel disseisin
Astbury
  Emme, w. of Nic., relict of Rog. Frank and of John Powell, 393, 424, 463, 625, 641, 650, 655, 713, 736, 771, 806, 826, 951
  Nic. (of), 771, 776, 778, 806, 826, 951
attorney, *see* Monk
Aubin
  Alice, w. of Phil. (d. by 1336), 121, 160, 223
  Phil. (d. by 1336), 100, 121, 160, 209, 223
  Phil. (fl. after 1336), ?citizen of Winchester, 385, 491, 496, 552, 646, 651, 1656–7, 1716
  Phil., s. of Phil., 651
Aubrey, maidservant, 816
Aubrey, John, 827–9
Augustinians, *see* Langford, John, s. of Maud; Winchester
Avery, John, mayor of Old Sarum, 1768, 1770–1
Avon, John, 2011
Avon (?in Stratford-sub-Castle), 1311, 1978
Axbey, Rob. (of), chaplain, clerk, vicar of cathedral church, 514–16, 531, 609, 704, 729, 737, 745
Axbridge (Som.), bailiff, *see* Tanner
Ayloff
  Emme, dau. of Rob., 111
  Margery, dau. of Rob., 111
Aynel
  John, clerk, chaplain of St. Martin's church, 1810, 1913–14, 1936, 1954
  John, priest (?same), 1954
A, P of, 1434

Bacon, Agnes, 740
Baggs, Wm., 578
Bailey
  Alice, w. of Wm., 1671, 2103
  Wm., draper, 1485, 1665, 1667, 1671, 1705, 1760, 1786, 1804, 2103; *and see* witnesses: coroner, reeve, citizen
Bailiff
  John, bro. of John of Britford, 553, 578
  John, s. of John, 553
  John, chaplain, 682, 689, 691, 1204
  Wm., taverner, 1456, 1584
  Wm. (?another), 1864, 2040
Baker
  Agnes, 1930
  Alice, relict of John, 1971
  her s. John, *see* Cann
  her s. Rob., 1971
  And., 604
  Clarice, 1379–81
  Gilb., 560, 719, 721
  John, clothier, draper, 1264, 1430, 1683 (*otherwise* Salisbury) John, grocer, s. of Nic.: *indexed as* Salisbury
  Maud, 897
  Nic., 588, 605, 621, 636, 744, 784, 802, 851–3, 862, 896–7, 912–13, 927, 933, 938, 940, 947, 1021, 1028, 1033, 1079, 1083, 1505, 1714, 1802–3, 1896, 2002–3, 2045, 2119
  Ric., *see* Upton
  Sim., 1888, 1893

bakers, *see* Bishopstrow;
  Bradley; Carpenter;
  Chubb; Cole;
  Fairwood; Grateley;
  Hampton; Hellier;
  Higdon; Isaac; Preece;
  Saddler; Sprot;
  Stapleford; Stonard;
  Taunton; Upton;
  West; Whichbury
Baldry
  Agnes, 614
  Agnes, dau. of John, *see*
    Warmwell
  Agnes, w. of Rob., 570
  Alice, 670, 1962–3
  Alice, dau. of Rob., 587
  Alice, relict of Hen.,
    24–5
  Douce, 570
  Geof., 265
  Hen., 24
  Hen., s. of Rob., 570,
    607, 614, 725–6, 762
  John, 7, 27, 362, 562,
    587, 631, 637, 643, 677,
    809, 2122
  Margt., relict of Ric.,
    353
  Ric., 314, 352–3
  Rob., 134, 315, 570,
    586–7, 628, 725–6,
    762, 777–8, 1658
  ygr. Rob., 552, 634, 702,
    785, 1656–7
  and see Fewster
Ball
  Agnes, 1820, 1871, 1887,
    2029, 2036–7, 2041,
    2052–3
  John, 764, 960, 1035,
    1039, 1060, 1216,
    1299, 1501, 1532,
    1693, 1695, 1745, 1747,
    1915–16, 2120, 2159
Ballingdon, John, 2029
Banbost, John, 817–18
Banner, Thos., 601
bar, at the, *see* Henry; John
Barber
  Alice, 1954
  Alice, relict of John (fl.
    1401), 2012; will, 2011
  her s. John, *see* Gosslin
  her s. Peter, and
    his daus. Alice and
    Christine, 2011
  Edith, 670, 1962–3
  Joan, w. of John, of
    Romsey, 567
  John (fl. 1367), 821
  John (fl. 1401), brazier,
    1754, 1836, 1951, 1990,
    2012; *and see* Belter;
    witnesses: reeve
barbers, *see* Catthorpe;
    Harnhill; Hellier
Barbours, Evette, 1720
Barfleet, Nic., apprentice,
    671
Barford
  Edith, dau. of Thos. (?d.
    by 1332), 270
  Ellen, w. of Thos. (fl.
    1363), 690, 843–4
  Gillian, w. of Thos. (?d.
    by 1332), 262
  John of, 665
  John, s. of Thos., 1174–5
  Ric. of, 126
  Thos. of (?d. by 1332),
    262, 270
  Thos. of (fl. 1363), 549,
    665, 690, 708, 843–4
  Thos., 1174–5
Barford St. Martin, parson
    of, *see* Erlestoke
Barnaby
  Alice, *see* Shearer
  John, 362–3, 428, 671
  John, s. of John, 671
  John (?same), 1663,
    1793, 1835, 1907, 1943,
    2060, 2062
Barnes, John, chaplain,
    1859
barns, 272, 690, 693, 789
Barnwell
  Adam (of), 331, 573, 603,
    615, 677, 705, 887
  Agnes, 887
  Michael, 233
  Rob., 233
Baron
  Emme, w. of John, of
    Westbury, 690, 971–2
  John, of Quidhampton,
    690, 1286
  John, of Salisbury, 1725–
    6
  John, of Westbury, 690,
    971–2
  Maud, 690
Barrett
  Amice, w. of John,
    weaver, 1681–2
  John (?more than one),
    1044, 1227, 1325–6,
    1777
  John, weaver, 1556,
    1681–2
  Wm., 1837
Bartlet
  Joan, 523
  John, friar, 1680
  Ric., 670, 1962–3
  Thos., chaplain, 1549
  Wm., 523, 564, 690, 739
  Wm. (?another), 1551,
    1891
Bash, Thos., tucker, 1762,
    1785
Basing
  John, 82
  Steph., 639
Basingstoke, John, 667,
    686, 715, 719–21, 869,
    1026
Bath and Wells diocese,
    bishop, *see* Erghum
Bathampton, Rob., 669
Batt, Ric., 573, 663
Battlesden (Beds.), 1000
Bayford, Wm., and his w.
    Joan, 1913–14
Baynard, John, chaplain,
    1720
Baynton
  John, 1786
  elder (*and unspecified*)
  Nic., 1511, 1559, 1701,
    1888, 1893, 1949,
    1951–2
  ygr. Nic., 1811–12, 1875
Beaminster
  Agnes, dau. of Wm. of,

see Beechfount
Joan, dau. of Wm. of, 649, 657
John of, s. of Wm. of, 572, 649, 657
Beauchamp
Joan, abbess of Wilton, 2169
Rog., kt., 2063
Becket, John, grocer, 2136, 2158; as mayor, 2158–9; *and see* witnesses: mayor, reeve, citizen
Bedfordshire, *see* Battlesden
Bedwyn, John of, 145
Bedwyn (*unspecified*), 1801
Beechfount
Agnes, w. of elder Rob., dau. of Wm. of Beaminster, 649, 657, 674, 684
Christine, relict of elder Rob., 1629, 1681–3, 1801
John, chaplain, 1682
Margt., 1681, 1683
Rob (of), 649, 657, 671, 674, 684, 696, 717, 725–6, 750, 761–2, 797, 850, 875, 881, 895, 946, 1019, 1034–5, 1216, 1369, 1629, 1681–3, 1801, 1808, 2112; *and see* witnesses: citizen
Rob., s. of Rob., 1681, 1683
Beek, the lord Wal., 329–30
Beer, Edm., 614
Beeton
John, draper, 798, 950, 1298, 1704, 1849, 1852, 1855, 1857, 1876, 1976
Thos., 1849, 1852, 1855, 1857, 1876, 1976
Belch, Sim., tucker, 1779, 1811–12, 1873–5
Belknap, Rob., justice of Common Pleas, 844
Bell, Nic., 1843, 1873–5,

2025; *and see* witnesses: reeve, citizen
bell-founder, *see* Gosslin; *cf.* brazier
Bellidge, Thos., 1969–70
Belter
John, 250–1
(?*otherwise* Barber) John, and his w. Alice, 1442
Rob., 250–1
Bemerton, 827–9, 898
Bennett
Alice, w. of Wm., 567
Christine of Ann, w. of Peter, 404, 426, 480, 534, 572, 599, 609, 616, 632, 637, 658, 681, 819
Edith, w. of John, 1260, 1264
John, 702, 751, 785, 872, 906–7, 934–5, 999, 1259–60, 1264, 1301, 1335, 1340, 1440, 1546, 1772; *and see* witnesses: citizen
John, canon of Wells, 980
Peter, 358, 394, 500, 548, 599, 625, 641–2, 644, 670, 1997, 1999–2000; *and see* witnesses: citizen
Thos., chaplain of St. Martin's church, 1936, 2160
Wm., 567
Berden, Thos., 171
Bergh, Hen., 947
Berkshire, *see* Garston, East; Kintbury; *and see, s.v.* ways: Wantage
Bernard
John, escheator of Wiltshire, 1782
(called Bower) Thos., draper, 2015, 2017
Bertins, Alice, *indexed as* Spicer
Berwick
Agnes (of), 551, 596, 710

Agnes, w. of Hen., 1586, 1928–9, 1943, 2010
Agnes, w. of Wm., *see* Woodford
Alice, *see* Stabber
Christine, w. of Wm., 113
Edith, w. of Ric., 623, 736, 756
Hen., weaver, 1228, 1585–6, 1643–4, 1849, 1852, 1855, 1857, 1870, 1906–7, 1928–9, 2010, 2060, 2062; will, 1943
John, bro. of Hen., *see* Smith
Maud, 1954
Ric. (of), 331–2, 416, 756, 1688; will, 623
Rog., 1944
Wm. (of), 18, 112–13, 233, 311, 590, 623, 673, 715, 742, 750; as mayor, 137
Berwick St. James, 2063
Berwick St. John, rector of, *see* Hackwell
Besil
John, 2061
Wm., esq., 2075
Best, Nic., and his w. Agnes, 437
Beveridge, Matt., 563, 732
Bide, Wm., commissary, 619
Bier, Edm., clerk, 427–8, 433, 470, 671
Binsmith, the binsmith, *see* Smith
Binstead (Hants), church of the Holy Cross, 626
Bishop
Edith, w. of Wm. (fl. 1320s), 175
John, 122, 190
Thos., clerk, 581
Wm. (fl. 1320s), 175
Wm. (fl. 1412), grocer, 1669, 1673, 1727, 1811–12, 1873–5, 1896, 1898–9, 1902, 1908, 1912, 1920–1,

1932–4, 1950, 1956–7,
1969–70, 2109, 2123–
4; *and see* witnesses:
mayor, reeve, citizen
Bishopstone (in Downton
hundred)
chaplains, 1943
church of St. John the
Baptist
beadsman, bell,
graveyard, lights,
tower, 1943
parochial clerks, 1943
crosses, 1943
Croucheston, *q.v.*
Faulston, *q.v.*
Flamston, *q.v.*
Throope, *q.v.*
vicar, 1943
and see 'Bolebergh'
Bishopstrow
Adam of, baker, 634
Wm., 634
Biston
Agnes, w. of Thos.,
1954, 2085
Thos., 1503–4, 1778,
1787, 1795, 1797,
1809–10, 1953–4,
1974–5, 2035, 2048,
2085
Blackhall, Sim., 2139
Blackmoor, Hen., 1957,
2037
Blake
Rob. (fl. 1365), 754, 763
Rob. (fl. 1413), 2162,
2164
Blakeney, Wm., spicer, 670
Bleacher
Alice, 800
Edith, w. of Thos. (fl.
1361): will, 698
John (d. by 1366), 800
John (fl. 1366), 800, 812,
823, 1965
Rog., 767
Thos., ironmonger, 1595,
1617–20, 1636, 1639,
1744, 1860, 1877,
1895, 1942, 1955, 1971,
1976, 2002–3; *and see*

witnesses: reeve
Thos. (another), *indexed
as* Play
Wm., 695, 823, 932,
1120, 1168, 1955
Wm. (two others), 1965
Blick
Maud, 588
Ric., 229
Ric., s. of Ric., 846
Blickling, John, chaplain,
1630–5, 1645, 1665,
1684, 1693, 1695,
1721, 1758, 1784
Blowers, Maud, 578
Bloxworth, Wm., chaplain,
1740
Blunt, Joan, relict of Thos.,
kt., 1951, 1967
Blyth
Rob., 1839
Wm., 816
Wm. (?another), 1839
Board, John, carpenter,
1165
Bodenham
Agnes, w. of John (d.
by 1360), 480, 568,
604, 612, 632, 658,
742, 772–3, 787, 801,
819–20, 824, 1089,
1096, 1130, 1217, 1772,
1801
Alice, w. of John (fl.
1365), sis. of Wm.
Gore, 772–3, 787, 835
Alice, w. of John (d.
1412), 2104
Christine, 632
Hen., 2104
Isabel, w. of John (d.
1412), 2104
John (d. by 1360), 479–
80, 590, 604, 612, 632,
658, 674, 683–4, 742,
772–3, 787, 819–20,
822, 824, 1089, 1772
John (fl. 1365, d. 1412;
?one man), 772–3,
775, 787–8, 835,
1178, 1472, 1740,
2032–3, 2051–3, 2076;

will, 2104; *and see*
witnesses: reeve
ygr. John, 1920–1, 1968,
1980, 2019–20
John, s. of John (d.
1412), 2104
Olive, dau. of Hen.,
2104
Olive, dau. of John (d.
1412), *see* Parch
Rob. of, 775, 788
Steph., chaplain, 623
Wm., 2104
Wm., chaplain, 2104
Body
Alice, w. of Rob.,
relict of Rob.
Woodborough, 1152,
2161, 2166–7
Rob., 1119, 1256,
1272, 1394, 1703–4,
1980, 1982–3, 2073,
2161, 2167; *and see*
witnesses: citizen
Bold
Cath., 1906, 1929
Gillian, 1882
Hen., 661, 789
Steph., 116
Wal., 259
'Bolebergh' (place, ?near
Bishopstone), 1943
Boltford, Ric., chaplain,
859, 866
Bond, Wm., 1783
'Bondham' (place), 2156
Bone
And., 743, 817–18, 1884
Joan, w. of And., 817
Joan, sis. of John, *see*
Amesbury
John, 694, 758–9, 817–18
Boney
Edith, relict of Hugh,
413
Hugh, 324–6, 378, 411,
413, 546, 629, 685,
732, 1186, 1658
John, 413
Bonham
Agnes, 1859
John, 1672, 1676, 1686–7

Nic., 678, 935
Thos., 1883, 1896, 2042–4, 2046–7, 2158–9
Thos., clerk, 2169
Thos., steward, 1939, 1941
Bonham (in Stourton), 2156
books
  children's manual, 1871
  collects, placebo, and dirge, 1882
  decretals, 1938
  Golden Legends, 1871
  host on high, 1938
  Hugucium, 619
  hymn book, 1882
  Innocent, 619
  matins, 1786
  Pars Oculi, 1871
  Passipon, 1938
  practice of bound paper, 1938
  Sextus Liber Doctrinalium, 619
  Trinities, 1938
  and see missals; porteouses; psalters
Boor
  John, 1211–12, 1536–8
  John, chaplain, clerk, 1054, 1379–80, 1408–9
  Nic., vicar of cathedral church, 440, 521, 569, 757
Boreham
  Agnes, relict of Wal., 448
  Wal., 448, 552
Borhams, Agnes, 555
Borley, John, 669
Boscombe, Rob. (of), tanner, 562, 631, 2122
Bosham
  Alice, w. of ygr. John, 1830–1
  Christine, w. of elder John, 1638, 1829, 1831
  Joan, 1831
  (called Pope) elder John, 1638, 1758, 1829, 1831, 1971
  (called Pope) ygr. John, 1830–1
  John, s. of elder John, 1971
Boss, John, 740
Bosset, (*otherwise* Snel) John, 557, 577, 744, 802, 1232, 1837
Bottlesham, Steph., chaplain, 567
Botwell
  John, chaplain, 116
  Steph., vicar of cathedral church, 1720
Bouch, Peter, 408, 801, 1768, 1770–1
Boughton, Thos., cordwainer, 1882, 1889–90
Bourchier, Thos., 834
Bourton
  John, chaplain, 1547
  John of, hellier, 671
Bowbar, John, tucker, 671
Bower
  Edm., 1787
  Rob., 1358
  Thos., *see* Bernard
  Wm., 1869, 2006–8
Bown
  Margt., w. of Wal., relict of Rob. Play, 895, 933, 940, 1079, 1561–2, 1564, 1646, 2002
  Wal., 1561–2, 1564
Bowyer
  Agnes, dau. of Rob., *see* Brown
  Christine, w. of Rob., 1396, 1937, 2108
  Rob., weaver, 1396, 1861, 1937, 1979, 2108
  Thos., *indexed as* Boyton
  Wm., *indexed as* Boyton bowyer, *see* Boyton
Boyce
  Margery, w. of Rob., 242
  Rob., 242, 2111
Boyland
  Edith, relict of Wm., 1589–90, 1595
  Wm., 580, 741, 1325,
1347, 1360–3, 1474, 1581, 1587, 1589–90, 1595, 1865
Boyton
  Agnes, w. of Thos. (d. 1400), 1786, 1792
  Gunnore, w. of Thos. (d. 1400), 1786, 1792, 1794–5, 1797, 1815, 1862–3, 1943, 1985, 2002–3, 2060, 2062, 2128, 2158
  her dau. Margt., nun of Amesbury, 1786
  her s. Rob., *see* Ogbourne
  Margery, and her husband John and s. John, 1786
  (*otherwise* Bowyer) Thos. (fl. 1361, d. 1400, ?same man), bowyer, 553, 572, 654, 759, 818, 843–4, 984, 993, 1008–10, 1055, 1073, 1143, 1149, 1163–4, 1483–4, 1521, 1534, 1666, 1671, 1691, 1728, 1767, 1792, 1794–5, 1797, 1815, 1978, 2002–3, 2103, 2168; will, 1786; *and see* witnesses: citizen
  (*otherwise* Bowyer) Wm., bowyer, 1786, 1916, 2005, 2015, 2017, 2028, 2068–70, 2113; *and see* witnesses: bailiff, reeve, citizen
  his bro. Thos. and s. Thos., 1786
Boyton, church, 1786
Braban, Hugh, tailor, 1779, 1811–12, 1873
Bradley
  Edith, w. of Sim., 1847
  Sim., baker, 1847, 1924, 2018
  Wal., *indexed as* Hoare
Bradley (*unspecified*), 1750
Bradley, Maiden, convent of, 1680

Bradley, North, 1729
  church of St. Nicholas,
    1729
  Southwick, *q.v.* (for cross-
    reference)
  vicar, see Budden
Bradwell, John (of),
  parochial chaplain of
    St. Edmund's church,
    442, 505, 537, 554,
    579, 585, 594, 598,
    627, 671, 703
Bramshaw, Edm. (of), 516,
    729, 745, 831, 1266,
    1275, 1312, 1882, 2079
Brawt
  Cecily, w. of Wm., 1753
  Wm., skinner, 1753
Brays, Joan, dau. of And.
  Bunt, 409
Brazier
  Adam, *indexed as*
    Bridgehampton
  Gilb., 580
  Peter, 1954
brazier, see Barber; *cf.* bell-
    founder
bread (given charitably),
    553, 668, 1719, 1783,
    1860, 1909, 1943, 2156
Breamore, Franciscan friar,
    671
Breamore
  Agnes, w. of Nic., 302
  Alice, w. of John, 2083
  Denise, 2080
  Edw., 1348–9, 1814,
    1864, 1993, 1995
  John, weaver, 2046–7,
    2066, 2080, 2083
  Nic. (of), 302, 544, 598,
    627, 718, 789, 794,
    797, 831, 2080
  Ric. (of), 135, 195, 553,
    1728
Breamore (Hants), priory
    of, 816
  prior, 2169
Bremhill, *see* Stanley
Brenchesley, Wm., justice
    of Common Pleas,
    1858

Breton, Nic., 2156
Brewer
  Alice, w. of John, 1650
  Edith, 157
  John, 1650, 1791
  Margery, 1938
  Ric. (fl. c. 1361), 532, 538
  Ric. (fl. 1406), 1985,
    2063
  Rob., *see* Jukes
brewers, *see* Hampton;
    Wade
Brice, Ric., and his w.
    Alice, 2039
Brickway, Wm., 216
Bride, Rob., weaver, and
    his w. Mabel, 1191
bridge, at the, *see* Richard;
    William
Bridgehampton
  (*otherwise* Brazier) Adam
    (of), 74, 205
  Gilb. of, 250, 571
  Thos. (of), 522, 588,
    633, 677, 697, 938,
    1024, 1166; *and see*
    witnesses: reeve,
    citizen
bridges (repaired
    charitably), 553, 577,
    671, 1859, 1909, 1979,
    1985, 2063, 2155
  'Grauniford' bridge, 1979
  Hayford bridge, 669
  and see Southampton;
    Upavon; Wilton;
    index 2: bridges
Bright, John, 831
Brightwhite
  Geof., 13
  Wm., 13
Brightwin, Hen., 811, 815,
    822, 825
Brigmerston, Mic. of, 591
Bristol
  Thos. of, and his w.
    Laurence, 55
  Thos. of, fisherman, 35,
    553
Bristol, 1786
  mayor, 1939–41
Bristow

  John, 1698, 1823–5
  Phil., 1703
  Ric., 1870, 2071–2
  Tamsin, w. of Ric., relict
    of Wm. Surr, 1624,
    1807, 1870, 2065,
    2071–2
Bristwin, Hen., 85
Britford
  Alice, w. of Thos. (d.
    c. 1379), 1274, 1276,
    1304, 1880, 1882
  Christine, w. of John (d.
    1361), 553
  John (d. by c. 1320), 134
  John of (d. 1361), fisher,
    fisherman, 644; will,
    553
  John, s. of John (d.
    1361), 553
  John, bro. of John (d.
    1361), *see* Bailiff
  Sanger of, 1882
  Thos. of (d. c. 1330s),
    284
  Thos. (of) (d. c. 1379),
    522–3, 554, 558, 598,
    618, 625, 627, 641–2,
    665, 667, 678, 680–1,
    686, 693, 697, 699,
    703, 709–10, 715, 722–
    3, 777–8, 803, 826,
    832, 838, 890, 1090–3,
    1117–18, 1135, 1274,
    1304, 1428, 1628,
    1731–2, 1798–9, 1880,
    1882, 1889; as mayor,
    673; *and see* witnesses:
    mayor, coroner,
    citizen
  Thos., s. of John (d.
    1361), 553
  Wm., 828
Britford, 1729
  church of St. Peter and
    St. Paul, 759
  farm, 749
  Harnham, East, *q.v.*
  vicar, 1882; *and see* Hook
    Norton
Brock
  Jas., 1461–2

John, chaplain, 2071–2
Bromham
  Isabel, relict of Jas., 879;
    cf. Marshall
  Jas. (of), 505, 530, 879
Bromley
  Alice, w. of John, relict
    of Thos. Eyre, 1217,
    2064, 2101
  John, 2101
Brond, John, and his w.
  Joan, 1229
brook, at the, *see* Gilbert;
  Ingram; John
Brown
  Agnes, w. of John,
    household servant,
    dau. of Rob. Bowyer,
    1937, 2108
  Joan, w. of John,
    butcher, 1835, 1907
  John, household servant
    of the college of St.
    Edmund's church,
    1871, 1937, 2108
  John, of Chute, 1971
  John, butcher, 1835,
    1863, 1907
  John, tucker, 1705
  Nic., chaplain, 1724,
    1826, 1871, 1879,
    1954; will, 1971
  Nic. (another), 1971
  Steph., 1178, 1225
  Steph., grocer, 1808
Brownrobins, Theobald,
  740
Brute
  Joan, w. of John, of
    Hindon, 1985
  John, of Hindon, 1874,
    1985
  John, of Swindon, 1219,
    2015
  Thos., tanner, 558, 562,
    631, 644, 741, 2122
Bruton
  Agnes, w. of Wm., 416,
    756, 1144
  Wm. of, 416, 466, 476,
    492–3, 549, 552,
    554–5, 579, 756, 831,

840, 1691, 2158; *and
   see* witnesses: citizen
Bruton (Som.), 619
  church, 619
  rector, *see* Paris
Bubble, Peter, 816
Buck
  Adam, 1882
  Nic., chaplain, 350–1,
    388–9, 451, 459, 523,
    578, 585, 594, 621, 735
  Wm., chaplain, vicar of
    cathedral church, 523,
    625, 641, 644, 676,
    679, 803, 838, 1037,
    1157, 1274–5, 1312,
    1378, 1428, 1510, 1550,
    1568, 1578, 1629–35,
    1645, 1665, 1684,
    1693, 1695, 1721,
    1731–4, 1736–7, 1758,
    1780, 1784, 1801,
    1879–81, 1883–5,
    1889–91, 1894–5,
    1903, 1924; will, 1882
Buckingham, archdeacon
  of, 1837
Buckinghamshire, *see*
  Amersham; Marlow;
  Wycombe
Buckland
  Joan, w. of ygr. Wm.,
    1045
  Margt., w. of Wm. (of),
    see Godmanstone
  Nic., 1880, 1915–16,
    2120, 2159
  Rog. (of), 752–3, 822,
    825, 2015, 2017
  Wm. (of), 457, 552, 555,
    582, 1900–1
  ygr. Wm., 568, 1045
  Wm. of, clerk, 728
Buckland (*unspecified*),
  17, 95
Budden, Ric., chaplain of
  Southwick, vicar of
  North Bradley, 1729
Buddle
  Amice, 237
  Cath., w. of John, 400
  Hugh, 237

Joan, *see* Pate
  (*otherwise* Prentice)
  John, 325, 400, 523,
    558, 613, 618, 664,
    741, 972, 1040–1,
    1197, 1319, 1949,
    2029, 2036–7, 2041,
    2123, 2159; *and see*
    witnesses: citizen
  Steph., 735
Buffing, Cecily, 1954
Bugger, Rog., 34
Bull, Hen., 550, 570
Bulmer, John, 2064
Bunt
  Agnes (d. by *c.* 1378), w.
    of Rob., 1053, 1093
  Agnes (d. by 1400), w. of
    Rob., *see* Lewisham
  Alice, relict of Hen. (d.
    by *c.* 1339), w. of John,
    432, 563, 631; will,
    559
  Alice, w. of Sim., 1078,
    1710
  Amice, w. of John (fl.
    1363), 677
  And., 409
  Christine, dau. of Hen.
    (d. by *c.* 1339), relict
    of Wm., *see* New
  Hen. (d. by *c.* 1339), 296,
    432, 559, 563, 565
  Hen. (fl. 1362), burgess
    of Wilton, 663, 2104,
    2169
  Joan, *see* Brays
  John, husband of Alice,
    432, 631
  John, husband of Amice,
    677
  John, s. of And., 409
  John, s. of Wm., 565
  John (*unspecified*), 653,
    688
  Peter, 663
  Ric., 615
  Rob., 405, 427–8, 433,
    456, 481, 484, 554,
    671, 677, 801, 816,
    846, 889, 956, 1003–4,
    1052–3, 1093, 1187,

GENERAL INDEX

1196, 1200, 1768,
1770–1, 1773, 1859,
1969–70, 2023; as
mayor, 818; *and see*
witnesses: mayor,
citizen
Sim., 1078, 1094, 1111–
12, 1123, 1128–9, 1158,
1449–51, 1516, 1644,
1710, 1770, 1904–5
Wm., 565
Burden, Agnes, 931, 1492
her s., *see* Cutting
Burford
Agnes, w. of Thos.,
1364, 1366
Joan, *see* Tull
Margt., sis. of Thos., *see*
'Prestempde'
Thos., 967, 1138, 1174–5,
1235, 1282, 1364–6,
1554, 1659, 1783,
1856, 1909, 2016,
2019–20, 2102; *and see*
witnesses: mayor
Thos., dyer, 2144–5
?his w. Joan, 2145
Burgess
John, mercer, 1777
Rob., 566
burgh, at the, *see* Henry;
John; Thomas; Walter;
William
Burton
the lord Peter, 1503–4
Wal., 2160
Bury, Hen., 100, 147, 160,
223, 255, 278, 770,
1658
Butcher, Ralph, 1836
butchers, *see* Brown;
Dinton; Manning;
Russell; Stalbridge;
Wallop; Wells;
Wilton; Winpenny;
Winterbourne
Butler
John, mercer, 1791, 1973,
2080, 2083
Ric., 1945, 1952
Butlingsey, Thos., 1328
Butt, John, cordwainer,

1767, 2168
Butterley
Agnes, w. of Thos. (d.
by 1361), 578
Alice, w. of John, relict
of ygr. Wm. Tenterer,
see Merriott
Christine, w. of John,
624
Christine, relict of Peter,
see Salisbury
Joan, relict of Thos. (d.
by 1361), 449–51, 605,
621, 636, 654; will,
578
her s. Thos., *see* Lea
John (of), 578, 605, 622,
624, 636, 654, 662,
817–18, 876, 884, 893,
928, 963, 967, 977,
1058, 1060–2, 1067,
1073, 1098–1101, 1138,
1155, 1246, 1248, 1278,
1283–4, 1294, 1296,
1315–16, 1350, 1364,
1403, 1428, 1431, 1471,
1483, 1485, 1519–20,
1526–7, 1534, 1554,
1665–6, 1684, 1708,
1721, 1758, 1760,
1805, 1842, 1882,
1896, 1935, 1938,
2046, 2052, 2124; *and
see* witnesses: mayor,
citizen
(called Upton) Peter,
1758; *and see* Upton
Thos. (of) (d. by 1361),
449, 578, 605, 621,
636, 654; *and see*
witnesses: citizen
Thos. (fl. *c.* 1387), 1345
Wal., 1628

Cabbel, John, 1740
Calabry, Reynold, 443
Cale, John, 2064
Calf, John, 1971
Callis
Ric., 362–3
Ric., *see* Marwood
Callow

Alice, *see* Gundy
Isabel, w. of Wm., 23
John, 23
Thos., 396, 399, 810,
1698, 1823–5
Wm., 23, 73
Calne
Hen., 749–50
Wal. (of), 551, 676, 679,
750; will, 749
Cambo, Peter, 707, 795
Camel
Agnes, w. of John,
hatter, relict of John
Hatter and of John
Mariner, 388, 459;
will, 735
Alice, relict of John,
grocer, 1751
Edith, 1938
Isabel, relict of John,
hatter, 1643–4
(*otherwise* Scammel) John
(d. by 1396), hatter,
735, 841–2, 851, 882,
1057–8, 1241, 1293,
1295, 1346, 1642–4,
1658, 1660, 1710,
1769, 1846, 1943,
2034–5
John (d. *c.* 1398), grocer,
[and John Camel,
unspecified], 1054, 1071,
1630–2, 1639, 1645,
1689, 1693, 1695,
1738–9, 1751, 1786,
1809–10, 1815, 1828,
1953, 2166
John, s. of John, grocer,
1739
Thos., 1862
and see witnesses: reeve
(?John Camel, hatter),
citizen (?John Camel,
grocer)
Candelan, Wm., chaplain,
514, 531, 609, 737, 745
Cann, John, s. of Alice
Baker, 1971
Canning
Christine, *see* Herring
Ellen, w. of John, 1218

Joan, w. of John, 1860, 1942
John, 1218, 1744, 1942; will, 1860
  his goddaughter Margt., 1860
Cannings, John, 748
Canon, Sim., 2064
Canterbury (Kent)
  (cathedral) church of St. Thomas, 1740
  prerogative court, 1979, 2011, 2063
  registrar, *see* Perch
Capon, Rog., 2065, 2072
Capp, Hen., 740
carders, *see* Hosey; Wallop
Cardmaker, (*otherwise* Chaffin) Thos., cardmaker, 2077, 2117, 2133–5, 2150
cardmakers, *see* Cardmaker; Newman
Carentham
  Agnes, w. of Rog., 1740
  Margt., w. of Rog., 1740
  Ric., *indexed as* Stoke
  Rog., 1740
Carmelites, *see* Winchester
Carmerdin, Sim., 1778
Carpenter, John, baker, 248, 714
carpenters, *see* Board; Cole; Crichel; Dunball; Hill; Pack; Poulshot; Somborne; Stalbridge; Wanstrow; Winterbourne
Carter
  Hugh, 1837
  Sim., 1837
  Wm., 1837
carter, *see* Ferrer
Carthusians, *see* Selwood; Witham
Cary
  John, 1932–4
  Margery, w. of John, dau. of John Thorburn (d. by *c.* 1396), 1932, 1934
Cass, Rog., 740

Castleton
  Goude, w. of Thos., 2151
  John, 1823–5, 1939–41, 2005, 2009, 2151
  Maud, w. of Thos., 1823–5
  Thos., mercer, (?and a namesake), 858, 1197–9, 1203–4, 1213, 1242, 1681–2, 1786, 1808, 1819, 1821–5, 1838, 1841, 1846, 1939–41, 2001, 2005, 2077, 2151; *and see* witnesses: citizen
Catherine, servant, 1979
Catthorpe, John, baker, 2154
Caundle
  Jas., 2027–8, 2105
  John, matins clerk in cathedral church, 2069–70; will, 1778
  his niece Edith, 1778
  Thos., 2105
  Wm., priest, chaplain in cathedral church, 1778, 2069–70
  Wm., s. of Thos., 2105
Cavenasser
  Wal., 538, 686, 774, 776
  Wm., 527, 532, 538
Caws, Thos., 581
cellar, at the, *see* Richard
Cerney, John, chaplain, 514–15
Chaffin, Thos., *indexed as* Cardmaker
Chalke
  Emme, 990
  John (of), clothier, 619, 729, 745, 990–1; *and see* witnesses: reeve
  John, s. of John, 990
Chalke, Broad, *see* Stoke Farthing
Chamber, John, 2104
Chamberlain, John, tailor, 1958, 1966, 1972
Champness, Edith, 137
Chancellor
  John, s. of Thos.

Hutchins, 2162, 2164
  Thos., *see* Hutchins
Chancery inquests, 1766, 1782, 1931, 2157
Chandler
  Agnes, relict of Laur., 507, 718–20, 731, 742
  John (d. by *c.* 1339), 309
  John (fl. *c.* 1360–1407, *often called* elder), 482, 582, 631, 658, 667, 670, 680–1, 686, 690, 701, 715, 719–23, 787–8, 835, 867, 869, 883, 952, 989, 994, 1103, 1106, 1143, 1147, 1154, 1156, 1164, 1185, 1217, 1237, 1241, 1271, 1277, 1292, 1300, 1370, 1372, 1374, 1388, 1390, 1422, 1425–7, 1438, 1441, 1465, 1472–3, 1479–80, 1489, 1496–1500, 1542, 1550, 1568, 1599, 1615–16, 1621, 1625, 1637, 1682, 1713, 1731–4, 1736–7, 1752, 1763–4, 1772, 1780, 1782–3, 1790–1, 1806, 1821, 1825–7, 1849, 1852, 1855, 1861, 1882–6, 1889, 1894–6, 1898–1901, 1903, 1905, 1917, 1920–2, 1924, 1946, 1962–4, 1968–70, 1973, 1981, 2024, 2027–8, 2061, 2104, 2122, 2152–3; as under-keeper of Holy Trinity hospital, 1952; *and see* witnesses: reeve, citizen
  ygr. John, s. of Wal., 1548, 1819, 1822, 1981
  John, s. of elder John, 1963, 1970, 1981
  John, clerk, dean of Salisbury, 1882, 1913–14
  Laur., 454, 507, 639, 670, 718–21, 731, 742
  Tamsin, w. of ygr. John,

1981
Wal., 817–18
Wal. (?another), 1822, 1981
Wm. (fl. c. 1360), 454, 543, 570
Wm. (fl. 1413), 2154
Chanter, Wm., 948
Chantrell, John, 147, 573, 615
chaplains (named), *see* Alexander; Algar; Alker; Allen; Arnold; Ashley; Axbey; Aynel; Bailiff; Barnes; Bartlet; Baynard; Beechfount; Bennett; Blickling; Bloxworth; Bodenham; Boltford; Boor; Bottlesham; Botwell; Bourton; Bradwell; Brock; Brown; Buck; Candelan; Caundle; Cerney; Chatt; Christchurch; Clark; Clement; Clifton; Codford; Cole; Cook; Coombe; Cottel; Crichel; Curl; Davitt; Dean; Dicker; Donnet; Edmond; Elion; Enterbush; Erlestoke; Farley; Farnborough; Ferrer; Fifield; Fowle; Fox; Foyle; Gilbert; Gould; Green; Groom; Hagbourne; Halwell; Hamish; Hampstead; Hatter; Heanor; Hellier; Herring; Hoare; Horningsham; Ilberd; Iwerne; Jacob; Jakes; John; Kendal; Liddington; Loddington; Longborough; Love; Manning; Marden; Mason; Medmenham; Mitchell; Netton; Newnham; Newton;
Pack; Pain; Passavant; Pentridge; Pope; Potterne; Purbeck; Quarrendon; Richard; Riggs; Russell; Self; Sexhampcote; Shalbourne; Shipton; Sireman; Skilling; Smith; Spicer; Spreed; Stafford; Stanton; Still; Stoke; Street; Swift; Thomas; Tucker; Uffcott; Upavon; Walbourne; Warin; Warwick; Wickham; Wild; Winslow; 'Wotthe'; Wraxall
Chaplin
  Joan, w. of Thos. (fl. 1361), 569
  Joan, w. of Thos. (fl. 1402), 1958, 1966, 1972
  Thos. (fl. 1361, d. by 1397), and his s. Thos. (fl. 1402), 355–6, 569, 604, 607, 634, 664, 680, 702, 723, 741, 785, 792–5, 797, 801, 814, 830, 876, 905, 908, 995–6, 1059, 1169, 1236–7, 1565, 1660, 1673, 1701, 1711, 1716, 1722–4, 1820, 1834, 1846, 1856, 1887, 1913–14, 1958, 1966, 1972, 2005, 2048, 2061, 2075, 2108; *and see* witnesses: mayor, citizen
  Thos., clerk, 1238
Chapman, Wm., weaver, 1791, 1959–60, 2004, 2065
Chapmans, Magote, 1729
Chardstock
  Cecily, relict of Nic., 946
  Nic., 832, 946
Charford, South (Hants), 816
Chark
  Edith, w. of Hen., relict
of Wm. Newman, 506, 581, 871, 880
  her dau. Maud, 581
  Hen., 871, 880
Charles, Rob., 2049–51, 2076
Charlton
  Wal., vicar of cathedral church, 516
  Wal., sheriff of Wiltshire, 2158–9
Charlton Musgrove (Som.), *see* Stavordale
Chasey, Hen., 1979
Chatt, John, collegiate chaplain of St. Edmund's church, 580, 582, 603, 653, 831–2, 845, 926
Chaucer, Nic., citizen of London, 827
Cheekwell, John, 1839
Cheese
  Agnes, w. of Edw., 1522
  Amice, 123
  Cecily, relict of John, 177
  Edw., 1522
  John, 114–15, 177, 179, 832
  John (?same), 142
  Rob., 28, 142, 697
  Steph., 177, 1689, 1695
  Wm., 46, 123
Cheltenham, Wal. (of), provost of the college of St. Edmund's church, 644, 659, 679, 845
Chelworth, Sim., and his w. Alice, 234
Chesham
  Joan, w. of Ric., 1890
  Ric., tucker, 1882, 1889–90
Cheyne
  Joan, 1913–14
  John, 1753
Child, Thos., mercer, 1870, 1873–5, 1906, 1929, 1935, 2126; *and see* witnesses: reeve,

citizen
Chilmark, 1253
Chilton, John, tucker, 639, 1012, 1014
chiminage, 317
Chippenham
  Alice, w. of Wal., 1987–8
  John, 1723–4, 1987–8
  Wal., 1903, 1987–8
  Wm., 1987–8
Chipper
  John, 238
  Wm., 238
Chirstoke, John, 1720
Chirton, John of, dubber, 26
Chitterne, John, clerk, canon of cathedral church, 1938, 1967, 1996, 1998, 2024, 2102, 2158
Cholderton, Osmund of, 571
Cholderton, rector of, *see* Geddington
Cholderton, East (in Amport, Hants), chapel of, 1971
'Chouch', Hugh, 16
Christ, the church of, 578, 1740
Christchurch
  Hen. of, 246
  Isabel, relict of Ric. of, 59, 154
  John, chaplain, 1200, 1239, 1994, 2054
  Ric. of, 59, 154
  Rog. of, 752–3
Christchurch (Hants), 822, 825
  church, 740
  priory, canon of, *see* Wimborne
Christine, servants of the name, 567, 2029
Christine at the wood, 578
Chubb
  Agnes, w. of Hen., 1910–11
  Hen., baker, 1910–11, 1933, 1950

Churchhay, Alice, w. of John, 1482
Chute, 1971
Cirencester
  Alice, *see* Sauter
  Gillian, *see* Cook
  Thos., 752–3
Cirencester (Glos.), 1729
Clarendon, *see* ways
Clark
  Beatrice, w. of Wm., 1342–3, 1419–20
  Benet, w. of David, 637, 1698
  Hen., 1991
  John (fl. *c.* 1348), 319–21, 402
  John (fl. 1403), 1837
  John, chaplain, 1838
  Peter, 652, 730
  Ric., 1336, 1909, 1939–41
  Steph., 1851
  Thos., 2044
  Wm., weaver, 1342–3, 1419–20
Clatford, John of, 673
Clement
  John, weaver, and his w. Alice, 1448, 1493–4, 1789
  Wm., chaplain, 1789, 1844–5
clerks, *see* Affpuddle; Ailward; Axbey; Aynel; Bier; Bishop; Bonham; Boor; Buckland; Chandler; Chaplin; Chitterne; Clowne; Cowage; Crichel; Curtis; David; Drury; Dunham; Dyer; Enfield; Enterbush; Felix; Fish; Fitton; Frank; Goslin; Harborough; Henry at the bar; Highworth; Hoare; Holhurst; Holyman; Homington; Hurle; Laurence; Lavington;

'Lenthorpe'; Lord; Man; Mason; Mottram; Mowlish; Ogbourne; Perch; Pitts; Poulton; Prentice; Ragenhill; Salisbury; Sauter; Sevenash; Spurgeon; Stallington; Sulham; Sydenham; Taunton; Thomas; Tidcombe; Walden; Winterbourne; *and see* scribes; witnesses: clerk
Clifton, Thos. of, chaplain, 603, 653
Clive
  Joan, w. of John, 2027–8
  John, tanner, 2027–8, 2105
Clopton, Wal., kt., 1475–6, 1742, 1813, 1979, 2056
cloth, clothes (given charitably), 553, 556, 648, 816, 1882, 1954, 2154
clothiers, *see* Baker; Chalke; Taylor; Wallop; Woodford
Clowne, Rog. of, clerk, archdeacon of Salisbury, 564, 578, 816
Coates
  John, 529
  Lucy, w. of John, 529
Cockerell
  Alice, w. of Wm., 1077, 1159
  Edw., 623
  Wm., 1077, 1158–9
Codford
  John, 5
  John, chaplain, 2003
  Wm., 5
Coffer
  Joan, w. of John, relict of John Luckham, 1255, 1714–15, 1802–3
  John, tanner, 1714–15, 1802–3

GENERAL INDEX

Cofford
  Alice, w. of Edm., 802, 1799, 1837; cf. Alice Monkton
  her s., see Monkton
  Edm., 557, 802, 1182–3, 1226, 1232, 1719, 1758, 1777, 1798–9, 1918–19, 1923; will, 1837
  Ellen, w. of Wm., 557
  John, 1837
  Maud, w. of Wm., 557, 744
  Nic., 557
  Thos., 1201–2, 1565, 1722
  Thos. (?another), tanner, 1944
  Wm., 738, 744, 802, 1232, 1837; will, 557
Cole
  Adam (fl. c. 1320), 28, 114–15, 142, 177
  Adam (fl. c. 1360), 489, 789
  Agnes, w. of John, baker, relict of Wm. Higdon, 1980, 1982–3
  Agnes, relict of Ric., 591
  Emme, 832
  Isabel (?relict of elder John), 1017, 1072, 1078, 1088, 1102, 1423–6, 1524–5, 1700, 1710, 1718, 1735
  Joan, w. of Rog., 122
  John, 269, 554, 573, 591, 605, 615–16, 636, 669, 675, 882, 1017, 1072, 1075, 1078, 1080, 1086, 1423–4, 1426–7, 1655, 1710; and see witnesses: citizen
  John, s. of John, 1423–4
  John or his s. John, 1709, 1740, 1944
  John, baker, 1982–3
  Maud, w. of Adam (fl. c. 1360), 489
  Parnel, w. of Adam (fl. c. 1320), 28, 114

Ric., carpenter, 1199
Rog. (?three of the name), 122, 258, 269
Steph., 1836
Wm., 271
Wm., chaplain, 1525, 1700
Colebrooke (Devon), see ways
Coleman
  Margt., 1039
  Wm., his maidservant Marion, his boy Wal., 816
Coleshill
  Rob., 352
  Wm. of, rector of Kington, 183
Collier
  Alice, w. of John, 1436
  John, tucker, 1245, 1436, 1527, 1800; and see witnesses: citizen
Collingbourne
  Peter of, 11, 60, 240, 245
  Ric. of, friar, 583
Collins
  Agnes, w. of Thos., dau. of Adam Wardour, 1992, 2000
  Thos., weaver, 2000
Comber, Wm., and his w. Cecily, 669
Comme, Nic., 1790, 1823–5
commissaries, 543, 648; and see Bide; Marston; Pain; Perch; Poulton
Common Pleas, see courts
Compton Chamberlayne, 233
Conning, Wm., 1729
Coof, Ric., and his inmate Alice, 1971
Cook
  Agnes, w. of Geof., 447
  And., 596, 666, 709–10
  his m. Gillian, 666
  Emme, w. of Ric., see Sivier
  Geof., 447
  Gillian, w. of Wal. (fl.

1365), dau. of Thos. of Cirencester, 752–3
John, 1184
Margery, w. of And., relict of Rob. Osborne, 551, 561, 596, 666, 709–10
Reynold, 1622–4
Ric., 507, 568, 952; will, 582
Rob., 447, 816
Thos., chaplain, 1097, 1099, 1113, 1253, 1365–6, 1483–4, 1666, 1945
Wal. (fl. 1365), 752
Wal. (fl. 1413), 2158; cf. Cox
Wm., 2026, 2031
cooks, see Melksham; Sherborne; Warin; William
Coombe
  John, weaver, 1974–5
  Steph., 472
  Thos., chaplain, 1573–5, 1865–6
  Wm., friar, 1836
Cooper
  Agnes, 720–1
  Alice, dau. of Rob., see Gomes
  Alice, w. of Wal., 1155
  Isabel, 1871
  Rob., 69
  Thos., 1719
  Wal., 556, 563, 685, 732, 837, 1155
cooper, see Green
Coppiner, John, 194, 645, 690, 693, 769
cordwainers, see Boughton; Butt; Ettshall; Harnham; Hathaway; Winchester
Corfe, John, rector of Radipole, 619
Cormell
  Agnes, w. of Ric., 1056
  Christine, sis. of Ric., mercer, see Dowding
  Joan, w. of Ric., mercer,

1201–2, 1258, 1912, 2155
John, 2155
Ric., 1056
(*otherwise* Knolle) Ric., mercer, 1201–2, 1258, 1806, 1882, 1902, 1908, 1912, 1962–3, 2061, 2075; will, 2155
Wm., tailor, 2064
Wm., elder s. of Ric., mercer, 2155
Wm., ygr. s. of Ric., mercer, 2155
Cornish, John, 2138–9
Corp, Wm., 694
Cosham
Joan, w. of Wal. of, 1796
Wal., 556, 661
Wal. of, 1796
Cosser, John, 1918
Costard
Alice, 666
Wm., 452–4, 467, 518, 522, 697, 803, 838, 1117–18
Cottel, Wm., chaplain, 47
Coulston
John, 1254, 1416–17
elder John (?another), 1729
Ralph of, 588, 711
Coulston (*unspecified*), 1930
Countwell
Adam, 1508–9
Agnes, w. of Adam, 1509
Courtier
Adam, 1171–2
Agnes, w. of Adam, relict of Rob. Langford, 1071, 1171–2
Courtman
Cecily, w. of elder John, 1719
Joan, 1719
John, 1084–5; will, 1719
John, s. of John, 1719
Margery, w. of elder John, 1084–5, 1719
courts
Common Pleas

(Common Bench, king's court), 68, 163, 269, 399, 880, 1049, 1858, 1958, 1972
justices (the king's justices), 68, 238, 399, 843–4, 1414, 1853–4, 1858; *and see* Belknap; Brenchesley; Hankford; Markham; Rickhill; Thirning; Thorpe
Exchequer, 278
King's Bench, *see* prisoners
and see Canterbury, prerogative court; London, husting court; index 2: court
Cousen, John, weaver, and his w. Alice, 901, 996
Coventry, Wm., 1769, 1793, 1813, 1835, 1896, 1907, 2025, 2034–5, 2124
Cowage, Anselm, clerk, 1680
Cox
Wal., 2064; *cf.* Cook
Wm., 2158
Crablane
Joan, w. of John, 1943
John, dyer, 1943, 2013–14, 2116, 2118, 2121
Crass, John, 1275–6, 1312
Creed
John, 549, 608, 953, 1015
(called Melksham) John, 1207, 1709
Sarah, w. of John, 953, 1015
Crewkerne (Som.), parish church of, 1709
Crichel
John (fl. *c.* 1319), 3, 61
John, s. of John, 61
John (of), chaplain, clerk, vicar of cathedral church, 407–8, 412, 514–16, 609, 644, 671, 700, 704, 724, 727, 729, 737, 745

John (fl. 1361, carpenter, 546
the master Wm. (of), clerk, 1–3
Cricklade
priory, 1938
Widhill, North, *q.v.*
Crier
Geof., 1519–21
Steph., 116, 415, 418, 517, 605, 636, 803, 838, 1684
Cripps
Denise, w. of Wm., 1880
John, 1979
ygr. John, 1979
Wm., 1880
cross, at the *see* Ralph Cross
Cross
Amice, w. of John, relict of John Webb, 653, 688
John, 688, 690
John, saddler: will, 2038
Thos., 2038
Croucheston (in Bishopstone, in Downton hundred), 192
Culpriest, Rog., 201
Cupping
Isabel, relict of John, *see* Alwin
John, 181, 291, 667
Curl, Thos., chaplain, 2063
Curtis
John, 1888
Ric., clerk, 2162, 2164
Cust, Thos., 567
Cutler
John, 619
Wm., *see* Upavon
Cutting, Thos., 1492
his m., *see* Burden
C...ssley, Wm., household servant, 816

Damerham, the master Nic., 619
Daniel, John, 2064
Dash
John, 277

Wm., 144
Daubeney, Adam, fisher, 1813, 1979
Dauntsey, Edm., 2125
David (fl. 1408), 2011
David, clerk, 602, 805, 810, 1823–4, 2067
　his w. Benet, 810
　cf. Laurence
Davitt, Rog., chaplain, 1729, 1750
Davy, Margt., 1828
Daw, Peter, mercer, 2054, 2082, 2149
Day
　Jas., 2031
　Pleasant, see witnesses: reeve
Dayson, Ric., 791
Deakin
　John, of North Widhill, and his w. Edith, 1152
　John, of Downton, 1721, 1860, 1874
Dean
　Gillian, relict of John, 245
　John, chaplain, vicar of cathedral church, 516, 774, 776, 806, 971, 1167, 1205, 1954
　Wal., chaplain, 1832, 2128
Dean (unspecified), 1954
Dean, West, rector of, see Pedwell
Deanbridge
　Adam, 599
　Agnes, w. of John, see Lea
　Edw. (of), 558, 664, 741
　John (of), 456, 602, 617, 751, 763, 807–8, 830; will, 599; and see witnesses: citizen
　Wal. of, 558
Debden, Wm., 2156
debtors (relieved charitably), 1938
Dedman, Hain, 1814
Delves
　Hen., 1895–6, 2045, 2136

Joan, w. of Hen., dau. of John Salisbury, kt., 1895, 2136
Denis, John, and his w. Agnes, 832
Denman
　Margt., 1778, 2069–70
　Rob., 1778, 2069–70
Dereham, Thos., 1975, 2144
Deverill
　Agnes, w. of elder Thos., 1004, 1154, 1185, 1513
　Alice, w. of John, see Rushall
　John, 1778
　Margery, 1954
　Rob. (fl. c. 1375) and Rob. (fl. 1413) [?two of the name], 956, 1221–2, 1341, 1555, 1605, 1658, 1681–2, 1688, 1694, 1703–4, 1713, 1767, 1791, 1949, 1951–2, 1967, 2168; and see witnesses: coroner, citizen
　Thos., 1004, 1154, 1185, 1220, 1513–14
　Thos., s. of Thos., 1154, 1185, 1513, 1515
Deverill, Hill, 1954
Deverill, Longbridge, 1533, 2103
Longleat, q.v.
Devizes, 564, 2001, 2005
　church of St. John, 2155
Devon, see Milton Abbatis; and see, s.v. ways, Colebrooke; Langford
Dewey, John, 327
Dicker, John, chaplain, 1508–9
Difford, Wm., 582
Diggon, Wm., 2011
Dinton
　Joan, dau. of John, 1230
　Joan, dau. of Ric., 831
　John, s. of Ric., 831
　John, butcher (and John unspecified), 840, 949, 1230, 1322, 1324, 1327,

1460, 1754, 1872, 1990
　Maud, m. of Ric., see Shearer
　Ric. (of), 602, 690, 693, 696, 804, 831; and see witnesses: citizen
Dinton, 2169
　rector, see Peakirk
Doder
　Agnes, w. of John, dau. of John Baldry, see Warmwell
　John, 497, 585–7, 594, 643, 683, 692; will, 556
　John, s. of John and Agnes, 556, 586, 643, 958
Doggett, John, rector of Preshute, 732
Dogskin
　Alice, see Webb
　Hen., 563, 732
　John, 1313, 1936, 2033, 2091–2, 2111
　Maud, relict of John, 2091–2, 2111
　Wm., 551, 666, 709
Dogton, John, 1773–4; and see witnesses: citizen; cf. Duckton
Doley, Adam, 2011
Doll, John, 1871
Dolling, John, and his w. Christine, 128
Dominicans, see James; Langford; Sprot; Weston; Wilton; Winchester; and see index 2: Dominicans of Fisherton
Donnet, John, chaplain, 567
Dorchester, Wm., 120
Dore, John, and his s. John, 619
Dorset, John, 2064
Dorset, see Christchurch; Handley; Iwerne; Pentridge; Shaftesbury; Sturminster Newton;

Tarrant; Tarrant
Gunville; Wimborne
Minster; *and see*
Milton *Abbatis*; *and
see (for cross-reference)*
Radipole
Dovedale
John, 474
Maud, 152
Maud *(another)*, relict of
Thos. Netheravon,
474
her dau. Agnes, *see*
Kilmeston
Maud *(either)*, 1733, 1736
Thos., 789
Thos. (?*another*), 1777,
1781
Dowden
John, 740
Thos., 740
Dowding
Christine, w. of Wm.,
sis. of Ric. Cormell,
1442, 1617, 1619, 2011,
2155
Rob., 964–5
Wm., merchant, 1617,
1619–20, 1665–6,
1721, 1956–7, 2045,
2063, 2114–15, 2117,
2119, 2135, 2155; *and
see* witnesses: mayor,
reeve, citizen
dower, 9, 435, 553, 556,
706, 1664, 1683, 1760,
1786, 1938, 2104
custom of the city, 14,
2154
pleas, 177, 237, 245,
843–4
Downton, John, draper,
2049–51, 2076
Downton, 445, 667, 816,
1874
church, 2063
vicar, *see* Turk
Drake, John, 51
Draper, John, 1729
drapers, *see* Bailey; Baker;
Beeton; Bernard;
Downton; Durrant;

Hart; Judd; Langford;
Mason; Melbury;
Nalder; Needler;
Pope; Shad; Snel;
Springham; Stabber;
Taylor; Tredinnick;
Wagain; Wallop;
Wells; Wishford;
Woodrow; *and see*
linendraper
Drew
Laur., *see* witnesses:
bailiff
Thos., 692
Drimmer, Thos., 663
Drury
Alice, sis. of John (d.
1404), 1859
Alice, w. of Reynold,
1649, 1746
John (fl. *c.* 1364, d. 1404:
?two of the name),
719–21, 1126, 1156,
1170, 1173, 1239, 1479,
1495–7, 1514–16, 1735,
1764, 1771, 1849,
1852, 1855, 1897; will,
1859
John, clerk, 1849, 1852,
1855, 1857
Reynold, 1649, 1746,
1849, 1852, 1855, 1928,
1976, 2010
Dubber
Christine, relict of John,
68
Edw., *see* Gilbert
Gilbert, 307, 644
John, 68
dubbers, *see* Chirton;
Gilbert; Shipton
Duckman
John, vicar of cathedral
church, 516
Wm., 564, 739
Duckton, John, 1969–70;
cf. Dogton
Dudmore
Margt., w. of Ric., 448,
539, 555
Ric., taverner, 448, 539,
555

Duke
Jas., w. of ygr. John, 831
elder John, 831
ygr. John, 831, 1467,
2079
Margery, 831
Wm., ironmonger, 1469,
2079
Dummer, Adam, 1829,
1831, 1984, 1989
Dunball
Edith, *see* Ferring
Maud, w. of Thos.,
2042–4
Thos., carpenter, 1087,
2043–4, 2046–7; will,
2042
his bro. John, *see* Pierce
Dunham, Wm. of, clerk,
1753
Dunkerton, Wm., *at* 555,
665, 759, 766, 793,
808, 820, 855, 894,
962–3, 1134, 1214,
1268, 1337, 1674,
1677–8, 1731–2, 1880;
and see witnesses: clerk
Dunn
Ellen, 816
John, vicar of Mere,
1680
Wm., 575–6, 652, 730,
1944
Dunning
Maud, w. of Wm.,
1892–3
Wm., weaver, 1892–3,
2018
Durkin
Agnes, w. of Bart., 1346,
1512
Bart., goldsmith, 1057,
1107, 1186, 1297, 1346,
1395, 1512, 1541, 1658,
1660, 1674, 1677–8,
1701, 1713, 1846,
1867–8, 1943, 1952,
2169
Edith, w. of Bart., 1057
Durley, Edm., 2011
Durnford
Hen., 1664

John, dyer, 1828, 1928,
    1993, 1995, 2010
Mabel, relict of John
    Langford, 288
Margt., w. of Thos.,
    relict of Rob.
    Hazelbury, 2007, 2163
Thos., 2163
Durnford, 1979
    church, 603, 1930
    Netton, *q.v.*
    Newton, *q.v.*
    prebendal jurisdiction,
        1930
    Salterton, *q.v.*
    vicar, see Maidenhead
Durrant
    Alice, w. of Rob.,
        relict of Ric. Hellier
        (*otherwise* Hawes),
        1909, 1961
    Jas., 1909
    Joan, 1909
    Rob., draper, 1830, 1909,
        1961, 2009, 2074
Durrington
    Agnes, see Smith
    Alice, relict of Thos. (d.
        by 1398), 1565, 1722
    Gillian, see Hoare
    John, 573
    Thos. (of) (d. by 1398),
        472, 668, 743, 1565,
        1722, 1884
    Thos. (fl. 1408), 2011
    Wm. (of), 165, 573
Dyer
    Adam, and his w.
        Beatrice, 999
    Edm., clerk, 553; *and see*
        witnesses: clerk
    John, weaver, 1533, 1887,
        2103
    Martin, 2073
    Nic., glover, 207
dyers, see Burford;
        Crablane; Durnford;
        Fyport; Hurn;
        Penton; Pope;
        Richard at the bridge;
        Scot; Sexhampcote;
        Sutton; William at the
            bridge; Winchester;
            Wootton
Dyke
    Alice, 789
    Edith, w. of Wm., 1851
    Joan, 789
    John (d. by 1366), 789
    John, s. of John, 863,
        1044, 1227
    John (either *or* another),
        1733, 1736, 1851
    Margery, w. of John (d.
        by 1366), see Ashlock
    Peter, 1851, 1960, 1974–5
    Wm., 1746, 1851, 1960
Dyne
    Christine, w. of Wal.,
        1787–8
    Reynold, 462
    Tho., 462
    Wal., 1787–8
    D, G of, 1434

Easton, Wm., and his w.
    Maud, 568
Easton, priory of, 2064
Ebbesbourne, Wm., 783
Ebeny, John, 666
Edendon, Wm., bishop of
    Winchester, 620
Edington
    Cath., w. of Steph., 1761
    Steph., 1255, 1714–15,
        1734, 1737, 1759, 1761,
        1776, 1780, 1798–9,
        1802, 1818–19, 1821–
        2, 1841, 1845, 1873–5,
        1879, 1881, 1911, 1916,
        1918–19, 1923, 1948–
        9, 1951, 1963, 1967,
        1970–1, 1988, 2029,
        2036, 2041, 2047,
        2071–2, 2093, 2102–3;
        and see witnesses: clerk
    Edith, household servant,
        2064
    Edith, maid, 1936
    Edith, servants of the
        name, 1778, 1836
    Edmond, Rog., chaplain,
        327
    Edward III, 661, 679, 704,
        729, 745, 844
        his w., see Philippa
    Edward, an apprentice,
        1836
    'Ele', Wm., see Woodford;
        cf. Heal
    Eling
        Parnel, 140
        Wm. of, 140
    Elion, Edw., chaplain,
        1259–60, 1373, 1386,
        1465, 1593–4, 1608–
        10, 1667–9, 1671–3,
        1676, 1685, 1687–9,
        1691–7, 1699, 1720,
        1727, 1773–4, 1786
    Eliot, Wal., 470
    'Elisett', servant, 1888
    Ellis
        Emme, w. of Wm., 1910
        John, limeburner, 1510
        John (?another *or* others),
            1978, 2061
        Margt., see Godmanstone
        Ric., parson of Sherfield,
            997
        Wm. (?two of the
            name), 136, 304, 1910
    Ely, John of, 1722; *and see*
        witnesses: coroner
    Enfield
        Alice, w. of Edm., 1440–
            1, 1535, 1546, 1832,
            1938
        Edith, w. of Edm., 1621,
            1670, 1690, 1706–7,
            1938
        the master Edm., clerk,
            1360–3, 1404–5, 1407,
            1440–1, 1483–4, 1486,
            1489, 1491, 1535,
            1542, 1546, 1561–2,
            1580, 1597–8, 1621,
            1630–5, 1645, 1665,
            1670, 1684, 1690,
            1693, 1695, 1701,
            1706–7, 1721, 1738–9,
            1742, 1744, 1751,
            1758, 1763–5, 1784,
            1832, 1860, 1944,
            1969–70, 1984, 1989,
            2156; will, 1938; *and*

see witnesses: mayor,
    reeve, citizen
Enfield (Mdx.)
    church, 1938
    altar of St. Nicholas,
      1938
    rector, 1938
Enford, the lord Thos., 569
Enford, church of, 2155
Enterbush
    Ric., chaplain, clerk,
      1463–4, 2013, 2026,
      2031
    Rog., 1852, 1857, 1957,
      1984, 1989, 2007,
      2026, 2029, 2031,
      2037, 2047, 2099, 2113
Erghum, Ralph, bishop
    of Bath and Wells,
    bishop of Salisbury,
    844, 1709
Erlestoke, Thos. (of),
    chaplain, clerk, parson
    of Barford St. Martin,
    324, 329–30, 407–8,
    412, 442, 452–3,
    463–4, 468, 477–8,
    502, 505, 507–8, 510,
    513–14, 522, 537, 560,
    566, 577, 580, 609,
    644, 649, 657, 663,
    671, 674, 684, 695,
    697, 700, 704, 708,
    718–21, 724, 727,
    729, 731, 737, 742,
    745, 792, 803, 806,
    899, 948, 966, 971–3,
    1023, 1048, 1098–1101,
    1117–18, 1133–4, 1137,
    1143–4, 1146–7, 1163–
    4, 1786, 2049–51, 2076
esquires, *see* Besil;
    Intborough, Merriott
Essington, John (of),
    taverner, 510, 519, 973
Etchilhampton, Rob. of,
    621
Ettshall
    John (fl. *c.* 1376),
      cordwainer, 997
    John (fl. 1413, same *or*
      another), 1295, 1297,
1367, 1495, 1499–1500,
  1616, 1625, 1640, 1819,
  1822, 1826–7, 1841–2,
  1895–6, 1935, 1981,
  2158
Maud, w. of John (fl. *c.*
  1376), 997
Everard
Agnes, w. of elder John,
  210, 692
Beatrice, w. of elder
  John, 625, 641, 692
Edith, 692
John, 210, 475, 497, 625,
  641; will, 692
John, s. of John, 692
Jordan, 692
Lucy, 692
Margery, 692
Rob., vicar [?of cathedral
  church], 1882
Wm., 692
Evesham, Wm. of, 673
Ewan
Joan, w. of John, 485
John, 485, 597
Wal., 485, 597
Exchequer, *see* courts
Exeter
Wm. of, 50
ygr. Wm. of, 54
Eyre
Alice, w. of Thos., *see*
  Bromley
Thos., 1217, 1585–6,
  1685, 1696, 1833,
  1888, 1892–3, 2101,
  2153; will, 2064; *and
  see* witnesses: reeve,
  citizen
Wm., 2064, 2101

Fadder, Rog., 1532
Fairwood
Margt., w. of Wm., 601,
  761
Wm., baker, 601, 761
Fakenham, Rog., 1020
Falconer, (called Leach)
  Ric., 1725–6; *cf.* Leach
false measure, 137
Faringdon, Rob. of, 543,
742, 813–14; *and see*
  witnesses: mayor
Farley
Alice, 566, 948
Edith, w. of Ric. of
  (d. by 1361), dau. of
  Geof. of Warminster,
  513; will, 566
John, chaplain, 1167,
  1194, 1205, 1238, 1370
Ric. of (d. by 1361),
  spicer, 513, 566, 948
Ric. (fl. 1361), 566, 692
Farnborough
Alice, w. of John, 1018
John (of), 665, 836, 900,
  1018, 2112–13; *and see*
  witnesses: citizen
Rog., chaplain, 1273,
  1285, 1518, 1561–2
Thos., 2011
Farrant
Christine, w. of Thos.,
  1876
Jac', w. of Thos., 1468
Thos., mercer, 1468,
  1470, 1784, 1816,
  1876, 1976, 2079
Farthing
Agnes, 698
John, and his w. Alice,
  92
John (another), 1778
Faulston (in Bishopstone,
  in Downton
  hundred), church of,
  1943
Felix, Thos., clerk, 1960,
  2004
Fernhill
Isabel, w. of Matt., 1437,
  1790, 1806
Matt. (of), 637, 651, 868,
  1437, 1790, 1806,
  1823–5
Ferrer
Cecily, w. of Ric., 2057
Isabel, w. of Wm. (fl. *c.*
  1392), 1421
John (fl. before 1367),
  832
John (fl. 1405), carter,

1779, 1811–12, 1860,
  1873–5
John (another), 1860,
  1942, 2104
Maud, w. of John, carter,
  1779, 1811–12, 1873–5
Ric., 2057
Rog., chaplain, 1760
Wm. (fl. before 1363),
  670
the master Wm. (fl. *c.*
  1392), 1421, 1472–3,
  1962–3
Wm. (fl. 1410, ?another),
  2061, 2075
Ferrers, Agnes, 707, 795
Ferring
  Edith, w. of Thos., dau.
    of Thos. Dunball,
    2043–4, 2046–7
  Thos., weaver, 2043–4,
    2046–7, 2080, 2083,
    2154
'Fetbien', John, 2055
Fewster
  Alice, w. of Rob., niece
    of Rob. Baldry, 628,
    1321
  Edith, w. of Wm., 1840,
    2142
  Rob., 599, 628, 683,
    813–14, 1321
  Wm., 1840, 2140–2; *and
    see* witnesses: reeve,
    citizen
Field, Thos., 1683; *and see*
  witnesses: citizen
Fifield, John, collegiate
  chaplain of St.
  Edmund's church,
  621, 845
Fifield (*unspecified*), parson
  of, *see* Toogood
Figheldean
  Hen. of, 97
  Joan, 619
  John, 619
  Thos., 619
Figheldean, 1664
  church of St. Michael,
    579, 1664, 2155
fines, 5, 90, 163, 244, 399,

880, 1049, 1414, 1854,
  1858, 1958, 1972
Fish
  John, 460, 1689
  John, clerk, 623
  John, weaver, 1915
  Sim., 35
  Thos., 740
Fisher
  Christine, w. of John,
    1786
  Edm., 1722
  John, 553, 1786
  Rob., 553
  Sim., 553
fishermen, fishers, *see*
  Bristol; Britford;
  Daubeney; Godfrey;
  Osborne; Pitt; Webb
Fisherton, Wm. of, 333–4
Fisherton Anger, 781
  address, 583, 589, 1878
  bridges, *see* index 2:
    Fisherton, lower
    bridge; Fisherton,
    upper bridge
  church of St. Clement,
    583, 1888
  image of St. Thomas of
    Canterbury, 583
  paupers, 1836
  property, 827–9, 898,
    1519
  rector (parson), 583; *and
    see* Gill
  Scammel's mead, 2063
  and see index 2:
    Dominican friary;
    Dominicans (of
    Fisherton)
Fittleton
  church, 2155
  Haxton, *q.v.*
Fitton, Ric., clerk, 2101
FitzPain, John, 266
Fivemark, John, 1985
Flamston (in Bishopstone,
  in Downton
  hundred), light of St.
  Anne in, 1943
Flanders, 578
Fleming

Agnes, w. of John, 2131
Hen. (d. by *c.* 1331), 226
Hen. (fl. 1365), 467, 471–
  2, 484, 567, 625, 641,
  644, 671, 701, 764–6
John, 2131
Fletcher
  Alice, relict of David,
    1404–6
  (*otherwise* Stook) David,
    924, 969–70, 973,
    991–2, 1095, 1097,
    1099, 1119, 1148,
    1365–6, 1376, 1404–5,
    1938, 2025
Florentine
  John, 512, 1477
  Thos., 186, 626
  Wm., 188
Focket
  John, 1765
  Margt., w. of Thos.,
    1179
  Ric., 1765
  Thos., 1013–14, 1024,
    1064, 1132, 1161–2,
    1165, 1179, 1192, 1203,
    1233, 1269, 1328,
    1690, 1765, 1954,
    1974–5, 2009, 2039
Foliot
  Edith, w. of Rog., 95
  Rog., 17, 33, 95
Fonthill, Rog., and his w.
  Maud, 651
Fool, John, 1725
ford, at the, *see* William
  Ford
Ford
  Isabel, w. of Laur. of,
    240
  Joan, w. of John of, 77
  John of, 77, 127
  Laur. of, 240
  Rog., 805
Ford (?in Laverstock),
  1722; *and see*
  Winterbourne Ford
Forest
  Christine, w. of elder
    John, 2029, 2032–3,
    2052–3, 2099
  elder John, weaver,

1262–3, 1348–9,
1384–6, 1585–6, 1605,
1718, 1748, 1777,
1796, 1833–4, 1843,
1850, 1896, 1923,
1991, 2001, 2005,
2032–3, 2036, 2045,
2052–3, 2096–9, 2111,
2123; will, 2029; *and
see* witnesses: citizen
John, elder s. of John,
2029, 2033
John, ygr. s. of John,
2029, 2042–4, 2053,
2096–7, 2099, 2159
ygr. John (?ygr. s. of
John), 1888
Rob., 2029, 2033, 2052–
3, 2096–9
Thos., canon, 2029
Wm., 616
forest, justice of the, 317
Forster
Peter, 2064
Ric., 2064
Fosbury
John (of), 775, 788, 810
John (of), s. of John (of),
612, 810
John (elder *or* ygr.),
847–8, 1180, 1823–5
John (?another), 1969–70
and see witnesses: citizen
Fountain
Edw. (fl. 1365), 755, 760
Edw. (fl. 1397, ?same),
1705, 1720, 1743
Joan, w. of Edw. (fl.
1397), 1705
John, 584
Rog., 755, 760
Fovant, Rob., 1755
Fowle
Agnes, *see* Langton
Christine, w. of Rog. (fl.
c. 1330), 238
John, 718, 721, 731, 746,
780–1, 787–8, 804,
831, 999, 1033, 1055,
1570–1, 2079, 2166;
and see witnesses:
citizen

John, chaplain, 1572
Rog. (fl. *c.* 1330), 238,
437
Rog. (d. by 1405), 1876,
1976
Rose, w. of John, 746,
780–1, 1571
Fox
Alice, 671
Christine, 1925–6
Hugh, 1843
Joan, w. of Rob., 1843
John, chaplain, 1318,
1377, 1444
Rob., 674, 684, 1843
Wm., 554, 608
Foyle, Wal., chaplain, 1549
Francis, John, rector of
Saltwood, 1725
Franciscans, 144
and see New;
Nottingham;
Southampton;
Winchester
and see index 2
Frank
Emme, w. of Rog., *see*
Astbury
Isabel, w. of John, 355,
521
John, 355, 521, 767
John, clerk, 2024
Rog., 463, 806
the master Wm., 1882
Franklin
Alice, w. of John,
wheeler, relict of
Wm. Woodrow, 1902,
1908, 1912
John, 1273, 1285
John (?another), wheeler,
1672, 1676, 1686–7,
1902, 1908, 1912
Wal., 566
frankmarriage, 1856
Freaks, Joan, 1828
Frear
Edith, dau. of Ric., *see*
Starr
Edith, w. of Ric., 554,
1945
Joan, 554

John, 554, 630
Ric., 492–4, 598, 627,
630, 1849, 1855, 1945;
will, 554
friars (named), *see*
Bartlet; Breamore;
Collingbourne;
Coombe; James;
Langford; Montagu;
New; Scammel; Sprot;
Till; Wallis; Weston
Friday
Edm., 1984, 1989
Joan, w. of Thos., 1984
John, 2156
Thos., 836, 900, 1266,
1984, 1989
Friend
Christine, relict of John,
570, 1457
her s. Wm., 1457
Christine, w. of Wm.,
see Wootton
Christine (either), 1132
John, 570
Wm., 431, 550, 604,
608; will, 570; *and see*
witnesses: reeve
Frith, Edw., 2093–4, 2104
Fromand, Rob., rector of
St. Thomas's church,
168
Frome, John, 1358
Frome (Som.), 11
Fry
Agnes, relict of Ric.,
591, 601, 761
John, weaver, 1946
John (?another), 2011
Ric., 591, 601, 761
Wm., 2063
Fuggles, Agnes, 62
Fugglestone, 1930
Quidhampton, *q.v.*
Fulham
Ebote, relict of Ric.,
1755
Ric., 1659, 1679, 1755
fulling, art of, 1992
furbisher, *see* Portman
Furmage, Wal., 1190, 2066
Fyfield (in Overton),

church of St.
Nicholas, 1971
Fyport, Thos., dyer, 1773–
4, 2138

Gage, Ric., weaver, 1928,
2009–10, 2060, 2062,
2064, 2074; *and see*
witnesses: reeve
Gallon, Adam, 967
Gardener, John (?three of
the name), 816, 1680,
1940
Garnet, Thos., 829
Garnon, Hugh, 1566
Garston, East (Berks.),
1979
church, 1979
Gatcombe
Joan, w. of John, 1111,
1449, 1451, 2016,
2020, 2104
(called Sergeant) John,
1111, 1128, 1389, 1391,
1449, 1451, 1747, 1776,
1798–9, 1829, 1831,
1852, 1856–7, 1901,
1911, 1914–16, 1918–
19, 1947–8, 2016,
2019–20, 2104
Gaunt
Joan, w. of elder Nic.,
relict of Thos. Long,
161, 386
Nic., 386–7, 406
Nic., s. of Nic., 406
Gaydon, tanner, and his w.
Alice, 57
Geddington, Wm. of,
rector of Cholderton,
72
Gifford, servant, 1979
Gifford
John, 65
the lord Nic., 2156
Wm., 550
Gilbert at the brook,
skinner, 1136, 1443,
1446–7, 1820, 1887
his w. Maud, dau. of
Alice Hammond,
1820, 1887

Gilbert
(*otherwise* Dubber) Edw.,
dubber, 1855, 1857,
1928, 1976, 2010,
2056, 2133, 2168
Joan, w. of Edw., 1855,
1857
(called Sumner) John,
1374, 1728, 1786, 1985,
2024
John, vicar of cathedral
church, 1777, 1996,
1998
Maud, relict of Thos.,
see Wallop
Rob., tanner, 2132
Thos., 694, 796, 799,
918, 1884, 1894, 1923,
1996, 1998, 2158
Wm., 1888
Gill
Adam, tanner, 1292
Agnes, relict of Wm.,
618, 664, 673, 741;
will, 558
her m. Agnes, *see*
Woodford
Agnes, dau. of Agnes,
558
Hen., rector of Fisherton
Anger, 509, 543, 589,
598–9, 627, 703, 1786
Maud, w. of Adam, 1292
Wm., 558, 571, 618, 664,
741, 786, 1551
Gillian, maid, 583
Gillingham, John, 1422
Gillmin, Sim., 633, 1900–1
Gitting, Alice, 1909
Glastonbury, Edw., s. of
Ric. of, 809
Glastonbury (Som.), 619
Gleese
Joan, relict of Thos., 568
Thos., 49, 568
Glendy
Alice, w. of Steph., 247
Steph., 247, 659
Thos., of Stratford, 328,
379, 740
Thos. (?another), s. of
Steph., 659

cf. 'Glondy'
Glinton, Wm., subdean of
cathedral church, 553
'Glondy', John, 1778; *cf.*
Glendy
Gloucester, Emme of, 1372
Gloucester (abbey), image
of St. Kyneburg the
Virgin, 2063
Gloucestershire, *see*
Cirencester; Hailes
Glover
Agnes, w. of Reynold,
1447
Agnes, w. of Thos., relict
of Rob. Harass: will,
1936
her dau. Agnes, 1936
her sis. Maud, *see*
Warin
her s. John, 1936
her s. Ric., 1936
her s. Wm., 1936
and see Harass
Nic., 1722
Reynold, 1447, 1449–51,
1720, 1910–11, 2150,
2156
Thos., 1936, 2111
glovers, *see* Dyer; Oword
Godfrey, John, fisherman,
470
Godmanstone
Joan, w. of Rob. (d. *c.*
1374), 504, 509, 555,
592–3; as relict of
Rob., 986, 1115–16,
1122, 1140, 1143, 1147,
1163–4
Margt., dau. of Wm.
Ellis, w. of Wm., 945,
1002, 1019; as relict
of Wm., 1661–2,
1706–7, 1727, 1791,
1842, 1896, 1910–11,
1915–16, 1935,
2027–8, 2040, 2105,
2112–13, 2120, 2159; as
w. and relict of Wm.
Buckland, 457, 1900–1
Rob. (of) (d. *c.* 1374),
364, 504, 509, 555,

585–7, 592–3, 625, 641–2, 671, 739, 780–1, 827–9, 832, 876, 891, 936, 975, 1144, 1146, 1188, 1745, 1747, 1978; *and see* witnesses: citizen
Rob. (fl. *c.* 1380), 1145
Wm., 945, 1002, 1019, 1106, 1110, 1142, 1145, 1231, 1333, 1431, 1456, 1463, 1471, 1661–2, 1994, 2054, 2102, 2112
Goldrom, Wm., and his w. Isabel, 121
Goldsmith
(called Ive) Jas., *see* Ive
Phil., 1688, 1694, 2013–14
goldsmiths, *see* Durkin; Harlwin
Goldston
Christine, w. of Wm., 568, 993, 1009–10, 1016
Wm., 457, 554, 582, 644, 832, 993, 1009–10; will, 568
Gollan
Agnes, w. of Rob., 1800
Rob., tucker, 1800, 1814, 1872
Gomeldon, John (of), 41, 196, 714
Gomeldon (in Idmiston), 1979
Gomes
Alice, dau. of Rob. Cooper, 69
Rob. (?two of the name), 66, 69
Goodall
Joan, relict of Wm., 1882
John, painter, 844, 866
Wm., 1882
Goodyear, Thos., smith, 554, 588, 782–3
Goosebeard, Hen., 867
Gore
Adam, vicar of cathedral church, 440, 521, 757, 786, 1041

Alice, *see* Bodenham
Clemence, w. of Rob., 786
Emme, w. of Rob., 688, 786, 837
Gillian, w. of Rob., 786
John, 775, 786, 788
Rob., 355–6, 558, 570, 644, 664, 688, 724, 727, 741, 775, 788, 837; will, 786
Rob., s. of Rob., 786
Wm., 835
Goslin
Agnes, w. of John (fl. 1408), 2011
John (fl. before 1363), 678
John (fl. 1408), bell-founder, s. of Alice Barber, 2011–12
Wm., clerk, 678
Goss
Adam, *see* Oxley
Agnes, dau. of elder Geo., 1529
Agnes, w. of elder Geo., 792
Alice, w. of elder Geo., dau. of Wm. Wishford, 671, 1150, 1246, 1248, 1342–3, 1419–20, 1436, 1526
elder Geo. (fl. *c.* 1359–1401), 405, 423, 456, 533, 544, 557, 610, 613, 616, 625–7, 635, 641, 644, 646, 671, 676, 678, 738, 744, 769, 792–4, 796–7, 799, 801–2, 831–2, 889, 937, 956, 1037, 1150, 1197, 1209, 1222, 1245–6, 1248, 1341–3, 1419–20, 1436, 1526, 1528, 1559, 1777, 1796, 1798–9, 1918–19, 1923, 1996, 1998; as mayor, 766; *and see* witnesses: citizen
ygr. Geo. (fl. 1397 and later), 1720, 1800,

1845, 1847, 1975
?ygr. Geo., tucker, 1834, 1894, 2158
Hugh, 1720
Maud, w. of Wal., *see* Shearer
Wal., 57, 696, 804, 810, 2067–8
Gough, John, canon of cathedral church, 421
Gould
Alice, w. of Rob., 18, 218
John, chaplain, 1888
Rob., 18, 187, 294
Gowan
elder John, 1306, 1308, 1703–4, 1939, 1941; *and see* witnesses: bailiff
John, of Norrington, 2036–7, 2041
John (*unspecified*), 1305, 1307, 1309, 1311, 1527–9, 1688, 1694, 1913–14, 2090, 2158–9
Laur., 1805, 1850, 1935, 2165
Grandon
John, 1589, 1786, 2017
John, rector of Kislingbury, 2017
Grant, Wm., and his w. Denise, 770
Grateley
John, 1914
Rog., baker, 1820, 1887
'Grauniford', *see* bridges
'Grauntpe', Thos., 1663
Green
Agnes, relict of John, sis. of John Sewin, 2118
Jas., parochial chaplain of St. Thomas's church, 2063, 2067–8, 2095, 2154
John, cooper, 2118
Greenleaf, Rog., and his w. Joan, 67, 71, 90
Greenway
Agnes, 760
John, 760

GENERAL INDEX

Wm., 755, 760
Grew
  John, hatter, 370
  Rog., 7
Griffin, servant, 816
Griffin, David, 816
Griffith, John, tailor, 1812
Grinder, John, 1900–1
Grisley, Wm., rector of
  Kelsale, 1725
grocers, see Baker; Becket;
  Bishop; Brown;
  Camel; Hyde;
  Mower; Newman;
  Pickard; Preston;
  Salisbury; Shirley;
  Spencer; Warin
Gromville, Alice, 1000
Groom, Laur., chaplain,
  vicar of cathedral
  church, 1882, 1889–91
Gundy
  Alice, sis. of Hugh, 1720
  Alice, w. of Hugh, dau.
    of Thos. Callow, 396,
    399, 1105, 1251, 1698,
    1741
  Hugh, 1105, 1251, 1265,
    1539, 1698, 1702, 1741,
    1743, 1838, 1847; will,
    1720
    his kinswomen Alice
    and Maud, 1720
  Parnel, w. of Hugh,
    1720, 1743
  Rob., 1720, 1741
  Thos., 486
Guyon, John, 1256, 1272
Guys
  Maud, relict of Wm.,
    2067–8, 2129
  Wm., 810, 815, 848,
    868, 1103, 1300, 1414,
    1591, 1659, 1679,
    1702, 1806, 1823–5,
    1838, 1925–6, 1964,
    1977, 2048, 2067–8,
    2122, 2129; and see
    witnesses: citizen

Habgood
  Beatrice, w. of Nic.,
    relict of John Knoyle,
    706
  Nic., 706
Hacker
  Agnes, w. of John, 442,
    537, 557, 744, 802,
    1112, 1123
  John, 442, 537, 557,
    744, 802, 1112, 1123,
    1798–9
Hackwell, [?*rectius* Halwell]
  John, rector of
    Berwick, 1506
Hagbourne, John (of),
  chaplain, 327, 792–3
Hailes (abbey, Glos.), abbot
  of, 1938
Haim, Steph., citizen of
  Winchester, 552, 1657,
  1716
Hain
  Adam, 567
  elder John, loader, 1979,
    2162, 2164
  ygr. John, 1979
  John (*unspecified*), 2052–3
hall, at the, see Peter
Halliday, John, skinner, 991
Hallum, Rob., bishop
  of Salisbury, 2100,
  2158–9
Halwell
  John of, 80
  John of, chaplain, 620
  Maud, see Tanner
  Rog., indexed as Tanner
  cf. Hackwell
Ham
  Alice, w. of Thos., 1517
  Thos., tailor, 1517, 1789,
    1844–5
Hamish, Nic., chaplain,
  430, 439, 465, 542,
  549, 671, 707, 755,
  760, 795, 987, 1705
Hammond
  Alice, w. of Thos., 1887
    her dau. Maud, see
    Gilbert at the brook
  Thos., 1887
Hampshire, see Alton;
  Amport; Andover;
  Charford, South;
  Cholderton, East;
  Christchurch;
  Lymington; Martin;
  Penton; Romsey;
  Sarson; Shirley;
  Snoddington;
  Somborne;
  Somborne, Little;
  Southampton;
  Stockbridge;
  Thruxton; Tidpit;
  Tytherley, West;
  Wallop; Weyhill;
  Winchester;
  *and see (for cross-
  references)* Ashley;
  Mottisfont; Sherfield;
  Walhampton;
  Wherwell
Hampstead
  Ralph, chaplain, 1573–5,
    1701, 1786, 1792,
    1794, 1815, 1865–6
  Thos., 1865–6
Hampton
  Adam of, skinner, 260
  John, brewer, 1848,
    1851, 1959–60, 2004,
    2071–2
  Maud, w. of Nic., 544,
    794, 797
  Nic., 544, 794, 797
  Wal. of, baker, 93, 256
Handley
  Adam, 1783
  Christine, w. of Wm.,
    tucker, 1685, 1783,
    1954, 2101, 2153
  John (of), 586, 1082,
    1783
  Margery, see Hayward
  Wm., tucker, 890, 1032,
    1082, 1696, 1833,
    1946, 2153; will, 1783
  Wm., tailor, 1811–12,
    1873–5
Handley (?Dors.), 319, 402
Hankford, Wm., justice of
  Common Pleas, 1854,
  1858
Harass

Agnes, relict of Rob., *or* her dau. Agnes, 1720; *and see* Glover
Gillian, 1540
Rob., 1415, 1431, 1471, 1936
Harborough, the master Hen., clerk, 2069–70
Harding
Agnes, w. of Nic., 1700
Nic., 1423–4, 1426–7, 1454–5, 1548, 1613–14, 1636, 1655, 1700, 1777, 1796, 1819, 1833–4, 1843, 1850, 1853–4, 1858, 1923, 1955, 1965, 1981, 1985, 1991, 2029, 2033, 2064, 2101, 2158, 2161, 2167; as mayor and master of Holy Trinty hospital, 1952; *and see* witnesses: mayor, reeve, citizen
Rob., 669
Hardy, John, mayor of Wilton, 2169
Hargreave, John, 1778
Hark, Wm., hatter, 353–5
Harlwin
Margery, w. of Ric., 1996
Ric., goldsmith, 1541, 1556, 1563, 1675, 1713, 1769, 1996, 2034–5
Harnham
Agnes, w. of John (d. by *c.* 1396), 1005
John (d. by *c.* 1336), 280
John [d. 1367, coroner of Wiltshire], 827
John (d. by *c.* 1396), cordwainer, 1005, 1601, 1675
John (fl. 1407), weaver, 1971
Oliver (of), 917, 1224, 1476; *and see* witnesses: bailiff
Rob. (of), 388–9, 459, 735
Thos., rector of Odstock, 1446

Harnham (*unspecified*), chaplain of, 1720
Harnham, East (in Britford), lepers, 569, 671
Harnham, West, 728, 842
Harnhill, Wm., barber, 2032–3, 2111
Harpenden
Christine, w. of Thos., 110, 161, 765
Galiena, relict of Steph. of, 110
Steph. of, 110, 765–6
Thos. (of), 110, 130, 161, 765
Wm. of, s. of Wm. of, 495, 656
Harrowden, Wm. of, 144
Hart
Alice, relict of Thos., 1597–8
Gillian, 740
Thos., draper, 1531, 1533, 1578, 1596–8
Hartell, Wm., 1837
Hartwell, Ric. (of), 560, 711
Harvey, Wal., archdeacon of Salisbury, canon of cathedral church, 93, 235
Hatfield
John, citizen of London, 827–8
Rob. of, 827–9
Hathaway, John, cordwainer, 1882, 1895
hatter, the, *see* Andrew
Hatter
Agnes, w. of John, *see* Camel
Edith, w. of Wm. (fl. *c.* 1319), 113
John, 735
John (fl *c.* 1319), chaplain, 112
John (fl. 1398), chaplain, 1740, 2104
Phil., 584
Wm. (fl. *c.* 1319), 113

Wm. (fl. 1413), 2154
hatters, *see* Andrew the hatter, Camel; Grew; Hark; Mariner; Newman; Whitehorn
Haversham, Olive, 2169
Haw, Eleanor, nun of Amesbury, 671
Hawes
Alice, w. of Ric., *see* Durrant
(*otherwise* Hellier) Ric., tiler, hellier, 676, 679, 1177, 1909, 1961, 2009, 2074
Thos., s. of Ric., *see* Hellier
Hawk
Agnes, w. of John, relict of Wm. of Winchester, 337, 347–9
John, 347–50, 414, 422, 543, 545, 548, 573, 615, 668, 711–16, 733–4
Hawkchurch, Ric. of, 119
Haxton
Adam (of), 465, 836, 2158; will, 549
Agnes, 549
Isabel, relict of Adam, *see* Ludwell
James, 549
John of, bro. of Adam, 458, 549
John, s. of Adam, 549
Maud, 564
Ric., 839, 1258
Wm., 549
Haxton (in Fittleton), 564, 739
Haydor, Thos. of, and his w. Cath., 234
Hayford, *see* bridges
Hayward
Agnes, 2064
Joan, w. of John, 1971
John, 1971
Margery, w. of Nic., dau. of Wm. Handley, 1783, 2153

GENERAL INDEX

Nic., merchant, 1783,
  1791, 1830, 1946,
  2064, 2153
Hazelbury
  Margt., w. of Rob., see
    Durnford
  Rob., 1627, 1733, 1736,
    1777, 1784, 1846,
    1869, 1881, 1917, 1924,
    1973, 1993, 2006–7,
    2163
Heal
  Alan, 839
  Christine, relict of Wm.,
    see Swift
  (*otherwise* Thatcher)
    Wm., smith, 758–9,
    839, 855, 1331, 1461,
    1674, 1677
  cf. Woodford, Wm. of
Heanor, John, chaplain,
  831, 835, 861, 926,
  1108–9
heath, at the, *see* John
Heath, John, 1225
Hellier
  Alice, w. of Ric., see
    Durrant
  John, ironmonger, 2079
  (*otherwise* Hawes) Ric.,
    indexed as Hawes
  Ric., barber, 1332, 1779,
    1811
  Thos., chaplain, 1909,
    2111
helliers, *see (for cross-
  references)* tilers
Hemby, John, 2063
Hemingby
  Alice, relict of John (d.
    by 1364), 728, 2025
  Alice, w. of John (fl.
    1409), 2025
  Isabel, w. of John (fl.
    1406), 1985
  Jas., 2025
  John (d. by 1364), 680–1,
    722–3, 728, 790
  John (fl. 1406), 1985
  John (fl. 1409, ?another),
    2025
  Henry III, 844

Henry IV, 1766, 1782,
  1931, 2157–9
Henry, servant, 1720
Henry at the bar, clerk,
  563, 732
Henry at the bar (?same),
  scribe, 138
Henry at the burgh,
  816, 1240; *and see*
  witnesses: citizen
Henry at the burgh, ygr.,
  (?another), 816
  his dau. Christine, 816
Henry at the weald, and
  his w. Alice, 82
Henshaw, Ric., and his
  dau. Margery, 619
Herring
  Christine, relict of Edw.,
    sis. of John Canning,
    1744, 1860
  her s. John, 1744
  Edw., 1744
  John, canon of
    Mottisfont (priory),
    1860
  Wm., chaplain, 1275–6,
    1312, 1734, 1737, 1780,
    1881
Hewet, Wal., 671, 740
Heytesbury
  Alice, w. of John, 630,
    960
  John (of), saddler, 630,
    960
  Wal. of, 76
Higdon
  Agnes, w. of Wm. (d.
    1398), *see* Cole
  John, 1980, 1983
  Wm. (d. by *c.* 1361), 455,
    1186
  Wm. (d. 1398), baker,
    1421, 1982–3, 1994,
    2054, 2106–7, 2161,
    2167; will, 1980
Highworth, John of, clerk,
  425
Hilary, Ric., skinner, 1443,
  1839
hill, at the, *see* John
Hill

Joan, w. of John (fl.
  1366), relict of Edm.
  Oisel, 790
Joan, w. of Thos., 608
John (fl. *c.* 1353),
  sheather, 365–6
John (fl. 1366), 790
John (fl. 1397),
  carpenter, 1582, 1600,
  1711, 1723
Maud, w. of John (fl. *c.*
  1353), 365–6
Thos., carpenter, 570,
  608, 1937
Wm., merchant, 1464–5,
  1717, 1805, 1896,
  1956–7, 2045, 2119,
  2158; *and see* witnesses:
  reeve, citizen
Hillmay, Wm., 1778
Hindon
  Alice, w. of Thos., 1455,
    1507, 1569
  Edith, w. of Rob., relict
    of John Robet, 564,
    739
  Isabel, w. of Rob., 1081
  Rob., 739, 1081
  Thos., 697, 819–20,
    822, 824–5, 838, 907,
    912–13, 916–17, 924,
    1017, 1095, 1217, 1315–
    16, 1425–7, 1454–5,
    1488, 1501–2, 1507,
    1569, 1670, 1689,
    1695, 1745; *and see*
    witnesses: citizen
Hindon, 338, 1874, 1985
Hinton
  Gunhild, w. of Nic., 84
  Nic of, 84, 249
Hitchcock, Wm., 656
Hoare
  Adam, chaplain, 648,
    675, 798
  Agnes, w. of Hugh, 1031,
    1041
  Ellen, 832
  Gillian, w. of John, dau.
    of John Durrington,
    sis. of Agnes Smith,
    573, 592–3, 615, 648,

832
Hugh, 1031, 1040–1, 1820, 1887
John, 489, 520, 556, 568, 573, 585, 592–4, 605, 615, 636, 648, 675, 699, 805, 1808, 1883, 1886; will, 832; *and see* witnesses: citizen
the master Wal. (*otherwise* Wal. Bradley), clerk, 1487, 1514–15, 1579, 1750; will, 1729
Wm. (fl. 1367–1412, ?one of the name), 832, 896, 1028–9, 1110, 1689, 1695, 1915–16, 1933, 1950, 2120, 2159
Hogman, John, weaver, 1382–3, 2080, 2083, 2105
Holbury
Alice, w. of Hugh Oliver, 849
Rob., 606
Wal., 579, 699, 854, 1200, 1206, 1239, 1495; *and see* witnesses: reeve
Wm., 53, 281
Holhurst, Ric., clerk, 2026, 2031
Holtby
John (of), 626, 728, 756
Nic., 545, 716, 733
Holyman, Wm., clerk, 1527–9
Homanton (in Maddington), 136
Homes
Alice, 543
Ellis, 494, 619, 729, 745, 1754, 1836, 1903; will, 543
Ellis, s. of Ellis, 543
Joan, 543
John, 543, 1211–12, 1738–9, 1903, 1990
Homington
Alice, relict of John (?d. by *c.* 1323), 841–2

John of (d. by *c.* 1323), 150, 487
John (of) (fl. *c.* 1362), clerk, 488, 542, 707
Ric., 841
Thos., 487
Homington, 464, 2061
Honeyland, Thos., 1231
Hook (*unspecified*), see ways
Hook Norton, Wm. of, vicar of Britford, 361, 463, 806
Hooper, Steph., 1733, 1736
hope, at the, *see* Thomas
Horingham
Agnes, w. of Rog., dau. of Edith, w. of John of Wells, 726
Rog., 726
Horn, Wm., and his w. Amice, 1898–9, 1920–1
Horningsham
John, chaplain, 1592
the lord Rob., 1680
Horsted, Ric. of, 228
Hosey, Ric., carder, 667
Hosier
John, 1753
John (?another), *see* Taylor
hosier, *see* Waite
hospitals, *see* Ludlow; Old Sarum; Wilton; *and see* index 2: Holy Trinity; St. Nicholas's
Howe, Rog., 1783
Howes
John, 578
Maud, w. of Ric., 578
Ric., 578
'Hoydon', Emme, relict of John of, 2
Hubert, Gilb., 198
Huggin, Wm., 1612
Hugh, vicar of Shrewton, 453
Hugon, John, 666
Huish
Agnes, w. of John, 2066
John, weaver, 2066, 2082
Humphrey, John, vicar

of Romsey, 1811–12, 1875
Hungerford
Alice, 1978
Rob. of, kt., 754, 763
Thos. (of) (d. by 1362), 494, 501, 509, 554, 557, 598, 627, 644, 686, 695, 703
Thos. (fl. 1367), 827; *and see* witnesses: bailiff
Thos. (fl. 1397), kt.: as bailiff, 1838; *and see* witnesses: bailiff
Hunt
Joan, 1046
John, 1888
Hurlbatt, John, 2156
Hurle, John, clerk, 2101
Hurn (at the hurn, in the hurn)
Agnes, *see* Watercombe
Joan, w. of Wm., *see* Killham
Joan, dau. of Wm., *see* Yeovil
John, 2051, 2076
Wm., dyer, 468, 909, 911, 1137, 1228, 2049–51, 2076
Hurst
Joan, w. of John, dau. of Rog. Wallop, 1580, 1742, 1869, 2006–7, 2055
John, 1580, 1742, 1869, 2006–7, 2056; will, 2055
Hussey
Alice (fl. 1331), 247
Alice (fl. 1361, ?another), 599
Hen., smith, 247, 2057
Joan, w. of Hen., 247, 2057
the lord Wm., 1729
Hutchins
Cecily, w. of Thos., dau. of Ric. Ryborough, 671, 717, 954–5, 2162, 2164
Joan, 1583

(called Chancellor)
Thos., 558, 574–6,
652, 664, 671,
717, 730, 741, 870,
875, 954–5, 1583,
2162, 2164; *and see*
witnesses: reeve
his s., *see* Chancellor
Huxtworth, Nic., 829
Hyde, Wm., grocer, 2114

Idmiston, Wal., 867
Idmiston
Gomeldon, *q.v.*
Porton, *q.v.*
vicar, *see* William
Ilberd, John, chaplain, 774, 776
Ildsley, Wm., 1971
Ingolf at the water, 553
Ingram at the brook, 124, 410, 608, 629, 657, 685, 732
his w. Alice, 124
his s., *see* John at the brook
Ingram, John, 668, 1065
Inkpen
Hen., 620
John, 620
the master Peter, 620
Rob., merchant, citizen of Winchester: will, 620
Intborough
Joan, w. of Wal., 2059
Wal., esq., 2023, 2030, 2048, 2058–9
Inways
Adam, burgess of Southampton, 1752, 1968; will, 567
Adam, bro. of Adam, 567
Rob. (fl. *c.* 1318), *see* Silvain
Rob. (d. by 1361), 567
Rob. (fl. 1361), 567
Ireland, Ric., tailor, 2038
Irish
Sim., 692
Wm., 1580, 1742

Ironmonger
Alice, 553
Lucy, 151
Martin, 1836
Thos., 361, 553
Wal., 361, 543
Wm., 255, 392
ironmongers, *see* Bleacher; Duke; Hellier; Play; Sewin; Sexton; Stockbridge; Swift
Isaac, Wm., baker, 1708, 1895, 1954
Isabel, servant, 2055
Ive
(called Goldsmith) Jas., 1651–2, 1848, 1851
Mary, w. of Ralph, 1649, 1746
Ralph, 212, 675, 1649, 1746, 1848, 1851, 1959, 2004
Thos., 789
Iwerne
Alice, 38–9
John of (d. by *c.* 1326), 178
John (d. by *c.* 1383), chaplain, vicar of cathedral church, 1167, 1191, 1208, 1579, 1750
Iwerne (Dors.), 652, 730

Jacket, little, 671
Jacob, Ric., chaplain, 1889
Jakes
John, chaplain, 1814, 1992, 2029, 2058–9
John (?same), 2148
John, tucker, 1718
James, Dominican friar, 1786
James, Ric., vicar [?of cathedral church], 1882
Janus, household servant, 1859
Jarvis
Agnes, w. of Thos. (fl. 1405), 1900–1
John, 964

Thos., bro. of John, 964
Thos. (fl. 1396, ?another), 1667–9, 1671–3, 1688–9, 1691, 1693–5
Thos. (fl. 1405, ?another), 1900–1
Jay
Edith, w. of Steph., *see* Pope
Steph., 805, 832, 1001, 1006–7
Jennway, John, 2154
Jerrard, Joan, 666
Jewell
Gillian, w. of Ric., 2061, 2075
Joan, w. of Ric., 1215, 2061
John, 1122
Ric., 1144, 1146, 1188, 1215, 1501, 1503, 1649–52, 1745–7, 1773, 1795, 1797, 1960, 1962–3, 2063, 2075; will, 2061; *and see* witnesses: coroner, reeve, citizen
Joan, servants of the name, 567, 1909, 1954
John, apprentices of the name, 566, 579
John, chaplain, 671
John, parochial chaplain of Amesbury, 648
John, servants of the name, 553, 1954
John, s. of Walter, 672
John at the ash, *indexed as* Nash
John at the bar, and his relict Alice, 300
John at the brook, 410
John at the burgh, 1786; *cf.* Walter at the burgh
John at the heath, 1178, 1189, 1641
his w. Alice, 1189
John at the hill, 597
John at the hurn, *indexed as* Hurn
John at the marsh, 1947–8

John at the mill, 1979
John at the New Inn, 831
John at the pit, 1938
John at the stone, 746; will, 740
   his goddaughter Lucy, and her dau. Agnes, 740
John at the 'vuere' (d. by 1362): will, 626
   his w. Agnes, 626
   his dau. Alice, 626
   his dau. Joan, 626
   his f., see Robert at the 'vuere'
John at the 'vuere' (fl. c. 1381), and two others of the name, 1195
John at the wick, 549, 564, 577
   his w. Agnes, dau. of John Wallop, 577
John at the wood, and his w. Joan, 49
John at the wood, and his dau. Margery, 566
John at the work, 12
   his relict Alice, 12
Jordan
   Joan, w. of John, 551
   John, mercer, 551, 561
Judd, John, draper, merchant, 1756, 1800, 1813, 1872, 1958, 1966, 1972, 1978–9, 1986, 2109; and see witnesses: coroner, reeve, citizen
Jukes
   Edith, relict of Rob., 85
   Gilb., 750
   (called Brewer) Rob., 85
Justice
   Geof., 1474
   John, 548, 580, 588, 711–14, 734, 757, 767, 811, 813–15, 824–5, 887–8, 939, 1261, 1303, 1325, 1360–3, 1626, 1754, 1809–10, 1836, 1904–5, 1938, 1944, 1953–4; and see witnesses: reeve

Margery, w. of John, 825, 1326, 1347, 1418, 1665, 1708, 1809–10, 1953, 2048; will, 1954
justices, see courts; forest

Keed, Wm., 96
Keevil, John, 619
Kelsale (Suff.), rector of, see Grisley
Kemp, Hoggett, 671
Kemps, Alice, 740
Kendal
   Agnes, 581
   Barnabas, chaplain, 581, 1262–3, 1345
   Margt., w. of Rob., 590
   Rob. (of), 498, 524, 581, 590, 638, 784, 856, 1042; and see witnesses: reeve, citizen
Kennet, John, 619
Kent, Thos., 1888
Kent, see Canterbury; and see (for cross-reference) Saltwood
Kerry, Wal., 575–6, 652, 730
Keyford
   Edith, w. of John, 1909
   John, 1909
Keynes
   Adam, 1371, 2040
   Joan, w. of Wm., 40, 140
   Wm., spicer, 40, 126, 140
Kilham
   Joan, w. of John, relict of Wm. at the hurn, 911, 2049–51, 2076, 2087
   John, 2049–51, 2087
Kill
   Alice, 2064
   John, 2064
Kilmeston
   Agnes, w. of Rog., dau. of Maud (relict of Thos. of Netheravon), 474, 796, 799
   Agnes, dau. of Rog., 799

   Agnes, dau. of Wm. (fl. 1366), 1749
   Ellen, 799
   Joan, 799
   Rog. (of), 554, 601, 645, 675, 769, 796, 798–9, 982, 1141, 1167
   Wm. of (d. by c. 1326), 174
   Wm. (fl. 1366), 799, 1749
   Wm. (d. 1399), vicar of cathedral church, 1320; will, 1753
   Wm. (either of last two), 1194, 1205
Kilpeck, Hen., 619
Kimble
   Agnes, 608
   John, 608, 650, 655, 761
   Phil., 601
Kimpton, John, weaver, 1660, 1720, 1846
King
   Alice, 1664
   Edith, w. of John, 1261, 1330, 1754
   Joan, 669
   John, roper, 1261, 1330, 1754
King's Bench, see prisoners
Kingbridge
   Alice, w. of John, 1797
   John, 1795, 1797, 1985
Kings, Joan, 1828
Kingsbury, John, 2156
Kington, Thos. of, 567
Kington (unspecified), rector of, see Coleshill
Kintbury (Berks.), 559
Kirkby, John, 2063
Kirtlingstoke
   Agnes, 1978
   Joan, w. of Rob., 1978
   Margt., 1978
   Rob., 937, 1000, 1036–7, 1405–6, 1718, 1748, 1791–2, 1794, 1986; will, 1978; and see witnesses: coroner, citizen
Kislingbury (Northants.),

rector of, *see* Grandon
Knight
  Joan, 1859
  John, 1271, 1599, 1659, 1679
  John (another), 1859
  Thos., 2169
  Wm., 469, 482, 640, 979, 1599, 1659, 1679, 1698, 1702
Knighton
  John (of), 77, 129, 166, 214–15, 225, 231, 276
  Ric. of, 805
Knights
  Agnes, 1828
  (called Shipster) Edith, shipster, 1888, 1892–3
knights, *see* Beauchamp; Blunt; Clopton; Hungerford; Peverell; Russell; St. Martin; Shove
Knolle, Ric., *indexed as* Cormell
Knottingley
  Eliz., w. of elder John, 1249–50
  John, 1249–50, 1576
  John, s. of John, 1576
  John (either), 1929
  Ric. (of), 578, 605, 636, 654
Knowle, Church (Som.), church, 619
Knoyle
  Beatrice, relict of John (d. by 1364), *see* Habgood
  Edith, relict of John (d. by *c.* 1318), 16, 619
  Edw. (of), 243, 660, 756, 772–3, 787
  Hen., *indexed as* Ludgershall
  Joan, w. of Thos. (fl. *c.* 1387–1410), 1316
  John (of) (d. by *c.* 1318), 16, 619
  John (d. by *c.* 1364), 414, 438, 531, 619, 706, 712, 737, 772–3, 787

Rob. (of), 44, 80, 87, 91, 95, 313, 570–1, 707, 791, 795
Thos., f. of Thos. (fl. *c.* 1355–67), 382–4
Thos. (fl. *c.* 1355–67), 382–4, 819–20, 824–5
Thos. (fl. *c.* 1387–1410, ?another), 1314–16, 1672–3, 1676, 1686–7, 1719, 1792, 1794, 1867–8, 1870, 1895, 1958, 1966, 1972, 1981, 2011–12, 2061, 2075, 2110
Wm., painter, 1453, 1510

Laccombe, Alice, 740
Lake, John, 1719, 1762, 1785, 1997, 1999–2000, 2061, 2075; *and see* witnesses: reeve
Lambard
  Alice, 2169
  elder John, 2169
  John, 2169
Landford, 578, 665, 708
  church of St. Andrew: altar, bell, chancel, cross, lights, vestment, 578
  rector, *see* White
Lane, Laur., 2048
Langford
  Agnes, relict of Rob., *see* Courtier
  And. of, 526, 690
  Hugh (of), linendraper, 103–4, 303, 581, 690, 693, 2049–51, 2076
  Joan, *see* Prior
  John (of), draper, linendraper, 102–3, 131, 628, 711
  John (of) (?same), 573, 615, 638, 662, 669, 687, 696
  John, tucker, 288
  John (?another), s. of Ralph, 564
  Mabel, w. of John, tucker, *see* Durnford

Marion, w. of Hugh, 103
Maud, relict of Hugh, 671, 693, 839, 1241; will, 690
  her sis. Christine, and Christine's dau. Maud, 690
  her s. John, canon of [priory of] St. Denis [Southampton], 690
  her s. Steph., friar, 690
  her s. Thos., a Dominican, 690
Ralph of, 564, 739, 789, 796, 799, 1781
Ric. of, 81
Rob., 1054, 1059, 1071, 1171–2
Wm., vicar of cathedral church, 135
Langford (Devon), *see* ways
Langford, Little, rector of, *see* Newton
Langport
  Rob. of, 29
  Wm., 1874
Langton, Agnes, dau. of Rog. Fowle, 1876
Latimer
  Nic., 2058–9
  Peter, 690, 693
Latners, Agnes, 1720
Latticemaker
  Rob., 1909
  Wm., w. of Rob., 1828, 1909
Laurence
  David, clerk, 811, 815; *cf.* David
  Isabel, 1230
  Nic., 613
Lavender, John, 749
Laverstock, Rob. of, 125
Laverstock
  Ford, Winterbourne Ford, *q.v.*
  vicar, *see* Ludwell
Lavington
  Alice, relict of Ric., *see* Spicer
  Christine, w. of Rob., 156

Ric. (of), 193, 292, 368
Rob. (of), 109, 156, 364, 707, 795
Rob. of (?same), clerk, 768
lea, at the, *see* William
Lea
  Agnes, w. of John, dau. of Alice Longenough (relict of John Deanbridge), 599, 602, 617, 751, 754, 763, 807–8, 830, 1860, 1942
  John, 677, 683, 748, 754, 763, 807–8, 830, 847, 939, 986, 1040–1, 1084–5, 1115–16, 1122, 1146–7, 1189, 1269, 1328, 1439, 1725, 1808, 1944; *and see* witnesses: citizen
  Phil., 1345
  Thos. of, s. of Joan Butterley, 578
Leach
  Alice, w. of Ric., 1786, 1871
  Margery, 633
  the master Ric., 821, 904, 955, 1117–18, 1144, 1151, 1220, 1406–7, 1490, 1530, 1541, 1560, 1566, 1661, 1663, 1675, 1688, 1694, 1727, 1768–71, 1773–4, 1786, 1793, 1815, 1835, 1862, 1871, 1907, 1943, 2023, 2029–30, 2058, 2146, 2148; *and see* witnesses: mayor, citizen
  Ric. (?same), *see* Falconer
Leacher, Wal., 1649, 1746
Leadbeater
  Agnes, w. of Thos., dau. of Thos. Stratford, 357
  Rob., 148
  Thos., 357
Legat, John, and his w.

Isabel, 241
Leicester, Thos., and his w. Agnes, 891
Leigh (*unspecified*), 1930
'Lenthorp', Geo. of, clerk, 1688, 1694
Leonard, Steph., tucker, and his w. Emme, 1977
lepers, *see* Harnham, East
letters patent, 704, 1766, 1782, 1931, 2157; *and see* index 2: city, mayor
Levenoth, John, and his w. Isabel, 2091–2, 2111
Lewisham
  Agnes, w. of John, relict of Rob. Bunt, 1200, 1768, 2023
  her s. Edw., 1768, 2023
  Alice, 1859
  John, 1200, 1768, 1820, 1859, 1887–8, 1892–3, 1897, 1979, 2023, 2162, 2164; *and see* witnesses: reeve, citizen
licences of the king, 421, 644, 661, 679, 704, 729, 745, 1536, 1782, 1931, 1952, 1966, 2088, 2100, 2157–9
Lichfield, Ric., 1414
Liddington, Wm. of, chaplain, 676; *cf.* Loddington
Lilley, Wm., 2063
Limeburner
  And., 567
  Wm., *see* 'Lytebrouth'
limeburner, *see* Ellis
Linden
  Alice, w. of Rob., 2130
  Rob., 1973, 2130
Line
  Amice, w. of Wm., 47
  John, 1753
  Wm., 47
linendraper, *see* Langford; *and see* drapers
Linford, Thos., 2125

Linnier, John, 535, 586
Lippiatt
  Alice, w. of John, 1804–5, 1896
  John, 1804–5, 1850, 1896, 2165
Little
  Benet, 1680
  Joan, w. of John, 2147
  John, mercer, 1108–9, 1480, 1574, 1865, 2029, 2066, 2099, 2137, 2147
  Maud, w. of John, 1480
  Sim., 1888
Littlefish, Rog., 289
Littles, Alice, 694, 758
Littleton
  John of, 649, 657
  Rog. of, 132–3, 169
loader, *see* Hain
Loddington, Hen. of, chaplain, 97; *cf.* Liddington
Lokebet
  Joan, w. of John, 671
  John, 598, 627, 703
London
  Hen., 1294
  John, 237, 2064
London, 827–8, 1686, 1979
  address, 543, 898, 1918, 1979
  aldermen, 316, 376
  citizens, *see* Arnold; Chaucer; Hatfield; Mund; Philpot; Pomfret; Rutter; Taylor; Thorney; Ward; Wilton
  collectors of murage, pannage, and passage, 316
  convent of St. Thos. of Acre, 1985
  gaols (Fleet, King's Bench, King's Marshalsea, Ludgate, Newgate), *see* prisoners
  husting court, 1671–3, 1688–9, 1691, 1693

mayor, 206, 316, 376
property in, 1647, 1671–3, 1688–9, 1691, 1693
sheriff, 206, 316
Long
  Alice, w. of Hen., 584
  Aubrey, w. of Peter, 215
  Hen., 430; will, 584
    his bro. Wm., see Salisbury
  Joan, w. of Thos. (d. by c. 1356), see Gaunt
  John, tailor, 1689, 1695
  Peter, 215, 225
  Ric., 566, 700, 724, 727
  Rob., 567
  Thos. (d. by c. 1356), 161, 371–2, 387
  Thos. (fl. 1361), 549
  Thos. (fl. 1397), 1689
  Thos., 584, 717
  Wm., 543; cf. Salisbury
Longbarber, Wm., 639
Longborough
  Nic., 680, 723
  Thos., chaplain, 701, 2024
Longenough
  Alice, relict of Phil. and of Wm. Whitehorn, 491, 496, 536, 552, 587, 602, 617, 751, 807–8, 830, 1656–7, 1716
    her dau. Agnes, see Lea
    her dau. Alice, 807–8, 830
  Edw., 481, 499, 981; and see witnesses: reeve
  Honour, relict of Edw., 981
  Phil., 435, 587, 643; and see Longenough, Alice; witnesses: citizen
Longleat (in Longbridge Deverill), convent of, 1680
Longstock
  Agnes, w. of Nic., 918, 1050–1, 1181, 1742, 1898–9, 1920–1

  Agnes (?another), 2056
  Nic., 918, 1050–1, 1181, 1742, 1898–9, 1920–1, 2104
Looseway
  Hen., 251
  Rog., 175, 241
Lopen (Som.), 1709
Lord
  Agnes, 1971
  Nic., clerk, 2154
  Wm. (?two of the name, fl. before c. 1361, d. by c. 1377), 554, 570, 579, 1005
  Wm. (?another, elder, d. 1396), (including all of the name in the period 1365–96 unless likely to be another) 773, 792–3, 851–2, 862, 918, 947, 962–3, 974, 979, 1005, 1021, 1029, 1033, 1052–3, 1069, 1072, 1074–6, 1083, 1094, 1096, 1102–4, 1107, 1175, 1210, 1237–8, 1259–60, 1268, 1377, 1388, 1390, 1402–3, 1410, 1454–5, 1459, 1484, 1516, 1524–5, 1530, 1541, 1546, 1549–50, 1556, 1563, 1567, 1592, 1605, 1608, 1622–3, 1660–2, 1667–9, 1675, 1685, 1700, 1760, 1767, 1769, 1777, 1846, 1876, 1964, 1969, 2122; and see witnesses: citizen
  Wm. (ygr., fl. 1408), (including all of the name after 1396 unless likely to be another) 1564, at 1656, 1686, 1702, 1744, 1786, 1792, 1794, 1815, 1826–7, 1840, 1848, 1895–6, 1904–5, 1960, 1974–5, 2002–3; and see witnesses: clerk,

citizen
Love
  John, 1210, 1753
  John (?another), chaplain, 1709
  Reynold, 827–9, 898–9
Lovel, Wal., 789
Luckham
  Gillian, nun of Wherwell, 671
  Joan, relict of John, see Coffer
  John, tanner, 607, 1121, 1255, 1714–15, 1802–3, 1925, 1927
Ludd
  Margt., w. of Ric., 1349
  Ric., 1348–9, 1742, 1869, 2006–8, 2163
Ludgershall
  (otherwise Knoyle) the master Hen., s. of John Knoyle, 619, 712
  John, 841–2
  Ric. of, 27, 89, 143
  R of, 27
Ludgershall, 414, 438, 531, 619, 706, 712, 737, 857
Ludlow (Salop.), hospital of St. John, 1938
Ludwell
  Adam (of), 605, 636, 836, 900, 944–5, 961, 1003, 1658; as mayor, 570; and see witnesses: mayor, citizen
  Cecily, w. of Adam, 945
  Hen. of, vicar of Laverstock, 564
  Isabel, w. of Adam, relict of Adam Haxton, 549, 836
Lutwich
  Geo., taverner, 483
  Joyce, taverner, 458, 791, 914
  Margt., w. of Geo., 483
  Margt., w. of Joyce, 791, 914–15
Lyme
  Hen. of, 69
  Wm. of, 341

Lymington, John, mercer, 1286, 1680
Lymington (Hants), 122
Lyneham
　Cath., 109
　John of, 109, 545, 716, 733
Lyner
　Emme, w. of Ric., 619
　John, 619
　Ric., 619, 668, 729, 735, 737, 745
'Lytebrouth', (called Limeburner) Wm., and his w. Agnes, 242

Mabley, John, tucker, and his w. Edith, 1964, 1977
Mack
　Hen., 2156
　Hugh, 2104
Mackinney, Thos., scribe, 698, 759
Maddington, John, 1223, 1432–3
Maddington, see Homanton
Magg, Ric., and his w. Edith, 125
Maidenhead
　John of, canon of cathedral church, keeper of de Vaux college, 1729
　Rog., vicar of Durnford, 1930
Man
　John, 1579, 1729, 1750
　Ric., clerk, 1680
Mandeville, Thos. (de), 757, 832
Manning
　John, butcher, 1895
　John, chaplain, 1399
　Thos., 1399, 1802–3, 1925–7, 1942, 2158–9, 2169; and see witnesses: citizen
Mansfield, Nic., 1791
March, Rob., 559, 562–3, 631

Marden, Thos., chaplain, 735
Margaret, servant, 1860
Mariner
　Agnes, w. of John, relict of John Hatter, see Camel
　John, hatter, 388–9, 459, 690, 735
　John, s. of John, 389
Marion, servant, 831
Marions, Maud, 1744
Mark the fair, see witnesses: citizen
Markham, John, justice of Common Pleas, 1858
Marlborough
　John of, 698
　Thos. (fl. c. 1348), 318
　Thos. (fl. 1400), 1685, 1692, 1696–7, 1699, 1786
Marlborough, 2001, 2005
　church of St. Peter, 1859
Marlow (Bucks.), 1837
　church of All Saints, 1837
marsh, at the, see John
Marshall
　Cecily, 1337
　Isabel, 894; cf. Bromham
　Joan, w. of John (d. 1362), 669
　John (d. 1362): will, 669
　John (fl. c. 1361–2), smith, 505
　John (?same, will approved c. 1374), (including all other references to men of the name) 533, 538, 543, 554, 583, 589, 646, 669, 735, 873, 894, 976; and see witnesses: reeve
　Rob. (d. by c. 1325), 172
　Rob. (fl. 1361), 583
　Rog., 583
　Thos., 976, 1337–9, 1367, 1393, 1968
　…, 874
Marston, Steph. of,

commissary, 1837
Martin (forename), 15
Martin
　the lord John, 1729
　Ric., 464
　Sibyl, 204
　Thos. (fl. before c. 1326), 204
　Thos. (fl. 1410), 2061
Martin (now Hants)
　chapel, 595
　church, 1909
　Tidpit, q.v.
Martival, Rog., bishop of Salisbury, 224, ?847
Marwood
　Ric., 805
　(called Callis) Ric., 1949
Mason
　Nic., chaplain, clerk, 1707, 1720, 1901, 1911, 1915–16, 2028, 2040
　Rob., collegiate chaplain of St. Edmund's church, 1871
　Thos., draper, 1851, 1918–19, 1923, 1996; and see witnesses: reeve, citizen
　Wm., 45
mason, see Nash
Matthew, servant, 1720
Matthew
　Agnes, w. of Rog., 644
　Christine, 2166
　Rog., 644
Matthey, Rog., 740
Maud, a maid, 1936
Maud, servants of the name, 831, 1720, 1971
Mawardine, Ric., and his w. Edith, 1925–7
May
　Adam, 359–60
　Rob. (fl. c. 1319), 67, 71, 90
　Rob. (fl. 1362), 622, 624
　Rog., 71
　Wm., 67, 71, 90
Mayhew, John, 653, 688, 837
Maynes, Eve, 831

Mayo, (called Wilkin)
  John, 1952
mead, at the, *see* Michael
Mead, Wm., weaver, 1984, 1989
Meager, Ric., 2066
Mealmonger, Ric., and his w. Christine, 417
Medmenham, John, chaplain, 1760, 1804
Melbury
  Agnes, w. of Wal., 96
  Nic., draper, 1843, 1955, 1965, 2016, 2019–20, 2098, 2104; *and see* witnesses: coroner, reeve, citizen
  Wal. of, 96
Melksham
  Hen. (of), 89, 173, 399
  John, 570, 826
  John of (?another), cook, 671
  John (another), *see* Creed
  Rob. of, 543
Mercer
  Edith, w. of Wm., 1979
  Joan, 1979
  John, *see* witnesses: citizen
  Jordan, 638, 662, 811, 815, 840
  Wm., 1793, 1813, 1835, 1907, 2108; will, 1979; *and see* witnesses: reeve
    his kinswoman Christine, 1979
mercers, *see* Burgess; Butler; Castleton; Child; Cormell; Daw; Farrant; Jordan; Little; Lymington; Woodford
Merchant
  Christine, relict of John, 2169
  John, 2169
merchants, *see* Daw; Dowding; Hayward; Hill; Inkpen; Judd; Newman; Preston; Russell; Ryde;
  Shirley; Wagain
mere, at the, *see* Thomas
Mere, Wal., 560, 579
Mere, 1558, 1680
  church, 1680
  parish priest, *see* William
  vicar, 1680; *and see* Dunn
  Woodlands, *q.v.*
Merriott
  Alice, 570
  Alice, w. of Geo., relict of ygr. Wm. Tenterer and of John Butterley, 764, 1061–2, 1483, 1485, 1665–6, 1708, 1717, 1721, 1760, 1853–4, 1858, 1895, 2063; will, 1985
  Alice, w. of Wm., 1805
  Christine, 2063
  Geo., esq., 1652, 1709, 1727, 1746, 1848, 1850, 1853–4, 1858, 1895, 1959, 1985, 2024, 2165; will, 2063; *and see* witnesses: reeve
  John, 570
  Maud, m. of Geo., 2063
  Maud, w. of Geo., 2063; will, 1709
  Ric., 2156
  Thos., 1721, 2024, 2063
  Wm., 1805
Merriott (Som.)
  chapel of St. Catherine, 2063
  church of All Saints, 1709
Messenger, Thos., and his w. Edith, 1844–5
Michael at the mead, *see* witnesses: bailiff
Middlesex, *see* Enfield; *and see* Westminster
Middleton, Thos., 1713
Milbourne, Reynold of, 176, 312, 673
Milcot, Ric., 738
Mildenhall
  Edith, w. of John, 885–6, 892, 989
  Joan, w. of John, 2034–5
  her s. John, 2034–5
  John, 885–6, 892, 989, 1156, 1305–6, 1653–4, 1703–4, 1735, 1768, 1770–1, 2023, 2030, 2034–5, 2058–9
mill, at the, *see* John; Richard; Robert
Millman, Wal., 599
Millward
  Alice, 1936
  Nic., 2156
Milton
  Maud, 595
  Rob., 2011
Milton *Abbatis* (Devon or Dors.), 666
missals, 1786, 1938, 1954
Mitchell, John, chaplain, 1882, 1889–91
Mohun, Wm., 677
Mondelard, Peter, 399, 487
Monk
  Ric., attorney, 844, 1066
  Wm., 214
Monkton
  Alice, w. of John, 580; *cf.* Alice Cofford
  John (of), 605, 636; will, 580
  Nic. (fl. 1361), s. of John, 580
  Nic. (fl. 1401, ?same), s. of Alice Cofford, 1758, 1798–9, 1837
Montagu
  Alice, w. of Wm. (fl. *c.* 1300), 1
  Clarice, w. of Wm. (fl. 1363), 671
  John, friar, 1836
  John, 1842, 1886, 1896, 1935
  Mabel, w. of Phil., 619, 729, 737, 745
  Phil., 619, 729, 737, 745
  Thos. (fl. *c.* 1319), 111
  Thos. (fl. 1396), dean of Salisbury, 1664, 1753
  Wm. (fl. *c.* 1300), 1
  Wm. (fl. 1363), 671, 921, 1038–9, 1060–2,

1665–6
Moore
  Denise, w. of Wm.,
    1318, 1444–5
  John, 2061
  Wm., tailor, 1318, 1377,
    1394–5, 1399–1401,
    1444–5, 1452,
    1615, 1637; *and see*
    witnesses: citizen
Moredon
  Cath., 325
  Wm. of, 149, 159, 325
Morris, Adam, 1680, 2162,
    2164
Morwelese, Wm., and his
    w. Joan, 770
Mottisfont (Hants),
    (priory of), canon, *see*
    Herring
Mottram, Wm., clerk,
    2101
Moulton, John, porter,
    1882
Mount
  John, and his w. Joan,
    485–6
  Ric., 578
Mower
  Cecily, w. of John, 1108,
    1575, 1628, 1633, 1865,
    1880
  John, grocer, 1048, 1108,
    1573, 1575, 1628, 1633,
    1681–2, 1691, 1759,
    1761, 1785, 1787–8,
    1817–19, 1841, 1853–4,
    1858, 1865, 1872, 1880,
    1882, 1884, 1889,
    1894, 1896, 1915–17,
    1922, 1937, 1939, 1941,
    1955, 1965, 1985, 2014,
    2045, 2082, 2109,
    2114–15, 2119–20,
    2123–4, 2127, 2140,
    2143, 2157–9; *and
    see* witnesses: mayor,
    citizen
  Wm., 1808
Mowlish, Martin, clerk,
    704, 729, 737, 745
Moyne

Ric., 475
Wm., 475, 1711, 1723–4
Mund
  John, 2063
  Thos., citizen of
    London, 1725
murage, 206, 316
Mussel
  Cecily (fl. 1361), 566
  Cecily (fl. 1397, ?same),
    1720
  Christine, relict of John,
    535
  John, 535, 586
  Thos., 535, 566, 586,
    1743, 1795, 1797
Mutton
  John, 673
  Rog. (?two of the
    name), 301, 551, 666,
    673, 709
  Wm., 728

Nalder
  Isabel, w. of Wal., 1408–
    9
  John, 522, 661, 697, 734,
    957; *and see* witnesses:
    reeve
  Wal., draper, 1408–9,
    1523, 1653–4, 1731–2,
    1734, 1737, 1769,
    1777, 1780, 1797, 1881,
    1897, 1903, 1906,
    1917, 1922, 1985,
    2034, 2111, 2126; *and
    see* witnesses: mayor,
    reeve, citizen
Napper, Hen., 803, 838
Nash (at the ash)
  Joan, w. of John (fl.
    1410), 2040
  John (fl. 1361), 603
  John (fl. 1410), mason,
    1371, 1895, 2040
Neale, John, 1979
Needham, Thos., rector of
    Stratford, 1725
Needler
  Agnes, w. of Wm., 2149
  elder John (fl. 1366, d.
    by *c.* 1396), (including

both of the name in
  the period 1366–96
  unless likely to be
  the other) 807–8,
  830, 1190, 1243, 1267,
  1300–1, 1481, 1502,
  1606, 1613–14, 1711,
  1723–4, 1964, 1980,
  1982–3, 1998
ygr. John, draper,
  (including both of
  the name from 1396
  unless likely to be the
  other) 1613–14, 1693,
  1695, 1718, 1749, 1850,
  1896, 1985, 1992,
  1997–2000, 2029,
  2063, 2066, 2082,
  2106–7, 2124, 2165;
  and see witnesses:
  mayor, citizen
Peter, 551, 561, 596, 666,
  710
Ric., 2107
Rob., 551
Wm., 2107, 2149, 2165
Netheravon
  Maud, w. of Thos., *see*
    Dovedale
  Ric., 739
  Thos., 474, 796, 799
Netheravon, 549, 574–6,
  600, 652
  church, 2155
  clerk, 2155
  vicar, 2155
Netton
  Hen., 650, 655
  John, 2104
  Rob., chaplain, 1640,
    1818
  Rog., under-treasurer of
    cathedral church, 1729
  the lord Wm. of, 578
Netton (in Durnford),
  1979
New
  Christine, w. of Rob.,
    dau. of Hen. Bunt,
    relict of Wm. Bunt,
    559; will, 565
  her dau. Amice, 565

her dau. Joan, 559, 565
her s. Steph., 565
elder John, tanner,
  587–8, 643, 705, 919,
  938, 943, 1045–7,
  1317, 1944; *and see*
  witnesses: reeve
John (?another), 663,
  1902, 1908, 1912
Rob., 549, 565, 836
Thos., Franciscan friar,
  554
New Inn, at the, *see* John
Newman
  Edith, w. of Rog., 31
  Edith, w. of Wm., *see*
    Chark
  Emme, w. of John (d.
    1413), 2154
  Hen., 581
  John (fl. 1361), 581
  John (fl. *c.* 1378,
    ?d. 1401 x 1404),
    cardmaker, (including
    some conjectured
    references) 1089, 1192,
    1203–4, 1213, 1233,
    1336, 1548, 1552, 1696,
    1801, 1819, 1833, 1843,
    1850, 1981, 2064, 2101,
    2153; *and see* witnesses:
    mayor, reeve, citizen
  John (d. by 1408),
    grocer, merchant,
    1805, 1991, 2045, 2119
  John (d. 1413), hatter,
    1787–8, 2154
  John (any of the above),
    1310, 1584, 1671, 1859
  Margery, w. of Wm., 581
  Nic., 1991
  Rog., 31, 155
  Thos. (d. by *c.* 1378),
    1063
  Thos. (fl. 1406), 1930
  Wm., 506, 581, 690, 871
Newnham, Adam (of),
  chaplain, 13, 70, 75
Newnham hill, *see* ways
Newport
  Agnes, w. of Rob., 1338–
    9, 1582, 1615, 1723,
    1925, 1927
  John, 580
  Rob., 1338–9, 1582,
    1615, 1723, 1925, 1927
Newrig, Nic., 668
Newton
  Rob., chaplain, 1726
  Steph., rector of Little
    Langford, 575–6, 652,
    730
Newton (*unspecified*), 760
Newton (?in Durnford),
  1979
Newton Tony, 1987–8
Nicholas, bondman, 816
Noble
  Alice, w. of John (fl. *c.*
    1318), 20
  Joan, 1828
  John (fl. *c.* 1318), 20, 130
  John (fl. 1402), 1777,
    1828, 1836, 1884
  Lucy, w. of John (fl.
    1402): will, 1828
Norridge (in Upton
  Scudamore), 1930
Norrington (in
  Alvediston), 2036–7
Northamptonshire, *see*
  Kislingbury
notary
  office of, 1938
  public, *see* Raby
Notley
  Constance, relict of
    Peter, 24–5, 38–9
  John of, 38–9
  Peter of, 24–5, 38–9
Nott, John, 827–9
Nottingham, Wm. of,
  general minister of
  Franciscans, 144
novel disseisin, 1838
  writs, 279, 1658
Nugg
  Hen., 515–16
  John (of), 170, 204, 275,
    328, 381, 514–16, 609
  John, s. of John, *see*
    Salisbury
  John (either), 1878
nuns (named), *see* Agnes;
Beauchamp; Boyton;
Haw; Luckham;
Romsey; Stone;
Weymouth
Nunton
  Adam, 320
  Alice, 321
  John (fl. *c.* 1348), 319
  John (?same), tanner,
    1733, 1736, 1924
  Nic. of, 319–21
Nursling, Hen. of, *indexed
  as* Spicer

oak, at the, *see* Richard;
  Severin
Oakden, Wm., 1786
Oakford, Rob., vicar of
  cathedral church, 516
obits, 543, 668, 690, 816,
  1729, 1753, 1778, 1783,
  1860, 1882, 1888,
  1938, 1943, 2011, 2104,
  2155–6
occupations, *see (for cross-
  references)* trades and
  occupations
Odiham
  Edm., 560
  John (fl. 1361), 560
  John (fl. *c.* 1386, ?same),
    1287
  Nic., 1772
  Phil. (d. 1361), 582, 701;
    will, 560
  Phil., s. of Phil., 560
Odstock, rector of, *see*
  Harnham
Ogbourne
  Rob., s. of Gunnore
    Boyton, 1786, 2002–3
  Wm., clerk, 962
Oisel
  Edm., 790
  Joan, relict of Edm., *see*
    Hill
Okehampton, Isabel of,
  182
Old Sarum
  borough, 801
  burgess, *see* Yate
  mayor, *see* Avery

mayoral seal, 1770–1
castle, *see* prisoners
castle (as a landmark), 110, 543, 746
church of St. Etheldred, 740
croft, 1187, 1768, 1770–1
fields, 197, 665, 708, 801, 1768, 1770–1
hospital of St. John, 671, 740
Newtown ward, 740
 croft, 740
 messuage, 740
 tenements, 386–7, 1082, 1783
 toft, 1778
Oliver
 Hugh, 564, 849, 854
 his w. Alice, *see* Holbury
 the lord John, 1943
Orme
 Agnes, w. of Wal., 1273, 1285, 2156
 Wal., 1273, 1285, 1706–7, 1741, 2114–15, 2117; will, 2156
 Wm., 1930
Osborne
 Cath., w. of Rob., 551
 Margery, w. of Rob., *see* Cook
 John, 1397–8
 Peter, 118
 Rob., fisherman, 561, 596, 709–10; will, 551
Otterbourne
 Agnes, 569
 Edith, 569
 Joan, m. of Ric., 569
 Joan, w. of Ric., 569
 Ric. of, 478; will, 569
  his sis. Christine, and her s. Ric., 569
Oword
 Alice, w. of Gilb., 1861
 Christine, 1861
 Gilb. (fl. 1362, d. 1404, ?one man), glover, 655, 833–4, 1746, 1807, 1839, 1937, 2065,
  2071–2, 2108; will, 1861
 John, s. of Gilb., 1861
 John (?same), 1882
 Margery, w. of Ric., 1518, 1861
 Maud, w. of Gilb., 655
 Ric., s. of Gilb., 1861
 Ric. (?same), keeper of St. Thomas's church, 1518, 2102, 2112–13, 2121, 2156; *and see* witnesses: reeve
Oxford
 Agnes, w. of John, 336, 362–3, 1097–9, 1354
 Ellen, *see* Pinnock
 John of, skinner, 335–6, 362–3, 398, 402–3, at 404, 419, 556, 585, 587, 594, 607, 643, 768, 807–8, 873, 968, 1090–2, 1354, 1752, 1968; as mayor, 776, 778, 783–4; *and see* witnesses: mayor, reeve, citizen
 Ric., 1871
 Sim. of (d. *c.* 1326), 55–6, 184, 264, 735, 841–2
 Sim. (fl. 1330s), 264
Oxford (university of), 1786
Oxley, (called Goss) Adam, 780–1

Pack
 Hen., chaplain, 859
 John, carpenter, 706, 841–2, 857
Packer
 John, 558, 567, 664, 741
 Ric., 558
Packing, Wm., and his w. Alice, 2021
Pain
 John, chaplain, 944
 John (?another), commissary, 2055
 Wm., 570, 572, 599, 602, 616–17, 632, 637,
  639, 658, 670, 681, 751
Painter
 Rob., 566, 690
 Wm., 470, 869
painters, *see* Goodall; Knoyle
Palmer
 John (d. by *c.* 1318), 19–20
 John (fl. 1367), tailor, 832, 926, 942
 John (two of the name, fl. 1408, ?others), 2011
 Maud, w. of John (fl. 1367), 832
 Maud (fl. 1409, ?same), 2029, 2033
Palting, Edith, 65
pannage, 206, 316
Pannett
 Emme, 606
 John, 606, 610, 635
 John (d. 1361), s. of John, 610, 635, 1777; will, 606
 John (either), 579, 699
 Margery, w. of John (d. 1361), 606, 610, 635
Parch
 John, weaver, 1784, 1978, 2104; *and see* witnesses: reeve, citizen
 Olive, w. of John, dau. of John Bodenham, 2104
Parchment
 Alex. (fl. *c.* 1318), 45
 Alex. (d. by *c.* 1336, ?same), 268
Paris
 Agnes, w. of John, 619
 Alice, 619
 John, 619
 (called Purbeck) John, chaplain, rector of Bruton, 438, 531, 737; will, 619
  his nephew Wm., 619
Park, Wal., 477–8, 502
Parlabean, Amice, 567
Parson

John (fl. c. 1386), 1290–1
John (fl. 1410, ?another), 2064
Pasker, Thos., 1324
passage, 316
Passavant, John, chaplain, 713–14
Patcham, John, 2011
Pate
  Joan, w. of Ric., dau. of John (Buddle called) Prentice, 2159
  Ric., 2159
paupers, relief of, 556, 560, 566–7, 569, 577, 581, 583, 648, 671, 690, 692, 740, 816, 1719–20, 1729, 1753, 1778, 1783, 1786, 1828, 1836, 1859–60, 1871, 1882, 1909, 1938, 1943, 1954, 1971, 1979, 1985, 2011, 2029, 2055, 2063, 2155–6; *and see (for cross-references)* hospitals
Paviour, Wm., vicar of cathedral church, 70, 75, 78
Paxhill
  Joan, w. of John (fl. 1400), 1728
  John (fl. 1361), 553
  John (fl. 1400, ?same), 1728, 1767, 2168
  Rob. of, 553
Pay, Hen., 1836, 1991
Peak, Joan, relict of John, 844
Peakirk, Wm. of, rector of Dinton, 575–6, 652, 730
Pechin
  Adam, 1663
  Joan, w. of Adam, 1663
  her dau. Agnes, 1663
  her dau. Christine, 1663
Pedwell, John, rector of West Dean, 2169
Penn, Phil., 579
Pensford (Som.), 1336,
1909, 1939–41
Penstone, Edm., 987, 2084
Penton
  Christine, w. of Wm., 2036–7
  Wm., dyer, 2036–7, 2041, 2123, 2159
Penton (*unspecified,* ?Hants), 1971
Pentridge
  Hen., chaplain, 1591
  Rog., 1823–5
Pentridge (Dors.)
  chaplain, 595
  church, 1979
Perch, John, clerk, commissary, registrar of [prerogative] court of Canterbury, 1979, 2011, 2063
Perrin, Wm., 1888
Peter, servant, 2064
Peter at the hall, 445
Petherton, South (Som.), church of St. Peter, 2063
Peutherer, Edith, w. of Ric., 1786
Peverell, Hen., kt., 720–1
Pewsey, John, 1971
Philippa, Queen, 704, 729, 745
Philpot, John, citizen of London, 827
Pickard
  John, 740
  Wm., grocer, 1787–8, 1805, 1846, 1850, 2005, 2114–15, 2156, 2165; *and see* witnesses: reeve
Pierce
  Alice, 1828
  Joan, 1828
  John (d. by c. 1339), 287
  John (fl. 1402), 1828
  ygr. John (fl. 1402), 1828
  John (fl. 1410, ?another), bro. of Thos. Dunball, 2042
Piercourt, Avice, 695
Piggesden, Ric., 345–6
Pill, And., 1851
Pilling, Margt., w. of John, 1139
pillory, judgement of, 137
Pilton, John, and his w. Agnes, 53
Pinch, John, 1896
Pinkbridge, Edm., 2011
Pinnock
  Edith, w. of Rob., 52
  Edw., 397, 403, 619, 690, 706, 768, 841, 859
  Ellen, relict of Edw., dau. of Sim. of Oxford (d. c. 1326), 841–2
  John, s. of Ric., 143
  John, s. of Wm., 5
  John (?another), 1375
  Lucy, 50–2
  Ric., 143
  Rob., 50–1
  Wm., 4–5
Pipards, Alice, 2011
pit, at the, *see* John
Pitt, Wm., fisherman, 153
Pitts
  Ric., canon of cathedral church, 1527–9
  Ric (?same), clerk, 1688, 1694
Play
  Alice, w. of Thos. (d. 1398), 1698, 1702, 1730, 1838
  her bro. John, 1730
  Edm., 1730, 2002
  Isoude, 1730
  John, s. of Rob (d. by c. 1394), 932
  John, s. of Thos. (d. 1398), 1730
  Margt., w. of Rob. (d. by c. 1394), *see* Bown
  Rob. (d. by c. 1394), smith, ironmonger, 562, 631, 649, 657, 660, 674, 684, 698, 765–6, 782–3, 791, 860, 881, 895, 920, 927, 932–3, 940, 1068, 1079, 1120, 1168,

1265, 1337–40, 1367, 1406–7, 1438, 1466, 1497–8, 1503, 1553, 1564, 1617–20, 1636, 1639, 1649–52, 1665–6, 1744, 1746, 1779, 1790, 1806, 1811–12, 1860, 1873–5, 1938, 1955, 1965, 1971, 2002–3, 2122
 Rob. (fl. 1398), 1730, 2002
 Thos., s. of Rob., 932 (*otherwise* Bleacher)
  Thos. (d. 1398), smith, 698, 860, 1224, 1698, 1702, 1755, 1838, 1896, 1958, 1966, 1972, 2002; will, 1730
pleas
 of *calumpnia*, 844
 of contract, 844
 of land, 69, 71, 90, 844
 of trespass, 844
 and see dower; fines; novel disseisin
Plebs, Maud, w. of Hen., 1680
Plowman, Geof., 1837
Plubel, Nic., 213
Plummer
 And., 1878
 John, 983
 Rog., 606, 610, 635, 742
Polling, Nic., skinner, 32
Polmond
 Alice, w. of John, relict of Ric. Alden, 682, 691
 Joan, relict of Wm., 1268
 John, 682, 691, 1210, 1221, 1323–4, 1333, 1475, 1511, 1949, 1952
 Wm., 682, 689, 691, 1268
Pomeroy, Alan, citizen of Winchester, 68
Pomfret, Wm., citizen of London, 1703–4
pontage, 376
Poole

Agnes, w. of Rob., 1943
 Rob., 1836, 1943
Poore, Ric., bishop of Salisbury, 844
Pope
 Cecily, w. of Hen., 905, 953, 957
 Christine, w. of (?ygr.) John, 2011
 Edith, w. of Hen., relict of Steph. Jay, 805, 1006–7
 Edith (?same), 1871
 Edith, w. of John, 1871
 Hen., dyer, 485, 564, 597, 605, 636, 712, 734, 786, 833–4, 839, 905, 953, 957, 1006–7, 1775–6, 1816, 1994, 2054
 Joan, dau. of (?ygr.) John, 2011
 Joan, w. of Rob., 1272, 1293
 John, tailor, 957, 1345, 1635, 1710
 elder John (?same), 2011, 2022, 2078, 2081
 ygr. John, 1909, 2011, 2074, 2153
 John, collegiate chaplain of St. Edmund's church, 1775–6; will, 1871
 John, kinsman of John, chaplain, 1871
 John (?others), *see* Bosham
 Maud, w. of Rob., 941
 Ric., chaplain, 965, 988
 Rob., draper, 941, 1256, 1272, 1293, 1704
 Sarah, 1871
Popham, Hen., 1195, 1786, 1815, 1862, 2063, 2073
Portbury (Som.), 88, 106
porteouses, 619, 671, 1729, 1786, 1871, 1882
Porter, Wm., 1741
porter, *see* Moulton
Portman, John, furbisher, 879, 894

Porton (in Idmiston), 671
Postle, Thos., 1717, 1805, 1896
Potterne, Nic. of, chaplain, 239
Pouchmaker, John, 671
Poulshot
 Isabel, 740
 John, carpenter, 562, 631
 John (two of the name), 603
 Wal., 603
Poulter, Rob., 99, 128, 180
Poulton
 Christine, 550
 Edith, w. of John (d. 1361), 550
 John (d. 1361), 1959–60, 2004); will, 550
 John of (?another), tucker, 743
 Margt., 550
 Thos., clerk, commissary, 1709
Powell
 Emme, w. of John, *see* Astbury
 John (d. by *c.* 1360), 318, 323, 343–4, 361, 390, 392–3, 420, 424, 587, 608, 625, 641, 643–4, 650, 655, 736, 771, 774, 776–9, 789, 826; as coroner, 436; *and see* witnesses: coroner
 John (?same), 1777
 John, s. of John (d. by *c.* 1360), 650
 Margt., w. of John, 323
 Ric., 826
 Rob., 777
 Thos., 736, 771, 774, 776–9
 Wm., 826
Poxwell, John, 1701
Pratt, Phil., 396
Preece, Ellis, baker, 262
Prentice
 Joan, *see* Pate
 John, clerk, 2110
 John, *indexed as* Buddle
 Ric., clerk, 1917, 1922

Preshute, rector of, *see* Doggett
'Prestempde'
  Margt., w. of Thos., sis. of Thos. Burford, 1856
  Thos., 1856
Preston
  John, grocer, merchant, 1169, 1683, 1801, 2026, 2031
  John, s. of John, 2031
  Wm. (fl. *c.* 1369), 874
  Wm. (fl. 1408, ?another), 2011
Prettyjohn, Hen., and his w. Agnes, 1637
Priddy, Ric., 1753, 1913–14
Priest, the lord Wm., 1729
priests (named), *see* Aynel; Caundle; William
Prior
  Joan, w. of Ric., dau. of John of Langford, 687
  Ric., 687
prisoners, relief of
  London: Fleet, King's Bench, King's Marshalsea, Ludgate, Newgate, 1979
  Old Sarum castle, 668, 671, 740, 1778, 1859, 1979, 1985, 2155
  Salisbury, 740
    Guildhall, 668, 1778, 1859, 1979, 1985
    serjeants (-at-mace), 1882, 1979, 1985
Prout, John, and his w. Agnes, 1170, 1173
psalters, 1786, 1882, 1943
Puddlemill
  Mabel, 1448
  Wm., 1006–7, 1032, 1344, 1448
Purbeck
  John, weaver, and his w. Alice, 667
  John, chaplain, *see* Paris
Purchase, Wm., tucker, 1786
Purdy
  Edm., weaver, 1876,

1897, 2126
  John, 1530
Purser
  Cecily, w. of Wm., 2077
  Nic., 1105, 1124, 1149, 1273
  Wm., 743, 768, 910, 1884, 2077; *and see* witnesses: reeve
Purvis, John, 1793, 1813, 1835, 1907, 1979
Pye, Wm., 359
Pyeleg, Ric., 567
Pyle, Abbot, 2064
P..., Wm., weaver, 983

Quarrendon, Ric., chaplain, 1450
Quarter
  Alice, w. of Thos., 548
  Thos.: will, 548
Quidhampton (in Fuggleston), 690, 827–9, 898, 1286

Raby, the master John, public notary, 1726
Radipole (Dors.), rector of, *see* Corfe
Ragenhill, Rob., clerk, provost of the college of St. Edmund's church, 1723–4, 1785, 1798–9, 1817–18, 1871–2
Ralph at the cross, and his w. Joan, 282
Ramsbury, Rob., 827
Randolph
  Lucy, w. of Wm., 274
  Thos., 1730, 1985, 2063
  Wm., 274; *and see* witnesses: bailiff
Rayner, Wm., 232
Read
  Alice, 1871
  Thos. (fl. 1361), 555
  Thos. (fl. 1404, ?another), 1871
Reading
  Agnes, relict of Ric., 68
  Cecily, w. of Rob., 1107,

1660, 1846
  Ric. of, 68
  Rob., 1107, 1660, 1741, 1846, 2005, 2077, 2114–15, 2117
Reaps, Agnes, 1909
Redenham
  Agnes, w. of Thos. (fl. *c.* 1370), 861
  Margt., 727
  Thos. (fl. *c.* 1370), 861
  Thos. (fl. 1399, ?another), tanner, 1680, 1759, 1761
Redhead, Sim., 639
Reynold, vicar of Shipton, 671
Reynold
  Agnes, w. of Wm., 2011
  Margery, 1954
  Wm., weaver, 1418, 1563, 1791, 1809–10, 1867–8, 1953, 2011
Rich, John, 553; *cf.* Richman
Richard II, 844, 1536
Richard, chaplain, 1828
Richard, household servant, 1871
Richard, servants of the name, 579, 1979
Richard at the bridge, dyer, 1153, 1184, 2116, 2118, 2121
Richard at the cellar, 1910–11
Richard at the mill, tucker, 1755, 1838
Richard at the oak, 619
Richard at the row, 1555
Richard at the stone, tucker, 524, 638, 662
Richman
  Agace, w. of John (d. 1361), 644, 679
  Edith, 1036
  John (d. 1361), 343–4, 525, 553, 557, 605, 625, 633, 636, 641, 644–5, 659, 679, 694, 740, 746, 769, 792, 937, 1037, 1684, 1978; as

mayor, 399; *and see*
    witnesses: coroner,
    clerk, citizen
John (fl. 1362), s. of
    John, 645, 769
John (fl. 1410, ?another),
    2064
cf. Rich
Rickhill, Wm., justice of
    Common Pleas, 1858
Rider, Cath., 1985, 2063
Riggs, John, chaplain,
    2013–14
Ringwood
    Joan, 1971
    John, 1226
    Peter of, 189
    Rog. (of), 598, 627
    Thos., 1898–9
Ripley, Wm., shearman,
    1958, 1966, 1972
Rise
    Edith, w. of Ralph, 30
    Ralph of, 30, 33, 79
    Rob., 647, 1267
River
    Joan, w. of Wm., 1278–
        84, 1697, 1699, 1701
    Wm., 1278–84, 1626–7,
        1630–5, 1645, 1665,
        1684, 1693, 1695,
        1697, 1699, 1701, 1713,
        1721, 1758, 1784,
        1791, 2085
Riveray, Rob., 816
Rivers, Ric., and his w.
    Denise, 543
Robbs, John, tailor, 2055–6
Robert, apprentice, 2064
Robert, household servant,
    1943
Robert, servants of the
    name, 668, 1954
Robert at the mill, 461–2
    his dau. Agnes, 462
    his w. Edith, 461–2
Robert at the 'vuere', 626
    his s., *see* John at the
        'vuere'
Robet
    Edith, relict of John, *see*
        Hindon

John, 739; will, 564
Rochelle
    Hen., 1680
    John, 816
Rodway
    Alice, w. of Wal., dau. of
        John Scot, 1219, 2015
    Wal., 1219, 2015
Roger, lad, 569
Roger, servant, 570
Roger at the well, 347–8,
    1777
Romsey, Margt. of, nun of
    Wilton, 2169
Romsey (Hants), 567, 665,
    708, 1184
    vicar, *see* Humphrey
Roper, Wm., 48
roper, *see* King
Roscombe, Lambert of,
    141
Rothwell, John, 1919, 1923
Round
    John, 2156
    Wal., 2156
Rous, Matt., 749
row, at the, *see* Richard
Rowde, Ric., 1685, 1697,
    1699
Ruddock, John, weaver,
    and his w. Joan, 1953
Rushall, Alice, w. of John
    Deverill, 1435, 1778,
    2069
Russell
    Edith, w. of Nic., 856,
        978, 1188, 1523, 1906
    Edith, relict of Wm., 74,
        91
    Edw., chaplain, 1684,
        1938, 1944
    Hen., 236, 329, 625, 630,
        641, 656, 671, 764–6,
        1665–6; *and see*
        witnesses: citizen
    Hen. (?another), kt.,
        2165
    Nic., butcher, 444, 629,
        685, 756, 779, 813–14,
        856, 888, 978, 1188,
        1257, 1429, 1523, 1906;
        and see witnesses:

        citizen
    Rob., 210, 587, 632, 643,
        658, 729, 745, 835,
        1839
    Rob. (another), kt., 1557,
        1805, 1850
    Wm., merchant, 8, 74,
        91
Rutter, Rog., citizen of
    London, 671
Ryborough
    Amice, 671
    Cecily, *see* Hutchins
    Joan, w. of Ric., 382,
        384, 671
    her dau. Maud, 671
    Joan, w. of Wal., *see*
        Warmwell
    John, bro. of Ric., 671
    John, s. of Ric., 382, 384
    Peter, 382, 384, 671
    Ric., 326–7, 364, 369–
        70, 373, 375, 377–8,
        380–5, 391, 394, 400,
        404–7, 412, 417, 434,
        445, 471–2, 479, 483,
        544, 552, 564, 577,
        599, 683, 690, 717,
        748, 794, 797, 801,
        830, 850, 875, 881,
        946, 1019, 1034–5,
        1216, 1526, 2112; will,
        671
    Wal., 974, 1057–8, 1207,
        1295, 1346, 1412, 1658,
        1685, 1898–9, 1920–1
    Wm., 671
Ryde
    Ric., 1309, 1368, 1704,
        1945
    Thos., merchant, 1945,
        2110, 2153; *and see*
        witnesses: reeve,
        citizen

Saddler, John, baker, 1889
saddlers, *see* Cross;
    Heytesbury
St. Honorine, John of, 545
St. Martin, Laur. de, kt.,
    730
Salisbury

GENERAL INDEX

Alice, w. of John (called Baker), 1895
Christine, w. of John, weaver, relict of Peter Butterley, 1758; will, 2160
Joan, see Delves
(*otherwise* Nugg) John, clerk, s. of John Nugg, 328, 379, 381, 514, 609; *and see* Nugg
John of (?same), parson of St. Thomas's church, 570
elder John, grocer, 1181
(*often called* Baker) John, grocer, s. of Nic. Baker, 947, 1225, 1493–4, 1618, 1665, 1730, 1751, 1789, 1805, 1826, 1846, 1882, 1895–6, 1930, 2029, 2032–3, 2124, 2158; *and see* witnesses: mayor, coroner, citizen
John *or* John, grocer (either of the two above), 1083, 1244, 1325, 1360–3, 1379–81, 1541, 1567, 1675, 1706–7, 1721, 1769
John, kt., 1895–6
John, weaver, 1758, 2160
Thos., kt., 827–9, 898
Wm., bro. of Hen. Long, 584; *cf.* Long
Wm., vicar of Ashley, 2055–6

Sall
Joan, w. of Wm. (?fl. 1413), 1397–8, 1400–1
elder Wm. (?d. by 1397), 1710
Wm. (fl. 1413), 1397–8, 1400–1, 1882, 1891, 1896, 1904–5, 1915–16, 1961, 2015–17, 2019, 2022, 2048, 2073–4, 2078, 2081–2, 2104, 2120, 2123–4, 2140–3, 2149,

2161, 2167; *and see* witnesses: mayor, reeve, citizen
Sallitt, Ellis, 340
Salter
Maud, relict of Ric., 782, 920
Ric., 634, 702, 782, 785, 920, 930
Rob., 1600, 1711, 1723, 1971
salter, see Sprot
Salterton (in Durnford), 1979
manor, 1979
Saltwood (Kent), rector of, *see* Francis
Sampson
Edith, w. of elder John, 1790, 1806
elder John, 1790, 1806
John (?same), 1823–5
Sand, John, and his w. Joan, 1066
Sandhurst (*unspecified*), church of, 1680
Santel, Wm., 118, 129, 164
Sarfy, Ric., 740, 746
Sarson (in Amport, Hants), 1600, 1711, 1723, 1919, 1923
Saucer
Denise, relict of Wm., 231
Wm., 230–1
Saunder, Wm., weaver, 1659, 1679
Saunders, Wm., 1719
Sauter
Alice, w. of Ric., dau. of Thos. of Cirencester, 752–3
Geof., clerk, 775
Ric., 752–3
Wal., clerk, 788
Sawyer, Malin, 740
Scammel
Joan, w. of Wm., 468, 909, 911, 2049
John, *indexed as* Camel
Thos., friar, 578
Wm., 468, 909, 911,

2049
Scot
Alice, dau. of John, *see* Rodway
Alice, w. of Wm., 6
John (d. by 1409), 2015
ygr. John (fl. 1412), 1896, 2124
John (?another), 1971
Thos., 821
Wm., dyer, 6, 197
scribes, *see* Henry at the bar; Mackinney; Thomas; *and see* clerks
Scriven
Rob., 668, 906
Phil., 668
Ralph, 219
Seager, Thos., tanner, 2027–8
Sealer
Alice, w. of Ric., 105
Ric., 105, 700, 724, 727
sealer, *see* Wardour
Self, John, chaplain, 2071–2
Selwood
Hen., 1296, 1499
John, 279
Selwood (Som.), Carthusian house in, 1729; *cf.* Witham
Sergeant, John, *see* Gatcombe
Sevenash, John, clerk, 811
Sever, Wm., 1729
Severin at the oak, 1976
Sewin
Agnes, *see* Green
Alice, relict of John, 2116, 2118, 2121
John, ironmonger, 1277, 1387, 2116, 2118, 2121
Sexhampcote
Agnes, 579
Joan, w. of Thos. (d. by c. 1396), 1125–7, 1603–4, 1756–7, 1840
Joan, w. of Wm., 579, 618
John, chaplain, vicar of Whiteparish, 918,

1664, 1756–7, 1840,
1864, 1928, 1993,
1995, 2010, 2130, 2132
Pauline, w. of Rob.,
1664
Rob., 579, 1125–6, 1746;
will, 1664
Rog., 1664
his dau. Alice, 1664
Thos. (fl. 1364), dyer,
703
Thos. (d. by *c.* 1396,
?same), 579, 833–4,
942–3, 977, 982, 1094,
1125–7, 1551, 1602–4,
1664, 1733, 1736,
1756–7, 1814, 1840,
1847, 1885, 1924, 1973,
2018
Wm. (of), 429, 618; will,
579
his sis. Edith, 579
Sexton
Gillian, w. of Thos., 1836
Gunnore, 1836
Maud, w. of Thos., 1836
Thos., ironmonger, 1257,
1330, 1460–2, 1588,
1674, 1677–8, 1754,
1832, 1990; will, 1836;
and see witnesses:
coroner, reeve
his sis. Alice, 1836
his sis. Maud, 1836
Seymour, Wal., 1522
Shad, John, draper, 1878,
2016, 2019–20, 2104
Shaftesbury (Dors.), 283,
1256, 1272
chaplain, *see* Alexander
Shalbourne, Thos. of,
chaplain, 495, 656
Shalbourne, 656
Shalford
John (of), 62, 681, 722
Wal., 62
Shearer
Alice (Barnaby), w. of
Ric., 374, 395–6, 401,
427–8, 831, 903–4,
984
Joan, w. of Steph., 831

Maud, w. of Steph.,
relict of Wal. Goss, m.
of Ric. Dinton, 528,
696, 756, 804, 831
Ralph, 432, 488
Ric., 374–5, 395–6, 401,
427–8, 433, 488, 831,
903
Ric. (another), s. of
Steph., 831
his dau. Amice, 831
Steph., 528, 696, 712,
729, 734, 745, 756,
789, 804, 2079; will,
831
shearman, *see* Ripley
sheather, *see* Hill
Shendlove, Alice, 208
Sherborne
And. of, 612
Edith, w. of John, 243
John (of), cook, 243,
625, 641–2
Sherfield, John, 840
Sherfield (*unspecified*,
Hants), parson of, *see*
Ellis
Shergold, Wm., 1783
Sherman, Ric., 1962–3,
2061, 2075
Shipster
Edith, *see* Knights
Maud, 698
shipster, *see* Knights
Shipton
John, dubber, 1393, 1735,
1832, 1859, 1897, 1971
Maud, w. of John, 1828,
1971
her dau., Agnes
Ric., 671
Rob., chaplain of
Stratford-sub-Castle,
740, 746
Thos. (of), weaver, 671,
1318
Wm., weaver, 1814,
1864, 1872, 1993, 1995
Shipton (*unspecified*), vicar
of, *see* Reynold
Shirley, Wal., grocer,
merchant, 1838, 1881,

1891, 1917, 1922,
2006–8, 2045, 2118,
2161, 2163, 2166–7;
and see witnesses:
mayor, reeve, citizen
Shirley (Hants), 1066
shoes (given charitably),
553, 581, 740, 1882,
2155
'Shorberd', John, 2095
Short, Wal., 1948, 1988,
2007, 2035, 2037, 2047,
2113
Shove
Agace, w. of Thos.,
1350–1, 1355, 1390–2,
1544–5, 2009, 2039
Gillian, w. of John, 1353,
1357
John *and* John, kt.,
(?same), 832, 1092,
1334, 1354, 1356–7,
2109
John (?another), s. of
Thos., 1350
Thos., 966, 1068–9,
1090, 1100, 1350–1,
1355, 1388–92, 1543–4,
2009, 2039
Shrewsbury, Ric. of, 644
Shrewton, John of, 415,
418
Shrewton, vicar of, 583;
and see Hugh
Shropshire, *see* Ludlow
Shute, ygr. John, weaver,
2044, 2099
Sibley
John, 2007
Rob., 136
Sidelinch, Adam, 86
Sifray
Joan, 1909
Ric., 1909
Silby, John, and his w.
Edith, 41
Silvain, (called Inways)
Rob., 44, 87
Silvester
John, 700, 724
Thos., 700, 724
Simmonds, Gillian, 1828

Sire
  Wm., 833–4, 1658
  Wm., s. of Wm., 1658, 1712
Sireman
  Hen., chaplain, 1740
  Wm., 1740
Sivier
  Emme, w. of John, relict of Ric. Cook, 582, 952
  John, 952
  Wm., 1860, 1942, 2011
Skilling
  Nic., 564, 739
  Thos., chaplain, 570
  Wal., chaplain, 1022
Skinner
  Alice, 740
  Bart., 669
  Edith, w. of Thos., 220
  Gilb., 1039, 1061–2
  John, 669
  Thos., 220
skinners, see Brawt; Gilbert at the brook; Halliday; Hampton; Hilary; Oxford; Polling; Way
Skinpain, Alice, 1936
Skutt, Alice, w. of Wal., 295
Slegge
  Thos., weaver, 1807, 1861, 2071–2; and see witnesses: citizen
  Wm., weaver, 1794, 1802–3, 1925–7, 1978, 2122, 2129, 2131; and see witnesses: reeve
'Smalmalet' see ways
Smarts, Maud, 667
Smith
  Agnes, dau. of Hen., see William at the bridge
  Agnes, relict of Thos., dau. of John Durrington, sis. of Gillian Hoare, 573, 592, 675, 798; will, 648
  Hen. (?one of the name), 748, 1182–3, 1777

Joan, w. of Hen., 748
John, bro. of Hen. Berwick, 1943
John, of Compton Chamberlayne, 233
John, chaplain, 1947–8, 2061, 2075, 2102–3
John (?another), 1951
Maud, w. of John, of Compton Chamberlayne, 233
Ric., tiler, 853
Rob., 1182–3
(called Binsmith, the binsmith) Thos., 489, 520, 592–3, 648, 675, 699, 798
Wal., 567
Wm., bro. of Wm. Thatcher, 1674
smiths, see Bleacher; Goodyear; Heal; Hussey; Marshall; Play
Snel
  John, draper, 415, 418, 556, 585, 594, 804
  (called Bosset) John, see Bosset
Snoddington (Hants), 2131
Snow, John, 2064
Somborne
  Edith, w. of John, 929
  John of, carpenter, 671
  John of (?same), 929–30
Somborne (unspecified, Hants), 690
  church, 690
Somborne, Little (Hants), 690
Somerset, see Crewkerne; Glastonbury; Frome; Knowle, Church; Lopen; Merriott; Pensford; Portbury; Selwood; Stavordale; Wells; Witham; and see (for cross-reference) Axbridge
Sorrel
  Agnes, relict of Rog., 738
  John, 305, 564, 678, 739,

908, 1918–19
Maud, relict of John, 678
Rog., 738, 1878
Sotts, Alice, 667
Souter, Evelotte, 1836
Southam, Thos., canon of cathedral church, 1779, 1811–12, 1873–5
Southampton (Hants), 217, 567, 620
  address, 682, 867, 1328, 1475, 1477–8, 1949, 2056
  Bull Street, 567
  burgess, see Inways
  churches: All Saints, Blessed Mary, Holy Cross, St. John, St. Laurence, St. Michael, 567
  rector of St. Michael's, 567
  dean, 567
  Franciscans, 569
  French Street, 1985
  messuages, 1066
  parishes
    St. John's, 567, 1985
    St. Michael's, 567
  priory of St. Denis, see Langford
  shop, 567
  tenements, 427–8, 511–12, 1985
  town wall, 567
  Wool bridge, 1985
Southmere, Thos., 11
Southwick
  Hen., 1235, 1278–81, 1411, 1542, 1670, 1790, 1806
  Isabel, w. of Hen., 1280–1
Southwick (in North Bradley), chaplain of, see Budden
Spaldwick, Wm., canon of cathedral church, 1971
Spearcock, Edm., 1359
Spencer
  Agnes, w. of Ric., 1345
  Edith, w. of Ric., 1944

Ric., grocer, 1345, 1396,
    1402, 1468–70, 1513,
    1531, 1574, 1597–8,
    1627, 1634–5, 1638,
    1691, 1700, 1751,
    1758, 1777, 1784–5,
    1796, 1800, 1817–18,
    1825, 1829, 1840,
    1853–4, 1858, 1865,
    1894, 1896, 1923,
    1932–4, 1944, 1950,
    1985, 2022, 2045,
    2048, 2066, 2078,
    2081, 2109, 2114–15,
    2119–20, 2123–4,
    2137, 2143, 2147–8,
    2153, 2156–9; *and
    see* witnesses: mayor,
    coroner, citizen
Wm., 1622–4, 2065
Spicer
    (*otherwise* Bertins) Alice,
        w. of Bertin, relict
        of Ric. Lavington,
        368–9, 656, 674
    Bertin, 368, 674, 2040
    Greg., 764
    (*otherwise* Hen. of
        Nursling) Hen., 72,
        661
    John, 42, 105, 283
    Maud, w. of John, 105
    Steph., 626
    Wm., chaplain of St.
        Martin's church,
        1867–8, 1938, 2160
spicers, *see* Blakeney;
    Farley; Keynes
Spindler, Ric., 2011
Spray
    John, 371
    Ric., 656
    Rob., 656
Spreed, Rob., chaplain,
    1859
Springham
    Agnes, w. of John, 78,
        277
    John, draper, 78, 277,
        580
    Peter, 60
Sprot

Edith, w. of John, 862
John, baker, 862, 1252
John, Dominican friar,
    2156
Marion, 102
Ric., 104
Wm., salter, 58, 104
Spurgeon, Nic., clerk, 1838
Stabber
    Alice, w. of Thos., dau.
        of Hen. Berwick,
        1929, 1943, 2010, 2062
    Thos., draper, 1816,
        1929, 1943, 2010,
        2034–5, 2049–51,
        2060, 2062, 2076
Stacy, Joan, relict of John,
    567
Stafford, Nic., chaplain of
    St. Thomas's church,
    2156
Staggard
    John, weaver, 1539, 1720,
        1733, 1736, 1847, 1924,
        1980, 2018; *and see*
        witnesses: citizen
    Ric., 2011
    Wm., 2018
Stalbridge
    Amice, w. of Thos. (d.
        by *c*. 1396), 884
    Hugh, butcher, 871, 880,
        936
    Joan, w. of John, 269
    John, 269, 1997, 1999–
        2000
    Thos. (d. by *c*. 1396),
        633, 884, 1279, 1283–
        4, 1611
    Thos. (fl. 1405),
        carpenter, 1882
Stallington, John (of),
    clerk, 569, 739, 837,
    at 841, 842, 901, 908,
    995, 1416–17, 1487,
    1729, 2042–4, 2046–7
Stangman, Wm., 1839
Stanley
    Agnes, w. of elder Wm.,
        566
    Joan, 566
    John, 1552

Wm., 550, 566, 609,
    668, 922; *and see*
    witnesses: reeve
Wm., s. of Wm., 566
Stanley (abbey, in
    Bremhill), abbot of,
    1760, 1804, 1850, 2165
Stanton, John, chaplain,
    690
Stapleford
    Alice, 660
    Edith, w. of Hen., 663
    Gilb. (of), baker, 660
    Hen. (of), 503, 532, 554,
        644, 663, 719–21,
        767, 885–6, 892, 950,
        1027, 1126, 1777,
        1809, 1900–1; *and see*
        witnesses: reeve
    Lucy, w. of Rog., 1134
    Rog., 1134, 1796
Starr
    Edith, w. of John, dau.
        of Ric. Frear, 554,
        1307–8, 1704, 1735,
        1849, 1855, 1945
    John, 1307–8, 1703–4,
        1735, 1828, 1849, 1855,
        1859, 1897, 1945
    Wm., 93
statutes
    Merchants, 570, 1395
    Mortmain, 704, 1766,
        1782, 1931, 2100, 2157
Stavordale (priory, in
    Charlton Musgrove,
    Som.), convent of,
    1680
Steed
    John, 283
    Lettice, w. of Rob., 583
    Margery, w. of John, 283
    Margery, w. of Rob., 589
    her s. John, 589
    Rob., 589; will, 583
Steer
    Thos., 1894, 1905, 1996,
        1998, 2158
    Wm., 1720
Steercock
    Edm., 410, 508, 540; *and
        see* witnesses: citizen

Wm., 1772
Stephen, servant, 1859
Stephens, John, weaver,
    1867–8
Steward
  Agnes, w. of Edw., see
    Woodford
  Edw., indexed as Upton
  John, 570
  steward, see Bonham
Stickbeard
  John (d. by c. 1336), 272
  John (fl. 1361), 606, 610,
    740
Still
  John, chaplain, 1066,
    1122, 1378
  Ric., 374, 524, 557, 568,
    605, 611, 613, 636, 638,
    662, 736, 779, 1186,
    1198, 1270, 1754,
    1836, 1883, 1886; and
    see witnesses: citizen
Stint, Phil., 554, 740, 746
Stints, Christine, 690
Stock, the lord John, 1680;
    cf. Stoke
Stockbridge, Wm. of,
    ironmonger, and his
    w. Agnes, 573
Stockbridge (Hants), 599
Stockton, John, 1176
Stockton, 566
Stoke
  Alice, w. of Hen., 9–10
  Hen. of, 9–10
  Joan, w. of Ric., 1740
  John, tailor, 1008, 1016,
    1074, 1076–7, 1136,
    1158–60, 1184, 1426,
    1445, 1644, 1655, 1752,
    1883, 1886, 1968, 2013
  John (?another), bro. of
    Ric., 1740
    his dau. Christine, 1740
  John (?another), s. of
    Ric., 1740
  Margt., w. of John,
    tailor, 1008, 1016,
    1074
  Nic., chaplain of St.
    Edmund's church,

1813, 1979
    (otherwise Carentham)
  Ric., burgess of
    Wilton, 882, 1727;
    will, 1740
  Rob., 1740
  Thos., 1450
  cf. Stock; Stokes
Stoke Farthing (in Broad
    Chalke), 695, 800,
    823, 1168
Stokes
  Alice, 698
  Thos., and his w. Joan,
    738
  cf. Stoke
Stonard
  Gillian, w. of Rob.,
    1982–3
  Rob., baker, 1980, 1982–
    3, 2106–7
stone, at the, see John;
    Richard
Stone
  Felice, 2169
  Joan, w. of elder John,
    dau. of John Ashley,
    1986, 2169
  Joan, dau. of elder John,
    2169
  John, 1986, 2071–2; will,
    2169
  John, s. of John, 2169
  Margt., nun of Wilton,
    2169
  Nic., 2169
  Olive, 2169
  Thos., 2169
Stook, David, indexed as
    Fletcher
Stourton
  Wm. of (fl. c. 1318), 40
  Wm. (fl. c. 1395), 1626–
    7, 1630–5, 1645, 1665,
    1684, 1693, 1695,
    1721, 1758, 1784,
    2158–9
Stourton, see Bonham
Stout, Wm., 1603–4, 2054,
    2074
Stoville, Ralph, and his w.
    Parnel, 239

Stratford
  Agnes, see Leadbeater
  And. (of), 708, 899
  John of (d. by c. 1332),
    257
  John (fl. c. 1382), canon
    of cathedral church,
    1193
  Nic. of, 43, 101
  Thos. (of), 132–3, 357,
    563 732
Stratford (Suff.), rector of,
    see Needham
Stratford-sub-Castle and
    Stratford (unspecified),
    328, 497, 665, 692,
    708, 746, 801, 1269
  Avon, q.v.
  chaplain, 740, 746; and
    see Shipton
  church of Holy Cross,
    692
  guild of St. James, 740
  light of the Blessed
    Mary, 740
  parishioners, 740
  parson, 740
  Street, John, chaplain, 1506
Stringer
  Agnes, 772
  John, 772
  Wm., 550, 552, 660,
    772, 787, 819–20,
    824–5
Studley, Ric. of, 267
Sturminster Newton
    (Newton Castle,
    Dors.), church of,
    1888
Sturmy, Ric., 191
Suffolk, see (for cross-
    reference) Kelsale
Sulham, Kentigern of,
    clerk, 626, 701, 754,
    763, 2024
Summer, Hen., 2023,
    2030, 2058–9; and see
    witnesses: citizen
Summerhill, Wm.,
    subdean of cathedral
    church, 2029, 2064,
    2160

Sumner, *see* Gilbert
Sunbury
  Geof., 1488, 1670
  Margery, w. of Geof., 1488, 1670
Surr
  Tamsin, w. of Wm. (d. 1404), *see* Bristow
  Wm. (fl. 1362), 650, 655
  Wm. (d. 1404, ?same), 1622, 1624, 1807, 1861, 1870, 1959–60, 2071–2; will, 2065
Sussex, *see* Twineham
Sutton
  Hen., dyer, 902
  Joan, w. of Hen., 902
  Nic., 1987–8
  Wm. of, vicar of cathedral church, 124
Swain
  Hen., 1255, 1714
  Ric., 580
'Swengedieu', John, 740
Swift
  Christine, w. of John, relict of Wm. Heal, 1461–2, 1674, 1677–8, 2112–13, 2116, 2118, 2121
  John, ironmonger, 1461–2, 1674–5, 1677–8, 1754, 1836, 1877, 1990, 2079, 2112–13, 2116, 2118, 2121; *and see* witnesses: reeve
  John, chaplain, 1056
  Ric., 192
Swindon (High Swindon), 1219, 2015
Swith, John, s. of John, 619
Swooper, Ric., 800, 823
Sydenham
  John, 1612, 2049–51, 2076
  the master Sim., clerk, 2049–51, 2076

tailors, *see* Agodeshalf; Braban; Chamberlain; Coffer; Cormell; Griffith; Ham; Handley; Ireland; Long; Luckham; Moore; Palmer; Pope; Robbs; Stoke; Waite; Wells; Yeovil
Talbot, John, 601, 672, 687, 736, 761, 771, 774, 776, 784, 1906, 2002–3; *and see* witnesses: citizen
tallage, 543, 1985, 2029
Tankard, Rog., 104
Tanner
  Edith, 1828
  John, bailiff of Axminster, 1851
  Maud, w. of Rog., 482
  (*otherwise* (of) Halwell, called the tanner) Rog., 482, 551, 561, 590, 596, 705, 710, 713, 874, 919
tanners, *see* Boscombe; Brute; Clive; Coffer; Cofford; Gaydon; Gilbert; Gill; Luckham; New; Newman; Nunton; Redenham; Seager; Tanner; Winterbourne
tan-turf, 2027
Tarrant, Rog., 364, 630, 2077
Tarrant (*unspecified*, ?Dors.), 2169
Tarrant Gunville (Dors.), church of, 2169
Taston, Wm., 816
Taunton
  Nic., baker, 297
  Ric., clerk, 2169
Tavente, John, 1233
Taverner
  John, 904, 984
  Joyce, and his w. Margt., 564, 782–3
taverners, *see* Bailiff; Dudmoor; Essington; Lutwich
Tawell, Rob., 2005
Taylor
  Ellen, w. of Nic., 699
  Felice, w. of Rog. (fl. 1407), 1971
  John (d. by 1397), 1671–3, 1688–9, 1691, 1693
  (called Hosier) John (another), 1680
  John (another), *see* Thorburn
  John (fl. 1410, another), 2063
  Lucy, w. of Nic., 1594, 1673
  Nic., draper, citizen and clothier of London and Salisbury, 460, 476, 549, 699, 832, 981, 1151, 1242, 1290–1, 1373, 1384–5, 1593–4, 1647, 1667–9, 1671–3, 1676, 1687–9, 1691, 1693–5, 1786, 1902, 1908, 1912, 2116, 2118, 2121, 2158; as mayor, 625, 641–2; *and see* witnesses: mayor, citizen
  Rob., 2156
  Rog. (d. by 1397), 1671–3, 1688–9, 1691, 1693
  Rog. (fl. 1407), 971
Teffont
  Adam, 1047, 1201–2, 1317, 1507, 1569, 1792, 1794, 2155; as mayor, 1766, 1782, 1791; *and see* witnesses: mayor, coroner, citizen
  Hen., 695
  John, 1179
  Maud, w. of Hen., 695
  Parnel, w. of Adam, 1047, 1317, 1507, 1569
Tenterer
  Alice, w. of ygr. Wm., *see* Merriott
  Christine, relict of John, 1760
  Gillian, relict of elder William, 1023
  Isabel, 1717
  John, 1717, 1760

Martin, 203
  elder Wm., 654, 661, 816, 876, 998, 1023; *and see* witnesses: mayor, citizen
  ygr. Wm., 401, *at* 404, 481, 487, 498, 500, 551, 561, 588, 611, 763–6, 809, 852, 921, 938, 970, 1025, 1484–5, 1717, 1760, 1804–5, 1985, 2045, 2063, 2119; *and see* witnesses: mayor, citizen
Tetsworth, Edm., 1249–50
Thatcham, Paul of, 99, 252
Thatcher
  Wm., *indexed as* Heal Wm., *cf.* Smith
Thirning, Wm., justice of Common Pleas, 1858
Thomas, apprentice, 831
Thomas, clerk, scribe, 580, 582
Thomas, household servant, 666
Thomas, parochial chaplain of St. Martin's church, 568, 582
Thomas, servants of the name, 668, 2011
Thomas at the burgh, 816
  his s. Rob., 816
Thomas at the hope, 88, 106
Thomas at the mere, 1253
Thomas at the wood, 578
Thorburn
  Alice, 1950
  Joan, w. of John (d. by *c.* 1396), 1351–3, 1356–9, 1932–4
  (called Taylor) John (d. by *c.* 1396), 1351–3, 1355–9, 1581, 1589, 1648, 1932–4, 1950, 2109
  John (fl. 1409), 2021
  John (fl. 1412, ?another), 2109
  Margery, *see* Cary
  Ric., 1950

Steph., 1816, 2021
Thornborough
  Thos., 583
  Wm., 583
Thorney, Thos., citizen of London, 827
Thornhill, John (of), 42, 123, 146, 167
Thorpe
  Hen., 2158–9
  Rob. of, justice of Common Pleas, 844
Thoytes, Gunhild, 669
Throope (in Bishopstone, in Downton hundred), 1943
Thruxton (Hants), church of, 2064
Thurman, Nic., 1506
Thurstan, Thos., 322, 325, 577
Tidcombe, Wm., clerk, 770
Tidpit, Wm., 694, 743
Tidpit (in Martin, *now* Hants)
  chapel, 595
  church of St. Peter, 1909
Tidworth
  Cath., w. of Ric., 334
  John (fl. *c.* 1351), 333–4
  John (fl. 1405), 1896
  Reynold (of), 68, 92–4, 97, 597
  Ric. (of), 97, 107, 117, 333–5, 564, 605, 636, 739, 758–9, 764
tilers *and* helliers, *see* Bourton; Hawes; Smith
Till
  John, friar, 1836
  Maud, 1689, 1695
  Wm., 832
Tinker, Agnes, relict of Sim., 1142
Tisbury, the master John, 2169
Titling, Ric., vicar of cathedral church, 2061
Tonner, Thos., 2011
Toogood, John, parson of Fifield, 1352, 1356

Toostrange
  Amice, w. of Thos., 558
  Thos., 558
Topp, Peter, weaver, 1781
Tosard
  Jarvis, 816
  Wm., 816
Tott
  Alice, relict of John, 574, 576
  John, 466, 549, 574–6, 600, 652, 2158
  Thos., 574–5, 652
trades and occupations, *see (for cross-references)* attorney; bakers; barbers; bell-founder; bowyer; brazier; brewers; butchers; carders; cardmakers; carpenters; carter; chaplains; clerks; clothiers; commissaries; cooks; cooper; cordwainers; drapers; dubbers; dyers; fishermen, fishers; friars; furbisher; glovers; goldsmiths; grocers; hatters; helliers; hosier; ironmongers; limeburner; linendraper; loader; mason; mercers; merchants; notary; painters; porter; roper; saddlers; salter; scribes; sealer; shearman; sheather; shipster; skinners; smiths; spicers; steward; tailors; tanners; taverners; tilers; tuckers; weavers; wheeler; *and see* index 2: bailiff
Tredinnick, Sim., draper, 1022, 1113, 1668, 1672, 1676, 1686–7, 1690, 1863, 1895, 1898–9, 1902, 1908, 1912, 1920–1, 2063, 2155;

and see witnesses: reeve
trentals, 565–6, 569, 579–80, 582, 584, 606, 671, 740, 832, 1836, 1839, 1930, 1936
Trippon, John, 2061
Tropenel
  Ric., 646–7
  Rog., 425
Trumper, John, 1836
Tucker
  Ellen, w. of Hen., 1311
  Hen., 1311
  Nic., chaplain, 1786, 1985
tuckers, *see* Bash; Belch; Bowbar; Brown; Chesham; Chilton; Collier; Gollan; Goss; Handley; Jakes; Langford; Leonard; Mabley; Poulton; Purchase; Richard at the mill; Richard at the stone; Wardour
Tull
  Joan, w. of Wm., dau. of Thos. Burford, 1856
  Wm., 1801, 1838, 1843, 1856, 2016, 2019–20, 2026, 2031, 2104; *and see* witnesses: reeve, citizen
Turk
  John, canon of cathedral church, 1193, 1536–8
  Thos., vicar of Downton, 1811–12, 1875
Twineham (Suss.), church of Christ, 668, 1938
Twyford, John, 1209, 1382–3
Tyldesley
  Hugh of, 2013
  Thos. of, 2013
Tyringham, John of, 298
Tytherley, West (Hants), manor of, 1066

Uffcott, Wm., chaplain, 503
Unwin, Sim., 1729
Upavon

Ric., vicar of cathedral church, 1560, 1566
(called Cutler) Wm. (d. by *c.* 1319), chaplain, 83
Wm. (fl. 1408), chaplain of St. Thomas's church, 1567, 1786, 1978, 1985–6
Upavon
  Cart bridge, 2155
  church, 2155
Uphill
  Alice, w. of Dominic, 1943
  Dominic, 1020, 1839, 1943, 2060
  Edith, w. of John (fl. before 1361), 692
  John (fl. before 1361), 595, 600, 692, 729, 745
  John (fl. 1406, another), 1943
Upton
  Agnes, w. of Edw., *see* Woodford
  Alice, 740
  Edith, w. of elder John, 341–4, 478
  (*otherwise* Steward) Edw. of, 332, 336, 603, 676, 705
  Hugh, 1486
  Joan, w. of Ric., 1247
  John (of), 341–4, 351, 356–8, 360, 424–6, 477–8, 502, 533, 535, 564, 569, 572, 586–7, 599, 616–17, 625, 628–9, 632, 637, 641–3, 646–7, 658, 664, 680–1, 685–6, 715–16, 719–23, 741, 751, 780–1, 785, 790, 929–30, 934–5, 989, 1093, 1193, 1211–12, 1244, 1254, 1458, 1486, 1754, 1795, 1797, 1832, 1836, 1895, 1954, 1990, 2048; *and see* witnesses: coroner, citizen; *see also* note on dating

John, s. of John, 1212
Margt., w. of elder John, 1212, 1486, 2048
Mary, w. of Wm., 1930
Peter of, 1254; *and see* Butterley
(called Baker) Ric., baker, 864, 878, 893, 914–15, 1114, 1247, 1400
Rog., 2048
the master Thos., 1486, 1729, 1930
Wm. of (fl. 1361), *see* witnesses: citizen
Wm. (d. 1405, ?another), 1944; will, 1930
Upton Scudamore, 477–8, 502, 1254, 1930
Norridge, *q.v.*
Upwell
  Maud, 441
  Nic., s. of John Winterbourne, 367, 429, 443
  Parnel, w. of Rog., 285
  Rog., 273, 285
  Wm., 365

Vellard
  Christine, 446
  Ellen, 117
  Thos., 446, 595, 673, 715
  Wm., 560
Viport, Thos., 1969–70
'vuere', at the, *see* John; Robert

Wade, John, brewer, and his w. Agnes, 1002
Wagain, Wm., draper, merchant, 365–7, *at* 404, 511, 546
Waite
  Hugh, 583
  John, hosier, tailor, 1320, 1432–3, 1481, 1759, 1761, 1784, 1819, 1821–2, 1841, 2094, 2106
  Maud, w. of John, 1432–3, 1481, 1759, 1761,

2094, 2106
Wm., 583
Walbourne, John, chaplain, 1399–1401, 1510
Walden, the lord Rog., clerk, 1688, 1694
Waldrich, Wm., 816
Walhampton (Hants), *see* ways
Wallingford, John of, 54
Wallington, Thos., 1373, 1386, 1593–4, 1667–9, 1671–3, 1676, 1688–9, 1691, 1693–5
Wallis
  Hen., friar, 1836
  John, 545
Wallop
  Agnes, *see* John at the wick
  Christine, w. of Rog. (?fl. 1398), 1869
  Edith, w. of John (d. 1361), 577
  Iseult, 108
  Joan, dau. of Rog. (?fl. 1398), *see* Hurst
  Joan, w. of Rog. (fl. 1377), 1049, ?1050
  John (fl. before 1361), carder, 604
  John (d. 1361, ?another), clothier, 577
  John of (fl. 1361, ?another), draper, 671, 718
  John of (fl. before 1365, ?one of above), 767
  John (of) (fl. 1377–1404, d. by 1405, ?another), draper, 1049–51, 1071, 1091, 1101, 1157, 1160, 1329, 1490, 1502, 1545, 1568, 1685, 1697, 1699, 1731–4, 1736–7, 1742, 1751, 1780, 1834, 1869, 1881–6, 1891, 1894, 1899, 1903, 1920–1, 1924, 1973, 1985, 1996, 1998, 2006–9, 2163; as mayor, 1491; *and see* witnesses: citizen

Maud, w. of John (d. by 1405), relict of Thos. Gilbert, 1329, 1884
Rog. of (fl. *c.* 1319), 108, 558, 618
Rog. (fl. 1377), 1049
Rog. (?fl. 1398, ?another), 1703, 1734, 1737, 1780, 1869, 1881, 1917, 1922, 2006–7
Thos., 577
Wm. of, butcher, 444, 629, 685
Wallop (*unspecified*, Hants), 47, 1882
Walrond, John, 20
Walsh, Hen., 767
Walter, 672
Walter, household servants of the name, 1680, 2029
Walter, provost of the college of St. Edmund's church, 625, 641
Walter, servant, 579
Walter at the burgh, 395, 399, 443, 579, 589; will, 816; as bailiff, 399; *and see* witnesses: bailiff
  his w. Isabel, 816
  his s. John, 816; *cf.* John at the burgh
Walter
  Parnel, w. of Wm., 1392
  Wm., 1392, 1777, 1796, 1841, 1853–4, 1858, 1867–8, 1878, 1883, 1886, 1896, 1923, 1932–4, 1945, 1950, 1985, 2039, 2081, 2109, 2124, 2127; *and see* witnesses: mayor, reeve, citizen
Waltham
  John, bishop of Salisbury, 1537
  Wm. of, 1688, 1694
Wansey, John, 1065, 1878
Wanstrow, Phil., carpenter, 1927

Wantage (Berks.), *see* ways
Warblington, Wm., escheator of Wiltshire, 2157
Ward
  Adam, *indexed as* Wardour
  John, citizen of London, 827
  Rog., 579, 668
Wardour
  (*otherwise* Ward) Adam, sealer, tucker, 1080, 1997, 1999–2000; will, 1992
  Agnes, dau. of Adam, *see* Collins
  Margt., w. of Adam, 1992, 1999
  Thos., 1992, 1997
Ware, John of, sequestrator of bishop of Winchester, 620
Wareham, Wm., 1676
Warin
  Gillian, w. of Rob., 149, 159
  Hen., collegiate chaplain of St. Edmund's church, 1871
  Maud, w. of Wm., sis. of Agnes Glover, 1936
  Rob., cook, 149, 159
  Wm., grocer, 1683, 1722, 1896, 1898–9, 1901, 1909, 1912, 1920–1, 1932–4, 1936, 1950, 1990, 2026, 2031, 2081, 2109, 2123–4, 2134–5, 2155; *and see* witnesses: mayor, reeve, citizen
Warlond, Thos., and his w. Maud, 1314
Warman, John, 566
Warminster
  Edith, *see* Farley
  Edw. of, 698
  Geof. (of), 566, 584
  John, 1930, 1944, 2061; *and see* witnesses: citizen
  Rob. of, vicar of

cathedral church, 510
Warminster, 1930
  address, 2027, 2117, 2133–5
Warmwell
  Agnes, w. of Wm., dau. of John Baldry, relict of John Doder, 556, 585–7, 594, 643, 832, 958
    her s. John, see Doder
  Joan, w. of Wm., relict of Wal. Ryborough, 974, 1697, 1699; will, 1685
  Rob., 1973, 2054; as keeper of St. Thomas's church, 2121
  Wm., 643, 725–6, 762, 832, 956, 958, 974, 992, 1087, 1161–2, 1222, 1229, 1243, 1288–9, 1301, 1315–16, 1321, 1335, 1341, 1403, 1410–11, 1437–8, 1459, 1484, 1516, 1527, 1612, 1655, 1685, 1697, 1699, 1711, 1717, 1723–4, 1746, 1750, 1760, 1783, 1806, 1817–18, 1859, 1882, 1885, 1890, 1896, 1898–9, 1920–1, 1924–6, 1959–60, 1962–3, 1971, 1973, 1985, 2004, 2042, 2046–7, 2069–70, 2080, 2082–3, 2085, 2104, 2122, 2153; as mayor, 1381; *and see* witnesses: citizen
Warneford, John, 597, 959
Warrener, Margt., w. of Ric., 200
Warwick, Wal., chaplain, 1741, 1743, 1760, 1804
water, at the, *see* Ingolf
Watercombe
  Agnes, w. of Rob., dau. of Wm. at the hurn, 2051, 2076, 2087
  Rob., 2051, 2076, 2087
Way
  Christine, w. of Rob., 1839

Edith, 1839
Joan, 1839
John, 1839
Margery, 1839
Rob., skinner, 1133, 1443; will, 1839
ways (repaired charitably), 553, 560, 566, 577, 671, 740, 1839, 1859, 1861, 1882, 1888, 1909, 1979, 1985, 2063–4, 2155
  Clarendon, 1979, 2011
  Colebrooke (Devon), 1979
  Hook (*unspecified*), 1979
  Langford (Devon), 1979
  Newnham hill (*unspecified*), 1979
  'Smalmalet' (*unidentified*), 1979
  Walhampton (Hants), 1979
  Wantage (Berks.), 1979
weald, at the, *see* Henry
weavers, *see* Barrett; Berwick; Bowyer; Breamore; Bride; Chapman; Clark; Clement; Collins; Coombe; Cousen; Dunning; Dyer; Ferring; Fish; Forest; Fry; Gage; Harnham; Hogman; Huish; Kimpton; Mead; Parch; Purbeck; Purdy; P...; Reynold; Ruddock; Salisbury; Saunder; Shipton; Shute; Slegge; Staggard; Stephens; Topp; Wells; Weston; Wickham; *and see* index 2: St. Edmund's church, light
weaving, art of, 2029, 2064
Webb
  Alex., 36–7
  Alice (Dogskin), w. of John (d. 1361), 653, 688
  Amice, w. of John (d.

1361), *see* Cross
John (d. 1361), fisher, 688; will, 653
John (fl. *c.* 1377), 1034
Ralph, 740
Sim., 740
well, at the, *see* Roger
Wells
  Agnes, w. of Ric., 1930
  Alice, w. of John (of) (fl. *c.* 1357), 397–8, 768
  Edith, w. of John of (fl. before 1364), 725–6, 762
    her dau. Agnes, *see* Horingham
    her s. Thos., 725, 762
  John (of) (fl. before and *c.* 1332, two of the name), 261
  John (of) (fl. *c.* 1357, ?another), tailor, 397–8, 768
  John of (fl. before 1361, ?another), 569
  John of (fl. before 1364, ?another), draper, 725–6, 762
  John (fl. *c.* 1381), 1156
  John (fl. *c.* 1391, ?same), weaver, 1466, 1496, 1504, 1795, 1797
  John (fl. 1404), butcher, 1863
  the lord John, 1871
  Ric., 1930
  Wm., 397–8, 768
Wells (Som.), 968, 1098
  cathedral church, canon of, *see* Bennett
  cloths of, 567
Wendover, Joan, w. of Ellis, 199
Werring, John, 1667–9, 1671–3, 1676, 1688–9, 1691, 1693–5
'Werton', Nic. of, and his w. Alice, 236
West
  Agnes, w. of Wm., 1535
  John, 1778
  Ric., 1380–1

Wm., baker, 1535, 1778, 2048
Westbury
 Joan, w. of John, 533
 John (of), 343–4, 533, 651, 798
 Rog. of, 550
 Wm., see witnesses: bailiff
Westbury, 690
Westminster, 703, 843–4, 1766, 1782, 1853–4, 1858, 1966, 2156
Weston
 Alice, w. of Ric., 1994, 2054
 John, Dominican friar, 668
 Ric., weaver, 1745, 1747, 1777, 1915–16, 1994, 2054, 2120, 2159
Westsby, Thos., 1851
Weyhill (Hants), church of, 1971
Weymouth, Cath., nun of Amesbury, 1871
Whaddon
 Margery, 1679
 Wm., 1271
Wheeler
 Ellen, 669
 Thos. (fl. before 1365), 770
 Thos. (fl. 1408), 2011–12
 Wm., 770
wheeler, see Franklin
wheelwrights, see index 2: market place where wheelwrights wait
Wherwell (abbey, Hants), nun of, see Luckham
Whichbury
 Agnes, relict of Gilb., 851–2, 862, 916
 Gilb. (of), 369, 371, 380, 390–1, 393, 434, 439, 465, 473, 479, 482, 490, 506, 549, 604, 607, 611–12, 614, 660, 667, 671, 680–1, 683, 686, 717, 719–23, 742–3, 767, 797, 822, 825, 850–2, 862, 916, 947,

1033, 1083, 1410, 1795, 1797; and see witnesses: reeve
 Nic., 607, 611, 614
White
 Adam, 1088, 2011
 Alice, 1888
 John (fl. c. 1318), 12
 John (fl. 1362), rector of Landford, 449–50, 578, 605, 636, 654, 715
 Maud, w. of Adam, 2011
Whitefoot, ygr. John, 98, 786
Whitehead, Agnes, 2011
Whitehorn
 Alice, dau. of Wm., 602, 617
 Alice, w. of Wm., see Longenough
 John (fl. before 1363), 696
 John (fl. 1413), 2169
 Olive, w. of John (fl. 1413), 2169
 Wm., hatter, 279, 602, 604, 617, 640, 670, 751
Whiteparish
 Alice, relict of Ric., 1609–10
 Ric., 1171–2, 1196, 1310, 1592, 1607, 1609–10
Whiteparish, vicar of, see Sexhampcote
Whitmore, John, 1750, 1938
Whitton
 Edith, 340
 John, 310
 Peter, 342
 Thos., 338–9, 342
 Thos., s. of Thos., 338–40
wick, at the, see John
Wick
 Gilb. of (fl. c. 1360), 469, 473, 637
 Gilb. (fl. 1406), 1940
 John, 739, 944, 961
Wickham
 Edith of, 1882
 Joan, relict of John (d. by c. 1387), 1288–9, 1291

 John, chaplain, 755, 760
 John (d. by c. 1387), 1288–9, 1291
 John (fl. 1409), 2029
Widhill, North (in Cricklade), 1152
Wight
 Mic. (of), 698, 776, 778
 Parnel, w. of Mic., 698
 Rog. of, 158
Wilcock, Nic., and his w. Christine, 1532
Wild, Wm., chaplain, 898
Wilkin, John, see Mayo
Willesden, Ric., 1938
William, apprentice, 1836
William, cook, 567
William, household servants of the name, 1859, 1936
William, parish priest of Mere, 1680
William, servants of the name, 567, 1909, 2011
William, vicar of Idmiston, 533, 646
William, workman, 1882
William at the bridge, dyer, 599, 747–8, 877, 923
 his w. Agnes, dau. of Hen. Smith, 748
 his s. Thos., 747–8, 877
William at the ford, 558
William at (in) the hurn, indexed as Hurn
William at the lea, and his w. Christine, 2146
Wilmington, John, 1549, 1925
Wilsford (?in Underditch hundred), church of, 1786
Wilton
 Joan, w. of Wm., butcher, 870, 1863
 John of, canon of cathedral church, rector of St. Thomas's church, 569, 599, 634, 671, 702
 Wm., butcher, 870, 1663, 1672, 1676, 1686–7,

1793, 1835, 1863, 1907
Wm., citizen of London,
    1287
Wilton (borough and
    suburbs), 655, 708,
    2104
  abbey
    abbess, see Beauchamp
    abbess and convent,
      690, 816
    altar, 690
    church of St. Edith,
      1740, 2104, 2169
    nuns, 2104, 2169; and
      see Romsey; Stone
    owner of property, 1740
  address, 613, 983, 1176,
    1920–1, 1968, 1980,
    1986, 2019–20, 2071–2,
    2104, 2169
  Bull bridge, 816, 2169
  burgesses, see Bunt; Stoke
  churches, 2104
    St. Giles, see Wilton:
      hospitals
    Holy Trinity, 1740
    St. Mary, 1740
    St. Michael, 1740, 1980,
      2104, 2169; rector's
      house, 2104
    St. Nicholas in Atrio,
      ?740, 1740
    St. Peter, 2169
  Dominicans, 1980, 2104
  Guildhall, 1740
  hospitals
    St. Giles, 671, 740,
      1861; church, 2104
    St. John, 2169
  mayor, see Hardy
  premises, 816, 1176, 1240,
    1740, 2104, 2169
    the Barns, 2169
    Boggle's Place, 2169
    Carentham's Corner,
      1740
    Castle mead, 2104
    Little moor, 2104
    Long ham, 2169
    Middle mead, 2104
    Scriven's mead, 1740
  streets

  Bullbridge, 1740
  Corn, 2169
  Kingsbury, 1740
  Little marsh, 1740
  Minster, 2104
  South, 1980, 2104, 2169
  West, 1740, 2104, 2169
Wiltshire
  John (of), 670, 705; will,
    603
  Maud, w. of John, 603
  Thos., 603, 705
Wiltshire
  coroner, see Harnham
  escheator, see Bernard;
    Warblington
  sheriff, 436, 843, 1853,
    2158–9; and see
    Charlton
Wimborne
  Hugh of, 755, 760, 1705
  John, canon of
    Christchurch, 1936
  Peter of, provost of
    the college of St.
    Edmund's church,
    1658
Wimborne Minster (Dors.),
  monastery of, 1720
Wimpler, Ric., 735
Wincanton (?surname),
  1864
Winchester
  Adam (of), 341–2, 345
  Agnes, w. of Wm., see
    Hawk
  Alice, w. of Wm., 299
  Cecily, w. of Wm., 346
  Edith, w. of John, dyer,
    56
  Edith, dau. of Wm., 286
  John of, cordwainer, 63
  John of, dyer, 56
  John (?another), 337–40
  Wm. of, dyer, 221, 293
  Wm. of (another or
    others), 286, 299,
    337–8, 346–7, at 360
  Wm. (?another), s. of
    Adam, 345
Winchester (Hants), 2055
  address, 496, 620, 1656–7

Augustinians, 567
bishop, see Edendon
Carmelites, 567, 584
(cathedral) church of St.
  Swithun
  dean, 584
  graveyard, 584
  relicts of St. Swithun,
    2055
church of St. Laurence,
  584
citizens, 68; and see
  Aubin; Haim; Inkpen;
  Pomeroy
cloths, 567
Dominicans, 567
Franciscans, 567
Hyde abbey, church, 626
Nunnaminster (nuns'
  monastery), 620
  chapel of Holy Trinity,
    620
Windsor
  Agnes, w. of Rob. of,
    169–70
  Rob. of, 169–70, 185
Winpenny, Hen., butcher,
  1588, 1740
Winslade, Hen., and his w.
  Margery, 689
Winslow, Wm., chaplain,
  1630–5, 1645, 1665,
  1684, 1693, 1695, 1721,
  1758, 1784, 1882
Winterbourne
  Agnes, w. of John (fl. c.
    1331), 227
  Alice, w. of Hugh, 1814,
    1864
  Alice, w. of John (fl. c.
    1323), 163
  Christine, w. of Hugh,
    1663
  Gillian, w. of John (fl. c.
    1360), 446
  Hugh (of), butcher, 627,
    703, 831, 941, 949,
    1015, 1131, 1663, 1762,
    1785, 1864, 1872, 1993,
    1995; will, 1814
  Isabel, w. of Hugh, 1864
  Iseult, w. of Rob., 59

Joan, w. of John (d. by *c.* 1354), 285, 367
John of (fl. *c.* 1323), 163
John of (fl. *c.* 1331, ?another), clerk, 227, 677
John (fl. *c.* 1332–6), 282
John (d. by *c.* 1354, ?same), tanner, 285, 367, 443
John (fl. *c.* 1360), 446, 569
John (d. by *c.* 1377, ?same), carpenter, 1030, 1076
Nic., *see* Upwell
Rob. of, 59, 211, 282
Winterbourne (*unspecified*), 130, 1875
Winterbourne Ford, Gillian, relict of John of, 640
Winterbourne Ford (in Laverstock), 1960; *and see* Ford
Winterslow
Hen. of, 31, 202
Hen. (?another), 290
Matt. of, 30
Wise
Alice, w. of John, 1781
Ellen, 1781
John: will, 1781
Margery, w. of Thos., 26, 48
Thos., 26, 48
Wishford
Alice, *see* Goss
John, 1452, 1492, 1517, 1545, 1665, 1692, 1749, 1755, 1772, 1786–8, 1909, 1961, 2009, 2024, 2057, 2061, 2063, 2073–5
Reynold, 2054
Wm. (of), draper, 369, 371–3, 377, 422–3, 461–2, 535, 557, 580, 585, 594, 600, 605, 622, 624, 636, 641, 645–7, 651, 654, 671, 715, 739–40, 744, 753, 769, 789, 802, 832, 865, 876, 893, 928, 977, 1067, 1246, 1350; *and see* witnesses: citizen
Witham (Som.), Carthusian priory of, 671; *cf.* Selwood
Withe, John, 31
Wither, Joan, 1971
Withes, John, 1719
Witts, Maud, 1954
Wolf, Rob., 1962–3, 1981, 2061, 2075
wood, at the, *see* Christine; John; Thomas
Woodborough
Alice, w. of Rob., *see* Body
Joan, 985, 1223, 1954
John, 504
Margt., 985
Rob., 1131, 1152, 1234, 2161, 2166–7
Wm. of, 504
Woodcock, Lucy, 1909
Woodford
Agnes of, w. of John, relict of Wm. Berwick and of Edw. of Upton (called Steward), 330, 332, 336, 417, 419, 558, 590, 618, 623, 625, 641, 644, 664, 673, 676, 679, 705, 741, 1011, 1693, 1695
her dau. Agnes, *see* Gill
Agnes, relict of Rob. (d. by *c.* 1351), 784
Alice, 1847
Cecily, w. of Rob. (d. 1362), 668
Edw. of, 22
Isabel, w. of Rob. (d. 1362), 668
John (of), 329–30, 336, 417, 419, 558, 590, 592, 625, 641, 644, 661, 664, 679, 741, 1011
Rob. (of) (d. by *c.* 1351), clothier, 163, 329, 572, 625, 641–2, 644, 654, 679, 692, 784
Rob. (of) (d. 1362), mercer, 545, 716, 733, 740, 1722; will, 668
Rog., 1733, 1736, 1840, 1847, 1924
(called 'Ele') Wm. of, 490; *cf.* Heal
Woodford
church of St. Margaret, 668
vicar, 668
Woodford, Little (in Woodford), church of, 1978
images, 1978
Woodhill
John of, apprentice, 671
Nic., 928, 951, 1148, 1566, 1693
Woodlands (in Mere), 1034
Woodroff, Wm., 1847
Woodrow
Alice, relict of Wm., draper, *see* Franklin
Beatrice, w. of Wm., weaver, 1888
Gillian, w. of Wm., weaver, 1888, 1893
Wm., draper, 1902
Wm., weaver, 1892–3, 2018; will, 1888
his sis. Agnes, and her dau. Margery, 1888
Woodway, Wm., 978, 1064
Woolbedding, Ralph, 601, 608
Woolmonger, Rog., 350–1
Wootton
Agnes, 1692, 1696
Alice, w. of Wm.: will, 571
Christine, w. of Wm., relict of Wm. Friend, 570, 608
Joan, relict of Wm., 1692, 1696–7
John (fl. 1361), 571
John (fl. 1409, ?same), 1710, 1758, 1829, 1831, 1904–5, 2011, 2022, 2078
Nic., 1692, 1696

Wm. (of), dyer, 558, 571,
    608, 618, 625, 641, 664,
    741, 744, 802, 925,
    974, 1551, 1685, 1692,
    1696; *and see* witnesses:
    citizen
Wootton (*unspecified*), 12
work, at the, *see* John
Wormell, Rog., 1909
Worms, 566
Worthy, Jarvis, 1714
'Wotthe', Hen., chaplain,
    668
Wraxall, John, chaplain,
    722–3, 785, 872, 883,
    966, 1332, 1779, 1873–
    5, 2025
writs, 68, 279, 316, 376,
    399, 436, 843, 1853,
    2026
    conventione, 247
    de cui in vita, 68, 223
    de dote, 177, 245
    ex gravi querela, 5, 66, 69,
        143, 204, 261, 282,
        1314
    de iudiciale, 147
    de libertate, 68
    de precipe, 238, 269, 277,
        283
    de precipe dum infra etatem,
        274
    de recto, 67, 71, 90, 126,
        130
    and see novel disseisin
Wrong
    Joan, 567
    Marion, 567
    Nic., 567
Wroughton, Thos., 1305
Wyatt, Wm., and his w.
    Gillian, 43
Wycombe (*unspecified*,
    Bucks.), church of,
    1837
Wylye
    Adam, 969
    Clarice, 166
    Isabel, w. of Nic., 86, 274
    John (fl. *c.* 1319), 86
    John (fl. 1379), 754, 763,
        969, 1104
    Nic. of, 36–7, 86, 253,
        274
Wymont, the lord Wm.,
    1680
Wyvil, Rob., bishop of
    Salisbury, 644, 661,
    679, 729, 745, ?847

Yate
    Joan, w. of John, 1290,
        1322–3, 1327, 1680
    John, burgess of ?Old
        Sarum, 1290, 1322–3,
        1327, 1558; will, 1680
Yeovil
    Joan, w. of Thos., dau.
        of Wm. Hurn, 1958,
        1966, 1972, 2050–1
    Thos., tailor, 1958, 1966,
        1972, 2050–1
Young
    Agnes, 1778
    John, 595

INDEX TWO

Salisbury: buildings, locations, and institutions

(Cottages, gardens, shops, and yards are indexed when they constitute the principal subject of a conveyance or devise. They are not indexed when they are specified only as appurtenances of a messuage or tenement separately indexed. Cross-references to forenames and surnames are to those listed in index 1; cross-references to witnesses are to the lists entered above index 1)

Almshouse, *see* Holy Trinity hospital
archdeaconry
 archdeacons, *see* Clowne; Harvey
 registrar's office, 1938
Avon, river (as a boundary), 476, 533, 841–2, 1516, 1691, 1767, 1869, 2013–14, 2158, 2168
Ayleswade bridge
 bequests, 566, 668–9, 671, 1786, 1979, 2063
 meadow towards, 140
 cf. bridge near St. Nicholas's hospital

bailiff, bishop's, 556
 presiding over the bishop's court, 66, 68–9, 71, 237, 241, 245, 247, 269, 274, 277, 279, 282–3, 399, 844, 1945
 and see court; witnesses
bakehouses, 604, 1635, 1880
Barnwell's cross, *see* New Street
bars, *see* Castle Street; Minster Street; New Street; Old Town; St. Martin's church (as a landmark)
 Milford bars, *see* Winchester Street

Beaminster Corner (Wineman Street), 864
Bedred Row (?Endless Street and Chipper Street), 1633
Bert's Corner (Culver Street and Wineman Street), 1807, 2065, 2071–2
bishop, 1985
 bailiff, *q.v.*
 chaplain (of the lord of the city), licence of, 1952
 court, *q.v.*
 liberties, 399, 844
 licences, 421, 679, 729, 745, 1537, 2088, 2100, 2158–9
 mill, 64, 2168
 owner of property, 64, 2168; *and see* Old Town
 surrenders into the hand of, 243, 262, 521–4, 601, 614, 632, 759, 766, 773, 776, 778, 783, 793, 818, 820, 834, 1665–7, 1707, 1747, 1774, 1776, 1787, 1810, 1812, 1818, 1845, 1852, 1857, 1901, 1911, 1914, 1916, 1948, 1957, 1963, 1970, 1975, 1988, 2007, 2028, 2035, 2037, 2044, 2047, 2068, 2113

 and see Erghum; Hallum; Martival; Poore; Waltham; Wyvil
bishopric, 224
Black bridge (in New Street), *see* Holy Trinity hospital; New Street
Brewery (on the way to the Dominican friary), 553
bridge near St. Nicholas's hospital, at the end of Drake Hall Street, bequest to, 1979; *cf.* Ayleswade bridge
bridges, *see* Ayleswade bridge; bridge near St. Nicholas's hospital; bridges in the market place; Fisherton, lower bridge; Fisherton, upper bridge; *and see (for cross-references)* Black bridge; *and see* index 1: bridges
bridges in the market place, bequest to, 1979
Brown Street
 common trench of running water, 1714–15, 1802–3, 1950
 cottages, 587, 643, 832, 884, 1211, 1283, 1410–11, 1436, 1549, 1790, 2048, 2073
 gardens, 832, 1714–15,

401

1802–3, 1925, 1927
gates, 585, 594, 1438,
  1790, 1932–4, 1950
kitchen, 1438
messuage, 661
piece of land, plot, 128,
  1711, 1714–15, 1723–4,
  1802–3
shops, 362–3, 472, 570,
  945, 1337; called
  Bakehouse, 1632
tenements, chief, 637,
  1790
tenements, corner, 20,
  72, 329–30, 423, 533,
  605, 623, 634, 636,
  702, 785, 865, 872,
  876, 928, 966, 1299,
  1337, 1339, 1350–9,
  1367, 1402–3, 1422,
  1435, 1535, 1693, 1695,
  1932–4, 1950, 2069–
  70, 2073; *and see* Bull
  Hall; Cheese Corner;
  Stint's Corner
tenements (other), 24,
  ?28, 38, 57, 125, 364,
  417, 473, 475, 489,
  497, 535, 587, 607,
  634, 637, 643, 646,
  651, 661, 670, 677,
  702, 725–6, 762, 785,
  1026, 1030, 1034,
  1045, 1063, 1074,
  1076–7, 1121, 1255,
  1289, ?1291, 1317,
  1437, 1440, 1532,
  1600, 1631, 1693,
  1695, 1711, 1714–15,
  1723–4, 1802–3, 1806,
  1925, 1927, 1933,
  1950, 1962–3, 2048,
  2069–70, 2073; on the
  way to St. Edmund's
  church, 752–3
tenement extending to,
  664, 741
Workhouse, *q.v.*
yards, 469, 1925, 1927
Buckland's Place (in Freren
  Street), 1300, 1964
Bug moor, meadow, 1764,

1896, 1964, 1977
buildings (named), *see
  (for cross-references)*
  tenements (other)
Bull Hall (Brown Street
  and Winchester
  Street), 100, 865, 876,
  1645, 1886, 1932, 1934
Bunt's Place (in Minster
  Street called Castle
  Street), 2023, 2030,
  2058–9
Butcher Row (called Pot
  Row), the butchers'
  street
shops, corner, 361, 392,
  434, 850
shops (other), 382, 384,
  535, 628, 756, 831,
  850, 870, 1079, 1143,
  1188, 1211–12, 1257,
  1521, 1588, 1618, 1786,
  1815, 1862, 2048
tenements, 92, 527, 672,
  831, 918, 1943, 2060,
  2062; opposite the
  butchers' stalls, 116;
  extending towards the
  market place, 2060,
  2062
and see Pot Row; ways
butchers' shambles, 1725
butchers' stalls, Butchery
shops, 240, 415, 418, 573,
  615, 626, 780–1, 851,
  882, 1520, 1534, 1556,
  1727, 1740, 1895
shops opposite, 17; *and
  see* Pot Row
tenements, corner, 573,
  615, 896, 1028; *and see*
  Chantrell's Corner
tenement, corner,
  opposite, 99
tenement (other),
  opposite, *see* Butcher
  Row

Carter Street
bakehouse, 604
cottages, 720–1
gardens, 868, 1698, 1843

meadows beside, 810
messuage, 1683
shops, 445, 491, 496,
  552, 604, 612, 731,
  810, 847–8, 891, 1146,
  1552, 1615, 1637,
  1656–7, 1659, 1679,
  1711, 1723–4, 1823–5,
  1843
tenements, chief, 479,
  637, 810, 1843
tenements, corner, 12,
  343–4, 445, 478, 502,
  720–1, 1236, ?1497;
  and see Dyne's Corner
tenements (other), 113,
  243, 313, 362–3, 468,
  478, 482, 502, 536,
  552, 604, 612, 617,
  637, 670, 672, 674,
  684, 751, 785, 877–8,
  810, 830, 872, 912–13,
  1056, 1089, 1147,
  1259–60, 1264–5,
  1271, 1284, 1430,
  1437, ?1497, 1591,
  1599–1600, 1606,
  1613–14, 1616, 1625,
  1628–9, 1656–7, 1659,
  1679, 1683, 1698,
  1702, 1711, 1723–4,
  1755, 1801, 1806,
  1838, 1843, 1962–3,
  1981, 2026, 2031,
  2061, 2075; beside the
  Close, 720–1; beside
  a trench, 731; *and see*
  Guys's Place
yards, 604
and see high street
Castle Street (beyond the
  bar)
cottages, 885, 892, 1156,
  1306, 1308, 1460,
  1496, 1655, 1703,
  1734–5, 1737, 1754,
  1836, 1859, 1903,
  1913–14, 1990
garden, 1903
gates, 1869, 1881–2,
  1891, 1917, 1922,
  2006–8, 2163

INDEX OF SALISBURY LOCATIONS, ETC

lane where horses are watered, 1731–2, 1734, 1737
messuages, 678, 1697, 1699, 1834, 1849, 1852, 1855, 1857, 1969–70, 2158; beside the graveyard of St. Thomas's church, 2158
plots, 1245, 1917, 1922
shops, 599, 1304, 1456, 1584, 1703, 1882, 1889–90
tenement, chief, 1734, 1737, 1780, 1891
tenements, corner, 1059, 1880, 1882, 1918–19
tenements (other), 164, 299, 472, 474, 540, 678, 892, 950, 961, 1050–1, 1070–1, 1141, 1152, 1187, 1194, 1208, 1233, 1238, 1289, ?1291, 1298, 1310, 1348–9, 1365–6, 1370, 1393, 1489, 1513, 1531, 1533, 1571–2, 1580, 1592, 1607–10, 1642–4, 1654, 1697, 1699, 1703–4, 1728, 1731–2, 1734–5, 1737, 1753–4, 1772–4, 1780, 1814, 1828, 1832, 1834, 1836, 1849, 1852, 1855, 1857, 1859, 1864, 1869, 1876, 1881–2, 1889–91, 1894, 1897–9, 1903, 1913–14, 1917–18, 1920–2, 1928, 1969–70, 1976, 1982, 1990, 1993, 1995, 2006–8, 2010, 2104, ?2126, 2128, 2130, 2132, 2138–9, 2144–5, 2158, 2163
tofts, 1881, 1903, 2006–7; extending to the Avon, 1869
yards, 885, 892
and see Minster Street
cathedral church
acolytes, bequests to,
1753, 1778, 1882
altars
bequest, 1938
matins, 648
St. Thomas the Martyr, 704, 729, 745; *and see* chapels
bells, 1778
bequests, 543, 548–51, 553–4, 556–9, 564–6, 568–71, 577–82, 595, 599, 603, 619, 623, 648, 666, 668–9, 671, 690, 692, 694, 698, 735, 740, 749, 786, 816, 831–2, 1664, 1680, 1719–20, 1729–30, 1740, 1753, 1778, 1781, 1783, 1786, 1814, 1836, 1838, 1859–61, 1882, 1888, 1909, 1936, 1938, 1943, 1971, 1979–80, 1985, 2011, 2029, 2038, 2042, 2061, 2063–5, 2104, 2154–6, 2160, 2169
canons
bequests to, 786, 1753, 1882, 1938
liberties, 844
owners of property, 1193
and see Citterne; Gough; Harvey; Maidenhead; Pitts; Southam; Spaldwick; Stratford; Turk; Wilton
chancellor, bequest to, 1753
chapels
St. Edmund's, 1882
of the Blessed Mary, 1753
(or altar) of St. Thomas the Martyr, 816; chantry, 816; *and see* altars
chaplains
annual, bequest to, 1882
vicar, bequest to, 671
and see Caundle
choristers
bequests to, 1753, 1882
owners of property, 613, 2005
Close
Common Hall, *q.v.*
east gate, 96, 362–3, 579, 588, 613, 673, 2040; fraternity of St. Anne's light, 579
dwelling house, 1882
as a landmark, *q.v. (for cross-references)*
north gate, 692
tenements, 235
trench, 731
crosses, bequests to
above the door of the choir, 666
above the door of St. Thomas's chapel, 666
and see fraternities, images, lights
dean, bequest to, 1753; *and see* Chandler; Montagu
dean and chapter, 224
endowment, 421, 704
licences, 2100, 2158–9
owner of property, 93, 439–40, 521, 549, 661, 729, 745, 757, 1538, 1730, 1805, 1850, 2005, 2165
fabric
keepers, 569
rent payable to, 105
fraternities, images, lights
altar cloth, 666
candle, 203
great cross, 551
high cross, 579, 581, 668–9, 735, 831, 1909; keepers as owners of property, 1703
Holy Cross above the door of St. Thomas's chapel, 666, 2064–5
of the Blessed Mary at the south door, 1778
of the Blessed Mary at

the west door, 566,
569, 579, 648, 666,
668
and see Close: east gate
graveyard, interments in,
569, 1729, 1778, 1882
matins clerk, *see* Caundle
precentor, bequest to,
1753
priests, chantry, bequest
to, 1753
sacristans, bequests to,
1753, 1778, 1882
their boys, 1753, 1778
subdeans, *see* Glinton;
Summerhill
treasurer, bequest to,
1753
treasury, 1729
under-treasurer, *see*
Netton
vicars
bequests to, 786, 816,
1720, 1753, 1778,
1786, 1882
owners of property,
138, 239, 1193, 1779,
1811–12, 1817–18,
1873–5, 1879, 1938,
2088–90, 2112–13
and see Axbey; Boor;
Botwell; Buck;
Charlton; Crichel;
Dean; Duckman;
Everard; Gilbert;
Gore; Groom;
Iwerne; James;
Kilmeston; Langford;
Oakford; Paviour;
Sutton; Titling;
Upavon; Warminster
Cavenasser's Corner, 980
cellars, 111, 160, 179, 393–
4, 404, 671, 735, 806,
816, 1727, 1823–5,
2056, 2103, 2158
Chantrell's Corner
(Butchery and
Winchester Street),
573, 615, 1110, 1727
Cheese Corner (?Brown
Street and Winchester
Street), ?28, 179, 345–
6, 350–1, 1506, 1522
Chipper Lane, 1865
cottages, 1468–70, 1648,
1816
tenements, 170, 1108–9,
1329, 1816
Chipper Street, 1856
cottages, 118, 712, 734,
738, 1111, 1128, 1182–
3, 1226, 1581, 1918,
2104
messuages, 694, 1796
shops, 442, 537, 1798–9
tenements, corner, 557,
744, 802, 1402–3,
1479–80, 1574–5,
1798–9, 1880, 1918–
19; beside a trench,
1775–6; *and see* Bedred
Row
tenements (other), 25,
39, 53, 557, 694, 712,
734, 738, 743–4, 802,
1796, 1884, 2021
yards, 118, 953, 1015,
1131
Chipping Place (street
called), tenements
opposite the market
place where grains are
sold, 1856
city (of New Salisbury)
bailiff, *see* bailiff, bishop's
bars, *q.v.* (for cross-
references)
beadsmen, bequest to,
2029
charters of liberties, 844
coroners, *q.v.*
council house, 476
court (bishop's), *q.v.*
customs, 14, 21
gaols, *see* index 1:
prisoners
Guildhall, 1928; *and
see* Guildhall (as a
landmark); index 1:
prisoners
liberties, 64, 68, 206,
217, 316–17, 376, 436,
844
mayor
bequest, 2064
examiner, 1945
letters patent, 1381
master of Holy Trinity
hospital, 1766, 1782,
1791, 1951
overseer, 577, 786,
1717, 1786, 1938, 2064
presiding over the
bishop's court, 237,
241, 247, 399
recipient of security,
553, 556, 671, 832
remainder man, 2051
trustee, 543, 625, 641,
1387, 1786, 1985, 2121
witness, 549
and see, Becket;
Berwick; Britford;
Harding; Richman;
Taylor; Teffont;
Wallop; Warmwell;
witnesses
mayor and commonalty
(citizens), 224
bequests, 543, 577,
1985, 1994, 2029
devise, 534
grants to, 642, 673,
2158
licences to acquire
property, 1931, 2100,
2157–9
owners of property,
784, 856, 865, 1896,
2158–9
remainder men, 1316,
1319
pillories, *q.v.*
serjeants (-at-mace), *see*
index 1: prisoners
ward, *see* Mead
and see ditches; trenches
Clark's Place (Gigant
Street and St. Martin's
Street), 1336, 1909,
2005
Close, canons', (as a
landmark)
cottages, *see* St. Martin's
Street

INDEX OF SALISBURY LOCATIONS, ETC

tenements, *see* Carter
  Street; Drake Hall
  Street; Minster Street;
  St. Martin's Street
Cold Corner, 1985
Common Hall (in the
  Close), 1882
Cordwainer Row
  messuages (shops)
    opposite, *see* Poultry
    shops, 441
  shops opposite Poultry,
    443
  tenement, 1377, 1452
coroners, 64; *and see*
  Powell; witnesses
court (bishop's, held for
  the city), 93, 163, 244,
  399, and *passim*; *and
  see* bailiff, bishop's;
  witnesses: clerk; *see
  also* note on dating
Cowhouse, 1806
cross called Powell's corner,
  tenement opposite,
  1093; *and see* Powell's
  Corner
cross (high cross) where
  fruit is sold, *see*
  Ironmonger Row
cross where fruit and
  vegetables are sold,
  tenements opposite,
  698, 860, 1730
cross (high cross) where
  fruit and other victuals
  are sold, corner
  tenement opposite,
  806, 971; *and see*
  Hampton's Corner;
  Powell's Corner
cross where hay is sold,
  tenements opposite,
  1725
Culver Street
  cottages, 91, 358, 383,
    414, 444, 480, 554,
    629, 685, 732, 774,
    776, 819–20, 824–5,
    951, 962–3, 1078,
    1138, 1148, 1155, 1186,
    1190, 1325–6, 1416,

1487, 1563, 1681–2,
  1701, 1704, 1709, 1713,
  1807, 1809–10, 1861,
  1867–8, 1904–5, 1937,
  1953, 2065, 2071–2,
  2110; extending to the
  city's ditch, 2110
gardens, 1710, 1974–5
gates, 649, 657, 1681–2,
  1809–10, 1953
messuage, corner, *see*
  Holy Ghost Corner
messuages (other), 494,
  601, 761, 789
plot, corner, 749–50
plot (other), 895
shops, 358, 774, 776,
  1681–2, 1791, 2065
tenements, corner, 413,
  440, 478, 502, 508,
  521, 629, 673, 685,
  732, 757, 1094, ?1418,
  1579, 1622–4, 1658,
  1701, 1709, 1713, 1729,
  1750; *and see* Bert's
  Corner; Holy Ghost
  Corner; Ive's Corner;
  Warr's Corner
tenements (other), 91,
  135, 234, 302, 313,
  601, 608, 633, 673,
  750, 761, 767, 774,
  776–8, 789, 819–20,
  822, 824–5, 886, 892,
  903, 1207, 1253, 1309,
  1368, 1417, ?1418,
  1654, 1658, 1701,
  1704, 1729, 1791,
  1807, 1809–10, 1937,
  1945, 1952–3, 2048
yards, 433, 633, 767, 984,
  1055, 1102, 1904–5,
  1952, 2022, 2078, 2081
Culver Street, called
  Mealmonger Street
messuage, 2080, 2083
tenements, 2066, 2080,
  2083

ditch (defensive), 1179,
  ?1472–3, ?1490, 1954,
  ?2146

city's ditch, 1665, 1708,
  1949, 1951, 1967, 2110
ditches (watercourses),
  ?1472–3,?1490, 1840,
  1895, 1968, ?2146
common ditch of the
  city, 2067–8
great ditch of the city,
  1765
new ditch of the city,
  1764
(called the Trench), 582
and see trenches
Dominican friary (in
  Fisherton Anger) (as a
  landmark)
Brewery, *q.v.*
plot on the way to, 553
tenement, chief, on the
  way to, 553
tenements (other) on
  the way to, 553, 1688,
  1694, 2013–14
and see ways
cf. Minster Street
Dominicans (of Fisherton),
  599
bequests, 543, 549, 554,
  565–7, 569, 578–80,
  583, 606, 668, 671,
  690, 692, 740, 786,
  831–2, 1664, 1719–20,
  1730, 1740, 1753,
  1778, 1783, 1814,
  1828, 1839, 1859, 1871,
  1888, 1909, 1936,
  1943, 1971, 1985, 2011,
  2029, 2063–4, 2104,
  2155–6
church, 599
altar, 1836
chalice, 543
choir, 1836
interments, 543, 599,
  1826, 2063
friars, bequests to, 671,
  1786, 1836, 1860–1,
  1882, 1985
friars (named), *see* James;
  Langford; Sprot;
  Weston
graveyard, 583

pittance, 671, 1786
priests, 1836
dovecots, 411, 449–51, 492, 543, 554, 558, 616, 618, 621, 885, 892, 1057, 1431, 1655, 1703, 1867–8, 1936
Drake Hall, 472
Drake Hall Street
  common ditch of the city, 2067–8
  cottages, 680, 723, 728, 916, 924, 1332, 1779, 1805, 1811–12, 1850, 1860, 1873–5, 2025, 2067–8, 2095, 2165
  gardens, 351, 478, 502
  meadow, 426, 477, 2048, 2067–8
  messuages, 519, 626, 973
  school, grammar, and schoolhouse, *q.v.*
  shops, 1488, 1670, 1805, 1850, 2165
  tenements, 472, 510, 680–1, 722–3, 728, 1340, 1670, 1744, 1779, 1811–12; opposite the east gate of the Close, 362–3; *cf.* Drake Hall
  yards, 347, 907, 917, 1211, 2048
  and see bridges; ways
Dyne's Corner (Carter Street and Winchester Street), 1645

End Street, *see* High Street
Endless Street
  cottage, corner, beside the street leading to St. Edmund's church, 800, 812, 823
  cottages in front of a trench, 2027–8
  cottages (other), 690, 800, 812, 823, 932, 1002, 1108–9, 1120, 1421, 1994, 2029, 2054
  messuages, 694, 871, 1223, 1433

shops, 485–6, 690, 964–5, 988, 1432, 1759, 1761, 1791, 2029, 2099; opposite the market place where pelts and fleeces are sold, 1689, 1695
tenements, chief, 558, 626, 2029, 2099
tenements, corner, 472, 516, 523, 558, 574–6, 610, 729, 745, 831, 932, 957, 1266, 1288, 1290–1, 1312, 1341–3, 1479–80, 1550, 1574–5, 1639, 1775–6, 1865, 1882, 1888, 1892–3, 2137, 2147; *and see* Bedred Row; Vellard's Corner
tenements (other), 489, 504, 506, 516, 558, 574–6, 579, 581, 587, 605–6, 610, 635–6, 652, 664, 690, 694–5, 729–30, 741, 745, 786, 804, 846, 849, 854, 867, 936, 954, 959, 985, 1000, 1037, 1168, 1200, 1209, 1239, 1268, 1286, 1292, 1322–4, 1327, 1347, 1382–6, 1467, 1474, 1495, 1530, 1559, 1583, 1587, 1589–90, 1595, 1636, 1680, 1753, 1759, 1761, 1777, 1787–8, 1791, 1865, 1888, 1955, 1965, 1978, 1994, 2027–9, 2054, 2079, 2093–4, 2096, 2099, 2105, 2154; opposite the market place where pelts and fleeces are sold, 1689, 1695
yards, 1002, 1112, 1123, 1129, 1142, 2027–8
and see high street

fish-yard, 543
fishermen's stalls

shops, 986, 1163–4
shops opposite, 460, 1689, 1695, 1786, 1792, 1794, 1978
tavern opposite, 1978
tenement, corner, opposite, 1978; *and see* Lime's Corner
tenements (other) opposite, 1122, 1689, 1695, 1792, 1794
Fisherton, tenement on the way to, 47
Fisherton, lower bridge, tenement beside (towards), 998, 1023, 1048; *and see* New Street
Fisherton, upper bridge, bequests to, 668, 671, 1786
Fisherton, upper bridge (as a landmark)
  gate in the street on the way to, 2116
  mill near, 2168
  shop in the street on the way to, 1767, 2168
  tenement, corner, *see* Wimpler's Corner
  tenements (other): at the east end of, beside, in the street on the way to, 35, 877, 994, 1153, 1184, 1277, 1387, 1767, 2013–14, 2116, 2118, 2121, 2168; on the way to, near the graveyard of St. Thomas's church, 1526–9
Fishmonger Row, tenement, corner, 502
Florentine's Corner (Minster Street and New Street), 512, 682, 689, 691, 1333, 1463–5, 1477–8
Focket Place (Gigant Street and St. Martin's Street), 1192, 2005
Franciscan friary (as a

INDEX OF SALISBURY LOCATIONS, ETC   407

landmark)
cottage beside, 935
ditch called the Trench opposite, 582
tenements opposite, 362–3, 582, 687, 1284
cf. Freren Street
Franciscans
  bequests, 549, 554, 565–7, 569, 579–80, 582, 606, 668–9, 671, 690, 692, 740, 786, 816, 831–2, 1664, 1719–20, 1740, 1753, 1778, 1783, 1786, 1814, 1828, 1836, 1839, 1859, 1871, 1888, 1909, 1936, 1943, 1971, 1985, 2011, 2029, 2063–4, 2104, 2155–6
  chantry, 816
  church, 816
  close, 446, 640
  friars, bequests to, 671, 1861, 1882, 1985
  friars (named), see Breamore; New
  gate, 935, 1301, 1896
  pittance, 671
  wall, 1964, 1977
fraternities, 577, 668–9, 735, 831, 1703, 1954, 1971, 2064
Freren Street
  cottages, 568, 582, 924, 992, 1690, 1763, 1765, 1896, 1964, 1969–70, 1977, 2156
  gardens, 568, 582, 993, 1124, 1149, 1763, 1765, 1896, 2156
  meadow, 810, 2067–8
  messuages, 570, 639, 905, 1204, 1969–70; and see Buckland's Place
  plot, 45
  shops, 507, 1621
  tenement, corner, 1896
  tenements (other), 297, 570, 582, 632, 639–40, 658, 775, 788, 1441; beside a trench, 82

tofts, 446, 482, 640, 883, 979
trench(es), 582; near Bug moor, 1964, 1977
yards, 470, 775, 788, 869, 924, 952, 1012–14, 1022, 1024, 1032, 1106, 1113, 1169, 1690, 1706–7, 1964, 1977
cf. Franciscan friary (as a landmark)

Gatehouse (in Winchester Street), 1719
gates, 96, 362–3, 579, 585, 587–8, 594, 613, 618, 649, 657, 673, 692, 719, 721, 935, 1301, 1438, 1681–2, 1734, 1737, 1742, 1780, 1790, 1806, 1809–10, 1869, 1881–2, 1891, 1896, 1917, 1922, 1932–4, 1949, 1952, 2006–8, 2011, 2039–40, 2116, 2118, 2121, 2163
George's Inn (in Minster Street), 1985, 2063, 2158
Gigant Street
  cottages, corner, on the way to St. Edmund's church, 1896, 2124
  cottages (other), 535, 586–7, 602, 643, 648, 669, 675, 683, 798, 832, 922, 931, 982, 1017, 1085, 1145, 1321, 1492, 1507, 1596, 1603–4, 1783, 1814, 1830, 1872, 1896, 1909, 2039, 2153; on the way to St. Edmund's church, 949, 2120, 2159
  gardens, 592–3, 1501, 1745, 1747, 1814, 1872, 1925–6, 2036–7, 2041; on the way to St. Edmund's church, 1915–16

gate, 2039
messuage, corner, 1830
messuages (other), 417, 853, 2039, 2153; on the way to St. Edmund's church, 2159
piece of land, 18
plots, 593, 1132, 1459
shop, corner, 335
shops (other), 607, 614, 945, 1321
tenements, corner, 215, 225, 319, 402, 607, 784, 832, 856, 974, 978, 1040, 1091, 1101, 1191–2, ?1388–92, 1560, 1566, 1634, 1685, 1696, 1717, 1789, 1833, 1844–5, 1909, 2036–7, 2041, 2064, 2101; and see Clark's Place; Focket Place; Ro Corner
tenements (other), 33, 49, 78, 129, 310, 457, 562, 591–3, 602, 607, 614, 631, 645, 648, 669, 675, 683, 696, 769, 798, 805, 813–14, 832, 835, 861, 897, 1006–7, 1021, 1029, 1096, 1103, 1150, 1344, 1448, 1493–4, 1501, 1517, 1567, 1685, 1696, 1700, 1717, 1745, 1747, 1783, 1789, 1820, 1833, 1844–5, 1887, 1925–6, 2039, 2064, 2101, 2122, 2129, 2131, 2153; on the way to St. Edmund's church, 1915–16, 2120
toft, 475
yards, corner, 514–15, 609, 1088
yards (other), 645, 769, 832, 1925–6; on the way to St. Edmund's church, 1915–16, 2120, 2159
Glasshouse, the, 749
Glastonbury's Corner (?in

Winchester Street: *cf.*
 Stratford's Corner),
 2127
Grandon's Corner
 (Wineman Street and
 opposite the market
 place), 1219, 2015,
 2017
Guildhall (as a landmark)
 messuage opposite, *see*
  high street
 shops: near, 566;
  opposite, 832
 tenement, chief,
  opposite, 832
 tenement, corner, on the
  south side, 69
 tenements (other)
  opposite, 467, 522,
  697, 1318, 1444–5,
  1454–5; *and see* high
  street
 gutters, 1434, 1926–7,
  2106–7
Guys's Place (in Carter
 Street), 1823–5, 2005;
 and see 810, 1591,
 1659, 1679, 1702,
 1806, 1838

Hampton's Corner
 (opposite the high
 cross where fruit and
 other victuals are sold;
 in Wheeler Row),
 623, 736, 806
high street
 (called Carter Street)
  tenement, 80
 (called End Street)
  tenements, 699
 (called Endless Street)
  messuage, opposite the
  Guildhall, 661
  shops, 63
  tenements, opposite
   the Guildhall, 661
 (called Minster Street)
  tenements, 841–2,
  2005
 (*unspecified*)
  shops, 142

  tenement, corner, 109
  tenements (other), 1, 3,
   31, 61–2, 112
Holy Ghost Corner
 (Culver Street and
 Winchester Street),
 1710, 2022, 2078, 2081
Holy Trinity hospital
 (hospital of the
 Holy Trinity and
 of St. Thomas of
 Canterbury, called
 Almshouse) (in New
 Street, beside Black
 bridge)
 bequests, 1719, 1783,
  1859, 1861, 1882, 1888,
  2011, 2104, 2154–5
 chaplains, 1979
 community, 1971
 paupers, 1720, 1778,
  1979, 1985, 2063–4
 endowment, 1766, 1782,
  1791
 masters, *see* city of
  Salisbury: mayors;
  Harding
 owner of property, 1848,
  1900–1, 1946, 1949,
  1952, 1977, 2027–8,
  2048, 2101
 overseer, *see* Agnes
 seal, 1952
 under-keeper, *see*
  Chandler
 and see New Street
hospitals, *see* Holy Trinity;
 St. Nicholas's; *and see*
 index 1: Old Sarum;
 Wilton
Hott Corner, tavern,
 (?Minster Street and
 New Street: *cf.* the
 Rose), 477

inns, *see* George's Inn;
 New Inn; Pinnock's
 Inn; *and see (for cross-
 references)* taverns
Ironmonger Corner (part
 of a street: ?Minster
 Street), 1895

Ironmonger Row
 shops, 782–3, 927, 933,
  940, 2002–3
 tenement, corner, 850;
  (?same) opposite the
  high cross where fruit
  is sold, 483
Ive's Corner
 (Mealmonger/Culver
 Street and Wineman
 Street), 533, 1746,
 1848, 1851, 1959–60,
 2004, 2071–2

kitchens, 1438, 1806, 1843,
 1882

lane where horses are
 watered, *see* Castle
 Street
Lime's Corner (opposite
 the fishermen's stalls),
 975, 1115–16

market place
 bequest for pavement,
  1786
 premises opposite, 908
 shop opposite, 1218
 tenement, corner,
  opposite, *see*
  Grandon's Corner
 tenements (other):
  extending towards,
  see Butcher Row;
  Pot Row; in, 122,
  877; opposite, 305,
  333–4, 468, 908, 968,
  1065, 1090, 1100,
  1137, 1139, 1185, 1228,
  1449–51, 1585–6,
  2015; opposite, *see also*
  Wheeler Row
 and see bridges
market place where fish are
 sold, corner tenement
 opposite, 567
market place where fleeces
 are sold, wool is sold
 tenement, corner,
  opposite, 572
 tenements (other)

INDEX OF SALISBURY LOCATIONS, ETC   409

opposite, 572, 625,
    641–2, 654, 1242, 1491
market [place] where
    fleeces and the yarns
    of wool are sold,
    tenements opposite,
    2005
market place where grains
    are sold
  shops opposite, 1860,
    2051, 2076
  tenement, chief,
    opposite, 564, 739
  tenement, corner,
    opposite, 1860, 1942
  tenements (other)
    opposite, 102–3,
    564, 599, 663, 739,
    909, 911, 1154, 1213,
    1364, 1860, 1878,
    1942, 2016, 2019–20,
    2049–51, 2076, 2087,
    2104; *and see* Chipping
    Place; Minster Street
market place where grains
    and linen cloth are
    sold
  tenement, corner,
    opposite, adjoining
    Minster Street, 2057
  tenement (other)
    opposite, 2057
market place where linen
    cloth is sold, tenement
    opposite, 748
market place where pelts
    and fleeces are sold,
    see Endless Street
market place where pewter
    is sold, tenement,
    chief, opposite, 543
market place where
    wheelwrights wait,
    tenements opposite,
    255, 770
market place where
    yarn, linen cloth,
    and woollen cloths
    are sold, tenements
    opposite, 1786
Martin's Croft
  cottages, 509; near

the graveyard of St.
    Edmund's church,
    1785; on the way to
    St. Edmund's church,
    1762
garden opposite the
    graveyard of St.
    Edmund's church,
    1756–7
messuage, *see* Rolleston,
    street called
racks, 557, 1837
tenements, 786
yards, 557, 1232; on the
    way to St. Edmund's
    church, 1800
mayor, *see* city of Salisbury;
    witnesses
Mead ward, 144
meadow land (located),
    see Ayleswade bridge;
    Carter Street; Drake
    Hall Street; St.
    Nicholas's hospital;
    and see Bug moor
Mealmonger Street
  cottages, 643, 736, 779,
    826, 831, 888, 972,
    1207, 1243, 1261, 1330,
    1746, 1754, 1836,
    1959–60, 1984, 1989,
    2004, 2046–7, 2082;
    on the way from a
    gate of the college of
    St. Edmund, 587
  messuage, corner, *see*
    Ive's Corner
  tenement, corner,
    1959–60; *and see* Ive's
    Corner
  tenements (other),
    779, 831, 983, 1754,
    1836, 1984, 1989,
    2082, 2149; *and see*
    Rolleston
  yard, 2038
  and see Culver Street,
    called Mealmonger
    Street
messuages, corner (named),
  see (for cross-references)
    tenements, corner

messuages (other) (named),
  see (for cross-references)
  tenements (other)
mill, *see* bishop
Minster Street
  building above a stile
    of the graveyard of
    St. Thomas's church,
    1691
  cottages, 1307, 1443,
    1749
  council house, *see* city
  gate, 618
  land, 1320
  messuages, ?421, ?644,
    1508, 1769; near
    the graveyard of St.
    Thomas's church,
    2112–13; opposite a
    field, 1768, 1770–1;
    and see George's Inn
  shops, corner, 589, 748,
    ?1477–8, 2104; near
    the graveyard of St.
    Thomas's church, 429
  shops (other), 23, 110,
    152, 335, 397–8, 403,
    421, 458, 464, 477,
    487, 500, 531, 549,
    579, 598, 619, 627,
    694, 729, 735, 737,
    745–6, 768, 816, 821,
    836, 873, 910, 1117–18,
    1133, 1151, 1196, 1220,
    1275–6, 1395, 1660,
    1674, 1677–8, 1688,
    1694, 1741, 1752,
    1839, 1846, 1943,
    1968, 2158; beside a
    stile of the graveyard
    of St. Thomas's
    church, 758–9; near
    that graveyard, 1019,
    2112–13
  tavern, 1769; *and see*
    Hott Corner
  tenements, chief, 549,
    729, 737, 745, 1630,
    1749
  tenements, corner, 477,
    505, 530, 557, 577,
    589, 744, 802, 879,

894, 1752, 1968;
and see Florentine's
Corner; Hott Corner;
market place where
grain and linen cloth
are sold; Rose, the;
Wimpler's Corner
tenements (other), 13,
16, 26, 48, 51–2, 55–6,
65, 70, 75, 88, 106–7,
172, 210, 214, 231,
236, 262, 305, 327–8,
379–81, 388–9, 395–6,
401, 427–8, 433, 437,
439, 459, 465, 484,
487, 527, 538, 544–5,
549, 557–8, 577, 579,
598, 605, 618–19, 627,
630, 636, 668, 690,
703, 706, 716, 718,
729, 733, 735, 744–5,
768, 792–4, 796–7,
799, 802, 821, 836,
841–2, 846, 859, 866,
886, 899–904, 906,
918, 925, 941, 944,
974, 995–6, 1003–4,
1018, 1020, 1052–3,
1105, 1107, 1124, 1136,
1167, 1171–2, 1187,
1241, 1256, 1273, 1285,
1293, 1302, 1428,
1434, 1447, 1481,
1514–15, 1551, 1565,
1642–4, 1660, 1674–5,
1677–8, 1684, 1688,
1691, 1694, 1749,
1769, 1777, 1781, 1839,
1846, 1895, 1943,
1968, 1980, 2034–5,
2077, 2114–15, 2117,
2150, 2156; above a
ditch, 1895; beside
the graveyard of St.
Thomas's church,
476, 549, 1691;
beside the north gate
of the Close, 692;
between two stiles of
the graveyard of St.
Thomas's church, 671;
near that graveyard,
2112–13; near a stile
of that graveyard,
694; on the south side
of that church, 89;
opposite the market
place where grains are
sold, 944; towards the
bar, 77; and see high
street; Pinnock's Inn;
'Riole', the
cf. Castle Street;
Dominican friary;
Ironmonger Corner
and see St. Thomas's
church (as a landmark)
Minster Street near the bar
tenements, 508, 1125–7,
1840
tenements beside a ditch,
1840
and see Castle Street
Minster Street beyond the
bar
cottages, 492, 543, 554,
1768, 1770–1
messuage, ?644
portion of land, 110,
161–2
shops, 493
tenements, 424, 492,
494, 532, 543, 553–4,
686, 740, 746, 1134,
1170, 1173, 1486;
beside a field, 1768,
1770–1
yard, 686
Minster Street, called
Castle Street
cottages, 2106–7; beyond
the bar, 2023, 2030,
2058–9
gate, 1742
messuage, 1671; or
tenement, 1996, 1998;
and see Bunt's Place
shops, 1671
tenement, chief, 1786
tenements, corner,
1798–9
tenements (other), 1671,
1685, 1722, 1742,
1786, 1798–9, 1923,
1983, 1996, 1998,
2103, 2106–7, 2161,
2166–7; beyond the
bar, beside a field,
2023, 2030, 2058–9
and see Castle Street

New Inn (in Winchester
Street), 369, 377, 717
New Street
almshouses beside Black
bridge, 1720
cellar, 111
cottages, 832, 1193, 1233,
1235, 1612, 1901, 1909,
1954, 1961, 1971, 2061,
2074–5; beside a ditch,
1179; on the way to
Barnwell's cross, 1946
garden, 365–6
house on the way to
Barnwell's cross, 1946
land beside a ditch, 1954
messuage, corner, 1830
messuages (other), 405–
8, ?421, 701, 755, 760,
929–30, 934, 1705,
2024, 2153, 2169;
towards Barnwell's
cross, 1791
plots, 754, 763, 1233
shops, corner, 335, 1477–
8
shops (other), 372–3,
?421, 454, 512, 570,
626, 875, 954, 970,
1073, 1295, 1297,
1760, 1791, 1804–5,
1850, 2165; beside the
hospital's trench, 1791
tavern, see Hott Corner
tenements, chief, 1630,
1895
tenements, corner, 319,
343–4, 402, 440, 478,
502, 521, 623, 634,
676, 679, 702, 719–21,
757, 785, 872, 966,
974, 1236, ?1388–92,
?1418, 1435, ?1497,
1535, 1543–5, 1554,
1634, 1685, 1696, 1833,

INDEX OF SALISBURY LOCATIONS, ETC 411

1971, 2009, 2064, 2069–70, 2101; beside Black bridge, 599; *and see* Florentine's Corner; Hott Corner; Rose, the
tenements (other), 42, 93, 96, 105, 120–1, 123, 136, 149, 159, 175, 250–1, 285, 314, 321, 331–2, 345–8, 350–6, 359–60, 365–7, 371, 419, 430, 447, 456–7, 477–8, 490, 502, 513, 546, 560, 566, 569–70, 584, 599, 626, 634, 676, 679, 700–2, 719–21, 724, 727, 742, 754–5, 757, 760, 763, 785, 790, 801, 832, 862, 887, 920, 948, 960, 987, 997, 1033, 1068–9, 1073, 1083, 1104, 1215, 1217, 1244, 1252, 1254, 1274, 1295, 1335, 1374, 1379–81, 1408–9, ?1418, 1457, 1466, 1485, ?1497, 1503–4, 1612, 1630, 1665, 1673, 1685, 1696, 1701, 1705, 1720, 1743, 1760, 1778, 1783, 1791, 1795, 1797, 1804–5, 1830, 1833, 1850, 1866, 1882, 1895, 1900–1, 1909, 1961, 1971, 1985, 2009, 2024, 2061, 2063–4, 2069–70, 2074–5, 2084–6, 2101, 2143, 2153, 2165; beside Black bridge, 742; beside the bridge, 2140–2; beside the lower bridge of Fisherton, 477; beside the river, 1910–11; beside a trench, 1573, 1866; beyond the bar, 573, 615; on the way to Barnwell's' cross, 1946, 2074; on the way to the bridge, 1930; on the way to the lower bridge of Fisherton, 1910–11; *and see* Fisherton, lower bridge
yards, 431; on the way to Barnwell's cross, 1946

Nuggeston
cottages, corner, on the way to St. Edmund's church, 1896, 2124
cottages (other), 584, 690, 693, 1275, 1882, 1992, 2042–4, 2046–7
cottages near, 922
messuages, 534, 616, 1997–2000
shops, 1882
tenements, 104, 458, 609, 616, 839, 974, 1087, 1248, 1882, 1896, 1992, 1997, 1999–2000, 2042–4, 2124
yard, corner, 514–15, 609
yards (other), 546, 616, 690, 693, 839, 1080, 1258
Nuggeston, street called, 831
tenements, yards, gardens, 1685, 1692

Old Town (the street called the Old Town), land of the bishop of Salisbury held in villeinage
cottage, beyond the bars, opposite, 563, 732, 1138, 1155
messuages: beyond the bars, on the way to St. Martin's church, opposite, 677; opposite, 1230
tenements: beyond the bar, in the street leading to St. Martin's church, 653, 688; beyond the bar, opposite, 85, 563, 732; opposite, 59, 811, 815, 837
yard(s) opposite, 963
and see St. Martin's church (as a landmark)

pillories, 478, 502
Pinnock's Inn (in Minster Street), 2005, 2077
Pot Row (*otherwise* Butcher Row)
shops, 390–1, 1210, 1249–50, 1429, 1523, 1742, 1863, 1906, 1929; opposite the butchers' stalls, 1870
tenements, 954–5, 1312, 1663, 1672, 1676, 1686–7, 1793, 1813, 1835, 1863, 1870, 1882, 1906–7, 1929, 1979, 2056, 2133–5; extending towards the market place, 2055–6
and see Butcher Row
Poultry
messuage (three shops) opposite Cordwainer Row, 1958, 1966, 1972
plot opposite, 1786
shops, 1896; opposite, 1786; *and see* Cordwainer Row
tenements, 1896, 1958, 1966, 1972, 2125; beside a lane, 1958, 1966, 1972; opposite, 1786
Powell's Corner
cross called, *see* cross
tenement called, opposite the high cross where fruit and other victuals are sold, 463, 623

racks, 294, 374–5, 493, 554, 557, 587, 593, 643–4, 659, 831, 943, 953, 1012–15, 1032, 1080, 1131, 1145, 1690, 1703,

1706–7, 1709, 1756–7, 1763, 1765, 1800, 1837, 1896, 1915–16, 1964, 1977, 1992, 1997, 1999–2000, 2038, 2120
'Riole', the (tenement in Minster Street), 816, 1895
Ro Corner (Gigant Street and St. Martin's Street), 529
Rolleston
　cottages, 884, 1627, 1784
　shops, 1627, 1784
　tenement near Mealmonger Street, 1234
　yards, 1627, 1784
Rolleston, corner called, 786
Rolleston, street called, street of, 1759, 1761
　cottages, corner, 1819, 1821–2, 1841
　messuage, in Martin's Croft, 659
　messuages, 644
　tenement, corner, 1819, 1821–2, 1841
　tenements (other), 644
　trench, 1819, 1821, 1841
　yard (corner), 644
　yard (other), 1819, 1821–2, 1841
Rolleston Lane, 1784
Rose, the (?corner tenement in Minster Street and New Street: cf. Hott Corner)
　shop beside, 1475–6
　tenement, corner, opposite, 1519

St. Edmund's church
　altars, 1971, 1979
　bequests, 569, 579, 581, 606, 668–9, 671, 690, 694, 786, 831–2, 1664, 1720, 1753, 1781, 1813, 1828, 1836, 1859–61, 1871, 1882, 1888, 1936, 1938, 1971, 1979, 1992, 2011, 2029, 2038, 2042, 2063–5, 2104, 2154–5
　boys wearing a surplice, bequest to, 1871
　chantry
　　endowment, 644
　　owner of property, 1680, ?2054
　chapel of the Blessed Mary, 1753
　　interment, 1871
　chaplains, annual, bequests to, 579, 1859, 1971, 2029
　chaplains, collegiate bequests to, 203, 579, 668, 740, 831–2, 1828, 1859, 1871, 1888, 1971, 1979, 2011, 2029
　　and see Chatt; Fifield; Mason; Pope; Warin
　chaplain, parochial bequests to, 549, 579, 606, 668, 688, 690, 786, 1781, 1859, 1861, 2011, 2038, 2042
　　and see Bradwell
　chaplains (unspecified) bequests to, 549, 558, 579, 831–2, 1786, 1814, 1828, 1861, 1871, 1888, 2011, 2154
　　and see Stoke
　college
　　bequest, 1871
　　household servant, see Brown
　college, provost, and provost and chaplains, as owners of property, 544, 570, 579, 613–14, 679, 1728, 1762, 1785, 1800, 1814, 1817–19, 1821–2, 1841, 1909, 1946, 1961, 2005, 2027–8, 2074, 2160
　deacon, bequests to, 549, 606, 668, 831, 1753, 1781, 1859, 1871, 1979, 2011
　fraternities, bequests to, 578, 668–9, 831, 2064
　graveyard, interments in, 549–50, 554, 556–8, 570–1, 577, 579, 581, 606, 666, 668–9, 690, 694, 786, 831–2, 1664, 1753, 1781, 1814, 1828, 1859, 1861, 1888, 1992, 2029, 2042, 2065, 2154
　interments, 1971, 1979, 2011
　light of the weavers' art, bequest to, 2064
　obits, 690, 2011
　priests, collegiate, bequests to, 786, 1753
　priests, stipendiary, bequest to, 1753
　priests (unspecified), bequests to, 666, 2065
　provost of the college, 832, 1871
　　bequests, 549, 668, 786, 831, 1753, 1828, 1859, 1861, 1871, 1888, 1971, 1979, 2029
　　trustee, 625, 641
　　as vicar of St. Martin's church, 1936
　　and see Arnold; Cheltenham; Ragenhill; Walter; Wimborne
　rector, bequest to, 1814
　sacristan, bequests to, 668, 831, 1753, 1781, 1859, 1871, 1979, 2011
St. Edmund's church (as a landmark)
　cottages, corner, see Endless Street; Gigant Street; Nuggeston
　cottages (other): near the graveyard, see Martin's Croft; on the way to, see Gigant Street; Martin's croft; opposite the graveyard, 926; and see Mealmonger Street
　croft opposite the graveyard, 164

INDEX OF SALISBURY LOCATIONS, ETC 413

gardens: on the way
  to, *see* Gigant Street;
  opposite the graveyard,
  831; *and see* Martin's
  Croft
messuage on the way to,
  241; *and see* Gigant
  Street
plot opposite the
  graveyard, 831
shops: in the street on the
  way to, 817–18; on the
  way to, 409
tenement, corner,
  opposite the graveyard,
  449–51, 605, 621, 636
tenements (other): in the
  street on the way to,
  817–18; in the street
  on the way to the pits
  opposite the graveyard,
  1685, 1692; on the
  way to, *see* Brown
  Street; Gigant Street;
  opposite, 578, 621;
  opposite the graveyard,
  605, 636, 845, 926
yard, corner, opposite the
  graveyard, 942
yards (other): in the street
  on the way to, 817–18;
  on the way to, *see*
  Gigant Street; Martin's
  Croft; opposite, 621;
  opposite the graveyard,
  374–5
St. Martin's church
  altars, 580, 1783, 1909
  bequests, 84, 565, 568–9,
    580, 582, 603, 653,
    668, 671, 832, 1719–20,
    1783, 1814, 1836, 1859,
    1882, 1888, 1909, 1936,
    1938, 1954, 1971, 1979,
    2011, 2029, 2063–4,
    2155, 2160
  chancel, interment, 1938
  chaplain, parochial
    bequests to, 565, 1719,
    1783, 1909, 1936, 1954,
    2064
    and see Thomas

chaplains (other),
  bequests to, 1719, 1783,
  1786, 1909, 1936, 1954,
  1971, 2064; *and see*
  Aynel; Bennett; Spicer
cross, 580
deacon, bequests to, 565,
  580, 653, 1719, 1783,
  1904, 1954
font, 1909
fraternities, bequests to,
  1954, 1971, 2064
graveyard
  cross, 568
  interments, 548, 550,
    565, 568, 580, 582,
    603, 623, 653, 1719,
    1936, 1954, 2160
  image of the Virgin, 2064
  interments, 1783, 1909,
    2064
  lights, bequests to, 580,
    1909
  sacristan, bequests to,
    580, 653, 1719, 1783,
    1909, 1954
  vicar, bequest to, 1936
St. Martin's church (as a
    landmark)
  cottages: in the street on
    the way to, 1896, 2029,
    2032–3, 2111; near,
    1471; on the way to,
    beside the graveyard,
    1936; towards, 981,
    1225, 1431; *and see* St.
    Martin's Street
  gardens: beyond the bar,
    towards, 1178; towards,
    1262–3
  gate of Bug moor, in the
    street on the way to,
    1896
  messuages, *see* Old Town
  tenement, corner,
    beyond the bar, on the
    way to, 603, 705, 1047
  tenements (other):
    beyond the bar, on the
    way to, 551, 603, 666,
    705, 709; in the street
    on the way to, 711,

713–14, (beside the
    graveyard) 840, 2111;
    near the graveyard,
    1540; on the way to,
    9–10, 874, 1936, 2029;
    towards, 918–19, 938–
    9, 1313, 1415, 2091–2;
    and see Old Town
  toft, towards, 1181
  and see St. Martin's Street
St. Martin's Street (on the
    way from the east gate
    of the Close towards
    St. Martin's church)
  cottage(s), corner, 1180
  cottages (other), 370, 551,
    596, 705, 710, 1011,
    1371, 1896, 1909, 2040,
    2151, 2160
  cout', 1482
  garden, 590, 1042
  messuages, 1360
  plots, 50, 54, 623, 749–50
  shop, corner, 1947–8
  shops (other), 1362, 1372
  tenements, corner, ?72,
    336, 673, 784, 856, 978,
    1064, 1191, 1561–2,
    1579, 1729, 1750;
    opposite the gate of
    the Franciscans, 1896;
    and see Clark's Place;
    Focket Place; Ro
    Corner
  tenements (other), 7, 27,
    40–1, 96, 165, 239,
    242, 350, 422, 482,
    498, 548, 551, 554,
    561, 570, 588, 590,
    596, 613, 705, 710, 715,
    750, 886, 946, 969,
    989, 1024, 1044, 1081,
    1161, 1180, 1197–9,
    1208, 1227, 1361, 1363,
    1453, 1498, 1500, 1510,
    1546–7, 1640, 1750,
    1817–18, 1879, 1909,
    1938, 1944, 1947–8,
    2005, 2151, 2160
  yards, 890, 1165
  and see St. Martin's
    church (as a landmark)

St. Nicholas's church
    [?*rectius* in Wilton], *see*
    Wilton
St. Nicholas's hospital
    bequests, 569
    chapel, 671
    chaplains, friar, 671
    fabric, 1836
    paupers, 671, 1836,
      1882, 2063
    sisters, 671
    owner of property, 1690,
      1763–4, 1964, 1977
    and see ways
St. Nicholas's hospital (as a
    landmark)
    meadow towards, 139
    and see bridges; ways
St. Thomas's church
    aisle, 1786
    altars, 569, 666, 671,
      1730, 1978, 2061, 2063
    bequests, 543, 553, 560,
      566, 569, 619, 666,
      668, 671, 698, 735,
      785, 1720, 1730, 1778,
      1786, 1814, 1836,
      1859–61, 1882, 1888,
      1971, 1978–9, 1985,
      2011, 2029, 2038, 2061,
      2063–4, 2104, 2154–6
    chalice, 569
    chantry, bequests to, 671,
      2061
    chapel, interment in,
      1985
    chapel of St. Stephen,
      bequest to, 2063
    chaplain, chantry, 671
    chaplain, parochial
      bequests to, 553, 698,
        1786, 1839, 2061,
        2063–4, 2154, 2156
      and see Green
    chaplains (other)
      bequests to, 1720, 1730,
        1786, 1836, 1971, 1985,
        2061, 2063–4, 2154,
        2156
      and see Stafford;
        Upavon
    deacon, bequests to, 543,
      553, 671, 698, 1786,
      1836, 2063
    graveyard, interments in,
      553, 560, 566, 698, 735,
      1720, 1730, 1839, 1860,
      2038
    image of the Blessed
      Mary, 2156
    interments, 671, 1685,
      1786, 1978, 2061, 2156
    keepers of the fabric and
      goods
      as trustees, 671, 2121
      and see Oword;
        Warmwell
      cf. wardens
    parish priest, bequest to,
      666
    parson
      as trustee, 543
      and see Salisbury
    rector, 671
      bequests to, 666, 1720,
        1778, 1836, 1839, 1978,
        2063
      and see Fromand;
        Wilton
    sacristan, bequests to, 553,
      671, 1786, 1836, 2063
    wardens
      as trustees, 1786
      cf. keepers
St. Thomas's church (as a
    landmark)
    messuages near the
      graveyard, 405–8;
      and see Castle Street;
        Minster Street
    room above a stile of the
      graveyard, 2158
    shop, corner, *see* Minster
      Street
    shops (other): near, 1331,
      1461–2, 1601; near a
      stile of the graveyard,
      855; opposite, 1224;
      and see Minster Street
    stiles, *see* Minster Street
    tenement, corner, near
      the graveyard, 2102
    tenements (other): near
      the graveyard, 394,
      404, 466, 1331, 1518,
      2102; opposite, 488,
      542, 707, 795; opposite
      the graveyard, 432; *and
      see* Fisherton, upper
      bridge (as a landmark);
      Minster Street
Salisbury
    archdeaconry, *q.v.*
    bailiff, *q.v.*
    bishop, *q.v.*
    bishopric, *q.v.*
    cathedral church, *q.v.*
    city of New Salisbury,
      q.v.
    court, *q.v.*
    school (grammar) and
      schoolhouse, 76, 472,
      1670
Scots Lane, 1731–2, 1888,
    1893
    cottages, 908, 1664
    messuages, 324–6, 378,
      400; on the south side
      of, 644
    shops, 564, 739, 1419–20,
      1847, 1888, 1892–3,
      2018
    tenements, corner, 523,
      564, 577, 610, 739,
      1290, ?1291, 1341–3,
      1680
    tenements (other), 474,
      564, 577, 671, 690, 739,
      789, 943, 977, 1157,
      1419–20, 1502, 1539,
      1680, 1733, 1736, 1847,
      1885, 1888, 1893, 1924,
      1973, 2018, 2162, 2164
    yards, 324–6, 378; on the
      south side of, 644
Shit Lane
    cottages, 2009, 2151
    tenement, corner, 1543–
      5, 2009
    tenement (other), 2009,
      2151
    tenement beside, 1738–9
    toft, 1162
Shit Lane, corner, 786
shop, corner (*unlocated*), 393
skillings, 1749, 1946

INDEX OF SALISBURY LOCATIONS, ETC

smiths (where smiths wait), see Winchester Street: shops, corner; shops (other)
sollars, 160, 397–8, 403, 415, 418, 429, 434, 460, 487, 552, 619, 626, 671, 720–1, 729, 745, 768, 791, 806, 1656–7, 1665, 1670, 1689, 1695, 1719, 1727, 1741, 1839, 1843, 1882, 1888, 1890, 1892–3, 1946, 2011, 2051, 2112–13, 2158
'Stapult' Hall, 1938
Stint's Corner (Brown Street and Wineman Street), 646–7
Stratford's Corner (in Winchester Street), 809; cf. Glastonbury's Corner
street where iron is sold, shop in, 318, 390–1

taverns, see fishermen's stalls; Hott Corner; Minster Street; and see (for cross-references) inns
tenements, corner, and messuages, corner, (named), see Beaminster's Corner; Bedred Row; Bert's Corner; Bull Hall; Cavenasser's Corner; Chantrell's Corner; Cheese Corner; Cold Corner; Dyne's Corner; Florentine's Corner; Focket Place; Glastonbury's Corner; Grandon's Corner; Hampton's Corner; Holy Ghost Corner; Hott Corner; Ive's Corner; Powell's Corner; Ro Corner; Rose, the; Stint's Corner; Stratford's Corner; Vellard's Corner; Warr's

Corner; Wimpler's Corner
tenements, corner (*unlocated*), 1035, 1278–82
tenements (other), messuages (other), and other buildings, (named), see Brewery; Buckland's Place; Bunt's Place; Common Hall; Cowhouse; Drake Hall; Gatehouse; George's Inn; Glasshouse; Guys's Place; New Inn; Pinnock's Inn; 'Riole', the; 'Stapult' Hall; Workhouse
trenches (watercourses), 82, 731, 1573, 1775–6, 1791, 1819, 1821, 1841, 1866, 1925–7, 1964, 1977, 2015, 2017, 2027–8
common, 567, 1665–6, 1673, 1714–15, 1721, 1738–9, 1802–3, 1950
Trench, the (ditch called), 582

(de) Vaux college
bequests, 1938
chaplains, 1729
fabric, 1836
fellows, 1729
library, 1938
scholars, 671, 1786, 1938
chapel, 1729
keeper, see Maidenhead
owner of property, 1729, 1866, 1879, 1882, 2158
Vellard's Corner (Endless Street and Wineman Street), 652, 730

Warr's Corner (Culver Street and Winchester Street), 2048
ways (repaired charitably) leading to Ayleswade

bridge, 1786
behind Butcher Row, 2063
opposite Dominican friary, 1786
Drake Hall Street, 1786
between St. Nicholas's hospital and a meadow, 1729
unlocated, see index 1: ways
Wheeler Row
shops, 736, 771, 1046, 1201–2
tenement, corner, see Hampton's Corner
tenements (other), 1672, 1676, 1686–7, 1902, 1908, 1912, 2155; opposite the market place, 1902, 1908, 1912
Wimpler's Corner (in Minster Street on the way to the upper bridge of Fisherton), 416, 694, 821, 1688, 1694
Winchester Street
cellar, 160
cottages, 358, 410, 1719, 1954
gardens, 1719, 2012
gate, 2011
Gatehouse, *q.v.*
houses, 789, 1719
messuage, corner, see Holy Ghost Corner
messuages (other), 114–15, 585, 594, 764, 1189, 1442, 2158; above the common trench, 1665–6; opposite the common trench, 1673, 1721
plots, ?764, 1231, 1270, 1719, 1721
rooms above a ditch, 1473
shops, corner, 589, 2104; where smiths wait, 434, 850
shops (other), 44, 87, 358,

832, 1079, ?1727, 2063;
above a ditch, 1968;
opposite the running
water, 567; where
smiths wait, 791
tenements, chief, 338–40,
342, 568, 571, 2011–12
tenements, corner, 215,
225, 413, 423, 478, 502,
508, 567, 589, 605,
636, 832, 850, 865, 876,
896, 947, 1078, 1350–9,
1367, 1709, 1717, 1805,
1883, 1886, 1932–4,
1950, 1968, 2045,
2158; *and see* Bull Hall;
Chantrell's Corner;
Cheese Corner;
Dyne's Corner;
Glastonbury's Corner;
Holy Ghost Corner;
Stratford's Corner;
Warr's Corner
tenements (other), 11,
?28, 43, 60, 74, 91,
124, 133–4, 310, 357,
369, 377, 382–5, 438,
448, 461–2, 471–2,
478, 481, 489, 495,
497, 524, 539–40, 543,
552, 555–6, 563, 568,
571, 580, 585, 594,
605, 611, 619, 636,
638, 649, 656–7, 660,
662, 671, 717, 729,
732, 745, ?764, 765–6,
772–3, 784, 787, 789,
809, 832, 852, 858, 881,
897, 921, 927, 933, 945,
947, 962–3, 1008–10,
1016, 1021, 1029, 1035,
1038–9, 1042, 1060–2,
1067, 1077, 1085, 1092,
1138, 1144, 1146, 1155,
1158–60, 1222, 1270,
1272, 1338, 1345, 1378,
1423, 1425–7, 1483–4,
1524–5, 1555, 1576,
1578, 1596–8, 1617,
1619–20, 1626, 1635,
1638, 1641, 1665, 1673,
1681–2, 1700, 1708–
10, 1717, 1719, 1721,
1738–9, 1751, 1758,
1805, 1808, 1829, 1831,
1842, 1883, 1886, 1896,
1932–5, 1950, 1954,
2011–12, 2022, 2045,
2048, 2063, 2078,
2081, 2119, 2158; above
the common trench,
1665; above a ditch,
1472, 1490; beside
the city's ditch, near
Milford bars, 1665,
1708; opposite the
common trench, 1673,
1721, 1738–9; *and see*
New Inn
workhouses, 2011
yards, 921, ?1951
Wineman Street
cottages, 1658, 1713,
1746, 1949, 1951–2,
2029, 2036–7, 2041,
2065, 2123, 2159;
beside the city's ditch,
1949
house, 108
messuage, corner, 1791;
and see Ive's Corner
plot, 1949
shops, 425, 1221, 2065;
beside the city's ditch,
1949
tenement, chief, *see* Ive's
Corner
tenements, corner, 20,
329–30, 533, 574–6,
595, 833–4, 914–15,
928, 1094, 1299, 1319,
1560, 1566, 1622–4,
1658, 1693, 1695, 1713,
1959–60, 2036–7,
2041, 2073, 2123, 2159;
and see Beaminster's
Corner; Bert's Corner;
Grandon's Corner;
Ive's Corner; Stint's
Corner; Vellard's
Corner
tenements (other), 30,
36–7, 132, 417, 425,
452, 550, 574–6,
600–1, 608, 646–7,
650, 652, 667, 730, 761,
803, 833–4, 838, 864,
878, 893, 937, 957, 967,
1036, 1041, 1095, 1114,
1119, 1216, 1249–50,
1267, 1294, 1296, 1344,
1396–8, 1423, 1499,
1649–52, 1693, 1695,
1718, 1746, 1791, 1861,
1952, 1959–60, 1967,
1979, 2004, 2029,
2052–3, 2071–3, 2098,
2108, 2123, 2159;
beside a trench, 2015,
2017
toft, 1658
yard beside the city's
ditch, 1951, 1967
Workhouse (in Brown
Street), 1714–15, 1802

WILTSHIRE RECORD SOCIETY
(as at November 2022)

President: Dr Negley Harte
Honorary Treasurer: Ian Hicks
Honorary Secretary: Miss Helen Taylor
General Editor: Dr Tom Plant

Committee:
Dr J. Hare
S.D. Hobbs
Mrs S. Thomson
S. Raymond
I. Slocombe

Honorary Independent Examiner: C.C. Dale

PRIVATE MEMBERS

Note that because of recent legislation the Society no longer publishes members' addresses in its volumes, as it had done since 1953.

Honorary Members
Ogburn, Senr Judge R W
Sharman-Crawford, Mr T

Adams, Ms S
Bainbridge, Dr V
Bathe, Mr G,
Bayliffe, Mr B G
Bennett, Dr N
Berrett, Mr A M
Berry, Mr C
Blake, Mr P A
Box, Mr S D
Brand, Dr P A
Brock, Mrs C
Brown, Mr D A
Brown, Mr G R
Browning, Mr E
Bryson, Dr A
Carter, Mr D
Cawthorne, Mrs N
Chalmers, Mr D
Chandler, Dr J H
Clark, Mr G A
Colcomb, Mr D M
Collins, Mr A T
Cooper, Mr S

Couzens, Mr T
Craven, Dr A
Crook, Mr P H
Crouch, Mr J W
Crowley, Dr D A
Cunnington, Ms J
Dakers, Prof C
d'Arcy, Mr J N
Dodd, Mr D
Dyson, Mrs L
Ede, Dr M E
Elliott, Dr J
English, Ms K
Forrest, Dr M
Gaisford, Mr J
Gale, Mrs J
Ghey, Mr J G
Ginger, Mr A
Goddard, Mr R G H
Griffin, Dr C
Grist, Mr M
Hare, Dr J N
Harte, Dr N
Hawkins, Mr D
Heaton, Mr R J
Helmholz, Prof R W
Henly, Mr C

Herron, Mrs Pamela M
Hickman, Mr M R
Hicks, Mr I
Hicks, Prof M A
Hillman, Mr R B
Hobbs, Mr S
Howells, Dr Jane
Ingram, Dr M J
Johnston, Mrs J M
Jones, Ms J
Kent, Mr T A
Kite, Mr P J
Kneebone, Mr W J R
Knowles, Mrs V A
Lansdowne, Marquis of
Lawes, Mrs G
Marsh, Rev R
Marshman, Mr M J
Martin, Ms J
Moles, Mrs M I
Morland, Mrs N
Napper, Mr L R
Newbury, Mr C Coles
Newman, Mrs R
Nicolson, Mr A
Nokes, Mr P M A
Noyce, Miss S

OGBOURNE, Mr J M V
OGBURN, Mr D A
PARKER, Dr P F,
PATIENCE, Mr D C
PERRY, Mr W A
PLANT, Dr T
POWELL, Mrs N
PRICE, Mr A J R
RAILTON, Ms A
RAYMOND, Mr S
ROBERTS, Ms M
ROGERS, Mr K H

ROLFE, Mr R C
ROSE, Mr A
SAUNT, Mrs B A
SHELDRAKE, Mr B
SHEWRING, Mr P
SKINNER, Ms C
SLOCOMBE, Mr I
SMITH, Mr P J
SPAETH, Dr D A
STONE, Mr M J
SUTER, Mrs C
SUTTON, Mr A E

TATTON-BROWN, Mr T
TAYLOR, Miss H
THOMSON, Mrs S M
WADSWORTH, Mrs S
WILLIAMSON, Mr B
WILTSHIRE, Mr J
WILTSHIRE, Mrs P E
WOODFORD, Mr A
WOODWARD, Mr A S,
WRIGHT, Mr D P
YOUNGER, Mr C

UNITED KINGDOM INSTITUTIONS

Aberystwyth
   National Library of Wales
   University College of Wales
Birmingham. University Library
Bristol
   University of Bristol Library
Cambridge. University Library
Cheltenham. Bristol and Gloucestershire Archaeological Society
Chippenham
   Museum & Heritage Centre
   Wiltshire and Swindon History Centre
Coventry. University of Warwick Library
Devizes
   Wiltshire Archaeological & Natural History Society
   Wiltshire Family History Society

Durham. University Library
Edinburgh
   University Library
Exeter. University Library
Glasgow. University Library

Liverpool. University Library
London
   British Library
   College of Arms
   Guildhall Library
   Inner Temple Library
   Institute of Historical Research
   London Library
   The National Archives
   Royal Historical Society
   Society of Antiquaries
   Society of Genealogists
Manchester. John Rylands Library
Marlborough
   Memorial Library, Marlborough College
   Savernake Estate Office
Norwich. University of

East Anglia Library
Nottingham. University Library
Oxford
   Bodleian Library
   Exeter College Library
St Andrews. University Library
Salisbury
   Bourne Valley Historical Society
   Cathedral Library
   Salisbury and South Wilts Museum
Swansea. University College Library
Swindon
   Historic England
   Swindon Borough Council
Taunton. Somerset Archaeological and Natural History Society
Wetherby. British Library Document Supply Centre
York. University Library

INSTITUTIONS OVERSEAS

AUSTRALIA
Adelaide. University Library
Crawley. Reid Library, University of Western Australia

CANADA
Halifax. Killam Library, Dalhousie University
Toronto, Ont Pontifical Inst of Medieval Studies
University of Toronto Library
Victoria, B.C. McPherson Library, University of Victoria

NEW ZEALAND
Wellington. National Library of New Zealand

UNITED STATES OF AMERICA
Ann Arbor, Mich. Hatcher Library, University of Michigan
Athens, Ga. University of Georgia Libraries
Atlanta, Ga. The Robert W Woodruff Library, Emory University
Bloomington, Ind. Indiana University Library
Boston, Mass. New England Historic and Genealogical Society
Boulder, Colo. University of Colorado Library
Cambridge, Mass. Harvard College Library
Harvard Law School Library
Charlottesville, Va. Alderman Library, University of Virginia
Chicago Newberry Library
University of Chicago Library
Dallas, Texas. Public Library
Davis, Calif. University Library
East Lansing, Mich. Michigan State University Library
Evanston, Ill. United Libraries, Garrett/Evangelical, Seabury
Fort Wayne, Ind. Allen County Public Library
Houston, Texas. M.D. Anderson Library, University of Houston
Iowa City, Iowa. University of Iowa Libraries
Ithaca, NY. Cornell University Library
Los Angeles Public Library
Young Research Library, University of California
Minneapolis, Minn. Wilson Library, University of Minnesota
New York Columbia University of the City of New York
Salt Lake City, Utah. Family History Library
San Marino, Calif. Henry E. Huntington Library
Urbana, Ill. University of Illinois Library
Washington. The Folger Shakespeare Library
Winston-Salem, N.C. Z.Smith Reynolds Library, Wake Forest University

LIST OF PUBLICATIONS

The Wiltshire Record Society was founded in 1937, as the Records Branch of the Wiltshire Archaeological and Natural History Society, to promote the publication of the documentary sources for the history of Wiltshire. The annual subscription is £15 for private and institutional members. In return, a member receives a volume each year. Prospective members should apply to the Hon. Secretary, c/o Wiltshire and Swindon History Centre, Cocklebury Road, Chippenham SN15 3QN. Many more members are needed.

The following volumes have been published. Price to members £15, and to non-members £20, postage extra. Most volumes up to 51 are still available from the Wiltshire and Swindon History Centre, Cocklebury Road, Chippenham SN15 3QN. Volumes 52-71 are available from Hobnob Press, c/o 8 Lock Warehouse, Severn Road, Gloucester GL1 2GA. Volumes 1-55 are available online, at www.wiltshirerecordsociety.org.uk.

1. *Abstracts of feet of fines relating to Wiltshire for the reigns of Edward I and Edward II*, ed. R.B. Pugh, 1939
2. *Accounts of the parliamentary garrisons of Great Chalfield and Malmesbury, 1645–1646*, ed. J.H.P. Pafford, 1940
3. *Calendar of Antrobus deeds before 1625*, ed. R.B. Pugh, 1947
4. *Wiltshire county records: minutes of proceedings in sessions, 1563 and 1574 to 1592*, ed. H.C. Johnson, 1949
5. *List of Wiltshire boroughs records earlier in date than 1836*, ed. M.G. Rathbone, 1951
6. *The Trowbridge woollen industry as illustrated by the stock books of John and Thomas Clark, 1804–1824*, ed. R.P. Beckinsale, 1951
7. *Guild stewards' book of the borough of Calne, 1561–1688*, ed. A.W. Mabbs, 1953
8. *Andrews' and Dury's map of Wiltshire, 1773: a reduced facsimile*, ed. Elizabeth Crittall, 1952
9. *Surveys of the manors of Philip, earl of Pembroke and Montgomery, 1631–2*, ed. E. Kerridge, 1953
10. *Two sixteenth century taxations lists, 1545 and 1576*, ed. G.D. Ramsay, 1954
11. *Wiltshire quarter sessions and assizes, 1736*, ed. J.P.M. Fowle, 1955
12. *Collectanea*, ed. N.J. Williams, 1956
13. *Progress notes of Warden Woodward for the Wiltshire estates of New College, Oxford, 1659–1675*, ed. R.L. Rickard, 1957
14. *Accounts and surveys of the Wiltshire lands of Adam de Stratton*, ed. M.W. Farr, 1959
15. *Tradesmen in early-Stuart Wiltshire: a miscellany*, ed. N.J. Williams, 1960
16. *Crown pleas of the Wiltshire eyre, 1249*, ed. C.A.F. Meekings, 1961
17. *Wiltshire apprentices and their masters, 1710–1760*, ed. Christabel Dale, 1961
18. *Hemingby's register*, ed. Helena M. Chew, 1963
19. *Documents illustrating the Wiltshire textile trades in the eighteenth century*, ed. Julia de L. Mann, 1964
20. *The diary of Thomas Naish*, ed. Doreen Slatter, 1965
21–2. *The rolls of Highworth hundred, 1275–1287*, 2 parts, ed. Brenda Farr, 1966, 1968
23. *The earl of Hertford's lieutenancy papers, 1603–1612*, ed. W.P.D. Murphy, 1969
24. *Court rolls of the Wiltshire manors of Adam de Stratton*, ed. R.B. Pugh, 1970
25. *Abstracts of Wiltshire inclosure awards and agreements*, ed. R.E. Sandell, 1971
26. *Civil pleas of the Wiltshire eyre, 1249*, ed. M.T. Clanchy, 1971
27. *Wiltshire returns to the bishop's visitation queries, 1783*, ed. Mary Ransome, 1972
28. *Wiltshire extents for debts, Edward I – Elizabeth I*, ed. Angela Conyers, 1973
29. *Abstracts of feet of fines relating to Wiltshire for the reign of Edward III*, ed. C.R. Elrington, 1974

30. *Abstracts of Wiltshire tithe apportionments*, ed. R.E. Sandell, 1975
31. *Poverty in early-Stuart Salisbury*, ed. Paul Slack, 1975
32. *The subscription book of Bishops Tounson and Davenant, 1620–40*, ed. B. Williams, 1977
33. *Wiltshire gaol delivery and trailbaston trials, 1275–1306*, ed. R.B. Pugh, 1978
34. *Lacock abbey charters*, ed. K.H. Rogers, 1979
35. *The cartulary of Bradenstoke priory*, ed. Vera C.M. London, 1979
36. *Wiltshire coroners' bills, 1752–1796*, ed. R.F. Hunnisett, 1981
37. *The justicing notebook of William Hunt, 1744–1749*, ed. Elizabeth Crittall, 1982
38. *Two Elizabethan women: correspondence of Joan and Maria Thynne, 1575–1611*, ed. Alison D. Wall, 1983
39. *The register of John Chandler, dean of Salisbury, 1404–17*, ed. T.C.B. Timmins, 1984
40. *Wiltshire dissenters' meeting house certificates and registrations, 1689–1852*, ed. J.H. Chandler, 1985
41. *Abstracts of feet of fines relating to Wiltshire, 1377–1509*, ed. J.L. Kirby, 1986
42. *The Edington cartulary*, ed. Janet H. Stevenson, 1987
43. *The commonplace book of Sir Edward Bayntun of Bromham*, ed. Jane Freeman, 1988
44. *The diaries of Jeffery Whitaker, schoolmaster of Bratton, 1739–1741*, ed. Marjorie Reeves and Jean Morrison, 1989
45. *The Wiltshire tax list of 1332*, ed. D.A. Crowley, 1989
46. *Calendar of Bradford-on-Avon settlement examinations and removal orders, 1725–98*, ed. Phyllis Hembry, 1990
47. *Early trade directories of Wiltshire*, ed. K.H. Rogers and indexed by J.H. Chandler, 1992
48. *Star chamber suits of John and Thomas Warneford*, ed. F.E. Warneford, 1993
49. *The Hungerford Cartulary: a calendar of the earl of Radnor's cartulary of the Hungerford family*, ed. J.L. Kirby, 1994
50. *The Letters of John Peniston, Salisbury architect, Catholic, and Yeomanry Officer, 1823–1830*, ed. M. Cowan, 1996
51. *The Apprentice Registers of the Wiltshire Society, 1817– 1922*, ed. H. R. Henly, 1997
52. *Printed Maps of Wiltshire 1787–1844: a selection of topographical, road and canal maps in facsimile*, ed. John Chandler, 1998
53. *Monumental Inscriptions of Wiltshire: an edition, in facsimile, of Monumental Inscriptions in the County of Wilton, by Sir Thomas Phillipps*, ed. Peter Sherlock, 2000
54. *The First General Entry Book of the City of Salisbury, 1387–1452*, ed. David R. Carr, 2001
55. *Devizes Division income tax assessments, 1842–1860*, ed. Robert Colley, 2002
56. *Wiltshire Glebe Terriers, 1588–1827*, ed. Steven Hobbs, 2003
57. *Wiltshire Farming in the Seventeenth Century*, ed. Joseph Bettey, 2005
58. *Early Motor Vehicle Registration in Wiltshire, 1903–1914*, ed. Ian Hicks, 2006
59. *Marlborough Probate Inventories, 1591–1775*, ed. Lorelei Williams and Sally Thomson, 2007
60. *The Hungerford Cartulary, part 2: a calendar of the Hobhouse cartulary of the Hungerford family*, ed. J.L. Kirby, 2007
61. *The Court Records of Brinkworth and Charlton*, ed. Douglas Crowley, 2009
62. *The Diary of William Henry Tucker, 1825–1850*, ed. Helen Rogers, 2009
63. *Gleanings from Wiltshire Parish Registers*, ed. Steven Hobbs, 2010
64. *William Small's Cherished Memories and Associations*, ed. Jane Howells and Ruth Newman, 2011
65. *Crown Pleas of the Wiltshire Eyre, 1268*, ed. Brenda Farr and Christopher Elrington, rev. Henry Summerson, 2012
66. *The Minute Books of Froxfield Almshouse, 1714–1866*, ed. Douglas Crowley, 2013

67. *Wiltshire Quarter Sessions Order Book, 1642–1654,* ed. Ivor Slocombe, 2014
68. *The Register of John Blyth, Bishop of Salisbury, 1493–1499,* ed. David Wright, 2015
69. *The Churchwardens' Accounts of St Mary's, Devizes, 1633–1689,* ed. Alex Craven, 2016
70. *The Account Books and Papers of Everard and Ann Arundell of Ashcombe and Salisbury, 1745–1798,* ed. Barry Williamson, 2017
71. *Letters of Henry Hoare of Stourhead, 1760–81,* ed. Dudley Dodd, 2018
72. *Braydon Forest and the Forest Law,* ed. Douglas Crowley, 2019
73. *The Parish Registers of Thomas Crockford, 1561–1633* ed. John Chandler, 2020
74. *The Farming Diaries of Thomas Pinniger, 1813-1847,* ed. Alan Wadsworth, 2021

Further details about the Society, its activities and publications, will be found on its website, www.wiltshirerecordsociety.org.uk.